COUNSELING AND PSYCHOTHERAPY

Theories and Interventions

FOURTH EDITION

David Capuzzi
Scholar in Residence, Johns Hopkins University
Professor Emeritus, Portland State University

Douglas R. Gross
Professor Emeritus, Arizona State University

PEARSON

Merrill
Prentice Hall

Upper Saddle River, New Jersey
Columbus, Ohio

Library of Congress Cataloging-in-Publication Data

Counseling and psychotherapy : theories and interventions / [edited by] David Capuzzi, Douglas R. Gross.—4th ed.

    p. cm.

Includes bibliographical references and indexes.

ISBN 0-13-198737-2

1. Counseling. 2. Psychotherapy. 3. Counseling—Case studies. 4. Psychotherapy—Case studies.

    I. Capuzzi, Dave.   II. Gross, Douglas R.   III. Title.

BF637.C6C634 2007

158′.3—dc22

2006018104

Vice President and Executive Publisher: Jeffery W. Johnston
Publisher: Kevin M. Davis
Associate Editor: Meredith Sarver
Editorial Assistant: Sarah N. Kenoyer
Production Editor: Mary Harlan
Production Coordinator: Penny Walker, Techbooks
Design Coordinator: Diane C. Lorenzo
Text Design: Techbooks
Cover Designer: Candace Rowley
Cover Image: Super Stock
Production Manager: Susan Hannahs
Director of Marketing: David Gesell
Marketing Manager: Autumn Purdy
Marketing Coordinator: Brian Mounts

This book was set in Berkeley by Techbooks. It was printed and bound by R. R. Donnelley & Sons Company. The cover was printed by The Lehigh Press, Inc.

Pearson Education Ltd.
Pearson Education Singapore Pte. Ltd.
Pearson Education Canada, Ltd.
Pearson Education–Japan

Pearson Education Australia Pty. Limited
Pearson Education North Asia Ltd.
Pearson Educación de Mexico, S. A. de C.V.
Pearson Education Malaysia Pte. Ltd.

10 9 8 7 6 5 4 3 2 1
ISBN: 0-13-198737-2

About the Authors

Meet the Editors

David Capuzzi, PhD, NCC, LPC, is a past president of the American Counseling Association (ACA) and is a Scholar in Residence and counselor educator at Johns Hopkins University. He is professor emeritus and former coordinator of counselor education in the Graduate School of Education at Portland State University in Portland, Oregon.

From 1980 to 1984, Dr. Capuzzi was editor of *The School Counselor.* He has authored a number of textbook chapters and monographs on the topic of preventing adolescent suicide and is coeditor and author, with Dr. Larry Golden, of *Helping Families Help Children: Family Interventions with School-Related Problems* (1986) and *Preventing Adolescent Suicide* (1988). In addition to this text he has coauthored and edited *Youth at Risk: A Prevention Resource for Counselors, Teachers, and Parents* (4th ed., 2004); *Introduction to the Counseling Profession* (4th ed., 2005); *Introduction to Group Counseling* (4th ed., retitled *Introduction to Group Work* in 2006) with Douglas R. Gross. He coedited, with Mark Stauffer, *Career Counseling: Foundations, Perspectives and Applications* in 2006. *Approaches to Group Work: A Handbook for Practitioners* (2003) and *Sexuality Counseling* (2002), the latter coauthored and edited with Larry Burlew, and *Suicide Across the Life Span* (2004) are three of his other texts. He has authored or coauthored articles in a number of ACA related journals.

A frequent speaker and keynoter at professional conferences and institutes, Dr. Capuzzi has also consulted with a variety of school districts and community agencies interested in initiating prevention and intervention strategies for adolescents at risk for suicide. He has facilitated the development of suicide prevention, crisis management, and postvention programs in communities throughout the United States; provides training on the topics of youth at risk, grief and loss, group work, and increasing therapeutic presence in counseling; and serves as an invited adjunct faculty member at other universities as time permits. He is the first recipient of ACA's Kitty Cole Human Rights Award and also is a recipient of the Leona Tyler Award in Oregon.

Douglas R. Gross, PhD, NCC, is a professor emeritus of Arizona State University in Tempe, where he was a faculty member in the counseling program for 29 years. His professional work history includes public school teaching, counseling, and administration. He has been president of the Arizona Counselors Association, president of the Western Association for Counselor Education and Supervision, chairperson of the Western Regional Branch Assembly of the American Counseling Association (ACA, formerly the American Association for Counseling and Development), president of the Association for Humanistic Education and Development, and treasurer and parliamentarian of ACA.

In addition to his work on this textbook, Dr. Gross has contributed chapters to many other texts: four editions of *Youth at Risk: A Prevention Resource for Counselors, Teachers, and Parents* (4th ed., 2004); four editions of *Introduction to the Counseling Profession* (4th ed., 2005); four editions of *Introduction to Group Counseling/Work* (4th ed., 2006); two editions of *Foundations of Mental Health Counseling* (2nd ed., 1996); *Counseling: Theory, Process and Practice* (1977); and *The Counselor's Handbook* (1974). His research has appeared in the following journals: *Journal of Counseling Psychology, Journal of Counseling and Development, Association for Counselor Education and Supervision Journal, Journal of Educational Research, Counseling and Human Development, Arizona Counselors Journal, Texas Counseling Journal,* and *AMCHA Journal.*

Dr. Gross currently serves as consultant to Corondolet Management Institute and does training in the area of bereavement, grief, and loss.

Meet the Contributors

Valerie E. Appleton (deceased), EdD MFCC, ATR, NCC, was a professor in the Department of Counseling, Developmental, and Educational Psychology at Eastern Washington University, Spokane. She was the director of the Counselor Education Program and two CACREP accredited emphases: mental health and school counseling. Dr. Appleton was a licensed marriage, family and child counselor and registered art therapist since 1981. She served as executive director of the editorial board for the journal of the American Art Therapy Association, *Art Therapy.* Her research included the use of art in trauma intervention and the broader area of counselor education.

Walter Breaux III, PhD, LMFT, LPC, NCC, is an assistant professor of counseling at Columbus State University, Columbus, Georgia. He received his bachelor's degree in psychology from Xavier University of Louisiana where he also earned his master's degree in mental health counseling. Dr. Breaux earned his doctorate in counselor education from the University of New Orleans in 2005. He has worked in various community agencies as a substance abuse counselor and marriage and family therapist. His current research interests include school violence, addiction counseling, and brief counseling techniques.

Jonathan W. Carrier, MS, is a doctoral student in counseling psychology at the University of Louisville. His published work has covered many topics within counseling and psychology, including behavioral interventions, group counseling suicide assessment, and adolescent employment. Mr. Carrier's current research focuses on the relationship of adolescent employment to family functioning and psychological well-being. He hopes to obtain a professorship in counselor education or counseling psychology upon the completion of his doctorate.

Cass Dykeman, PhD, is an associate professor of counselor education at Oregon State University. He is a national certified counselor, master addictions counselor, and national certified school counselor. Dr. Dykeman received a master's degree in counseling from the University of Washington and a doctorate in counselor education from the University of Virginia. He served as principal investigator for a 1.5 million federal school-to-work research project. In addition, he is the author of books, book chapters, and scholarly journal articles. Dr. Dykeman is past president of both the Washington State Association for Counselor Education and Supervision and the Western Association for Counselor Education and Supervision. He is also past chairperson of the School Counseling Interest Network of the Association for Counselor Education and Supervision. His current research interests include school violence, addiction counseling, and brief counseling techniques.

Tim Evans, PhD, is a licensed marriage and family therapist in South Tampa, Florida, where he counsels individuals, couples, and families and works in the area of substance abuse. He is executive director of the Florida Adlerian Society and has taught for the Adler Institute in Riga, Latvia. Dr. Evans received his doctorate from the University of Georgia and completed an APA counseling psychology internship at the University of Delaware. Dr. Evans served on the board of directors for the International Committee for Adlerian Summer Schools and Institutes where he has taught Adlerian psychology. Dr. Evans is a diplomate in the North American Society of Adlerian Psychology. He has served on the editorial boards for the *International Journal of Action Methods: Psychodrama, Skills Training and Role Playing* and the *Journal of Individual Psychology.*

Mary Lou Bryant Frank, PhD, received her training as a family therapist and a counseling psychologist at Colorado State University. At Arizona State University in Tempe, she coordinated the eating disorders program, co-coordinated the master's and doctoral practicum training program, and concurrently taught in the counseling department. She established and taught in the master's program in community counseling at North Georgia College & State University. She contributed a chapter to Capuzzi and Gross's *Introduction to Group Counseling* (first and second editions) and has published in the *Journal of Counseling and Development.* Dr. Frank received a Distinguished Service Provider Award in Counseling for 1989–1990. She has been a consultant and speaker at eating disorders conferences, private hospitals, and universities. She has served as assistant academic dean and associate professor of psychology at Cinch Valley College of the University of Virginia. She was a professor and head of the Department of Psychology, Sociology, Philosophy, and Community Counseling at North Georgia College & State University. Currently, she serves as dean of undergraduate studies and general education at Kennesaw State University.

Melinda Haley, MS, NCC, is a nationally certified counselor and doctoral student at New Mexico State University. At NMSU, Ms. Haley teaches educational psychology and conducts research regarding the cultural factors that affect attitudes toward inmates. She has published in many different counseling subject areas. Her current research interests include, but are not limited to, personality disorders and personality development over the life span; criminology; the psychology of repeat offenders and variables that contribute to individual perceptions of inmates; multicultural issues in counseling, including racial bigotry; the psychology of ethnic cleansing; and posttraumatic stress disorders and efficacious factors in trauma counseling.

Richard J. Hazler, PhD, is a professor of counselor education at Penn State University. He earned his PhD at the University of Idaho. Previous professional work included positions as an elementary school teacher and counselor in schools, prisons, the military, and private practice. Dr. Hazler is editor of the Student Focus column for the American Counselor Association's *Counseling Today,* is on the editorial board of the *Counselor Education and Supervision Journal,* and is widely published on a variety of counseling and human development issues. His books include *The Emerging Professional Counselor: Student Dreams to Professional Realities,* 2nd edition (2003), *The Therapeutic Environment: Core Conditions for Facilitating Therapy* (2001) with Nick Barwick, *Helping in the Hallways: Advanced Strategies for Enhancing School Relationships* (1998), and *Breaking the Cycle of Violence: Interventions for Bullying and Victimization* (1996).

Barbara Herlihy, PhD, NCC, LPC, is a professor in the Counselor Education Program at the University of New Orleans. Dr. Herlihy has worked as a professional counselor in schools, community agencies, and private practice. Her scholarly work has focused primarily on ethics in counseling and reflects her additional interests in counseling theory, multicultural counseling, and clinical supervision. She has published many articles and book chapters on these topics. She is the coauthor of five books, most recently *Ethical, Legal, and Professional Issues in Counseling* (2005; with Ted Remley) and the *ACA Ethical Standards Casebook* (6th edition, in press, with Gerald Corey) Her work as a teacher, scholar, and counselor is grounded in feminist philosophy and practices.

Cynthia R. Kalodner, PhD, is associate professor and director of training of the counseling psychology doctoral program in the Department of Counseling, Rehabilitative Counseling, and Counseling Psychology at West Virginia University. She received her doctorate in counseling psychology from Pennsylvania State University in 1988. Previously, she was an assistant professor in the counseling psychology program at the University of Akron. Dr. Kalodner also completed a postdoctoral fellowship in public health at Johns Hopkins University. Her present research focuses primarily on eating disorders, including cognitive-behavioral approaches to understand and treat women with eating disorders, media influence on eating disorders, and prevention issues.

Vivian J. Carroll McCollum, PhD, is a professor of counseling and program chair at Albany State University. She received her doctorate in marriage and family therapy from St. Louis University. Her professional specialty is multicultural issues in counseling and the effects of client-counselor interaction in school counseling, career counseling, and family therapy. Dr. McCollum is active in the American Counseling Association, receiving the Ohana Award at the 2005 convention for her work in social justice. Dr. McCollum has over 20 years of experience as a college counselor, school counselor, private practitioner, and counselor educator. She has made contributions recently to the *Journal of Counseling and Development* and the *Journal of School Counseling.*

Al Milliren, EdD, is professor of counseling education in the School of Education at the University of Texas of the Permian Basin. He is also the director of education for the West Texas Institute for Adlerian Studies in Odessa. Dr. Milliren earned his bachelor's degree from

Bradley University where he also earned a master's degree in counseling and guidance. He received his doctorate in educational psychology from the University of Illinois, Urbana–Champaign in 1971, specializing in elementary school counseling. Dr. Milliren is a diplomate in the North American Society of Adlerian Psychology (NASAP) and is currently the vice president of NASAP. Dr Milliren has more than 40 years of experience working with Adlerian psychology as a professional school counselor, as a counselor in private practice, and as a university professor. He has many publications and presentations to his credit in the areas of both counseling and education.

Nathanael G. Mitchell, MEd, is a doctoral student in counseling psychology at the University of Louisville. Mr. Mitchell recently copresented research on the psychological correlates of bullying and victimization as well as research on the family functioning of adolescent workers. His current research activities include childhood obesity and critical thinking. Upon completion of his doctorate, he hopes to obtain a professorship in counseling psychology.

John F. Newbauer, EdD, is a health service provider in psychology and holds diplomates in the North American Society of Adlerian Psychology and the American Board of Psychological Specialties (psychological testing). He is also a member and fellow of the American College of Forensic Examiners. Dr. Newbauer is director of treatment and diagnostic services for the Allen County Juvenile Center in Fort Wayne, Indiana, a division of the Allen Superior Court. His practice focuses on older children and adolescents and their parents, and he performs forensic evaluations related to juvenile delinquency issues. Dr. Newbauer is also on the core faculty of the Adler School of Professional Psychology and on the faculty of the International Comittee of Adlerian Summer Schools and Institutes. Dr. Newbauer is a past president of the North American Society of Adlerian Psychology.

Gregory J. Novie, PhD, has been in private practice as a psychologist since 1986. His areas of research interest include countertransference with borderline and narcissistic conditions. Dr. Novie received his master's degree in rehabilitation counseling from Southern Illinois University and his doctorate in educational psychology from Arizona State University in Tempe. He received his psychoanalytic training from, and is a member of, the Southwest Center for Psychoanalytic Studies. He also is a member of the division of psychoanalysis of the American Psychological Association and regularly contributes clinical research writing to the division's quarterly publication. His latest article (March, 2005) is titled "The long good-bye: Successful termination in a borderline patient."

Manivong Ratts, PhD, received his doctorate in the counselor education and supervision program at Oregon State University (Corvallis, Oregon). His areas of research include social justice, school counseling, advocacy competencies, career development, and cultural competence. Mr. Ratts received his master's degree in counseling from Oregon State University. He is a licensed school counselor, licensed professional counselor (Illinois), and national certified counselor. He is also the counselor representative of Counselors for Social Justice, a division of the American Counseling Association.

Donna M. Roy, BA, MS, received a bachelor of arts in German from the University of Maine at Orono and a master's degree in international administration from the School of International Training in Brattleboro, Vermont. She has 20 years of experience in teaching, training, and mentoring adolescents and adults. In her private counseling practice, she draws from advanced professional training in Hakomi body-centered psychotherapy as well as experiential study of dream states, ritual, and ceremony. Ms. Roy also received a master's degree in counselor education, specializing in community counseling from Portland State University.

Deborah J. Rubel, PhD, is an assistant professor of counselor education at Oregon State University. She received her master of counseling degree in mental health counseling and her PhD in counselor education and counseling from Idaho State University. Her primary interest is diversity issues in group work. She also has a passion for counseling theories and a commitment to teaching counseling students how to critically evaluate traditional theories from a multicultural and social justice perspective and to adapt them for use with a variety of populations.

Susan E. Schwartz, PhD, is a Jungian analyst trained at the C. G. Jung Institute in Zurich, Switzerland, with a doctorate in clinical psychology. She is a senior analyst, teacher, and secretary at the C. G. Jung Institute in New Mexico. She gives lectures and workshops worldwide on various aspects of Jungian analytical psychology and has a private practice in Scottsdale, Arizona.

Ann Vernon, PhD, LMHC, is professor and coordinator of counseling at the University of Northern Iowa. Dr. Vernon also has a private practice where she specializes in working with children and adolescents. She has published many books, chapters, and articles, including *Counseling Children and Adolescents, What Works When with Children and Adolescents,* and *Thinking, Feeling, Behaving.* In addition to teaching and doing therapy, Dr. Vernon presents workshops throughout the world on applications of rational emotive behavior therapy with children and adolescents and on other topics related to working with children. Dr. Vernon has assumed professional leadership roles in state, regional and national counseling associations.

Robert E. Wubbolding, EdD, clinical counselor and psychologist, is the director of the Center for Reality Therapy in Cincinnati, the director of training for the William Glasser Institute in Chatsworth, California, and professor emeritus of counseling at Xavier University. Author of 10 books on reality therapy, including *Reality Therapy for the 21st Century, Counselling with Reality Therapy,* and *A Set of Directions for Putting and Keeping Yourself Together,* he has taught reality therapy in North America, Asia, Europe, Australia, and the Middle East. His work has focused on making reality therapy a cross-cultural approach with other applications to management, addictions, and corrections. He has extended the central procedure of self-evaluation to include 22 applications based on choice theory. At the present time, Dr. Wubbolding's interest is to review research studies validating the use of reality therapy, thereby rendering reality therapy respected as a freestanding and validated system of counseling. In the past, he has been an elementary and high school counselor, a high school teacher, an administrator of adult basic education, and a correctional counselor.

Preface

Counseling and Psychotherapy: Theories and Interventions, Fourth Edition, presents a variety of theories and conceptual frameworks for understanding the parameters of the helping relationship. These parameters can include models for viewing personality development; explaining past behavior; predicting future behavior; understanding current behavior; diagnosing and treatment planning; assessing client motivations, needs, and unresolved issues; and identifying strategies and interventions for use during counseling and psychotherapy processes.

Theories help organize data and provide guidelines for the prevention and intervention efforts of counselors and therapists. They direct a professional helper's attention and observations and offer constructs, terminology, and viewpoints that can be understood by colleagues and used during supervision and consultation sessions. Theory directly influences the interventions used by counselors and therapists to promote a client's new insight, new behavior, and new approaches to relationships and problem solving. The greater a counselor's or therapist's awareness of the strengths and possibilities inherent in the many theoretical frames of reference, the greater the potential for understanding the uniqueness of a particular client and for developing the most effective treatment plan.

This book is unique in both format and content. All the contributing authors are experts who provide state-of-the-art information about theories of counseling and psychotherapy (see the Meet the Contributors section for their backgrounds). In addition, each chapter discusses applications of the theory as it relates to one particular case study—a hypothetical client named Jonathan who is introduced on page 71. This book also includes information that is sometimes not addressed in other counseling and psychotherapy textbooks, such as a chapter that focuses on the importance of achieving a personal and professional identity before beginning work with clients, a chapter on feminist theory, a chapter on body-centered counseling and psychotherapy, and a chapter on transpersonal theory. The book's unique approach enhances its readability and should increase reader interest in the material.

Features of the Text

This book is designed for students who are beginning their study of individual counseling and psychotherapy. It presents a comprehensive overview of each of the following theories: psychoanalytic, Jungian, Adlerian, existential, person-centered, Gestalt, cognitive-behavior, rational emotive behavior therapy, reality, family, feminist, body-centered, and transpersonal. Each theory is addressed from the perspective of background, human nature, major constructs, applications (including a discussion of the goals of counseling and psychotherapy, the process of change, traditional intervention strategies, and brief intervention strategies), clients with serious mental health issues, cross-cultural considerations, evaluation (which evaluates both the supporting research and the limitations of the theory), a summary chart, and a case study consistent with the theoretical model under discussion.

One text cannot adequately address all the factors connected with a given theory; entire texts have been written on each of the theories in this book. This text does, however, attempt to provide a consistent approach to analyzing and studying each theory and includes examples of how to apply the theory to a case study.

The format of this text is based on the contributions of the coeditors, who conceptualized the content and wrote the first two chapters, as well as the contributions of 21 authors selected for their expertise in various theories. Each chapter contains theoretical and applied content. The text is divided into the following four parts: Foundations for Individual Counseling and Psychotherapy, Theories of Counseling and Psychotherapy, Nontraditional Approaches, and Integrative Approaches.

Part I, Foundations for Individual Counseling and Psychotherapy, consists of chapters 1, 2, and 3. Chapter 1 offers a general perspective about the helping relationship and individual counseling as well as descriptions of brief approaches to counseling and psychotherapy. This introductory information is followed by chapter 2, Achieving a Personal and Professional Identity, emphasizes that it is not possible for a counselor or therapist to make use of a theory or conceptual framework unless he or she is self-assured and clear about personal boundaries. Chapter 3, Diversity and Social Justice Issues in Counseling and Psychotherapy, sets the stage for developing awareness of the limitations of traditional Western theories and subsequent cross-cultural discussions in each of the theory chapters.

Part II, Theories of Counseling and Psychotherapy (chapters 4 through 14), focuses on 11 major approaches to working with individuals. Each of these chapters—Psychoanalytic Theory, Jungian Analytical Theory, Adlerian Theory, Existential Theory, Person-Centered Theory, Gestalt Theory, Cognitive-Behavior Theories, Rational Emotive Behavior Therapy, Reality Therapy Theory, Family Theory, and Feminist Theory—presents the theory and then applies the theory to the case study of Jonathan.

Part III, Nontraditional Approaches (chapters 15 and 16), introduces theoretical approaches that stem from Eastern philosophy and transpersonal psychology.

Part IV, Integrative Approaches, considers how the expressive arts, narrative, and symbolism can be used within the context of any theoretical orientation of the counselor or therapist.

New to This Edition

This fourth edition features new material that enhances overall content. A new chapter on diversity and social justice issues in counseling and psychotherapy (chapter 3) presents state-of-the-art information and perspectives for counselors and therapists who will be practicing with increasingly diverse client populations. The updated chapter on feminist theory (chapter 14) traces the evolution of feminist theory and addresses issues involved in theories that are based on male developmental models. The revised chapter on family theory (chapter 13) discusses how counselors and therapists engaging clients in individual work must keep in mind the systemic variables that influence clients and the fact that some clients may need family counseling and psychotherapy as part of a comprehensive treatment plan.

In response to the increasing interest in alternative approaches to counseling and psychotherapy, this edition includes a revised chapter on body-centered counseling and psychotherapy (chapter 15) as well as a new chapter on transpersonal theory (chapter 16). Few textbooks of this nature address conceptual frameworks that are nontraditional or external to the mainstream models usually adopted by practitioners and academicians in Western culture. The concluding chapter of this edition describes integrative approaches to counseling and psychotherapy. The possibility of using expressive arts, narrative, and symbolic modalities within the context of a given theoretical framework is new to this text.

Readers of the fourth edition will find the Companion Website (www.prenhall.com/capuzzi) helpful in the process of mastering the content of the text. This site is designed to assist the reader in a variety of ways. For each chapter, the following information is provided: a chapter overview, lists of key terms and key people, suggested classroom exercises designed to enhance instruction as well as to provide experiential components for the learning experience, individual exercises that can be completed, questions for study and discussion, and URLs. Some professors who adopt this text may tie some of the course assignments and requirements to the content of this website. In addition, PowerPoint® slides are available for use by professors who have adopted the text.

We, the coeditors, and the 21 other contributors have made every effort to present current information and content focused on both theory and applications. It is our hope that the fourth edition of *Counseling and Psychotherapy: Theories and Interventions* will provide the foundation that students need to make decisions about follow-up study of specific theories as well as about the development of their own personal theory of counseling and psychotherapy.

Acknowledgments

We would like to thank the other 21 authors who contributed their time and expertise to the development of this textbook for professionals interested in individual counseling and psychotherapy. We also thank our families who supported and encouraged our writing and editing efforts. Thanks to our editors and other staff members at Merrill/Prentice Hall for their collaborative and thorough approach to the editing and production of this textbook. Without the dedicated efforts of this group of colleagues, we know this book could not have been published.

We are also grateful to the reviewers for their helpful comments and suggestions for improving this edition: Markus Bidell, University of New Mexico; James A. Gold, State University College at Buffalo; Constance R. Matthews, Pennslyvania State University; Susan Sears, Ohio State University; and Jennifer Walker, Saint Louis University.

Brief Contents

Contents

Note: Every effort has been made to provide accurate and current Internet information in this book. However, the Internet and information posted on it are constantly changing, so it is inevitable that some of the Internet addresses listed in this textbook will change.

Part I

Foundations for Individual Counseling and Psychotherapy

Chapters

Counseling and psychotherapy encompass a number of relationship and personal and professional modalities in which the counselor or therapist needs to be proficient. These modalities include the creation of essential core conditions that serve as a foundation for the establishment of a helping relationship and as prerequisites to change on the part of the client. These modalities also include the achievement of a personal and professional identity that will enable the counselor or therapist to facilitate the process of counseling and psychotherapy. This part of the text addresses two other modalities: (1) brief approaches to counseling and psychotherapy, which are a rapidly developing area that has been encouraged by managed care; and (2) counselor awareness of diversity and social justice issues, which is important in the context of the counseling and psychotherapy process.

The helping relationship is the foundation on which the process of counseling and psychotherapy is based. It is not possible to use the concepts and associated interventions of a specific theory unless such applications are made in the context of a relationship that promotes trust, insight, and behavioral change. Chapter 1, "Helping Relationships: From Core Conditions to Brief Approaches," is designed to aid you in the development and delivery of the helping relationship. To achieve this purpose, the helping relationship is presented in terms of definitions and descriptions, stages, core conditions and personal characteristics, helping strategies, and applications in diverse populations. Chapter 1 also introduces the importance of considering brief approaches to counseling and psychotherapy. The chapter shows how traditional theories can be adapted for briefer, more focused work in the counseling and psychotherapy process. In chapters 4 through 17, authors provide follow-up information by discussing both traditional and brief interventions in the applications sections of their chapters.

Chapter 2, "Achieving a Personal and Professional Identity," discusses why the personal and professional identity of the helping professional must be addressed before and during the process of studying and applying individual approaches to counseling and psychotherapy. The chapter addresses the importance of health and wellness for the helping professional, recognition of values and cultural bias in theory and practice, awareness of the daily world of the practitioner, and achievement of perspective and balance between the helping individual as a person and as a professional. The chapter also includes a discussion about developing a personal theory.

In a discussion of the limitations of traditional counseling theories and practices, Chapter 3, "Diversity and Social Justice Issues in Counseling and Psychotherapy," enhances counselor or therapist awareness of the many diversity and social justice issues that need to be addressed in the context of the counseling and psychotherapy process. The chapter provides this context in several ways: by clarifying key concepts and reviewing the history of diversity and social justice issues in counseling; by increasing understanding of how diversity influences individual and group functioning; by increasing awareness of how diversity may influence the counseling and psychotherapy process; by providing several perspectives on diversity-appropriate interventions; and by suggesting how counselors and therapists can develop self-awareness, knowledge of diverse populations, and counseling skills relevant to diversity and social justice.

As these chapters indicate, counselors and therapists must achieve high levels of competence, effectiveness, and expertise to create a helping relationship beneficial to clients. They must also develop the ability to know themselves from both personal and professional perspectives and to become sensitive to diversity and social justice issues as they affect their work with clients. We have made every attempt to introduce these topics in the chapters included in this section of the text. You are encouraged to do additional reading and follow-up course work and to commit to personal counseling or therapy to achieve the purposes outlined in these chapters.

CHAPTER 1

Helping Relationships: From Core Dimensions to Brief Approaches

Douglas R. Gross
Professor Emeritus
Arizona State University

David Capuzzi
Johns Hopkins University
Professor Emeritus
Portland State University

The **helping relationship** appears to be a cornerstone on which all effective helping rests (Bertolino & O'Hanlon, 2002; Combs & Gonzalez, 1994; Halverson & Miars, 2005; Miars & Halverson, 2001; Purkey & Schmidt, 1987; Seligman, 2001). Words such as *integral, necessary,* and *mandatory* are used to describe this relationship and its importance in the ultimate effectiveness of the **helping process.** Even though different theoretical systems and approaches use different words to describe the helping relationship (see chapters 4 through 17), each addresses the significance of the relationship in facilitating client change. Kottler and Brown (1992), in their *Introduction to Therapeutic Counseling,* made the following comments regarding the significance of this relationship:

> Regardless of the setting in which you practice counseling, whether in a school, agency, hospital, or private practice, the relationships you develop with your clients are crucial to any progress you might make together. For without a high degree of intimacy and trust between two people, very little can be accomplished. (p. 64)

In further support of the significance of the helping relationship, Brammer and MacDonald (1996) said:

> The helping relationship is dynamic, meaning that it is constantly changing at verbal and nonverbal levels. The relationship is the principle process vehicle for both helper and helpee to express and fulfill their needs, as well as to mesh helpee problems with helper expertise. Relationship emphasizes the affective mode, because relationship is commonly defined as the inferred emotional quality of the interaction. (p. 52)

The ideas expressed in these two statements describe the essential value of the helping relationship in the process of counseling or psychotherapy and the significant role that the counselor or therapist plays in developing this relationship. Through this relationship, client change occurs. Although the creation of this relationship is not the end goal of the process, it certainly is the means by which other goals are met. The relationship serves as the framework within which effective helping takes place.

This chapter serves two purposes. First, it will aid you in understanding the various factors that affect the helping relationship: definitions and descriptions, stages, core dimensions, strategies, and issues of diversity. Second, the chapter will introduce you to brief approaches to counseling and therapy. In subsequent chapters, authors discuss brief approaches as applied to their specific theory. The information presented in this chapter is intended to help you understand the dynamics of the helping relationship and their application in both theory-specific and brief approaches and to aid you in incorporating these dynamics into your chosen theoretical approach.

HELPING RELATIONSHIPS: DEFINITIONS AND DESCRIPTIONS

Although agreed-upon definitions and descriptions of the helping relationship should be easy to find, such is not the case. Despite the importance of this relationship in the overall helping process, a perusal of textbooks and articles dealing with counseling and psychotherapy shows the lack of a common definition. **Rogers** (1961), for example, defined a helping relationship as one "in which at least one of the parties has the intent of promoting the growth, development, maturity, improved functioning and improved coping with life of the other" (p. 39). Okun (1992) stated that "the development of a warm, trustful relationship between the helper and helpee underlies any strategy or approach to the helping process and therefore, is a basic condition for the success of any helping process" (p. 14). According to Miars and Halverson (2001), "the ultimate goal of a professional helping relationship should be to promote the development of more effective and adaptive behavior in the clients" (p. 51).

It is easy to see the difficulty in categorically stating an accepted definition or description of the helping relationship, regardless of which of these statements you choose to embrace. Yet despite differences, each description carries with it directions and directives aimed at a single goal: the enhancement and encouragement of client change. The following definitive characteristics of the helping relationship embrace this goal and describe our conceptualization of this relationship:

- A relationship initially structured by the counselor or therapist but open to cooperative restructuring based on the needs of the client
- A relationship that begins with the initial meeting and continues through termination

- A relationship in which all persons involved perceive the existence of trust, caring, concern, and commitment and act accordingly
- A relationship in which the needs of the client are given priority over the needs of the counselor or therapist
- A relationship that provides for the personal growth of all persons involved
- A relationship that provides the safety needed for self-exploration of all persons involved
- A relationship that promotes the potential of all persons involved

The major responsibility in creating this relationship rests initially with the counselor or therapist; demands for client involvement and commitment increase over time. It is a shared process, and only through shared efforts will the relationship develop and flourish. Development evolves in stages that take the relationship from initiation to closure.

HELPING RELATIONSHIPS: STAGES

The helping relationship is a constant throughout the counseling or psychotherapeutic process. The definitive characteristics we presented in the previous section indicate that the relationship must be present at the initial meeting between the client and the counselor or therapist and continue through closure. Accepting the helping relationship as a constant throughout the helping process leads to visualizing this process from a developmental perspective. This development can best be viewed in terms of a narrow path whose limits are established by the client's fear, anxiety, and resistance. Such client reactions should not be seen as lack of commitment to change; rather, they need to be understood in terms of the unknown nature of this developing alliance and the fact that this may be the first time the client has experienced this type of interaction. These reactions are often shared by the counselor or therapist, based on his or her level of experience. The path broadens through the development of trust, safety, and understanding as the relationship develops. The once narrow path becomes a boulevard along which two persons move courageously toward their final destination—change. Movement along this broadening path is described by various authors in terms of stages or phases. Osipow, Walsh, and Tosi (1980), in discussing the stages of the helping relationship, stated:

> Persons who experience the process of personal counseling seem to progress through several stages. First, there is an increased awareness of self and others. Second, there is an expanded exploration of self and environment (positive and negative behavioral tendencies). Third, there is increased commitment to self-enhancing behavior and its implementation. Fourth, there is an internalization of new and more productive thoughts and actions. Fifth, there is a stabilization of new behavior. (p. 73)

Brammer (1985) divided this developmental process into two phases, each with four distinctive stages. Phase 1, titled "Building Relationships," includes preparing the client and opening the relationship, clarifying the problem or concern of the client, structuring the process, and building a relationship. Phase 2, titled "Facilitating Positive Action," involves exploration, consolidation, planning, and termination.

Purkey and Schmidt (1987) set forth three stages in building the helping relationship, each containing four steps. Stage 1, "Preparation," includes having the desire for a relationship, expecting good things, preparing the setting, and reading the situation. Stage 2 is "Initiating Responding" and includes choosing caringly, acting appropriately, honoring the client, and ensuring reception. The third and final stage, "Follow-up," includes interpreting responses, negotiating positions, evaluating the process, and developing trust.

Egan (2002) stated that the helping relationship minimally can be broken down into three phases: relationship building, challenging the client to find ways to change, and facilitating positive client action. The goal in the first phase is to build a foundation of mutual trust and client understanding. In the second phase, the counselor challenges the client to "try on" new ways of thinking, feeling, and behaving. In the third phase, the counselor aids the client in facilitating actions that lead toward change and growth in the client's life outside the counseling relationship.

Authors such as Corey & Corey (1993), Gladding (2003), Hackney & Cormier (1996), and Halverson & Miars (2005) provide other models of the developmental nature of the stages of the helping relationship. Although the terms used to describe stages may differ, there seems to be a consistency across these models: Movement occurs from initiation of the relationship through a clinically based working stage to a termination stage. The following developmental stages show our conceptualization of this relationship-building process and are based on the consistency found in our research and our clinical experience.

- *Stage 1: Relationship development.* This stage includes the initial meeting of client and counselor or therapist, rapport building, information gathering, goal determination, and informing the client about the conditions under which counseling will take place (e.g., confidentiality, taping, and roles of counselor or therapist and client).
- *Stage 2: Extended exploration.* This stage builds on the foundation established in the first stage. Through selected techniques, theoretical approaches, and strategies, the counselor or therapist explores in depth the emotional and cognitive dynamics of the person of the client, problem parameters, previously tried solutions, decision-making capabilities, and a reevaluation of the goals determined in Stage 1.
- *Stage 3: Problem resolution.* This stage, which depends on information gained during the previous two stages, is characterized by increased activity for all parties involved. The counselor's or therapist's activities include facilitating, demonstrating, instructing, and providing a safe environment for the development of change. The client's activities focus on reevaluation, emotional and cognitive dynamics, trying out new behaviors (both inside and outside of the sessions), and discarding behaviors that do not meet goals.
- *Stage 4: Termination and follow-up.* This stage is the closing stage of the helping relationship and is cooperatively determined by all persons involved. Methods and procedures for follow-up are determined before the last meeting.

Keep in mind that people do not automatically move through these four stages in a lockstep manner. The relationship may end at any one of the stages based on decisions made by the client, the counselor or therapist, or both. Nor is it possible to identify the amount of time that "should" be devoted to any particular stage. With certain clients, much more time will need to be devoted to specific stages. Brown and Srebalus (1988), in addressing the tentative nature of relationship stages, issued the following caution:

Before we describe a common sequence of events in counseling, it important to note that many clients, for one reason or another, will not complete all the stages of counseling. The process will be abandoned prematurely, not because something went wrong, but because of factors external to the counselor-client relationship. For example, the school year may end for a student client, or a client or counselor may move away to accept a new job. When counseling is in process and must abruptly end, the participants will feel the incompleteness and loss. (p. 69)

Viewing the helping relationship as an ongoing process that is composed of developmental stages provides counselors and therapists with a structural framework within which they can function effectively. Inside this framework fit the core conditions and strategies that serve the goals of movement through the relationship process and enhancement and encouragement of client change. These core conditions and strategies are discussed in the following two sections.

HELPING RELATIONSHIPS: CORE CONDITIONS

The concept of basic or **core condition** related to the helping relationship has its basis in the early work of Rogers (1957) and the continued work of authors such as Carkhuff and Barenson (1967), Combs (1986), Egan (2002), Ivey (1998), Patterson (1974) and **Truax and Carkhuff** (1967). The concept incorporates a set of conditions which, when present, enhance the effectiveness of the helping relationship. These conditions, which vary in terminology from author to author, generally include the following: **empathic understanding, respect and positive regard, genuineness and congruence, concreteness, warmth,** and **immediacy.**

In reviewing this listing, note that the concept of core or basic conditions relates directly to various personal characteristics or behaviors that the counselor or therapist brings to and incorporates into the helping relationship. It is difficult to pinpoint how such characteristics or behaviors develop. Are they the result of life experiences, classroom instruction, or some combination of both? Our experience in education favors the combination explanation. Core conditions or behaviors must already be present to some degree in our students for our instruction to enhance or expand them.

The remainder of this section deals with core conditions and relates them directly to the personal characteristics or behaviors of counselors or therapists that should enhance their ability to effectively use these conditions in the process of helping. Although definitions, emphases, and applications of core conditions differ across theoretical systems, there appears to be agreement about their effectiveness in facilitating change in the overall helping relationship (Brammer, Abrego, & Shostrom, 1993; Brems, 2000; Gladding, 2001, 2003; Murphy & Dillon, 2003; Prochaska & Norcorss, 2003; Sexton & Whiston, 1994; Thompson, 1996).

Empathic Understanding

Empathic understanding is the ability to feel *with* clients as opposed to feeling *for* clients. It is the ability to understand feelings, thoughts, ideas, and experiences by viewing them from the client's frame of reference. The counselor or therapist must be able to enter the client's world, understand the myriad of aspects that make up that world, and communicate this understanding so that the client perceives that he or she has been heard accurately.

Egan (2002) identified both primary and advanced levels of empathic understanding. At the primary level, empathic understanding is the ability to understand, identify, and communicate feelings and meanings that are at the surface level of the client's disclosures. At the advanced level, it is the ability to understand, identify, and communicate feelings and meanings that are buried, hidden, or beyond the immediate reach of a client. Such feelings and meanings are more often covert rather than overt client expressions.

Personal characteristics or behaviors that enhance a counselor's or therapist's ability to provide empathic understanding include, but are not limited to, the following:

- Knowledge and awareness of one's own values, attitudes, and beliefs and the emotional and behavioral impact they have on one's own life
- Knowledge and awareness of one's own feelings and emotional response patterns and how they manifest themselves in interactive patterns
- Knowledge and awareness of one's own life experiences and one's personal reactions to those experiences
- Capacity and willingness to communicate these personal reactions to one's clients

Respect and Positive Regard

Respect and positive regard are defined as the belief in each client's innate worth and potential and the ability to communicate this belief in the helping relationship. This belief, once communicated, provides clients with positive reinforcement relative to their innate ability to take responsibility for their own growth, change, goal determination, decision making, and eventual problem solution. Respect and positive regard form an empowering process that delivers a message to clients that they are able to take control of their lives and, with facilitative assistance from the counselor or therapist, foster change. Communicating and demonstrating respect for clients takes many forms. According to Baruth and Robinson (1987), it "is often communicated by what the counselor does not do or say. In other words, by not offering to intervene for someone, one is communicating a belief in the individual's ability to 'do' for himself or herself" (p. 85).

Personal characteristics or behaviors that enhance a counselor's or therapist's ability to provide respect and positive regard include, but are not limited to, the following:

- Capacity to respect oneself
- Capacity to view oneself as having worth and potential
- Capacity to model and communicate this positive self-image to clients
- Capacity to recognize one's own control needs, and the ability to use this recognition in a manner that allows clients to direct their own lives

Genuineness and Congruence

Genuineness and congruence describe the ability to be **authentic** in the helping relationship. The ability to be real as opposed to artificial, to behave as one feels as opposed to playing the role of the helper, and to be congruent in terms of actions and words are further descriptors of this core condition. According to **Boy** and **Pine** (1982),

> the counselor's genuineness is imperative if the client is to achieve genuineness. If the counselor is truly genuine, he or she engages in counseling attitudes and behaviors that influence clients to be genuine. The authentic counselor feels compelled to be involved in facilitative behaviors that have

meaning and relevance for clients rather than to adopt superficial and mechanical behaviors that have little or no value. (p. 8)

Implicit in this statement is the idea of the counselor's ability to communicate and demonstrate this genuineness, not only to enhance the relationship but also to model this core condition so that clients can develop greater authenticity in their interactions with others.

Personal characteristics or behaviors that enhance a counselor's or therapist's ability to prove genuineness and congruence include, but are not limited to, the following:

- Capacity for self-awareness and the ability to demonstrate this capacity through words and actions
- Understanding of one's own motivational patterns and ability to use them productively in the helping relationship
- Ability to present one's thoughts, feelings, and actions in a consistent, unified, and honest manner
- Capacity for self-confidence and ability to communicate this capacity in a facilitative way in the helping relationship

Concreteness

Concreteness is the ability not only to see the incomplete picture that clients paint with their words, but also to communicate to clients the figures, images, and structures that will complete the picture. In the process of exploring problems or issues, clients often present a somewhat distorted view of the actual situation. Concreteness enables the counselor or therapist to help clients identify the distortions in the situation and fit them together in such a way that clients are able to view the situation in a more realistic fashion. Concreteness helps clients clarify vague issues, focus on specific topics, reduce degrees of ambiguity, and channel their energies into more productive avenues of problem solution.

Personal characteristics and behaviors that enhance a counselor's or therapist's ability to provide degrees of concreteness include, but are not limited to, the following:

- Capacity for abstract thinking and ability to read between the lines
- Willingness to risk being incorrect as one attempts to fill in the empty spaces
- Belief in one's own competence in analyzing and sorting through the truths and partial truths in clients' statements
- Ability to be objective while working with clients in arriving at the reality of clients' situations

Warmth

Warmth is the ability to communicate and demonstrate genuine caring and concern for clients. Using this ability, counselors and therapists convey their acceptance of clients, their desire for clients' well-being, and their sincere interest in finding workable solutions to the problems clients present. The demeanor of the counselor or therapist is often the main avenue for communicating and demonstrating warmth. Often it is through nonverbal behaviors—a smile, a touch, tone of voice, a facial expression—that genuine caring and concern are communicated. The counselor's or therapist's capacity for transmitting concerns and caring to clients, either verbally or nonverbally, enables clients to experience, often for the first time, a truly accepting relationship.

Personal characteristics or behaviors that enhance a counselor's or therapist's ability to demonstrate warmth include, but are not limited to, the following:

- Capacity for self-care and ability to demonstrate this capacity in actions and words
- Capacity for self-acceptance, basing this acceptance on one's assets and liabilities
- Desire for one's own well-being and ability to demonstrate this desire through words and actions
- Desire to find, and successful personal experience in finding, workable solutions to one's own problems, and ability to communicate this desire through words and actions.

Immediacy

Immediacy is the ability to deal with the here-and-now factors that operate within the helping relationship. These factors are described as overt and covert interactions that take place between the client and the counselor or therapist. A client's anger at a counselor or therapist, the latter's frustration with a client, and the feelings of the client and counselor or therapist for each other are all examples of factors that need to be addressed as they occur and develop. Addressing such issues in the safety of the helping relationship should help participants in two ways: to gain insight into personal behavioral patterns that may be conducive or not conducive to growth, and to use this insight in relationships outside the helping relationship.

Dealing with interactions can be threatening, as it is often easier to deal with relationships in the abstract and avoid personal encounters. A counselor or therapist needs to be able to use the factor of immediacy to show clients the benefits that can be gained by dealing with issues at they arise. According to Egan (2002), immediacy not only clears the air but also is a valuable learning experience.

Personal characteristics or behaviors that enhance a counselor's or therapist's ability to use immediacy effectively include, but are not limited to, the following:

- Capacity for perceptive accuracy in interpreting one's own feelings for, thoughts about, and behaviors toward clients
- Capacity for perceptive accuracy in interpreting clients' feelings for, thoughts about, and behaviors toward the counselor or therapist
- Capacity for and willingness to deal with one's own issues related to clients on a personal as opposed to an abstract level
- Willingness to confront both oneself and clients with what one observes to be happening in the helping relationship

HELPING RELATIONSHIPS: STRATEGIES

The previous section identified the core conditions that need to be present for the effective development of the helping relationship. Differences between these core conditions and **strategies** are the subject of this section.

The core conditions relate to specific dynamics present in the personality and behavioral makeup of counselors or therapists that they are able to communicate to clients. The term *strategies* refers to skills gained through education and experience. These skills define and direct what counselors or therapists do within the relationship to attain specific results and to move the helping relationship from problem identification to problem resolution.

Various terms have been used to address this aspect of the helping relationship. Some authors prefer the term *strategies* (Combs & Avila, 1985; Cormier and Cormier, 1991; Gilliland, James, & Bowman, 1989; Hackney & Cormier, 1994); others prefer *skills* (Halverson & Miars, 2005; Hansen, Rossberg, & Cramer, 1994; Ivey, 1998); still others prefer the term *techniques* (Belkin, 1980; Brown & Pate, 1983; Osipow et al., 1980). The terms, however, are interchangeable.

We decided to use the term *strategies,* which denotes not only deliberative planning but also action processes that make the planning operational. We think that both factors are necessary. For the purpose of discussion, we grouped the strategies in the following categories:

- Strategies that build rapport and encourage client dialogue
- Strategies that aid in data gathering
- Strategies that add depth and enhance the relationship

Note that specific strategies, such as those stemming from various theoretical systems, are not included in this section. They will be presented in chapters 4 through 17, which deal with specific theories. It is also important to understand that much overlap occurs between these arbitrary divisions. Strategies designed to build rapport and encourage client dialogue may also gather data and enhance relationships.

Strategies That Build Rapport and Encourage Client Dialogue

This group of strategies consists of the active listening strategies that enhance the listening capabilities of counselors and therapists. When used effectively, active listening strategies provide an environment in which clients have the opportunity to talk and to share their feelings and thoughts with the assurance that they will be heard. By using such strategies, counselors and therapists enhance their chances of providing such an environment.

Active listening strategies include **attending** and **encouraging, restating, paraphrasing, reflecting content** and **perception checking,** and **summarizing.** The following paragraphs present explanations and examples of these strategies.

Attending and Encouraging. In these strategies the counselor's or therapist's posture, visual contact, gestures, facial expressions, and words indicate to clients that they are being heard and that the counselor or therapist wishes them to continue sharing information.

Example

Encouraging	COUNSELOR/THERAPIST (*smiling*): Please tell me what brought you in today.
	CLIENT: I'm having a hard time trying to put my life in order. I'm very lonely and bored, and I can't seem to maintain a lasting relationship.
Attending and Encouraging	COUNSELOR/THERAPIST (*learning forward*): Please tell me more.
	CLIENT: Every time I think I have a chance of developing a relationship, I screw it up by saying or doing something dumb.
Encouraging	COUNSELOR/THERAPIST (*nodding*): This is helpful, please go on.

Restating and Paraphrasing. These strategies enable a counselor or therapist to serve as a sounding board for the client by feeding back thoughts and feelings that clients verbalize. Restating involves repeating the exact words used by the client. Paraphrasing repeats the thoughts and feelings of the client, but the words are those of the counselor or therapist.

Example

	CLIENT: I don't know why I do these dumb things. It's almost as if I did not want a relationship.
Restating	COUNSELOR/THERAPIST: You don't know why you do dumb things. It may be that you don't want a relationship.
	CLIENT: I do want a relationship, but each time I get close I seem to do everything in my power to destroy it.
Paraphrasing	COUNSELOR/THERAPIST: You are very sure that you want a relationship, but each time you have the opportunity you sabotage your chances.

Reflecting Content and Reflecting Feeling. These strategies enable the counselor or therapist to provide feedback to the client regarding both the ideas (content) and the emotions (feelings) that the client is expressing. By reflecting content, the counselor or therapist shares his or her perceptions of the thoughts that the client is expressing. This can be done either by using the client's words or by changing the words to better reflect the counselor's or therapist's perceptions. By reflecting feelings, a counselor or therapist goes beyond the ideas and thoughts expressed by the client and responds to the feelings or emotions behind those words.

Example

	CLIENT: *Sabotage* is a good word. It's like I see what I want, but instead of moving toward it, I take a different path that leads nowhere.
Reflecting Content	COUNSELOR/THERAPIST: You have a good idea of what you want, but when you see it developing, you turn and walk the other way.
	CLIENT: I am not sure *walk* is the right word. *Run* is more descriptive of what I do, and all the time I'm looking back to see if anyone is following.
Reflecting Feeling	COUNSELOR/THERAPIST: You're afraid of getting close to someone, so you put as much distance between the other person and yourself as possible. I also hear that you're hoping that someone cares enough about you to run after you and stop you from running away.

Clarifying and Perception Checking. These strategies enable a counselor or therapist to ask the client to define or explain words, thoughts, or feelings (clarifying) or to request confirmation or correction of perceptions he or she has drawn regarding these words, thoughts, or feelings (perception checking).

Example

	CLIENT: If what you say is true, I'm a real jerk. What chance do I have to be happy if I run away every time I get close to someone else?
Clarifying	COUNSELOR/THERAPIST: You say you want to be happy. What does *happy* mean to you?
	CLIENT (*long pause*): I would be happy if I could let someone care for me, get to know me, want to spend time with me, and allow me to just be me and stop pretending.
Perception Checking	COUNSELOR/THERAPIST: Let me see if I'm understanding you. Your view of happiness is having someone who cares enough about you to spend time with you and to allow you to be yourself. Am I correct?

Summarizing. This strategy enables the counselor or therapist to do several things: (1) to verbally review various types of information that have been presented to this point in the session; (2) to highlight what the counselor or therapist sees as significant information based on everything that has been discussed; and (3) to provide the client with an opportunity to hear the various issues that he or she has presented. Therefore, summarizing provides both the client and the counselor or therapist with the opportunity not only to review and determine the significance of information presented but also to use this review to establish priorities.

Example

	CLIENT: Yes, I think that's what I'd like to have happen. That would make me happy. I would be in a relationship, feel cared about, and yet be able to be myself without having to either run or pretend.
Summarizing	COUNSELOR/THERAPIST: We've talked about many things today. I'd like to review some of this and make plans for our next meeting. The parts that stick out in my mind are your loneliness, boredom, desire to have a lasting relationship, your behaviors that drive you away from building such a relationship, and your need for caring and the freedom to be yourself. Am I missing anything?
	CLIENT: Only that I want someone who wants to spend time with me. I think that's important.
Summarizing	COUNSELOR/THERAPIST: So now we have a more complete picture that includes loneliness, boredom, desire for a relationship, desire for someone to spend time with, desire for someone who cares, and the need to be yourself. On the other side of the picture, we have your behaviors that keep this from happening. Where do you think we should begin next week?

Strategies That Aid in Data Gathering

This group of strategies includes all of the active listening strategies plus three strategies designed to extract specific information and gain greater depth of information in areas that are significant in the client's statements. As with active listening strategies, a counselor or therapist who uses the following strategies enhances his or her chances of gaining significant information. This set of strategies includes **questioning**, **probing**, and **leading**; the following paragraphs present explanations and examples of each.

Questioning. This strategy, when done in an open manner, enables the counselor or therapist to gain important information and allows the client to remain in control of the the information presented. Using open questioning, the counselor or therapist designs questions to encourage the broadest client responses. Open questions, as opposed to closed questions, generally cannot be completely answered by a yes or no response, nor can they be answered nonverbally by shaking of the head. This type of questioning places responsibility with clients and allows them a degree of control over what information will be shared.

Example

	CLIENT: I've thought a lot about what we talked about last week, and I feel I have to work on changing my behavior.
Open Questioning	COUNSELOR/THERAPIST: Would you tell me what you think needs to be done to change your behavior?
	CLIENT (*short pause*): I need to stop screwing up my chances for a relationship. I need to face what it is that makes me run away.
Open Questioning	COUNSELOR/THERAPIST: Would you please talk more about the "it" that makes you run away
	CLIENT: I can't tell you what it is. All I know is that I hear this voice saying, "Run, run."

Probing and Leading. These strategies enable a counselor or therapist to gather information in a specific area related to the client's presented concerns (probing) or to encourage the client to respond to specific topic areas (leading). Each of these enables the counselor or therapist to explore at greater depth areas that are seen as important to progress within the session.

Example

Probing	COUNSELOR/THERAPIST: I want you to be more specific about this "voice." Whose voice is it? What does it say to you?
	CLIENT (*very long pause*): I guess it's my voice. It sounds like some thing I would do. I'm such a jerk.
Leading	COUNSELOR/THERAPIST: You told me whose voice it is, but you didn't tell me what the voice says. Would you talk about this?
	CLIENT (*raising voice*): It says, "Get out or you're going to get hurt. She doesn't like you and she'll use you and drop you just like the rest."

Strategies That Add Depth and Enhance the Relationship

This group of strategies is used to enhance and expand the communication and relationship patterns that are established early in the counseling or therapeutic process. When used effectively, these strategies should open up deeper levels of communication and strengthen the relationship patterns that have already been established. Counselors or therapists using these strategies model types of behaviors that they wish their clients to emulate. Such behaviors include, but are not limited to, **risk taking, sharing of self, demonstrating trust**, and **honest interaction**. Strategies that add depth and enhance a relationship include **self-disclosure, confrontation**, and **response to nonverbal behaviors**. The following paragraphs present explanations and examples of each strategy.

Self-Disclosure. This strategy has implications for both clients and counselors or therapists. In self-disclosing, the counselor or therapist shares with the client his or her feelings, thoughts, and experiences that are relevant to the situation presented by the client. The counselor or therapist draws on situations from his or her own life experiences and selectively shares these personal reactions with the client. Note that self-disclosure could have both a positive and a negative impact on the helping relationship, and care must be taken in measuring the impact it may have. From a positive perspective, self-disclosure carries with it the possibility of modeling self-disclosure for the client or helping the client gain a different perspective on the relevant problems. From a negative perspective, self-disclosure might place the focus on the counselor's or therapist's issues rather than on those of the client. When self-disclosure is used appropriately, gains are made by all persons involved, and the relationship moves to deeper levels of understanding and sharing.

Example

Self-disclosure	COUNSELOR/THERAPIST (*aware of the client's agitation*): The anger I hear in your voice and words triggers anger in me as I think of my own lost relationships.
	CLIENT (*smiling*): I am angry. I'm also glad you said that. Some times I feel like I'm the only one who ever felt this way.
Self-disclosure	COUNSELOR/THERAPIST (*smiling*): I am very pleased with what you just said. At this moment, I also do not feel alone with my anger.

Confrontation. This strategy enables the counselor or therapist to provide the client with feedback in which discrepancies are presented in an honest and matter-of-fact manner. A counselor or therapist uses this strategy to indicate his or her reaction to the client, to identify differences between the client's words and behaviors, and to challenge the client to put words and ideas into action. This type of direct and honest feedback should provide the client with insight as to how he or she is perceived, as well as indicate degree of caring by the counselor or therapist.

Example

	CLIENT (*smiling*): I feel angry at myself a great deal. I want so much to find a person and develop a relationship that lasts.
Confrontation	COUNSELOR/THERAPIST: You've said this several times in our sessions, but I'm not sure I believe you, based on what you do to keep it from happening. Make me believe you really want this to happen.
	CLIENT: What do you mean, you don't believe me? I just told you didn't I? What more do you want?
Confrontation	COUNSELOR/THERAPIST: Yes, I've heard your words, but you haven't convinced me. I don't think you've convinced yourself, either. Say something that will convince both of us.

Responding to Nonverbal Behaviors. This strategy enables a counselor or therapist to go beyond a client's words and respond to the messages that are being communicated by the client's physical actions. Care must be taken not to overgeneralize regarding every subtle body movement. The counselor or therapist is looking for patterns that either confirm or deny the truth in the words the client uses to express himself or herself. When such patterns become apparent, it is the responsibility of the counselor or therapist to share these patterns with the client. Then it is the client's responsibility to confirm or deny the credibility of the perception.

Example

	CLIENT (*turning away*): Yes, you're right. I'm not convinced this is what I want. (*smiling*) Maybe I was never meant to be happy.
Nonverbal Responding	COUNSELOR/THERAPIST: What I said made you angry and, I would suspect, hurt a little. Did you notice you turned away before you began to speak? What were you telling me when you turned away?
	CLIENT (*smiling*): What you said did hurt me. I was angry, but I'm also embarrassed not to be able to handle this part of my life. I don't like you seeing me this way.
Nonverbal Responding	COUNSELOR/THERAPIST: I've noticed that on several occasions when you talk about your feelings such as anger, embarrassment, or hopelessness, you smile. What does the smile mean?
	CLIENT (*long pause*): I guess I want you to believe that it isn't as bad as it sounds, or that I'm not as hopeless as I think I am.
	COUNSELOR/THERAPIST: It is bad, or you wouldn't be here, and *hopeless* is your word, not mine. Our time is up for today. Between now and next week, I want you to think about what we've discussed. See you next week?

The strategies outlined in this section enable a counselor or therapist to achieve more effectively both the process and outcome goals related to counseling or therapy. Choosing which strategy to use, when to use it, and its impact in the helping relationship is based on the education, experience, and personal dynamics that a counselor or therapist brings to the helping relationship.

CROSS-CULTURAL CONSIDERATIONS

Another factor that affects the helping relationship is cultural diversity. Awareness of cultural diversity involves the counselor's or therapist's openness and motivation to understand more about his or her own culture as well as the cultural differences that clients bring to the helping relationship (Arciniega & Newlon, 2003; Montgomery & Kottler, 2005; Sue and Sue, 2002). Such understanding is often characterized as the cornerstone on which the helping relationship rests. This understanding, which is based on education and life experience, should enable counselors or therapists to increase their sensitivity to the issues that confront clients, should enable them to develop insight into the many variables that affect clients, and should enable them to place clients' issues, problems, and concerns in proper perspective. The key word in these three statements is *should*. Experience indicates that the key factor in the development of cultural awareness is the individual's receptiveness, openness, and motivation to gain such awareness. Without these characteristics, education and experience will have little value. The combination of these characteristics with both education and experience enhances the chances of changing the *should* to *will*.

According to Weinrach and Thomas (1998), the emphasis on issues of diversity goes by several names: cross-cultural counseling, multicultural counseling, counseling for diversity, and diversity sensitive counseling. Included under these names is not only racial diversity but also diversity in areas such as age, culture, disability, education level, ethnicity, gender, language, physique, religion, residential location, sexual orientation, socioeconomic situation, trauma, and multiple and overlapping characteristics of all of these. Indeed, the portrait titled "Diversity" is painted with a very broad brush.

Within each racial grouping exist areas of diversity such as age, disability, sexual orientation, gender, religion, and so forth. True complexity surrounds the subject of diversity. Patterson (1996) points out that "because every client belongs to numerous groups, it does not take much imagination to recognize that the number of combinations and permutations of these groups is staggering. Attempting to develop different theories, methods and techniques for each of these groups would be an insurmountable task" (pp. 227–228).

The insurmountablity suggested by Patterson (1996) could leave the counselor or therapist believing that there is little one can do to individualize the helping process via theories, methods, and techniques to better meet the needs of such a diverse client population. However, it may not be the theories, methods, and techniques that need to be changed but the counselor's or therapist's knowledge, attitudes, values, and behaviors that relate to diversity. If counselors or therapists enter into helping relationships *aware* of the degree of diversity that exists within each client, have taken the time and effort to better *understand* the factors surrounding these diversities, have come to *accept* and *appreciate* their own diversity and the values they place on diversity in others, and are able to *communicate* understanding, acceptance, and appreciation of this diversity to clients, then perhaps the insurmountable becomes surmountable.

For example, counselors or therapists who work primarily with older people must become *aware* that this population (65 years and older) brings to counseling or therapy diversity in race, gender, culture, and language. In addition, counselors or therapists must *understand* the diversity specific to this stage of life, that is, increased disability, more health problems, increased trauma due to loss of significant others, lowered socioeconomic status as a result of retirement and living on a fixed income, and decreased self-importance stemming from living in and with a society that places a more positive emphasis on youth,

Awareness and understanding are the first steps. Counselors or therapists must not only *accept* and *appreciate* their own diversity and the part it plays in their evaluation of others but also learn to accept and appreciate this diversity in others. Counselors or therapists are not free from **ageism** (society's negative evaluation of older persons) and its attitudes and values that impede both acceptance and appreciation. Confronting and changing negative attitudes and values in oneself and being able to demonstrate to clients, through words and behaviors, that such negative attitudes and values have no place in the helping relationship, provide counselors and therapists with the tools to accomplish *communication*—the final step in the process of understanding cultural diversity (Lemoire & Chen, 2005; Sanders & Bradley, 2005).

How does one communicate understanding, acceptance, and appreciation in the helping relationship? A look back at the core conditions presented earlier in this chapter is a good starting point. Conditions such as empathic understanding, respect and positive regard, genuineness and congruence, concreteness, warmth, and immediacy all address ways of communicating understanding, acceptance, and appreciation, and they are basic to the helping relationship. According to Patterson (1996), the nature of this relationship, as prescribed by the core conditions, has been known for a long time and can be applied across groups regardless of diversity. Therefore, a helping relationship based on the identified core conditions is applicable not only to older people but also to clients with other issues of diversity (e.g., sexual orientation, disability, religion). According to Weinrach and Thomas (1998), "the core conditions are nondiscriminatory" (p. 117).

Pedersen (1996, 2000) further contends that the counselor's or therapist's competence in providing a cross-cultural therapeutic relationship rests in the personal qualities he or she brings to the relationship. Developing the personal qualities and gaining the awareness, understanding, acceptance, appreciation, and "competence" to communicate these can only be achieved through education, life experiences, work experiences, self-evaluation, and the counselor's or therapist's willingness to be open to the learning inherent in these experiences.

According to McFadden (1996), counselors and therapists must strive to be "culturally competent." The culturally competent counselor or therapist "not only implies recognition of and respect for members of diverse populations but also fosters an outcome that enables clients to function effectively in their own culture and with the majority population while promoting biculturallity" (p. 234).

Pedersen (1996) uses the term *culture-centered approach* to describe counseling or therapy that

> recognizes that the person herself or himself has internalized patterns of behavior that are themselves culturally learned. If the emphasis is placed—as it should be—on accuracy of assessment, appropriateness of understanding, and competence of practice, then the counselor will need sensitivity to the cultural context. (p. 237)

Cultural diversity addresses the counselor's or therapist's openness and motivation to gain awareness, understanding, acceptance, and appreciation of client diversity and to develop the skills necessary to communicate this to the client in the helping relationship. Personal characteristics or behaviors that enhance a counselor's or therapist's ability to become culturally aware include, but are not limited to, the following:

- Need and the personal motivation to understand one's own cultural diversity as well as that of others
- Need to seek out education, work experiences, and life experiences that will afford one the opportunity to gain greater awareness of cultural diversity
- Need to be open to new ideas and differing frames of reference as they relate to cultural diversity
- Need for self-assurance to admit what one does not know about the diversity of clients and willingness to learn from clients
- Need to be aware of one's own cultural stereotypes and biases and be open to changing them through education and experience

BRIEF APPROACHES

Overview

Tracing the exact beginnings of brief approaches to counseling and therapy is not an easy task. Did they become part of the therapeutic world during World War II, as suggested by Herman (1995) when he stated that military clinicians devised a "menu of creative psychotherapeutic alternatives and shortcuts" to ensure that the maximum number of soldiers could be returned to active duty in a minimum of time (p. 112)? Was it the pioneering work at the Mental Research Institute in the 1950s and 1960s under the direction of **Don Jackson** and **Gregory Bateson,** with consultation and collaboration with **Richard Fisch, John Weakland, Jay Haly, William Fry, Jr., Virginia Satir,** and **Milton Erickson** that provided the real thrust in the development of brief approaches to counseling and psychotherapy? Regardless of where one places the responsibility, brief approaches are now a major part of the therapeutic picture.

According to Lewis (2005) approximately 50 brief approaches exist in the literature. Many of these are tied to existing theoretical systems, that is, rational emotive behavior therapy, reality therapy, psychodrama, Adlerian therapy, and so forth. A few stand alone as developing theoretical and therapeutic approaches: **brief problem-focused therapy, brief solution-focused therapy,** and **solution-oriented and possibility therapy** (Palmatier, 1996; Shulman, 1989). Brief approaches are a rapidly developing area, and development has been encouraged by the response from managed care systems, which are attracted to brief approaches because their focus on symptom relief and increased function is pragmatic and cost-effective (Hoyt, 1995).

Lewis (2005) has stated that "the overemphasis on length of treatment may take those interested in brief counseling approaches down the wrong path" (p. 176). When discussing brief approaches to counseling and psychotherapy, the emphasis should not be on *brief* but on the concepts of counseling and therapy. Mahoney (1997) has stated that "indeed, the actual number of hours logged in psychotherapy is much less important . . . than is the significance of the experiences that transpire during that time" (p. 14). There appears to be no hard and fast rule regarding how long brief counseling and psychotherapy should take. According to Sharf (1996), 3 to 40 sessions could be the range. Generally, brief counseling and therapy ranges from 1 to 25 sessions, with 25 considered the maximum number of sessions. Hoyt (1995) perhaps best captured the essence of this numbers debate when he stated that brief counseling and psychotherapy are not defined by "a particular number of sessions but rather the intention of helping clients make changes in thoughts, feelings, actions in order to move toward or reach a particular goal as time-efficiently as possible" (p. 1).

Because of the many different brief approaches, it is important to consider factors that seem to be common across the approaches. Cooper (1995) has offered the following eight technical features found in various forms of brief counseling:

- Keep a clear and specific treatment focus.
- Use time conscientiously.
- Limit goals and clearly define outcomes.
- Place emphasis on the present—here and now.
- Assess rapidly and integrate assessments into treatment.
- Review progress frequently and discard ineffective interventions.

- Maintain a high level of collaboration between therapist and client.
- Be pragmatic and flexible in use of techniques.

Addressing the issue of basic elements in brief approaches, Fisch (1994) has provided counselors or therapists with the following four principles:

- Narrow the database regarding counselor-client focus.
- Use interactional rather than intrapsychic concepts.
- Develop a task orientation rather than an insight orientation.
- Define goals in order to know when to stop therapy.

Common factors in brief approaches are further supported by Bertolino and O'Hanlon (2002) and Hoyt (2000) when they suggest that brief counselors or therapists (1) embrace pragmatism and parsimony, (2) see human change as inevitable, (3) build on client resources and competence, (4) focus on work outside of counseling and psychotherapy, (5) recognize that sometimes counseling and therapy do not help, and (6) view counseling and psychotherapy as more effective when based on specific contexts and problem areas. Lewis (2005) further states that brief counselors or therapists shift their efforts from concentrating on deficits to looking for strengths, from exploring problems to creating solutions, and from fixation on the past to active construction of a preferred future.

The following sections build on the common factors and provide comparative discussions of the three brief approaches mentioned previously, namely, brief problem-focused therapy, brief solution-focused therapy, and solution-oriented (possibility) therapy. These three brief approaches have developed from a common theme rooted in client competence and strengths (De Jong & Berg, 2002; Fisch, 1994). Each draws on client strengths in solving problems, finding solutions, or discovering possibilities. According to Lewis (2005),

> the strength based approaches do not embrace a normative model that prescribes which is normal and healthy or abnormal and deviant; the approaches move away from viewing the client as pathological and resistant, and concentrate on working with clients to find out what works in their own lives. (p. 178)

These three approaches were selected as they seem to be representative of the current brief counseling and psychotherapy movement.

Brief Problem-Focused Therapy

Brief problem-focused therapy had its beginnings at the Mental Research Institute in Palo Alto, California. In 1966, Richard Fisch opened the Brief Therapy Center with the express purpose of finding what therapeutic results could occur in a period of a maximum of 10 one-hour sessions. The sessions focused on the main problem, used active techniques to promote change, and searched for the minimum change required to resolve the problem (Lewis, 2005). The therapeutic goal was to resolve the problem as it occurred between people; emphasis was placed on change and outcomes, not knowledge, insight, or other such concerns. It was assumed that change would be easier if people did something differently.

According to Fisch, Weakland, and Segal (1982), clients come to therapy for the following reasons: (1) clients are concerned about behavior, actions, thoughts, or feelings of themselves or someone with whom they are involved; (2) clients describe the problem as deviant in the sense of being unusual or inappropriate; (3) clients' efforts to stop or change the behavior have been unsuccessful; and (4) clients seek professional help because they have not been able to make changes on their own. Clients want change but problem formation and problem maintenance form a vicious circle that leaves clients stuck. In fact, clients' misinterpretation of ordinary difficulties in life and their unsuccessful attempts at solutions often aggravate the problem. The therapeutic goals of brief problem-focused therapy are to interrupt this vicious circle and initiate resolution of the problem by assessing where clients are stuck and what they are doing to get unstuck and by stopping them from doing what they see as logical or necessary (Fisch, 1990). Reframing, which is the infusion of new meaning into a situation, is a technique often used in this initial process.

During the initial stages of treatment, assessment via data gathering is important. The counselor or therapist, who is acting persistently, firmly, and politely, works within the client's position, language, and values in attempting to answer the following questions:

- What is the essential complaint, to whom does it belong, who is doing what that presents a problem to whom, and why does such behavior constitute a problem?
- What solutions have been attempted to solve the problem?
- What are the client's minimal goals and how will the client evaluate the achievement of these goals?
- Who is most invested in change?

According to Fisch et al. (1982), counselors or therapists should keep their options open and avoid taking positions prematurely. It is important to take time and encourage clients to be specific in committing to a position. Counselors or therapists need to put clients at ease by asking for their assistance. It is also important to determine who is most discomforted by the problem, clients or other persons.

When the solutions attempted by clients have maintained and perpetuated the problem, interventions are directed toward helping clients step away from these solutions by stopping the problem-maintaining behavior or by altering their view of the problem so that it is no longer considered a problem. Counselors or therapists who use this approach see problems arising from the following five basic solutions that clients tend to maintain: (1) attempting to force something that can occur spontaneously; (2) attempting to master a feared event by postponing it; (3) attempting to reach accord through opposition; (4) attempting to attain compliance through volunteerism; and (5) confirming the accuser's suspicions by defending self.

Counselors or therapists also try other interventions such as these: (1) going slow—directed at clients whose main solution is trying too hard; (2) recognizing the dangers in resolving the problem too quickly; (3) making a U–turn or going in an opposite direction because the strategy being used is not working; and (4) continuing the ineffective approach at arriving at solutions, which is used with clients who are having difficulty changing what they are doing (Fisch et al., 1982). Termination is done without fanfare and includes assessing goals in a cautionary way.

Brief Solution-Focused Therapy

Brief solution-focused therapy was developed by **Steve de Shazer** and **Insoo Kim Berg** at the Brief Family Therapy Center in Milwaukee, Wisconsin. It has its foundation in the theoretical ideas of Bateson, the clinical work of Erickson, and the pioneering work conducted at the Mental Research Institute. According to Lipchik (2002), brief solution-focused therapy looks closely at the pattern of interaction surrounding the problem, approaches for changing the pattern, and creation of outcomes. Its focus shifts from concentration on problems to concentration on solutions, and it draws on client strengths by using all the client brings that can promote change. For solution-focused counselors or therapists, the solution-finding process holds therapeutic promise and helps clients develop expectations of change and solutions.

In brief solution-focused therapy, little attention is paid to the details of the problem. More attention is directed at highlighting how the client will know when the problem is solved. The key to this approach is using what clients have, in terms of strengths and resources, that will meet their needs in such a way that they will be able to find satisfactory solutions to problems. The approach emphasizes that counselors or therapists must do more than assess how problems are maintained or how to solve them. Solutions arise when people involved in problematic situations are required to do something different, even if the action seems irrational, irrelevant, bizarre, or humorous. No one problem or group of problems occurs all the time. A goal of this approach involves getting clients to envision their future without the problem; when this happens, the problem is diminished (de Shazer, 1991, Lipchik, 2002, Walter & Peller, 2000).

According to Miller (2001), solution-focused brief therapy is based on the assumption that solutions are constructed rather than that problems are solved. Thus, knowing a lot about problems may not be necessary to formulating solutions. In fact, problems may be unconnected and even irrelevant to the change process (Lewis & Osborn, 2004). In this approach a small change in one area can lead to greater changes in other areas; this is often referred to as the ripple effect, whereby problem irregularities, or times when the problem is not a problem, are identified (Berg & Miller, 1992).

Brief solution-focused therapy assumes that clients want to change, so client resistance is not an issue. Counselors or therapists compliment clients on positive steps they have taken, suggest things for them to do that might be good for them, and often assume the role of student and place clients in the role of teacher. Clients are encouraged and trusted to know and make decisions regarding what is best for them.

de Shazer (1985) provided a list of categories (building blocks) under which client complaints could be grouped, together with basic assumptions to help counselors or therapists understand these complaints and construct solutions. The building blocks are as follows:

- A bit or sequence of behavior
- Meanings ascribed to the situation
- Frequency and location in which the complaint happens
- Degree to which the complaint is involuntary
- Significant others involved in the complaint
- Question of who or what is to blame
- Environmental factors
- Psychological or feeling state involved
- The past
- Dire predictions of the future
- Utopian expectations

The assumptions include the following:

- Recognize that clients' complaints are brought on by the clients' worldview.
- Realize that complaints are maintained based on the clients' belief that the original decision was the only thing that could be done. Clients remain trapped because they keep doing the same thing.

- Initiate minimal change; once this process begins, clients will provide additional changes for resolving the complaint.
- Focus on the clients' view of what reality would look like without the complaint; use this viewpoint to generate ideas for change.
- Promote problem resolution by suggesting new frames of reference and new behaviors based on the clients' view of reality.
- View change holistically, that is, a change in one part of the system will bring about changes in other parts of the system.

Intervention in brief solution-focused therapy takes many forms. Because of the nature of the relationship between the counselor or therapist and the client, establishing rapport and promoting cooperation are crucial. Based on the interactional process of change and the belief that clients can solve their own problems, counselors or therapists must fit into the worldview of clients. When this is achieved, counselors or therapists begin a technique called **change question** which involves seeking exceptions to the problem or exploring the solutions that clients have attempted. Questions such as, "Since the last time we met, have you been noticing some changes in yourself or discovering a new way of looking at the problem?," "When did you manage this problem in the past?," "What did you do differently?," and "When were things just a little bit better?" create an expectation for change, emphasize the client's role in this change, and stress the fact that change occurs outside of the counselor's or therapist's office.

The **miracle question** is another intervention that helps clients to clarify goals and to identify exceptions to the problem. Clients are encouraged to imagine a solution and to remove constraints to solving the problem, thereby building hope for change. Clients are asked, "Suppose that one night, while you were asleep, there was a miracle and this problem was solved. How would you know? What would be different?" (de Shazer, 1991, p. 113). This type of question allows clients to visualize their life without the problem.

Scaling questions is an intervention designed to make the abstract concrete by quantifying intangibles, placing power with clients, and demonstrating change (Lewis, 2005). In this intervention, clients are asked, "On a scale of 1 to 10, where 1 means you have no influence over your problem and 10 means you have total influence, where would you place yourself today?" This question is often followed by questions such as, "Where would others place you on this scale?" and "What do you need to move a fraction of a point up the scale?"

The foregoing examples highlight interventions that attempt to induce doubt regarding the severity and dominance of the problem and aid clients in finding both exceptions to the problem, define goals that concentrate on constructing solutions. Brief solution-focused therapy concentrates its techniques and interventions on creating the expectation that solutions exist or are imminent.

Solution-Oriented and Possibility Therapy

Solution-oriented and possibility therapy, developed by **O'Hanlon** and **Weiner-Davis**, was influenced not only by the work of the Mental Research Institute and the Brief Family Treatment Center but also by that of Milton Erikson and narrative therapists such as White and Epston. The term *possibility* was coined by O'Hanlon to reduce the confusion that often exists between solution-focused and solution-oriented approaches. Solution-oriented and possibility therapy emphasizes clients' competence in acting with counselors or therapists to create solvable problems. This approach to therapy has a future goal orientation and focuses on bringing about small but positive outcomes for clients. It emphasizes the clients' internal experiences and stresses that clients must be heard and understood if change is to occur.

Solution-oriented and possibility counselors or therapists view clients as being stuck not only because of how they are doing the problem but also because of how they are viewing the problem. Therefore, views, actions, and context are crucial, and practitioners are encouraged to attempt the following actions (O'Hanlon & Weiner-Davis, 1989):

- Change what clients are doing, as this relates to the situation seen as problematic.
- Change the clients' frame of reference and their view of the problem.
- Bring resources, solutions, and strengths to bear on the problematic situation.

The solution-oriented approach begins the therapy process by looking at clients' strengths, solutions, and competence. It moves the process away from purist thinking toward diverse ideas found in the literature using terms such as *constructivist, narrative, postmodern, collaborative, competency based, interactional,* and more (Bertolino, 1999; Bertolino & O'Hanlon, 2002; De Jong & Berg, 2002). Solution-oriented therapy validates clients' emotional experiences and it is flexible rather than formulaic. In this approach, the political, historical, and gender influences that impinge on clients' problems are considered. Solution-oriented therapy is heuristic in nature and is open to ideas and perspectives from differing approaches. O'Hanlon (1999) offers the following three principles to guide the work of the solution-oriented counselor or therapist:

- Acknowledge and validate clients' perceptions and experiences.
- Facilitate clients in changing how they view things or do things.
- Acknowledge clients' resources, expertise, and experiences and collaborate with them about the direction of counseling.

In solution-oriented therapy, assessment and intervention are not separated into distinct steps. Often, the initial interviewing process is seen as an intervention because through the use of solution-oriented techniques (e.g., presuppositional questioning), clients come to view their situations differently. In place of asking, "Did anything good come from the relationship?," one might ask, "What were the good things that came from the relationship?" This approach focuses on the way clients perceive and talk about their problems. It also aids the counselor or therapist who is looking for exceptions to the problem in an attempt to normalize the problem by making it simply a natural response to life events. O'Hanlon and Weiner-Davis (1989) offer the following eight techniques for changing the patterns of doing or viewing problems:

- Change the frequency or rate of performance of the problem.
- Change the time when the problem occurs.
- Change the length of time the problem occurs.
- Change where the problem takes place.
- Change the pattern of the problem by adding something to it.
- Change the sequence of events in the problem pattern.
- Change the problem pattern by breaking it down into smaller parts or elements.
- Change the problem pattern by linking it with some burdensome task.

In each of these eight change processes, interventions are negotiated collaboratively with clients in a relationship where change is expected. The goal is to help clients identify possibilities rather than problems, and the processes involve using what is going right rather than focusing on what is going wrong. Solution-oriented counselors and therapists use stories, anecdotes, parables and humor to help clients change. Narrative therapists act similarly in aiding clients to move from problem-saturated stories to more hope-filled stories. Narrative therapists believe that the client is never the problem; rather, the problem is the problem. **Problem externalization** has been embraced by solution-oriented and possibility counselors and therapists and has been refined in such a way that the problem is placed outside the clients. For example, if a client's problem is feelings of inferiority, the counselor or therapist might ask, "How long has this inferiority been controlling your life?" Thus, the problem becomes a controllable entity outside of the client instead of an internalized entity within the client. Solutions and possibilities are sought to work effectively with this external visualization.

CONCLUSIONS

The helping relationship is the foundation on which the process of counseling or psychotherapy rests. It is best viewed in terms of developmental stages, the first of which begins with the initial meeting of the client and the counselor or therapist and is characterized by rapport building, information gathering, goal determining, and information sharing. Building on the foundation established in the first stage, later stages address extended exploration and problem resolution; the final stage in this process is termination and follow-up.

The helping relationship, when viewed from this developmental perspective, progresses from stage to stage due to the presence of certain components that the counselor or therapist brings to the relationship. The first of these are the core conditions of empathic understanding, respect and positive regard, genuineness and congruence, concreteness, warmth, and immediacy. These conditions are personality characteristics of a counselor or therapist which he or she is able to incorporate into the helping relationship.

The second component in the process of developing a helping relationship is a set of strategies aimed at building rapport and encouraging client dialogue, data gathering, and relationship enhancement. These strategies are skills and techniques that a counselor or therapist gains through education and experience and is able to use effectively in the helping relationship.

The third component focuses on issues of cultural diversity and the counselor's or therapist's motivation and willingness to develop awareness, understanding, acceptance, and appreciation of client diversity. These factors, when communicated effectively, often are viewed as the cornerstone on which the helping relationship is based.

In combination, the developmental nature of the helping relationship, the presence of the core conditions, the implementation of the various strategies, and attention paid to issues of diversity create a facilitative environment in which both the client and the counselor or therapist have the strong potential for positive growth. Potential exists, guarantees do not. Achieving the true potential of the helping relationship depends on what the client and counselor or therapist bring to the relationship and what each takes from it.

Brief therapies, regardless of the name, the emphasis, or the techniques and interventions used, are a major player in today's counseling and therapy marketplace. Spurred on by third-party payers, by research regarding the effectiveness of brief approaches, and by a client population wanting to be helped as quickly as possible, brief approaches to counseling and psychotherapy have challenged professionals to evolve. This evolution is not one of instant cures but one of timely and efficient provision of service to clients.

CHAPTER 2

Achieving a Personal and Professional Identity

David Capuzzi
Scholar in Residence
Johns Hopkins University
Professor Emeritus
Portland State University

Douglas R. Gross
Professor Emeritus
Arizona State University

How well do I really know myself, and how effective will I be with clients? Do I really understand my chosen profession and the stressors involved? These are just two of the questions we believe each of you should ask yourself as you progress through your graduate education and clinical supervision experience. Some careers can be pursued without a high level of self-awareness, but the profession of counseling or psychology is not one of them. Knowledge of theory and research and expertise in translating that knowledge into strategies and interventions can be delivered only through the being and personhood of the provider. Each member of the helping professions is given an enormous amount of responsibility every time client interactions occur. This responsibility can be upheld only if each counselor or therapist maintains a sense of **health** and **wellness** to ensure that the understanding and support, assessment, and treatment planning that a client receives are the best they can possibly be. The more a counselor or therapist has developed, integrated, and accepted an identity as a person and as a professional, the better that individual is at giving the incredible gift of helping another human being develop a unique sense of self.

Personal and **professional identity** must be addressed before and during the process of studying and applying individual approaches to counseling and psychotherapy. It is not easy, for example, for the beginning graduate student to be receptive to peer and supervisor feedback as it relates to individual work with clients. The student must have enough self-awareness and a great enough sense of well-being to be receptive to suggestions for changes that are needed to maximize therapeutic effectiveness. On-site observations of individual sessions and required videotaping and playback for supervisory purposes escalate the stress level of any graduate student. If students can develop high levels of self-acceptance and self-understanding, they will receive more benefit from the supervision process and have greater potential for developing clinical skills.

Many students are enrolled in graduate programs that require participation as a client in either individual or group counseling for the purpose of facilitating their continued personal growth. This requirement helps students avoid the confusion that arises when client issues are similar to unresolved personal issues. Such personal issues often surface during the practicum or internship experiences required of students. For this reason, many graduate programs expect enrollees to complete requirements for counseling or therapy before initiating practicum and internship courses and placements. At times, supervisors may recommend that students seek additional counseling or therapy at the same time they are enrolled in a practicum or internship.

Because of the stresses and complexities of the helping professions, faculties in counseling and psychology departments are becoming more definitive and assertive about expectations for the wellness and functionality of potential counselors and therapists. Many educators and clinical supervisors are stressing the need for counselors and therapists to involve themselves in consultation and counseling or psychotherapy after graduation to maintain personal growth, wellness, and treatment-planning ability. Many experienced professionals stress the importance of involving significant others in ongoing couples or family counseling, so that as the counselor or therapist grows and changes, friends and family members can participate in and understand that process of change.

This chapter addresses the importance of health and wellness for the counselor or therapist, as well as the importance of recognizing values and cultural bias in theory and practice, becoming aware of the daily world of the practitioner, and achieving perspective and balance between personal and professional roles. It also includes a discussion about developing a personal theory.

IMPORTANCE OF HEALTH AND WELLNESS

The personal qualities, traits, and characteristics of the counselor or therapist have long been recognized as an extremely important component of the helping relationship (Brems, 2000; Carkhuff & Berenson, 1977; Egan, 1975; Evans, 1997; Myers, Mobley, & Booth, 2003; Rogers, 1961). As Okun (1987) has noted, a continually increasing database supports the concept that counselors and therapists are effective only if they are self-aware and able to use themselves as the instruments through which change occurs. One way of conceptualizing this role in the relationship is to compare the contribution the counselor or therapist makes to a client's growth and maturation to that of a painter working on a canvas, an architect designing a building, or a sculptor chiseling a statue. The client presents possibilities and options, which are much like the raw materials of canvas and paint, building site and construction materials, or chisels and stone. The artist approaches the task with a database of information and the expertise to translate a concept or mental image into something beautiful or functional. Whether the database and expertise of the artist can be fully accessed most often depends on the mental, emotional, physical, and spiritual sensitivities with which the artist approaches the work. Creativity can be compromised or never actualized if the being of the creator is impaired, tired, or dysfunctional, because everything the artist has to contribute is conveyed through the person of the artist.

The counselor or therapist is the conveyer of possibilities and potentials to the client. If the being or personhood of the counselor or therapist is impaired at the time of an encounter with a client, it may be difficult to see the client's potential and use those possibilities for engaging in a mutually rewarding relationship to achieve desirable outcomes. The health and wellness of the counselor or therapist have much to do with the art form inherent in the helping relationship.

There are a number of approaches to health and wellness that are described, researched, and prescribed by those wishing to sensitize counselors and therapists to the importance of self-care as a prerequisite to caregiving. We have grouped these approaches into three categories for discussion and presentation: **personal characteristics models, psychological health models**, and **multidimensional health and wellness models**. Each category provides counselors and therapists with concepts that are helpful and applicable to the maintenance of their own sense of well-being and their ability to cope successfully with both personal and professional responsibilities.

Personal Characteristics Models

Person-centered counseling theory offers a well-researched analysis of how counselors and therapists might work with clients. The person-centered school identifies accurate **empathy,** nonpossessive **warmth, positive regard,** and **genuineness** as the "necessary and sufficient conditions" for therapeutic change (Corey, 2004, 2005; Rogers, 1957; Truax & Carkhuff, 1967). Empathy—often defined as the capacity to view and understand the world through another person's frame of reference (Egan, 1975)—is one of the most extensively studied personal characteristics or variables in process-outcome research. Most reviews of studies that analyze the relationships between empathy and outcome show positive relationships in one half to two thirds of the research under scrutiny (Orlinsky & Howard, 1978, 1986). Genuineness—described as consistency in values, attitudes, and behaviors on the part of the counselor or therapist—is also the focus of therapeutic process research and is generally related positively to therapeutic outcomes (Orlinsky & Howard).

Counselor or therapist **affirmation**—the ability to communicate positive regard, warmth, and acceptance to the client—is also significantly associated with positive therapeutic outcomes (Orlinsky & Howard, 1978). In addition, Carkhuff and his associates have stressed the importance of concreteness or specificity of expression (Carkhuff & Berenson, 1977). As we noted in chapter 1, concreteness means that the practitioner's response serves to clarify the meaning the client is communicating so that the client's self-understanding is actually enhanced.

Personal characteristics models for addressing the health and wellness of the counselor or therapist have been discussed from perspectives other than that of Carl Rogers. A number of writers and researchers have focused on the importance of the personal characteristics of the counselor or therapist on the outcome of counseling or psychotherapy (Goldfried, Greenberg, & Maramar, 1990; Hanna & Bemak, 1997; Hanna & Ottens, 1995; Myers, Mobley, & Booth, 2003; Seligman, 2001; Whiston & Sexton, 1993). Combs and his colleagues (1969) conducted a series of studies resulting in the conclusion that the personal beliefs and traits of the counselor or therapist differentiated between effective and ineffective helping. Effective helpers seem to perceive others as able, rather than unable, to solve their own problems and manage their own lives. Effective helpers also perceive others as dependable, friendly, worthy, able to cope, and able to be communicative and self-disclosing. In general, effective helpers maintain a positive view of human nature and approach family, friends, colleagues, and clients in a trusting, affirming way. A **composite model of human effectiveness** has been suggested by George and Cristiani (1990) as a means of **analyzing the personal characteristics of effective helpers.** The elements of this composite model include openness to and acceptance of experiencing, awareness of values and beliefs, ability to develop warm and deep relationships with others, willingness to be seen by others as one actually is, willingness to accept personal responsibility for one's own behaviors, and development of realistic levels of aspiration. Meier and Davis (2001) have suggested that helpers who are the most effective strive to apply the four following principles to assess characteristics and traits that affect their own ability to assist others and may reflect their own level of health and wellness: (1) become aware of your personal issues, (2) be open to supervision, (3) avoid hiding behind the use of too many tests, and (4) consult when presented with an ethical dilemma.

The literature related to personal characteristics models that is available to counselors or therapists is voluminous (Capuzzi, Gross, & Stauffer, 2006; Seligman, 2001; Schmidt, 2002). Characteristics such as assertiveness, flexibility, tolerance of ambiguity, honesty, emotional presence, goal-directedness, and self-respect have been addressed to the point that the beginning counselor or therapist may find the suggested profile somewhat overwhelming and threatening. The important thing to remember is that no one can achieve the perfection that such idealized models suggest. All of us have flaws and imperfections that can obstruct our ability as helpers, just as all of us have unique strengths and capabilities that enable us to influence others positively. We believe that effective counselors and therapists are able to maintain a sense of personal well-being and happiness despite flaws or inadequacies, and we stress the importance of a perspective that ensures that personal issues do not diminish the capacity to engender personal growth on the part of clients.

Psychological Health Models

The following provocative scenario (Kinnier, 1997) can be used to introduce some of the dilemmas inherent in suggesting criteria for psychological health. Imagine a psychological health contest between the John Wayne persona of the 1950s silver screen and the Leo Buscaglia persona of the 1990s lecture circuit. Which persona would win? Among John Wayne's celluloid traits were his stoicism and his readiness to fight. He rarely displayed any weaknesses or "shared his feelings" with anyone. In contrast, Leo Buscaglia's most salient public traits have been his readiness to cry and share his feelings with everyone. Is "strong and silent" healthier than "vulnerable and expressive"? For men? For women? Does the answer depend entirely on the biases of the judges and the context of a specific time and place?

To cope with dilemmas such as the one posed by Kinnier, most mental health practitioners have focused on identifying symptoms of psychopathology instead of criteria for mental health. It has been easier to identify undesirable behaviors and emotions (note current approaches to diagnosis and treatment planning) than it has been to identify and agree on behavior and emotions indicative of mental health. Cross-cultural differences have further complicated attempts to delineate the traits of a psychologically healthy client. (See the multicultural counseling competencies developed by the Association for Multicultural Counseling and Development on the Web site of the American Counseling Association at www.counseling.org.) It is difficult to establish acceptable criteria for psychological health because such criteria are intricately woven into a particular cultural and temporal background. Nevertheless, a number of theoreticians and practitioners have emphasized psychological health models as approaches to promoting the health and wellness of clients.

About 50 years ago, Jahoda (1958) proposed six criteria for mental health: a positive attitude toward self, continual movement toward self-actualization, purpose or meaning in life, ability to function independently and autonomously, accurate perception of reality, and mastery of the environment. Basic self-esteem was viewed as essential by luminaries such as Allport (1961), Erikson (1968), Jung (1954), Maslow (1970), Rogers (1961), and Sullivan (1953). Personal autonomy and competence were emphasized by Fromm (1955), Horney (1950), Maslow (1970), and Rogers (1961). The capacity to give and receive love as a criterion for psychological health has been endorsed by Adler (1978), Allport (1961), Erikson (1968), Freud (1930), Fromm (1955), Maslow (1970), and Sullivan (1953). More recent discussions of a variety of criteria for the psychological health of the practicing counselor or therapist can be found in Brems (2000), Campbell (2000), Schmidt (2002) and Skovholt (2001).

After conducting a survey of psychological literature to determine what criteria for psychological health had been identified by theoreticians and researchers, Kinnier (1997) proposed nine criteria for psychological health. We believe these criteria apply to counselors and therapists as well as to their clients.

1. *Self-acceptance.* Self-esteem seems to be a prerequisite for developing other important components of psychological health. Psychologically healthy individuals experience strong feelings of self-acceptance and self-love. Individuals who love and respect themselves have the capacity to love and respect others and possess the foundation for becoming self-actualized.

2. *Self-knowledge.* The importance of self-exploration and self-knowledge cannot be overemphasized. Psychologically healthy individuals know themselves well and stay aware of their feelings, motivations, and needs. They are introspective and committed to understanding themselves.

3. *Self-confidence and self-control.* Individuals who are psychologically healthy have confidence in themselves and can function independently of others. They have appropriate skills for assertive behavior but do not unnecessarily impose their views or will on others. Such individuals have an internal locus of control, believe that they can exert reasonable control over their lives, and feel capable of achieving their goals.

4. *A clear (though slightly optimistic) perception of reality.* Perceptions of the people, events, and objects around us are always subjective, but there is usually enough societal consensus about the nature of reality to provide beneficial comparisons with our own point of view. Psychologically healthy individuals have a clear perception of

reality and an optimistic view of life. They view themselves, their present circumstances, and their futures accurately and positively, which enhances possibilities and potentials.

5. *Courage and resilience.* Danger and risk surround the daily lives and decision-making opportunities of most individuals; therefore, failures, crises, and setbacks are inevitable. Psychologically healthy individuals are aware of this reality, adapt well to challenges and changed circumstances, and can bounce back from disappointments and setbacks. As Kinnier (1997) notes, "psychologically healthy individuals bravely confront their fears and accept their responsibility. They are prepared to take risks when appropriate. They accept setbacks and failures as part of life, and as the once popular song says, after a fall they 'pick themselves up, dust themselves off, and start all over again'" (p. 55).

6. *Balance and moderation.* The theme of balance and moderation is one that recurs in psychological literature. Psychologically healthy individuals work and play, laugh and cry, enjoy planned and spontaneous time with family and friends, and are not afraid to be both logical and intuitive. They are rarely extremists or fanatics, and usually they do not do anything in excess.

7. *Love of others.* The capacity to care deeply about the welfare of another person or the condition of humanity in general is another characteristic of the psychologically healthy person. Mental health professionals from a number of theoretical orientations believe that the ability to give and receive love, the desire to develop close ties to another person or persons, and the need to belong to another person, family, or group are fundamental to mental health. Psychologically healthy individuals are not reticent about loving and caring for others. They need to experience close interpersonal relationships and are intimate with at least one other person.

8. *Love of life.* The psychological benefits of humor, spontaneity, and openness have been touted by many professionals. People who are active, curious, spontaneous, venturesome, and relaxed have traits that promote their capacity to partake of and enjoy life. Psychologically healthy people embrace the opportunities that life presents, do not take themselves too seriously, and look forward to the unexpected with the vitality to cope, solve problems, and move on to the future with a positive perspective.

9. *Purpose in life.* Individuals vary in their choice of the most meaningful aspects of life. Work, love, family, intellectual or physical accomplishment, or spirituality may become the primary focus for one individual or another. Although variation among individuals is bound to exist, the important achievement for each person is to develop a purpose—an investment—that creates a sense of meaning and satisfaction. The joy and sense of exhilaration and accomplishment that result from finding meaning and purpose in life are prime factors in the maintenance of psychological health.

Multidimensional Health and Wellness Models

As noted by Myers (1991), several different wellness models have been proposed for use by counselors and therapists. One of the most common models defines wellness holistically by considering it from spiritual, mental, and physical aspects of functionality. Other models describe dimensions such as spirituality, physical fitness, job satisfaction, relationships, family life, nutrition, leisure time, and stress management (Ardell, 1988; Brems, 2000). Quite often, physical wellness is given more attention than other dimensions of wellness because physical illness cannot be as easily ignored (Evans, 1997). Most systemic models of wellness, however, suggest that all the identified dimensions of wellness interact and that they must all be evaluated in the process of assessing a person's state of wellness (Skovholt, 2001).

In 1984, Hettler proposed six dimensions of wellness—intellectual, emotional, physical, social, occupational, and spiritual—as components of a lifelong paradigm to promote health and wellness. These characteristics are represented graphically in a hexagon in which each component is equal in size. Hettler's model has been used frequently in the physical and public health professions to promote the importance and understanding of wellness. Even though Hettler emphasized the importance of each component of the hexagon, when the model is used in the health professions, the emphasis has been on physical well-being. In addition, emphasis has been placed on present functioning instead of development across the life span.

Chandler, Holden, and Kolander (1992) suggested modifying Hettler's model from a hexagon to a pentagon. In their model, spirituality is not a separate component; instead, it is an integral component of each of the other five areas of a pentagon. Spirituality is viewed as the core of wellness that is inseparable from the other five dimensions of wellness. In addition, Chandler et al. proposed that spirituality develops over time as the individual matures and develops openness to the importance of spiritual wellness.

Wilbur's (1995, 1997, 2000) integral model is another multidimensional model that counselors and therapists can draw from to increase their effectiveness as healers in the context of a counseling relationship. Wilbur's model emphasizes the integration of body, mind, soul, and spirit in self, culture, and nature. Its primary strength is increasing awareness of the multiple facets of reality or truth. Wilbur points out that many individuals may not develop body, mind, soul, and spirit symmetrically. For example, a person who is well educated and read may not have spent equal time developing his or her body or in establishing a sense of meaning or purpose in life.

There are other multidimensional or holistic models of health and wellness. Health has been defined as the absence of illness. Wellness goes far beyond the absence of illness and incorporates a zest and enthusiasm for life that results when the dimensions of wellness (intellectual, emotional, physical, social, occupational, spiritual) have been addressed, developed, and integrated. "With a holistic focus, wellness incorporates not just the whole person, but the whole person throughout the totality of the life span" (Myers, 1991, p. 185). A person can be "well" even when undergoing treatment for physical illness, because the physical dimension is just one dimension of the wellness model. One of the best discussions of holistic models was published in the *Journal of Counseling and Development* (Myers, Sweeney, & Witmer, 2000). This discussion extends and modifies the original model, based on Adlerian concepts, presented by Sweeney and Witmer in 1991 and Witmer and Sweeney in 1992. The discussion of 2000 describes the revisions of the original model, reviews research that supports each component of the revised model, and describes the use of the Wheel of Wellness as a basis for working holistically with clients. The five major life tasks discussed in conjunction with the revised model are spirituality, self-direction, work/school, friendship, and love.

Makinson and Myers (2003) defined these life tasks and noted that individual mastery of these five major tasks is not static but develops across the life span. *Spirituality* addresses an individual's awareness of a being or a force that transcends the material world and provides a sense of wholeness or connectedness to the universes as well as a feeling of optimism, meaning, and purpose to life and the future. *Self-direction* includes 12 subtasks: those of sense of worth; sense of control; realistic beliefs; emotional awareness and coping; intellectual stimulation, problem solving, and creativity; sense of humor; nutrition; exercise; self-care; stress management; gender identity; and cultural identity. The subtasks are the means through which individuals regulate themselves and engage in intentional behavior to successfully meet the three remaining life tasks. Adler viewed work as one of the essential aspects of a positive, functional lifestyle, and the third major life task of *work/school* is a major component of the Wheel of Wellness model. Use of leisure time complements this life task and is an important component of it. *Friendship* relates to close relationships with others and social support; it is considered essential to optimal functioning across the life span. The fifth major life task is *love,* which is considered to be critically important to each of us. It is a primary component in the development of close relationships and prerequisite to the establishment of healthy couples and family systems. Note that these life tasks are interactive and that change in one area can effect changes in another. In general, individuals who choose healthy behaviors may be expected to experience wellness in multiple areas, and persons who experience a lack of wellness in one area may experience lack of wellness in multiple areas.

The importance of health and wellness models should be understood by all those undertaking the study of theories of counseling and psychotherapy. The counselor's or therapist's role in facilitating the wellness of clients creates a natural link between counseling and psychotherapy and wellness; however, the emphasis in the link is on counselors or therapists helping clients. Little emphasis is placed on the importance of counselors or therapists helping themselves, and even less attention is given to the wellness behaviors of counselors or therapists (Evans, 1997; Myers et al., 2003). In addition to the fact that counselors and therapists need to address wellness with respect to both their clients and themselves, counselors and therapists should assess what the various theories of counseling and psychotherapy offer with respect to the dimensions of health and wellness. Some of the theories and approaches included in part II of this book do not encourage the counselor or therapist to approach clients from a wellness perspective, nor do they encourage the practitioner to engage in personal care from a holistic frame of reference. One of the tasks of a beginning counselor or therapist is to think about developing a theory or approach to the helping relationship. This may entail the adoption of one of the theories presented in this textbook, the development of an integrated model, or the conceptualization of a personalized theory or approach based on the study of theory and research as well as experience with clients. We encourage you to consider a number of perspectives before conceptualizing a personal theory of counseling and psychotherapy, for no single theory provides a perspective that could be described as completely adequate.

VALUES AND CULTURAL BIAS IN THEORY AND PRACTICE

As you read the theory chapters in parts II and III of this book, think about the way the values and cultural biases of the chief proponents of each theory may have influenced the development of the theory. In addition, assess your personal values and understandings of cultural differences. This section of the chapter introduces the subject of values and cultural bias in theory and practice.

Values in Theory and Practice

Everyone has a set of beliefs that guides decisions, determines one's ability to appreciate the people and things in the environment, governs conscience, and influences perceptions of others (Belkin, 1984; Robinson, 2005; Pederson, 2000; Schmidt, 2002, 2006). Because the **values** of a counselor or therapist are an integral part of what is brought to a relationship with a client, it is important to consider the role values play in theory and practice and in achieving a personal and professional identity.

One of the key issues to consider is whether, during the process of counseling or psychotherapy, counselors or therapists can avoid conveying their values to their clients (Corey, 2001; George & Cristiani, 1990). Some maintain (especially professionals associated with the orthodox **psychoanalytic** point of view) that a counselor or therapist must remain neutral with clients and avoid communicating value orientations. In such circumstances, a counselor or therapist would strive to appear nonmoralizing, ethically neutral, and focused on the client's values. If topics such as pro-choice versus pro-life, religion, physician-assisted suicide, or gay, lesbian, and bisexual orientation were to arise during the counseling or psychotherapy process, the counselor or therapist would not take a position. The reason for such neutrality is the belief that it is important for clients to move from an external to an internal locus of control during the counseling or psychotherapy process. Values introduced by the counselor or therapist would be detrimental to such an objective.

As early as 1958, however, Williamson voiced an opposing position and promoted the idea that counselors and therapists cannot avoid letting clients know about their values and should be open and explicit about the nature of those values. Williamson reasoned that counselor or therapist neutrality may be interpreted by clients to mean that the professional is supporting client behavior that is not acceptable by social, moral, or legal standards. Samler (1960) went further and encouraged counselors and therapists to develop an awareness of their own values and of how these values relate to and influence the development of client values. Samler believed that assisting clients to change their values is a legitimate goal and a necessary component of the helping relationship. In 1958 and 1989, Patterson pointed out that the values of the counselor or therapist influence the ethics of the helping relationship and the goals, techniques, and interventions used in the context of helping. Kelly's (1995) study focused on the value orientations of counselors in these domains: universal values, mental health values, individualism-collectivism values, and religious-spiritual values. Kelly's purpose was to identify values that characterize counselors or therapists and may represent values taught to clients during the counseling or psychotherapy process.

We believe it is imperative for counselors and therapists to be aware of their own values and to consider the influence that these values have on clients. The following questions may be useful to the helper in the process of examining values issues:

- Am I completely cognizant of my own values?
- Do my values influence my preference for particular theoretical frameworks (such as rational emotive behavior theory or Jungian concepts) and associated techniques and interventions?
- How will I resolve dilemmas that arise when my values and those of my client are opposed?

- What is my belief about whether a counselor or therapist can remain neutral and avoid communicating value orientations to clients?
- What is my role in helping clients delineate their values more clearly?

Cultural Bias in Theory and Practice

In 1962, C. Gilbert Wrenn was one of the first to suggest that practitioners were providing counseling and psychotherapy from a narrow cultural perspective. Wrenn (1962) encouraged counselors and therapists to broaden their **monocultural** perspectives and be more responsive to clients from different cultural backgrounds. By the mid-1970s, more emphasis on the issue of **cultural bias** in theory and practice began to appear in the literature. For example, Katz (1985), Pedersen (1987), and Sue (1997) pointed out that traditional counseling or psychotherapy is based exclusively on White culture and fails to meet the needs of culturally diverse client populations. Today, it is widely acknowledged that current theories are derivatives of Western culture and are not universally applicable to cross-cultural counseling and psychotherapy situations (Corey, 2001; McFadden, 1988; Richardson & Molinaro, 1996; Schmidt, 2002, 2006; Vontress, 1988).

Because the United States is becoming increasingly diversified, recognition of the cultural bias that exists in theories and techniques of counseling and psychotherapy has become even more important in the process of achieving a personal and professional identity. Christopher (1996) addresses diversity issues through the concept of **moral visions.** He notes that moral visions are constellations of cultural values and assumptions that shape our experience of life and the stances we take toward life. Christopher points out that different cultures provide different moral visions. The ideal person in traditional Confucian China was first and foremost characterized by filial loyalty and being a dutiful son or daughter. In contrast, in North American culture, attributes such as authenticity and autonomy are reinforced. Moral visions both prescribe and describe what a person should be or become, and they influence the development of theories of counseling and psychotherapy. Most Western counseling or psychotherapy theories are moral visions that presuppose the importance of individualism. For example, **behaviorist, cognitive-behavior,** and **reality** theories emphasize utilitarian individualism. They stress rationality, control over emotions, enhanced human liberty, the importance of achieving self-defined goals, and opposition to irrational authority. **Humanistic** theories, such as **person-centered** and **Gestalt** theories, promote the importance of turning inward, of making contact with inner experiencing, and of identifying and expressing feelings. Such emphases may not be congruent with the moral visions of clients from other cultures.

Usher (1989) provided some helpful guidelines for assessing the cultural bias inherent in theories of counseling and psychotherapy. We include those guidelines here to extend the discussion of cultural awareness and diversity that began in chapter 1, to preview the content of chapter 3 on diversity and social justice issues, and to alert you to some of the pitfalls associated with attempts to apply Western frames of reference to all clients, irrespective of their cultural identity and experience. We do not intend to discourage counselors and therapists from making appropriate use of current theory; rather, we want to sensitize practitioners to the importance of cultural differences as determiners of approach selection and development of a personal theory of counseling and psychotherapy.

Assumptions About Normal Behavior. A real source of cultural bias is the assumption that *normal* means the same thing to members of various social, political, economic, and cultural backgrounds. Although some clients may believe that being reasonably assertive or responsibly individualistic is a normal goal, such traits may be considered inappropriate in other cultures. Pedersen (1987) argued that "what is considered normal behavior will change according to the situation, the cultural background of a person or persons being judged, and the time during which a behavior is being displayed or observed" (p. 16). He pointed out the danger of diagnostic errors when using definitions of normality grounded in the perspective of the culture in which a particular theory or conceptual frame of reference was developed.

Emphasis on Individualism. A number of theories (e.g., **person-centered** and **rational emotive behavior theories**) emphasize the welfare and centrality of the individual and deemphasize the importance of obligation and duty to family, organizations, and society. Because such themes are central to some cultures' value systems, it would be a mistake for the counselor or therapist to promote individualism on the part of a client for whom such a focus would be contrary to cultural or ethnic identity. For example, an Asian American client might not return to a counselor or therapist who did not respect what the client communicated about deference to the wishes of parents or other older members of the extended family.

Fragmentation by Academic Disciplines. Many theories of counseling and psychotherapy have been developed without considering the potential contributions of other academic disciplines such as sociology, anthropology, theology, and medicine. A counselor or therapist who uses a theory that has been developed from a narrow perspective may be handicapped in attempts to facilitate the helping relationship with a client who is culturally different. It is important for all counselors and therapists to take courses or participate in training experiences offered by other disciplines or by those who maintain a different cultural perspective.

Dependence on Abstract Words. Counselors and therapists with a Western frame of reference live in a low-context culture (i.e., less emphasis on how the meaning of a statement is affected by the context). They may depend on abstract words associated with theory and practice and assume that these abstractions will be understood by others—including clients—in the same way they are understood by the professional. Such abstractions may have little meaning, or take on different meanings, when used outside the cultural context in which they were initially developed. For example, would all clients understand the concepts of self-actualization or fictional finalism? Many clients are not receptive to abstractions or conceptualizations, which, in a culture not based on Western values, worldviews, or protocols, may seem removed from the reality of life.

Overemphasis on Independence. Usher (1989) cited Pedersen (1987), who criticized theories and practices that devalue necessary dependencies inculcated by certain cultures. Most counselors and therapists in the United States view the independence of the client as desirable and neglect the function of healthy dependencies in some cultures; therefore, many of the theories they use do a disservice to clients who have grown up and continue to function in a different cultural context. Many cultural groups value a person's capacity to subjugate individual desire to the overall welfare of the family, community, or organization. Counselors and therapists need to be sensitive to and respectful of such a perspective.

Neglect of Client Support Systems. Many theoretical orientations do not recognize the role that family and peers play in providing support for a troubled client to the same extent that they recognize the role of the professionally prepared counselor or therapist. (Neither do the proponents of many approaches to counseling and psychotherapy.) It may be necessary for counselors and therapists to incorporate the client's natural support system into a treatment plan. In some cultures, talking with family members or friends may be more acceptable than talking with a trained professional who is usually a total stranger.

Dependence on Linear Thinking. Most theories make the assumption that clients relate to linear thinking. Linear thinking emphasizes cause-and-effect relationships, whereas the non-linear or circular thinking characteristic of some cultures does not separate cause and effect, does not follow a singular stream of thought, and invites free association. It is important for counselors and therapists to realize that for some clients, conversation about topics seemingly unrelated to counseling or psychotherapy may be an essential element of a productive helping relationship.

Focus on Changing the Individual Rather Than the System. Quite often, counselors and therapists who use Western theory as the sole basis for practice assume that their role is to make the client more congruent with the system. Such a role can be quite problematic when Western culture-bound paradigms, such as the American Psychiatric Association's *Diagnostic and Statistical Manual of Mental Disorders,* are used to assess the behavior of clients who are culturally different (Lewis-Fernandez & Kleinman, 1995). If counselors or therapists do not question whether the "system" is in the best interests of a culturally different client, are they simply serving as agents of the status quo?

Neglect of History. Some counselors and therapists minimize the relevance of a client's personal and cultural history; instead, they focus more intensively on present behavior, the current problem, and immediate events. Clients from some cultures, such as Native American cultures, see themselves as closely connected to their ancestors. Their current problems cannot be fully understood without consideration of their history. Such clients might not return to a counselor or therapist who did not provide opportunities to explore the present in terms of past experience as well as present needs.

Cultural Encapsulation. Counselors and therapists need to guard against the possibility of becoming **culturally encapsulated** by the mainstream group with which they are associated. When such encapsulation occurs, assumptions and beliefs may not be questioned, and clients from diverse cultural backgrounds may not be treated effectively because of the operation of certain biases on the part of the professional. The more counselors and therapists can experience and learn about other cultural groups, the less likely they will be to approach clients with biases that prevent effective helping. Both the American Counseling Association and the American Psychological Association have endorsed the importance of all counselors and therapists developing multicultural awareness knowledge and skills so they can be more effective and avoid making incorrect or culturally inappropriate assumptions about working with clients. We encourage you to begin reading in this area (Abreu, Gim Chung, & Atkinson, 2000; Ariel, 1999; Locke, Myers, & Herr, 2001; Pederson, 2000; Schmidt, 2006; Smith, 2004) and to evaluate the theories described and discussed in parts II and III of this text in the context of working with clients whose history and experience are different from yours.

DAILY WORLD OF THE PRACTITIONER

There is no doubt that a complex relationship exists between elements of the therapeutic process and the demands experienced by the counselor or therapist on a daily basis (Hannigan, Edwards, & Burnard, 2004; Moursund & Kenny, 2002). The clients with whom the practitioner works, the setting, the expectations of colleagues and supervisors, personal life, and significant others are constantly interacting and, at times, reciprocally influencing outcomes. We believe that an important part of developing a personal and professional identity is becoming as aware as possible of the daily world of the practitioner and the stresses that sometimes impede the counselor's or therapist's well-being and the services provided to clients.

The demands inherent in most work environments (e.g., school, college, university, mental health center, hospital, private practice, rehabilitation clinic) are tremendous. Concerns about having enough clients, students, supervisees, research funds, publications, involvements in professional and community organizations, collected fees, and malpractice and liability insurance are just a few examples of the demands that converge on counselors and therapists. Coping with the restrictions precipitated by funding cuts, mandated short-term counseling, practicing in the context of evidence-based outcomes, and expectations to remain current and keep up with changing certification and licensure requirements present additional stresses and expectations. Freudenberger (1983) has noted that the very nature of the therapeutic personality often makes it difficult to say no, and many people engaged in counseling and psychotherapy find themselves overextended, tired, and overly involved with work. For some professionals, the drive to develop a reputation for excellence, coupled with the need for success, must be monitored carefully to avoid chronic discontent and eventual **burnout** (Hannigan et al., 2004; Skovholt, 2001).

The demands that clients place on counselors and therapists are a significant factor in a practitioner's daily world. In the span of a few days, many counselors and therapists find themselves confronted with the problems of people who are chronically mentally ill, terminally ill, physically or sexually abused, suicidal, or substance abusers or who have eating disorders, or a host of other concerns and issues. Most research to date (e.g., Finch & Krantz, 1991; Hellman & Morrison, 1987; Pines & Maslach, 1978) and some literature reviews (Osborn, 2004) indicate that counselors and therapists in settings that serve large numbers of clients who are seriously disturbed experience higher rates of personal depletion, less career satisfaction, and more impaired working relationships with colleagues. This information is quite pertinent for those planning to place themselves in settings in which there is a high probability of working with challenging clients.

The ominous shadow of malpractice hovers all too often over the daily world of the practitioner (Remley & Herlihy, 2005). Rates for liability insurance have risen as clients have become more litigious and counselors and therapists have become fair game. Because many clients enter the counseling or psychotherapy process with expectations about becoming better—perhaps in an unrealistically short period of time—counselors and therapists are vulnerable to having client disappointments or frustrations worked out in court rather than in a therapeutic environment. More and more lawyers have chosen to specialize in personal injury and malpractice cases and actively seek clients who are discontented with the results of counseling and psychotherapy (Kaslow & Schulman, 1987). Even when the counselor or therapist is innocent, the insurance carrier or one's own legal counsel may suggest an out-of-court settlement to avoid the trauma of a trial, the possibility of a guilty verdict, the accompanying censure by professional organizations, and the possibility of losing required state licensing. To the beginning—and even to the experienced—counselor or therapist, such a settlement can seem like an admission of guilt; yet preparing for and going through a trial can pose an even greater ordeal and create a high level of stress. In addition, such trials may attract a great deal of unwelcome media attention. Because counselors and therapists believe in the sanctity and privacy of the therapeutic encounter, such public exposure can be a bitter experience that has negative impacts on personal well-being as well as on the lives of family members.

More than any other professional, the counselor or therapist must continually deal with the reality of terminations. Whether the treatment process has been successful or not, the ending of a helping relationship may be experienced as another separation and, quite often, as a permanent loss. Despite the fact that counselors and therapists are prepared during their educational and supervisory experiences for the inevitability of terminations with clients, endings may be difficult and force practitioners to deal with unresolved personal losses (e.g., departure of adult children, death of significant others, divorce).

Terminations can also become transformations when clients appear in different roles in the life of the counselor or therapist. For example, former clients may later reenter as trained mental health professionals or, as is often the case in small communities, may become part of the social milieu of the counselor or therapist. The reality of termination or transformation can be a source of satisfaction or stress depending on how the counselor or therapist views the nature of the posttreatment void or the posttreatment relationship.

In many ways, the daily world of the counselor or therapist may threaten relationships outside the workplace. For example, in the process of striving to improve working relationships with cotherapists, colleagues, and supervisors, counselors or therapists may share much of their inner selves and, in so doing, develop satisfying relationships built on trust, respect, and mutual understanding. These relationships may supplant or replace other significant relationships outside the workplace. As a result, a marriage or long-term relationship may begin to seem less interesting and rewarding unless steps are taken to prevent this from happening.

The expression of admiration by clients, trainees, and colleagues may also result in some unexpected fallout. Significant others outside the workplace may begin to resent the attention that the counselor or therapist receives from clients and colleagues, or the counselor or therapist may begin to expect the same level of admiration from significant others. In either situation, resentment, frustration, and anger may result. Again, counselors and therapists need to take steps to prevent this from occurring.

The basic principle of confidentiality may also create problems for the counselor or therapist in relationships outside the workplace. Counselors and therapists cannot talk about their clients except in the context of receiving supervision or consultation or in situations when the best interests of the client or society are at stake. Significant others may feel shut out, especially when they know that others have access to information unavailable to them.

ACHIEVING PERSPECTIVE AND BALANCE

Our previous discussion of the daily world of the counselor or therapist is necessarily limited in scope; nevertheless, we believe the discussion does convey the fact that counselors and therapists deal with demands and stresses that can place them at risk for burnout (Schulz, Greenley, & Brown, 1995; Skovholt, 2001) and personal depletion. Because it is important to maintain a high level of personal health and wellness, we think the following guidelines may be useful to individuals in training as well as to other members of the profession.

Know the Warning Signs for Burnout

How do graduate students or practicing counselors or therapists know they are heading for difficulty when striving to develop and maintain a high level of professional competence? Kaslow (1986) identified some of the signs of burnout:

- Not wanting to go to work
- Constantly complaining about disliking practice or feeling overwhelmed by it
- Experiencing a sense of foreboding or imminent doom
- Viewing life as dull, heavy, and tedious
- Experiencing an increasing number of negative countertransference reactions to patients or students
- Being extremely irritable, withdrawn, depressed, or intolerant at home
- Suffering frequent illnesses of inexplicable origin
- Wanting to run away from it all or having periodic suicidal ideation

Kaslow (1986) notes that when two or more of these indicators appear periodically and with gradually increasing frequency, intensity, and duration, a counselor or therapist has entered a warning zone and should seek personal counseling and psychotherapy, take a vacation, cut back on obligations, and so on until he or she reexperiences perspective and balance. Beginning counselors or therapists can consult a variety of additional sources that either describe or discuss the topic of burnout (Corey, 2001; Moursund & Kenny, 2002; Skovholt, 2001). One of the most interesting and thought-provoking treatments of the topic appears in a text by Brems (2000), *Dealing with Challenges in Counseling and Psychotherapy* (2000).

Consider Networking Options

It is not always necessary to enter a counseling or psychotherapy relationship to achieve balance and perspective. Counselors and therapists can use a number of beneficial options to renew and revitalize their ability to function in a positive way. They can establish a network of professional contacts to provide different options for support and continued professional development. For example, working with a cotherapist, asking a colleague to view a client session through a one-way mirror and then offer feedback, or seeking clarification and assistance from a supervisor can provide valuable support and ideas for treatment options when working with a difficult client. Any one of these networking options can help a counselor or therapist to share the burden of providing counseling or psychotherapy or to break through an impasse in a client-practitioner relationship (Kaslow & Schulman, 1987).

Most communities provide opportunities for professionals to join a support group to share personal or professional concerns. Often there are local opportunities to attend workshops and training sessions to enhance expertise or develop new skills. Such workshops also allow practitioners to meet and talk with other counselors and therapists who share similar interests. It is always important to participate in some combination of local, state, regional, or national professional organizations such as the American Counseling Association, the American Psychological Association, or the American Association of Marriage and Family Therapists. Professional organizations provide a myriad of opportunities for continued learning and networking with other members of the helping professions (Brems, 2000; Glosoff, 2005; Skovholt, 2001). An excellent resource for graduate students is a local chapter of Chi Sigma Iota, an international honor society for students, alumni, and supporters of counselor education programs and departments.

Refer Clients When Appropriate

Another way to maintain perspective and balance is to be amenable to the possibility of referring clients who are difficult or chronic or whose issues fall outside your ability to provide adequate care. A referral can be done in a positive way from the vantage point of a client, and colleagues will view the referral as a sign of professional integrity and wisdom. When a client is struggling with issues too close to those of the counselor or therapist, referral of the client is preferable to undertaking or prolonging work in which one becomes overly involved.

Disengage from the Professional Role

The experienced counselor or therapist knows how to disengage from the role of being a professional so that time with friends and family members, social engagements, vacations, and avocational interests can be enjoyed. Disengaging provides opportunities for rest, relaxation, and rejuvenation while relieving the practitioner from obligations. Counselors and therapists need to experience nurturing interpersonal relationships, just as clients need to spend time with significant others. At times, counselors and therapists can become so enmeshed in the demands of the profession that they find it difficult to enjoy opportunities for fun and relaxation.

Cultivate Strengths and Develop Stamina

Osborn's (2004) article, "Seven Salutary Suggestions for Counselor Stamina" presents a refreshingly proactive approach to developing perspective and balance by cultivating inner resources to avoid burnout, instead of eliminating or "remediating" the signs of burnout after burnout occurs. Osborn proposed that counselors can maintain their therapeutic effectiveness by developing the stamina to approach the challenges connected with the profession of counseling with enthusiasm, persistence, confidence, and endurance. The following seven suggestions encompass on- and off-the-job activities, ways of thinking, and dispositions and represent a holistic approach.

1. *Selectivity.* Selectivity refers to being intentional about setting boundaries and limits about what one can and cannot do and avoiding the pitfalls of submitting to a relentless workload. It also means carefully selecting professional specializations and how

and with whom one wants to practice. "It is not possible to be all things to all people" is a common saying. The same concept can be applied to the counselor's role as a professional helper. In addition, counselors who are selective and intentional about their professional roles are less likely to accept employment in settings that place unrealistic expectations on their employees and reinforce and reward an exhaustive approach to work-related obligations.

2. *Temporal sensitivity.* Time-sensitive counseling, or temporal sensitivity, is the second suggestion for developing stamina. This means that time is not only something to be managed but also something that is viewed realistically. It means starting and stopping counseling sessions on time, leaving space between sessions, and staying focused. One of the implications is that time should be viewed as a precious commodity and as a collaborator rather than as an adversarial aspect of life. Acknowledging the limitations of time can enhance the counselor's or therapist's focus on the moment and the ability to be therapeutically present with clients.

3. *Accountability.* Accountability as an aspect of developing stamina means practicing from a theoretically evidence-based and ethical point of view. It means thinking through and being able to "own" the decisions made on behalf of clients and practicing within professional guidelines for standards of care. Accountability also means being open to evaluation and consultation. When a professional is able to adopt such a perspective and act from an internal locus of control, it is likely that a higher level of job satisfaction and less burnout will occur.

4. *Measurement and management.* This fourth component of stamina is related to the first component, that is, selectivity. Measurement and management entail daily decisions that support, protect, and accentuate the limitations and boundaries already selected (e.g., specializations, workload, credentials, type or setting of practice). In addition, measuring and managing off-the-job time seems to be crucial for enhancing stamina. Engaging in satisfying, meaningful activities and relationships strengthens a practitioner's stamina and helps sustain professional longevity.

5. *Inquisitiveness.* A certain degree of curiosity about the life narratives of others and a desire to engage in meaningful and therapeutic conversations with clients is essential for those who choose to be a counselor or therapist. Stamina, in this context, implies that counselors and therapists approach clients and their experiences as unique; as individuals whose life narratives are to be honored, respected, and understood; and as human beings who should not be judged or stereotyped. Stamina also means being curious and interested in professional developments and maintaining an ongoing interest in learning about new theories, research, and practices. This means participating in professional associations and taking pride in the profession of counseling.

6. *Negotiation.* Counselors and therapists need to be responsive to and cooperative with colleagues; at the same time, they need to remain steadfast in the process of upholding certain standards, values, and guidelines. Often they must negotiate with colleagues, team members, insurance carriers, or supervisors on behalf of clients, themselves, or both. Negotiation requires being assertive, confident, and enthusiastic about the professional role. Negotiation also necessitates vigilance to make sure that one does not become entrapped in a work situation that becomes so restrictive that it prevents a reasonable negotiation process from taking place.

7. *Acknowledgment of agency.* The term *agency* often is used to refer to the setting or place in which counseling takes place. Agency, however, can refer to an inherent capacity to sustain movement along an envisioned path. Agency means that in the midst of challenges, the counselor or therapist can draw from inner resources and the will of the human spirit to maintain resilience and professional and personal perspective.

Consider Possible Options for Renewal

We began our careers in the 1960s as members of the profession of counseling and human development. At that time, the daily world of the practitioner was quite different from what it is today. Standards for credentialing, education, and supervision, although reasonably demanding, were not as specific, time consuming, and exacting as they are currently. As the profession has matured, the expectations for graduate work, **credentialing**, practice, and **continuing education** have become decidedly more demanding and stress producing. Because of these demands, many professionals develop a pattern of overload that can be traced back to graduate education and, quite often, to some inherent needs and predispositions that make overload seem acceptable as a way of life. We do not believe that it is possible to continue indefinitely as an effective counselor or therapist unless options for renewal are considered and pursued. Such options are unique for each counselor or therapist and can only be identified on an individual basis. Exercise, time with friends, participation in a choral group, leaves of absence or sabbaticals, travel, gardening, white-water rafting, massages, time with significant others, and time alone are examples of the hundreds of options and combinations of options that may have appeal as well as potential for practitioner renewal.

Mackey and Mackey (1994) analyzed the impact of personal therapy on the outlook of the practicing professional. Results indicated that counselors and therapists emerged from the experience with new ideas for therapeutic techniques, enhanced empathy, better understanding of the therapeutic process, higher levels of self-awareness, and greater ability to set limits, establish boundaries, and maintain an appropriate balance between closeness and distance in professional relationships. All of these outcomes are pertinent to renewal and to the avoidance of or overcoming of burnout.

It is not possible to nurture others unless we provide the self-nurturance and renewal that maintains and restores our capacity as helpers. The health and wellness of the helper has much to do with the art form inherent in the helping relationship. Consult Coster and Schwebel (1997), Dupree and Day (1995), and Skovholt (2001) for additional information.

IMPORTANCE OF A PERSONAL THEORY

After you finish reading this chapter and the one that follows, you will begin a fascinating exploration of theories of counseling and psychotherapy. Some theories will have more personal appeal than others; all of them will present some stimulating perspectives about human nature and about providing help to those who seek assistance. In addition, each theory will suggest a variety of theory-congruent strategies or applications designed to help clients achieve desired changes in behavior, outlook, motivation, and so on. We want the content of this book to help you think about a personal theory of counseling and psychotherapy. We hope you give considerable thought how the formulation of a personal theory of counseling and psychotherapy could be helpful to you as you work with clients.

From time to time, the topic of developing a personal theory of counseling and psychotherapy is addressed in the professional literature. Three of the earliest discussions of this topic were put forth by Lister (1964), Passons (1975), and Shoben (1962). More recently, developing a personal theory of counseling and psychotherapy has been addressed briefly by Corey (2005) and Seligman (2006). We think it is important for counselors or therapists to understand how a personal theory can be helpful in the process of working with clients.

A counselor or therapist can use a personal theory to provide a framework for understanding the meaning of a client's behavior. This statement will have added meaning as you read chapters 4 through 17 and notice that each theory is discussed from the perspective of the same paradigm. One aspect of the paradigm is focused on how clients develop as personalities across the life span; the associated information directs the observations of the counselor or therapist and helps the counselor or therapist assess the client's behavior in relation to how the theory suggests that behavior has developed. This process of observation also helps the counselor or therapist discriminate between relevant and irrelevant aspects of client behavior as well as connect what, at first, may seem like disjointed pieces of information about client behavior.

Developing a personal theory should assist the counselor or therapist in understanding how change in client behavior might be precipitated. If a counselor or therapist uses a framework that addresses how personality and behavior has developed, then he or she should also have ideas about how to modify that behavior during the counseling and psychotherapy process. Note that the change process is addressed in conjunction with discussing and evaluating each of the theories in this text. Suggestions for interventions that can be used to modify behavior are connected to the assumptions the theory makes about human development across the life span and the change process as described. In a similar vein, the goals of counseling and psychotherapy are derivatives of the conceptual framework provided by the theory and used by the counselor or therapist to guide the counseling and psychotherapy process.

A personal theory should provide reasonable guidelines for the clinician as observations and assessments are made and treatment plans are developed. A personal theory, however, should never be adhered to rigidly; rather, personal theory should always be modified as the expertise and experience of the counselor or therapist accumulates over time. The following suggestions for circumventing problems in the development and application of a personal theory are worth noting:

- Stay cognizant of your own feelings, values, beliefs, expectations, and personality traits that influenced, and continue to influence, your personal theory.
- Study existing theories of counseling and stay updated on new developments, including research data, which can be applied to existing theories as well as your personal theory.
- Be open to the use of alternative and Eastern approaches to counseling and psychotherapy.
- Do not incorporate elements of existing theory into your personal theory if they are incongruent with your belief system and personality traits.
- Assess your personal theory in the context of using it with diverse populations and make modifications to meet the needs of clients whose life experiences and values are different from yours.

- Modify your personal theory as time and experience accrue.
- Use the six-point paradigm, as presented in Chapters 4 through 17 of this text, as the organizational structure around which you develop the conceptual framework you plan to use with clients.

The personal theory you decide to develop will be refined gradually as you accumulate knowledge about theory, research, and practice and build experiences with clients through practicum, internships, and volunteer and paid positions. We encourage you to begin thinking about the conceptual frame of reference with which you plan to approach clients, but we discourage you from adopting a position until you carefully explore possibilities and participate in a variety of clinical opportunities with associated one-to-one and group supervision experience.

As you read the introduction to part II of this text, consider the paradigm that is used to present each theory addressed in the text: background, human nature, major constructs, applications, evaluation, and a case study ("The Case of Jonathan"). Use these dimensions as you begin to formulate and "draft" your own personal theory of counseling. At first, you may just want to outline your thoughts, and you will probably make revisions as you reflect on the content of this text and begin to counsel clients. We believe that it is important for every professional counselor or therapist to think through his or her belief system related to how clients develop the behavioral patterns that are observed and how behavioral change can be facilitated. In addition, we believe that interventions used by the counselor or therapist to facilitate change must always be tied to what the counselor or therapist believes about the inherent nature of the clients being served and any associated constructs that inform the theoretical set the counselor or therapist uses to guide *practice*. Theory, research, and practice should always be closely aligned, and each of us has an obligation to think through our way of working with clients. We must be willing to revise and modify our preferred way of doing our work as we, as individual professionals, grow and mature and as new theory and research are made available for our use.

CONCLUSIONS

This chapter stressed the importance of achieving a personal and professional identity as you begin to study theories of counseling and psychotherapy and gain experience in translating theory into practice. We believe that personal identity and professional identity are interrelated and fundamental to being able to understand, evaluate, and apply the theories presented in this text. Because the health and wellness of the counselor or therapist is a prerequisite to effectiveness, we addressed this topic through descriptions of personal characteristics, psychological health, and multidimensional health and wellness models.

The values and cultural biases of each counselor or therapist have an impact on the use and application of theory as well as the structuring of the helping relationship. We hope you will make personal assessments of your values and sensitivity to culturally diverse client populations as well as evaluate the values and cultural biases on which the theories presented in subsequent chapters are based.

Some students enroll in college and university programs for preparing counselors and therapists without being totally aware of the demands they will encounter. Through its description of the daily world of the counselor or therapist and the importance of achieving perspective and balance, this chapter provided an initial overview of the stresses and expectations of the profession as well as the importance of learning how to cope with professional demands. We believe that each person needs to develop a realistic understanding of the profession and that this knowledge is an essential component for the development of personal and professional identity.

Finally, this chapter stressed the importance of thinking about the conceptual frame of reference with which to approach clients. Although some practitioners may adopt an existing theory, many will develop a personal theory to inform and guide their practices with clients. We hope you will obtain benefits from the information in this book and will develop analytic and evaluative skills that will enable you to apply this information effectively to client populations. Effective application will result when a practitioner is able to find a compatible balance between theoretical tenets and the personal and cultural characteristics that serve as a basis for his or her uniqueness. When you reach that point, you will have answers to the two questions that began this chapter.

CHAPTER 3

Diversity and Social Justice Issues in Counseling and Psychotherapy

Deborah J. Rubel
Oregon State University

Manivong Ratts
Seattle University

Increasing concern regarding the ethical and effective treatment of diverse populations requires that counselors and therapists begin to consider the effects of culture and societal dynamics on counseling and psychotherapy processes. The purposes of this chapter are to (1) introduce the background of the multicultural and social justice movements in counseling and psychotherapy, (2) outline a variety of frameworks for understanding diverse clients, and (3) explore the implications of diversity on counseling and psychotherapy processes. The chapter emphasizes the necessity of both interpersonal and systemic interventions, such as advocacy, to adequately address the mental health needs of diverse populations. The chapter also includes suggestions for building counselor and therapist diversity competence following the American Counseling Association's Multicultural Counseling Competencies, which focus on gaining practitioner self-awareness, knowledge, and skills.

BACKGROUND

The changing composition of the U.S. population, along with an increased commitment to providing competent counseling to diverse populations, has brought issues of diversity to the forefront of discussions among counselors and therapists (Sue & Sue, 2003). Although there is widespread acceptance within the helping professions that counselors and therapists must provide competent treatment to diverse clients, traditional theories of counseling have been criticized for their limitations for this purpose (D'Andrea, 2000).

To answer the limitations of traditional counseling theories and practices, a variety of models, theories, and concepts have been created that address needs of diverse clients during the counseling process. These theories are not meant to replace existing theories but to add to the ways in which counselors and therapists understand themselves and diverse clients, to broaden practitioners' views of the counseling process, to add to practitioners' repertoire of techniques and strategies, and most importantly, to assist practitioners in seeing themselves, clients, and the practice of counseling within a broad cultural context (Sue & Sue, 2003). This chapter provides a context for diversity issues in counseling in the following ways:

- Clarifying key concepts and reviewing the history of diversity issues in counseling
- Increasing understanding of how diversity influences individual and group functioning
- Increasing awareness of how diversity may influence the counseling process
- Presenting several perspectives on diversity-appropriate interventions
- Suggesting ways to develop self-awareness, knowledge of diverse populations, and diversity-relevant counseling skills.

Definitions

Issues of diversity, multiculturalism, and social justice are often confusing and frustrating to discuss. Part of the difficulty is the lack of clear, common language and meanings with which to communicate important ideas. In this chapter definitions will be provided for key concepts as they are discussed; initially, however, several terms should be clarified.

Use of the terms **multiculturalism** and **diversity** interchangeably when discussing group and individual differences may cause confusion (Arredondo, Toporek, & Brown, 1996). Within the counseling profession, the term *multicultural* most often refers to individual and group differences based on race and ethnicity (Helms & Cook, 1999). **Race** is as a categorization of individuals based on skin color and other physical attributes, historical geographic origin, and the perceptions of the dominant group; **ethnicity** is an individual's identification with a group based on culture, nationalism, citizenship, or interactions of race, religion, and sociopolitical history (Smith & Kehe, 2004). More inclusive definitions of multiculturalism have been criticized for diverting discussion away from issues related to race and ethnicity to other issues when discussion becomes uncomfortable (Helms & Cook; Sue & Sue, 2003).

The term *diversity* is used to describe group and individual differences based on other dimensions of differences, as well as race and ethnicity (Arredondo et al., 1996). The dimensions of difference commonly used include race, ethnicity, **gender, sexual orientation, socioeconomic status, disability status**, age, and **spirituality** (Adams, Bell, & Griffin, 1997), though other dimensions may also be relevant (Arredondo et al., 1996).

Discussions about counseling diverse clients often refer to cultural differences. **Culture** is the "characteristic values, behaviors, products, and worldviews of a group of people with a distinct sociohistorical context" (Smith & Kehe, 2004, p. 329). Cultural differences may be readily observable as differences in clothing, foods, customs or traditions, and languages, or as subtler but crucial differences in parenting beliefs, family structure, social hierarchy, gender role expectations, communication style, and relationship to time and space. Some do not consider diverse groups such as women or gay, lesbian, bisexual, and transgender (GLBT) persons to have a distinct group culture (Sue & Sue, 2003); nonetheless, the experience of these groups within surrounding cultures is significant to the counseling process.

Discussing diversity also requires the use of terms to describe social or cultural groups that are numerically superior or hold more power and status versus groups that have fewer numbers or less power and status. The terms **majority, dominant culture**, and **agent** refer to groups and members of groups who are more numerous or hold more power. The terms **minority, nondominant culture, underrepresented**, and **target** refer to groups and members of groups who have fewer numbers, less power, or both. In this chapter, all terms will be used to reflect the literature from which the information was drawn; however, the term *diverse clients* will be used to indicate clients who differ significantly in experiences, culture, or social identity from the counselor or therapist or who identify predominantly with minority, nondominant culture, underrepresented, or target groups.

Diversity in Today's Society

The increasing diversity of the U.S. population is often mentioned in the rationale for giving increased attention to the impact of social and cultural differences on the counseling process (D'Andrea, 2000). Racial and ethnic minority populations will rise from approximately 30% to near 50% of the population by the year 2050 according to census projections (U.S. Census Bureau, 2004). In the same 2000 census, persons over the age of 65 accounted for nearly 13% of the population, and 20% of the population was identified as having a disability. And though the U.S. Census does not track sexual orientation, by some estimates people who identify as gay, lesbian, or bisexual account for up to 15% of the population. These numbers, coupled with the relatively low status and power of these groups and women in U.S. society (Sue & Sue, 2003), indicate that understanding diversity and working toward **social justice** are major issues facing this society.

Diversity has the potential to strengthen society, but it may also contribute to misunderstanding, conflict, and oppression (Bell, 1997). Although the counseling profession is often cited as a resource for promoting the well-being of diverse people, it has often failed in this capacity (Sue & Sue, 2003). Some evidence suggests that minority populations underutilize counseling services, terminate services prematurely, and suffer psychological harm when treated according to traditional models (D'Andrea, 2000) and that counseling that does not acknowledge culture issues and societal power dynamics may promote an unjust status quo (Katz, 1985).

These criticisms are generally linked to **cultural bias** in counseling practice. Issues contributing to cultural bias were introduced in chapter 2 and include such counselor or therapist issues as (1) adhering to culturally determined definitions of normal behavior and language, which can impede communication between counselor or therapist and client; (2) minimizing or ignoring the impact of a client's group sociopolitical history; and (3) underutilizing client support systems and systemic interventions. The goal of addressing such limitations to provide competent counseling to diverse clients continues to be the focus of both the multicultural and social justice counseling perspectives (Ratts, D'Andrea, & Arredondo, 2004).

MULTICULTURAL AND SOCIAL JUSTICE COUNSELING PERSPECTIVES

The need to address issues of diversity in counseling has given rise to two emerging but complementary perspectives. The multicultural counseling perspective has been the predominant perspective represented in the professional literature and organizations. As this perspective has developed and matured, critics have noted its limitations, and the social justice counseling perspective has gained credibility as a complementary perspective that answers the limitations. Although the two perspectives differ, they share many foundational values, concepts, and skills. To more fully understand both perspectives, it is useful to review their histories, similarities, and differences.

Multicultural Counseling

Many researchers have attempted to define multicultural counseling during its evolution. Vontress (1988) defined multicultural counseling as "counseling in which the counselor and the client are culturally different because of socialization acquired in distinct cultural, subcultural, racioethnic, or socioeconomic environments" (p. 74). More recently, Sue and Sue (2003) described multicultural counseling as a helping process that relies on both universal and culture-specific techniques to meet goals that are consistent with client values; recognizes individual, group, and universal dimensions of client identity; and integrates client worldview into the assessment, diagnosis, and treatment of clients and client systems.

These definitions share the assumptions that counseling professionals should recognize the impact of cultural differences on client life experiences, client-counselor or therapist relationships, and the counseling process. Before the development of a multicultural counseling perspective, counseling was most often viewed as a culture-free process in which cultural differences between client and counselor or therapist were largely ignored (Ivey, D'Andrea, Ivey, Simek-Morgan, 2002).

The multicultural counseling movement originated in the 1950s (Jackson, 1995) in response to recognition that the United States had become increasingly diverse in race, culture, and language (Sue, Arredondo, & McDavis, 1992). Racial segregation, systematic discrimination, and prejudice were widespread during this era, and as an extension of societal inequality, counseling with clients of color during this time focused primarily on assimilation into the White dominant culture. Though professional literature at the time had begun to address these issues, people of color were underrepresented as counselors, counseling scholars, and members and leaders of counseling-related professional organizations (Jackson). The inequalities served as painful motivation for society and the profession to change as they entered the 1960s.

The 1960s were a time of social and political unrest; open challenge of the White establishment and racist institutions became commonplace. During this time mental health scholars and practitioners began to question the racist counseling practices that were prevalent in the field (Pope-Davis, Coleman, Liu, & Toporek, 2003). This questioning led to positive changes in the profession, such as increased numbers of publications and studies dedicated to issues of race counseling and the formation of professional groups to raise awareness (Jackson, 1995).

The end of the 1960s marked the formation of the Association of Non-White Concerns (ANWC), which consisted mainly of African American members of the American Personnel and Guidance Association (APGA), the predecessor of the American Counseling Association

(ACA). Initially, AGPA rejected recognition of ANWC as an official division, and it was not until 1972 that official divisional status was granted (McFadden & Lipscomb, 1985). This led to the creation of the ANWC journal, the *Journal of Non-White Concerns*. The 1970s also began to bring a broader focus to counseling that included other racial and ethnic groups, as well as women and people with disabilities.

During the 1980s and 1990s multicultural issues became a priority in the counseling profession with unprecedented numbers of publications devoted to the subject (Jackson, 1995). During this era, the ANWC changed its name to the Association for Multicultural Counseling and Development (AMCD; Parker, 1991), which reflected a desire to widen the focus from primarily African American concerns to concerns of Latino and Latina Americans, Asian Americans, and Native Americans (Jackson).

The 1990s and the new millennium brought legitimacy to multicultural counseling (Sue & Sue, 2003). Part of this legitimacy can be attributed to AMCD's 1991 approval of the Multicultural Counseling Competencies (MCCs) as standards for counselor training and practice (Sue et al., 1992). The original MCCs contained 31 competencies that emphasized counselors must actively seek to understanding themselves, their clients, and clients' environments and must use their understandings to provide services that fully respect, embrace, and utilize diverse clients' unique life experiences.

Along with increased credibility came debate about the scope of multicultural counseling and its limitations (Pope, 1995). Two prominent criticisms are that the multicultural counseling movement has emphasized cultural awareness within counseling sessions but has placed less emphasis on systemic social change strategies and social justice (Vera & Speight, 2003) and that the movement has emphasized issues of race and ethnicity over other social identity variables such as gender, sexual orientation, religion, class, and disability status (Weinrach & Thomas, 2002). The perceived limitations of multicultural counseling have led to increased calls for inclusion of a social justice perspective in counseling (Vera & Speight, 2003).

Social Justice Counseling

The social justice counseling perspective has at its core the goal of full and equal participation of all groups in society (Bell, 1997). Goodman (2001) further described social justice as a process of seeking dignity, self-determination, and safety for all people by addressing issues of equity, power, and oppression. Thus, social justice-oriented counselors or therapists facilitate client well-being by seeking to establish a more equal distribution of power and resources in society through macrolevel interventions such as advocacy, as well as addressing client issues in sessions through microlevel intervention (Goodman et al., 2004).

Although emphasis on social justice counseling is recent, the origins of social justice within the counseling professions are much earlier. According to Kiselica and Robinson (2001), social justice has been an integral part of the counseling profession since the early 1900s when counseling pioneers Frank Parsons and Clifford Beers responded, respectively, to the exploitation of immigrants to the United States and the inhuman treatment of people with mental illness. Both believed that counseling should address the larger social, political, and economic issues that contribute to clients' problems (Kiselica & Robinson).

Despite these deep roots, social justice concepts made few appearances in the counseling literature until the 1970s. Articles published during that time addressed such topics as systemic barriers to client well-being (Dahl, 1971) and advocacy for marginalized groups

(Gardner, 1971). Psychological problems, which had been viewed as originating inside the client, were now linked with factors outside the client (Jackson, 1995).

Calls for adoption of a social justice counseling perspective continued in the 1980s. Katz (1985) argued that all counseling theories and practices emerge from limited cultural contexts; thus, they are not value neutral. Moreover, she claimed that adhering to traditional counseling paradigms promoted a White, middle-class status quo and that counselor denial of the value-laden nature of the helping process was a significant barrier to understanding diverse client concerns.

Several key events occurred during the 1990s that advanced the social justice counseling perspective. In 1999, **Loretta Bradley** was elected ACA president, and during her tenure Bradley selected "Advocacy: A Voice for Our Clients and Communities" as her presidential address theme. That same year the formation of Counselors for Social Justice (CSJ), a division of ACA, served to legitimize the social justice counseling perspective (Kiselica & Robinson, 2001).

During the new millennium, the social justice counseling perspective continues to gain support. Since 2000, Division Seventeen of the American Psychological Association (APA) has published two special issues of *The Counseling Psychologist* dedicated to social justice issues in counseling. Additionally, the ACA Advocacy Competencies, which serve as a how-to manual for addressing issues of social justice and oppression in counseling, were finalized in 2003 by a task force of CSJ leaders (Counselors for Social Justice, 2005).

Both multicultural and social justice counseling perspectives share core assumptions:

- Counselors or therapists must consider clients' social and cultural context during the counseling process.
- Oppression significantly affects the lives of many diverse clients.
- Counselors or therapists must go outside the boundaries of traditional counseling theory and technique to serve these clients.

Given the historical, philosophical, and practical connections that exist between the two perspectives, counselors or therapists should understand that both perspectives are necessary to adequately address the impact of social and cultural differences and oppression on diverse clients (Ratts et al., 2004). Accordingly, the following sections address diversity in a broad sense and discuss macrolevel and microlevel conceptualizations and interventions for diverse clients and their environments.

KEY CONCEPTS OF COUNSELING WITH DIVERSE CLIENTS

Becoming a diversity-competent counselor or therapist means learning to view self, others, and the world in new ways. The process of stepping outside one's life experience to understand and interact differently with others is inherently difficult. Counseling theories assist counselors or therapists in this process by providing a framework for understanding clients and their concerns, defining the counseling relationship, suggesting the goals and overall process of counseling, and describing interventions and strategies to achieve these goals. No comprehensive counseling theories exist that address all aspects of diversity. This section reviews a range of useful theories, concepts, and suggestions for understanding and working with diverse clients.

Constantine (2001) concluded that the ability to understand diverse clients and their concerns in terms of sociocultural and systemic factors is necessary for counselors or therapists to adequately treat them. However, most traditional counseling theories do not account for these factors and contain culturally determined assumptions about behavior that tend to skew judgments of abnormality toward diverse clients (Sue & Sue, 2003). Fortunately, the diversity, multicultural, and social justice counseling literature provides theories and concepts that help integrate sociocultural and systemic factors into the understanding of diverse clients and their concerns. Three such concepts are the oppression model, social identity development, and worldview.

Understanding Diverse Clients Through the Oppression Model

Both multicultural and social justice counseling perspectives stress the importance of understanding clients and their concerns in terms of the systems in which they develop and live. This type of understanding allows counselors or therapists to see themselves, clients, and the counseling relationship as part of societal systems, envision external barriers to client well-being, and implement systemic interventions such as advocacy. One way to conceptualize societal systems is through the oppression model (Bell, 1997).

Social identity groups are a collection of people who share physical, cultural, or social characteristics within one of the categories of social identity. The common social identity group categories included in discussions of diversity are race, ethnicity, gender, sexual orientation, class, disability, age, and religion (Hardiman & Jackson, 1997). According to the oppression model, within each identity group category specific identity groups are valued more highly and, consequently, have more power than other groups. Social identity groups with more power are known as dominant or agent groups. Currently in the United States, agent groups include Whites, heterosexuals, males, the "able-bodied," the upper class, and young or middle-aged adults (Hardiman & Jackson, 1997). Social identity groups that have less power are known as target groups and include, but are not limited to, people of color; gays, lesbians, or bisexuals; females or transgender people; people with disabilities; the working class or poor; and older persons or the very young (Hardiman & Jackson, 1997).

Oppression begins with agent groups systematically devaluing the values, beliefs, and experiences of target groups. A multileveled socialization process that occurs both overtly and covertly perpetuates this devaluation. Many social and psychological processes contribute to the devaluation process, but the basic dynamics can be understood through examining the roles of stereotypes, prejudice, discrimination, and privilege.

Stereotypes are negative generalizations about social identity groups and group members. Stereotypes allow people to selectively attend to negative group attributes, which may or may not exist, and form simplistic, negative views that deny the complexity of human identity. Many prejudices are based on stereotypes. **Prejudices** are judgments of social identity groups or group members made without adequate information or contact (Smith & Kehe, 2004). Prejudices serve individual and group psychological needs by contrasting with another group or by justifying unequal treatment of other groups. This, the active form of prejudice, is called **discrimination**.

Discrimination is behavior by one social identity group that causes harm to members of other social identity groups (Smith & Kehe, 2004). Discrimination can take several forms.

Individual and **institutional discrimination** result from the actions of individuals and institutions and are intended to discriminate against target social identity groups and individuals. **Structural discrimination** results from policies and practices that unintentionally discriminate against target social identity groups.

Related to structural discrimination is **privilege**, which is defined as unearned access to resources that is readily available to members of agent groups (Smith & Kehe, 2004). Because of their access to resources and power, members of agent groups can function without understanding the needs of target groups and group members; consequently, agent groups are blinded to their own privilege and to the experiences of target groups. Thus, privilege is much more difficult to identify and eradicate than overt discrimination. Because of its association with agents in decision-making positions, ability to blind agents to the needs and experiences of target groups and group members, and invisibility, privilege allows for the creation of policies, laws, organizations, and institutions that are discriminatory. These structures socialize generations of agents to privilege while socializing targets to oppression, powerlessness, and discrimination.

The material, emotional, and relational results of oppression are relevant to counseling process. Clients may lack access to resources such as basic human needs and education and suffer discriminatory treatment by banks, law enforcement, and employers. The experience of being oppressed profoundly affects how target groups and individuals view themselves and others. The emotional results of oppression include internalized oppression, learned helplessness, and functional paranoia (Sue & Sue, 2003). Additionally, the relational results of oppression may manifest in the therapeutic relationship as mistrust and anger (Helms & Cook, 1999).

The oppression model gives counselors or therapists a basic framework to understand the large and small systems in which practitioners and clients function, to understand agent and target client experiences, and to understand themselves as people who have also developed within these systems. The oppression model also reminds practitioners to be vigilant for oppression, discrimination, and privilege and to assume that all dominant culture systems may have some oppressive aspects.

Understanding Diverse Clients Through Social Identity Development

Traditionally, counselors or therapists have understood client identity through human theories such as Erikson's psychosocial theory and Freud's psychoanalytic theory (Quin & Comstock, 2005). However, these theories do not adequately assist practitioners in understanding how social, political, and cultural contexts influence diverse client identity. Social identity development models have emerged, in part, to answer this need. According to Sue and Sue (2003), racial/cultural identity models, a form of social identity development model, represent some of the most useful frameworks for better understanding and treating clients with diverse identities. The following paragraphs describe a process of social identity development, identify prominent social identity models, and discuss the usefulness of these models.

Identity is profoundly affected by the socially assigned designations of culture, race, ethnicity, gender, religion, sexual orientation, ability or disability, and class, among others. Identity, or sense of self, begins with the individual characteristics and social identity group memberships with which that person is born (Tatum, 2000). Throughout life, family, institutions such as schools, churches, and legal systems, and the cultural environments of communities, regions, and nations influence identity. Within these contexts, social identity group memberships are valued differently. For instance, in one family males may be valued more highly than females or in a community heterosexuality may be valued more highly than being gay, lesbian, or bisexual. Each valuation may be internalized by a person to some degree as part of his or her identity. In this way, social identity development affects how people view and feel about themselves, members of their identity groups, and those in other groups (Helms & Cook, 1999).

Social identity development models emerged for the purpose of simplifying the complexities of identity development. Most social identity development models characterize individuals as having varying degrees of awareness and acceptance of their social identities. These models describe individuals' level of identification with social identity groups through the behaviors and attitudes they display (Helms & Cook, 1999). This variability validates that members of a social identity group may share characteristics and experiences but also may vary significantly in their identification with that group, which allows counselors to conceptualize diverse clients without stereotyping (Sue & Sue, 2003).

The predominant social identity development models describe minority racial, ethnic, and cultural group members' experiences as they develop within the dominant, White culture. Examples of these models are Atkinson, Morten, and Sue's racial/cultural identity development model (R/CID) (Sue & Sue, 2003) and the people of color racial identity model (Helms, 1995). These models and others share a progression of statuses from dominant culture acceptance, to minority culture acceptance, to a complex state of minority culture acceptance that allows connection to and valuing of other cultures, including the dominant culture.

The stages of the R/CID (Sue & Sue, 2003) provide an example of this progression. In the initial stage, conformity, minority group individuals prefer dominant culture values over those of their own groups. In the dissonance stage, these individuals become increasingly aware of racism and discrimination and experience conflict as their dominant culture values are challenged. Individuals in the resistance and immersion stage may strongly commit to minority values and beliefs, reject dominant culture, and become passionate about combating discrimination against their own group. Individuals in the introspection stage may experience discomfort with the rigid views they held before, reevaluate dominant culture, and struggle with how to integrate dominant culture with minority culture. During the final stage, integrative awareness, individuals develop an appreciation of their own culture and dominant culture, critically evaluate all cultures, and commit to ending all forms of oppression.

Models have also been developed to describe the social identity development of dominant group individuals. Helms' White racial identity model is an example of this type of model (Helms & Cook, 1999). The assumption that healthy identity development for dominant group members involves becoming aware of privilege and its affect on other groups forms the basis of this model. Seven stages describe White individuals as they move from ignorance of and contentment with the racist status quo (contact stage) through stages of increasing awareness, varying attitudes toward group identity, and increasing personal responsibility (disintegration, reintegration, pseudo-independence, immersion, and emersion stages). By the final stage, autonomy, White individuals have developed a positive, White, nonracist identity, value diversity, and take an active stance toward combating racism.

Although many social identity models are structured around race and ethnicity, some models describe the identity development process of other social identity group categories. An example is Cass's (1979) model of gay, lesbian, and bisexual sexual identity formation. Hardiman and Jackson (1997) described a generic model of social identity development that includes all target and agent groups in society. This model, like the aforementioned racial/ethnic models, moves from target and agent individuals having little or no consciousness of their group identity, to acceptance, to resistance, to redefinition, and finally to a stage called internalization.

Understanding clients through social identity development is complicated by the reality that each person has multiple social group memberships spanning many dimensions of diversity. For example a person may identify as lesbian, female, Asian American, and working class. Reynolds and Pope (1991) suggested that people experience several stages of social identity development simultaneously, thereby living a blend of social identities that result in complex experiencing of themselves and the world. Thus the aforementioned person may experience varying levels of identity development with respect to each of her identities and have disparate feelings about each aspect.

Social identity development models offer counselors or therapists several benefits. Foremost, these models allow practitioners to better understand clients' experiences, issues, and needs. Each phase of development is associated with different behavior and feelings, which may influence the process of counseling. For instance, African American clients in the conformity stage and those in the immersion stage, as described by the R/CID model, will likely have different feelings toward the dominant culture and different views about the role of racism. They will have different levels of comfort with discussing issues of race, and they may express different levels of comfort and trust with a White therapist or with an African American therapist. All these factors influence the process of counseling.

Social identity development models also allow counselors or therapists to better understand themselves. Whether counselors or therapists have agent or target identities, or a combination of both, their relationships with these identities will affect how they view and interact with clients during the counseling process (Helms & Cook, 1999). Self-assessment of social identity development enables counselors or therapists to better identify their own vulnerabilities with regard to diversity and target knowledge and experiences and to identify counsel that may assist them in better serving diverse client populations.

Social identity development models can be great tools for counselors or therapists, but they have limitations. Reynolds and Pope (1991) caution against oversimplifying the use of identity development models and suggest that rigidly ascribing one identity to a client may result in an inaccurate view of client experience. Others caution that social identity theories should not be used to stereotype clients; instead, they should be used to help understand clients in their current context (Kwong-Liem, 2001; Sue & Sue, 2003).

Understanding Diverse Clients Through Worldview

In addition to understanding diverse clients' systems and social identities, counselors or therapists need to understand clients as individuals with their own unique experience of the world (Ibrahim, 1991). The concept of **worldview** is useful for this purpose (Ibrahim, 1991; Sue & Sue, 2003). Worldview is related to social identity but includes (1) individual, group, and universal dimensions; (2) cultural upbringing and individual life experiences; and (3) all client conceptions that guide their meaning making, decisions, and behavior (Ibrahim, 1991; Sue & Sue, 2003). Worldview encompasses clients' individual, social, and universal contexts, including dimensions of family, social identity, history, language, and biological, ecological, and environmental factors (Smith & Kehe, 2004).

Although worldview is complex, models such as Kluckhohn and Strodtbeck's (1961) value-orientation model may simplify understanding its important dimensions. This model highlights four dimensions where counselor and client worldviews may differ significantly: experiences and values of time, attitudes toward activity, views of social relationships, and beliefs regarding the essential nature of people. Ibrahim (1991) expanded the model into a theory, developed a measurement instrument—the Scale to Assess Worldviews, and described the categories to more specifically express a wide range of worldviews:

- View of human nature—good, bad, and a combination of good and bad
- View of social relationships—lineal-hierarchical, collateral-mutual, and individualistic
- View of nature—subjugate and control nature, live in harmony with nature, and accept the power and control of nature over people
- Time orientation—past, present, and future
- Activity orientation—being, being-in-becoming, and doing

Ibrahim suggested that orientation within this framework must be understood in the context of history of the client's identified groups, languages, gender, religion, family history as well as current family life, ethnic/cultural and majority culture perspectives, and neighborhoods in which the client grew up.

Some authors have focused on three other dimensions of worldview: locus of control, locus of responsibility, and collectivism or individualism (Oyserman, Coon, & Kemmelmeir, 2002; Sue & Sue, 2003). Locus of control refers to beliefs about the degree to which a person can influence his or her own life and ranges from internal where the person can exert control to external where external factors control the individual. Locus of responsibility describes beliefs about where responsibility for a problem lies, generally in terms of attributing responsibility to either the individual or to the system (Sue & Sue, 2003). Most counseling theories that emphasize intrapsychic phenomena demonstrate an individual locus of responsibility, whereas theories that emphasize family, organizational, or societal dynamics demonstrate a systemic locus of responsibility.

Worldview can be characterized in terms of individualism or collectivism. An individualistic worldview places the individual and her or his goals, uniqueness, and power at the center of importance. A collectivistic worldview places the social (family, community, nation) at the center (Oyserman et al., 2002). A primary concern for autonomy of the individual demonstrates a high level of individualism; in contrast, attention to the influence of choices on family and community demonstrates a high level of collectivism. Clients with a primarily collectivistic orientation have different priorities and choices during therapy from clients who are more individualistic.

Counselors or therapists who gain knowledge of their own and clients' worldviews will more accurately understand diverse clients' experiences, issues, goals, and ways of being during the counseling process. The concept of worldview allows counselors or therapists to understand clients in terms of clients' universal, group, and individual identities (Sue & Sue, 2003). Practitioners who adopt the worldview concept can be both culturally sensitive and client specific, thereby avoiding stereotypic understanding and treatment of clients that may be damaging (Ibrahim, 1991).

DIVERSITY AND THE COUNSELING PROCESS

Adequate understanding is only part of providing competent counseling to diverse clients. Differences between counselor or therapist and client affect the counseling process from relationship formation to goal setting to implementing strategies and techniques. Counselors or therapists must be aware of and manage the influence of diversity on the counseling relationship, collaborate with diverse clients to form appropriate goals, and implement socially and culturally sensitive interventions and strategies to meet those goals. The following sections discuss the implications of diversity on the counseling relationship, goals, and diversity-appropriate counseling interventions.

The Counseling Relationship

A strong relationship is necessary for effective counseling to take place. The qualities of such a relationship were summarized in chapter 1 as empathic understanding, respect and positive regard, genuineness and congruence, concreteness, warmth, and immediacy. A strong counseling relationship becomes even more important when working with diverse clients; however, forming a strong relationship may be challenging. Issues that deserve particular attention during formation and maintenance of the counseling relationship are developing cultural empathy (Chung & Bemak, 2002) and trust (Helms & Cook, 1999; Slattery, 2004; Sue & Sue, 2003) and striving for an egalitarian relationship when appropriate (McWhirter, 1991; Slattery, 2004).

Cultural Empathy. Empathy is accepted as one of the core conditions in the counseling relationship. Chung and Bemak (2002) described empathy as the counselor's ability to view and experience the world cognitively and emotionally as the client does. Attaining and communicating this level of understanding when counseling diverse clients requires special consideration, and the term **cultural empathy** is used to describe this experience and process. Ridley and Lingle (1996) defined cultural empathy as a counselor's learned ability to understand and communicate understanding of the culturally diverse client's experience, as well as to experience and communicate concern for the culturally diverse client. Cultural knowledge is a prerequisite; however, cultural empathy moves a step beyond cognitive understanding to include emotional understanding, concern, and, especially, communication.

Several authors have discussed concrete ways to establish cultural empathy. The following list summarizes the suggestions of Chung and Bemak (2002) and Ridley and Lingle (1996). To establish cultural empathy, counselors or therapists should communicate these elements in clear but culturally appropriate ways during the counseling process:

- Understanding of the client's experience for clarification
- A humble but realistic sense of how well the counselor may or may not understand the client's cultural background and experience
- A sincere interest in learning more about the client's cultural background and experience
- Openness to clarifying verbal and nonverbal communication, checking out assumptions, and adapting the counseling process and techniques to be more culturally appropriate
- Affirmation of the client's cultural experience as well as cultural differences between counselor or therapist and client

Trust. Trust is an important component of effective counseling relationships. Slattery (2004) indicated that cultural mistrust can be a barrier to effective counseling relationships and may be based on personal experience, group history, association of counseling with the establishment, or therapist behavior. This may be especially true when clients have predominantly target group identities and counselors have predominantly agent identities. Because of experiences with institutional discrimination, clients from target groups may tend to view mental health professionals as representatives of the dominant establishment and as not to be trusted unless there is evidence to the contrary.

Sue and Sue (2003) reported that counselors or therapists who are perceived as trustworthy by clients have more influence and potential effectiveness during the counseling process. Responsibility for developing trust in the diverse counseling relationship rests on the practitioners. Counselors or therapists should not immediately characterize mistrust as pathological on the part of the client. Diverse clients may test dominant-culture practitioners for sincerity and openness. Even subtle verbal or nonverbal behavior by the counselor or therapist that indicates prejudice will lower levels of trust; responses that are honest, and genuine, include some self-disclosure, and acknowledge obvious differences will more likely be perceived as trustworthy (Sue & Sue, 2003).

Egalitarian Relationships. Egalitarian relationships, when consistent with client expectations and needs, are ideal for work with diverse populations, especially with persons who have been disempowered by chronic oppression (Cheatham et al., 2002; Slattery, 2004). Many of the ideas regarding egalitarian counseling relationships are derived from feminist therapy and are counter to some traditional counseling theories that place the bulk of power in the counseling relationship with the counselor. Egalitarian counseling relationships occur when power between the client and counselor is somewhat equalized. McWhirter (1991) suggested the following techniques for developing egalitarian relationships:

- Do not use psychological jargon, blame the client for lack of improvement, or refuse to share knowledge or educate the client. These acts mystify the process.
- Define problems and identify goals collaboratively.
- As practitioners, present yourselves realistically—as fallible human beings with specialized knowledge and skills that may be helpful.
- Allow clients to present themselves as experts on themselves and their environments.
- Educate clients so that they can participate in an informed manner as well as increase their power to deal with issues on their own.

Many diverse clients, due to their issues, stage of development, and worldview, may require a direct or authoritarian style (Sue & Sue, 2003). Counselors or therapists must be sensitive to cues that indicate a client may need a more direct style, for example, frequently requesting and accepting feedback, verbally or nonverbally; expressing displeasure with lack of direction or authority; and needing prompting before expressing opinions (Slattery, 2004).

Counseling Goals

Previous sections have described some ways in which clients' experiences of oppression, social identity and level of development, and worldviews may influence the formation and prioritization of counseling goals. Above all, counseling goals that are inconsistent with a diverse client's values, beliefs, and current environment are to be avoided (Helms & Cook, 1999). For example, a common counseling goal is autonomy or independence, but this may not be an appropriate goal for a client who is deeply socialized in a collectivistic culture or a culture in which families are viewed as central. To avoid this kind of mismatch, the goals of counseling should be coconstructed with the client and should reflect the client's worldview and cultural orientation, as well as the client's current environment (Slattery, 2004).

Authors have presented various general counseling goals for diverse clients. Helms and Cook (1999) described symptom remission, social identity development, bicultural identity development, and cultural congruence as potentially appropriate counseling goals for many such clients. From a social justice perspective, D'Andrea (2000) suggested removal of exterior barriers, such as discriminatory policies and practices, that impede client well-being as important goals of counseling. Empowerment is a commonly mentioned goal of both multicultural and social justice counseling (McWhirter, 1991; Slattery, 2004). According to McWhirter, empowerment within the context of counseling is

> the process by which people, organizations, or groups who are powerless (a) become aware of the power dynamics at work in their life context, (b) develop the skills and capacity for gaining some reasonable control over their lives, (c) exercise this control without infringing upon the rights of others, and (d) support the empowerment of others in their community. (p. 224)

Empowerment may be an especially appropriate goal for those whose self-determination is limited, who are members of stigmatized or oppressed social identity groups, and who are distressed by their own dependency and sense of powerlessness (McWhirter).

Appropriate Counseling Interventions with Diverse Clients

Socially and culturally appropriate interventions are the consequence of counselor or therapist awareness and knowledge of self and diverse clients. Culturally appropriate interventions take into account clients' communication styles, values and beliefs, and life experiences and result in formation of functional counseling relationships and attainment of appropriate goals. These interventions can range from the skills and strategies of traditional counseling approaches to indigenous or folk healing methods to a synthesis of both. Interventions may be delivered conventionally in a one-on-one mental health setting or may be delivered in the context of group, family, community, or other systems. The list of recommendations that follows was adapted from Sue and Sue (2003) and Arredondo et al. (1996). Counselors or therapists who wish to use socially and culturally appropriate interventions skills should consider these actions:

- Become familiar with a variety of theoretical orientations and approaches, because a flexible counseling approach is necessary to meet the needs of diverse clients.
- Be open to interventions that are outside the scope of traditional counseling, such as systemic interventions and indigenous or folk healing methods.
- Become knowledgeable of the effects of all dimensions of diversity on communication style.
- Become aware of your own communication style. Feedback from varied sources that are knowledgeable about diversity is especially useful.

- Assess all counseling interventions for strengths and weaknesses with respect to clients' social, cultural, spiritual, and political dimensions.
- Focus on actual skill building.
- Be mindful of the goals of interventions. Successful adaptation of skills is more likely if client needs are clear and interventions are designed to meet those needs.

Several aspects of appropriate counseling interventions are discussed next: adapting traditional interventions, incorporating indigenous or folk methods, communication issues, empowerment, and advocacy.

Adapting Traditional Interventions. Adapting traditional skills and interventions for diverse clients can range from using the skills as is but providing context to members about the purpose of the skill or intervention, to incorporating cultural variations. Working with diverse clients does not mean throwing out all traditional counseling skills (Sue & Sue, 2003); however, these skills will be much more useful if counselors or therapists orient clients to the counseling process and explain the purpose of specific skills and interventions (Arredondo et al., 1996). Diverse clients may become comfortable with skills and interventions if they understand the purpose. Provision of this type of context may also be helpful if the practitioner and client decide to brainstorm alternative interventions, and it will also assist the practitioner in finding appropriate cultural adaptations.

Range of adaptation can be demonstrated using as an example the common counseling skill, reflection of feeling. The counselor or therapist may choose to use reflection of feeling with a diverse client without much explanation or adaptation if the client is verbally expressive of feelings, seems comfortable with the counselor or therapist commenting on feelings, and responds to the reflection by agreeing, correcting, or expanding. The counselor or therapist may also choose to explain the purpose of feeling reflections. For example, "I will say what I believe you are feeling because it is important for me to understand what you are feeling and for you to know that I understand. I would like to know if you feel differently or if my words make you uncomfortable." Some diverse clients may not be comfortable challenging the counselor, so the counselor or therapist should monitor client verbal and nonverbal behavior for signs of shutting down or discomfort with feeling reflections.

If the client does not respond well to feeling reflections or if the counselor or therapist anticipates a poor response, the counselor or therapist may choose to adapt the skill to meet the client's needs. The practitioner should consider, and possibly explore with the client, (1) if verbal expression of feeling is discouraged by the client's cultural group or (2) if the client is uncomfortable discussing feelings in an individualistic context versus a family or community context. In the first instance, the practitioner and client can collaborate to find a suitable option, perhaps nonverbal techniques for expression (Arredondo et al., 1996). In the second instance, Cheatham et al. (2002) suggest rewording feeling reflections to include relationship and context, for example, "You feel anxious in relations to your family." If use of or adaptation of a customary skill or intervention does not seem to meet the diverse client's needs, then use of indigenous or culturally based interventions is another alternative.

Incorporating Indigenous or Folk Methods. Many authors consider the incorporation of indigenous and folk healing into counseling to be a potentially effective treatment option for culturally diverse clients (Koss-Chioino, 2000; Sue & Sue, 2003; Yeh, Hunter, Madan-Bahel,

Chiang, & Arora, 2004). Incorporation of these methods may be particularly useful if clients are deeply involved in their culture and request or mention these methods (Koss-Chioino). Additionally, Sue and Sue contend that becoming familiar with indigenous healing practices may help counselors or therapists better understand the worldview of diverse clients and assist counselors or therapists in anticipating potential conflicts in belief systems that may affect the therapeutic process.

Every society and culture has its own versions of healing and healers that address physical and psychological disturbances (Sue & Sue, 2003). According to Koss-Chioino (2000) alternative healing methods are a part not only of communities of underrepresented groups but also of dominant groups. Examples of indigenous or folk healing include Asian practices such as *reiki*, *quigong*, and *pranic* healing (Yeh et al., 2004); use by some Mexican Americans of a *curandero*, or spiritual advisor; and Native American healing traditions such as those of the Native American Church as well as more regional tribal traditions (Koss-Chioino).

The following actions are a summary of suggestions by Koss-Chioino (2000), Sue and Sue (2003), and Yeh et al. (2004) for counselors or therapists who are considering incorporating indigenous or folk methods or who are consulting with or referring to indigenous or folk healers:

- Become aware of your attitudes toward indigenous healing practices. Clients may hesitate to disclose interest in these methods if they sense negative attitudes.
- Become familiar with the beliefs and healing practices of different cultures.
- Extend knowledge of these practices by engaging in different communities and personalizing the information.
- Be willing to form respectful relationships with indigenous and folk healers. These relationships may provide useful information, build counselor credibility in the community, and facilitate future referral and consultation.
- Recognize the importance of spirituality in the lives of many diverse clients. Know your clients views on indigenous healing.
- Be aware of the ethical and practical challenges of consulting with indigenous healers or incorporating their healing methods into treatment.
- Become aware of new practices that synthesize indigenous methods with traditional counseling.

Communication Issues.   Therapy is a process of interpersonal interaction and social influence that relies on effective communication (Sue & Sue, 2003). Both counselor or therapist and client must communicate adequately, in both verbal and nonverbal realms, for effective therapy to take place. In particular, the practitioner's communication should be accurate and appropriate. Sue and Sue discussed several aspects of communication style that may affect counseling intervention. Differences between counselor or therapist and client **proxemics**, **kinesics**, and **paralanguage** may contribute to miscommunication during counseling. Proxemics involves individuals' culturally influenced sense of personal space; kinesics involves use of movement such as facial expressions, posture, gestures, and eye contact to communicate. Paralanguage relates to use of voice loudness, pauses, silences, speech rate, and inflection to express differences in meaning. Counselors or therapists should also consider whether the client's cultural communication style is **low context** or **high context**. Low-context communication relies largely on the message relayed by verbal communication, whereas high-context communication relies less on the verbal communication and more on additional shared understanding, nonverbal techniques, and paralanguage to convey the full meaning of the message. Counseling interventions for diverse clients should consider all of these dimensions (Sue & Sue, 2003).

Skills and Interventions for Empowerment. Empowerment is a commonly mentioned goal of counseling, particularly with diverse clients who may have experienced oppression (Lee, 1991; McWhirter, 1991; Slattery, 2004). For empowerment to occur, counselors or therapists need to use empowering interventions throughout the counseling process. According to McWhirter, empowering interventions start with the attitudes, belief, and person of the counselor or therapist. To be empowering, counselors or therapists should believe in the client's ability to make positive changes. Thus, empowering interventions should give no more "help" than is required.

Empowering interventions may be used early in counseling. Slattery (2004) suggested that the counseling process will be most empowering if clients are offered the least restrictive effective treatment possible and are given choices about receiving treatment. Clients should be educated about the rationale for treatment and interventions during informed consent, and clients should be aware that counseling is as much about learning to solve problems as it about solving problems. Additionally, the therapeutic relationship should be egalitarian and collaborative within culturally appropriate boundaries.

Empowerment continues through the phase of problem identification (McWhirter, 1991; Slattery, 2004). To maximize empowerment during this phase, counselors or therapists should listen to and respect client views of problems and desired outcomes (Slattery). Empowering conceptualizations (1) take into account the social, political, and economic context; (2) resist blaming the client for things beyond their control; and (3) clearly differentiate between responsibility for the problem, which may be environmental, and responsibility for coping with the problem, which is the client's (McWhirter). Ineffective or problem behavior should be viewed as best attempts to cope with the situation (Slattery).

Helping clients become aware of personal resources is also critical to empowerment. Identification of problem-free times and areas of life is essential to empowerment. Counselors or therapists should recognize and validate clients' strengths such as support networks. Clients' attempts at solutions should be acknowledged and used as building blocks for further problem solving (Slattery, 2004).

Education is one of the most empowering interventions, and it can be used throughout the counseling process. Exposing the client to the power dynamics that surround them empowers them in three ways (1) by making overt the external influences that have hindered them, (2) by helping them see themselves as less damaged; and (3) by encouraging more active and effective problem solving. Within the counseling session, clients should be taught and encouraged to identify their own patterns and environmental barriers rather than relying on the counselor. Helping clients to become assertive and to gain decision-making skills, and social skills is also empowering, although it is important to consider the impact of these skills on other parts of the client's life (Slattery, 2004).

Advocacy Skills and Interventions. Both the multicultural and social justice counseling literature have called on counselors and therapists to include advocacy in the scope of their practice (Arredondo et al., 1996; Sue et al., 1992). However, advocacy is not an intervention that has been a focus in counseling education or training programs. In this section we define advocacy and its forms, and identify advocacy skills and their use with diverse clients.

Ezell (2001) defines advocacy as "purposive efforts to change specific existing or proposed policies or practices on behalf of or with a specific clients or group of clients" (p. 23). Thus, advocacy is distinct from traditional counseling interventions in that its focus is ultimately the system and not the client. Ezell suggests that advocacy, in some form, is appropriate for clients who have little power and may not be able to advocate for themselves within the necessary systems without assistance.

Growing acceptance of advocacy as a counseling intervention has increased discussion of its scope and targets. Advocacy may be undertaken for a specific client (case advocacy) or for a group of clients with similar issues or identity (class advocacy) (Ezell, 2001). Targets of advocacy may also vary. The ACA Advocacy Competencies describe advocacy as occurring at microlevels and macrolevels, which include the client-student level, community-systems level, and the public information, social, and political levels (Lewis, Arnold, House, & Toporek, 2005).

- At the client-student level, counselors identify and facilitate client understanding of social, political, economic, and cultural barriers to client well-being, and they advocate with or on behalf of clients to respond to these barriers.
- At the community-systems level, counselors advocate for clients within the clients' communities and relevant institutions using nontraditional interventions to change attitudes, policies, rules, and structures that are detrimental to client well-being.
- At the macrolevel level, counselors intervene on a larger scale to raise awareness of broad societal issues, change attitudes and beliefs of the general public, and change public policy and laws that are harmful to groups of clients.

To make the variety of advocacy targets and interventions more concrete, here are several examples adapted from Ezell (2001) that represent different advocacy types and targets:

- Teaching a client advocacy skills so she can advocate for fair work conditions for herself (client level, case advocacy)
- Representing a student client at an administrative hearing to decide if he will be reinstated to school (community-systems level, case advocacy)
- Presenting a rationale to the board of directors of a private, nonprofit counseling center for providing translators and bilingual counselors for non-English-speaking clients (community-systems level, class advocacy)
- Gathering data about disparities in mental health services for immigrants to the United States (macrolevel, class advocacy)

According to Kiselica and Robinson (2001), advocacy requires special skills and attributes such as verbal and nonverbal communication skills, understanding of how systems work, awareness of group dynamics, technology and research skills, and a commitment to human rights issues. Ezell (2001) suggests that counselors or therapists who undertake advocacy need to be persistent, persuasive, collaborative, assertive, and resourceful.

Many counselors and therapists are relatively unfamiliar with advocacy; therefore, they need to be vigilant about ethical issues (Ezell, 2001). Counselors and therapists should make every attempt to receive informed consent from clients or client groups before undertaking advocacy activities. Similarly, clients have the right to refuse advocacy. Counselors and therapists should also evaluate if advocacy for one client or client group will harm another client or client group. As advocacy is often meant to help clients from diverse groups, the methods and outcomes of the advocacy should be evaluated carefully for consistency with clients' values and beliefs (Ezell).

BECOMING A DIVERSITY-COMPETENT COUNSELOR

Sue and Sue (2003) contend that in the changing world of counseling there is no clinical competence without multicultural competence. Sue et al. (1992) have described three necessary characteristics of culturally competent practitioners: (1) awareness of own assumptions, values, and biases; (2) understanding of the worldview of the culturally different client; and (3) ability to develop appropriate intervention strategies and techniques. The preceding sections of this chapter have discussed various ways to understand and work with diverse clients. However, acquiring the awareness, knowledge, and skills necessary for diversity competence extends far beyond this chapter. The next two sections discuss gaining self-awareness and gaining additional knowledge and skills.

Gaining Self-Awareness

As the MCCs have outlined, counselor or therapist awareness of self is critical is critical to providing competent services to diverse clients (Sue et al., 1992). Practitioners' views of themselves and others are shaped by their experiences as members of multiple social identity groups. Without awareness of stereotypes, biases, and culturally based reactions, practitioners will unwittingly view diverse clients' experiences, issues, goals, and interactions in counseling from their own perspective, which may be inaccurate or harmful to the client. This phenomenon is called **cultural encapsulation** (Sue & Sue, 2003).

To minimize cultural encapsulation, counselors or therapists need to develop a clear sense of their place in society, cultural background and influences, beliefs and values, and interpersonal impact on others. Counselors or therapists should know their cultural background and how it has influenced their attitudes, values, and biases toward normal and abnormal behavior. They also must be able to recognize the limits of their competence, recognize the sources of their discomfort with diverse clients, and understand how the dynamics of oppression affect them personally and their interactions with others (Arredondo et al., 1996). To achieve these goals, authors suggest that counselors or therapists attend to their personal growth, seek out professional workshops, actively seek a nonracist identity, maintain personal and professional relationships with individuals different from themselves, and seek feedback regarding behavior (Arredondo et al.). Counselors or therapists can also become more aware of their socialization through a variety of learning activities, such as completing a social group membership profile (Bell, 1997) or analyzing their level of social identity development using a relevant model (Cheatham et al., 2002). Helms and Cook (1999) suggest that practitioners answer the following questions in exploring their assumptions about human functioning and the counseling process:

- What do you consider to be normal counselor or therapist and client behavior during therapy?

- If group goals are in conflict with the client's individual needs or desires, how do you resolve the conflicts?
- At what age do you believe that a child should leave his or her parents and make a life independent of them?
- What strategies do you use to include a client's support systems as allies?
- Can you describe an instance in which you intervened to change a system to fit the client's need rather than requiring the client to change to fit the system?

Gaining Additional Knowledge and Skills

As described in preceding sections, knowledge of client worldview is critical for counselors or therapists to understand clients' experiences, issues, goals, and best path to healing and functioning. However, the complexity of worldview and the breadth of diversity make this a monumental task. Counselors or therapists should begin by collecting knowledge about their own social and cultural background. Exploration and gathering of knowledge should then extend to populations or cultural groups with whom they will commonly work and those about whom they have little knowledge. Exploration involves the group's history in the society, including impact of oppression, and knowledge of the group's culture, including common beliefs and values regarding parenting, family, spirituality, social hierarchy, gender roles, communication styles, and relationship to time and space. Knowledge of a group's areas of strength, resistance, and resilience is also critical (Arredondo et al., 1996; Slattery, 2004).

Hanna, Bemak, and Chung (1999) indicate that book knowledge is not sufficient for developing adequate knowledge and skills. Receiving supervision from clinicians who are knowledgeable about diversity or differ in social identity has the potential to increase awareness, knowledge, and skills related to counseling diverse clients (Lum, 2003). In addition, Lum suggests making book knowledge and skills come alive by "contacting" diverse communities by becoming familiar with community demographics, reading local alternative news sources, and interviewing community leaders. Lum also suggests spending time in the community—observing, patronizing businesses, attending social functions, talking with community members, and shadowing helping professionals who have developed effective relationships in the community.

CONCLUSIONS

The counseling profession is committed to providing competent treatment to diverse clients; however, traditional approaches are limited in their usefulness for this purpose. The multicultural and social justice counseling perspectives share these two assumptions: (1) Counselors or therapists must integrate diverse clients' social and cultural context and experiences of oppression during the counseling process, and (2) counselors or therapists must go outside the boundaries of traditional counseling approaches to adequately serve these clients. The multicultural and social justice perspectives highlight the importance of using broad definitions of diversity in counseling, as well as a dual focus on microlevel and macrolevel counseling interventions.

Human diversity affects nearly every aspect of the counseling process; therefore, counselors or therapists need to use new frameworks to understand themselves and diverse clients and to guide them in the counseling process. The oppression model, social identity development, and the concept of worldview are frameworks that can help practitioners integrate sociocultural and systemic factors into their understanding of diverse clients. Counselors or therapists who view themselves and their clients through these frameworks will better understand the experiences and concerns of diverse clients and have a solid foundation for understanding the influence of diversity on the rest of the counseling process.

The counseling process is affected by diversity through the counseling relationship, counseling goals, and the appropriateness of interventions and strategies for diverse clients. Developing trust and empathy may be challenging; nevertheless, the initial challenges can be overcome with sufficient knowledge of client worldview and appropriate communication. Egalitarian counseling relationships may be beneficial for diverse clients, although client needs and expectations for structure need to be considered. Counselors or therapists should collaborate with diverse clients to set counseling goals, because worldview and environment may influence what is need and desired outcomes.

One of the most important ways that diversity affects the counseling process is through skills and interventions. The skills and interventions used should reflect diverse clients' communication styles, values and beliefs, and life experiences. Although traditional techniques and strategies may be effective with diverse clients, adaptation or incorporation of culturally based methods may be necessary. In addition, systemic interventions such as advocacy may be necessary to fully address the issues of diverse clients.

Finally, continuing practitioner development is an absolute must to attain diversity competence. Attaining necessary self-awareness, knowledge, and skills goes far beyond reading. Counselors or therapists will not be able to adequately work with diverse clients until they fully understand themselves as social, cultural, and political beings. Acquisition of knowledge and skills should extend beyond book learning to actual experience of differences and personal change.

Theories of Counseling and Psychotherapy

Chapters

Part II contains 11 chapters, each of which addresses a selected theoretical system that has direct application to the counseling or therapy process. We selected the theoretical systems based on their current use in the field of counseling and therapy, and we chose the chapter authors based on their expertise and their current application of the theoretical system in their work with clients. To provide you with a consistent format, each chapter contains information dealing with the following areas:

- *Background.* Historical information related to the development of the theoretical system and the individuals responsible for its development
- *Human nature.* A developmental perspective—the process of individual development over time, as defined by the theoretical system
- *Major constructs.* Structural components that comprise the theoretical system
- *Applications.*

  Overview. Introduction to the six areas that follow

  Goals of counseling and psychotherapy. Description of desired client outcomes based on the tenets of the theory

  Process of change. Factors in the theory that address what brings about change in the individual

Traditional intervention strategies. Techniques for implementing the process of change

Brief intervention strategies. Techniques for implementing the process of change using a brief approach

- *Clients with serious mental health issues.* Discussion of how each theory can be used with clients who have serious mental health issues
- *Cross-cultural considerations.* Discussion of cross-cultural considerations in using the theory
- *Evaluation.*

Overview. Introduction to the three areas that follow

Supporting research. Current research studies that form the bases for continued use of this theoretical system

Limitations. Description of the factors that limit the use of this theoretical system

Summary chart. Summarization of the material presented

- *Case study:* Case analysis and treatment based on the theory

Chapter Content

The first three chapters in part II deal with the theoretical systems, often classified as *analytical,* developed by Sigmund Freud, Carl Jung, and Alfred Adler. Chapter 4, "Psychoanalytic Theory," provides background information relative to counseling and psychotherapy in a psychoanalytic framework and emphasizes current use of this framework for individual counseling and therapy. Chapter 5, "Jungian Analytical Theory," describes the development and definition of the major constructs of Jungian psychology and applies the constructs in the case of Jonathan, the subject of the hypothetical case study that occurs in each chapter. Chapter 6, "Adlerian Theory," highlights the contributions of Alfred Adler and demonstrates the application of his major constructs in current approaches to counseling and psychotherapy.

The second three chapters in part II deal with the theoretical systems often classified as *humanistic.* Chapter 7, "Existential Theory," sets forth the philosophical underpinnings of existential counseling and psychotherapy and demonstrates how this philosophy translates into approaches that can be used by the counselor or therapist in working with clients. Chapter 8, "Person-Centered Theory," deals specifically with the work of Carl Rogers. The chapter highlights the continual development of this theoretical system from Rogers' work in the early 1940s to the last years of his life, when he traveled to troubled places in the world and used his person-centered approach to promote peace among warring groups. Chapter 9, "Gestalt Theory," emphasizes the pioneering work of Frederick Perls and his development of Gestalt counseling and psychotherapy. Major concepts and interventions are presented in combination with their current use in counseling and therapy

The next three chapters in part II deal with the theoretical systems, often classified as *behavioral, cognitive behavioral,* or *rational emotive,* that were developed by the following theorists: Beck, Ellis, and Glasser. Chapter 10, "Cognitive-Behavior Theories," provides a general background about both the behavioral and cognitive-behavior theoretical views and discusses how the cognitive-behavior approach developed from the behavioral point of view. Emphasis is given to the work of Aaron Beck. Chapter 11, "Rational Emotive Behavior Theory," focuses on the work of Albert Ellis, with special attention directed to the A-B-C-D-E model for understanding how thoughts and behaviors are related. Contributions to counseling and psychotherapy made by Ellis and his colleagues are stressed. Chapter 12, "Reality Therapy Theory," highlights the work of William Glasser. The chapter places special emphasis on his delivery system for reality therapy, which helps persons remediate deficiencies, make better choices, and become more fully self-actualized.

Chapter 13, "Family Theory," suggests ideas for working with families, because individual approaches do not adequately address the patterns of communicating and relating that connect individuals to each other in families. The chapter indicates ways to add systems-level interventions to the individualistic approaches studied in previous chapters.

Chapter 14, "Feminist Theory," shows how feminist theory has evolved gradually as a response to women's rejection of traditional psychotherapies. The chapter addresses some of the sexist, oppressive aspects of many of the currently used theories of counseling and psychotherapy, and it encourages counselors and therapists *not* to apply theories based on male developmental models to women.

We think that the theoretical systems included in part II provide a comprehensive and current review of major counseling and psychotherapy approaches to working with individuals. Our conviction is strengthened by our selection of authors, who not only have expertise in the specific theoretical systems, but also practice these approaches in working with clients.

We asked each author or set of authors to address the following case study information in the development of a treatment or counseling plan that is consistent with the specific theoretical system presented. This approach gives you the opportunity to view the theoretical systems from a comparative perspective as you search for the theoretical system that is most appropriate for your future work as counselors or therapists.

THE CASE OF JONATHAN

Client Demographics

The client, Jonathan, is a 36-year-old Native American male. He is the youngest of six children and was raised on the Navajo reservation in New Mexico. He attended the Bureau of Indian Affairs school on the reservation, dropped out when he was 16, and returned the following year and earned his high school diploma. He attended the University of New Mexico for 2 years where he pursued a degree in nursing. At the age of 20, he dropped out of the nursing program and returned to the reservation. He secured a job at the Bureau of Indian Affairs hospital and worked in several positions during his time there. He has been married twice and is currently separated from his second wife. He has four children, three from his first marriage (two boys and a girl) and one from his second marriage (a girl). The four children range in age from 6 to 15. He has been separated from his second wife for approximately 7 months, and at the time of the separation he left the reservation. He is currently living in Phoenix, Arizona, where he works in a residential treatment facility that specializes in providing alcohol and drug treatment for adolescents.

Presenting Problem

Jonathan arrived 10 minutes late for his initial appointment. He was apologetic and explained his difficulty in finding the mental health agency. He appeared uncomfortable and somewhat apprehensive as he explained that his supervisor had suggested that he talk with someone at the agency regarding some of the difficulties he was having at work. During the intake process, he said that he was having difficulties getting along with his coworkers and his supervisor. He stated that he could not seem to relate to the people he worked with. They always seem to expect more that he can deliver. They are always on his back. His work is never good enough to suit his supervisor. He describes the supervisor as a perfectionist who wants everyone else to be the same.

Jonathan explained that the situation at work is making him very depressed; he is having difficulty sleeping and his sleep is often interrupted with disturbing dreams. He is lonely and misses seeing his children and his family, but he feels that he has no future on the reservation. He is having financial difficulties due to the cost of living in Phoenix and his need to pay child support to his first wife and provide financial support to his second wife and daughter. He is drinking more than he should and is having a difficult time controlling his anger and frustration. He has had several arguments with coworkers and his supervisor, the last of these resulting in his being suspended for 3 days without pay. He has tried to find other employment but nothing seems to work out. He feels this is due to the fact that he is a Native American and most employers are prejudiced; this has added to his anger. It scares him when he thinks of what he might do if something does not change. He refused to elaborate on that statement but feels that he is trapped. In his words, he is not wanted in the "White man's world" and has no future in his own.

Family Background

Jonathan describes his family of origin as close knit, held together by cultural and tribal values. He was raised to be proud of his Native American background, his language, and tribal traditions. He had three older brothers and two older sisters. One brother was killed in a traffic accident and one sister died during childbirth. His remaining siblings and his parents continue to live on the reservation. His two older brothers manage a trading post on the reservation and his sister is a full-time mother to her three children. His parents continue to farm, although due to declining health, they now require much more assistance from their children. His parents and siblings were very upset when he left the reservation and have put a lot of pressure on him to return. The pressure has increased because of the declining health of his parents.

Early Adult Years

Jonathan's decision to quit school at the age of 16 occurred at the time of the death of his brother. Jonathan had been driving the car and always felt that there was something that he could have done to avoid the accident. The car had been struck by a drunk driver who had crossed the median and hit them head on. If only he had been able to swerve, his brother might still be alive. Jonathan had been thrown from the car and sustained only a broken shoulder. His guilt and grief over his brother's death, and the reaction of his family, had all added up to Jonathan leaving school and spending the year trying to figure out what he was going to do about all of this. His parents and siblings were upset by his leaving school, but they were dealing with their own grief and tolerated his decision not to return to school.

Jonathan did not seem to be sure about whether his family blamed him for the accident. He went back to school the following year and earned his high school diploma.

His 2 years at the University of New Mexico were difficult in terms of relationships and finances. He had received a scholarship, but he was away from the reservation and away from his girlfriend. During his 2nd year at the university, his girlfriend announced that she was pregnant. Jonathan left school at the end of the year, returned to the reservation, and got a job at the local hospital. He and his girlfriend married a month after his return. The marriage resulted in three children and lasted 6 years. During the last year of the marriage, Jonathan began drinking heavily and seeing another woman. He and his wife divorced 6 years ago.

Postdivorce Years

Six months after the divorce, Jonathan married again and within 4 months he and his new wife had a daughter. Things went well during the first few years of the marriage, but earlier patterns returned. Jonathan began to drink again and his wife began to suspect that he was seeing another woman. Six months ago, they agreed to a trial 2-month separation, which has been continued three times. From Jonathan's perspective, the chances of reconciliation do not look good. He states that he loves his wife but does not know how to live in this type of relationship. He feels that the same thing happened in his first marriage; no matter what he tries to do to make the relationship work, it is never good enough. His reaction is often to get angry and walk away. He often turns to drink and other women for solace. He feels that if he and his wife cannot salvage their marriage, he will never again place himself in this type of relationship. He feels guilty for being an absent father to his children, and he thinks there is something that he should do or could do to make all of this better.

Jonathan decided to leave the reservation at this time, hoping that he could find answers to his problems. He also felt that the reservation could not provide him with the professional or financial opportunities necessary. Shortly after his move to Phoenix he began to have disturbing dreams. According to Jonathan, these dreams generally entail the following:

> I am on a long bus filled with very noisy people. We all seem to be going to different places. When I talk with other people on the bus, I get the impression that they think that the bus is going to California; others think that it is going to New York. I bought a ticket to Albuquerque. As the bus moves along, the passengers get more irritated and begin to argue as to where the bus is going and when it will reach its destination. The more the passengers argue the faster the bus goes. We pass signs indicating California, New York, and Albuquerque, but the bus never stops long enough for anyone to get off. At each stop the bus seems to get much longer and no one can reach the exit before the bus starts again. I do my best to explain the problem to the bus driver but she doesn't seem to hear me or ignores me. I end up shouting at the driver and she ends up laughing at me. I pick up a piece of pipe and start pounding the steering wheel to stop her from laughing. I also realize, as I look back from the front of the bus, that all of the other passengers have disappeared. I am all alone with the laughing driver. It is about this time that I wake up and find that I am not able to get back to sleep. I have had this same type of dream about four times in the past 6 weeks.

These dreams, coupled with the situation at work and the marital separation, seem to leave Jonathan very depressed, angry, lonely, and without any direction. In his words, "I have little to live for. I have ruined the lives of three families plus my own life and who knows what I am doing to my children."

CHAPTER 4

Psychoanalytic Theory

Gregory J. Novie
Southwest Center for Psychoanalytic Studies

This chapter briefly outlines psychoanalytic theory and technique. Its purpose is to introduce the beginning clinician to a complex psychotherapeutic process and metapsychology. Its goal is to interest you in further exploring psychoanalysis as a treatment option and personal theoretical orientation. (A suggested reading list appears at the end of the chapter for those who wish to go beyond the basic information of the chapter.)

Beginning with the work of Sigmund Freud, the chapter reviews a history of psychoanalysis and then presents the psychoanalytic movement from the perspective of three historical periods. The first period was dominated by Freud and continued through the end of World War I. The second period, which followed the end of World War I, was dominated by the establishment of training institutions and the emergence of the American Psychoanalytic Association. In the third period, which began with the end of World War II and continues into the present, psychoanalysis has expanded worldwide.

Building on this historical background, the chapter presents a developmental perspective of human nature that emphasizes unconscious dynamics and the processes involved in change. These dynamics include psychic determinism or causality, consciousness as an exceptional rather than a regular attribute of the psychic process, displacement, condensation, psychosexual stages, and defense mechanisms. The developmental theory espoused by Freud is used to explain not only the etiology of human behavior but also the etiology of human neuroses and psychoses. This developmental perspective explains client dynamics and provides a framework for the intervention strategies used by the counselor or therapist.

BACKGROUND

The history of psychoanalysis begins with **Sigmund Freud** (1856–1939). Freud had collaborated with his mentor, Josef Breuer, to write the first psychoanalytic paper, "Studies in Hysteria," in 1895. This paper was about the "founding case" (Gay, 1988, p. 63) of psychoanalysis, a patient referred to as Anna O. Before Freud, the field of psychology was considered a speculative philosophy on one hand and an empirical study of psychophysiological processes on the other, and the study of the human mind was limited to religious and magical thought. With psychoanalysis, psychology took a definite first step in the direction of scientific thinking about human motivation. As Fenichel (1945) observed, "An understanding of the multiplicity of everyday human mental life, based on natural science, really began only with psychoanalysis" (p. 4).

Fine (1979) divides the history of psychoanalysis into three periods. The first period is dominated by Freud and covers his early work through the end of World War I. During this period, Freud drew adherents to his cause, many of whom became the early pioneers of the psychoanalytic movement. The context of Western European and Viennese society during this period involved strict social norms and mores regarding sexuality. In such a Victorian setting, sexuality—and particularly female sexuality—was permitted very limited expression. It was the blocking or **repression** of such sexuality that led to Freud's (and Breuer's) conception of **hysteria**. Repression is a **defense mechanism**, a mental process that "defends" our conscious mind from unwanted and painful thoughts and feelings. In hysteria, patients reported vague complaints of paralysis and pain without organic causes—the present-day psychosomatic disorders. What Freud discovered was that such patients transferred feelings and thoughts about important people in their life onto the therapist. **Transference** continues as a fundamental concept in psychoanalytic thought.

The first psychoanalytic society was formed in Vienna at the dawn of the 20th century years later, as psychoanalysis gained recognition, the International Psychoanalytical Association was founded. This first historical period led to the emergence of psychoanalysis, which has since evolved into a dynamic psychology and a philosophy of cultural relevance.

The second historical period, which dates from 1918 to 1939, was dominated by the establishment of training institutions and the emergence of the American Psychoanalytic Association. Many new psychoanalytic societies were organized in democratic countries and specific regulations were adopted for the training of psychoanalysts. The training system that is now almost universally standard involves a tripartite model, the foundation of which is the candidate's personal analysis. "It may be assumed that since about 1930 every practicing analyst has been through a training analysis" (Fine, 1979, p. 3). The training also includes theoretical instruction that lasts about 4 years and control analyses in which the candidate in training is supervised in the conduct of several analyses. Candidates are typically drawn from the mental health professions, especially in the United States, which has the largest membership of psychoanalysts belonging to the International Psychoanalytical Association. The significance of this second historical period is marked not only by the proliferation of psychoanalytic education worldwide, but also by the expansion of psychoanalytic thought through the creation of a sizable body of scientific literature. Such literature typically uses the case study method of one or a few patients.

The third historical period began with the end of World War II and continues into the present. In this period, psychoanalysis has expanded worldwide. The 1992–93 roster of the

International Psychoanalytical Association, the latest one available, lists 8,197 members, 45 component and provisional societies, and 1 regional society (American Psychoanalytic Association). The roster includes 18 societies in Europe, 16 in Latin America, 3 in the Middle and Far East, 1 in Australia, and 8 in North America. This third historical period has also seen the expansion of psychoanalytic theory beyond classical Freudian metapsychology. Pine (1985) enumerates four distinct psychoanalytic psychologies that have developed within psychoanalytic metapsychology: Freud's drive theory, and the newer theories of **ego, object relations**, and **self psychology**.

Recent developments in U.S. health care are also affecting the perception of modern psychoanalysis. The contemporary psychotherapeutic scene has been greatly influenced by modern health care marketing. Rising health care costs have engendered the development and promotion of a variety of abbreviated psychotherapeutic strategies. Managed care programs such as health maintenance organizations, preferred provider agreements, and employee assistance programs typically rely on interventions designed to keep costs to a minimum. Accordingly, the field of psychotherapy has become a veritable "convenience market" in which reducing the total number of contacts between the counselor or therapist and the client is a priority. Similarly, the choices available to persons who decide to get help are limited by the health care option to which they subscribe. It is not surprising, therefore, that a precise definition of psychotherapy has been further obscured by rapidly expanding methods designed to limit costs. Wolberg (1977) lists no fewer than 36 definitions that "generally do not agree on the techniques employed, the process included, the goals approximated or the personnel involved" (p. 14).

Amidst these "innovations," psychoanalysis has lost favor as a treatment option, except perhaps in a few urban areas. Because it is recognized as a depth psychology, and because the analytic method involves multiple weekly sessions over an extended period of time, psychoanalysis has little short-term economic advantage in the contemporary marketplace of managed health care. Nevertheless, despite the predicted demise of psychoanalysis, new training institutes continue to form in major metropolitan areas, which indicates continued interest in psychoanalysis on the part of professional counselors and therapists. In part, this interest may be the result of dedication to a dynamic theory and method that seeks to understand and change psychopathology as well as the forces operative in the therapeutic process. It may also reflect counselors' and therapists' dissatisfaction with technique-oriented strategies and their wish to increase the use of the therapist's thoughts and feelings (countertransference) as a tool in the therapeutic process. (Personal analysis is a requirement for psychoanalytic training.)

What distinguishes psychoanalysis as a psychotherapeutic theory and method? Wolberg (1977) divides the varieties of psychotherapy into three main groups: **supportive therapy, reeducative therapy**, and **reconstructive therapy**. His schema depicts a gradation from lesser to greater complexity in the perceived objectives of each therapeutic strategy. For example, whereas in supportive therapy the object "is to bring the patient to an emotional equilibrium as rapidly as possible" (p. 68), reeducative therapy attempts to achieve more extensive goals through an "actual remodeling of the patient's attitudes and behavior in line with more adaptive life integration" (p. 101). The difference is in the specific therapeutic technique used. In supportive strategies, reassurance, suggestion, relaxation, and persuasion may be used. In contrast, reeducative approaches rely more on reconditioning. The counselor or therapist introduces behavioral reinforcers or the therapeutic relationship (approval-disapproval) to modify, liberate, or promote self-growth.

The objectives of reconstructive therapies offer the greatest complexity. The goal of reconstructive psychotherapy is to bring the client to an awareness of crucial unconscious conflicts, their permutations, and how these limit his or her daily life. In addition, it is also to become more aware of one's desires and needs. In contrast, supportive efforts toward this kind of insight are minimal, and the reeducative emphasis is less on searching for unconscious causes than on promoting new and better forms of conscious behavior through conscious action. Counselors or therapists who direct their efforts toward reconstructive changes within the client have typically turned toward psychoanalytic methods and theories because of their emphasis on creating the optimal conditions for deep, lasting change.

HUMAN NATURE: A DEVELOPMENTAL PERSPECTIVE

(*Note:* In order to give examples of major constructs in the next two sections of this chapter, the following brief case history was created.)

CASE HISTORY—*Juanita*

The client is a 43-year-old Latina female. She is the oldest of five children and was raised in a large metropolitan area in the southwestern United States. Religion plays a very significant role in her life. She is a college graduate, has taught math and science in a middle school for the past 4 years, and tends to pour all of her energy into her students, which often causes a strained relationship with her own children. She is divorced from her husband of 5 years; the divorce was opposed by her parents and family. She was referred for analysis by her physician because she has not been eating properly and she has experienced frequent, unexplained crying spells, depression, inability to maintain meaningful relationships with various males, and lack of concentration. She has sought help from her priest, coworkers, and mother. Juanita took care of her brothers and sisters while growing up due to the demands of her mother and father's business. She has had the following dream on several occasions:

> I am always running and there are shadowy figures behind me. I am in a large warehouse type of structure with lots of boxes and crates. The boxes and crates are all marked with arrows reading "exit." The arrows are all going in different directions; therefore, I never find my way out, and the figures keep getting closer. I wake up in a cold sweat, breathing rapidly, heart pounding, and a scream stuck in my throat. I can't sleep so I usually go to the kitchen and drink coffee.

The Freudian Unconscious

In the late 19th century, medically oriented approaches assumed that neuroses were caused by some unknown organic factor, and therapeutic measures were limited to electric shock and hypnotism (Fine, 1979). Freud isolated himself from this mainstream position, as Fine observes, and in the process made his first major discovery: "The key to neuroses lies in psychology, and all neuroses involve a defense against unbearable ideas" (1979, pp. 21–25). In an attempt to understand clinical data, Freud arrived at two fundamental hypotheses concerning mental development and functioning, hypotheses that can apply to normal as well as pathological activity. According to Brenner (1974), these two hypotheses, "which have been abundantly confirmed, are the principle of psychic determinism or causality, and the proposition that consciousness is an exceptional rather than a regular attribute of psychic processes" (p. 2).

According to the first principle, **psychic determinism**, mental activity is not meaningless or accidental; nothing in the mind happens by chance or in a random way, and all mental phenomena have a causal connection to the psychic events that precede them. An example of this principle can be drawn from the case study of Juanita. The information obtained at the initial meeting with the analyst and the client's childhood history are organized in such a way as to develop a context of continuity between early psychic experiences and the symptoms we assume to be a consequence of these experiences. We ask ourselves, "What caused this?," and we organize our data around this question because we are confident that a coherent answer exists that is connected to the rest of the client's psychic life. We assume that each neurotic symptom is caused by other mental processes. For example, Juanita complains of insomnia and difficulty concentrating and perhaps feels these are signs of some spiritual problem; hence, her first effort at seeking help is with her priest. As counselors or therapists, however, we presume that there are psychological causes outside of the client's conscious awareness.

Freud first noted the principle of psychic determinism in relation to dreams. He discovered that "each dream, indeed each image in each dream, is the consequence of other psychic events, and each stands in coherent and meaningful relationship to the rest of the dreamer's psychic life" (Brenner, 1974, p. 3). This principle contrasts with the notion that dreams are products of random brain activity during sleep, an idea popularly held by neurologists and psychiatrists 70 years ago and by some organic theorists today.

The second principle, that of **unconscious mental processes**, is closely linked to the first. This principle accounts for the apparent discontinuities in the client's perception of symptom and cause, for the causal connection has become part of the unconscious process. In the case study, Juanita has repressed her mental conflicts into the unconscious, thereby causing her symptoms. It follows, then, that if the unconscious cause or causes can be discovered through the therapeutic process, the causal sequence becomes clear and the client's insight leads to cure. Note that this brief explanation is a simplified version of what in actuality is a long and complex treatment process in which the client examines through free association a variety of unconscious mental processes. This simplified explanation also ignores the role of interpersonal influence, that of the client-therapist relationship, as a mutative factor in psychoanalysis.

Freud (1938/1940) argued that "the governing rules of logic carry no weight in the unconscious; it might be called the Realm of the illogical" (pp. 168–169). He also declared: "We have found that processes in the unconscious or in the Id obey different laws from those in the preconscious ego. These laws in their totality are named the primary process, in contrast to the secondary process, which governs the course of events in the preconscious ego" (p. 164). In other words, Freud called attention to the fact that a portion of the mind, which is particularly active in our dreams, our emotional life, and our childhood, works within a framework of timelessness, spacelessness, and the coexistence of opposites. For example, timelessness is implied in our clinical work when we take for granted the simultaneous presence of an adult client and his or her expressions of infancy such as dependency. Freud's notions of **displacement** (an idea's emotional emphasis becomes detached from it and is superimposed on some other ideas) and **condensation** (several ideas are expressed through a single idea) exemplify spacelessness. Feelings expressed toward an uncaring employer may be an unconscious replication of childhood feelings toward a parent in the past or toward the counselor or therapist in the present. These feelings are displaced onto the employer as a defense against a painful memory or onto the counselor or therapist against the threat of awareness. Displacement is essentially a disconnecting of some feeling toward someone and a reconnecting of it to someone else (who had nothing to do with the original feeling), without being aware of it. Usually people displace such affect onto those who bear some resemblance to the original person. For example, if a man goes through a bitter divorce, he may displace onto the next woman he dates the resentment he feels toward his ex-wife.

Condensation is a more difficult and abstract concept. Think of it as a mosaic in which many parts are put together in a disorganized way, so that the end product is an amalgam of images, shapes, and colors. The mechanism of condensation is the mind's way of unconsciously keeping from awareness disturbing affects and thoughts by rendering them confusing and distorted. It is perhaps similar to an abstract artwork in which the themes depicted by the artist are blended together in a strange and logic-defying way. Freud and his followers identified a number of defensive strategies, or **defense mechanisms**, unconsciously used by the mind; these defy normal logic but act to protect the subject from awareness of unwanted feelings.

In *The Ego and the Mechanisms of Defense* (1966), **Anna Freud** (his daughter) specified such defense mechanisms as **regression, repression, reaction formation, isolation, undoing, projection, introjection,** and **displacment**. Repression and projection, commonly seen in clinical practice, are unconscious defensive processes. Repression refers to "an operation whereby the subject attempts to repel, or to confine to the unconscious, representations (thoughts, images, memories) which are bound to an instinct" (Laplanche & Pontalis, 1973, p. 390). Projection is an "operation whereby qualities, feelings, wishes or even 'objects,' which the subject refuses to recognize or rejects in himself, are expelled from the self and located in another person or thing" (p. 349). The other mechanisms operate similarly by unconsciously protecting the subject from awareness of repressed conflict and subsequent anxiety.

Prejudice, for example, represents a culturally defined projection of one group's disavowed aspects of itself onto another (usually subordinate) group. For example, in American culture Blacks were seen as overly sexual, dishonest, and lazy—projections of unwanted traits of the dominant cultural group. Groups of young men attacking male gays is another example. These young men refuse to accept loving or tender feelings toward other men; they find it too threatening to consider such feelings and hence need to defend by projecting the unwanted traits onto others and then attacking. Reaction formation is a process whereby an individual takes the opposite stance (unconsciously) to protect from awareness one's gratification in the abhorred position. For example, a man may become a preacher and rail against "sins of the flesh" as a way to defend against his own sexual impulses. What is often a sign of a reaction formation is the zeal with which someone embraces a position and simultaneously attacks the opposite—expressed in Shakespeare's words "he doth protest too much." Table 4.1 presents a discussion of the main defense mechanisms.

Freud's Developmental Theory

"In psychoanalytic treatment, the client regresses and recapitulates, in a modified form, early developmental phases. Both neuroses and psychoses are based on a series of fixations on and regressions to these past ego stages and orientations" (Giovacchini, 1987, p. 87). Freud postulated the **psychosexual stages** of infantile sexuality as oral, anal, and phallic, which

Table 4.1
Defense Mechanisms

Regression
Regression is a process whereby a client decompensates and becomes less rational; literally the client moves backward in terms of reasoning, judgment, and thinking. For example, an adult client had been severely depressed and suicidal for a number of weeks. One session she began to refer to herself by another name, that of a 9-year-old girl. She spoke in a young girl's voice and language. Typically, regression is not so extreme, but usually there is some form of a loss of reasoning and judgment.

Repression
Repression is the first and foremost defense mechanism. Repression seals off and pushes down into the unconscious and out of awareness unwanted thoughts and feelings. For example, after working a year with a client, a therapist remarked that the client had said nothing about his mother. The client told her, with anger and surprise, "We don't talk about her in here!" The client was demonstrating that he had repressed—or sealed off or pushed beneath awareness—any negative thoughts or feelings about her.

Reaction Formation
Reaction formation involves the denial of faulty impulses by going to the opposite extreme. For example, an evangelist who has a history of sexual acting out rails against immorality. The evangelist finds defense against his own sexual desires by taking the offensive and condemning such desires and behaviors in others.

Isolation (Isolation of Affect)
Isolation involves avoiding painful feelings by detachment from the source of such feelings. For example, a person may avoid feelings of guilt about some act or behavior through lengthy cognitive speculations regarding the differences between good and bad.

Undoing
Undoing involves taking back, softening, or restructuring statements or admissions because of the anxiety produced by the original statement or admission. For example, a client may express affection for the counselor or therapist but, due to the anxiety this produces for the client, she states that she has feelings such as these for a lot of people.

Projection
Projection involves the shifting of blame or the assigning of one's faults to others. Think of a movie projector inside one's head. It projects onto a screen (another person or group) one's own fears, fantasies, and conflicts. For example, a highly prejudiced person often denies his prejudice by stating, " I do not hate them, they hate me."

Introjection
Introjection involves the adoption of other people's attitudes or behaviors as if they were one's own. Introjection is best viewed as partial identification, as the individual adopts only that which lowers anxiety. For example, a child may incorporate her parents values and standards into her personality not because they are correct but because they protect her from the negative outcomes possible in opposing those same standards and values.

Displacement
Displacement involves transferring emotional reactions from one person or situation to another. For example, the person who has had a difficult day at work because of the demands of his supervisor, arrives home and yells at his spouse or children. The home situation produces less anxiety than the work situation.

Rationalization
Rationalization involves the provision of rational explanations for irrational or unacceptable behaviors. For example, after an athletic event, a person takes part in damaging property and explains away the behavior by stating that she did it because everyone else was doing it.

linked developmental theory with sexual impulses. This meant that Freud believed sexual expression went beyond what is ordinarily considered sexual, for he postulated infantile activities as erotic, centered around bodily zones beginning with the mouth.

In essence, psychosexual stages refer to a sequential acquisition of progressively sophisticated modes of gratification from various bodily zones that are necessary for growth and development. The term **libido** describes instinctual energy that belongs to the sexual drive. The discharge of this energy leads to pleasure, and the part of the body that leads to such pleasure is referred to as an **erogenous zone**. Erikson (1963) elaborated on these erogenous zones: "oral-sensory, which includes the facial apertures and the upper nutritional organs; anal, or the excretory organs; and the genitalia" (pp. 73–74). He posited modes of functioning within each zone: incorporation, retention, elimination, and intrusion. The following examples show how modes may interplay in each zone.

Orality represents a method of relating to the external world. The infant's smiling is an indication of ability to recognize objects in the external world as separate from the self. The first mode of approach in the oral zone is incorporation, that is, to "take in" in a dependent fashion what is offered by the mother. Modes of incorporation dominate this stage, yet other modes are also expressed. According to Erikson (1963),

> There is in the first incorporative stage a clamping down with jaws and gums; there is spitting up and out (eliminative mode); and there is a closing up of the lips (retentive mode). In vigorous babies even a general intrusive tendency of the whole head and neck can be noticed, a tendency to fasten itself upon the nipple and, as it were, into the breast (oral intrusive)." (p. 73)

In clinical work, one might refer to orally dependent clients, which indicates that extreme dependence is the result of a predominance of oral elements in adult functioning. This functions as a metaphor to describe a fixation at the oral stage of development, wherein the overly dependent adult client tends to relate to the world in terms of a need to be nurtured. Whereas the child actually requires this nurturing to survive, the adult client wants to be taken care of, to be soothed and nurtured in a psychological sense. A client described as an oral character may use any or all of the modes described previously: spitting out what the counselor or therapist offers or intrusively penetrating into the counselor or therapist's space, demanding to be "fed." Erikson (1963) saw the primary conflict at this level as one of developing the sense of basic trust versus the sense of mistrust.

To Freud, control of the anal sphincter initiates the anal stage of development and is seen as an important contributor to adult structure. Control of the sphincter, which is part of the total muscle system activated at this stage, places an emphasis on the duality of rigidity and relaxation, flexion and extension. As noted by Erikson (1963),

> The development of the muscle system gives the child a much greater power over the environment in the ability to reach out and hold on, to throw and to push away, to appropriate things and to keep them at a distance. This whole stage, then, which the Germans called the stage of stubbornness, becomes a battle for autonomy. For as he gets ready to stand more firmly on his feet the infant delineates his world as "I" and "you," "me" and "mine." Every mother knows how astonishingly pliable a child may be at this stage, if and when he has made the decision that he wants to do what he is supposed to do. (p. 82)

Accordingly, conflict at this stage involves the antithesis of letting go and holding on, of autonomy versus shame and doubt.

The **Oedipus complex,** which is one of the most controversial and best-known of Freud's theories, dominates the phallic stage. At this stage, the child has moved away from a two-person system of mother-child interaction to a triangular relationship with both mother and father. The Oedipus legend, from Greek mythology, assumes the child's wish to possess the parent of the opposite sex, which creates a conflict with the parent of the same sex. In more graphic terms, and truer to the original legend, incestuous feelings are combined with patricidal impulses. In the case of the boy who wishes to possess his mother, he fears retaliation by the father and fantasizes the father's revenge of castration (i.e., the father's retaliation will be directed at the boy's penis), which is termed *castration anxiety*. This complex is necessary for later development, because the threat of castration leads the child to internalize, as a permanent part of his psychic structure, a prohibiting, controlling superego that is the foundation of morality. In the case of a girl, the unconscious wish is to marry the father and to take care of him in a much better way than she imagines the mother is capable of doing. Although these theories remain controversial today and are seriously questioned by modern developmental theorists, they continue to be used as important metaphors in understanding clinical material.

Post-Freudian Psychoanalytic Theory

According to Pine (1990), it was Fairbairn (1941) who coined the term **object relations theory** and focused attention not on the pleasure-seeking motivation (Freud's drive theory) but on the object-seeking nature of motivation. Pine also described how it was a new method of clinical work—infant and child observation—that added momentum to this shift in emphasis from an internal drive based on instinct to seeking an object (person). Others contributing to this shift and expansion of knowledge and theory included Melanie Klein, Donald Winnicott, and Heinz Kohut. Kohut (1977) developed a theory and technique that came to be known as **self psychology,** which emphasized the concept of self as the organizing construct of experience, rather than innate drives and instincts.

These post-Freudian theorists, taken together, can be seen as expanding psychoanalytic theory from Freud's one-person system to a two-person system. Rather than seeing the individual as a closed and separate system attempting to negotiate a balance between inner needs striving for gratification on the one hand and the constraints of society (the reality principle) on the other, the scope widened to include another person (the analyst). Freud's metaphor for psychoanalytic treatment was the surgeon removing a tumor (repressed memory). In addition, Freud conceived the analyst as a mirror (nonreactive, noncontributory) reflecting back only those unconscious desires and fears emanating from the client. Winnicott (1958), who was a pediatrician before becoming a psychoanalyst, considered therapy more like the relationship between a mother and an infant, where there is a highly attuned emotional sensitivity, first on mother's part and then, as the infant develops, of a more reciprocal nature. To underscore how important the object relation is in development and in psychotherapy, Winnicott would say there is no such thing as an infant. These object relations theorists did not discard Freud's drive theory but tended to add to it the significance of interaction with important others in the formation of personality and pathology.

Rabin (1995) described a paradigm shift in psychoanalysis that can be characterized by a number of different terms such as *intersubjectivity theory* (Stolorow, Brandshaft, & Atwood, 1987), *relational theorizing* (Mitchell, 1988), and *social constructivism* (Hoffman, 1991). Rabin argued that this shift is

> from the positivistic belief that there are ultimate truths to be found within the intrapsychic structure of the patient, with the analyst as the arbiter of reality, to the 'postmodern' perspective, where all knowledge is perspectival, contextual and nonuniversal. *The analyst and the patient together create or construct* what is clinically useful [emphasis added]. (p. 467)

This paradigm shift is away from Freud's metaphor of analyst as archeologist sifting through strange symbols (e.g., dreams, slips of the tongue, symptoms) to decipher meanings and present them to the client via an interpretation. This shift has also entailed a greater awareness of and use of the therapist's feelings and thoughts during a therapy session, data referred to as **countertransference**. Freud viewed such reactions as contaminating therapy and saw them as a function of unrecognized neurotic conflicts within the analyst. However, recent trends are toward the recognition and use of countertransference as a tool to facilitate therapy (Lecours, Bouchard, & Normandin, 1995). Table 4.2 compares the drive, ego, object relations, and self theories just discussed.

Table 4.2
Comparison of Theoretical Approaches

	Drive	Ego	Object relations	Self
Motivating force	Instincts	Instincts and growth	Seeking object to satisfy instincts	Feelings of inadequacy
Goal of therapy	Uncovering unconscious conflicts	Uncovering methods of defending against conflicts, developing inherent potential	Uncovering the way one relates to others in getting needs met	To enable clients to better meet their needs for feeling worthwhile
Role of counselor	Mirror	Mirror	Participant observer	Participant observer
Central agent of change	Interpretation	Interpretation	Experience of therapeutic relationship	Experience of therapeutic relationship

MAJOR CONSTRUCTS AND PROCESSES OF CHANGE

The assumptions on which the system of psychoanalytic theory rests are referred to as **metapsychology** (Rapaport & Gill, 1959). As noted by Greenson (1967), "The clinical implications of metapsychology intimate that in order to comprehend a psychic event thoroughly, it is necessary to analyze it from six different points of view—the topographic, dynamic, economic, genetic, structural and adaptive" (p. 21).

The **topographic** point of view is the first major construct. It contrasts unconscious and conscious mental processes. The deeper layer of the mind, the unconscious, has only the aim of discharging impulses. Both conscious and unconscious expressions are present in clinical material and can be described as manifest and latent. Consider the dream material presented in the case study of Juanita. The client reports recent occurrences of dreams such as the following:

> I am always running and there are shadowy figures behind me. I am in a large warehouse-type of structure with lots of boxes and crates. The boxes and crates are all marked with arrows reading "exit." The arrows are all going in different directions; therefore, I never find my way out, and the figures keep getting closer. I wake up in a cold sweat, breathing rapidly, heart pounding, and a scream stuck in my throat. I can't sleep so I usually go to the kitchen and drink coffee.

In psychoanalytic clinical work, it is essential to have the client's association to a dream in order to verify assumptions about the latent, or unconscious, meaning of a symbol or the dream itself. To interpret the meaning of a dream without these associations would be to impose our own thoughts onto the client, a process derogatorily called **wild analysis.** Because we do not have Juanita's associations in this case, we will guess at some possible associations to illustrate the metapsychological points of view. We might assume, for example, that the **manifest symbol** of the warehouse unconsciously represents (i.e., has a latent meaning of) a place that holds things, as could the boxes and crates. A large warehouse gives the feeling of much open space, perhaps emptiness. The structures that could hold things (as in comfort in being held) are all marked in different directions. Juanita has turned to many people for support and has found no way out of the emptiness and depression (warehouse). The conscious representation of a warehouse with labeled boxes and crates represents order and control, but the unconscious representation stands for chaos without exit. Both stand in topographic relation to the other: one conscious, the other unconscious. A further elaboration, and much more presumptive, is that the warehouse is not only symbolic of her depression and emptiness but also at a deeper level of intestine and bowel. We might assume that at this level Juanita's not eating is about control versus chaos, a desperate attempt to deny her need to put something into her, be it need for food, relationships, or sexual intimacy.

Dynamic and **economic** points of view are the second and third major constructs of psychoanalytic metapsychology. To understand these two points of view, it is necessary to explore Freud's idea of the **psychoeconomic hypothesis.** This hypothesis requires a construct of **psychic energy,** much like physical energy, with principles of pleasure-pain and constancy. The following explanation of the idea of psychic energy is necessary before defining the dynamic and economic points of view.

For Freud, the development of instincts necessitated conflict. For example, when the two primary instincts of sexual and aggressive drives strive toward expression, they clash with the reality principle, which leads to states of pent-up tension. As noted by Giovacchini (1987),

> Psychoanalysis requires a concept of psychic energy to explain the various movements of the psychic apparatus, those involved in action, problem solving, reestablishment of emotional equilibrium, and growth. A hypothesis of psychic energy must be based on certain general principles that dictate the distribution and production of energy and how it is to be used. (p. 62)

Giovacchini further noted:

> Freud relied on two principles on which he built his concepts of psychic energy, the principle of constancy and the pleasure principle, more specifically, the pleasure-pain principle. The constancy principle is based on the hypothesis that the function of the nervous system and the psychic apparatus is to keep the level of excitation at its lowest point. The pleasure principle is related to the constancy principle in that it asserts that lowering the level of excitation, which connotes release and relief, leads to pleasure, whereas increased excitation creates tension and disruption and is experienced as pain. (p. 63)

This **tension-discharge hypothesis** supports the dynamic point of view, which assumes that mental phenomena are the result of the interaction of psychic forces seeking discharge. This reasoning was based in part on the theories of hydraulic systems in physics during Freud's time. Greenson (1967) states that "this assumption is the basis for all hypotheses concerning instinctual drives, defenses, ego interests, and conflicts. Symptom formation, ambivalence, and over-determination are examples of dynamics" (p. 23).

The way in which psychic energy is distributed, transformed, or expended defines the economic point of view. To illustrate the dynamic and economic points of view, assume that Juanita was in a state of dammed-up instinctual tension before the recent outbreak of her depressive symptoms. However, her ego was beginning to lose the ability (in the dream the shadowy figures are getting closer) to carry out defensive operations so that she could function without obvious debilitating symptoms. These operations seemed to be consistent with a compulsion for activity such as was exemplified by her pouring all of her energy into her students. Her need for activity and control was probably bolstered by a variety of stereotypical rituals and repetitions, not only as they concerned herself (i.e., her thoughts and her body, as in not eating) but also as they involved her interpersonal interactions (not letting men get close). This coping style would be necessary to contain instinctual forces such as intense rage and fear of abandonment from explosive expression. The client's strained relationship with her children precipitated the most recent outbreak of symptoms (i.e., nightmares and insomnia).

Juanita's ego has lost the ability to cope with this influx of affect seeking discharge, and she didn't think she could have waited much longer for an appointment with an analyst. The impulse to rage is frozen in its attempt for expression, as in her dream "a scream stuck in my throat." This frozen image reflects the conflict around intentionally holding onto and involuntarily letting go of something from within. In this instance, the something within happens to be a scream, which unconsciously could be equated with Juanita's sense of self, a self she struggled to find in the midst of family and cultural pressures to be what was expected of her.

The fourth major construct of psychoanalytic metapsychology is the **genetic** point of view, which concerns an understanding of the origin and development of psychic phenomena. It explains how the past is being brought to the present and why a certain compromise solution has been adopted. To return to the case example, Juanita's history and associations expressed in analytic sessions would no doubt highlight the importance her mother played in her adopting a particular defensive style as well as in the psychic conflicts already noted.

The fifth major metapsychological construct is the **structural** point of view, which assumes that the psychic apparatus can be divided into several persisting functional units. "The concept of the psychic apparatus as consisting of an ego, id, and superego is derived from the structural hypothesis" (Greenson, 1967, p. 25). The id is the agency from which all instincts derive; the ego is the agency that mediates these drives with the external environment. Based on a signal of anxiety, the ego brings a number of defensive operations into play. It works as an agency of adaptation with functions such as control over perception, voluntary motility, and the setting up of affective memory traces, to name just a few. The superego is the agency of the personality within which develops a framework of conscience, self-observation, and the formation of ideals. It acts as a judge or censor for the ego.

To illustrate the structural point of view as it applies to Juanita, assume that the ego's defensive functions have weakened under the pressure of her divorce and her family's criticism and shunning of her. Her action of pouring herself into her students to the neglect of her children has mobilized the conflict she likely experienced as a child when her parents "poured" themselves into the family business to the neglect of Juanita (as she became mother to her younger siblings). This conflict centers in part around the expression of anger (the trapped scream, the depressive shutting down). Further assume that as she progresses in analysis she will no longer regress in this way when confronted with similar situations, for her ego functions will have replaced inadequate defenses with new insight and greater freedom of choice in responding.

Thus far, all the examples from the case study reflect attempts at **adaptation**, the sixth major metapsychological construct. A person's relationship to his or her environment, objects of love and hate, and society are based on the adaptive point of view.

APPLICATIONS

Overview

The following sections present information dealing with the goals and intervention strategies that have application to psychoanalytic theory. The goals of psychoanalytic theory stress changing the personality and character structure of the individual through resolving unconscious conflicts and developing more effective ways of dealing with problems, particularly in relationships. The intervention strategies that are part of psychoanalytic theory place special emphasis on free association, dream analysis, analysis of transference, analysis of resistance, interpretation, and the interactions that take place between the client and the counselor or therapist. The goals and intervention strategies that follow are designed to enhance the change process for the individual.

Goals of Counseling and Psychotherapy

The goals of psychoanalysis place emphasis on (1) resolution of clients' problems to enhance the clients' ability to cope with life changes (i.e., to make their way of relating to self and important others more meaningful and enriching); (2) their working through unresolved developmental stages; and (3) their ability to cope more effectively with the demands of the society in which they live. Although goals vary with the client and with the psychoanalytic approach (drive theory, ego psychology, object relations, self psychology), each approach seeks the attainment of its goals through the exploration of unconscious material, particularly as it relates to the client-analyst relationship.

Traditional Intervention Strategies

Freud's technique for uncovering hidden psychic processes evolved over a period of several years, and despite some relatively minor variations it is still in use today. The classical technique entails a process of **free association** (letting thoughts drift over events of daily life, past history, and dreams) on the part of the client, who is typically in a recumbent position with the counselor or therapist sitting behind and out of sight. The practitioner maintains a position of neutrality, referred to as the **rule of abstinence**, to deny the client's wish for gratification of instinctual demands, such as wanting to have a more personal relationship with the analyst by asking about his or her personal life or to have the analyst agree with him or her. These techniques of neutrality minimize the actual presence of the counselor or therapist and allow the client to focus more freely on intrapsychic matters such as fantasies, dream analysis, childhood-based conflicts, and defensive or resistive operations that block awareness of unconscious processes. More important, they facilitate the development of the **transference**, defined by Laplanche and Pontalis (1973) as

> infantile prototypes that re-emerge and are experienced with a strong sensation of immediacy and are directed toward the analyst within the analytic situation. This is the terrain on which all the basic problems of a given analysis play themselves out: the establishment, modalities, interpretation and resolution of the transference are in fact what define the cure." (p. 455)

In other words, transference involves the client's reliving, in the presence of the counselor or therapist, the repetitious and rigid defenses of the past. It is the analysis and the eventual understanding of these defenses within the transference that make change possible. For example, if a client says something and the analyst is silent, the client might feel that the analyst is critical of what was said—not only feel but be convinced that this is what the analyst thinks. The analyst would likely find that one or both parents often reacted with indifference to the client and that this pattern was being reactivated as a here-and-now experience for the client. The early pattern of experience with the parent was being "transferred" onto the analytic relationship. It is strategic on the part of the analyst to maintain enough of a neutral and anonymous presence, sort of like a blank screen, onto which the client can project these transferences. The analyst can then help the client become aware of such patterns (i.e., of expecting criticism or needing approval) and how these cause problems in living.

The aim of the analytic technique, primarily through the analysis of transference, is to increase clients' insights into themselves. The analysis also seeks to strengthen ego functions, such as being able to look at oneself realistically, that are required for gaining understanding. The most important analytic procedure is **interpretation**—making unconscious phenomena conscious. In a classic paper, Strachey (1934) stated that interpretation modifies existing psychic structure, where structure is conceived as stable and enduring ways of relating to oneself and others. Greenberg (1996), however, wrote that the client-therapist interaction is mutative "because structure itself consists of internalized interactions represented in a particular way" (p. 36).

Empathy, intuition, and the counselor's or therapist's own unconscious and theoretical knowledge all contribute to the construction of an interpretation. Other analytic procedures include confrontation, clarification, and working through. The procedure of working through is of great significance because it involves the continued analysis of resistances brought about after an insight has been achieved. It refers to the broadening and deepening of insight that leads to permanent change. An example of a **resistance** would be a client who takes great pains in coming to sessions exactly on time, not a minute before or after. This behavior would be thought of as a resistance to whatever experience the client might fear in being late or early. Being late could represent aggression toward the therapist (making him or her wait), and being early could mean a feeling of need of the therapist and fear the therapist will be disapproving. Working through in this case would involve confronting the client with this behavior and helping him or her sort through feelings, thoughts, and fears about the behavior. As such resistance often continues for some time, the process of working through takes several weeks or months to reach the point where the client does not act or frees oneself from acting in this case. The client works to put his or her feelings into words, and perhaps fantasies, images, or daydreams, and arrive at an understanding that would obviate the necessity of the particular resistance.

Gill (1996) described what he believes to be a major shift in conceptualizing therapeutic action or change. The shift is away from the emphasis on interpretations to an emphasis on what he calls the "experiential factor." He means that the experience between the client and the counselor or therapist is what is mutative. This shift has meant a greater awareness of and appreciation for how the therapist experiences the therapeutic interaction and how this experience (which includes countertransference) influences the course of change or lack thereof. In training analysts, the shift is occurring this way: Instead of helping analyst trainees find the "right" interpretation, supervising analysts are helping trainees understand what is happening in the experience of a therapy session, not only with the client but also within the analyst. Interpretations are less about the there and then and more about the here and now.

Brief Intervention Strategies

Brief intervention strategies are the hardest topic to write about in the context of psychoanalytic practice, primarily because they are not well applicable in psychoanalytic technique. Indeed, if the sine qua non of psychoanalytic technique is free association with unfolding of feelings and thoughts toward the analyst, then time restrictions are not relevant. Debate continues within psychoanalysis about what separates psychoanalysis from psychotherapy as a treatment, and duration of treatment is one major difference. Among the major therapies, psychoanalysis is the least effective in brief interventions that require the therapist to be more directive and to keep an eye on the prize, meaning the specific goal the client wants to accomplish. In addition, a core technique in psychoanalysis is the interpretation of the client's thoughts and feelings toward the analyst. This is a phenomenon of the transferring of thoughts and feelings from past important relationships of the client. But to offer an interpretation that the client has a certain feeling or thought toward the analyst requires previous laying of groundwork. This groundwork is the attentive and patient listening of the analyst, the nonintrusiveness and anonymity of the analyst, and the analyst's open mind about where the client might be heading in treatment. Such strategies or ways of thinking cannot be easily condensed or shortened. It takes time to develop trust, and it is on the client's terms and schedule not the managed care entity or another third party that has designated the therapy as brief from the start.

Consider this example. At his initial session, Mr. D said he wanted to work on feeling less anxious. He had read various self-help books and had gone to a therapist once before but he did not improve. He wanted to spend only a few sessions on this problem, so he himself wanted to make it a brief therapy. This is not unusual, as most people seeking therapy hope to get results quickly. After taking his history for a session, I told him that the way I worked took longer than a few weeks and he may not be interested in that. When I tried to ask why he wanted to spend such a short time on his problem when it seemed to be greatly limiting his life, he did not have an answer. However, he said he would think about it. Several days later he called and said he wanted the "full program," his words for the longer approach. He came in for a second interview and kept asking what specifically he should be doing at home to get better, citing various self-help methods he had read about. Finally, I told him I didn't think I could help him and told him why. He needed to have someone tell him what to do. Free association was his "enemy" in that his obsessive thoughts were clogging up his mind and making him anxious all the time. I sensed he did not want to get at what was underneath this anxiety. I did not think he wanted to risk the peeling away of his defenses and the temporary increasing of his anxiety as we got closer to the issues underlying it. He did not want this, and it was going to take him a lot of time to trust my word that this could eventually help. It was too big of a leap of faith for him.

One can argue that psychoanalytic thought informs even the briefest intervention. Thinking like an analyst, however, means to delve beneath the surface of words and feelings and to believe in an unconscious aspect of the mind. What do we mean when we say a brief intervention? Is the patient busy and can only attend a handful of sessions? Should an analyst accept this limitation at the first session and go about trying to help in the amount of time available? A psychoanalytic strategy should address these questions first, even before addressing the issues that brought the patient in. In other words, if the problem is serious enough to come to a first session, why would a patient limit the amount of time spent on solving the problem?

Brief strategies are perhaps a relative term. Within psychoanalysis there is a general demarcation between less severe and more severe pathology. The less severe is based on the assumption that repressed and unresolved inner conflicts are the cause of distress; illuminating and working through these conflicts is the course of therapy. In more severe pathology, there exists in the client more of a deficit or incompleteness. For example, there is a distinction between a client whose mother was demanding and perfectionistic (conflict) and a client whose mother was severely abusive and neglecting. A conflicted relationship with a mother assumes some experiences of good enough mothering, hence the conflict (Jorgensen, 2004).

CLIENTS WITH SERIOUS MENTAL HEALTH ISSUES

According to Seligman (2004), today's counselors and therapists are treating clients with increasing numbers of severe disorders. Problems such as anxiety, depression, obsessive-compulsive disorders, panic disorders, phobic disorders, schizophrenia, and borderline personality disorder are becoming more and more common. How applicable is psychoanalysis to this changing scenario?

Up until the 1950s, many traditional analysts believed that psychoanalysis could only be applied to intelligent, motivated, and fairly high functioning clients. The process of psychoanalysis was thought to induce a regression in the client, and such instability and turmoil was not considered weatherable by the more disturbed clients. Many papers were written on the subject of **analyzability**, which is essentially deciding whether a client can benefit (and will not be harmed by) a psychoanalytic approach. Since the 1950s, applications to more disturbed clients have been increasing. Indeed, if psychoanalysis is the therapy that attempts fundamental and profound change shouldn't this process be applied to those clients who are in the greatest despair of mental disorders?

There are no hard and fast rules that state which mental disorders are most successfully treated by a psychoanalytic approach. It does seem, however, that serious mental health issues are particularly suitable to psychoanalytic theory and practice, the only method that trains therapists in treating clients with these types of issues with a goal beyond supportive maintenance. Several years ago I attended a seminar on psychoanalytic treatment of schizophrenia. Some therapists would say this is a waste of time, that such clients cannot benefit from any psychotherapy, let alone one so insight-based as psychoanalysis. But such clinical applications have been going on since the late 1950s. It was during that time that the analyst Leo Stone (1954) wrote a seminal article titled "The widening scope of indications for psychoanalysis." This change in thinking occurred during an era when psychoanalysis was pre-eminent as a treatment. Many analysts believed then and now that analysis is the most powerful treatment available for the most seriously disturbed clients.

Since the 1950s many theorists have argued that the strategies used by the analyst need to adapt to the client, not the other way around. The so-called classical analytic strategy was to be neutral and impassive, a blank canvas that would be painted with the client's neurotic conflicts. Freud's metaphors for the stance of the analyst were the mirror and the surgeon. In a mirror, the client's reactions to the analyst reflect the client's conflicts. These reactions do not penetrate the surface of the mirror/analyst; indeed, a mirror has no feelings toward the person looking at it—it is inanimate! By remaining unknown, this position or stance encouraged clients to transfer their past feelings and attitudes toward others (mainly mother and father) onto the analyst. This is like projecting a movie onto a blank screen, and the psychic process is termed *projection*. Psychoanalysis has evolved a long way from these Freudian metaphors. Now there is a much greater appreciation of how the analyst's feelings and thoughts about a client are not only inevitable but also extraordinarily helpful (DeCastro, 2003).

The most seriously ill clients need to be medicated so that delusions, hallucinations, and agitated fear are at a minimum. With patients who have severe conditions, the analytic stance has a chance to make some sort of therapeutic connection. One reason is that through their extensive training and own analysis, analysts have a deep, experience-near understanding of psychopathology. The understanding is not just intellectual and theoretical but experiential. In their own analysis, as well as those they conducted in training, analysts experience first-hand the intense fear and anxiety of facing the deepest conflicts. No matter how well adjusted a person is, the intense and long process of psychoanalysis erodes those cherished means of self-denial and self-preservation and lays bare the intense conflicts each human has experienced in the process of development. Knowledge of this process in theoretical and experiential terms enables analysts to deal with a disturbed client from minute to minute and session to session (Almond, 2003). In the confusing labyrinth of the seriously disturbed client, such grounding is essential; analysts need to know where the client is and what would be the best thing to say or do at the time. It is the accumulation of small, empathic attunements over time (the glacial time of years, not weeks) that gradually fosters trust in such clients, and often trust alone is the primary success of the treatment.

Ms. G came to therapy with a history of cutting herself. She had been hospitalized for one suicide attempt. These facts plus others indicated that Ms. G was a client with serious mental health issues. Another therapist referred her and I have wondered from time to time why this therapist did not treat the patient. I would describe this therapist as cognitive-behavioral in approach and I suspect (though never confirmed) that he felt Ms. G would be demanding, draining, and likely an unsuccessful case. After having Ms. G in therapy now for 5 years, I think I can see how another therapist could have those feelings. Indeed, Ms. G had been through two periods of brief solution-focused therapy with positive results that faded over time. This is typical for clients who have been diagnosed borderline personality, a condition particularly noted for self-mutilation and stormy relationships, including therapeutic ones.

How could psychoanalysis work for Ms. G? In the movie *The Horse Whisperer,* Robert Redford treats a young girl and her horse for serious "mental" health issues—they have gone through the severe trauma of being hit by a huge truck. Once the therapy has begun, there is a scene in which the horse attacks Redford and runs off into a meadow. Redford walks to the edge of the meadow and waits. All day he waits, unmoving, just watching the horse. Over the course of the day the horse moves closer and closer until by the end of the day he's brushing up to Redford. Redford's skill was in realizing and accepting that he had to go at the horse's pace; he had to wait for the horse to trust on its own. There was nothing Redford could say; he had to act out and prove his accepting and patient attitude. Redford also realized that the horse's owner, the teenage girl, needed to watch the sequence in the meadow if she were to believe that she could also trust Redford. Part of Redford's success as a "therapist" was that he acted in a way that was significantly different from what the girl expected (Fonagy, Gergely, Jurist, & Target 2002). His act gave the girl hope, and in clients with serious mental health issues, it is often a loss of hope that precludes therapeutic engagement and progress (Helm, 2004).

CROSS-CULTURAL CONSIDERATIONS

According to Lee and Chaung (2005), counselors and therapists enter what they term the *cross-cultural zone* when working with people representing different cultures. This "zone" is described in many ways, and professional associations such as the American Counseling Association (ACA), the Association for Multicultural Counseling and Development (AMCD), and the American Psychological Association (APA) provide competencies and objectives for their members. Included in such competencies and objectives are directives regarding awareness of one's own cultural values and biases, (2) awareness of clients' worldviews, and (3) use of culturally appropriate intervention strategies. Each of these is further broken down into areas such as attitudes and beliefs, knowledge, and skills. Based on these as guidelines, theoretical orientations can be compared with one another with respect to their awareness of and understanding of cultural differences.

Two major areas of psychoanalytic technique are relevant to a discussion of cultural diversity. One is free association, which creates a climate in which what comes to the client's thoughts is what gives direction to the analysis. It is not the analyst's decision to pursue this or that goal; instead, the analyst "bears witness" to what unfolds from a client's unconscious.

This unfolding is truly unique for each client; hence the process emphasizes individual differences. The analyst tries to keep an open mind to the unfolding and does not find it important to place a client in a diagnostic category—in one sense, a denial of differences within the category. In fact, a client's therapy may be described by a recurring theme rather than a diagnosis. Freud labeled one of his early cases "The Wolf Man" because of a client's recurring dream involving wolves.

The second area of psychoanalytic technique that relates to cultural differences is countertransference, which essentially means the reactions the analyst has toward the client. If one of the purposes of discussing cultural differences is to guard against reacting negatively toward a client who is from a culture other than the therapist's, then psychoanalysis has tried to make such a strategy an institutional foundation. To become an analyst—unlike a counselor, psychologist, or psychiatrist—an individual must undertake his or her own psychoanalysis with an approved analyst. Such an undertaking does many things, one of which is to help the analyst in training understand his or her own particular ways of reacting to people. Reacting to people involves the many forms of diversity, that is, age, gender, race, national origin, class, type of psychological problem, and so forth. In addition, part of psychoanalytic training requires analysts in training to individually supervise client cases, usually three or four. The clients have been coming to analysis at least three times a week for at least a year and usually longer. Each weekly supervisory session focuses solely on one client and the sessions of that week. This in-depth look at the interaction between client and analyst always considers the analyst's thoughts and feelings toward the client and what they signify in the treatment at that particular time.

EVALUATION

Overview

This section of the chapter deals with the research that supports psychoanalytic theory and its application to counseling and therapy. Limitations that affect the use of this theoretical approach are also discussed. Thousands of research studies have been conducted on the scientific status of psychoanalysis, and research is ongoing. Limitations are related to cost of treatment and geographic setting.

Supporting Research

Psychoanalysis shares with other fields of study in the social sciences the problem of demonstrating itself as scientific. In addition, because it is a method of therapy, research limitations are imposed on it that do not exist in other fields. For example, a simple research design of treating one person analytically while having a similar person act as a control would be unethical. Therefore, the empirical value of psychoanalysis has to be founded on clinical investigations; that is, the empirical testability of psychoanalytic theory must be demonstrated in the treatment situation. Grunbaum (1984) notes, "The naturalistic setting or 'psychoanalytic situation' is purported to be the arena of experiments in situ, in marked contrast to the contrived environment of the psychological laboratory with its superficial, transitory interaction between the experimental psychologist and his subject" (p. 100). The following paragraph is a cursory review of research findings from studies of the psychoanalytic theory and method.

In *The Scientific Credibility of Freud's Theories and Therapy*, Fisher and Greenberg (1977) compiled a synthesis of almost 2,000 individual studies on the scientific status of psychoanalysis. They concluded that Freudian theory had been subjected to more scientific appraisal than any other theory in psychology and that results had borne out Freud's expectations. Similarly, Luborsky and Spence (1978) emphasized that the psychoanalytic session has epistemic superiority over validity obtained from the more artificially controlled conditions of an experiment and supports Freud's general theory of unconscious motivation.

Despite these affirmations, particularly as they relate to the clinical observation of the major motivational forces of mental life, current criticism of psychoanalysis focuses on its use of multiple sessions and overall length of treatment. Opponents of psychoanalysis point to the efficacy of briefer models of treatment, especially in contemporary health care settings where cost of care is a major concern. They argue that brief, technique-oriented psychotherapy may be just as effective in alleviating a specific symptom without uncovering unconscious dynamics. The debate is not so much about the empirical testability or value of psychoanalysis as it is about the economics of treatment.

Limitations

Psychoanalysis in the United States has traditionally been limited to educated middle- to upper-class clients who can afford the cost of treatment. Counselors or therapists using psychoanalysis have tended to practice mainly in areas of large urban populations. Therefore, the urban and rural poor, as well as the rural middle class and upper class, have not had access to psychoanalytic services. Even if this limitation were alleviated by a national health care plan, the overall cost of educating a counselor or therapist, and the personal sacrifices involved in analytic training automatically tend to limit the availability of practitioners certified in psychoanalysis. Analytic training is a rigorous process that severely taxes interested candidates both financially and emotionally. The unfortunate outcome is a limited pool of psychotherapists whose training includes—in fact, mandates—personal therapy of considerable duration.

It is not surprising that counselors and therapists, on occasion, harbor disturbing feelings toward their clients. Strong passions of love and hate can skew how well the therapy is conducted. Sometimes a practitioner is aware of these strong emotions, but sometimes the emotions are buried in the unconscious, which makes an understanding of the source and usefulness of these feelings unavailable as a means of improving the therapeutic process. In this regard, psychoanalytic training provides an advantage that could be offered to any counselor or therapist who wishes to go beyond a method of brief or technique-limited therapy. Those who do not have an understanding of the source and rationale for emotions experienced in therapeutic situations may be shortchanging themselves and their clients.

The limitations of psychoanalytic methods as applied to large populations of both rural and urban poor may never be alleviated. In contrast, greater strides may be made toward offering counselors and therapists, through psychoanalytic training, a sound procedure for better understanding themselves and their clients, thereby improving their overall therapeutic skills.

SUMMARY CHART—*Psychoanalytic Theory*

Human Nature

Human nature is dynamic, based on the flow and exchange of energy within the personality. This view is based on two fundamental hypotheses concerning mental development and functioning: psychic determinism or causality (nothing happens by chance or in a random way, and all mental phenomena have a causal connection to the psychic events that precede them); and unconscious mental processes (a portion of the mind works within a framework of timelessness, spacelessness, and the coexistence of opposites).

Major Constructs

- The topographic hypothesis means that there exists a conscious and unconscious mind.
- The dynamic hypothesis sees the mind as a closed energy system in which every effect has a cause.
- The economic hypothesis entails the pleasure-pain and constancy principles.
- The structural hypothesis divides the mind into id, ego, and superego.
- The adaptive hypothesis describes how the individual attempts to cope with societal demands.

Goals

The goals of psychoanalysis emphasize resolution of clients' problems so as to enhance clients' personal adjustment, their working through unresolved developmental stages, and their ability to cope more effectively with the demands of the society in which they live.

Change Process

The changing of the personality and character structure of the individual involves resolving unconscious conflicts, working through unresolved developmental issues, and developing skills to cope with particular demands of societal relationships.

Interventions

- Free association encourages the client to say whatever comes to mind.
- Analysis of dreams is important because dreams reflect the status of the analytic relationship.
- Analysis of transference attempts to state what is happening between client and analyst.
- Analysis of resistance involves putting into words what is blocking the client's awareness.
- Interpretation refers to the analyst's formulation of what is taking place in the analysis.

Limitations

- More than any other treatment, psychoanalysis requires the client's commitment in terms of time, money, and personal effort.
- Psychoanalysis is a long-term treatment.
- Psychoanalysis is generally available only in urbanareas because of limited availability of trained analysts.
- A rigorous training program that requires time, money, and emotional commitment of practitioners is a formidable obstacle.

THE CASE OF JONATHAN: *A Psychoanalytic Approach*

To better understand the psychoanalytic method and theory outlined in the preceding sections, imagine a session unfolding. Recall that, the research material of psychoanalysis is drawn from the productions of clients in therapeutic settings, that is, free association, dream analysis, and so on. This material is used to substantiate psychoanalytic theories regarding mental functions. Accordingly, this case study provides clinical material as it might unfold to serve as an example as well as to explain ideas about unconscious processes. The word *therapist* is used as this is a more common term for those who practice psychoanalysis.

In the case of Jonathan, it may be hard to distinguish a psychoanalytic approach from other positions. The client is experiencing severe symptoms of depression, alcohol abuse, severe guilt, and suicidal ideation. Indeed, Jonathan says he has little to live for and feels responsible for "ruining" the lives of most everyone with whom he is close. He is in jeopardy at his job after having been suspended for angry arguments. It seems clear that turmoil is reaching the boiling point and that to encourage him to explore unconscious conflicts and dynamics at this point is ill-timed. As in most any other approach, the first step in treatment with Jonathan would be problem solving in nature, including a possible psychiatric referral for medication to lessen the severity of his anger and depression.

What would distinguish a psychoanalytic approach at this beginning phase of treatment? Not so much what could be directly observed in a session but more what is in the mind of the psychoanalytically oriented therapist: the hypotheses and questions generating in the therapist's mind about what is happening inside the client's mind. In engaging in such internal theorizing, the therapist can guide his or her interventions. For example, with Jonathan there seems to be a great risk that he will leave therapy abruptly. His solution attempt for his problems on the reservation was to leave. He seeks the immediate amelioration of depressed feelings with alcohol, and this speaks to his limited tolerance for frustration. Therapy is not likely to afford him the immediate gratification that alcohol would and he will likely become easily disenchanted. Add to this that he feels non-Native Americans are prejudiced against him, and assuming the therapist is not Native American, basic issues of trust are immediately present. The therapist might ask Jonathan if he feels he could work with a non-Native American or if he would prefer to be referred to someone else. At this early stage and with this type of client, analyzing the client's feelings about prejudice is premature. The classically Freudian technique is one of such analyzing, but in this day and age that would be a caricature more befitting a Hollywood movie. An analytic approach would recognize that the first and pressing need therapeutically is to build trust. Asking about

Jonathan's desire regarding the ethnicity of the therapist is an intervention toward that goal. It recognizes Jonathan's belief and concern without interpreting it as some expression of neurotic conflict.

Another strategy to develop trust would be to attempt to establish a working alliance. For example, could the therapist engage Jonathan as an ally in trying to figure out what he could do to minimize the tension on his job? If so, the therapist would ask many questions about the job and in particular Jonathan's thoughts and feelings about coworkers and his supervisor. At every opportunity the therapist would make comments to indicate an empathic understanding of Jonathan's perspective—to see it and feel it through his eyes. With a client as guarded, angry, and depressed as Jonathan, such empathic attachment is the greatest challenge to the therapist. What makes this so challenging is that a client such as Jonathan elicits emotional reactions from others, including the therapist. Jonathan is likely to express anger early on to the therapist, perhaps by being 10 minutes late for the first session. Perhaps as a sign of his conflict around anger, he would have been apologetic. Also, he was also coerced into coming to the appointment, so perhaps he is even more guarded and resentful than he usually is.

How do therapists develop skill in empathic attunement? One defining feature of therapists with psychoanalytic training is that they undergo analysis; they have been in Jonathan's position as a client. Such therapists have not only talked the talk, they've walked the walk. This helps immensely to know, not intellectually but at a gut level, what it feels like to be vulnerable, to not know, to seek help from another, to admit failure, and so on. As therapy progresses with Jonathan, more defining features of a psychoanalytic position will emerge. Perhaps chief among these are transference-related comments. For example, if Jonathan came late to a session and apologized profusely, the therapist might say something like, "You know, I had the feeling that you were apologizing for more than just being late, that you seemed to feel very badly about it, more so than what one would expect for 10 minutes. Any thought about that?"

As therapy progresses, more observations and interpretations about Jonathan's feelings toward the therapist (his transference reactions) will be commented on and explored. The purpose is to help Jonathan see and understand, in the here-and-now relationship with the therapist, how and why he relates to people the way he does. This opportunity seems crucial for a client like Jonathan, as so much of his history and reported problems have to do with a fundamental breakdown in relating to other people.

No psychoanalytic approach would be complete without a discussion about a client's dreams. Dreams and slips of the tongue in everday speech were seen by Freud as windows into the unconscious. In psychoanalytic therapy, dreams are most important for what they communicate about a client's hidden (unconscious) thoughts and feelings about the therapist. In time, the therapist becomes the object of the client's thoughts and feelings, and long-standing fears and hopes from important others (mainly parents) get transferred onto the therapist. A dream in the course of therapy can only be understood and be useful if one sees the context in which the dream originated. In other words, what was going on in the session or sessions prior to the dream? In the case of Jonathan, there is a recurring dream at the beginning of treatment, which would not involve the therapist. Nevertheless, this dream would be of interest because it is a recurring dream that might change over the course of treatment to reflect conflicts that might arise, in particular conflicting feelings toward the therapist.

My first reaction to Jonathan's this dream is that he is trapped and that there is movement. In a movie titled *Speed*, a bus was wired with a bomb and if the speed of the bus dropped below 50 mph the bomb would go off. This speaks to the urgency Jonathan feels: things are hurtling along and he is losing control. I would be concerned about suicide, given that he already said he has got little to live for. Another striking feature of the dream is that the bus driver is a woman. A woman is in control of his fate. She laughs at him, sadistically, as he is impotent with his banging with a pipe on the steering wheel. At the end of the dream, it is just Jonathan and the laughing driver but he feels alone.

The usefulness of such a dream lies in what associations the client and the therapist make while talking about the dream. Such associations are a continuation of the dream and help to flush out some of its meanings. Of particular significance are meanings regarding the client's feelings and thoughts about the therapist. If this dream occurred months into treatment, it might be speculated that the laughing bus driver is the therapist, taking the client places he does not want to go (painful feelings and memories) and never stopping long enough so the client can get off (three or four sessions a week).

Suggested Readings

Bollas, C. (1990). *The mystery of things.* New York: Routledge.

Caspi, A. (2000). The child is father to the man: Personality continuities from childhood to adulthood. *Journal of Personality and Social Psychology, 78,* 158–172.

Eagle, M. N. (1999). A critical evaluation of current conceptions of transference and countertransference. *Psychoanalytic Psychology, 17,* 24–37.

Galatzer-Levy, R. M., & Barach, H. (2000). *Does psychoanalysis work?* New Haven, CN: Yale University Press.

Jones, E. E. (2000). *Therapeutic action: A guide to psychoanalytic therapy.* Northvale, NJ: Aronson.

Kaley, H., Eagle, M., Wolitzky, D. (Eds.). (1999). *Psychoanalytic therapy as health care: Effectiveness and economics.* Hillsdale, NJ: Analytic Press.

Kirshner, L. (1999). Toward a postmodern realism for psychoanalysis. *Journal of the American Psychoanalytic Association, 47,* 445–463.

Meissner, W. W. (2000). On analytic listening. *Psychoanalytic Quarterly, 69,* 317–367.

Mitchell, S. (2000). *Relationality: From attachment to intersubjectivity.* Hillsdale, NJ: Analytic Press.

Teicholz, J. G. (1999). *Kohut, Loewald, and the postmoderns.* Hillsdale, NJ: Analytic Press.

CHAPTER 5

Jungian Analytical Theory

Susan E. Schwartz

C. G. Jung Institute, New Mexico

Everything good is costly, and the development of personality is one of the most costly of all things. It is a matter of saying yea to oneself, of taking oneself as the most serious of tasks, of being conscious of everything one does, and keeping it constantly before one's eyes in all its dubious aspects—truly a task that taxes us to the utmost. (Jung, 1967, p. 24)

Jungian analytical psychology is an approach to an individual's symptoms and problems that looks at the total person—mind, body and soul. The approach links the conscious and unconscious in the exploration for the meaning of life for each individual in a personal way that also takes into account collective influences. There are many ways to uncover the unfolding of the psyche for example, dreams, synchronicities, complexes, life situations. All these contain the symbols that reveal the process of becoming oneself.

BACKGROUND

Jungian analytical psychology originated with the Swiss psychiatrist **Carl Gustav Jung**. An early member of Freud's psychoanalytic circle, Jung had at one point been designated by Freud to head the psychoanalytic movement. However, through a series of events, dreams, and interactions with Freud, it became clear to Jung that he could not agree with Freud about the primacy of the sexual trauma theory and Freud's approach to psychological phenomena. Their differences were accentuated in Jung's book *Symbols of Transformation*. The ideas Jung articulated in this book were pivotal to his being ostracized by Freud and the psychoanalytic organization, as Jung proposed different interpretations of psychological processes.

After resigning from teaching psychiatry at the University of Zurich and leaving his position at the Burkholzi Psychiatric Clinic in Zurich, Jung spent 6 years with no outer production but his private analytical practice. All his energy was absorbed in a psychological crisis, a personal and professional journey precipitated by the break with Freud. Through deepening psychological work involving his journals and dialogues with dreams, constructing figures and cities in sand; drawing; chiseling in stone; and researching myth, Eastern religions, and ancient cultures, Jung developed the concepts that later appeared in his writings and methodology of personality transformation, which he called the **process of individuation**.

Jung's work at the Burkholzi Clinic, under Eugen Bleuler (famous for his studies in schizophrenia), included development of the word association test. This psychological test revealed the **complexes** with their **archetypal core** and confirmed the influence of the unconscious on conscious life. The research had brought Jung and Freud together, because both were unearthing evidence about the existence and effects of the unconscious. Jung also discovered what he later termed the **collective unconscious** from working with patients with schizophrenia. The dreams and actions of these patients reflected the images and symbols in ancient religions, alchemy, myths, and tales of the world. Jung said,

> At a time when all available energy is spent in the investigation of nature, very little attention is paid to the essence of man, which is his psyche, although many researches are made into its conscious functions . . . yet deciphering these communications seems to be such an odious task that very few people in the whole civilized world can be bothered with it. Man's greatest instrument, his psyche, is little thought of, if not actually mistrusted and despised. "It's only psychological" too often means: "it is nothing." (1964, p. 102)

Jung's basic premise resonated with his belief in the reality of the **psyche**.

Jung, born in 1875, descended from a heritage of clergymen. His father was a minister in a small town outside of Basel, Switzerland. During preparation for his confirmation in the Protestant church, Jung was dismayed by his father's lack of faith and inability to convey his spirituality. This lacuna led to Jung's lifelong search for spiritual components within the psyche (*spiritual* refers to a connection to the meaning of one's life and to whatever is beyond one's life). Other disappointing experiences with his father also contributed to Jung's projection of the father image onto Freud, 20 years his senior. On their trip to the United States to lecture at Clark University in 1907, Freud refused to share his dreams and interpreted Jung's dreams in personalistic modes. As a result of the disappointment in this experience, Jung began the process of eventual severance of their friendship, which propelled him on a different path. The psychological struggles in their relationship portray aspects of the initiation process when a son separates from his father.

Jung was significantly influenced by observing the two personalities of his mother. He perceived her outward compliance with social rubrics, while privately she expressed

---

Note: The author of this chapter used only Jung's original writings as references for the chapter; see References section at the end of the book. A listing of current publications is provided in the Suggested Readings section at the end of the chapter.

Anima   Constellation of feminine qualities in a man

Animus   Masculine side of a woman

Archetype   Typical, universal, human manifestation of life—whether biological, psychological, or spiritual. An archetype reflects instinctive reactions that have an inherited mode of psychic functioning and arise from the collective unconscious.

Complex   Energic constellation composed of a cluster of images with a similar feeling tone. The complex manifests as more or less well-organized and autonomous parts of the personality.

Ego   Center of the field of consciousness. The ego's role is to maintain relation with other psychological contents. It establishes boundaries between a person and others.

Persona   Person's presentation put forth to the world. The persona is structured from parental introjects, social role expectations, and peer expectations.

Psyche   Essence of a person, the totality of all psychic processes. The psyche is composed of the conscious and unconscious.

Self   Provider of the blueprint of life and center and guide to the personality. The Self expresses the unity of the personality and encompasses the experiencable as well as the not yet known. It contains the uniqueness of each person entwined with the entirety of life—human, plant, animal, inorganic matter, and the cosmos.

Shadow   The "not I" subpersonality. The shadow symbolizes the other, or dark, side that is an invisible but inseparable part of the psychic totality. It has positive and negative forms and can be manifest in both personal and collective figures.

Figure 5.1   Jungian Vocabulary

contrasting opinions. Jung later used this concept in his theoretical distinction between the **personal unconscious** and collective unconscious and the **ego** and **Self**. His mother and father, whose relationship was emotionally distant, represented the dichotomies of **spirit** and **matter**, **anima** and **animus**, **persona** and **shadow**.

Jungian analytical psychology derived from Jung's life, and its theories and substantiations came from his clinical work. He said, "My life is what I have done, my scientific work; the one is inseparable from the other. The work is the expression of inner development" (1963, p. 211). Jung found parallels to his psychological explorations in the various religions and symbols of the world, the medieval science of alchemy, and myths and fairy tales. They all delineated the classic psychological patterns evident in his clinical practice and supported two of Jung's contributions to psychology—the collective unconscious and the process of individuation. Figure 5.1 is presented to aid you in better understanding the special terminology used by Jung in explaining various aspects of his theories.

HUMAN NATURE: A DEVELOPMENTAL PERSPECTIVE

The psyche, the essence of a person, is composed of the conscious and unconscious, and it is the matrix from which consciousness arises. The personal unconscious is composed of the forgotten, repressed, and subliminally perceived events and reactions in a person's life. The collective unconscious includes symbols, images, and **archetypes** common to all people. The foundation of every individual contains these deposits of human reactions to universal situations that have occurred since primordial times. The personality is composed of the ego, persona, shadow, anima, animus, and Self.

Ego

The **ego** is the center of the field of consciousness, and its role is to maintain relation with other psychological contents. It is personally oriented with the task of developing subjective identity and self-worth; it establishes boundaries between a person and others. The ego must be functional for the inner gifts to be actualized.

The ego's archetypal core is the Self, the director of the whole personality. The first half of life involves ego separation from the Self. In the second half of life, ego and Self reunite and assimilate alienated aspects of the personality. The process of individuation requires giving up the will of the ego for a resilient relationship with the Self.

Persona

In Jungian psychology the word *persona* (from the Greek, meaning "sounding through a mask") denotes the presentation put forth to the world. The **persona** is structured from parental introjects, social role responsibilities, and peer expectations. Although the genuine nature of a person comes through the public face, the persona can be a cover for personality weaknesses and conjoin with the need for protection and acceptance. The persona either prevents the inner conflicts and insecurities from attaining visibility or leads to growth through its creative aspects.

The persona is like a skin mediating the inside and outside and functioning in dynamic and compensatory relation to the ego, shadow, anima and animus, and Self. The persona bridges the gap between the ego and the outside world, whereas the animus and anima, the inner masculine and feminine images, mediate between the ego and the core of the Self. The persona corresponds and is compensatory to the habitual outer attitude, and the animus or anima reflects the habitual inner attitude. If rigid, the persona severs a person from the natural instincts, and the anima and animus remain undifferentiated and the shadow is repressed. In this situation, the ego lacks flexibility and adaptation.

Problems occur when the individuality of a person is suppressed or neglected to fit **collective ideals**; that is, outer expectations substitute for a person's individual standpoint. If external values are artificially adapted, a person acts in false and mechanistic conduct to himself or herself and others. Inordinate dependence on the persona denotes self-distrust and inauthenticity.

Shadow

The **shadow**, or "not I" subpersonality, and its differentiation from the ego are part of the movement into personality awareness. Jung said,

> The shadow . . . usually presents a fundamental contrast to the conscious personality. This contrast is the prerequisite for the difference of potential from which psychic energy arises. Without it, the necessary tension would be lacking. . . . One is flat and boring when too unsullied and there is too much effort expended in the secret life away from the eyes of the others. Without its counterpart virtue would be pale, ineffective, and unreal. Their impact on consciousness finally produces the uniting symbols. (1963, p. 707)

The shadow confronts a person with dilemmas arising from being a part of the collective consciousness. Jungian psychology warns of the danger of blind obedience to the collective that results in neglect of the individual. Jung brought attention to the shadow because he lived through two world wars where the **collective shadow** brutally ruled. Facing the shadow promotes reflection on human nature and reveals individual values. Living the shadow consciously implies taking responsibility for oneself and others, owning talents and problems, and taking back projections. The moral obligation to live one's potential appears in dream figures that signify repressed personality aspects.

Humans are often ambivalent about the shadow, which contains the worst and best in the personality. The dark side gains strength when potential is denied. Although it is bitter to accept the shadow—the black, the chaos, the melancholia—doing so can be the start of psychological work. Jung thought of the shadow as the first complex to personalize in analysis. The shadow also contains material with the potential for healing.

The shadow is difficult to confront and assimilate due to the ease of unconsciously projecting it onto others. People prefer to entertain idealized images of themselves rather than acknowledge weaknesses or shame. Recognizing the shadow means giving up the ideal or perfect. The shadow gives dimensionality to life, makes one real, and allows the ego to use its strength. Owning one's shadow makes it easier to solve relationship and family problems rather than projecting the unwanted or rejected contents. By taking back projections, the personality attains definition, style, and inner unity.

Integration of the personal shadow provides a bridge from the ego to the **contrasexual** part of the personality. Jung stated that a person

> will have every opportunity to discover the dark side of his personality, his inferior wishes and motives, childish fantasies and resentments, etc.: in short, all those traits he habitually hides from himself. He will be confronted with his shadow, but more rarely with the good qualities, of which he is accustomed to make a show anyway. He will learn to know his soul, his anima. (1963, p. 673)

(Note that Jung's use of the masculine pronoun reflects the bias of his era.)

Anima

In Jungian psychology the **anima** (from the Greek, meaning "soul") connotes the constellation of feminine qualities in a male. It personifies the male's relation to these aspects, the image of woman inside himself, and his projections onto females. In each era the feminine image changes. The anima initially is experienced from a male's psychological life with his mother or the primary female figure in his life and is influenced by his personal and archetypal experience of the feminine. Becoming conscious of this sexual polarity is essential for personality completeness and psychological union of the masculine and feminine aspects. This concept of the anima applies to all people, regardless of sexual orientation.

The anima is an archetype and, like all archetypes, it is never wholly comprehended. It is discovered with inner work. If separated from his feminine nature, a male can become uneasy, uncommitted, avoid conflict, and drift. Disconnected from the feminine and his emotions, he pays sparse attention to his psyche, and this constricts inner and outer freedom. Flat and monotonous moods signify anima neglect and cause various reactions such as depression, impotence, and even suicide. When out of touch with this aspect of his personality, a male might use drivenness, accomplishment, or physical performance to avoid inner reflection. Fearing the feminine, he becomes distant from inner and outer relationships, and the anima cannot sufficiently function as the bridge to the ego and the Self.

The inner feminine becomes known through images from the unconscious, which are associated with the instinctual part of life, the flow of emotion, the rhythm of nature, and the physicality of pleasure. The anima can take the forms of the creative muse, lover, caregiver, and so on. Jung defined the anima as implying the "recognition of the existence of a semiconscious psychic complex, having partial autonomy of function" (1953a, p. 302). He described the anima as expressing spiritual values and being close to nature. As the anima becomes increasingly differentiated, a male assumes an active rather than a passive role in relation to the feminine. In reference to this, Jung describes consciousness arising from the anima: "it lives of itself, makes one live, and cannot be fully part of consciousness" (1959, par. 57). This statement refers to the transcendent and archetypal aspects that extend the personality beyond ego consciousness.

Animus

The **animus** (from the Greek, meaning "spirit" or "breath") refers to the masculine side of a female. It is influenced by the collective image of male that a female inherits, her experience of masculinity from contact with her father or other primary male figures, and the masculine principle in the culture. If the animus is undeveloped, without sufficient room for expression or growth, it hinders the female through internal castigations and sufferings, undermining her participation in life. Classically interpreted, the animus signifies a female's feeling relationship to the male, culture, and spiritual life, reflecting the predominance of the masculine deity in Western culture.

Feminine nature is pushed into the background by the negative animus. Unassimilated, unacknowledged, or projected, the negative animus causes chronic self-esteem problems, power struggles, and self-alienation. The negative animus manifests in a voice of critical commentary or issues excessive commands and prohibitions. If drawn to a destructive fascination with the animus, a person may sever contact with the world, give up her or his soul, be dreamy and without focus, or be driven to accomplishment.

Problems occur if a father has no limits and is either all-giving or a rigid disciplinarian. If he is encased in a distant and foreboding authority structure, a daughter is not personally affected in a positive way. If his emotion is absent or he is physically unavailable, a negative father complex forms. Activating the masculine principle brings courage, determination, force, and authority. These qualities from a positive father complex enable a person to be effective and competent in the world.

The anima and animus together form a **heiros gamos**, or an internal union of opposites in the personality, that appears in dreams, ancient symbols like yin and yang, and relationships. In current Jungian thought, the anima and animus characteristics are found in both males and females to different degrees depending on the person.

Self

Behind all psychological patterns lies the **Self**, the blueprint of life and the unfolding center and guide for the personality. The Self contains the uniqueness of each person entwined with the entirety of life—human, plant, animal, inorganic matter, and the cosmos. The Self is a synthesis for personality emergence, a cohesive force establishing balance and well-being and guiding the whole personality. It causes us to be what we are and is based on the innate drive toward self-realization.

The Self is personal, yet its striving nature affects the progress of humanity. The empirical symbols of the Self are identified with an aura of numinosity (i.e., connected to the spiritual), and its images have strong emotional value. They appear in dreams in many forms such as animals, hermaphroditic figures, jewels, flowers, and geometric concentrically arranged figures known as **mandalas**. *Mandala* is a Sanskrit word meaning "magic circle," and it is one of the oldest religious symbols. Jung discovered the mandala in the dreams of his patients, where it functioned as a creator and preserver of development and pushed the personality through chaos toward potential wholeness.

The question is not how the Self is created during the course of life, but the extent of its attaining consciousness. The Self is a **temenos**, a center for the source and ultimate foundation of being, transcending personal vision. It is a metapsychological concept referring to the entirety of the psyche and containing the whole range of psychic phenomena. The Self, composed of archetypes and instincts, is supraordinate to the conscious ego. This center of the personality, the midpoint that embraces the conscious and the unconscious psyche, is also the whole circumference. "The beginnings of our whole psychic life seem to be inextricably rooted in this point and all our highs and ultimate purposes seem to be striving toward it" (Jung, 1967, p. 67). The Self is without bounds, an illimitable and indeterminable unconscious where one is simultaneously oneself and connected beyond the personal.

Humans are born with the Self as the matrix of potential faculties waiting to be actualized. "In the last analysis," Jung said, "every life is the realization of a whole, that is, of a self, for which reason this realization can also be called individuation" (1953b, p. 330). The Self is paradoxical: It contains both positive and negative polarities for the organizing of experiences, operating through the ego, and having continuity throughout time.

MAJOR CONSTRUCTS

When **psychic energy**, or **libido**, is lost from consciousness, it passes into the unconscious and activates the contents of the archetypes and complexes. Jung's concept of **enantiodromia**, a term he borrowed from the Greek philosopher Heraclitus, means "flowing into the opposite." The psyche is a dynamic, self-regulating system governed by opposition; it is based on complementary or compensatory factors pulsing through all psychological constructs. The point is not to radically convert from one side to the other, but to integrate personality aspects.

Jungian psychology is teleologically oriented, based on a philosophy of human development as proceeding from childhood though adulthood. Each stage of life requires new attitudes, renewed orientation, and reanchoring to different contexts. The major constructs that undergird this development are **psychological types**, complexes, archetypes, symbols, and the personal and collective unconscious.

Psychological Type

Jung's notion of typology is oriented toward conscious life. The terms **extravert** and **introvert** originated with Jung. They represent the two attitudes for perceiving the world and one's relationship to it. An extravert looks at the world and then to himself or herself, whereas an introvert uses the perspective of the inner world and then perceives the outer. The extravert is influenced by collective norms, the introvert by subjective factors. Jungian analysts are predominantly introverts, as often are those who seek this kind of counseling or psychotherapeutic treatment. The work emphasizes the mix of conscious and unconscious and appeals to people who are searching the psychological depths to find their way.

In addition to the two attitudes, there are four functions that determine a person's psychological perception of the conscious world: **sensation**, perceiving through the senses; **thinking**, giving order and understanding; **feeling**, which weighs and values; and **intuition**, the leap to future possibilities. In each person, one function, called the **superior function**, predominates and takes its particular form according to social and cultural influences. Another function, called the **inferior function**, remains mostly unconscious and is connected to the shadow. The functions are limited to four, a number regarded throughout cultural history as designating wholeness and totality.

The main, or superior, function becomes the most developed and the two accessory functions become reasonably so; the fourth, or inferior, function remains undifferentiated, primitive, impulsive, and out of conscious control. Human nature is not simple; therefore, an absolutely pure type is rare. The functions change in dominance depending on the activities at different life stages. The attitudes do not change but are realized as a person progresses through life. For example, a child may appear to be an introvert in a quiet and withdrawn family, but later in life the adult may uncover adaptation and release pent-up extraversion.

Each attitude can be paired with each function, which allows eight psychological combinations. For example, a person may be introverted sensation thinking, extraverted sensation feeling, and so on. The complementary, or compensatory, relation between the opposite functions is a structural law of the psyche. In the second half of life the inferior function gains attention as the psychological situation naturally alters to round out the personality.

A sensation-type person takes life as it comes, focusing on the conscious daily perception of physical stimuli. Intuition and sensation are called irrational functions; thinking and feeling are associated with the rational and logical. Intuition is the opposite function to sensation, and the intuitive-type person is imbued with creative capacities and inspirations. Intuitive types of people perceive possibilities, but they can be so removed from the present and the senses that they forget the physical world. Thinking is apparent in persons ruled by intellectual motives; their life actions are based on objective data. Such people prefer logic and order, and emotion and feeling are repressed. A thinking person tends to be cold and has difficulty understanding human relationships. In contrast, a feeling type of person is especially concerned with human relationships. Feeling, however, is not to be confused with emotion. Any function can lead to emotional reactions. A feeling person weighs, accepts, or refuses by evaluating what something is worth.

The Myers-Briggs Type Indicator is a popularized adaptation of Jung's principles of **typology**. It is not taught in Jungian institutes because it is solely oriented to conscious functioning.

Complex

A complex is an energic **constellation** with varying degrees of autonomy, ranging from hardly disturbing ego functioning to attaining predominance over the personality. A complex is composed of a cluster of images or ideas with a similar feeling tone, and it manifests as well-organized and autonomous parts of the personality. The psyche's inherent tendency to split into complexes brings dissociation, multiplicity, and the possibility of change and differentiation.

Jungian counseling or psychotherapy aims to separate the complexes from the unconscious into conscious awareness. Jung said we all have complexes and the real issue is whether they are controlling us. Complexes either repress or promote consciousness, inhibit or inspire, hinder development or provide the seeds for new life. Complexes are like magnets that draw psychological and archetypal experience into a person's life. They occur where energy is repressed or blocked, point to unresolved problems and weaknesses, and develop from emotional wounds. When a complex is touched, it is accompanied by exaggerated emotional reactions and may also be experienced physically.

A complex does not completely disappear, but the arrangement of energy changes with awareness. The psychic energy caught in the complex is accessed for personality development. No complex should entirely control the personality, but the ego complex dominates during waking life. The particular makeup of a complex is apparent through images pertaining to the unconscious psychological situation occurring in dreams and the synchronous events of waking life. A person's destiny can be adversely affected by a complex, and psychological issues can remain unresolved for generations. For example, a woman with a negative father complex transfers a limited purview onto everything male and operates from negatively biased perceptions.

Archetype

The personal unconscious consists of complexes and the collective unconscious is composed of archetypes. The word *archetype* originated with Plato and means "ideal form" or "first imprint." The archetype is at the core of the complex. It is imbued with the tendency to form images rich in emotional content with infinite possibilities for analysis. The repetitions and clusterings of archetypes are called **motifs**.

The archetype is a formless structure with infinite varieties, enmeshed in history and more or less pertinent to a time or place in the evolution of the psyche. The archetype is expressed and comprehended through mythological and sacred images in cultural and personal life. Jung commented on this when he said that

> it is only possible to come to a right understanding and appreciation of a contemporary psychological problem when we reach a point outside our own time from which to observe it. This point can only be some past epoch that was concerned with the same problems, although under different conditions and in other forms. (1954, p. viii)

Humans inherit a tendency to structure experiences of psyche and **soma** in typical and predictable ways called archetypes. These archetypes have a basic form, express the human psyche, and define a pattern of development. Yet Jung stated,

> No archetype can be reduced to a simple formula. It is a vessel which can never empty and never fill. It has a potential existence only, and when it takes shape in matter it is no longer what it was. It persists throughout the ages and requires interpreting anew. The archetypes are imperishable elements of the unconscious, but they change their shape continually. (1959, p. 301)

These building blocks of the psyche operate in basic psychological, instinctual patterns that are counterparts to the biological instincts. Instincts are impulses of action without conscious motivation. Like a snake appearing in a dream, instincts are collective, universal, and regularly occurring phenomena—without individuality yet having personal significance.

Jung described the archetype as composed of two poles. The "psychic infra-red," or the biological psyche of one end, gradually passes into the "psychic ultra-violet" on the psychic end. The archetype describes a field both psychic and physical. The essence of the archetype forms a bridge where spirit and matter meet.

Jung stated that the archetype "represents or personifies certain instinctive data on the dark, primitive psyche, the real but invisible roots of consciousness" (1959, p. 271). An archetype cannot be described but is circumscribed by the opposites of its spectrum. Archetypes are impersonal personifications of human potential encompassing the deeper currents of life. Their images in dreams, mythology, religions, and fairy tales gain relevance with personal application. The remembrance of a favorite fairy tale or myth and its archetypal journey help a person glean meaning from life's sorrows and joys. Archetypes inform everyday life. They are at work in relationships, organizations, family systems, and the way life is experienced and interpreted.

Symbol

The Jungian definition of **symbols** includes the personal and collective, conscious and unconscious. A symbol is felt, often viscerally, as in an important dream. Jung described this feeling as "numinous," giving significance and depth to life and connecting with the transcendent.

Each symbol has two sides, one related to the conscious ego and one turned toward the archetypal contents of the collective unconscious. The unconscious produces answers to psychological problems through its symbolic images, which are compensatory to the conscious mind. A symbol takes energy from the unconscious and transforms it to resolve conflicts and channel self-expression. It unfolds as a working metaphor throughout life. Symbols are spontaneous psychic manifestations pertinent for individual and societal change.

It seems logical that if people are biologically related, they are psychologically related, especially on collective and archetypal levels. Jung studied myths, the fundamental symbolic expressions of human nature, as representing typical psychic phenomena. Mythological patterns reflect the distinctive psyche of a given culture or religion and contain universal symbolic relevance. Myths and their symbols help bring order out of psychological chaos.

The word *symbol* comes from the Greek *symbolon*, which means "coming together." A symbol arises from conflict or disorientation, joins two separate elements, and mobilizes energy. Symbols spontaneously arise from the unconscious psyche, transform it into conscious experience, and energize the ego. Signals in the form of symbols are received through dreams every night.

Psychic contents not yet conscious express themselves in symbolic ways. Because the unconscious contains the germs of future psychological situations and ideas, Jung called the transmutation of libido or energy through symbols the **transcendent function**. Conscious and unconscious confront each other, and the symbol provides a bridge to a third possibility which is transcendent. The symbol is activated after an experience of disintegration, when the personality is jarred by psychological threats to the status quo.

Because the psyche is as real as the body and encompasses the spiritual and biological realms, the unconscious is the matrix of psychogenic symptoms signaling disharmony with conscious life. To the extent that persons are unaware of the symbolic dimension of existence, they experience the problems of life as symptoms. The ability to recognize the symbolic images behind the symptoms transforms the experience.

Personal Unconscious

The unconscious is continually engaged in the grouping of unconscious contents and is normally coordinated with consciousness in a compensatory relationship. The personal unconscious is composed of the memories that can be accessed from childhood and past events, fantasies, and wishes and desires that are related personally and are acquired during life. The personal part of the unconscious holds those qualities that due to trauma, time of life, and outer situations are just below the surface of consciousness and are accessible to consciousness through dreams, in counseling or therapy, and as they show up in daily life. The personal unconscious defines individuals as uniquely themselves, but it is limited in content. Jung described it as the subjective psyche and demarcated it from what he called the collective unconscious, or the objective psyche, which goes beyond the personal sphere and is unlimited. The point is to become conscious of the unconscious contents as they appear first through the personal unconscious and then in the collective unconscious—their combination facilitates getting to the roots of the complexes.

Collective Unconscious

The collective unconscious encompasses all previously discussed aspects of the psyche. This concept distinguishes Jungian analytical psychology from other approaches. The unconscious is not only personal but also collective and impersonal. The collective unconscious consists of the sum of the instincts and their correlates, the archetypes. This storehouse of potentially energizing, enriching, and also abhorrent material brings the understanding and knowledge that furthers development of each human being. The complexity of the psyche means that comprehension of it is, at the most, partial, because there is no finite knowledge of its boundaries or complete nature.

CONSCIOUS COMPONENTS—COLLECTIVE AND PERSONAL

PERSONA
EGO—center of the field of consciousness
   TYPOLOGY
     ATTITUDES
       Introvert, Extravert
     FUNCTIONS
       Thinking, Feeling, Sensation, Intuition
SHADOW

UNCONSCIOUS COMPONENTS

COLLECTIVE COMPONENTS	*PERSONAL COMPONENTS*
ARCHETYPES	COMPLEXES
Images, myths, symbols	Personal memories
	(repressed, forgotten,
	traumas)
SHADOW	
ANIMUS/ANIMA	

Figure 5.2   Jungian Picture of the Psyche—Body, Mind, and Soul

The collective unconscious goes beyond the individual ego, and its nature is revealed through cultural myths, religious images and symbols, dreams, drawings, active imagination, dance, or any creative work. The collective unconscious contains the deposit of human reactions to universal situations, initiations, and rites of passage through the stages of life operating since primordial time.

Figure 5.2 provides an overview of the major constructs that explain the developmental process inherent in Jungian analytical psychology.

APPLICATIONS

Overview

The following sections present information dealing with the goals, process of change, and intervention strategies that apply to Jungian analytical psychology. The goals of Jungian psychology stress the processes of individuation, personality unity, and transcendence. The transformation of personality depends on the potential for growth inherent in each person. Intervention strategies are designed to both meet the goals and enhance the change process for an individual, with concurrent ramifications for society.

Goals of Counseling and Psychotherapy

Individuation and personality unification are central to Jungian psychology. Individuation, the differentiation of the various components of the psyche, addresses the development of the unique elements of an individual. As a person gains knowledge of various personality aspects, he or she synthesizes into what Jung termed the *transcendent function*. Transcendence involves a constant striving for wholeness, integration of the personality, and realization of the Self.

Process of Change

Jungian psychology is conceptually broad and attempts to address the isolation and confusion of modern times. Uneasy ambience and aimlessness impel the search for fulfillment. The illnesses of society—the boredom, joylessness, and inability to love—adversely affect interpersonal and intrapersonal relationships.

The transformation of character follows the potential for growth inherent in the human psyche. When the conscious attitude is at an impasse, psychic energy is drawn into the unconscious and emerges in dreams, images, and synchronous events. Jung's concept of **synchronicity** involves the acausal and meaningful coincidences that impart order in the world, opening the way toward experiencing the Self. For example, the *I Ching*, the ancient book of Chinese wisdom, is based on synchronicity. Asking a question and throwing yarrow sticks or coins provides a symbolic answer to the problem at hand.

Over a lifetime, psychic energy transforms. The individuation process, or the way a person comes into his or her uniqueness, requires the differentiation and reintegration of the unconscious. The process reflects the archetypal, spiritual, and religious activities of the psyche. Jungian counseling or psychotherapy is a method encompassing the phases of education, catharsis, rebirth, and transformation. The process recaptures developmental difficulties where growth is stopped. Renewal comes with initiatory experiences reactivating the psyche.

Jung found the individuation process repeated in history, religious rituals, tribal ceremonials, and initiatory practices. He studied Eastern religions and mystical wisdom literature, the spiritual disciplines of the Kabbalah, Gnosticism, Kundalini yoga, and so on, as analogous methods to the individuation process. He extensively researched alchemy, a medieval science and precursor to modern-day chemistry. The symbols and goals of alchemical work, or symbolically turning lead into gold, parallel the individuation process, the stages of psychological development, dream symbols, and issues of the transference and countertransference.

A person can proceed, often until midlife, functioning reasonably well, but part of the personality remains undeveloped and dormant. A crisis comes, relationships alter, and life becomes tumultuous. Beliefs become challenged, a terminus is reached, and change must occur—some new direction taken. The energy stored in the unconscious pushes to be known. The prospective, or forward-moving, function of the psyche leads to further development and finding a sense of purpose in life. Jung is noted for recognizing the significance of the second half of life as a time for deepening the personality.

Jungian analysts use the chair or couch or both. People are seen weekly, and preferably two or more times a week. A higher frequency of sessions encourages depth, concentration, and activation of the unconscious influence on conscious functioning. Because the process of individuation plays out differently for each person, there are no prescribed techniques, no formal treatment goals set by the Jungian counselor or therapist, no reliance on traditional categories of pathology.

Problems develop due to an ossified approach to life and disunity with the Self. Although disorder is painful, it becomes an impetus for personality growth. The issue is not whether difficulties exist but the way they are handled. Psychological illness is simultaneously a warning and a natural attempt at healing. The process of change is not quick or easy. Consciously suffering the psychic pain of the past allows energy from past wounds to transform so that the person gains a more satisfying present and future life. This approach is applicable to people of all ages, including children.

Traditional Intervention Strategies

Dreams. Dreams are a natural way to discover and unravel the mysterious workings of the personality. More than just bizarre images that come with sleep, they are as real as waking life. Dreams address core issues, and throughout history they have been recognized as a source of inspiration.

The belief that dreams are a means of divine communication or an occult way of discerning the future was pervasive in the ancient Near East. In biblical times dreams were considered the agents of God's word, announcing God's will to the dreamer. Dream interpretation was an important part of the spiritual life of the ancient Greeks and Egyptians, whose word for *dream* was derived from the verb meaning "to awaken." In all races and at all times, dreams were regarded as truth-telling oracles.

Attending to dreams is a way to obtain information about unknown and untapped psychological areas. Dream information enhances the day world and shines a light on the repressed qualities and contents that rob the individual of actualizing potential. Big dreams occur at significant life markers or crisis times, with dream messages that provide inroads to the psyche. Dream books do not suffice as ready-made guides for interpretation, because the dream and its symbols cannot be separated from the dreamer. Following dreams leads to recovery of one-self as dreams weave together current experiences with those from the past and future.

Dreams keep people from straying from the truths of the body. Their images are symbolic portrayals of an actual unconscious situation, bringing the potency of the situation to life and triggering emotional reactions. Physical disorders in dreams express psychological issues and may serve as an early warning system for illness. Dreams often suggest treatment, contain methods and tools for psychological and physical healing, and crystallize a problem into something workable and understandable.

The Jungian form of counseling or psychotherapy involves not only treatment of a symptom but also reconstruction of an individual and restoration of human dignity. Jung wrote, "One should never forget that one dreams in the first place, and almost to the exclusion of all else, of oneself" (1964, p. 312). What the dream has to say is always seen in light of the attitude of the conscious mind of the dreamer. When inner potential is negated or ignored, pathology appears; when the gold of the personality becomes stuck and repressed into the unconscious, things go badly.

Recurring dreams, nightmares, and childhood dreams are all crucial expressions of the unconscious and relate to factors primary in the life of the individual and his or her culture. Through personal associations, the dreamer is led deeper into the psyche and finds similar motifs repeated in religions, legends, myths, and fairy tales. Although contemporary societies have lost the formal rites of initiation, all people have a psychological need to access the spirit that cultural lore imparts. These initiatory processes are stored in the unconscious and emerge through dreams and fantasy material to replenish the personality.

The dream is not merely the ego reflecting on itself; rather, a dream is a communication from the unconscious—beyond, yet in relation to the ego. To concern oneself with dreams is a way of accessing one's true nature and gaining knowledge to free the complexes. Children are easily in touch with their dreams because they are psychologically closer to the uncon-scious. For adults, work is needed to get back to this state. Too often the rational world takes over and the inner life is negated.

The dream is like a play with an opening scene, statement of the problem, action, climax, and resolution. The dream characters represent compensatory expressions of the personality. Awareness of the projection of one's qualities onto dream figures is a way to reclaim them. On the subjective level, the figures in dreams are personified features of the dreamer's personality. On the objective level, they represent an actual person or someone in close relation, such as a partner, child, or parent. It is worth noting in the dream where the dreamer stands, the position and action of the dreaming ego, and whether the dreamer is an observer, a participant, or not present. There is meaning in the sequential order of events, the people who appear, and those named or unnamed. The unnamed represent qualities remote from consciousness and, therefore, less identifiable. A dream placed in a familiar or foreign country, or not on earth, reveals the distance of the psychological information from conscious awareness. Holding the living relationship between the conscious and unconscious, called by Jung the **tension of the opposites**, helps sustain and organize a person while he or she pursues what Jung called the psychological treasure hard to attain in the unconscious.

The dream is an important means of facilitating inner work and addressing the blind spots of a personality. Dream images arise from involuntary psychological processes that are not controlled by the ego or will. In working with the dream, the Jungian counselor or therapist and client stay consonant with the facts and do not distort or change the information. They stick to the dream images, which leads to gradual emergence of the reasons for psychological blocking and resistance. The counselor or therapist uses theory to create a flow of information without distorting the dream into an intellectual venture.

In dreams, nothing is absolute; not everything is analyzable at the time of the dream, and clarification may occur with later dream material. Personality definition develops through its aspects being named; the dream retains a mystery by keeping some things hidden. Dreams are self-regulating and depict the psyche's forward and regressive movements. Dreams are more or less synchronous with daily life, and they parallel or anticipate actual occurrences. Dreaming produces growth by synthesizing psychological aspects. When understood, this natural process reinforces reliance on the psyche and its wisdom. Concentration and value placed on the dream world foster personality integration and individuation.

Transference and Countertransference. Jungian analytical psychology reweaves the personality through the container, or temenos, of the counseling or psychotherapeutic relationship. Transference relates to past personal dramas as well as the archetypal struggle of each person on the path toward self-realization.

During a Jungian session, a client discusses dreams, active imagination, personal relationships, current problems, childhood development, transference, synchronous occurrences, and so forth. All of these are worked on additionally outside of the sessions through recording feelings, emotions, and thoughts and by engaging in creative endeavors that make the unconscious conscious. Initial problems vary, and treatment usually goes beyond the first symptoms. People naturally become intrigued with themselves as they awaken to the meaning of their existence.

Addressing transference and countertransference is part of the art of Jungian counseling or psychotherapy. "The unrelated human being lacks wholeness, for he can achieve wholeness only through the soul, and the soul cannot exist without its other side, which is always found in a 'you'" (Jung, 1966, p. 454). Through the attention and reflection of the Jungian counselor or therapist, clients learn to regard themselves psychologically and to comprehend and honor the reality of the psyche. The discourse between two individuals is actually a discourse among four. Present are the Jungian counselor or therapist and his or her anima or animus, as well as the client and his or her anima or animus. Treatment involves exploring how all the characters interact within the therapeutic vessel as the archetypal process of individuation unfolds.

Transference portrays the inner situation, expectations, complexes, fantasies, and feelings of the client. Part of the psyche looks for a bridge from the past into present reality. Transference is defined by its phenomenon of **projection**, or seeing oneself in an other, and it occurs in all relationships. Split-off or unintegrated parts of the client are projected onto the counselor or therapist, who embodies the family, the unused aspects of the personality, and the potential of the client—until the client begins to take back the projections. The relationship enacts the unconscious drama as it holds the client through exploring current and past issues, discovers what archetype colors the person, and finds the hints at solution present in dreams and fantasies. The counselor or therapist needs emotional clarity to differentiate the client's projections from his or her own. The treatment relies on the totality of the psyche of both participants.

To be aware of his or her complexes and psychological composition, a Jungian counselor or therapist has intensive personal analysis before and during formal training at a Jung institute. Each engages in his or her own psychological work to facilitate psychological transformation with others. Countertransference reflects the counselor or therapist reacting to the client and gives useful information. The nonverbal communication, timing, and sensitivity of the counselor or therapist relies on the psychological and physical signals received from the client. The counselor's or therapist's personality corresponds to the unconscious of the client in this shared interactive space. Each counselor or therapist must ask whether feelings about the client stem from his or her unconscious and unintegrated conflicts, or whether the reaction is to the unconscious drama of the client. The mutual transformation that occurs through this process demands honesty and perseverance from both participants. Jung said, "The doctor is therefore faced with the same task which he wants the patient to face" (1954, p. 167).

Jung commented about the transformative process, "I have no ready made philosophy of life to hand out . . . I only know one thing: when my conscious mind no longer sees any possible road ahead and consequently gets stuck, my unconscious psyche will react to the unbearable standstill" (1954, p. 84). Jung described the counselor or therapist as a wounded healer, reminiscent of the shaman, or medicine man, in various cultures who can activate the healing powers of the sick.

Active Imagination. In a state of *abaissement du niveau mental* (a lowering of consciousness), the ego loses energy and a person receives information from the unconscious. An individual approaches active imagination with the intent to accept whatever arises from the psyche and without the ego assuming control. From this state, a person creates or makes sense of the unknown material that floats up from the unconscious by writing, drawing, dancing, and so forth. A person takes the symbols and images and communes with them without the pressure of producing something rational.

Brief Intervention Strategies

Jungian theory is basically an in-depth approach to life situations. The approach always depends on how extensively a person wants to go. The therapist or counselor does not operate in cookbook-like fashion, as in-depth work pertains to the complexity of the soul as it operates within the client. The process depends on the interactive conscious and unconscious space between counselor or therapist and client. The interventions listed previously can all be applied to brief therapeutic work and are useful in getting to the heart of the matter as well as in teaching people to become independent and self-reliant. The use of dreams, recording in journals, and attending to synchronicities are ways to create dialogue with personality parts and can be used in brief work for accessing problems, solutions, and strengths.

CLIENTS WITH SERIOUS MENTAL HEALTH ISSUES

People with problems such as personality disorders, psychotic reactions, borderline disorders, chronic depression, and narcissistic and schizoid diagnoses respond to Jungian forms of treatment because of the intense and early wounding typically associated with these diagnoses. It takes time to comprehend these complex psychological situations. Connections and meaning must be established between the inner and outer, past and present, and personal and collective experiences. Often people with these serious diagnoses tend to have an internal impetus to delve deeply into the psyche wherein lay both the wounds and the healing.

As mentioned earlier in the chapter, Jung began his work with patients at a mental hospital and was one of the first psychiatrists to heed the meaning in the symbolic language of delusions and hallucinations. Therefore, Jungian thought is based on personalities at the psychological edge. Jung discovered that people with severe disorders were expressing personal and collective issues and solutions, which he corroborated through his research into the collective unconscious. The ways for making sense of these precarious psychological places are many—dreams, drawings, poetry, literature, religion, spirituality, and anything that promotes finding meaning in the suffering.

CROSS-CULTURAL CONSIDERATIONS

The cross-cultural aspects of the many cultures in the United States have been magnified by the shrinking world. These cross-cultural aspects appear in the realm of religious, ethnic, and transgenerational influences. The Jungian counselor or therapist takes into account how background contributes to lifestyle, psychological attitudes, relationships, and so forth. In Jungian therapy or counseling, cross-cultural considerations are a given due to the collective unconscious that contains information from all cultures. People of different cultures understand each other because they share collective fundaments, which are part of the bedrock on which lives are built.

When clients see a therapist or counselor of a different background, the experience may be beneficial, as clients have to explain their background and it becomes clearer through the elucidation process. It is not enough to merely have joint similarities between therapist and client, because this can cause unconsciousness. Jungian thought supports the concept that treatment works when there is a change in both client and therapist or counselor. The openness and egalitarian nature of this theory means the relationship and the various levels of interaction (conscious and unconscious, similar and different) and the personal and collective cultures traveling in the space between the therapist and client provide a breadth of healing.

EVALUATION

Overview

This section of the chapter deals with research supporting Jungian analytical psychology as well as the limitations of this approach. Note that based on the nature of Jungian analytical psychology, little traditional research has been done with this approach to counseling and psychotherapy. Nevertheless, clinical results gleaned from a heuristic perspective provide support for the continued use of Jungian analytical psychology. The limitations addressed in this section occur according to choices of the client who seeks to embark on the journey of self-discovery.

A misconception exists that people who participate in Jungian treatment are already fairly healthy. This is not necessarily the case. Many people seek Jungian counseling and psychotherapy for urgent problems and emotional disturbances, severe or otherwise. Once these clients regain some personality balance, they begin attending to their personality and the original disturbance becomes the symptom leading them deeper into themselves. Jung was an early proponent of the mind, body, and soul connection, and he has influenced many subsequent psychological and physical theorists. The connections Jung made with the physical and the symbolic meaning in body symptoms are helpful in understanding and using the body and mind conjunction. In fact, Jung used many creative approaches to heal the psyche. It is fallacious to assume that Jungian therapy and counseling treatment is not crisis oriented or is not for people with urgent problems because there are no outlined or linear steps or procedures to follow.

Supporting Research

Little statistical research exists about Jungian analytical psychology. The process is non-replicable, confidential, and based on individual and archetypal processes. Tests are not usually administered in this depth approach to the psyche. The heuristic approach from personal and archetypal research validates the transformative process. Jung claimed that scientific proof resided in his empirical research into myth themes, world tales, primitive cultures, and religious ceremonies and rituals. The growing popularity of Jungian psychology correlates with the cultural need to compensate for emptiness and loss of meaning by reconnecting with unconscious realms.

Jung made significant contributions to the fields of sand play therapy, art therapy, and psychology. He advocated analysts' coming from a wide background, the crucial point being that they have a personal analysis. His interest in Eastern philosophy, mystical religions, and mythology brought him in contact with many of the great thinkers of the 20th century. Jungian counselors and therapists lecture and write on topics ranging from classical Jungian thought to music, mathematics, philosophy, Eastern and Western religion, and modern psychological developments.

As in all fields of counseling and psychology, analysts in Jungian psychology are currently engaged in outcome studies to assess the effect of this psychological approach. Several Jungian journals publish articles referring to the results and supporting the value of this more intensive approach to solving the problems of life.

Limitations

Jungian analytical psychology has limitations in the sense that most people who embark on this path are often of an intellectual bent, have reached a certain level of accomplishment, and are looking not only for crisis intervention but also for ways to enhance the meaning of their lives. Their outer functioning may look sufficient to others, but they know they are living below their level of satisfaction and must plumb the psychological depths to stretch their personality. This is not an elitist approach, but some people do have an impetus for deeper psychological development as well as having more time, money, and personal effort to expend. The approach requires more than a cursory look at oneself, and the psyche is rigorous in its demand for attention once it is discovered. Although the approach is useful for all ages and backgrounds, internal desire and the ability for strenuous work are requirements and set the limitations. At the beginning, people often do not know what is entailed in the process, yet some part of their psychological makeup agrees to take a long and arduous internal look. Sometimes it is surprising to discover who remains in the work and who finds it inappropriate.

Essentially, the Jungian approach is useful for those who want to invest in themselves over time and not for the short term, and for those who wish to go beyond the symptoms and proceed into the psyche. These people have wonder, fear, and a need to work out their underlying malaise, depression, anxiety, or other problems through discovering what lies in the unconscious. Those who fit this approach will naturally find this way.

SUMMARY CHART—*Jungian Analytical Theory*

Human Nature

The foundation of every individual contains deposits of human reactions to universal situations that have occurred since primordial times. This foundation is reflected in the concepts of the ego, persona, shadow, anima, animus, and Self.

Major Constructs

The complex is a cluster of impressions with similar feeling tones that function autonomously. The archetype, or inherited mode of psychic functioning, is at the core of the complex. It becomes known through symbols arising from the collective unconscious. Symbols contain answers to psychological problems. The collective unconscious contains deposits of the human psyche from the beginning of time. Psychological types are oriented to conscious life. People who are introverted view the world from a subjective standpoint; people who are extraverted look outward before registering their inner reactions. The four functions are the ways libido, or psychic energy, manifests: sensation, what is happening now; intuition, the leap to future ideas; thinking, intellect and logic; and feeling, the valuing of a person or thing.

Goals

Individuation is the unification of the personality by incorporating the conscious and unconscious realms.

Change Process

The transformation of character follows the potential for growth inherent in the human psyche. When the current conscious attitude is at an impasse, psychic energy is drawn into the unconscious and emerges in dreams, images, and synchronous events. The individual process, or the way a person comes into his or her uniqueness, requires the differentiation and reintegration of unconscious psychological complexes.

Interventions

Dream analysis provides an important way to understand the unconscious and its impact on conscious life. Transference and countertransference are part of the dynamic process that occurs in the therapeutic relationship. Active imagination and other creative productions support the movement of the psyche from problems to solutions.

Limitations

The Jungian approach requires the client's serious and usually long-term commitment in terms of time, money, and personal effort. Clients, select this theoretical approach for themselves because their personality is suited to it.

THE CASE OF JONATHAN: *An Analytical Approach*

Psychological problems call attention to one-sided attitudes and create possibilities for movement. A crisis brings change because the resulting personality disunity activates the unconscious and spurs on the need to examine oneself. Conflict in personal and collective values and the arousal of basic needs are touchstones for growth and the ingredients for developing authentic self-definition. Being involved in Jungian work equips people to become their own interpreters of life and to decipher meaning from their experiences.

The beginning paragraph of the case study described Jonathan's cultural background, which influences his personality development, his emotional and spiritual life, and family relationships, all of which are in turmoil. Family and tribal values seemed to have meaning for him in the past, and he is experiencing a tension of opposites between the predominant White urban culture and the culture of the Native American reservation. This tension creates emotional suffering both in himself and in relationships with others, and it is pulling him into psychological exploration.

Childhood issues, unresolved grief around separation, as well as his current situation of loneliness contribute to Jonathan's use of ineffective behaviors exhibited by the complexes operating autonomously and taking over his ego functioning. His current work with adolescents seems a good situation for him, as he is developmentally stuck at this age and is acting out in similar ways to them. The work can provide a mirror for him and might be a place to gain the self-awareness he needs to function more effectively with himself and others. The initial information about Jonathan reveals that his ego lacks sufficient connection to the Self, or core of his being, as he is easily distracted by fighting with others and is unable to find direction professionally, relationally, or internally. These reactions signal a damaged ego-Self connection that negatively affects his confidence and ability to function or access enough internal support.

Because we develop an image of our Self as a child, Jonathan's treatment will explore childhood history, adolescence, and the grief and mourning from incomplete connections and unresolved separations. The death of his brother and the subsequent guilt and grief may be part of why Jonathan does not complete things or commit to his life. There is a repeat of the number 6 throughout his history that is curious and may be a clue for him. He quit school at 16 when his brother died, divorced 6 years ago, married for 6 years, and 6 months ago separated from his second wife who he married 6 months after the divorce. There were 6 children in his family. It could be interesting and helpful for him to follow this thread into his life.

Jonathan has not learned that he is good enough and keeps on reinforcing that he cannot do it. He is not using his heritage or its myths and legends, which could sustain him. Rather, an internal rift has formed a disconnection from his spiritual heritage leaving him bereft of his moorings. Jonathan's alcoholism shows he is drinking the wrong kind of spirit and it is downing him. He seems also to be using alcohol to disconnect from his physical self, to deny consciousness, and as a calling for help. Current conflicts are heightened as is his drinking, so he will start to pay attention to the issues of relationships, commitment to himself, and how to handle the cultural conflict. Jung said,

> But if we can reconcile ourselves with the mysterious truth that the spirit is the life of the body seen from within, and the body an outer manifestation of the life of the spirit—the two being really one—then we can understand why the striving to transcend the present level of consciousness through acceptance of the unconscious must give the body its due, and why recognition of the body cannot tolerate a philosophy that denies it in the name of the spirit. (1968, Par. 2142)

Use of Dreams

Part of Jungian counseling or psychotherapy involves exploring childhood, recurrent, and present dreams. The dream emanates from the unconscious and is compensatory to consciousness for personality adjustment and rectification. Taken alone, a dream is ambiguous and contains a multiplicity of meanings; a series of dreams, however, shows an arrangement around a particular problem, a circumambulation (walking around) to gain different perspectives. Few or no associations demonstrate repression and difficulty accessing the material due to resistance. The initial dream presented by a client depicts the prognosis for the course of the counseling or psychotherapy. The dream is a useful instrument for opening dialogue with the inner dimensions of the psyche. It expresses psychological truths about the dreamer, often differently than the dreamer can comprehend or acknowledge consciously.

Rather than associations supplied by the counselor or therapist, a correct dream interpretation is what fits for the dreamer. As a therapeutic relationship is established, Jonathan will benefit from having a dialogue with the dream figures, drawing them, or writing his reactions and amplifications. The first session is a time to establish rapport and build a place where Jonathan can begin to share material. His efforts, along with those of the Jungian counselor or therapist, aim to translate the conflicts in his life into means for developing consciousness and different approaches to his issues.

In this instance, Jonathan's repetitive dream gives some clues about his major issues but at the same time presents no definitive answer about whether he will get through his dilemmas. The dream shows Jonathan swamped by unconscious contents—mostly associated with the feminine side—that call for a deepened relationship to them. Recurrence demonstrates that the problem is not solved. Jonathan does not give an emotional reaction after the dream except to say he is unable to go to sleep. The unconscious obviously is disturbing him and wants him to pay attention, but part of Jonathan's personality does not listen and he seems powerless against it. As his ego position has weakened, he is depleted and his self-esteem decreases. Substituting the unhealed wounds with a persona adaptation, such as blending into the White culture, is not possible.

The dream portrays shadow aspects erupting from repression, and the other people on the bus represent Jonathan's unknown psychological parts. They, too, are held hostage by the bus driver and cannot find a way out. Having no exit denotes an existential crisis. Jonathan is in the midst of a cultural and personal identity crisis demonstrated by the turmoil in the dream. The bus in the dream represents a collective way of travel and here it is driven by the feminine. However, the masculine should be running a man's personality, not the feminine. The dream shows Jonathan has to get in contact with the driver so he can take charge. The complex related to Jonathan's self-worth is activated and the ego's networking capacity with other parts of the personality is disjointed and has no direction or focus, and Jonathan's destructive impulses are taking over. Unable to listen to the interior parts of himself creates the violence and rage portrayed in the dream. Unrecognized personality elements turn against his personality, become destructive, and negatively affect his urge for life. The feminine side can lead to transformation and renewal, but when it is obfuscated and laden with repressed guilt and shame, conflict results. The spirit darkens and the unconscious assumes a devouring nature, forcing attention inward. Jonathan's external and current situations replicate earlier experiences, just as the dream itself keeps repeating. Depressive illnesses are often caused by painful losses inadequately mourned and summarily repressed. In many mythologies, dealing with death and dismemberment represents the transitory stage leading to rebirth and new growth.

At the moment and for a long time, Jonathan has been disabled by depression, which can be a force stopping him or initiating him toward individuation. It corresponds to the nigredo, or the dark beginnings of the alchemical process. This darkness is necessary to regain the treasure in his personality. These steps are part of Jonathan's overcoming his psychological inertia and facing reality rather than being crushed by it.

The Jungian counselor or therapist sits with a client to cultivate the therapeutic alliance, develop rapport, and mutually explore messages from the dreams and the client's reactions. Every rent in a client's psychic life adds to the client's burdens but also can illuminate the path to be taken. Jonathan's dream stimulates encountering these problems, yet Jonathan has not developed a means for internal communication. The affirmative feeling to his Self is absent and his emotional needs are unmet. Dreams are part of the Native American culture and consulting them a time-honored tradition. Jonathan knows to attend to them but not how to use them. His spirit, which could be found in the dreams, is lost in his pursuit of the alcoholic spirits. Being off the reservation seems to have separated him from his Native American cultural traditions that can heal. The intensity of Jonathan's suffering raises questions of timing and technical ability for the Jungian counselor or therapist to consider in careful observation and evaluation of his capacity to comprehend.

Identification of Issues

According to the fourth edition of the American Psychiatric Association's *Diagnostic and Statistical Manual of Mental Disorders* (1994), Jonathan's problem is a depressive disorder with alcoholism. Inner emptiness, undifferentiated feelings, and the being run by the anima denote internal estrangement. Jonathan's dark feelings overtake the ego and disturb his ability to function. He gets drunk, fights, leaves relationships and retreats, all of which signify grief, avoidance, and confusion in his life. Jung stated,

> Over against the polymorphism of the . . . instinctual nature there stands the regulating principle of individuation. . . . Together they form a pair of opposites . . . often spoken of as nature and spirit. . . . This opposition is the expression and perhaps also the basis of the tension from which psychic energy flows. (1960, p.58)

What mixture of emotions does Jonathan carry about his family and the pressures he internalized from childhood? An authentic sense of Self is rooted in a well-developed identity based on identification with the parent of the same sex; hence, the important influence in a son's early years of his father's presence. Is there some discord between the inborn archetype of father which Jonathan acts out by leaving his role as a father? The child perceiving his parents tends to repeat the pattern in himself and with subsequent partners. Jonathan lives at a distance from his children who symbolize the future, potential, and new life, and he has problems with love and intimacy. Therapy would explore what Jonathan experienced with his parents and their relation to him, especially during traumatic times and when he was the same age as his children are now.

Leaving home represents separation from the "participation mystique" that binds Jonathan to his family and Native American culture. This is a phrase Jung used to denote the interpersonal and unconscious melding between people. It is necessary to be close enough to gain rootedness and become internalized. Although seemingly identified with his background, Jonathan radically broke from it by leaving the reservation and entering the White culture. If he is not yet released from the parental complex, Jonathan cannot access his own position. If father, mother, family, or culture is insufficiently attached to, a hole in the psyche of a son forms and fills with splits and confusions that destructively affect work, relationships, and self-regard.

Jonathan is not consciously aware of any of the archetypal energies flowing through him nor does he access his natural powers. Jonathan's story can be likened to the Native American vision quest a boy takes as part of his initiation into manhood, but this one has gone awry. Jonathan is not using his cultural wisdom or its rituals that could solidify his sense of identity as a man. Most likely his behavior reflects an internal situation of the shadow in union with the anima, his inner feminine side, which is blinding his perception of his world. In many fairy tales the hero must be able to fight his battles to gain strength but not to just rebel. If he accomplishes the necessary tasks, he can have the princess. Jonathan must learn this lesson or else he is in danger of losing his courage and resolution, and he will not develop his Eros, or sense of relatedness.

The development of Jonathan's feeling side arises from an innate need for balance to his thinking. Jonathan does not know how to be intimate and keeps on repeating the same relationship problems. These factors indicate an introverted attitude in a man who is a thinking sensation type. Adaptation to the environment fails with an overdeveloped superior function, in this case thinking. The blocked libido causes his inferior feeling function to be activated. The immaturity of the psyche makes itself apparent in crisis situations. As the problem becomes acute, the lack of internal solidity is increasingly perceptible. The opposite sides of Jonathan's nature are embattled and unable to be contained within himself. Jonathan needs to learn to access the fundamental inner structures and be able to handle his anxiety if he is to gain psychological growth. Jung referred to this as the **canalization of libido**, or the energy transformation of psychic intensities or values from one psychological aspect to another. This is a process of progression and regression and creates internal adaptation so that the personality flow recommences.

Aspects of Treatment

Jungian treatment includes use of transference and countertransference. Jonathan's psychological work will be affected by the conscious and unconscious impressions, input, and reactions of the counselor or therapist. For Jonathan, the therapy or counseling relationship will no doubt be affected by the conflict he exhibits with men and women and within himself—the difficulties with trust and intimacy. As with dreams, the Jungian counselor or therapist does not direct but listens to the way Jonathan's psyche leads them both. Jung stated, "No one can overlook either the dynamism or the imagery of the instincts without the gravest injury to himself. Violation or neglect of instinct has painful consequences of a physiological and psychological nature for whose treatment medical help is required" (1959, p. 57)

No capacity is more terrible and difficult to break than the one an individual imposes on himself or herself. As Jonathan's dream warns, captivity by the anima is what he must confront. The situation may be released through developing a conscious and responsible attitude to the anima and the shadow, making the contents knowable and the energy usable. Jonathan's situation of distress, blackness of feeling, and intimations from the unconscious signal that he needs a reconciliation of the warring elements and a conscious differentiation in his psyche.

Collective answers cannot satisfy the individual, as each person has a unique psychological complexity. The path involves turning to the unconscious and gleaning its resources for creativity and knowledge in a process of differentiating and integrating unconscious contents. Emergence of the personality is fraught with the struggle to separate the chaos that begins any psychological endeavor. Relationships with oneself and others rest on the dynamism inherent in the psychological quest for individual identity. By going though the suffering, people discover the meaning of personal destiny, which entails taking the total Self seriously.

Suggested Readings

Bair, D. (2003). *Jung: A biography.* Boston: Little, Brown.

Bolen, J. S. (2005). *Tao of psychology: Synchronicity and the self.* San Francisco: Harper.

Cambrey, J., & Carter, L. (Eds.). (2004). *Analytical psychology: contemporary perspectives in Jungian analysis.* London: Routledge.

Edinger, E. (2002). *Science of the soul: A Jungian perspective.* Toronto: Inner City Books.

Fordham, M. (2002). *Technique in Jungian analysis.* London: Karmac Books.

Hannah, B. (1999). *The inner journey: Lectures and essays on Jungian psychology.* Saratoga: Bookwood Services

Hawker, C., & Samuels, A. (2000). *The interpretation of realities: Jung and the postmodern.* London: Routledge.

Harding, M. E. (2003). *The parental image: Its injury and reconstruction.* Toronto: Inner City Books.

Hillman, J. (1997). *Soul's code: In search of character and calling.* New York: Warner Books.

Hollis, J. (2003). *On this journey we call our life: Living the questions.* Toronto: Inner City Books.

Jacoby, M. (2002). *Jungian psychotherapy and contemporary infant research: Basic patterns of emotional exchange.* London: Routledge.

Kalshed, D. (1997). *The world of trauma: Archetypal defenses of the personal spirit.* London: Routledge.

Perry, J. (1998). *The trials of the visionary mind: Spiritual emergency and the renewal process.* New York: State University of New York Press.

Schwartz-Salant, N. (1998). *The mystery of human relationship: Alchemy and the transformation of the self.* London: Routledge.

Singer, T., & Kimbles, S. (Eds.). (2004). *The cultural complex: Contemporary Jungian perspectives on psyche and society.* London: Routledge.

Stevens, A. (2003). *Archetype revisited: An updated natural history of the self.* Toronto: Inner City Books.

Shorr, A. (1999). *The essential Jung.* Princeton: Princeton University Press.

Ulanov, A. (2000). *Religion and the spiritual in Carl Jung.* New Jersey: Paulist Press.

Von Franz, M. L. (1999). *Archetypal dimensions of the psyche.* Boston: Shambhala.

CHAPTER 6

Adlerian Theory

Alan P. Milliren
The University of Texas of the Permian Basin

Timothy D. Evans
Tampa, Florida

John F. Newbauer
Adler School of Professional Psychology

Individual Psychology, which was founded by **Alfred Adler,** is a cognitive, goal-oriented, social psychology interested in a person's beliefs and perceptions, as well as the effects that person's behavior has on others. It is one of the few psychologies interested in democratic processes in the home, school, and workplace. Individual Psychology promotes social equality, which means granting each other mutual respect and dignity regardless of our inherent differences. It is not a set of techniques but a comprehensive philosophy of living. The three most fundamental principles are (1) behavior is goal oriented; (2) humans are fundamentally social, with a desire to belong and have a place of value as an equal human being; and (3) the individual is indivisible and functions with unity of personality (Ferguson, 1984). These principles, which make Individual Psychology unique from other approaches, are described in Adlerian psychology as **purposiveness, social interest,** and **holism.** Together, these principles describe the person as moving in unity toward self-chosen goals that reflect a human value for belonging and social contribution.

    The term *Individual Psychology* (Adler, 1935) is often misunderstood. In his theory, Adler stressed the unity or indivisibility of the person; thus, he named it Individual Psychology. The term *individual* was used to focus on the whole individual at a time when others, like Freud, were focusing on a divided and, therefore, conflictual personality. The word *individual* differed significantly from Freud's concept of duality where everything is in conflict, such as the id, ego, and superego or the conscious, subconscious, and preconscious. Instead, Adler developed a holistic theory of psychology that emphasized the unity of the individual working toward a goal (Ferguson, 2000b). This holistic approach, along with other fundamental components, characterizes contemporary Adlerian psychology.

BACKGROUND

Alfred Adler was born on February 7, 1870, in a small suburb of Vienna (Ellenberger, 1970). He was Hungarian by birth and later became a citizen of Vienna, Austria. Alfred was the second son in a family of six children, not counting two who died in early infancy. His older brother's name was Sigmund, and Alfred seemed to view Sigmund as someone who was always ahead of him, a true firstborn with whom Alfred felt he could never catch up. Later in his life, another Sigmund (Freud) would also seem to serve as a rival. Despite the rivalry in childhood between Alfred and his brother, they seemed to remain friendly toward each other as adults.

Adler was a sickly child and suffered from rickets and fits of breathlessness. His illness as well as the death of his younger brother Rudolf, when Alfred was about 4 years old, seemed to strengthen his goal of becoming a physician. In 1895, he graduated from the Medical School of the University of Vienna and established his medical practice. In December 1897, Adler married Raissa Epstein, a woman who had come from Russia to study in Vienna. According to Furtmueller (1946), Adler met Raissa at a socialist political meeting and was very impressed with her. Later, she continued to be active in the socialist party and the Adlers frequently entertained the Trotskys, who lived in Vienna from 1907 to 1914. Perhaps because of his association with socialism and his wife's influence, Adler was very much in favor of women having equal rights and the same privileges as men. Alfred and Raissa had four children: Valentine, Alexandra, Kurt, and Cornelia (Nelly).

In 1898, Adler published the *Health Book for the Tailor Trade,* a forerunner of health psychology, which was consistent with a stress/diathesis model of disturbance. This publication associated the health problems of tailors with the unhygienic conditions under which they worked. "Adler's purpose in *Health Book for the Tailor Trade* was clearly not to provide a dispassionate, scholarly tome. Rather, in a pattern that was to become characteristic of Adler throughout his career, he explicitly linked his writing to the need for definite action" (Hoffman, 1994, p. 36). In this 31-page monograph, many of the roots of Adler's later psychological theory can be found, especially regarding the "role of physician as social activist and reformer" (p. 37).

In 1902, Adler served for a brief period in the Hungarian army as a general physician. Later that year, Adler received a postcard from Sigmund Freud inviting him to join the Wednesday evening study circle, which eventually became the Viennese Psychoanalytic Society. Adler was one of the first four physicians to be invited by Freud to attend this group although "how Adler and Freud first came to know each other has never been satisfactorily determined" (Hoffman, 1994, p. 41). According to Hoffman, Adler was invited by Freud to attend the study group, and it seems clear that Freud sought him out. Thus, it is probably accurate that Adler was never a pupil of Freud's. This one point, alone, became a significant element in the relationship between Adler and Freud, which eventually terminated with considerable bitterness. From 1902 until 1911, Adler was a central part of that Viennese Psychoanalytic Society, becoming its president in 1910. Adler published his famous paper on organ inferiority in 1907.

Adler came to disagree with Freud over the role that sexuality and social factors played in motivation and development. Adler had developed a social theory that emphasized personal beliefs or "fictional finalism," a concept that is similar to subjective perception. This differed from Freud's view of behavior as being biologically or physiologically determined. Freud branded Adler's emerging social theory of Individual Psychology as "radically false" and insisted that it failed to contribute a "single new observation" to science (Hoffman, 1994, p. 90). Eventually, the differences with Freud became so intense that Adler and several members of the Viennese Psychoanalytic Society left in 1911. They founded their own group, known as the Society for Free Psychoanalysis, which ultimately became the Society for Individual Psychology.

In 1911, Adler became a Viennese citizen. He also read Hans Vaihinger's book, *The Philosophy of the As If*, which seemed to have a strong impact on his developing theory. In 1912, he produced his second book, *The Nervous Character*, which was followed 2 years latter by the introduction of the *Journal of Individual Psychology*. During World War I, Adler served in a neuropsychiatric unit of the Austro-Hungarian army. It was his experience in the war that seemed to significantly shape his ideas about human nature.

After the war, Vienna was in great turmoil. What once had been a proud city was now full of orphans and in need of establishing order. Adler worked as a consultant in the schools of Vienna, holding clinics with teachers, parents, and students in what has become known as the **open forum** model of counseling (Evans & Milliren, 1999). In this model, Adler would meet in an open, public forum with the teachers and parents and ask them about the child. He would then interview the child and eventually make recommendations for the teachers, the parents, and sometimes the child. "By involving the audience in the counseling session, Adler emphasized helping the family through education" (Evans & Milliren, p. 135). These "public counseling demonstrations challenged the then-traditional practices of individual therapy" (p. 135) and can be viewed as a milestone in the development of community mental health programs. Adler "believed that therapy was not for an elite but should be made available to everyone. His public demonstrations reflected this desire to make psychology available to what Adler considered the 'common man'" (p. 135).

In the late 1920s, Adler began to travel to the United States to give lectures in public and academic settings. He was well received and had considerable coverage in the popular press. In fact, he was considered one of the most prominent psychiatrists of his day, and people would flock to his lectures. In 1927, Adler published *Understanding Human Behavior* and discussed the important concept of **social interest**, which was only suggested in his early writings. His ideas of the inferiority complex, birth order, community feeling and social interest became popular psychological concepts.

The Nazis came to power in Germany in the 1930s and soon became a powerful force in Austria as well. Adler envisioned the upcoming conflict and made plans to leave his homeland. He began to spend more and more time in the United States and planned to move there after his lecture tour in the summer of 1937. Adler had an ambitious tour planned with lectures in The Hague, England, and Scotland. He was to be accompanied on this tour by his daughter, Alexandra, who was also a psychiatrist. Alfred Adler died during the first part of that tour in Aberdeen, Scotland, on May 28, 1937 (Hoffman, 1994).

Rudolf Dreikurs was influenced by Adler's teaching and practice in Vienna (Terner & Pew, 1978). Dreikurs, in his early days of practicing psychiatry in Vienna, became involved with Adler and his child guidance centers. Both Adler and Dreikurs were convinced that Individual Psychology should focus on the education of children in the home and school, which would increase the level of the child's functioning, develop the child's citizenship, and be preventive instead of remedial. In 1937, Dreikurs moved to the United States where he helped to promote and further develop Adlerian psychology.

As much as the popularity of Adler's psychology grew in the United States in the early to mid-1930s, it was Rudolf Dreikurs who "popularized" the approach and contributed significantly to the further development of the theory. In the late 1930s and early 1940s, Dreikurs worked in Chicago to initiate the child guidance centers. Open-forum family counseling or therapy was practiced, and the concept of democratic family relationships was stressed in these centers. "Dreikurs' dream was to establish child guidance centers all over the world and his understanding of children was of unique importance" (Hooper & Holford, 1998, p. 142). It was the setting of the child guidance centers that "helped inspire one of Dreikurs's most important contributions in psychology, the **four goals of misbehavior** in children" (Terner & Pew, 1978, p. 155).

In 1962, Dreikurs established the first International Summer School for the study of Adlerian psychology. This is now known as the International Committee for Adlerian Summer Schools and Institutes (ICASSI). After a long career promoting and teaching Adler's psychology and philosophy of life, Dreikurs died in 1972.

HUMAN NATURE: A DEVELOPMENTAL PERSPECTIVE

Adlerian psychology is interested in understanding the **lifestyle,** or the law of psychological movement, of the individual. Each person comes into this world dependent on others for food, clothing, shelter, and nurturance. Our survival as a species depends on our ability to cooperate and be our brothers' and sisters' keeper. Beecher and Beecher (1966) described how baby turtles are capable of surviving from the moment they are hatched. A turtle never sees his father, only briefly encounters his mother, and is not affected by this lack of contact. Most animals are able to provide for themselves as adults within 2 years. Human beings require at least 12 years before achieving the minimum capability for meeting the challenges of living. Unlike the turtle, the human infant cannot survive on his or her own. Thus, humans must develop the skills of cooperation and will always find it necessary to live in a group. To develop properly, the human infant must be protected, fed, and educated and have human relationships for about a fourth of his or her life span. As the growing child learns to become more competent, he begins to gain a sense of mastery over the environment.

The pattern or style that characterizes how the individual "goes about going about" becomes useful in assessing why that individual behaves as he or she does. Understanding the client's lifestyle gives the counselor or therapist a better understanding of behavior and serves as a useful guide as counseling or therapy progresses. Although the emphasis in this process is on understanding the individual's behavior, it is always done from the client's subjective viewpoint. The counselor's or therapist's role is not to establish the facts of the client's experience but to investigate the client's perception of the experience.

> Early experiences, no matter how dramatic or potentially traumatic, are not specifically causative of personality traits because each child will determine for himself or herself the significance of the experience. The power of subjective interpretation of reality is apparent, for example, if one interviews adult identical twins about some incident that occurred quite early in their lives and that they shared. It is clear from their recollections that the twins do remember the same incident. But when they are asked to pinpoint which was the most vivid moment in the incident and how they felt at that moment, their answers are likely to indicate that they experienced the incident in totally different manners (Dinkmeyer, Pew, & Dinkmeyer, 1979, p. 26).

Successful counseling or therapy helps the individual understand his or her subjective psychological movement, or private logic.

Early Development

From the moment of birth, each child acts "as if" he or she is attempting to answer this question: How do I fit in? The family is the first social group to which the child belongs. Thus, the child begins to make many assumptions about who he or she is, how others are, how the world should be, and how the world will treat him or her. The child's ordinal position in the family plays a role in developing this view of self and world and has a significant impact on the child's developing pattern of living or lifestyle. Because no two human beings have exactly the same reaction to the same situation, each child interacts with and interprets experience in the family differently. No two children, born into the same family, grow up in exactly the same situation. This is true even for twins.

The perception of the family environment differs from one child to another and can change over time for a variety of reasons. For example, the family structure changes considerably with the birth of each child. Not only is each new child born into an increasingly larger family, but also the age differences and gender of each of the children significantly affect the position of every other child. This is even more pronounced in families in which a certain child may be accorded a more important position, such as an eldest son or daughter. Ernesto, a sixth grader from a fairly large family, describing himself as the oldest, proceeded to list three or four younger brothers and sisters. Later, when the family was observed while attending a meeting, it appeared that Ernesto also had two older sisters. When asked about it, the boy remarked, "Oh yeah, but they don't count!" Ernesto was the eldest son in a family where such a position was highly valued. It was "as if" no one else counted. The older sisters became "invisible."

Many factors significantly affect the family environment. Parents are older and more experienced as each child enters the family. Family finances may shift and change, and the family may relocate. Extended family members or other significant individuals may move in and out of the family group. Death or divorce of the parents are important factors that influence the family environment. Remarriage of one or both of the parents adds the presence of a stepparent and possibly stepbrothers or stepsisters. Specific family values and the general psychological atmosphere of the family are extremely influential, such as in families where all the children are involved in athletics, are all musical, or all earn advanced educational degrees. In each case, these specific activities were highly valued by the parents, and it was "as if" one could not "belong" without pursuing and developing competence in these areas.

The counselor or therapist should pay attention to health and development issues that exist for different family members. It is not uncommon for the oldest daughter in a family to assume the mothering role when the real mother is sickly, out of the home, working full time, or otherwise unable to function in that capacity. A child with developmental disabilities may overshadow brothers and sisters because the family devotes more time to this particular child. The death of a child may create a phantom sibling that the other children must live up to in terms of accomplishments because of parental expectations. Although there are a number of typical characteristics that seem to be more or less universal, interpreting birth order is not a cut-and-dried process.

Birth Order and Family Constellation

Although Adler is known for emphasizing birth order, his views are often misunderstood. The position of the child in the birth order is not deterministic. It only provides probabilities that a child will have particular types of experiences (Shulman & Mosak, 1977). Adlerian psychology considers not only individual development but also the social context in which it occurs. The social field of the child includes parents, siblings, and other significant individuals that create the multitude of relationships influencing the child. Although there are many factors that would indicate exceptions, there are some general characteristics of various birth order positions. Counselors or therapists are cautioned, however, to use this information in the context of what they know about the individual and the individual's family of origin.

Only Children. Only children are unique; they grow up in a world that is heavily populated with adults. There are no other children with whom to compete, so the only child may work extremely hard to achieve an adult level of competence. When the parents are extremely capable, the child sometimes finds it far too difficult to compete with any measure of success, may become discouraged, and may give up or look for alternative pursuits where he or she might be outstanding. If a child cannot be good enough in positive and constructive ways, he or she may become "good" at misbehaving. Such children have given up hope of ever being responsible and capable. In contrast, some only children receive so much attention and service from the adults in their world that they attempt to remain helpless and irresponsible. These children have not given up, they just never got started!

It is not unusual for only children to become quite egocentric. After all, they never had to contend with sharing anything. Ed and Sally, a young married couple, constantly squabbled about whose things belonged to whom. She complained that he was far too stingy, while he complained that she was always taking his things without permission. Sally had grown up in a large family where the general attitude was "what is yours is ours," and she saw no need to ask to use things that, to her, were community property. Ed, on the other hand, had grown up in an atmosphere of "what is mine is mine." He related that on occasions when other children were coming over to play, his mother had a cabinet where he could lock up the toys he wanted to keep away from others. As they grew to understand the attitudes each developed as a result of growing up in their respective families, the squabbling began to cease and each attempted to be more respectful of the other's attitude.

Another fairly typical characteristic of only children is that they often grow up enjoying being the center of attention. This is particularly true when the child is the first or only grandchild and, therefore, is valued just for existing. In many instances, only children develop a talent of one sort or another and expect to be able to take center stage as the star. When only children have been catered to or have often been given their own way, they may refuse to be cooperative when others do not give in to them. Barbara, an only child, commented that she would often call her mother to pick her up if, when playing at a friend's house, the other child would not play or do what she wanted. Only children often develop skills for relating only to adults, especially if the adult world is their primary social environment, and not to their peers. As a result, they become content being loners and feel no need to develop relationships with other children.

Oldest Children. Oldest children have had the good fortune of being only children for some period of time, whether one or several years. If a gap of approximately 5 years exists between two children in one family, then each of the children appears to be more like an only child. When the birth of the second child occurs, the oldest child often feels dethroned. Sometimes this generates feelings of being unloved or neglected and the child tries to compensate. Often, oldest children try to regain a position of superiority through good deeds (e.g., becoming overly responsible, serving as the caretaker of the rest of the children, taking on extra chores or activities, excelling at academics). If this does not work, oldest children may achieve superiority through being the best of the worst! It is not unusual to find that gender issues become significant. For example, when a firstborn male is followed closely by the birth of a female sibling, the situation can easily lead to a more or less permanent dethronement of the male child.

Richard, the oldest child in his family, developed into the responsible child—almost to the point of being excessive. He took it on himself to look after everybody and everything, and he became especially involved in this activity as a 9-year-old when his father divorced his mother. Richard took over the chores that had previously been his father's. Richard was already mature beyond his years and this further defined his role as the man of the house, a role that his mother regularly reinforced because she was so grateful for having such a good son. Richard devoted so much of his time and effort to taking care of things at home that he refused to participate in athletics and other social activities at school. As a consequence, he ignored his peers and did not develop the necessary skills for relating to them. As he got older, he complained of lack of friends and closeness in relationships, but he justified the situation on the basis that he had to take care of his family.

Juanita was the oldest in her family as well. As her mother was working two jobs to support the family, Juanita's stance in the world was to become "a better mother than her mother." From the young age of 5, she recalls many occasions in which she told the younger children that they had to mind her because she was the mother in this house! When she was 12, her mother remarried, quit working, and stayed home to take care of the children. Juanita was not prepared for this change of events, and because she had not developed social skills for participation in activities outside the home, she did not know what to do. At 14 she resolved to quit school as soon as she could and have a family of her own. She became promiscuous, and by the time she was 16 she had given birth to a son and was pregnant with her second child.

Second Born. Second-born children often find themselves in an uncomfortable position. During the early years, the second born always has someone in front who is more advanced. The situation may be mitigated if the oldest is a boy and a girl is born in a year or so. However, if the eldest child is successful, second borns are easily discouraged and give up hope of achieving a place in any area or activity occupied by the oldest. As a result, the second-born child usually develops characteristics opposite of the firstborn. If a third child is born, the second born may feel "squeezed."

Ruth, a second-born child in a family with five children, indicated that she always felt that she was in the shadow of her sister. When she was interviewed about her family constellation, Ruth said Emily was 27 months older. The interviewer asked Ruth why it was important to her to be so specific about the age difference. Ruth commented, "Because she really *is* more than two years older than I am." She indicated that those extra months gave Emily an unfair advantage, which was why Emily was so much better.

Raul, also a second born, had an older brother, Juan, who was developmentally delayed. Raul excelled academically and became the valedictorian of his high school class, but he never felt as though he was given full attention or acknowledgment by his parents for his achievements. Meeting Juan's learning needs required considerable time and attention from his parents. Although it would have been easy for Raul to revert to the "useless side" and achieve recognition through misbehavior, he found academics to be a means for expressing his capabilities and receiving encouragement outside the family.

Middle Children. Like second borns, middle children have a sibling who is in the lead, but they also have a sibling who is close on their heels. Not only do they have to keep up, but also they feel that they have to run as fast as they can to stay ahead. Depending on the capabilities of the other siblings, middle children may often feel like Nathan, who indicated that he was never sure of his abilities or himself. His major strength was being social, with many friends and contacts, a characteristic not possessed by his older brother or younger sister. However, Nathan had academic difficulties in high school, which limited his college choice. Consequently, he believed that his undergraduate degree was not the same quality as the degrees held by his siblings. For the most part, Nathan was extremely unsure of how he measured up, and this played out in his career where he has been unable to stay in any job for more than 2 years. He was never fired but he was always dissatisfied with not being given enough recognition for the things he achieved. Of the three children, however, Nathan, had the most empathy for others.

Youngest Child. Youngest children often find themselves in an enviable position in the family because they may be pampered and spoiled by parents and older siblings. Too many things may be done for them, including making decisions and taking responsibilities. Because of their unique position, youngest children may easily become discouraged and develop feelings of inferiority, perhaps because there are limited expectations for their success, youngest children often become the most successful child in the family. Gary conveyed an easygoing, laid-back style of life and seemed never to get caught up in struggles for superiority or accomplishment. The youngest of three boys, he never had a chance to be first at anything; nevertheless, he maintained a strong, positive attitude about his childhood and the fact that his brothers always seemed to be competing to be first. When asked why it didn't bother him, he explained that he was always the *first* to vote that he would go *last!*

Youngest children, no matter how capable they are, tend not to be taken seriously by others. Sondra, at age 46, was the youngest child in a family of six children. She regularly complained that no one in the family would consult her or listen to her ideas, even though she was the primary caregiver for her aging parents. Her older siblings would question all of the decisions she made regarding the care, and when major health issues were to be decided, her input was "always," according to Sondra, discounted. Sondra, an extremely capable woman, was easily discouraged and harbored considerable feelings of inferiority.

Early Recollections

In addition to collecting information about the client's birth order and family constellation information, it is important to note the memories or recollections that the client holds about early experiences. Recollections are different from reports of experiences; the most significant memories have an "as if" component to them. The individual recalls the experience *as if* it were occurring at the moment. The counselor or therapist is not interested in the exact nature of the individual's experience but in the perception of it. From a myriad of experiences, the client chooses to select only certain ones that support or influence current functioning. These memories exist for the individual as little "life lessons" kept available as guides for decision making about the challenges of living. It is the interpretation of these selected events that the individual carries with him or her as reminders of the goals and limits for participation in life.

Adler (1931) noted:

> Among all psychic expressions, some of the most revealing are the individual's memories. Her memories are the reminders she carries about with her of her limitations and of the meaning of events. There are no "chance" memories. Out of the incalculable number of impressions that an individual receives, she chooses to remember only those which she considers, however dimly, to have a bearing on her problems. These memories represent the story of her life, a story she repeats to herself for warmth or comfort, to keep her concentrated on her goal, or to prepare her, by means of past experiences, to meet the future with a tried and tested approach. (pp. 58–59)

Powers (1975) stated that the early recollections tend to be quite consistent with the individual's current worldview regarding life, self, and others.

> Adler was among the first to notice that memory is selective and creative. Each of us recalls events and occurrences from the past as if they illustrated a certain meaning of life. By this active recollection, we rehearse in private parables the attitudes which characterize our responses to current challenges and which caution us against or encourage us toward the possibilities of the future. (p. 1)

As one's worldview changes, so will the nature of the various recalled memories. Early recollections have embedded in them beliefs about self, others, and the world, as well as ethical convictions and plans of action.

From early recollections, it is possible to identify the goal toward which the person is directed. Recurrent dreams and even favorite fairy tales and childhood stories are also considered part of the database for understanding a lifestyle. When working with parents, Walton (Walton, 1996a; Evans & Milliren, 1999) explores their most memorable observation (MMO). The MMOs provide clues to the dynamics of the family and are decisions that the parent made in adolescence about how family life was *going to be* when he or she had the opportunity to have a family.

> Use of this technique can allow the counselor to help a parent see how he/she: (1) overemphasizes the likelihood of occurrence of a situation the parent guards against; (2) overemphasizes the negative influence of such a situation if it should occur; and (3) underestimates his/her ability to deal with the situation in an effective problem-solving way if it should occur." (Walton, 1996b, p. 4)

Wingett (W. Wingett, personal communication, November 26, 2001) suggests that counselors or therapists listen for key words as the client describes the problem. Often, clients will use the words *lost* or *stuck* to describe the situation that brought them into counseling: "I am *stuck* in this mess and don't see any way out," or "I'm just *lost* in this and don't know where to turn." In response, the counselor or therapist follows up by asking the client about the experiences: "Tell me about a time in your life when you were lost or stuck. Maybe you were lost while traveling or were lost and could not find your way home or were lost in a shopping mall," or "Tell me about a time in your life when you were stuck in the snow or sand or mud." By getting the details of these experiences in terms of what the client was thinking and feeling and how the client handled the situation, the counselor or therapist will be able to ascertain the nature of the client's problem-solving approach to life.

MAJOR CONSTRUCTS

One of the difficulties encountered when attempting to study Adler's theory is the unsystematic manner that characterized his writing. On rare occasions did Adler present his mature theory in an organized or concise form; most of his writings focused on topics or subtopics related to his theory. However, there is one paper that appeared in the first volume of the *International Journal of Individual Psychology* (Adler, 1935) wherein Adler presented a short overview of the basic principles of Individual Psychology.

Basic to an understanding of Individual Psychology is the concept that the individual has the **creative power** to interpret experiences, both internal and external, influenced by both heredity and environment, in an individualistic, subjective manner. From these interpretations, the individual develops an attitude toward life, or **life style**, that is expressed in one's relationships to oneself, others, and the world. Adler discussed the belief that the individual "relates himself always according to his own interpretation of himself and his present problems" (Adler, 1935, p. 5). "Man does not merely react. He adopts an individual attitude" (Dreikurs, 1950, p.4).

Each individual is uniquely different from others with an approach to life that is entirely his or her own creation. However, no one can escape the necessity of solving a great number of problems, and complications arise from inability to solve these problems adequately. Three general types of problems arise: work, friends, and family. Dreikurs (1950) described these as **three life tasks:**

> The human community sets three tasks for every individual. They are: work, which means contributing to the welfare of others; friendship, which embraces social relationships with comrades and relatives; and love, which is the most intimate union with someone of the other sex and represents the strongest and closest emotional relationship which can exist between two human beings. (pp. 4–5)

Meeting these challenges of living involves the **social embeddedness** of the individual. "The individual cannot be considered apart from society. He is inextricably embedded in it. His very thinking, using language as the main tool, is socially determined, since language is a social product and is socially acquired" (Ansbacher, 1965, p. 341). Adler often spoke of the **ironclad logic of social living**, in essence indicating that all human problems were social problems. To be successful, the individual cannot operate in terms of **private logic** but has to function in keeping with the **common sense**.

As a social evolutionist, Adler believed progress could be made only through the conscious efforts of the individual. If people were not willing to contribute, or if they functioned in a manner contrary to the concept of evolution, then "the psychological decline and fall of the individual" (Ansbacher & Ansbacher, 1964, p. 39) would surely occur. Thus, an individual's efforts at cooperation and contribution were essential elements of a mentally healthy lifestyle.

Adler believed that the whole individual could not be understood by only looking at parts or individual characteristics. Life is characterized by movement—the **psychological movement** of the individual in pursuit of a goal. In this movement, the whole of the personality is expressed; the individual's mind, body, emotions, perceptions, and all functions move toward the chosen goal. Without recognizing this goal-directed nature of the individual, one cannot see the individual as a whole (Dreikurs, 1950). As Adler described it, the individual functions **as if** he or she were striving to compensate for a **felt minus** situation by attempting to achieve a plus.

Thus, the Adlerian view of the person is that of an indivisible, social being whose behavior occurs as an interaction within the social setting. However, the individual is not just reactive but is proactive, that is, acting on the environment *in order to* make things happen or to achieve a desired outcome. There is freedom of choice and **goal-directedness** of behavior. The individual is perceived as being able to *choose* those behaviors that will move him or her toward a desired objective. Motivation is viewed as more of a pull than a push, with the individual moving toward those immediate and long-range outcomes or objectives that are important in the frame of reference of the individual.

There are as many variations of personally acceptable goals of success as there are individuals. "In my experience I have found that each individual has a different meaning of, and attitude toward, what constitutes success" (Adler, 1935, p. 6). As long as the individual has a feeling of belonging and is prepared to meet the tasks of life, he or she will have a positive or healthy view of life and behaviors will be directed toward the *useful* side of life. It is only when the individual is ill-prepared to meet the challenges of living that he or she switches to the *useless* side. In these latter instances, the individual has a negative view of life and behaves in a manner in opposition to the logic of social living. What better argument is there for early involvement with children and parent education programs?

Adler was not one to present typologies of human beings, for he believed that each individual had to be described according to his or her own unique pattern. Although Adler did develop some general principles to describe the nature of the individual, "his main interest was in the description, understanding, and modification of the unique individual" (Ansbacher & Ansbacher, 1964, p. 660). Therefore, the focus of Individual Psychology is predominately on the ideographic description of behavior—on the specific psychological movement involved in the individual's personal orientation to life. However, on several occasions Adler did indicate four different general types, although he did so only for purposes of teaching to show "the attitude and behavior of individuals toward outside problems" (Adler, 1935, p. 6).

> Thus, we find individuals whose approach to reality shows, from early childhood through their entire lives, a more or less dominant or "ruling" attitude. This attitude appears in all their relationships. A second type—surely the most frequent one—expects everything from others and leans on others. I might call it the "getting" type. A third type is inclined to feel successful by avoiding the solution of problems. Instead of struggling with a problem, a person of this type merely tries to "side-step" it, in an effort thereby to avoid defeat. The fourth type struggles, to a greater or lesser degree, for a solution to these problems in a way which is useful to others. (Adler, 1935, p. 6)

Each individual, with a unique orientation to life, retains and maintains this approach "from childhood to the end of his life, unless he is convinced of the mistake in his creation of his attitude toward reality" (Adler, 1935, p. 6). This process is similarly described by Combs and Snygg (1959) in that the individual strives to maintain and enhance the phenomenal self—a self that is a product of the individual's own creation. Thus, Adler not only considered the human being as a totality but also as a **unity**. This unity, or what Adler termed the *life style*, is comparable to what is often noted as the ego and is expressed in the individual's "thinking, feeling, acting; in his so-called conscious and unconscious—in every expression of his personality" (Adler, 1935, p. 7).

Of the four types presented by Adler, the first three—"the 'ruling' type, the 'getting' type, and the 'avoiding' type—are not apt, and are not prepared to solve the problems of life. These problems are always social problems. Individuals of these three types are lacking in the ability for cooperation and contribution" (Adler, 1935, p. 7). When those who lack the ability to cooperate and contribute in meeting the external problems of living, they are confronted with a form of inadequacy or shock. "This shock leads up to the individual's failures—which we know as neurosis, psychosis, etc. Significantly, the failure shows the same style as the individual" (Adler, 1935, p. 7). Thus, the first three types of individuals are inadequately prepared for life. Although they may be able to function somewhat effectively as long as they are not faced with a critical situation, they will eventually encounter a problem demanding more cooperation and contribution, or **social interest**, than they are prepared to offer.

> In the fourth type (the socially useful type), prepared for cooperation and contribution, we can always find a certain amount of *activity* which is used for the benefit of others. This activity is in agreement with the needs of others; it is useful, normal, rightly embedded in the stream of evolution of mankind." (Adler, 1935, p. 7)

Adler believed that the individual was firmly embedded in society. Only within the social milieu could the individual be understood; the degree of social interest was the measure of mental health. Adler wrote in terms of the ironclad logic of social living, and only those who were able to cooperate with and contribute to the general welfare were capable of achieving **significance** or, in terms of contemporary writers, self-actualization.

For Adler, life was movement, and it was the nature of this movement on the part of the individual that was of interest to the Individual Psychologist. For some, this movement might be described as active in form; for others, this movement may be more passive. Such movement is easy to observe in children. For example, one child may tend to be more energetic in his or her behavior or activity level, whereas another may be content to sit by and observe what is going on. For the most part, degree of activity remains constant throughout one's life, but it may only become apparent when the individual experiences favorable or, particularly, unfavorable situations. "But it is the individual shade of interpretation that matters in the end. And when reconstructing the unity of a personality in his relationships to the outer world, Individual Psychology fundamentally undertakes to delineate the individual form of creative activity—which is the life style" (Adler, 1935, p. 8).

Development of Concept of Belonging and Fundamental Human Striving

Adler's theory of Individual Psychology might best be described as a work in progress, as the development of his theory took place in three separate, though not mutually exclusive, phases (Dreikurs, 1967a).

First Phase. The first phase covered the period from 1907 to about 1912 (Shulman, 1951). During that time, Adler emphasized the role of *organ inferiority.* A review of Adler's writings from these earlier years indicates that three basic elements of his mature theory were developed. First, Adler postulated the concept of the unity of the individual, although at this early time the context was physiological. He talked about the confluence of drives—that every drive is connected with one or more other drives; more directly, however, he was still concerned with the drives as physiological processes (Ansbacher & Ansbacher, 1956).

Adler also began to postulate his motivational principle. Originally, in 1908, Adler wrote about the *aggression drive,* which served as the superordinate force that provided the direction for the confluence of drives. Apparent here is the dynamic nature of his early theoretical development wherein the individual strives for a level of success or satisfaction. In 1910, the aggression drive was replaced by the concept of *masculine protest;* the physiological, objective psychology of Adler was shifting to a psychological, subjective one. Adler viewed the masculine protest as "the striving to be strong and powerful in compensation for feeling unmanly, for a feeling of inferiority" (Ansbacher & Ansbacher, 1956, p. 45).

The third element of Adler's early theory, proposed in 1908, was the need for affection— the goal toward which the confluence of drives is struggling. The need for affection was Adler's idea that an *inner disposition* of the individual required other people and social relationships to be satisfied. This element described the nature of the striving of the individual; however, Adler cautioned that the satisfaction or blocking of the gratification of this need should only be done for culturally useful purposes. Thus in this first phase, the beginnings of Adler's emphasis on community are apparent, as are the beginnings of his approach to working with children. However, in this phase Adler's psychological theory basically reflected a strong biological orientation, which lasted until around 1912 when his theory began to shift "toward a socially oriented, subjectivistic, holistic psychology of attitudes" (Ansbacher & Ansbacher, 1956, p. 76).

Second Phase. The second phase of development in Adler's theory lasted about 4 years, from 1912 to 1916, when Adler placed increased emphasis on the feeling of inferiority. By now, Adler had established his own psychological "school," having withdrawn from Freud's psychoanalytic circle in 1911. The break with Freud coincided with the appearance of Vaihinger's *The Philosophy of "As If,"* which served as a major impetus to the direction of Adler's theoretical development (Ansbacher & Ansbacher, 1956). With the introduction of *The Neurotic Character* in 1912, it was obvious that Adler was considerably influenced by Vaihinger and that a major modification had taken place in Adler's theory of neurosis.

Vaihinger's greatest influence on Adler's Individual Psychology was in respect to the concept of the **fictional goal,** which is a subjective creation of the individual that offers a basis for action *as if* such were a true and logical assessment of reality. The fictional structure, when combined with a teleological orientation, resulted in Adler's concept of the fictional goal (or fictional final goal, or guiding fiction). This fictional goal is an ever-present creative product of the individual and serves as the end state to be achieved by the individual's strivings. The concept of the fictional goal also "became the principle of unity and self-consistency of the personality structure" (Ansbacher & Ansbacher, 1956, p. 90) and was a means by which the individual could compensate for feelings of inferiority.

After the principle of the unity of the personality was established in terms of a *fictional finalism,* striving for this goal became the dynamic force in Adler's theory. The general description of this force, from 1916 on, remained predominately the same: The psychological movement of the individual took place in terms of a striving for perfection, from below to above, from a felt minus to a plus, from inferiority to superiority. In the early days, though, Adler wrote from the frame of reference of

> the neurotic patient; it was the neurotic whom Adler showed as striving for enhancement of his self-esteem or for the safeguarding of it. When he generalized from the neurotic, he described the normal individual as behaving in the same way, only less clearly so and to a lesser degree. (Ansbacher & Ansbacher, 1956, p. 101)

During this second phase in theory development, Adler called the striving for superiority the *will to power,* a will that increased proportionately in strength with the extent of the strength of the feeling of inferiority. "In effect, the pleasure of *feeling* powerful was directly related to the displeasure of feeling powerless" (Ansbacher & Ansbacher, 1956, p. 111). At this time in Adler's theory development, the neurotic person served as the frame of reference for describing the normal individual. This orientation changed as Adler's theory continued to mature.

Third Phase.   When Adler returned to Vienna in 1916 after serving in World War I as a doctor, he presented the concept of **Gemeinschaftsgefühl**, or social interest, to his old group. Although this was not a totally new idea for Adler, the weight he attached to it was, "for he knew *now* that it was the one question at issue between man and his fate" (Bottome, 1957, p. 122). The period from 1916 until Adler's death in 1937, marked the last major modification to be introduced to the theory of Individual Psychology. During these years, Adler's efforts were spent, in part, in an attempt to develop the simple theme of social interest. "What Adler was in search of was a reconciliation between individual and society, a means of effecting a reintegration of the maladjusted neurotic with his environment through a simple and rational code of conduct that would satisfy the demands of both" (Way, 1962, p. 186).

By the 1930s, Adler recognized that feelings of inferiority were not a fundamental condition of human nature but a mistaken approach to life. Adler shifted his notion of the individual's striving for superiority to a fundamental desire to belong, to feel worthwhile as a human being and be part of the human community (Ferguson, 1989). Not only had Adler found the concept for describing the ideal state of the individual's relationship to his or her environment, but also he had changed his frame of reference from the neurotic individual to humankind in general. He had developed a criterion for normalcy—social interest—and could now rewrite his theory in terms of the normal individual.

Neurosis was now defined as the extent to which the individual possessed a discouraged attitude toward life. The "normal" individual functions courageously, cooperating and contributing to the extent of his or her social interest. Thus, the process of curing neuroses, as well as the process of educating children toward "normal adjustment," requires a program of help that is aimed at expanding and strengthening the individual's social interest. In this final phase, Adler established the most important and major element in his theory: The concept of social interest became the sole criterion of mental health and the increase of social interest was the major therapeutic goal.

Social Interest

For Adler, the criterion for "success" in life, in essence the healthy personality, is inherent in the extent to which the individual embodies social interest (Gemeinschaftsgefühl) in his or her characteristic approach to life and life problems. It is this conceptualization that describes the ideal state of the individual's mental health. Adler's term *Gemeinschaftsgefühl* presents considerable difficulty in terms of translation into English and, much like the terms *Gestalt* or *Vorstellung*, there is no available English equivalent that conveys the same meaning. A number of terms—"social feeling, community feeling, fellow feeling, sense of solidarity, communal intuition, community interest, social sense, and social interest (Ansbacher & Ansbacher, 1956, p. 134)"—have been used. Adler seemed to prefer the latter term, *social interest*, which he used in most of his later writing (Ansbacher & Ansbacher, 1956; Dreikurs, 1950).

Although the term *Gemeinschaftsgefühl* presents translation problems, Ansbacher (1966) pointed out that these are minor difficulties compared to the problem of understanding what the concept really means. In Adler's own words, "it becomes clear that the difficulty with this term is not one of the translation from German into English, but one of the definition, no matter which language or which particular term one might choose" (Ansbacher, 1966, p. 14)." To advocate sole use of the term *Gemeinschaftsgefühl* does not solve the problem, because the term would still convey little or no meaning, particularly to those with few or no skills in the German language.

In the original German, Gemeinschaftsgefühl is a composite of *Gemeinschaft* which is "a community, an aspect of the cosmos" and *Gefühl* which is a "subjective state, an attitude, a state of the organism preparatory to action" (Buchheimer, 1959, p. 242)—two words conveying a two-part or two-dimensional whole. In this view, Gemeinschaftsgefühl becomes a mediating factor that provides for the reconciliation of the individual's internal, personal, subjective environment or frame of reference with the demands of the person's external, common, objective environment or surroundings. Ansbacher (1968) indicated that these two parts can be considered as the psychological *process* dimension and the *object* (outside world) dimension at which the process is directed.

Adler used and described Gefühl, or "interest," in "social interest," in terms of three different aspects: of its being an aptitude or innate potentiality; of its being a set of abilities; and of its being a generalized attitude. Ansbacher (1968) describes these as three developmental steps:

> In Step 1, social interest is an assumed *aptitude* for cooperation and social living which can be developed through training.
>
> In Step 2, this aptitude has been developed into the objective *abilities* of cooperating and contributing, as well as understanding others and empathizing with them.
>
> In Step 3, social interest is a subjective *evaluative attitude* determining choices and thus influencing the dynamics of the individual. When not backed up by the skills represented in Step 2, such an attitude of social interest may not be sufficient to meet all contingencies. (p. 132)

If social interest, then, is an aptitude or innate potentiality, it must be consciously developed until, as Bottome (1957) quotes Adler as saying, it becomes "as natural as breathing or the upright gait" (p. 168). The next step—the function of education and training—is the development of this potential, that is, converting the aptitude into an ability or skill. Just as a potential for music, numbers, or artistic productions must be trained, so must the social interest be trained. The development of the capability for social interest makes an excellent argument for implementing character education training and comparable programs. With training in social interest comes the development of the capacities for cooperation and contribution. In brief, these capacities can be described, as the ability to accept *what is* (the implication here being one of cooperation) with a view of *what could be* (the implication being the element of contribution).

Emphasizing the abilities of cooperation and contribution as basic elements of the "interest" in social interest, Dreikurs (1950) indicated

> each individual has to make an adjustment to two social levels which oppose each other. Fulfilling the social tasks which confront us means meeting not only the acute obligations presented to us by the needs of the groups around us, but also the needs for improvement and social development. (p. 9)

Social interest requires that the individual have enough contact with the present to make a move toward the future meaningful and enough vision of the future to go beyond mere conformity. "The ideal expression of social interest is the ability to play the game with existing demands for cooperation and to help the group to which one belongs in its evolution closer toward a perfect form of social living" (p. 8).

The social interest dimension described by cooperation is best exemplified by the ability of the individual to give and take. The person not only must feel a part of life as a whole but also must be willing to accept the good and the bad aspects of living. The person might be described as being neither optimist nor pessimist but being one who functions effectively within the realities of the situation. He or she operates as a part of life in conjunction with others. One of the measures, then, of the degree of social interest developed by the individual is expressed by the extent to which the individual is willing to cooperate. Although many individuals may have a limited capacity to cooperate, life does not present them such demanding problems that their cooperation is found to be in short supply. Often they are never called on to cooperate to such an extent that they would be found lacking in their ability. It is only under difficult situations and stress that the cooperative ability of an individual can be assessed.

In addition to developing a capacity for cooperation (step 1), individuals must develop a capacity for contribution, that is, a willingness to consider the welfare of others in their personal striving for overcoming and perfection (step 2). Humans do not live an isolated existence; every action and feeling has some effect and impact on others. Adler considered it to be a major function of each individual that he or she become his or her "brother's keeper" (Bottome, 1957). A major aspect of the dimension of contribution is the idea that there is no one-to-one correspondence between contribution and reward, and individuals must be able to give far more than they receive. This willingness to contribute must take place in a context of primary concern for others and the general welfare. Concern for personal benefit can only be secondary and must follow solely as "spill out" from the primary concern (Dreikurs, 1950).

The individual must be able to function on two planes—a horizontal and a vertical. The horizontal plane consists of the day-to-day demands of social living and is part of the here and now. This plane includes the individual's immediate relationships to all elements of this environment; all things and all persons with which the individual comes in contact, either directly or indirectly, are involved. Thus, the horizontal plane is not restricted solely to social relationships, as may be implied by the term *social interest*; rather, the horizontal plane is the totality of the person's environment. This plane might be adequately described as a *continuum of cooperation*, the extremes of which can be characterized in terms of the cooperative movement displayed by the individual—whether it be *with* in a synergistic relationship or *against* in a hostile, fighting relationship toward the total spectrum of environmental elements.

The second plane, which is vertical in nature, consists of a type of evolutionary movement that is continuous and upward in direction. This plane can be designated as a *continuum of contribution* and refers to a general striving for improvement and social development. At the extremes of the two planes, individuals move *toward* improvement in a constructive manner inclusive of the welfare of others or move *away* from social development in a destructive manner ignoring the social good. To remain solely on the horizontal plane constitutes a type of conformity in an individual that has no element of a futuristic or evolutionary orientation. Devoting sole attention to the vertical constitutes striving for superiority without a concomitant interest in the immediate environment. A balance, or equilibrium, must be maintained between the two directions of these planes if the social interest is to exist to any high degree in an individual.

In the third developmental step, an individual moves closer to achieving a subjective, evaluative attitude toward life. However, without the development of the previously mentioned capacities for cooperation and contribution, the arrival at such an attitude on the part of the individual would be inadequate to meet all the challenges of living. The development of freedom, for example, without the concomitant attitudes of commitment and responsibility, is as disastrous for the individual as it is for him or her to have feelings of insecurity or inferiority. A mentally healthy attitude toward life not only allows for a feeling of value and self-worth but also influences the nature and direction of the activities the individual proposes to undertake—a direction of moving ever closer to a more adequate form of social living.

Life, as viewed by Adler, presents the individual with two often contradictory demands. On the one hand, the individual has to be capable of meeting the acute demands of the existing environment; he or she has to have the capacity to cooperate. On the other hand, the demands for social improvement and development require the individual to possess the capacity to make a contribution. To resolve this dilemma, the individual must find that balance between present needs and the demands of evolution (Dreikurs, 1950). Fortunately, there seems to exist in all human beings a recognition of the "necessity of being human, of contributing and cooperating in human society" (Wolfe, 1930, p. 26). Even the neurotic person exemplifies this awareness by spending his or her life justifying the reasons for avoiding humanity and humanism. The social interest cannot be avoided and, in its ultimate form, it establishes an ideal and a direction for the strivings of the individual and the group as a whole.

The meaning of *Gemeinschaft*, or the "social" in "social interest," is too often viewed from the limited perspective of social relations. The German term, in fact, has a much broader meaning than that implied in the word *social* (Ansbacher, 1968). While describing the difficulty that *Gemeinschaftsgefühl* creates for translation, Dreikurs (1950) indicated that the main difficulty lies in the term *Gemeinschaft*: "It is not identical with any of the many English words which are used for it . . . although all the various terms, 'community,' 'society,' 'group,' have some of the connotations implied in 'Gemeinschaft.' It is perhaps closest to the term commonweal which contains some of the significant aspects" (p. 4). "Even Adler extended the meaning of *Gemeinschaft*, the social in social interest, to a variety of 'objects' one would not necessarily assume under this term. In fact nearly all objects in the world are potentially included" (Ansbacher, 1968, p. 133).

> Social interest remains throughout life. It becomes differentiated, limited, or expanded and, in favorable cases, extends not only to family members but to the larger group, to the nation, to all of mankind. It can even go further, extending itself to animals, plants, and inanimate objects and finally even to the cosmos. (Ansbacher & Ansbacher, 1956, p. 138)

Thus, *Gemeinschaft,* as Adler used the term, is not restricted solely to the social community; rather, it describes a holistic relationship between humankind and the cosmos. Way (1962) described this relationship: "The feeling for the *Gemeinschaft* is wider than the term 'society' suggests. It embraces a sense of relatedness, not only to the human community, but to the whole of life" (p. 201). As a person's horizons expand, relationships begin to include more and more of life; ultimately, there is a feeling of connectedness with the whole of the universe, society, and nature.

Social interest is a blending of the Gemeinschaft with the Gefühl; it describes a picture of what *can be* rather than what *is.* Social interest establishes an ideal rather than a norm or median as the direction for the strivings of humankind. It is more than a concept of adjustment because it implies courage, initiative, and creativity. It places the whole of existence on a dynamic foundation of movement and improvement, belonging and cooperation. Social interest represents an *ideal norm;* therefore, it can be used as a standard to which the functioning of the individual can be compared. It serves as a relative index of the individual's mental health status.

Emotions and Feelings

Adlerians view emotions as an element of motivation. "Without strong emotions, no strong acts are possible" (Dreikurs, 1967b, p. 213). The psychological movement of the individual is goal directed and in addition to a lifestyle goal, the individual has immediate goals. Emotions are the fuel that helps attain those goals. Emotion comes from two Latin words, *ex* or *e* which means "out of" and *movere* which means "to move." Hence, emotions help an individual "move out" of a situation in a way that is consistent with that person's lifestyle and immediate goals. As Adler explained:

> They depend on his goal and his consequent style of life. The feelings are never in contradiction to the style of life. We are no longer, therefore, in the realm of physiology or biology. The rise of feelings cannot be explained by chemical theory and cannot be predicted by chemical examination. In Individual Psychology, while we presuppose the physiological processes, we are most interested in the psychological goal. (Ansbacher & Ansbacher, 1956, p. 226)

Adler divided emotions into conjunctive and disjunctive emotions. Conjunctive emotions, such as joy, love, excitement, and caring, serve the purpose of bringing people closer together. Disjunctive emotions, such as anger, jealousy, bitterness, hatred, and loathing, distance people from each other. Ansbacher and Ansbacher (1956) provided an excellent example of this movement from Adler's writings:

> The emotion of joy, for example, cannot stand isolation. In its expressions of seeking company and embracing another, it shows the inclination to play the game, to communicate, and to share the enjoyment. The entire attitude is engaging. It is extending the hand, so to speak, a warmth which radiates toward the other person and intended to elevate him as well. All the elements of union are present in this emotion. (p. 227)

Depending on lifestyle goal and immediate goals, a person chooses the type of emotion that will serve his or her purpose. Joe was angry a lot. He reported that he had been abused by his mother and father and was determined not to be abused by others. The question to be asked is what use does Joe's anger serve. Joe admitted that he thought others would try to hurt him eventually, so he created a shield of anger to minimize that potential hurt and to keep people at a distance from him. The anger also served the purpose of intimidating others and getting them to acquiesce when there was a quarrel, because most people backed down when they saw how upset Joe became. Typically, anger is chosen on occasions when the individual believes himself or herself to be powerless. Although there is no guarantee that anger will make another person cooperate, it is self-reinforcing because it creates the illusion of being in power. Emotions are purposive and serve the goals of the lifestyle and of the immediate situation.

Amy, a 17-year-old, was described by school personnel as "being out of control." She had learned to use her emotions to suit her goal of power ("I am equal to you by being more powerful"). Whenever Amy did not like something that others were doing, or when she did not want to give in to the demands of the school, she had "fits of temper." On one occasion when Amy was in the school library, her teacher asked her to put her book on the shelf and get ready to leave. Amy did not respond so the teacher continued to tell her to put her book on the shelf. As the teacher got frustrated and demanded that Amy comply, the school director stepped in to force the issue. Amy "blew up," yelling at them to leave her alone and proceeded to sweep the books off the shelves of the bookcase that was nearest to her. As Amy was clearing off the shelves, she completely missed a full cup of coffee the director had set down on top of the bookcase she was clearing. Amy had emptied everything else from that bookcase, but why did she miss the coffee cup? From an Adlerian perspective, the answer is clear. Amy was not driven by the anger but was using it; she was able to decide what she would destroy and what she wouldn't. In this case, she seemed to know that the director's coffee was off limits! As a rule, when Amy responded by "being out of control," the faculty and staff in the school would back off and leave her alone to do whatever she wanted. Amy was not *out of control*; she was using her anger to be *in control*.

Emily might be best described as thin-skinned and oversensitive. Her friends are careful around her in terms of what they say or might suggest. They all comment that being with Emily is like walking on eggs all of the time. They avoid discussion of subjects that have a tendency to upset her and constantly check in with her to make sure she is "okay" with the activities they are engaged in. Although Emily does not have the awareness, it is clear that she uses her "sensitivity" to control her environment and her friends. As a consequence, Emily has a difficult time keeping friends and does not understand why. Fred, on the other hand, is easygoing, enjoys life, and always has something positive to say to and about others. He is inquisitive and curious about his world and others are naturally drawn to him; he is never at a loss for being with friends.

After describing a person without emotion, Dreikurs (1967b) commented:

> We can see now why we need emotions. They provide the fuel, the steam, so to speak, for our actions, the driving force without which we would be impotent. They come into play whenever we decide to do something forcefully. They make it possible for us to carry out our decisions. They permit us to take a stand, to develop definite attitudes, to form convictions. They are the only basis for strong personal relationships to others, for developing interests and for building alliances of interests with others. They make us appreciate and devaluate, accept and reject. They make it possible for us to enjoy and dislike. In short, they make us human beings instead of machines. (pp. 207–208)

Depending on lifestyle goal and the immediate goals, a person chooses the type of emotion that will serve his or her purposes. No matter how it appears, emotions are not something that control the individual; rather, the individual learns to use emotions to pursue goals. As a way of preserving self-esteem, it may feel as if the emotion dominates the person; however, closer analysis indicates that the reverse is true.

APPLICATIONS

Overview

Adler identified three phases of the counseling or therapy process: (1) understanding the client; (2) explaining the client's behavior to him or her in a way that makes sense; and (3) strengthening social interest, the "working through" part of counseling or therapy (Ansbacher & Ansbacher, 1956). Dreikurs (1956) expanded the three phases to four with the addition of building relationships as an initial step, which was consistent with the research on counseling and psychotherapy that was current in his time. Adler never discussed the "relationship" element of the counseling or therapy process, other than to say it was similar to talking with a good friend. Dreikurs referred to the four phases as building a *relationship* of mutual trust and respect; psychological *investigation* to understand the client's lifestyle and present area of operation; *interpretation* to help the client learn about his or her unique motivations, intentions, and goals, which are often unconscious or unaware; and *reorientation* or reeducation, which has encouragement as a central ingredient. Dreikurs emphasized that these phases often overlap.

Mozdzierz, Lisiecki, Bitter, & Williams (1986) expanded on the roles and functions of an Adlerian counselor or therapist and emphasized that these are not stages or phases of counseling and therapy in any chronological sense; rather, they are processes or elements that the counselor or therapist needs to attend to with different degrees of emphasis at different times. Rapport is usually one of the first processes or elements requiring attention by the counselor or therapist, but understanding the client is also an important step in the initial part of treatment and may actually enhance rapport building by helping clients feel that someone actually understands them. A more important emphasis for the Adlerian counselor or psychotherapist is that the patterns of living that the client has adopted be disclosed to the client in a way that makes sense. At various times during counseling or therapy (e.g., after a particularly discouraging week or difficult confrontation), the role of rapport building may again be emphasized while the other three processes temporarily take a backseat. Similarly, at some point it may be useful to explore additional early recollections or solicit other information typically thought of as part of understanding the client in an effort to help the client learn about himself or herself.

Although considerable information is available about Adlerian theory and diagnostic technique, little is available to illustrate Adler's therapeutic style. Stein (1991) described the problem this way:

> Adler demonstrated his therapeutic approach; he did not write about it at length. The people who studied with him learned his style of treatment by observing him and absorbing it first hand. He insisted that Adlerian psychotherapy had to be creative, that it could not be made into a system or procedure.
>
> Many therapists, students, and university professors are not aware of the original Adlerian approach. One reason is that most of Adler's writings have been out of print for some time and

his two most important clinical works, *The Neurotic Constitution* and *The Theory and Practice of Individual Psychology*, are very poorly translated. The other reason is that the classical Adlerian technique of psychotherapy has not been comprehensively documented or widely demonstrated. (p. 241)

Adler was always reluctant to define or delineate typologies of personality and treatment technique.

The possible ways in which the individual can relate to life's questions are as infinite as the possible patterns of individuality. Even if some patterns of answers are similar, if this leads to the assumption that we might be able to create a typology, it would be very wrong, even theoretically, to organize cases into typical categories and force these various living forms into types. In order for a person in our profession to meet the demands of his work responsible and fairly, he must be able to feel the nuances of every variation and recognize the uniqueness of every individual. (Adler, 2005b, p. 80)

Adler conceived of therapy as a subjective, creative activity—the "artistry of Individual Psychology"—that "is bound to differ with the individual case" (Adler, 2005a, p. 80). As a result, he did not care to describe his technique in treatment "because a written description of the technique of treatment involves laying down the law upon a matter that cannot be standardized, measured, and categorized" (Adler, 2005a, p. 80). De Vries (2005) commented that Adler's style had to be seen to be appreciated. "Here was a therapist who, in a careful approach, quickly came to the core of the problem and used very simple everyday language from the patient's own vocabulary" (p. 1).

Stein has presented the opportunity to observe Adler's conversational style through some recently translated lectures, *Lectures to Physicians & Medical Students* (Adler, 2005b). This particular work contains a series of lectures that Adler delivered "at what was identified only as an 'Urban Hospital,' somewhere in Europe" (p. iv).

All of these never-before-published manuscripts add to our appreciation of Adler's remarkable understanding of human nature and the cure for mental suffering. His unique synthesis of psychological and medical knowledge, as well as his exceptional, creative intuition, provide us with a timeless, profound resource in our continuing quest for improving our therapeutic abilities (p. iv).

A brief excerpt from an interview found in Lecture No. 12 (Adler, 2005b) concerning a woman with a neck spasm is illustrative of Adler's manner.

DR. A: When you have fully recovered and your neck is well again, then what would you like to do?

PATIENT: Perhaps learn to become a housekeeper to work in a home or on a farm, but I have not improved, so I don't give this any thought.

D: Are you depressed because you are not getting better? Perhaps you take life too hard, is that so?

P: I don't know.

D: As a child or a young girl, did you have hopes that you would do well?

P: Yes.

D: Then you were brave, and now you want to lose courage? Tell me, who do you think will get further, she who faces life courageously or the person who always fears that this and that will never work?

P: Certainly the first.

D: You see, if you know this now, then when you leave here you will be able to remember: To be a human being means to have courage. Whatever we begin to do, we can never know how it will come out. However, if we dare with courage, we shall certainly attain more than if we have no confidence from the outset. Would you like to talk a few more times with the lady who wrote down your medical history, so that she can help you when you start out anew?

P: Yes, if that is possible.

D: That's fine, you will do well and don't forget: She who dares, wins! (pp. 131–132)

This example illustrates Adler's encouraging, conversational style. Bottome, Adler's biographer, wrote in her own autobiography of how Adler enjoyed making jokes during therapy. When she discussed this with him, he replied; "'Yes, that is true . . . but I am sometimes at my most serious when I make jokes.' . . . 'Seif,' Adler used to say with a twinkle, 'practises what I preach.' But this was only a joke, for Adler never preaches; but he was a man whose whole personality bore the imprint of his philosophy" (Bottome, 1962, p. 223).

After reviewing various accounts of how Adler worked and the dialogues included in *Lectures to Physicians & Medical Students*, Milliren and Wingett (2005) developed a process called RCI/TE. RCI identifies the inquiry element, **respectfully curious inquiry**, which includes the process of reflective, Socratic exploration, and TE indicates **therapeutic empowerment**. There are seven elements, or FLAVERS, of effective RCI:

F = *Focusing* on what it is the client wants and arriving at mutually agreed on goals

L = *Listening* attentively, empathetically, and reflectively

A = *Assessing* client's strengths, resilience, and social interest

V = *Validating* client resources and "character"istics; encouraging client growth

E = *Engaging* in the humor that abounds in the ironies of social living

R = *Replacing* information gathering ("factophilia") with appropriate clarification, creative intuition, imaginative empathy, and stochastic questions

S = *Socratic* dialoguing (what? who? where? when? how?) that serves as the *key* element of the RCI process.

The RCI process develops more as a conversation about the client's life journey in the areas of work, friendships, intimacy, self, and spirituality. It is designed to discover where the client has been, what is currently happening for the client, and where the client would like to be. As this exploration progresses, observations of the client's behavior are connected to speculations about the client's logic. With this process, the client is assisted in bringing his/her beliefs to awareness. (Milliren & Wingett, 2004, p. 1)

Therapeutic empowerment is based on the four elements of equality, empathy, encouragement, and education. The focus here is similar to

the re-education/re-orientation phase of the Adlerian counseling process in which the client's beliefs are co-evaluated by the client and counselor to assess the usefulness of the behavior that evolves from the belief. Therapeutic empowerment involves replacing useless behaviors with creative alternatives. Prescriptions for more effective options may be suggested, more functional or useful behaviors are encouraged, and, throughout, social interest is enhanced. (Milliren & Wingett, 2004, p. 1)

Goals of Counseling and Psychotherapy

Dreikurs (1967a) distinguished counseling and psychotherapy from each other based on the idea that each of these has different objectives. Counseling was described as focusing on an acute situation aimed at the solution of immediate problems. It was viewed as a process of learning to adapt to the challenges presented by the tasks of life. The goal was not to change lifestyle as much as to help the client understand how his or her lifestyle may interfere with completing the tasks of life. Therapy, on the other hand, had a goal of changing the lifestyle and was designed to affect the whole personality and lead to the reorganization of the client's life. Both counseling and psychotherapy, however, are accomplished in light of the overarching goal of enhancing the client's social interest.

Contemporary Adlerians tend to see counseling and psychotherapy as more similar, as do clinicians and counselors in general. The goal of counseling and psychotherapy for Adlerians is to assist clients to understand their unique lifestyles and help them learn to think about self, others, and the world and to act in such a way as to meet the tasks of life with courage and social interest. Although Adlerian counseling and therapy may vary from a short-term to a rather long-term process, they are generally considered to be forms of brief therapy, primarily because of their emphasis on interpretation, confrontation, and working with the client to understand and explain the client to himself or herself. The reorientation phase of psychotherapy emphasizes the development of social interest and involves a great deal of encouragement; a variety of strategically planned learning experiences over an extended period of time are included, particularly for clients who have severe deficits (Stein & Edwards, 1998).

Process of Change

Change seems to occur in Adlerian psychotherapy and counseling because of a variety of mechanisms. Dreikurs (1956) posited that insight was an important part of change, although it was not the only therapeutic agent. He believed that change occurred as the patient began to recognize his or her goals and intentions. Dreikurs spoke of a process Adler called "spitting in the patient's soup" as a way of helping the client become aware of his or her motivation. Once the patient becomes aware of his or her motivation for the behavior, the behavior becomes less desirable. One can continue to eat soup that has been spat in, but it may not be as appetizing. Dreikurs believed that it was not only making the person aware of goals and motivation that helped a person to change, but also making the person aware of his or her own power, of the ability to make decisions, and the freedom to choose directions. Encouragement is an essential element in counseling and therapy. Encouragement begins in therapy with a relationship based on mutual respect and trust. It is the process of restoring the patient's faith in self and the realization of strength and ability as well as dignity and worth. According to Dreikurs, "without encouragement neither insight nor change is possible" (Dreikurs, 1956, p. 118).

Shulman (1973) wrote about the process of confrontation and credits it as an important ingredient in change and success of Adlerian counseling or therapy. He sees confrontation as a way of provoking therapeutic movement. Because a major goal of Adlerian counseling or psychotherapy is to recognize and change mistaken goals and beliefs and their associated moods and actions, confrontation is frequently used as a way of holding the mistaken goals and beliefs up in front of the client, as with a mirror. Confrontation presents an opportunity to the client to make an immediate change in beliefs, behaviors, or mood. Confrontation is an active method, so the counselor or therapist has to make the client aware of his or her private logic and goals, the ownership of these, and the ability to change them.

Adler's emphasis on understanding the interpersonal nature of behavior and facilitating change processes rather than on analyzing intrapsychic processes contributed to the split between him and Freud. Adler's focus became one of empowering discouraged individuals to resolve problems by recognizing their strengths and assets rather than focusing on their weaknesses. For Dreikurs, all psychotherapy involved the correction of faulty social values and attitudes. He saw psychotherapy as a way of teaching cooperation.

> We find four attitudes essential for cooperation, with their counterparts disrupting it. These are: (1) social interest—hostility; (2) confidence in others—distrust and suspicion; (3) self-confidence—inferiority; (4) courage—fear. Social interest is an expression of a sense of belonging; lack of social interest limits or impedes cooperation and makes an opponent appear as an enemy. Fear seems to be the chief obstacle to adequate social functioning in a democratic atmosphere; it can be regarded as the sin of free man. (Dreikurs, 1967a, p. 152).

Traditional Intervention Strategies

Lifestyle Analysis. Lifestyle analysis is the process of learning to understand the goals and motivation of the client. This is a mutual process in which both the client and counselor or therapist learn more about the beliefs and patterns of behavior that the client has developed in a creative attempt to address life's challenges. Lifestyle is a cognitive blueprint a person has developed that includes ideas about self, others, and the world. It also includes ethical convictions (e.g., what I should be, what life should be) and a unifying fiction or goal toward which all movement is directed. Lifestyle is an ongoing process. It is similar to "personality" but slightly different in that it includes patterns of behaviors as well as beliefs and perceptual schema. A person's lifestyle not only affects what the person does but also how the person sees the world, other people, and the self. If a person has a lifestyle that includes the belief that other people are hostile, that person will find validation on a daily basis of other people's hostility through the apperception of reality. Apperception is the process of experiencing or perceiving things mediated by attribution of meaning and significance to those experiences or perceptions.

Methods of doing lifestyle analysis range from a more formal or structured approach to the less formal and structured. Shulman and Mosak (1988) developed a standardized way of collecting lifestyle data and suggested ways of interpreting that data. Powers and Griffith (1987) proposed another standardized method of data collection and emphasized slightly different aspects in interpreting data. Other Adlerians see lifestyle analysis unfolding as therapy or counseling continues and do not gather data in as systematic manner as do these authors.

Other than in brief counseling or therapy, data for lifestyle analysis usually involves the collection of information in some or all of the following areas:

Family Constellation. The family constellation includes the ordinal and psychological position in the family of reference along with an understanding of relationships between the siblings, the parents, and the parents and children as the client perceives them. These evaluations on the part of the client form a part of the basic convictions on which the client's anticipations of life, self, and others are based.

Family Atmosphere. The family atmosphere is set by the relationship between the parents. The client's evaluation of this atmosphere as a child becomes important to the decisions he or she makes about how life and relationships should be and is retained and used in later life. To explore the general climate of the household, climate-related terms may be used (e.g., *sunny, partly cloudy, tornadic, icy*). The participation of each parent in the creation of the family atmosphere is a significant aspect of the child's **gender guiding lines.**

Family Values. Family values represent what both parents want for the children. These are the values that are shared by both the mother and father and, typically, are indicated by the ways in which all children in the family are alike. Each child in the family must take a position with respect to these values that operate as "family imperatives." Although most children are likely to support the family standard, it is not unusual for one child to ignore it, defy it, or take a contrary position. Exploration of family values can be accomplished by asking a child, "What is important to mother? To father?" With an adult, one might say, "Growing up as a child, what was important to mother? To father?" Asking for mottoes is another means of ascertaining family values: "If mother had a motto, something she might put on a plaque or a poster, what would it be? If your father had a motto, what would it be?"

Gender Guiding Lines. The values not shared by the parents but held by only one take on a different significance. The child experiences these as elements of the gender guiding lines—what it means to be a "real" man or a "real" woman. These unshared values form the rules and patterns for a person's expectations regarding gender, and they are often perceived by the person as if they are destiny.

Family Role Played by Each Child. In a discussion of family roles assumed by children of alcoholics, Reed (1995), identified the following four roles: the hero, the scapegoat, the lost child, and the mascot. Milliren (1995) discussed the need for educators (and counselors and therapists) to "recognize the almost driven nature of the 'hero,' to understand the purposes of the behaviors of the 'scapegoat,' to have insight into the aloneness of the 'lost child,' and to know the need for affiliation on the part of the 'mascot' (p. xvii)." Other role descriptors have also been suggested (Typpo & Hastings, 1984): the responsible one, the caretaker, the family pet, the forgotten child, the problem child, the acting-out child, and the adjuster. All of these are lifestyle patterns adopted by children to cope with the family situation. These roles become so ingrained that they continue through life, even after the need for the coping style is no longer required.

Early Developmental Experiences. It is sometimes useful to explore the nature of early development experiences, that is, early experiences with peers, adults, school, and sex, to obtain an additional dimension about the conclusions the client drew about how life should be. Sometimes these take the form of early recollections.

After the data are collected, a report is usually prepared. The discussion and modification of the report becomes a collaborative activity between the counselor or therapist and the client. This process takes the form of a dialogue that allows the counselor or therapist and client to begin to examine the beliefs the client holds about life and living. The purpose of lifestyle assessment is to help clients understand who they are, how they became who they are, and to bring their unconscious goals to a level of greater awareness. Note here that Adlerians use the term *unconscious* only as an adjective. There is no such thing for them as "the unconscious," and it may be more accurate to use the concept "out of awareness" when describing unconscious processes. Because the lifestyle is the set of rules that the individual lives by, it is important for him or her to come to understand his or her movement through life. Once these rules are clarified, the person is in a better position to change disliked or unproductive elements.

Encouragement. Encouragement is the key in promoting and activating social interest and psychological "muscle" or hardiness. Social interest and psychological hardiness are required to take life in stride without becoming discouraged and to create meaning and purpose in life (Evans, 1997b). Encouragement is a fundamental Adlerian concept for helping parents (Meredith & Evans, 1990) and teachers (Evans, 1995, 1996) improve relationships with children and create an atmosphere of cooperation and democracy in the family and school. Encouragement is probably the universal therapeutic intervention for Adlerian counselors and therapists. Encouragement is not a technique; rather, it is a fundamental attitude or "spirit."

Although the concept of encouragement is simple to understand, it is difficult to define. Simply stated, encouragement is the process of drawing out and expanding the courage. Encouragement is not a special language used to gain compliance or cooperation. Rather, it is a fundamental attitude regarding human nature. Encouragement is a spirit, conveyed through interactions with others. Human beings are worthwhile merely because they exist. It is their birthright to belong. Belonging is not something to achieve through accomplishments. Thus, encouragement was Mr. Rogers telling children, "I like you just the way you are," not "I like you when you do it well enough, fast enough, and get it all correct." The most fundamental encouragement an adult can give a child is the sense that he or she has significance, even when things go poorly. The most fundamental encouragement a spouse can convey to his or her partner is that the partner counts by the mere fact of his or her existence. Communicating this spirit will develop an individual's capacity to withstand adversity and the willingness to function when things go poorly. Involving oneself in living life, especially in times of adversity, is an act of courage.

Courage is the willingness to move forward, one step at a time, in the face of adversity and in spite of how you feel. It is produced through encouragement and comes from a feeling of belonging and contribution. A major source of courage comes from acceptance and recognition of competence rather than focus on failure. To instill courage, the therapist or counselor must stimulate a sense of belonging on the part of the client and impart an appreciation for the ironclad logic of social living. Instilling courage involves recognizing the strengths and abilities of the client, assisting the client in setting goals that are attainable in a reasonable amount of time, and helping the client identify the steps and methods by which these goals may be attained. Some clients need more help with the process of identifying steps and methods for goal attainment, whereas others may need more assistance with identifying goals. Still others have been so discouraged that they feel like they don't belong to the human race.

Encouragement is the single most important quality in getting along with others. It is so important that the lack of it could be considered the basic factor in misbehavior, divorce, job loss, suicide, and other human problems. Encouragement is the key ingredient in all positive professional and personal relationships. The ability to function in today's world rests on the ability to nurture and convey concern for others. Encouragement is desperately needed today because fear, power, and threat of punishment are not effective in developing responsible, capable, and fully functioning individuals. Dreikurs (Terner & Pew, 1978) said that human beings need encouragement like plants need water. Yet so few of us know how to encourage ourselves and others. The mark of an encouraging person is someone who infuses life into the world. Encouragers are so comfortable with human nature that they convey faith in a person just because he or she exists.

Fear, worrying, and obsession are all forms of negative thinking that create discouragement. Conjuring up fears taints present opportunities. Fear puts a stranglehold on the ability to function. Some individuals worry so much that they develop a negative attitude and go around reacting, obsessing, and pointing out all the dangers of life in an attempt to control the world. None of this activity solves the problem—it just makes people difficult to be around. After a while, others either avoid or minimize their contact with people with this negative outlook. The discouragement that flows from their tongues poisons the well. They send admonitions of doom and gloom that extract the joy from life. Fear and excessive worry convey a vote of no confidence. In this way, people treat themselves as inferior and reflect doubt in their ability to handle life. Fear is diminished by developing a more adequate and trusting view of self.

Half the job of encouragement lies in avoiding being discouraging. All criticism and external control, like rewards and punishment, are viewed as discouraging. Criticism is the poison that sours a marriage and destroys relationships between adults and children. According to Evans (1997a), there are five general ways to discourage:

- Setting high expectations or unrealistic standards
- Focusing on mistakes in a misguided attempt to motivate
- Making comparisons among people
- Making pessimistic interpretations
- Dominating by being overly responsible

No corrective effort of a person's behavior is possible without encouragement. The worse the behavior, the more encouragement is needed. Yet individuals who misbehave are most likely to receive the least amount of encouragement. Instead of building on a discouraged person's strengths, we tear him or her down; instead of recognizing the person's efforts and improvement, we point out his or her mistakes; instead of allowing the person to feel like he or she belongs and can become responsible through shared decision making, we control and punish.

To become encouraging, we need to abandon our feeling of the need for external control (Glasser, 1999) and stop focusing on mistakes. We need to make the relationship a priority and develop a friendly and respectful atmosphere. Encouragement is often mistaken as praise, but praise is external control. Praise focuses on outcomes (doing well), uses superlatives, and is conditional. Encouragement focuses on effort or improvement rather than results. It highlights strengths and assets, rather than identifying weaknesses, limitations, deficits, or disorders. Encouragement can be given anytime, no matter how poorly things are going; praise, rewards, and punishment can only be given with good or bad results. Encouragement separates the deed from the doer. A particular behavior can be disturbing, but the individual is not labeled as being "bad." Encouragement points out specific behaviors that contribute, improve, or display strength. Encouragement is focused on intrinsic motivation so that encouraging someone is also a means for helping him or her develop self-control (Evans and Milliren, 1999).

Every person with whom we come in contact feels better or worse by how we behave toward him or her. Our attitude toward others either brings out their very best or very worst. Encouragers contribute, cooperate, and help out in life. They have discovered that the meaning in life is to help, not burden. Inappropriate behavior is the result of discouragement and derives from feeling alienated, different, or as if one does not belong.

> All symptoms of neuroses and psychoses are forms of expression of discouragement. Every improvement comes about solely from encouraging the sufferer. Every physician and every school of neurology is effective only to the extent that they succeed in giving encouragement. Occasionally, a layman can succeed in this also. It is practiced deliberately only by Individual Psychology. (Adler, 1926)

Brief Intervention Strategies

There are probably as many forms of brief counseling and therapy as there are practitioners who are doing it. Any discussion of brief counseling and therapy first requires a definition. Shulman (1989) approached it this way:

> Any full discussion of brief psychotherapy should distinguish between the attempt to shorten the length of psychotherapy for the treatment of neuroses and character disorders (the first application of psychotherapy) and special procedures for special cases, i.e., crisis intervention, changing behavior patterns in a family, child guidance, marriage counseling, specific symptom removal, and the other special applications. (p. 14)

In addition to the preceding differentiation, Shulman also indicated that some clients require a longer time in therapy than others. He indicated, for example, that clients with better developed social interest will be helped more quickly than those without.

Manaster (1989) concluded that there have been essentially two ways to limit therapy to a shorter time frame: "limiting goals and limiting time (p. 242)." Bottome (1962) described the following instance of an unemployed man who came to consult with Adler:

> A man who had hunted fruitlessly for a job in a time of great unemployment in Holland came to Adler in despair. He told him all he had done to find work, and added that he was now in the verge of suicide. Adler listened to his story without sympathy or comment. When the man, hurt and astonished, rose to go, Adler said reflectively, 'I find that what you need is a job.' The man left him in a rage, but came back within a week to say that he had found a job. (p. 224)

This is a classic example of goal-limited therapy.

From an Adlerian perspective, it is important for the individual to gain an understanding of how he or she moves through the world. Much of the focus is on helping the client gain perspective on the beliefs he or she holds. In a meeting with a client who was having trouble connecting with her in-laws, she commented that they had more pictures around the house of their "other" granddaughter (not her daughter), and this was an aggravation every time the client visited. A quick check of the client's birth position revealed that she was an oldest child who had all the responsibility for caring for her younger siblings. When asked how that was for her, her spontaneous comment was, "It wasn't fair!" In a matter of seconds, the client followed that comment with an "Oh my gosh!" What she realized in that moment was that she was counting the pictures and deciding how it wasn't fair. Once she understood this and quit counting, the situation seemed to miraculously resolve itself.

In goal-limited counseling and therapy, often only data regarding the relevant lifestyle elements are obtained. Milliren and Eckstein (2005) proposed that a relevant "thin slice" is sufficient for developing a sense of a client's lifestyle beliefs. In essence, thin-slicing is a process of rapidly sorting and selecting, from a wide range of information, the more relevant factors.

> It is striking, for instance, how many different professions and disciplines have a word to describe the particular gift of reading deeply into the narrowest slivers of experience. In basketball, the player who can take in and comprehend all that is happening around him or her is said to have "court sense." (Gladwell, 2005, p.44)

Thin-slicing is particularly valuable when working with a client from a goal-limited perspective. Consciousness, being holistic, seems to remain focused around all facets of the immediate concern. Therefore, conducting a brief lifestyle analysis provides information that is particularly relevant to understanding the client's attitudes and orientation about life that connect to that concern.

Walton (1996c) suggested five questions for brief lifestyle analysis:

- Complete the following statement: "I was the kid who always . . ."
- Which sibling did you think was most different from you when you were a child? How? (If the client is an only child, ask, How were you different from other kids?)
- When you were a child, what did you think was most positive about your mother? Father? Was there anything you rejected about mom or dad?
- Unforgettable or most memorable observations: When you were growing up, can you recall any conclusions you made about life? For example, "When I get to be an adult, I certainly will always . . ." or "I will never let this happen in my family (or in my life)?"
- Two early memories (recollections); What was the earliest specific incident you can recall? (Record these in the present tense in the precise words of the client.) What moment was most vivid? What feeling is connected with the incident?

Walton indicated that not all of the questions are required to be effective in helping the client. However, use of this set of five questions can help the counselor or therapist achieve considerable insight into the client—how he or she approaches others and how he or she is affected by the situation.

Although Adler may have been one of the first to offer a brief or time-limited approach to therapy, he did not concern himself with the length of therapy. After leaving the psychoanalytic movement in 1911, Adler concerned himself more with the development of his own approach (Shulman, 1989). The emphasis was on being of help to the client rather than defining the length of treatment. Ansbacher (1989) maintains that "Adlerian psychology represents the tradition of brief psychotherapy" (p. 32). In their recent book on adlerian therapy, Carlson, Watts, and Maniacci (2006) concluded that "Adlerian therapists have had a long history of doing brief, time-limited psychotherapy" (p. 274). Whether Adler was the first to offer brief therapy may be less important than the fact that the Adlerian approach fits nicely in a context of contemporary brief therapy.

CLIENTS WITH SERIOUS MENTAL HEALTH ISSUES

At first, Adler attributed all psychopathological behavior to exaggerated feelings of inferiority. Later, both Adler and Dreikurs believed that serious mental disorders reflected a tremendous sense of inadequacy and an inability to develop a quality human relationship, along with a lack of social interest. The greater the social interest, the greater the level of functioning. To feel equal and adequate to the task at hand results in being able to participate in a constructive and useful manner. This willingness to cooperate is social interest. A person who lacks it feels less than others and, instead of moving toward others as a member of the human community, moves toward self-elevation. The movement away from others may be toward personal glory, which can be a useful compensation; if the inadequacy is too great, movement will be toward the useless side of life. All serious mental disorders can be reduced to this analogy (Dreikurs, 1961).

Adlerians view behavior as occurring on a continuum rather than as a dichotomy; they do not believe it is "either/or" but "degree of" that differentiates one person from another. Some theories of counseling and psychotherapy propose a categorical difference between those who are "seriously mentally ill" and those who are "normal," but Adlerians believe that people act in ways that are consistent with their lifestyle goals. Adlerians believe that the only reliable diagnosis of symptoms, particularly psychosomatic symptoms, is to ascertain their function or use. Behavior is purposive, so there is usually some payoff or outcome toward which the behavior is directed, even though the individual may be unaware of it. If a symptom has no function or particular gain, the Adlerian counselor or therapist would conclude that the problem has organic origins and needs to be treated by a physician (Dreikurs, 1956).

One of the most important things an Adlerian counselor can do is to continually ask, "What's the use for this behavior?" Richard, a therapist in private practice, consulted with one of the authors about a case because he could not understand what was going on with his client. Martha, a fourth grader, had been referred for having difficulty at home and at school. As Richard discussed the case, he related two incidents that occurred while he was interviewing this little girl. First, Richard had asked about an incident involving Martha and her younger brother in which Martha had refused to share her drawing materials. When asked to explain, Martha immediately began to cry, and Richard said that he thought she was being remorseful and that she must have felt really bad about not sharing with her brother. Later in the interview when Richard was discussing what she might do differently in these situations with her brother, Martha began to cry again. He asked why she was crying and Martha said she felt like she was such a bad person for not sharing with her brother.

What Richard forgot to do was ask, "What's the use?" He failed to look for the purpose of the behavior; as a result, he believed that this was a sweet little girl who felt extremely sorry for the fact that she had not shared her things. However, after initiating a discussion of what the possible purpose might be, Richard happened to mention that Martha's mother was extremely demanding in her expectations of Martha's behavior, for example, "After all, Martha is the oldest and needs to set the example!" With this background information, the purpose of Martha's crying was suddenly clear. Martha was acting as if she believed that crying would allow her to avoid being punished for misbehaving. Richard mentioned that when Martha cried, he dropped the subject and went on to talk with her about other things. Richard further shared that the mother had told him that her response, whenever Martha burst into tears, was to tell her to not do it again. The mother was afraid of Martha's extreme sensitivity about everything and did not want to do anything to upset her further. Rather than being extra sensitive, however, Martha was using "water power" to manipulate the situation.

Shulman (1962) talks of persons with schizophrenia or bipolar disorder as sharing three characteristics: extremely low self-esteem; extremely high-flown goals in life, and drastic measures for narrowing the gap between the self-image and the self-ideal. There are, of course, some genetic or organic factors that are often involved in what is commonly called serious mental illness (e.g., schizophrenia, bipolar disorders, major depression). However, these are viewed as dispositions or propensities that increase the potential for developing these types of behavioral patterns rather than determining factors. Environment and learning history need to be taken into consideration. Persons with schizophrenia are not all alike. Neither are all persons with bipolar disorder alike. Some lead lives that are more productive than others, whereas some have totally given up and feel isolated, totally different from other human beings. The purpose of counseling and therapy, whether it be individual, group, or milieu treatment, is to foster the sense of belonging, of competence, and of courage to participate in life.

For Adlerians, having a serious mental illness such as schizophrenia or bipolar disorder is a part of life that must be dealt with through education, medication, socialization, and encouragement rather than stigmatization and isolation. Community support programs such as Fountain House in New York, Thresholds in Chicago, and other community-based programs around the world exhibit a philosophy that is similar to Adler's: "We are not alone." This was the emphasis of the first members at Fountain House who bonded together to assist each other in their reentry into society after years of hospitalization and isolation from others. This movement has made it clear that the principles of belonging, helping each other, useful contribution, and support are essential elements in the intervention process (Beard, Propst, & Malamud, 1982).

A person with a serious mental illness still has to decide what to do about the illness and about the tasks of life. Like a physical illness, serious mental illness of organic etiology may need medical intervention. If medication is necessary to allow one to function better, then its importance needs to be addressed as part of treatment. For many who have serious mental illnesses, learning to recognize the onset of stress and alternatives to cope with stress are important aspects of treatment. For Adlerians, social treatment and involvement in community activities are frequently the focus of interventions. Group therapy and community drop-in centers, in which a sense of belonging, membership, and useful contribution are encouraged, help the person with serious mental illness to develop social interest and to learn to address the tasks of life in a constructive manner.

CROSS-CULTURAL CONSIDERATIONS

Earlier in this chapter, it was noted that Adler's first publication, *Health Book for the Tailor Trade,* focused on the working conditions of tailors and how these affected their physical health. In 1898, Adler initiated his public career focused on the role of the physician in social issues and reform activities (Hoffman, 1994). This orientation of concern for others continued through his life and culminated in the development of Adler's concept of Gemeinschaftsgefühl—an expression of "social feeling: compassion, altruism, and selflessness" (Hoffman, 1994, p. 101). Bottome (1962), one of Adler's biographers, commented in her autobiography in recalling a chance observation of Hitler in 1932 that "Adler was a man who really minded if a single baby in China had a headache, and he had taught us that we also were responsible for this child in China, or any other children anywhere, but what we possessed was hope; and we had seen it at work upon human material" (p. 193).

Adler enjoyed the camaraderie of the coffeehouses in Vienna and after the break with Freud, he met regularly with others at the Cafe Central. These meetings were open to any and all who attended. As Dreikurs noted (Hoffman, 1994), it was quite simple to join in the group and the discussions. "You just went. No one was excluded, and the door to the weekly Monday meetings was characteristically left wide open" (p. 120). Such openness characterizes all of Adlerian psychology, which is a socially oriented approach to individuals and groups that is inclusive, respectful, and focused on social equality. "Adler campaigned for the social equality of women, contributed much to the understanding of gender issues, spoke against the marginalization of minority groups, and specifically predicted the Black power and women's liberation movements" (Carlson et al., 2006, p. 32).

Arciniega and Newlon (2003) stated that "strict Adlerian theory would have some limitations for minority clients who want quick solutions, for the clients would have little interest in exploring early childhood memories, or dreams" (p. 435). The word *strict* as applied to the conduct of a detailed lifestyle analysis would probably create limitations for many clients, minority or not. We live in a culture of fast food and brief therapy, and there is probably less interest in the use of lifestyle assessment on the part of both clients and professionals. This does not mean that lifestyle assessment is not of value. In fact, many Europeans, who are part of a more insightful, slower paced, pondering culture, enjoy and find value in lifestyle assessment. The issue may be more importantly focused on the manner in which the theory is applied by the practitioner rather than on the appropriateness of the theory itself. Many of the assumptions inherent in Adlerian psychology are an excellent match with the beliefs and values of many minority groups. As Arciniega and Newlon (2003) pointed out,

> Adlerian assumptions that people are equal, social, and goal-centered, that they seek cooperation, and that they contribute to the common good of the group are holistic and are congruent with the cultural values of these racial and ethnic groups. The individual's unique subjective interpretation and perception are part of Adlerian theory, and the client's culture, values, and views are honored and accepted. Adlerian goals are not aimed at deciding for clients what they should change about themselves, Rather, the practitioner works in collaboration with clients and their family networks. (p. 436)

Carlson et al. (2006) concluded that "Adlerian psychotherapy is clearly relevant for working with culturally diverse populations in contemporary society" (p. 32).

EVALUATION

Overview

Of all of the personality and counseling theories, Alfred Adler's Individual Psychology is probably among the least well-known but has had the greatest influence on current approaches to counseling and psychotherapy (Corey, 1996). Willingham, writing about the status of

Adlerian Psychology in 1986, indicated that Adler had an influence on various theories and methodologies in counseling, psychotherapy and education. He quoted Wilder as stating: "most observations and ideas of Alfred Adler have subtly and quietly permeated modern psychological thinking to such a degree that the proper question is not whether one is Adlerian but how much of an Adlerian one is (p. xv)" (Willingham, 1986, p. 165). "Modern applied psychology is increasingly congruent with Individual Psychology in that many applications in organizational psychology and counseling with families and school utilize concepts and methods that strongly resemble Adlerian ideas and practices" (Ferguson, 2000a, p. 14).

In many respects, Adler developed a personality theory and approach to counseling and psychotherapy that was far ahead of his time. Watts (2000) stated "that many contemporary approaches have 'discovered' many of Adler's fundamental conclusions, often without recognition of his vision and influence" (p. 11). Watts also believes that as much as Adlerian counseling may be viewed as antiquated by students, educators, and practitioners, it "solidly resonates with postmodern approaches to counseling" (p. 16). In fact, "Adlerian theory addressed social equality and emphasized the social embeddedness of human knowledge long before multiculturalism became chic in the counseling profession" (p. 16).

The simplicity of Adlerian psychology is often used as its major criticism, of which Adler was apparently aware. The simplicity and commonsense approach of Adlerian theory is illustrated by a story told about Adler when he was scheduled for a series of lectures in Aberdeen, Scotland:

> His host was psychology professor Rex Knight, who came to greet Adler at the Caledonia Hotel. After exchanging mutual greetings in the lobby, the two men sat down briefly to chat on a sofa. Suddenly, a handsome young man swaggered over. "I hear that you two gentlemen are psychologists. I bet there's nothing that either of you can tell me about myself."
>
> Knight looked quizzically to Adler for an answer, who raised his eyes and gazed deliberately at the young man. "Yes, I think there's something that I can tell you about yourself." As the stranger smiled expectantly, Adler continued, "You're very vain."
>
> "Vain!" was the startled reply. "Why should you think that I'm vain?"
>
> "Isn't it vain," Adler said simply, "to come up to two unknown gentlemen sitting on a sofa and ask them what they think of you?"
>
> As the young man left baffled, Adler turned to Knight and commented, "I've always tried to make my psychology simple. I would perhaps say that all neurosis is vanity, but that might be too simple to be understood." (Hoffman, 1994, p. 322)

Simple solutions such as recommending that a teacher and parent encourage a student who is doing poorly in school or removing the parent from sibling fights to reduce the conflict are strategies that work. Results, many times, are what validate the theory for the practitioner and the client.

Supporting Research

Adler developed his theory for the common person, offering common solutions for dealing with the day-to-day problems of living. It was a therapeutic, educational, and rehabilitative model that was a part of the pioneering work taking place in modern psychiatry. By the 1930s, the theory was being applied to everyday, real-life problems in parenting, schools, marriage, and the workplace. Empirical evidence for the theory came from case results rather than experimental designs (Ferguson, 2001). In the 1950s and 1960s most cited studies involving Adlerian psychology were conducted by non-Adlerians (Mosak & Dreikurs, 1976). Until the past 30 years or so, however, little research emerged on the effectiveness of Adlerian psychology. Watkins (1982) wrote:

> Admittedly, as theoretical and practical interests grow, so must the body of research which supports and extends one's theoretical and practical understanding. The decade of the seventies saw more research studies being done to test the usefulness of Adlerian constructs and concepts than had been done in many preceding years. (p. 90)

Watkins (1983) reported that during the years from 1970 through 1981, there were 75 research studies in the *Journal of Individual Psychology*. Birth order "and its effects on personality development and functioning" (p. 100) was the most researched area with 24 studies. "Social interest is examined in 19 studies (25 percent), early recollections in 6 (8 percent), and lifestyle in 4 (5 percent)" (p. 100). Watkins concluded his survey by indicating that "research on Individual Psychology has flourished during the period examined (and, as a side note, has been quite confirmatory)" (p. 103). He cautioned, though, that the study of clinical populations is extremely limited and "there is a definite need for further Adlerian-oriented research on inpatients and outpatients alike" (p. 104).

In a follow-up study, Watkins (1992) examined the research activity with Adlerian theory appearing in the *Journal of Individual Psychology* during the years 1982 to 1990. He noted that 103 studies appeared during this 9-year period. This was a marked increase over the previous 12 years that he had reported on (Watkins, 1983). Although he did not attempt to evaluate the quality of the studies reported, Watkins (1992) concluded "that research into Adler's theory is still on the increase (at least in *IP*) and suggests it is a vital theory that lends itself to empirical inquiry" (p. 108). Since 1990, the reported research has continued to grow; the *Journal of Individual Psychology* has published additional studies on marriage, children, substance abuse, classroom management, behavioral problems in children and youth, and offenders. A number of other professional journals have included research articles on Adlerian theory as well.

A number of university faculty (e.g., Dr. John Dagley, University of Georgia; Dr. Roy Kern, Georgia State University; Dr. Eva Dreikurs Ferguson, Southern Illinois University, Edwardsville) have guided their doctoral students toward researching and refining Adlerian concepts. A leading figure in the development and validation of Adlerian research on lifestyle is Dr. Roy Kern, who set out to validate Adler's psychology and develop a number of instruments based on Adlerian principles. For the past 25 years, Kern has been developing objective instruments for the assessment of lifestyle that are designed to be used in clinical and educational consultation as well as research. This has led to the publication of 50 or more research articles and more than 40 dissertations. As a result, Kern has provided a means to validate many of the Adlerian constructs. Some of the instruments now available include the Lifestyle Questionnaire Inventory, the Kern Lifestyle Scale, Lifestyle Personality Inventory, Basic Adlerian Scales for Interpersonal Success—Adult Form (BASIS-A) (Kern, Snow, & Ritter, 2002).

Perhaps the best ways to validate Adlerian theory have been the results experienced by clients and practitioners and the way theory and writings have become international and cross-cultural. Dreikurs started the International Committee for Adlerian Summer Schools and Institutes (ICASSI) in 1962 with the first school being held in Denmark. The ICASSI has provided rich international social experiences wherein long-term relationships have emerged among people from many nations. The ICASSI meets in a different country each year and has at least 24 different nationalities represented at each summer institute.

Limitations

One of the issues regarding Adlerian theory and practice is the lack of research demonstrating its specific effectiveness in counseling and therapy. Although this could be addressed as a major limitation, the problem plagues not only Adlerians but also all approaches to counseling and therapy. An early problem with experimental research was that the European Adlerians were, at times, unduly suspicious of research based upon statistical methods. To further complicate matters, the idiographic (case method) approach on which Adlerians relied did not lend itself to conventional research methodology. Statistical methods tend to be more appropriate for group research but they were not considered particularly applicable. Adlerian psychology also rejects the notion of causality and focuses on intent and the social field in which behavior takes place. These are hard concepts to measure with statistics.

Much of the research derived from many studies was not designed to examine Adlerian counseling or psychotherapy, but the research is clearly applicable to it. Ferguson's book, *Motivation: A Biosocial and Cognitive Integration of Motivation and Emotion,* does a thorough job of examining significant research and how it applies to Adlerian theory.

> The book integrates Adlerian principles and methods with contemporary scientific psychology, especially in the areas of motivation and emotion. The book presents a vast amount of studies in scientific psychology that support Adlerian theory. The book provides evidence, in support of Adlerian psychology, that scientific psychology increasingly shows the validity of Adlerian concepts, of holism, psychic/mental determinants influencing neurochemical and physiological processes, and the impact of social processes on psychological well-being. The book integrates Adlerian ideas in line with research in modern scientific psychology. (E. D. Ferguson, personal communication, November 28, 2001)

Adler and Dreikurs both have been criticized personally as well as for their theoretical formulations. Both individuals were extremely forceful personalities whose "conceptualizations and insights were rich in insights. These insights contrasted with ideas then currently espoused, and rejection of these ideas often became confounded with rejection of the person as well as his ideas" (Ferguson, 2001, p. 325). Part of the criticism came from the sphere of the depth psychologists who argued that the methods of Adler and Dreikurs were too superficial; the other part came from the cognitive-behavioral theorists who viewed them "as too dynamic, too concerned with inner motivation" (Ferguson, 2001, p. 325). So to some, Adlerian theory appears to lack the depth that the more analytic approaches offer and to others Adlerian theory is not as scientific as the more behavioral approaches might prefer. "The cognitive-social personality theory and methods of Adler and Dreikurs are very different from behavioristic approaches and, by criteria of broad and long-term health-providing effects, the theory and methods are indeed deep" (Ferguson, 2001, p. 337).

Another possible limitation in the application of Adlerian theory is the emphasis on social connectedness and individual responsibility. Individuals who are mentally healthy or fully functioning possess high levels of cooperation and contribution, and they are perceived as being in charge of the decisions they make about life. There is no room for blaming others or society for one's situation in life. However, these beliefs run contrary to the general cultural thinking regarding human behavior and human relationships.

> Thus, Individual Psychologists find themselves becoming agents of change for the community and the culture. As community values change, Adlerian methods become easy to apply. Until such changes in community beliefs occur, however, *Adlerian methods and Individual Psychology will be ahead of their time.* (Ferguson, 2000a, p. 19).

The Individual Psychology of Adler and Dreikurs, with its emphasis on relationships and not on symptoms, is more relevant today than ever, especially given current controversies surrounding the use of medication. Adlerian psychology has never been an approach to focus on symptoms and a search for causes. To discuss or focus on symptoms only strengthens the symptoms. Adler, today, would agree with what is being written by Whitaker (2002), *Mad in America*, and Glasser (2005), *Treating Mental Health as a Public Health Problem*. Just as Glasser sees the unifying problem that all people who are "mentally ill" share as unhappiness—specifically involving unhappy relationships—Adlerians view all problems as social problems (relationships). The unifying answer to the individual's well-being and happiness is the development of social interest; emphasis is placed on developing a quality relationship or relationship of equals. As Glasser wants to teach people how to get along well with each other, Adlerians want to teach people how to create democratic relationships that are not based on a psychology of external control.

SUMMARY CHART—*Adlerian Theory*

Human Nature

Adlerian psychology is interested in understanding the lifestyle, or law of psychological movement, of the individual. Early experiences and birth order and family constellation play a major role in the development of the lifestyle personality, although these factors are solely formative and not deterministic. As the individual pursues the need to belong and find a place of significance, he or she draws conclusions about the world and his or her personal worth. These conclusions combine to form a system of beliefs that guides all of the person's future interactions.

Major Constructs

The most fundamental principles of Adlerian Psychology include the following:

- *Purposiveness.* All behavior is goal directed or purposive. Although not always aware of the purpose, each individual moves through the world in such a way as to make things happen or to achieve a desired outcome. The person is not pushed by causes; rather, the person is pulled by his or her goals and dynamic striving.
- *Social Interest.* People are social beings who want to belong; they want to be able to find a place in the group. Because participation in a group requires a high level of cooperation and contribution, the development of social interest, or Gemeinschaftsgefühl, is a necessity for success in life. All of life's problems are basically problems of interactions with others and require a high level of social interest for resolution.

- *Holism.* The person is a dynamic, unified organism moving through life in definite pattern toward a goal. The person cannot be understood in part but must be viewed in totality.

In combination, these three principles describe the person as moving in unity toward self-chosen goals that reflect a human value for belonging and social contribution.

Goals

Problems arise in three general areas: work, friendship, and family. The primary goal of counseling or therapy is to assist the client in the development of social interest, for this is required for effective resolution of life's problems.

Change Process

The lifestyle of the individual serves as a road map that governs his or her journey through life. If a person holds a number of mistaken beliefs about self, others, and the world, then the process of change involves helping that individual to reassess and reorient his or her belief system. The counseling or therapy process emphasizes four elements: (1) relationship and rapport building, (2) information gathering, (3) interpretation and goal setting, and (4) reeducation and reorientation. The counselor or therapist works in an atmosphere of encouragement wherein the client is empowered to use his or her strengths to make new decisions about how to achieve significance.

Interventions

The primary interventions in Adlerian counseling and therapy include lifestyle analysis and encouragement. Lifestyle analysis is the process of discovering the goals and motivation of the client. Because lifestyle contains the person's beliefs and perceptual schema about self, others, and the world, the aim of lifestyle analysis is to help the client identify elements that are working well and those that are not. Encouragement is viewed as the universal therapeutic intervention designed to assist the client in developing the courage to face life's problems. Adlerians may use a variety of additional techniques and methods as long as they are philosophically consistent with the basic theoretical premises of the approach.

Limitations

Many of the beliefs in Adlerian theory tend to run counter to the prevailing general thinking in the culture regarding human behavior and relationships. Adlerian theory is neither analytic, dynamic, or behavioral/scientific. It is a cognitive, goal-directed social psychology. It is a simplistic and commonsense approach. Nonetheless, a growing body of research seems to indicate that Adlerian theoretical concepts are consistent with contemporary scientific psychology. Studies of outcome effectiveness with this approach will help to expand the acceptance of the ideas of Adler and Dreikurs. Adlerian theory continues to be ahead of its time.

THE CASE OF JONATHAN: *An Adlerian Approach*

There are probably as many different styles of counseling or therapy as there are individual Adlerians; however, certain principles will always be in evidence. As mentioned in the introduction to this chapter, three basic principles will be present: purposiveness, social interest, and holism. These principles will be explored using the four elements of the counseling or therapy process: relationship and rapport building, information gathering, interpretation and goal setting, and reeducation and reorientation.

Relationship and Rapport

It is essential that the counselor or therapist develop rapport with Jonathan and take the time, both initially and throughout counseling or therapy, to understand the world as Jonathan sees it.

Information Gathering

Although it is essential to build rapport and create a therapeutic relationship through the use of listening and reflecting skills, during the information-gathering phase the counselor or therapist must ask the client questions that generate meaningful responses. Most Adlerian counselors or therapists are quite active directing the counseling or therapy process; however, the content of the process and the client's story are left to the client. During this phase, the counselor or therapist is seeking to gain a picture of Jonathan's worldview and will direct the process of discovering how Jonathan sees himself, how he believes others should treat him, and how he views his place in the world. The nature of the questions asked would be open-ended to seek expanded information rather than being closed-ended, which would lead to only a 'yes' or a 'no' response. The counselor or therapist would probably begin by exploring Jonathan's family constellation and birth order. A sample question might be as follows: "Tell me about your childhood. What was it like growing up in your family? Did you have brothers and sisters and what was you relationship to each of them?"

Jonathan is the youngest of six children. It would help to know how he dealt with being the youngest, and this could be found out by exploring in more detail the family of origin in regard to relationships among the siblings, the family atmosphere, and Jonathan's early recollections. His self-statement regarding his referral problem had to do with getting along with others, so it may be that he was a youngest child who developed a sense of entitlement. He may have developed a life position where he expects others to do for him and treat him as someone who is special. As a result, he may have developed a discouraged lifestyle and ended up feeling that he was not as competent as others, that he could only do things if others were very supportive. Although complete information is not available, this conclusion is consistent with other elements of the story Jonathan presented.

The dream represents a similar situation. Jonathan is on a long bus, being carried along by someone else. A passive approach to life is involved. Everyone on the bus (everyone in the world in his way of thinking perhaps) is heading for a place of promise: New York, California.

He's going to Albuquerque. In the cultural context of a Native American, the driver is an image of the trickster, a part of life that is represented frequently by the coyote or by the raven among some peoples. This bus driver has led Jonathan on a journey seeking big adventure and payoff. But as is always true of life, there is no payoff when one lets someone else drive the bus, only irritation and argument when the vehicle of life does not take the individual where he or she wants to go. Jonathan's response is the typical spoiled child's response to try to use force to keep the bus driver from laughing at him. Notice that he does not seem to be concerned any longer about where his journey is taking him, only that he is being laughed at. The trickster, by leading him on with promises of the big city, has left him alone, lonely, and now unable to sleep. The trickster tries to teach a lesson. What might the lesson be for him?

Interpretation and Goal Setting

Jonathan believes that others seem to expect more than he can deliver, a sad commentary as far as his own feelings of self-efficacy are concerned. He feels inferior to others and seems to see them as being critical. He reports that his work is never good enough and that others are always on his back. His boss is a perfectionist. These are all symptoms of the discouragement. His marriages have gone the same way, and he has the same complaint. He reports that things went well during the first few years of marriage, but he feels that no matter what he tried to do to make the relationship work, it was never good enough. The question becomes good enough for whom? More than likely the answer is for him. He struggles with his own uncertainty.

Guilt seems to be one theme that runs through this man's journey. Jonathan seems to use guilt to make himself feel better. Although it appears that outwardly he is "suffering" from guilt, in fact, his guilt does not lead to constructive action but only passive acceptance of his ruined life. He complains that he feels guilty for being an absent father and yet he has moved away. To feel guilty that one is not living by one's children does not change the behavior. It does serve the purpose of making one feel better, however. He can say to himself, "At least I feel badly about not being with my children. Look how I suffer from my guilt."

Guilt is an artificial way of making himself feel better, to feel more noble than his actions would indicate he might be. This represents a neurotic solution to the life task of intimacy or sex. Rather than actually remaining in a marriage that may be difficult, remaining close to his children so that he can see them grow and participate in their lives, he moves away. By creating guilt in himself, he makes it seem like he is suffering because it is impossible to be with them. In reality, he left his wife and children, moved to a big city for the "professional or financial opportunities necessary." One must ask necessary for what? If he wants to be a father to his children, he needs to be near them, not hundreds of miles away. There are similar jobs on the reservation. He also has his parents who are dying. More than likely he feels put upon by these demands, demands that he resents, having been the youngest in the family with older siblings and parents who took care of all his needs. He feels entitled to a better life, to someone who will comfort him like the "other women" he runs to when the challenge of marriage becomes more than he feels capable of handling.

Resolving his guilt over his brother's death is an issue that needs to be dealt with as a trauma. Exploration of the event and the responses of those who were close to him and to that event and to him after that event may help clarify the meanings that he attributed to this life experience. Adler was fond of paraphrasing Epictetus by saying that what happens to us is not as important as what we make of what happens to us. Exploring what did happen, remembering his thoughts and feelings about the event, is an important way of approaching the issue of what sense he made of this accident. An extremely important part of this is how he remembers his parents and siblings reacting to the event. How did those he loved and whose judgment he valued react? How did this change his opinions of himself, others, or life? Most important, how did this affect his sense of belonging?

Jonathan's drinking is a problem for him, as is his seeking comfort of other women. These issues may be exacerbated by Jonathan's pride in being a Native American and acceptance of the cultural and tribal values that he said were so important for him when he was growing up. In addition, many tribal groups do not approve of the use of alcohol by their members. Attendance at Alcoholics Anonymous may be an important part of his treatment.

Evans (Evans, 1997b) suggests that counselors or therapists work with the client to identify a starting point by asking what the client would like to get better at or improve on. At a minimum, the counselor or therapist can ask about life tasks and have the client rate himself or herself on a scale of 1 to 10 as to feelings about how well he or she is accomplishing each of these.

Work	1 — 2 — 3 — 4 — 5 — 6 — 7 — 8 — 9 — 10
Love and marriage	1 — 2 — 3 — 4 — 5 — 6 — 7 — 8 — 9 — 10
Friendships (male)	1 — 2 — 3 — 4 — 5 — 6 — 7 — 8 — 9 — 10
Friendships (female)	1 — 2 — 3 — 4 — 5 — 6 — 7 — 8 — 9 — 10

Other areas might include the following:

Leisure	1 — 2 — 3 — 4 — 5 — 6 — 7 — 8 — 9 — 10
Finances	1 — 2 — 3 — 4 — 5 — 6 — 7 — 8 — 9 — 10
Parenting	1 — 2 — 3 — 4 — 5 — 6 — 7 — 8 — 9 — 10
Getting along with self	1 — 2 — 3 — 4 — 5 — 6 — 7 — 8 — 9 — 10
Finding a meaning in life	1 — 2 — 3 — 4 — 5 — 6 — 7 — 8 — 9 — 10

Relationships with

Spouse	1 — 2 — 3 — 4 — 5 — 6 — 7 — 8 — 9 — 10
Children	1 — 2 — 3 — 4 — 5 — 6 — 7 — 8 — 9 — 10
Boss	1 — 2 — 3 — 4 — 5 — 6 — 7 — 8 — 9 — 10
Coworkers	1 — 2 — 3 — 4 — 5 — 6 — 7 — 8 — 9 — 10

When the ratings are complete, the counselor or therapist might ask the client which of these he or she is most satisfied with and which he or she might want to work on for improvement. After the client selects an area, then the development of a goal can proceed. For example, if the client selects an area which was rated as a 6, the counselor or therapist might ask what it would take to move that to a 7 or 8.

Reeducation and Reorientation

Therapy or counseling with Jonathan will involve a lot of confrontation, not just passive listening, within a relationship that is based on mutual respect. The Adlerian counselor or therapist will actively attempt to hold up a mirror to Jonathan so that he can see himself, his behavior, and his strengths. Recognizing who he is and what decisions he actually has power over will be an important part of counseling or therapy. "Spitting in the soup" of his guilt and other feelings that he uses to enable him to escape responsibility will allow him to rely on his own sense of strength and empower him to make different decisions. To him, many of his current problems (e.g., loneliness, being away from his children) are the result of his attempt to solve his problems. A person's problems are the solutions attempted in the past that failed; the failed solutions involve behaviors that the person continues in a way that adds to the problems. Jonathan needs to be aware of the decisions and choices he has made; then he can be empowered to make different choices. Encouragement will be important with Jonathan, as he seems to be convinced that he has no power. Holding up the mirror of his life will help him see that he had power but that it was misdirected. Mistakes can be corrected and new directions can be chosen.

CHAPTER 7

Existential Theory

Mary Lou Bryant Frank
Kennesaw State University

Psychological theories are an intimate reflection of the values and biases of the real people creating the theories, and existential theory is no exception. A behavioral approach reflects a theorist to whom science and logic are the organizing factors for existence. An existentialist is a theorist to whom science is complementary to **meaning**, for whom relationships are as important as the scientific advancement of a theory, for whom the subjective individual experience is as important as the objective, factual report, and for whom the theorist is as much involved in the **process** as in the product (May, 1983; Gazzola, Iwakabe, & Stalikas, 2003). For an existentialist, the journey is as important as the destination (Bugental, 1978; Maddi, 2004), and the existential journey is not superficial (Wilber, 2004; Yalom, 1980):

> To explore deeply from an existential perspective does not mean that one explores the past; rather it means that one brushes away everyday concerns and thinks deeply about one's existential situation. It means to think outside of time, to think about the relationship between one's feet and the ground beneath one, between one's consciousness and the space around one; it means to think not about the way one came to be the way one is, but that one is. . . . The future-becoming-present is the primary tense of existential therapy. (Yalom, 1980, p. 11)

Unlike traditional psychoanalytic and psychodynamic counselors and therapists, existentialists are not deficiency focused. As reflected in Seligman's theory of positive psychology (M. Seligman, 2004), existentialist thought is focused on potentialities. Existentialists want to aid individuals in developing schemas to understand and cope with their lives. Szasz (2005) contends that it is the existential belief in the inherent worth and capability of individuals that uniquely leaves harsh diagnostic lables for deficiency-based therapies. Likewise, existentialists represent a diverse population. In as many ways that meaning can be gleaned from life, there are avenues to describe the process of finding meaning. Just as some existentialists are more psychodynamic in their orientation (Maunder & Hunter, 2004; Yalom, 2005), others are more humanistic (Bugental, 1978; Colaizzi, 2002; Maslow, 1968). Another circle of existentialists seems to be a part of the newest wave in psychology—**transpersonal theory** (Wilber, 1997, 2004), whereas other approaches address existential issues through **spirituality** (Epple, 2003; Gibbs, 2005; Hinterkopf, 1998; D. Miller, 1997).

For some individuals, meaning emerges from the struggle with life and death, destiny and freedom, isolation and connection. Anticipated by **Maslow** (1971), transpersonal psychology and the religiously based counseling approaches offer a haven for those individuals who find meaning in the spiritual realm. The existential philosophers **Buber** (1970) and **Tillich** (1987), as well as the psychological theorists Maslow (1968) and Wilber (2000), were explicit that from an existential quest a spiritual awakening could unfold. For some people, hope emerges from despair. Not all existentialists, however, find meaning through spirituality. Some find that the quest for meaning is always filled with the anxiety of ultimate death (Maunder & Hunter, 2004; Yalom, 1980, 1999). Nevertheless, transpersonal psychology and the approaches emphasizing spirituality are frameworks for examining the process of spiritual development that may surface after scratching the existential veneer.

The purpose of this chapter is to outline the background of **existentialism**, explore the developmental nature of the quest for meaning, examine the major constructs of existential thought, describe applications of the theory, summarize the evaluation of the theory, and explore the theory's limitations. The theory is summarized by an applied case analysis. In the process of understanding a theory about existence, it is my hope that the you will gain a deeper sense of self, an appreciation for what it means to be alive, and a heightened respect for the human struggle of which we are all apart.

BACKGROUND

Arising from the philosophic roots of **Kierkegaard, Nietzsche, Camus,** and **Sartre,** existentialism gained an audience in the post-World War II European community where it found form and voice. Emerging from the atrocities of war, vanquished idealism, and fragmented family life, the philosophers of this period developed a perspective that reflected the realities of their harsh existence. In the midst of the destruction, people reverberated to the philosophical writings of Nietzsche (1889) almost 50 years earlier: God must also be dead. People saw death as the core event permeating their existence. These experiences with mortality reflected a new perspective that, although not always optimistic, was full of realism.

Kierkegaard was a primary influence on other existentialists such as **Heidegger,** Buber, and Nietzsche. Kierkegaard (1944) pursued scientific truth from the landscape of the human perspective. The great problems of humanity were not a result of lack of knowledge or technology, he believed, but lack of passion, love, and commitment (May, 1983; R. Miller, 2004). Kierkegaard was convinced that the goal of pure objectivity was not only unattainable but also undesirable and immoral. These beliefs foreshadowed findings in physics (Bohm, 1973; Evans, 1996; D. Miller, 1997; Ord, 2005; Tart, 2005) and gender studies (Broussard, 2005; Goldberg; 2005; Kalpana, 2005), and they also were reflected in the antireductionistic concept of consilience proposed by biologist E. O. Wilson (1998). Kierkegaard had the revelation that unless science is examined in a relational context, truth is not possible (Bretall, 1951). Objective, detached understanding is an illusion; a subject can never be truly separated from the process of being observed and the context of that observation. It is no small wonder that Kierkegaard was not favored among the more objective, cognitive, and behavioral theorists who were influenced by Descartes.

According to Descartes, an objective, rational examination was crucial to the development of empirical science. Consistent with this viewpoint was the prevailing thought of Copernicus who provided the scientific model of a detached observer that is embodied in current scientific research methodology. From Descartes emerged a mechanistic theory of mind and body only causally interacting. In the midst of a Cartesian mind-set, Heidegger (1949) developed an alternate paradigm. Building on Kierkegaard, Heidegger continued to develop existential thought. Heidegger's concept was antimechanistic and antitheoretic in a Cartesian sense. To Heidegger (1962), theories and humans were imperfect, and an objective reality was not reality at all. Existence is only understood in terms of being in the world through subjective participation. Heidegger noted that in striving for exactness, the Cartesian system was missing reality.

Heidegger's (Cohn, 2002) notions of choice also influenced the existential psychologists. Heidegger reasoned that each choice an individual makes represents the loss of an alternative. The past becomes important in terms of lost opportunities. Future choices are limited because of past choices and the time remaining to fulfill them. People have the freedom to choose but must balance this with responsibility for choices. By encountering these limitations, persons may experience **nothingness, guilt,** and **anxiety**. These core concerns reverberated among authors around the world. The field of literature was ripe for existential development (e.g., Dostoyevsky, Tolstoy, Kafka, Sartre, Camus, Hemingway, Eliot, Fitzgerald, Stein, Ellison, Faulkner, Wolfe, Pound, Blake, Angelou, Kidd, Martel, Hosseni, Rand, Doctorow, Walker, and Frost). Both in the United States and Europe, the best literary minds echoed existential rumblings.

North American psychologists initially reflected the focus on universal concerns through **humanism**. The **third force** arose as an answer to the limitations of the Freudian and behaviorist approaches. The positive aspects of humanness (e.g., love, freedom with responsibility, self-actualization, potential, transcendence, uniqueness, choice, creativity) were missing from Freudian and behavioral theories. The development of the Association for Humanistic Psychology spawned a positive arena for collaboration. The humanistic element focused on human capacities and potentialities (Kernes & Kinnier, 2005). As part of a natural evolution from humanistic to existential, many humanistic theorists (e.g., Maslow, Bugental, Frankl, and May) moved into an existential position. Although humanism was the initial paradigm, existentialism built on the respect for the individual and added the dimensions of **ontology**, experiential awareness, and responsibility.

The many works of **May** (1953, 1969, 1979, 1983, 1992) are noteworthy because of May's major contributions to the emergence of existential counseling or psychotherapy from the humanistic perspective. The subtle differences between humanism and existentialism are evident in his description of the goal of counseling or psychotherapy (May, 1961):

> In my judgment, the existential approach is the achieving of individuality (including subjective individuality) not by passing or avoiding the conflictual realities of the world in which we immediately find ourselves—for us the Western world—but by confronting these concerns directly and through the meeting of them, achieving one's individuality. (p. 51)

Through his honest, direct confrontation with anxiety, will, freedom, meaning, and myth, May forged the basis of the development of existential counseling and therapy in the 20th century.

Existentialism also has roots in contemporary religious thought. Religion's differing perspectives kindle a conflict. The disagreement is one between essence (representing the scientific, objectivity, and facts) and existence (representing what is real for each individual). In Western culture, essence has triumphed over existence (May, 1983). However, this battle takes place on holy ground, as indicated by Tillich:

> The story of Genesis, chapters 1–3, if taken as myth, can guide our description of the transition from essential to existential being. It is the profoundest and richest expression of man's awareness of his existential estrangement and provides the scheme in which the transition from essence to existence can be treated. (1987, p. 190)

The quest for knowledge and understanding is what eventually separates humanity from the safety of objectivity. Islam (Gibbs, 2005) is equally affected by the struggle to understand **angst** and must make peace with the existential questions if it is to flourish. Descartes may have won the battle, but Tillich would contend that the war is not resolved.

Existential questions themselves have a religious flavor. Some existentialists have said that religion is a superficial defense against the ultimate reality of death (Yalom, 1980), because it has nothing to do with the worldly questions of **meaninglessness**, anxiety, and existence (Tillich, 1987). However, the dichotomy may be more one of semantics than substance. As Tillich (1987) wrote:

> Whenever existentialists give answers, they do so in terms of religious or quasi-religious traditions which are not derived from their existential analysis, [but] from hidden religious sources. They are matters of ultimate concern or faith, although garbed in a secular gown. Existentialism is an analysis of the human predicament. And the answers to the questions implied in man's predicament are religious, whether open or hidden. (pp. 187–188)

Tillich contended that the existential dilemmas are religious questions in secular terms. Buber (1970) similarly emphasized the religious lineage within existential ancestry through the reverence implicit in some relationships. When "a man addresses with his whole being the You of his life that cannot be restricted by any other, he addresses God" (p. 124). When an individual no longer relates to another as an object, as an extension of himself or herself, or as a means to an end, he or she enters a relationship expressed by "I to Thou" (p. 124). The essence of the ideal existential encounter embodies respect, honor, and divinity.

The religiosity that develops from the existential quest is developmental. From an individual's struggle with consciousness and responsibility, and from unconscious existential choices, a third stage of development emerges as a "**spiritual unconscious**" (Frankl, 1975). In an interview, Frankl and Skully (1995) discussed that although *logotherapy* (the first form of existential psychotherapy) was imbued with "spirit," Frankl was called to heal but not save the individual soul. Unconscious religiosity is intrinsic to our ability to transcend our situation and transform our perspective and emotional reaction. Whether the spiritual dimension is labeled, inherently perceived, or ignored, it is a component of existential development.

Beginning from a philosophical approach to the world, existentialism has evolved to an approach that helps people cope with the uncertainty and complex pressures of their lives. Recognizing the individual nature of experience in the context of an objective, scientifically oriented society, existential counselors and therapists validate the anxiety people experience. The importance of choice and responsibility in coping with these pressures has led existentialists today to honor the individual's experience and realize the religiosity embedded in existential questions. Central to the development of this approach and to working through the existential concerns is the importance of connecting with others. Following the path of early existential theorists, existentialism is grounded in realism—attempting to acknowledge the authentic human experience, the importance of meaning, and the reality of change.

HUMAN NATURE: A DEVELOPMENTAL PERSPECTIVE

The universality of existential concerns is evident in children as well as adults. May (1992) was the first to propose an existential developmental model that moved from a naive stage of innocence, to adolescent rebellion and struggle, to embracing conventional tradition, and finally to developing beyond the ego and self-actualizing. Neither discrete nor linear, these "stages" are evident in many of May's myths (1992); for instance, May used them to exemplify the stages of female development through myths such as the one titled "Briar Rose" (p. 194). In defining strategies for helping troubled adolescents, Hanna, Hanna, and Keys (1999) perceived existential approaches as valuable in establishing and maintaining the therapeutic relationship as well as in addressing issues of freedom and responsibility. Kerr, Cohn, Webb, and Anderson (2001) validated these stages in their exploration of the reasons why boys do not achieve their potential and often become depressed. Maunder and Hunter (2004) indicated that it is in initial attachments that persons develop understanding of themselves and reality. Existential counseling was also the focus of Rusca (2003) in a study of adolescant females with anorexia and Fisher (2005) who studied adult survivors of sexual abuse. In both situations, presence, authenticity, awareness, and responsibilty were vital elements in the healing process. These elements are also essentials of existential counseling. In all instances, the authors cited suggested that it is important to find meaning, especially at critical points in our lives. Although existentialism does not have discrete stages, finding meaning has developmental implications.

A Focus on Potentials

Addressing core existential concerns helps to promote health and further development. Not addressing these core concerns causes individuals to become "stuck" and develop mental health problems. Existential counseling focuses on the possibilities that are available and presses the client and counselor or therapist to become more alive, aware, and sensitive while coming to terms with the realities of mortality and aloneness (Bauman & Waldo, 1998; Imes, Rose Clance, Gailis, & Atkeson, 2002). Roysircar (2004) and Yalom (1980) examined the development of existential concerns with death. The anxiety produced by awareness of nonexistence is overwhelming, even to a young child. Most children cope with death by denying it. Parents and other adults foster this denial in the first phase of life by avoidance and hesitant confrontation.

By the time of adolescence, however, denial becomes ineffective. Initiation into adulthood reintroduces the reality of death and isolation and necessitates a search for new meaning. Adults find that aging offers the ultimate loss. As individuals age, the reality of death has an increased complexity and is in danger of being minimized by health care professionals (Maunder & Hunter, 2004). Through each developmental stage, it is easy to encounter denial and avoidance of death. Rather than avoiding the realities of mortality, existentialists see death and aging as the ultimate opportunity to grow. Dass (2000) found that the loss of ability he experienced after a stroke and coming to terms with his own aging provided him with an increased awareness and appreciation of life:

> This culture sees life as collecting experiences. But, aging is an emptying out and beginning to experience the moment, what's happening right now. In our culture, we value old people who act young. We don't value old people for acting old, for their wisdom. For them to hear their own wisdom, they have to experience their own silence. That's one of the ways the stroke was a blessing—it increased my silence. (p. 12)

By facing our mortality in the various stages of our existence, we can more fully live.

Despite contemporary focus on superficial, commercial fulfillment, many people still search for existential meaning as they reach critical developmental stages. In studying older adults, Kraus and Shaw (2000) discovered that perceived control over the most important life role was the main factor reducing the odds of death. Moreman (2005) found that existential angst is a normal part of aging and that finding personal meaning is also important. Stressful health problems were the focus of a study by Lantz and Gregoire (2003); they found that existential psychotherapy was beneficial to individuals who had a heart attack and their partners. Likewise (Kissane, et al., 2004) reported that a group of patients with cancer who were ambivalent about their cancer therapies became more compliant and developed a more positive attitude after existential counseling. Furthermore, low-income women with HIV (Mayers, Naples, & Nilsen, 2005) were more likely to have positive outcomes if they found meaning in their stressful situation.

In a survey of mental health workers in Hong Kong (Yiu-kee & Tang, 1995), existential variables (e.g., death, freedom, responsibility, anxiety, isolation, meaninglessness) were found to be correlates of burnout, emotional exhaustion, and depersonalization. A review of implications of treating dying patients (Kaut, 2002) indicated that it was important for all health care workers to be aware of and open to the patient's existential and spiritual issues. Without this sensitivity, the dying person will have greater emotional, psychological, and physical distress. For individual development to be complete, there must be a sense that we have found meaning and, consequently, peace in our lives.

Gaining understanding about the meaning of life and taking responsibility for one's life serve to influence and inspire development. The process of development, whether spiritual or secular, is characterized by anxiety, for which death is the primary cause (Cappeliez & O'Rourke, 2002; Deurzen-Smith, 1991; Lantz & Gregoire, 2003; O'Connor, 2004). Existential concerns permeate human existence.

Hillman (1996) stated that it is denial and fear of death that lead to theories that focus on development, parents, social conditions, genetic predispositions, and other concerns arising out of human perceptions. As Krueger and Hanna (1997) wrote, "Death has a paradoxical quality in that the fear of it is paralyzing to the individual who avoids it, while at the same time acceptance of its inevitability can free the individual from the trivial life that results from that avoidance" (p. 197). Whether individuals transcend (Längle, 2004), develop heightened awareness (Miars, 2002), or are shaken by the struggle (May, 1983), they are forever changed by their confrontation with or their denial of death.

A Worldview

Unique among theorists, existentialists have conceptualized their philosophy in context. They suggest that all theories have usefulness, but they are useful depending on the individuals and the issues. As indicated by Bugental (1996), in a discipline that is at odds with itself, it is unique in being able to identify the usefulness of other approaches.

Professional theorists seldom see value in approaches that do not fit personal or prevailing preferences. Bugental (1978) was the first to see theories in perspective. According to Bugental, there are six levels of helping goals, extending from behavioral change to spiritual development. Corresponding to the six goals are six different types of helping, from behavioral to transpersonal.

Others have also seen the value of a broader perspective. Vontress, Johnson, and Epp (1999) indicated that existential counselors or therapists need to be flexible, integrating other counseling approaches as appropriate for a given client. Wilber (1997) and Davis (2003) also offered broader viewpoints by incorporating other theoretical orientations into a developmental schema. Wilber's theoretical model is transpersonal and more reflective of Eastern religion than Tillich's (1987) focus on the Western perspective. Wilber (1997) views an individual's pathology as a matter of degree, beginning with psychotic symptoms and advancing to spiritual struggles. Like Bugental, Wilber sees each theory as subtly answering the questions raised at various levels of dysfunction. Physiological and biochemical interventions (psychiatry) are more effective for psychotic symptoms. Psychodynamic and existential therapies are the bridge to transpersonal techniques. Each theory makes a contribution, but none has the answer for all people or all issues. Besides viewing itself in the context of other counseling or psychotherapy theories, existential theory also perceives the individual in an ever-changing environment. Within a family, a gender, a language, a culture, a time period, and a system, individuals struggle to find identity and meaning.

Existentialism strives to help honor the pain that occurs at many levels of experience. As described by Van Kaam (1966), "Existential psychology sees man as living in a human world; therefore when my counselee enters my room, he is not alone, but rather brings with him a whole world . . . nothing exists for any human being that does not have a certain meaning for him" (p. 61). Unique among theories (Buxton, 2005), existentialism directly addresses the contextual elements that shape the individual's reality.

MAJOR CONSTRUCTS

Approaches to Existentialism

Existentialism embodies differing perspectives and approaches. Three forces can be found within the existential perspective: **dynamic existentialism, humanistic existentialism,** and **transpersonal existentialism.** Common to all approaches is the nature and quality of the existential relationship. However, dynamic existentialists (Maunder & Hunter, 2004; Yalom, 1980), like their Freudian predecessors, focus attention on the resolution of inner conflict and anxiety. Humanistic existentialists emphasize unconditional acceptance, awareness of personal experience, and authenticity. In the transpersonal existential approach, death is perceived as an opportunity for the individual to rise above the given circumstances; the approach is grounded in a belief that humans are spiritual beings. According to this approach, most people experience tragedy, but in equal proportion, they experience joy (Maslow, 1968). Health is the ability to transcend the environment, drawing from the joyful aspects of existence.

Death

Death is the ultimate truth. Both in myth and in reality, it is ever present. In *The Cry for Myth,* May said that "we are able to love passionately because we die" (1992, p. 294). How people accept this mortal condition—or find ways to ignore it—determines psychological well-being. Death is encountered in all counseling or psychotherapeutic experiences. Concerns such as grief need to be addressed, but most existential healing also involves letting go of the unhealthy or dysfunctional parts of self, relationships, or ideals.

Well-being involves becoming more honest and authentic. In working through resistance to authenticity, clients watch as parts of themselves die. Suicidal and homicidal feelings are common during this period. Drawing from Horney's notion of idealized and despised images of self, Bugental (1978) asserted that both images are false and must die for the real person to emerge: "But there is a fearful wrenching involved in that relinquishment. The nakedness seems, and indeed is, so terribly vulnerable and so truly mortal. Usually the 'killing' of the old self occurs in some kind of break out experience" (p. 79). **Death anxiety** can cause people to connect as well as cause feelings of isolation and despair (Beshai & Naboulsi, 2004). Wisman and Koole (2003) showed that individuals with different world views connect with each other when faced with impending death. Rodriguez (2004) reported how death anxiety can actually signal a creative period in life. A confrontation with death signals the rebirth of a more aware and more authentic being.

Freedom

Freedom comes after our confrontation with our inaccurate representation of ourselves. It emerges only after we realize that the world is an arbitrary construction of our awareness. Hence, we can make each moment the way we wish and make our future different from any moments in our past. Although we can choose each thought we have, there are costs and benefits for each decision. Several studies (Blinderman & Cherny, 2005; Mayers et al., 2005) linked the type of concentration camp struggle described by Frankl (1984), where he outlined his existential approach called **logotherapy,** and the situation facing individuals who have AIDS and cancer. In both cases, people have the freedom to choose their reaction to these deplorable situations. Survivors of victimization have the power to choose their reaction to the injustice, just as those individuals hurt by society, others, or themselves can regain their dignity by honoring their pain and choosing not to be dominated by it (Kaut, 2002). Maddi (2004) proposed that a person's choice for his or her future requires courage built on commitment, control, and challenge. Courage to be and to do is existential. The emotional readiness to make decisions and the choice of reactions to them are keys to the meaning gleaned from the encounter. Freedom is silhouetted by responsibility.

Isolation

Isolation is a separation from oneself as much as from others. The isolation from our true self keeps us from connecting and contributing to the larger social order in more productive ways. People are isolated and defended by their own false identities. Out of their fears, people erect walls to prohibit the connections they most desire. As Bugental (1978) stated, "When I begin to realize that my truest identity is as process and not as fixed substance, I am on the verge of a terrible emptiness and a miraculous freedom" (p. 133). The therapeutic encounter provides individudals a dress rehearsal (Yalom, 2002) for life, with the potential pitfalls, conflicts, and losses that can occur. Although individuals are ultimately alone, they have the potential to connect and share meaning in life.

Culture

Sartre defined culture as the "objective mind" (Cannon, 1991). It is the context of the world that concurrently shapes individuals as they construct it. Existential counseling or psychotherapy, by definition, addresses the cultural, contextual dynamics of counseling or psychotherapy. Solomon, Greenberg, and Pyszczynski (1991) indicated that a person's culture gives his or her world meaning and protects him or her from anxiety regarding death. Montuori and Fahim (2004) found that culture in the United States is overshadowed by the precepts of individualism. However, through open, authentic encounters, people can develop cultural understanding. Rosenblatt, Greenberg, Solomon, Pyszczynski, & Lyon (1989) showed that when individuals are asked to think about death or are faced with death anxiety, they tend to adhere more to their cultural values and biases. Likewise, race (Meissner, Brigham, & Butz, 2005) appears to affect people's phenominological perceptions of themselves and others. Culture can become a means of escape when an individual is faced with fear of demise.

Other existentialists believe that connecting with others individually and within their culture helps individuals to heal from their isolation (Maslow, 1954). Buxton (2005) described existential counseling or psychotherapy as uniquely able to address the cultural dynamics in relationships. However, the more we force a connection, the further we are pushed apart. The more we struggle to understand our feelings, the more they elude our realization. When we begin acknowledging and accepting who we are in our cultural context, we can start to connect with others and then, again, with ourselves.

Meaninglessness and Meaningfulness

Out of the will to love and live, people arrive at meaning in their lives (May, 1969). In gaining a deeper awareness of themselves, people also gain a deeper sense of others. Efforts to gain understanding involve confronting aspects of ourselves before we develop the heightened sense of the world that gives our lives meaning. Yalom (1980) and Bugental (1978) described the despair of the reality of meaninglessness in the world. Ventegodt, Kandel, Neikrug, and Merrick (2005) indicated that working through this despair can have positive results. "Existential pain is really a message to us indicating that we are about to grow and heal. . . . Existential problems are gifts that are painful to receive but wise to accept" (p. 300).

Blinderman and Cherny (2005) agreed that addressing existential issues and finding meaning does not result in more suffering. Likewise, Mascaro and Rosen (2005) indicated that hope emerges when existential meaning is addressed. People transcend—that is, find meaning in their world—by being fully aware of themselves. Truly being oneself involves being more integrated within and without. Paradoxically, as people become more open to their true feelings, they are better able to join with others and be one with the world. The person is more able to love. Through transcendence, the person also becomes more capable. When people are most truly themselves, they are also more creative, aware, and productive. Life is not as painful a struggle. People are more aware of the potentialities in their lives and within themselves. Meaning is implicit in discovering ourselves and in our awareness of others.

Authenticity and Vulnerability: Two Sides of the Existential Self

Becoming a more authentic person means that an individual lives intentionally (Utne, 2004), with compassion (R. Miller, 2004) and awareness (Miars, 2002). Existential authenticity is the context for freedom and responsibility. The authentic individual is not needy in relationships but is able to benefit from them. Likewise, existential counselors respect the challenge of being **authentic** and **vulnerable** and honor the person's power to change. Miars (2002) indicated that it is imperative that the counselor or therapist be emotionally authentic to facilitate the emergence of authenticity in the client. People need to feel safe to be real. Ultimately, the courage to "be" human and authentic rests with both the counselor and the person being counseled. Both can benefit from the encounter.

Existential Relationships

Outcome research indicates that the helping relationship is the most important aspect of the counseling or psychotherapy process (R. Miller, 2004). Across all of the applications of existential thought, the form and quality of the relationship are consistent. Yalom (Jacobsen, 2003) indicated that the role of the counselor is to "put yourself into the skin and the experience of the other person . . . and to embrace a relationship while you have it" (pp. 350–351). The relationship is professional, but the client and counselor are but two travelers in life, with the counselor having skills in empathy as well as knowledge of the journey. Although skilled, the counselor or therapist is present with the client in a very real and immediate existence. But the therapeutic relationship describes only the functions not the substance of the encounter.

The diversity and substance of relationships were probably best described by Buber (1970). According to Buber, relationships may be experienced at several levels or at a combination of different levels. Some individuals relate to the world and to others as "I to I." People speak at or about others but seldom to them. These individuals take and never give. "I to it" relationships depict an individual relating to another as an object. Another level of relationship is among people who relate to others and the world as "it to it." For these individuals, "I" has little meaning, for they do not have much sense of self. The next relationship level is called "we to we." In this relationship, no one has any individuality or objectivity. "Us to them" describes a relationship between the chosen few and the damned. All the good attributes are wrapped up in "us"; all the negative ones are represented by "them." The "I to you" relationship implies treating the other individual as a person. The encounter involves two, rather than one to an object or one to a despised part.

The profound meeting, the core of the existential connection, is the "I to Thou" relationship. This relationship involves an encounter with God and a deeper respect for the individual. The notion of transcendence is a part of the connection at this level. The most potent form of help involves being present in a respectful, honoring encounter (Dass & Gorman, 1985).

In the final analysis, "I to Thou" relationships provide hope for genuine understanding. In the "I to Thou" relationship, the counselor or therapist is merely a guide on a voyage (Bugental, 1978). The counselor or therapist who offers respect to the client is a traveler on the same road. At the "I to Thou" level, the whole person is considered and honored. Yalom (2002) validated the importance of relational process as the central element of therapy. The counseling or psychotherapeutic relationship may reflect several levels of encounter at a given time for the client and the counselor or therapist. Whatever the level, both counselor and therapist are affected by the relationship.

Hazards on the Journey

The journey through the "dark night of the soul" can be difficult for counselors and therapists (Bugental, 1978, p. 77). They must protect themselves, their time, and their private lives. Making several such painful journeys with clients is bound to affect practitioners at a personal level. Kopp wrote:

> Doing counseling is like remembering all the time that you are going to die. Because the counseling hour has a definite beginning and ending, we are kept aware of its being temporary. There is only me, and you, and here, and now. We know in advance that it will not last, and we agree to this." (1972, p. 42)

Being an existential counselor or therapist means being open to continued learning and awareness, because existential helping operates at an intense level of involvement.

May (1979) suggested that there is a potential for losing scientific focus when working with people at an existential level. In rebelling against the rationalistic tradition of contemporary psychology, existential counselors and therapists might be detached from philosophical or technical realities. The trend toward transpersonal theory and spirituality underscores the danger. Spiritually focused therapies (Richards & Bergin, 2002) are nonnaturalistic; that is, they want to base their interventions and approaches on scripture and they are not solely grounded in science. If the existential counselor or therapist ignores the need to delineate therapeutic interventions, he or she may be professionally vulnerable.

Despite the concerns and warnings, there is value in taking the risk to truly encounter another person. Existentialism is one alternative and the only viewpoint solidly grounded in theory (May, 1983) and philosophy (Buxton, 2005). Most significant, clients find this approach helpful (Yalom, 1980, 2002).

APPLICATIONS

Overview

Existential counseling and psychotherapy have been applied in diverse settings and among diverse individuals and groups. The field of family counseling (Lantz, 2004) has embraced existentialism as providing a contextual approach based on choice, responsibility, and growth. Group counseling also has been an arena for applications of the existential model. The interpersonal relationships of a group are directly addressed by an existential approach (Maglo, 2002; Yalom, 2005). A group provides a safe environment to address human struggles in the context of others. An existential model has also been applied to the following: children (Floyd, Coulon, Yanez, & Lasota, 2005; Roysircar, 2004); sexual abuse (Feinauer, Middleton, & Hilton, 2003); physical disorders (Goldberg, 2005; Lantz & Gregoire, 2003; Maunder & Hunter, 2004); body image disorders (Broussard, 2005; Kaplana, 2005; Rusca, 2003); AIDS (Mayers, Naples, & Nilsen, 2005); cancer (Blinderman & Cherny, 2005; Kissane, Grabsch, Clarke et al., 2004; Kissane, Grabasch, Love et al., 2004; Morita et al., 2004; Raveis & Pretter, 2005); serious mental disorders (Coker, 2004; Fisher, 2005; Kiser, 2004; Mascaro & Rosen, 2005); culture awareness and issues (Heisel & Flett, 2004; Zhao, 2005); end of life and terminal illness (Albinsson & Strang, 2003; Breitbart, Gibson, Poppito, & Berg, 2004; Kaut, 2002; Imes, Rose Clance, Gailis, Atkeson, 2002; Mak & Elwyn, 2005; O'Connor, 2004); public administration leadership (Purkey & Siegel, 2003; Waugh, 2004); career counseling (Maglio , Butterfield, & Borgen, 2005); and individuals in supervision (Worthen & McNeill, 1996). Although existentialism may not be the primary theory adopted by many counselors and therapists, it does have considerable impact.

Goals of Counseling and Psychotherapy

The existential goals of counseling or psychotherapy and change are "tragically optimistic" (Frankl, 1984, p. 161). Existential counseling or psychotherapy has the following core principles (Frankl, 1984): (1) suffering is a human achievement and accomplishment; (2) guilt provides the opportunity to change oneself for the better; (3) vulnerability motivates a person to become authentic; and (4) life's unpredictability provides an individual incentive to take responsible action. Although steeped in philosophy, these principles hardly provide a working primer for the beginning existential counselor or therapist. Existential change is a process whereby meaning is gleaned from common, worldly endeavors. The goal of counseling or therapy is to be aware of potentials within a realistic backdrop. Clients are transformed through courageous and subtle encounters with aspects of their humanness in the context of a counseling relationship.

Process of Change

Change evolves from a client's willingness to participate in the interpersonal encounter by confronting loneliness, experiencing individuality, encountering true connection, and developing the inner strength to transcend the life situation (May, 1953). Discussing and working through these issues can increase insight, improve relationships, and lead to a more aware sense of being (Yalom, 2005). But the process of change begins much earlier. By reaching out to be with another person authentically, the client has begun the process of transformation. Anxiety loses its power, and clients change as their fears melt into vital energy. Tillich (1980) said that courage to be oneself evolves out of personal anxiety.

The process of existential change involves coming to terms with anxiety through awareness of responsibility and choice. Yalom (1992) wrote: "Don't underestimate the value of friendship, of my knowing I'm capable of touching and being touched. . . . I realize I have a choice. I shall always remain alone, but what a difference, what a wonderful difference, to choose what I do—choose your fate, love your fate" (p. 301). Through increased awareness of self and experience of the world, combined with awareness of choice and responsibility, clients can experience their potential. Instead of a veiled existence, they can live consciously and responsibly; they can connect with others as well as with aspects of themselves. The actual process of change may move rapidly; clients may bloom into creative, energized individuals able to self-actualize. The process may also unfold more gradually. Regardless, the catalyst for change is the relationship facilitating the development of awareness, acceptance, responsibility, vulnerability, and authenticity in the individual.

The change process discussed thus far has been in the context of individual counseling or psychotherapy. But as indicated in a text about group counseling (Yalom, 2005), many people have found the existential model useful for understanding and implementing the group process. The multiple relationships provided by the group can promote a change toward greater awareness and genuineness through an awareness provided by the relationships. The existential treatment perspective, which directly addresses the meaning found in relationships, is a central focus of group development. Waugh (2004) used existentialism to develop a method of studying ethics and management. Individual process and group development have been transfomed by the existential approach.

Traditional Intervention Strategies

Although supported by a fully developed theory and philosophy, existentialism offers no set of techniques (May, 1983). Lantz (2004) explained that most therapies focus on science and research, and counselors, because of their advanced knowledge of best interventions, apply these approaches in the counseling context. However, existential counseling has a different approach; "the process of treatment is an artistic process rather than a process of science" (Lantz, 2004, p. 8).

> The therapist realizes that the current clinical situation has never-ever previously occurred, will never exactly occur again in the future, and that no valid, reliable, and scientific procedure and understanding can be accurately and predictably utilized to create change. (Lantz, 2004, p. 178)

In most theories, understanding follows technique, but the existential counselor or therapist allows the approach to flow from the clients and the theory rather than from a generic intervention. Existential theory is steeped in phenomenological awareness. Therefore, the following intervention strategies flow from a respectful understanding of individual clients.

Telling the Story: Finding the Meaning of Myth. In his last work, May (1992) viewed myths as central to gaining existential meaning: "Each one of us is forced to do deliberately for one-self what in previous ages was done by family, custom, church, and state, namely, form the myths in terms of what we can make some sense of experience" (p. 29). In his book, May discussed the ways in which myths provide insight and meaning. In the counseling or psychotherapy session, stories may be facilitative in helping clients understand events in their lives. Clients also create their story as they detail their past and future.

Binswanger and Boss (1983) articulated the intervention of canvassing a client's experience. The client's history is gathered but is not explained or categorized. Instead, the existential intervention "understands this life history as modifications of the total structure of the patient's being in the world" (p. 284). The practitioner is viewing the client's history through the client's being and awareness rather than focusing on pathological development. As the story unfolds, the client can see the patterns from a larger perspective. "Healing through narration and opening up involve an existential act of self-transcendence of an embodied person who organizes his or her experience in time" (Mishara, 1995, p. 180). Life myths literally order and focus the world, giving life meaning and value.

Sharing Existence in the Moment. The existential relationship is the primary therapeutic intervention, and the client is an existential partner. The client is viewed with compassion not met with pity or sympathy (Dass, 2000; Dass & Bush, 1992; Dass & Gorman, 1985; R. Miller, 2004). The counselor or therapist must be genuinely present on the "sharp edge of existence in the world" (Binswanger & Boss, 1983, p. 285). As Bugental (1978) asserted

> Presence is the quality of being in a situation in which one intends to be as aware and as partici-pative as one is able to be at that time and in those circumstances. Presence is carried into effect through mobilization of one's inner (toward subjective experience) and outer (toward the situation and any other person in it) sensitivities. . . . Presence is being there in the body, in emotions, in relating, in thoughts in every way. (pp. 36–37)

Lantz (2004) used the terms "participatory subjectivity" and "empathic understanding" to capture the connectedness that exists in the therapeutic relationshsip. Emerging from the intervention is a deep sense of relatedness, which Heuscher (1987) and R. Miller (2004) call love. As part of the relatedness, and therapeutically significant, the counselor or therapist must be able to use himself or herself as an indicator of what is occurring within the client. "It is not possible to have a feeling without the other having it to some degree also. . . . The use of one's self as an instrument requires a tremendous self-discipline on the part of the therapist" (May, 1979, p. 122). *Being* implies presence but it also restrains the counselor's or therapist's own distortions, thoughts, and feelings as he or she participates in the client's world.

Centered Awareness of Being. The existential counselor or therapist helps the client become more centered, more aware. The key is becoming consistently aware. "Analysis and confrontation of one's various inauthentic modes . . . particularly extrinsically oriented, non-autonomous, or death denying . . . seems to be the key therapeutic technique on this level" (Wilber, 1986, p. 137). By eliminating the extrinsically focused aspects of themselves, clients become more aware of themselves in the environment. The subjectivity gained in centering (Bugental, 1978) can lead to other levels of understanding or transcendence (Letunovsky, 2004; Maslow, 1968). Only by looking inward does the client develop insight and a keener awareness of being. The most important first step is becoming more conscious of reality and authentically examining the various aspects called *self*.

Self-Responsibility. Taking responsibility for growth is important, but taking responsibility for self-destructive actions is not easy. This intervention involves helping clients take owner-ship of their lives. First, they must be accountable for their choices. Equally important, they must let go of the responsibility that others own in the process of relating (Wilber, 1986; Yalom, 2005). Being responsible acknowledges that obligation can be assumed, shared, and owned by others.

Dream Work. Counselors and therapists working in a variety of approaches have considered dreams as the window to the unconscious. In existential counseling and therapy, dreams have an additional usefulness. The focus is on the client's "dynamic, immediately real and present" (May, 1983, p. 152) existence viewed through the dream rather than the set of dynamic mechanisms at work. "In the dream we see the whole man, the entirety of his problems, in a different existential modality than in waking, but against the background and with the structure of the a priori articulation of existence, and therefore the dream is also of paramount therapeutic importance for the existential analyst" (Binswanger & Boss, 1983, p. 285).

Through dream work, the counselor or therapist is better able to help the client see the pattern of being in the world and know the possibilities of existence through the dream (Binswanger & Boss, 1983). At the end of life (Bulkeley & Bulkley, 2005), dreaming may help resolve existential issues and bring peace. Although unsettling, the existential experience of dreams moves the individual closer to authenticity. Existential dreams "deepen self-perception" (Kuiken, 1995, p. 129). Dreams are like insight. They provide a reflection of inner vision, and the dreamer is compelled to discover their meaning.

Disclosing and Working Through Resistances. Addressing resistances to awareness requires a sensitive intervention, and the counselor or therapist is most effective when addressing issues supportively. This intervention creates both anxiety and joy for the client (May, 1983). Bugental (1978) suggested that counselors and therapists use comments such as "You can feel how much that way of being has cost you all of your life" and "You have wanted so much to be loved that you have often forgotten to take care of your own needs" (p. 90). The client owns the responsibility and the power to address the issues blocking awareness and authenticity. The counselor or therapist serves as the midwife in the birth of a more authentic being.

Body Work. One of the more recent approaches (Letunovsky, 2004) using existential counseling involves the here and now in the physical context. Examples of this approach include painting, working with clay, working with wooden swords, and body awareness exercises. Through the use of different artistic mediums, graphics, and physical movement, existential counselors have helped individuals express immediate, concentrated meaning. In so doing, clients get beyond resistences to authenticity and greater awareness of being.

Confronting Existential Anxiety. Probably the most important intervention is being aware of the client's existential issues. The complex societal and individual reaction to death stirs complex emotions in most individuals (Kubler-Ross, 1975). It takes courage to discuss the forbidden subject of death. As Yalom (1980) said, "If we are to alter therapeutic practice, to harness the clinical leverage that the concept of death provides, it will be necessary to demonstrate the role of death in the genesis of anxiety" (p. 59). Sometimes this may be accomplished by a review of the client's life (Mills & Coleman, 2002). In such interventions, individuals are encouraged to examine and resolve issues by focusing on their life stories. By confronting ultimate losses (e.g., relationships, life, and self) and by being present through the resultant anxiety, counselors and therapists have a powerful tool to help individuals work through fear.

Closure. Facing the end of the helping relationship is the final confrontation with reality. It is expected that additional issues will arise to delay the inevitable ending. The intervention of termination requires continued authenticity and willingness to be present. The counselor or therapist and the client may never meet again. Paralleling every other loss in the lives of both the client and the counselor or therapist, termination represents a real death to both people. It is critical that the practitioner help the client by processing the ending of counseling or therapy, by creating a good parting. The difficulty with this intervention is that it exposes the reality of ending that is present in all relationships.

Brief Intervention Strategies

Most existential counselors and therapists resist the thought of brief therapy because it runs against their very grain. An approach that values deep relationship processing also values a long-term model of working through these issues. However, life is not always long-term process. As such, brief existential approaches actually mirror the intense, transitory existence of life. Several counselors and therapists have struggled to create brief existential counseling. Cooper (2003) compiled a number of the approaches. Although some therapists understand that structuring the existential questions (Strasser & Strasser, 1997) can facilitate a shorter term of therapy, others (Van Deurzen, 2002) believe that issues will only become revealed but may never be completed. Cooper outlined a traditional therapeutic approach that includes assessing, identifying the core problem, teaching individuals how to search for answers, identifying client resistances, addressing the key concern, and terminating.

All counselors and therapists have been forced to realize that focusing on the larger potential of human growth and development will not fit into the world of limited insurance coverage and dwindling resources. Of necessity, existential counselors and therapists are faced with the same struggle. Additionally, brief existential counseling or therapy may even have benefits other approaches lack. In a short-term authentic experience, individuals are necessarily led to address death, anxiety, isolation, and meaning. Brief existential counseling mirrors reality.

CLIENTS WITH SERIOUS MENTAL HEALTH ISSUES

Existential counseling has been used with clients with a wide variety of problems. A mental disorder is always a potential consequence of feeling alone in an isolating culture and context, living without meaning, suffering with loss and death, confronting anxiety, and struggling with responsibility and freedom. Whatever the reason, mental disorders represent the loss of an individual's potential. In the confrontation with life and death, many people develop a desperate sense of isolation (Albinsson & Strang, 2003; Feinauer, Middleton, & Hilton, 2003; Mascaro & Rosen, 2005). Still, existentialists offer promise and hope.

In a culture that is increasingly electronically distancing, it is a normal reaction for people to feel alone and disconnected. Isolation can also suggest the separation of self from the inner experience. Cultural overvaluing of individualization creates detached, unaffected people who often cover up problems by living cognitively and intellectualizing the human experience. Instead of being in the world, individuals feel alienated and forsaken. Until they have come to terms with their struggle, these individuals have literally lost their world and their community. Similarly, problems arise when people experience world changes and then have to readjust and find new meaning for their lives. Equally difficult is the loss of relationships, jobs, and potential. In every case, individuals can experience hopelessness and despair.

The full spectrum of anxiety disorders are a direct result of existential struggles and can be addressed through existential counseling or therapy. Existentialists have varying approaches to angst, or existential anxiety, but they all would concur with Tillich (1980) that "the basic anxiety, the anxiety of a finite being about the threat of nonbeing, cannot be eliminated. It belongs to existence itself" (p. 38). Anxiety is a universal experience of being "thrown" into existence (Heidegger, 1962), of being alive in a threatening time and being aware of the predicament. Viewing the center of the panic as something to be explored and understood rather than escaped serves to disempower the anxiety. Without recognition and understanding, fear may serve as the focus of existence and create other, more serious psychopathologies (e.g., major depression, psychotic disorders, and somatic disorders).

Hansen (1999) specifically noted the usefulness of existential counseling and therapy in working with individuals with borderline personality disorder, schizophrenia, depression, and mania. Resistance to addressing struggles with relatedness is natural. It is important to realize that empathically understanding the pain can help facilitate understanding existential possibilities (Heisel & Flett, 2004). Existentialists believe that relationships can be transformed through counseling and therapy to allow a person to live more authentically (Buxton, 2005). In spite of everything, relationships and the resulting anguish and stress are always present in struggling to understand one's purpose in life.

The existential crisis and confrontation of it also produces depression and dysthymia. Often, depression is a last attempt to hold on to the defenses against anxiety (Bugental, 1978), as well as being a natural reaction to a lack of meaning in life (Breitbart et al., 2004). **Anomic depression** (Frankl, 1984) is the term used to describe the affective reaction to meaninglessness. To find meaning, the path is often filled with despair, hopelessness, and longing. Working through existential issues can be a struggle. Through this journey, the client gains insight, understanding, and responsibility, which allow him or her to be more resilient in the face of new life pressures.

The more individuals are satisfied with life, the more at peace they are with death. Research with seriouosly ill clients (Lantz & Gregoire, 2003) has shown that gaining meaning helps alleviate depression and seems to improve prospects of their prognosis (Kissane, Grabsch, Clark et al., 2004). Existential counseling or psychotherapy has been seen as the critical variable in working with suicidal clients (Heisel & Flett, 2004; Mascaro & Rosen, 2005). By understanding the ways clients construct meaning, counselors or psychotherapists have a theoretical basis for understanding the dynamics of the desire to die. Although depressed, the person is not really prepared for the emotional confrontation with death. The fear of approaching the universal questions is as strong as the fear of not approaching them. The individual is estranged in a chasm of existential depression.

Individuals with bipolar disorders represent the combined struggle with anxiety and depression. Combining the fear and anxiety of being and nonbeing with the conflict over meaninglessness can produce the dually conflicted individual diagnosed as bipolar. Existential counseling or therapy addresses the pain experienced at both extremes in a manner that allows the individual an increased sense of self-awareness and the ability to affect this dualistic struggle.

A wide variety of disorders result in problems in being false with one's self. These problems range from personality disorders to substance abuse disorders and eating disorders. In discussing the problems arising from inauthenticity, Heidegger (1962) described the genuine person as one who has a profound awareness of existence. The lack of *Dasein,* of "being there," implies that the person is unauthentic—avoiding presence, accessibility, responsibility, and expression. The individual adopting a "false self" is disconnected and wooden (Letunovsky, 2004). But living an inauthentic existence does not happen in isolation.

We all live in relationships, in a culture, and in a time period. Finding our authentic self is accomplished by "being there" and by "being with" others (Miars, 2002). Likewise, inauthentic existence is characterized by difficulty with interpersonal relationships as well as with oneself. By increasing our awareness, we become more authentic and more present, and we allow ourselves to learn to be comfortable with ourselves and with others. For instance, the counselor or therapist who views clients as individuals in a cultural system, not just as individuals defined solely by psychological diagnoses and treatment plans, is beginning to live authentically. Conversely, the inauthentic person pathologically resists being known. It is impossible to experience a veiled life. Everything that makes the person alive and allows the individual freedom remains imprisoned behind the mask of inauthenticity.

Maslow's (1954) seminal work with self-actualized people provided additional insight into the psyches of creative individuals who were unable to fulfill their true potential. Not everyone with capability becomes self-actualized. Maslow (1968) cited three reasons why people do not achieve their potential: lower instinctive pressure to self-actualize, cultural institutions that control or inhibit creativity, and tendencies toward fear and regression. Without these constraints, Maslow suggested, actualization is a natural process. But individuals who do not actualize experience shame, anxiety, and defeat. Remorse may be a guide back to actualization; but if the warning is not taken, individuals live knowing they did not reach their potential. In contemporary Western culture, women and members of underrepresented groups represent repressed individuals; these groups have often been discouraged to self-actualize and encouraged to self-doubt. Although taking responsibility is ultimately the solution (Letunovsky, 2004), it may not be deemed worthy of effort. When self-actualization is aborted, individuals see their lives as meaningless, but this may be an indicator that a breakthrough is possible.

Before the final stage of transcendence that seems to characterize most existential breakthroughs (Maslow, 1968; May, 1979; Tillich, 1987), some people get bogged down with existential guilt and despair; often, attempts at suicide occur. As indicated by Tillich (1987),

> Life is marked by ambiguity, and one of the ambiguities is that of greatness and tragedy. This raises the question of how the bearer of the New Being is involved in the tragic element of life. What is his relation to the ambiguity of tragic guilt? What is his relation to the tragic consequences of his being, including his actions and decisions, for those who are with him or who are against him and for those who are neither one nor the other? (p. 228)

For a person who is on the verge of understanding meaning in life, guilt may prove the ultimate undoing. Heidegger (1949) described the guilt flowing from heightened awareness and questioned the right of anyone to let himself or herself be killed for the truth. "He who does so," said Tillich, "must know that he becomes tragically responsible for the guilt of those who kill him" (1987, p. 229). Existential guilt is not irrational; rather, it is grounded in responsibility. Guilt is the "worm in the heart of the human condition, an inescapable consequence of self-consciousness" (Loy, 1996, p. 9). Still, it prohibits the individual from joining and participating in the awareness of reality. When struggling to work through this existential crisis, the individual is left with the consequences of unremitting shame and responsibility.

Of all the mental disorders discussed thus far, possibly the most unsettling is a loss of self in the world, or **existential isolation**. (This can be seen in avoidant, dependent, obsessive compulsive personality disorders as well as in major depression.) When individuals fail to develop inner strength, worth, and identity, they move beyond being isolated to feeling a profound sense of loneliness. Existential isolation occurs when an individual fails to develop an authentic sense of self in the world (Colaizzi, 2002). The person instead internalizes anxiety and searches for any available sanctuary. Because existentialism embodies hope, even the most serious disorder holds the promise of breakthrough. The sanctuary may provide an authentic connection with another person and then with the lost aspects of self.

CROSS-CULTURAL CONSIDERATIONS

Existential counseling and psychotherapy are grounded in culture. Culture is an integral consideration of the core individual concerns, and this is unique among the approaches to counseling and psychotherapy. Zhao (2005) described the importance of understanding the layers of self: the universal and existential human experiences and those experiences influenced by culture and society. Cultural context is one important aspect of self-understanding. Existential concerns are addressed across cultures (Blinderman & Cherny, 2005; Coker, 2004; Zhao, 2005) because they are universal. Montuori & Fahim (2004) found that existential psychotherapy provides the basis through which to understand individuals in cultural situations. Throughout this chapter, culture has been integrated into the various components of existentialism, in the same ways as it is in existential counseling and psychotherapy. We are a product of our culture, our situation, and our unique experiences, and existentialism addresses each facet.

EVALUATION

Overview

Trying to evaluate the efficacy of existential counseling and psychotherapy runs against their very assumptions. May (1961) indicated that "methodology always suffers from a cultural lag. Our problem is to open our vision to more of human experience, to develop and free our methods so that they will as far as possible do justice to the richness and breadth of man's experience" (p. 35). The counselor's or psychotherapist's intuitive abilities and knowledge, although subjective, contribute to a better understanding of the process. Unfortunately, existentialists tend to be congruous. The theory that focuses on **existence** over **essence** is more centered on theory, counseling or psychotherapy, and people than on generating testable hypotheses, research design, and advancing the theory through scientific analysis (Lantz, 2004).

Supporting Research

Counseling or psychotherapy outcome research has led to some interesting developments. It is becoming clearer that one theoretical approach to counseling or psychotherapy is not measurably more effective than any other. L. Seligman (2004) implied that all approaches have value. Wertz (2005) summarized the methods of phenomenological research and illustrated that there is much to be gained by looking beyond traditional assumptions. For example, the possibility that clients may be primarily looking for connection may supersede the focus of interventions that assume clients want to understand their symptoms. The process variables common to humanistic and existential psychodynamic studies tend to be the areas in which research continues to focus.

Concurrently, others have found the same phenomenon. In *The Heart and Soul of Change: What Works in Therapy*, Hubble, Duncan, and Miller (1999) brought together research that shows that 85% of client change is due to nonspecific counseling or psychotherapeutic factors. Issues such as spiritual faith and community membership account for 40% of client change, relationship factors account for 30%, and hope and expectancy account for 15%. These variables are addressed in existential counseling or psychotherapy. By addressing the personal encounter, which validates the process as much as the content, existential counseling or psychotherapy offers the framework that counselors or psychotherapists and clients are most seeking.

Moreover, Abrams and Loewenthal (2005) indicated that existentialism is an ethical and a moral approach. It is a counselor's or therapist's responsibility to acknowledge the subjective experience of the individual, to acknowledge the value of the relationship, and to acknowledge the human encounter with choice. It is important that the integrity of the individual and of the counseling relationship supersede political and scientific argument. Existentialism uniquely focuses on elements of the human experience that have been ignored, but these elements may be the most important factors in facilitating growth and change.

Efforts to apply existentialism to specific populations have been significant, and research is growing. Blinderman & Cherny (2005), Gibbs (2005), and Montuori and Fahim (2004) found that existentialism is easily applied to multicultural and international clients, because the counselor or psychotherapist focuses on the subjective experience of the client's perspective and background. Research done by Torres-Rivera et al. (2001) noted the importance of personal awareness and realistic training in developing multiculturally aware counselors or psychotherapists. They found that the existential counseling or psychotherapy model is vital to training multiculturally sensitive counselors or psychotherapists.

The need for increased research has led to expanded existential scales. Lyon and Younger (2005) developed an existential meaning scale (EMS) that was used to look at a population with HIV. The Grief Evaluation Measure (GEM) developed by Jordan, Baker, Matteis, Rosenthal, and Ware (2005) was useful in working with many psychiatric symptoms and measured adjustment to life after a significant loss. Lester and Abdel-Kahelek (2003) developed a scale to measure existential insecurity. Harville, Stokes, Templer, and Rienzi (2004) studied the Life Attitude Profile in connection with the Death Depression Scale. Beshai and Naboulsi (2004) used a Death Anxiety Scale to study anxiety about life and existential being. In all cases, more research is necessary. Having instruments in a world where instrumentation leads to additional research will advance existential theory and counseling.

Single or group case studies have proved helpful in examining existential concerns. Wertz (2005) approached schizophrenia using an existential perspective, and results were dramatic. Mascaro and Rosen addressed existential meaning and hope in relation to depression. Sexual abuse was studied using existential counseling (Feinauer et al., 2003; Fisher, 2005). Rusca (2003) found that anorexia and existential issues were reflected in the superficial struggle of understanding self. Likewise, Broussard (2005) found that bulimia reflected isolation and existential guilt. Medically unexplained symptoms were positively addressed through an existential approach (Maunder & Hunter, 2004). All studies indicate the need for further investigation. Despite recent gains, more work needs to be done to fully understand and apply existential theory.

Wong (2004) indicated a need for increased research on the healthy aspects of existentialism and the search for meaning. He thought that better understanding of the antireductionistic, subjective, existential approach would lead to the advancement of this theory. Wertz (2005) focused on the importance of research methods that are available to assess the existential approach. In addressing each research challenge, the focus of assessment must remain on the subjectively human person even though qualitative and quantiatitve methods are used. But the psychotherapeutic community has not yet arrived at this level of awareness. From a traditional, scientific viewpoint, assessing existential counseling or psychotherapy is like trying to measure psychotherapeutic progress with a yardstick, knowing that the progress is neither linear nor unidimensional.

Limitations

Existentialism is not for everyone. It proposes a worldview in which each theoretical approach has a place. Systemic concerns, by their nature, deserve a family approach. Individuals with serious ego deficits will benefit from the psychoanalytic model. Each theoretical model reflects different levels of goals and needs of the client. Although existentialism may be used with a wide spectrum of concerns, it requires that individuals be ready to look at their fears, anxieties, and responsibilities. An existential approach also focuses on the interpersonal nature of counseling and psychotherapy and provides the client insight into other relationships. Miars (2002) addressed concerns about existential counseling by looking at existential authenticity as being valuable for all counseling approaches. Nevertheless, an approach that does not provide clients with specific direction and solutions to their problems may be unsettling to those who want a more prescriptive, objective approach.

Existentialism faces the world acknowledging the subjective experience. Because subjectivity runs counter to much of current thought, it is understandable that existentialism may not answer clients' perceived needs. For example, Kendler (2005) argued that truth from an existential perspective is not the same as objective, scientific truth, and because they are so compelling, phenomenological approaches can actually harm society. Cartesian science has a powerful hold on our way of thinking and viewing each other.

Some clients may also be skeptical about existentialism because of the lack of clearly defined steps involved in treatment. Existentialism is not for the client who wants to avoid pain or experience immediate relief from struggle. Whether or not existential counseling or psychotherapy is brief, the existential search tends to go beyond four or five sessions.

Existential counseling or psychotherapy relies heavily on the verbal encounter. The underlying assumption of healing for existentialists is rooted in the helping relationship. Individuals who avoid contact with others will find this approach intrusive. Silence has its uses in existentialist counseling or psychotherapy (Dass & Gorman, 1985), but most existential counselors and therapists rely on the verbal exchange.

Probably the most obvious challenge for existentialism is the lack of scientific exploration specifically focused solely on existential interventions. While cognitive behaviorists are generating incremental, specific research to validate their theory, existential research is being evidenced in different forms. In medicine, counseling or psychotherapy, and related health care fields, existential concerns are being discussed and studied in outcome research, in developmental studies, and in studies of supervision and training. There is not a lack of research, but a lack of focus on the term *existentialism* specifically. Existentialists seem to be defenseless in a battle of science, but in actuality they are being woven into the fabric of the healing process.

Nevertheless, the studies mentioned in this chapter show that the struggle over theoretical validation has not yet been resolved. The lack of proof of the specific theoretical approach is problematic. In addition, individuals without a solid sense of integrity are attracted to a model that lacks a sequence of techniques and guidelines. Existential counselors or psychotherapists need to continue to find palatable ways in which to study their unique approach (albeit inconsistent with their subjective model). If they do not, existentialism will be a haven for critical scientific scrutiny and unusual and fanciful approaches with no substance.

Because most strengths also embody weaknesses, the underlying faith in a client's potential for growth may appear shallow and unprofound. At a concrete level, the question of who am I appears inconsequential. Existentialism's strength in honoring the person may be comprehended as a cursory gesture.

SUMMARY CHART—*Existential Theory*

Human Nature

Existential theory is realistically optimistic about human nature. People exist in a culture and context, and all struggle with the universal concerns of death, freedom, isolation, and meaninglessness.

Major Constructs

Existentialism addresses the following constructs: confronting universal fears of death, understanding ultimate isolation, finding purpose in a predominantly meaningless existence, coming to terms with anxiety, accepting the burden of freedom of choice, realizing the responsibility for living, and living authentically.

Goals

The goal of existential counseling and psychotherapy is to confront anxieties about the givens of existence. Existentialism involves learning to live more authentically and gaining meaning from common, everyday endeavors and pain. Clients are transformed through courageous and subtle encounters with aspects of their humanness and through the interpersonal relationship with the counselor or therapist.

Change Process

Change evolves from a client's willingness to participate in the interpersonal encounter by confronting loneliness, experiencing individuality, encountering true connection, and developing the inner strength to transcend the life situation.

Interventions

Interventions in existential counseling and psychotherapy include understanding the client's world, sharing existence in the moment, fostering a centered awareness of being, encouraging self-responsibility, working with dreams, confronting existential anxiety, and learning to put closure on relationships.

Limitations

Existential theory uses a subjective approach to understand a world that is currently most popularly understood within an objective system. Existentialism relies on verbal exchange and authenticity. The theory does not rely on scientific testing to validate it. Because most strengths also embody weaknesses, the underlying faith in a client's potential for growth may appear shallow and unprofound.

THE CASE OF JONATHAN: *An Existential Approach*

Jonathan's concerns reflect an existential struggle with death, isolation, freedom, and meaninglessness. The death of his brother caused an early trauma that Jonathan has not been able to fully address. He has not been able to find himself in a satisfying relationship and has battled depression and loneliness. No one has validated his pain or acknowledged his loss of self in the world. Jonathan challenged cultural traditions by leaving the reservation. He seems torn between two worlds that are incompatible. Cultural and family expectations have affected his work and the recent pressure to return home to the reservation and care for his aging parents. Confronting this loss of self, of identity, Jonathan experiences existential isolation and despair. To find meaning—or to escape from finding it—he has become depressed, developed problems at work, moved from relationship to relationship, disconnected from his family, and abused alcohol. Still, his anger, fear, and frustration are clearly a result of a crisis of selfhood.

The life Jonathan has constructed is fragile and he realizes the exigency of the situation. His nightmares reflect his lack of purpose and direction in life and his angry and helpless reaction to it. He has difficulty in maintaining a job or relationships. In the past, Jonathan has been able to cope by finding meaning in and through others (new relationships). Ultimately, his choices have never filled the void left by the death of his brother.

The potential loss of his freedom that would follow a return to the reservation seems to have intensified the nightmares, as well as his deteriorating relationships at work, financial problems, drinking, and likely permanent separation from his current wife. However, his flight through others has never been fulfilling, and now he is alone with building responsibilities he feels unable to handle. The problems in being able to find other meaningful work are compounded by encountering prejudice.

Although Jonathan attempts to distance himself from his culture, he continues to be faced by it. In trying once more to escape his problems, he is having increased difficulty and is "alone with the laughing driver" on a bus going nowhere he wants to go. For Jonathan, alcohol has also proven ineffective in helping him find respite. In facing his life without culture and with increased pressures to create a new meaning out of his painful past, Jonathan has no way to turn to escape. He is left alone and afraid.

Treatment and Intervention Plan

Jonathan's desire to work on these issues is of paramount importance. His current depression and hopelessness could be paralyzing. A medication consultation may be necessary if his depression does not abate. Alcohol abuse needs to be assessed. Because his current defense of withdrawal and escape were not working, he was asked to come to counseling by his supervisor.

His lateness to the session indicates he is reticent and careful, but the amount of information he provided shows openness to the process. His current pain may be a positive factor in motivating him to change.

The goal of counseling will be to help gain an understanding of Jonathan's current condition. (In this process, Jonathan will also gain perspective on his situation.) First, it will be important to discuss his cultural background and any feelings he has about the counseling or psychotherapy experience as well as any cultural differences or similarities that may exist between Jonathan and the counselor or psychotherapist. Also, it will be important to discuss the gender of the counselor or psychotherapist with Jonathan. If he has any concerns about this, a referral will need to be made immediately. Next, it will be important to hear Jonathan's story. In telling his struggle and pain, Jonathan needs to be heard and validated. He will be facing his fears while he focuses on the issues prompting the depression: the death (and his responsibility for it) of his brother, the separation from his family, separation from his current wife (and any feelings he has about the problems in these relationships), the difficulty living in a predominantly White culture, the relationships with his children, the use of alcohol to escape, and his career identity (currently working in a residential drug and alcohol treatment program for adolescents).

In all areas, Jonathan experienced loss and meaninglessness (leading to hopelessness). In spite of everything, however, he has persisted. Ultimately, he will gain freedom and understanding by acknowledging his struggle and being heard and respected by the counselor or psychotherapist. He will also have his counselor or psychotherapist with him as he confronts his anxiety about having to decide what to do next and whether to return to the reservation. Jonathan has made choices that were unpopular with his spouses, family, and culture.

Jonathan's withdrawal has occurred over several years and relationships and has been in reaction to external pressures, which are now increasing as a result of family issues, problems at work, financial issues, relationship problems, increased drinking, and his general affect. Jonathan has not been able to move beyond his feelings of responsibility over his brother's death when Jonathan was 16. He has developed a pattern of detaching from relationships, which has been difficult in view of the pressures from his culture to be intricately connected. Jonathan has not been true to himself or others and that has left him isolated in a world without meaning or direction.

Case Analysis

The first phase of treatment will be developing a therapeutic relationship. Because Jonathan has been victimized by his culture and the majority culture, developing trust and groundwork for the "I to Thou" relationship is important for counseling or psychotherapy to begin. A concurrent component is helping to assess the extent of alcohol use and abuse. Counseling or psychotherapy will not be effective if Jonathan is under the influence of alcohol. In the past, he has sought to detach in relationships; now Jonathan will need to be committed to working through these issues that continue to follow him from relationship to relationship and job to job. By addressing this core aspect of self, he can gain power over his life and his choices.

The dream seems to be a revealing of his sense of powerlessness, frustration, and lack of direction. The ideal and final interpretation will be made by Jonathan, but the following discussion emerges from an existential interpretation. Jonathan's real self is confronting his sense of lack of direction and ultimate aloneness in a situation where he feels powerless (alone with a bus driver who does not listen and laughs at him). The culture (bus that the riders feel is going everywhere) seems to be going nowhere in particular, although he had a ticket to Albuquerque (home). He feels trapped (no one has time to get off at the bus stops). His anger (pounding on steering wheel) only serves to make everyone else disappear. He is left alone and unable to have any power over where he is going on a bus with a driver who laughs at his desire for help. It could be that he is the bus driver, detached from his own desire to find his way home. He cannot figure out how to escape from his situation and is afraid and angry. This shows that Jonathan is focused and motivated to confront these aspects of himself and his world. He would welcome someone to help him to deal with his helpless feelings. Escape no longer is providing solace. He has not been able to find "home." There is a sense he may be ready to change.

The counselor or psychotherapist will need to help Jonathan confront the anxiety of death. By meeting his fears of loss and engulfment and encountering the aspects of himself that are painful and angry, he will sense all that he has encountered and survived. Jonathan will also develop a stronger sense of himself and his responsibility for making his own choices. He can find a place in the world that is not bound by the bus, the driver, or the people without direction. By continuing to flee from relationships, work, and life, Jonathan avoids being and living. He is trapped in his fears by his substance abuse, depression, and isolation.

Counseling or psychotherapy will involve helping Jonathan on his journey as he encounters the fears embodied by the individuals on the bus and the frustration of not having control over his life. It will be important for the counselor or psychotherapist not to fall into the easy pattern of offering him insight or direction (giving another voice to where the bus is destined). Instead, Jonathan needs to integrate his own voice and sense of self. This will occur through the process of validating his losses and his pain, understanding his cultural pressures, and helping him to find meaning in himself and his existence. The path (bus) he has taken thus far has not gotten him where he wants to go or provided any relationships or understanding. He has felt alone, out of control, angry, and afraid.

The counselor or psychotherapist is providing a context of relating that will help Jonathan to learn that his escape from others through drinking, his not staying committed in relationships, and his not knowing how he wants to deal with his family only keep him mired in anxiety and depression. By facing his insecurities and losses, he will gain a sense of inner strength, awareness, and self. By taking responsibility (getting behind the wheel), he can realize the freedom he has to be himself and choose as well as to be responsible for his choices. Once he has recognized his power and responsibility, he can be himself in relation to others. He will no longer be alone.

Group counseling and support for alcohol abuse, especially with others struggling with cultural issues, might be helpful when Jonathan has developed a better sense of himself. The group would allow Jonathan to connect with others with similar struggles, to validate his pain and his struggles to make peace with himself, and to develop healthier ways of relating to others and making choices.

CHAPTER 8

Person-Centered Theory

Richard J. Hazler
Penn State University

The person-centered theory of **Carl R. Rogers** is one of the most popular in the fields of psychology, counseling, and education. Rogers' perceptions of people and of how a supportive environment can assist in their development have had an immense impact on a wide variety of professions and on parenting. This approach to people was a major deviation from the psychoanalytic and behavioral models for working with people that were predominant in the early part of the 20th century.

Person-centered theory offered a new way to look at individuals and their development, as well as how people can be helped to change. From this frame of reference, people were viewed as fully in charge of their lives and inherently motivated to improve themselves. The responsibility for personal behaviors and the ability to choose to change them were also seen as belonging fully to the individual. Here was a way to view and deal with human beings that did not rely on other people (counselors, psychologists, parents, teachers, etc.) as the primary directors of change. People could control their own change if the right conditions were offered.

Rogers saw all individuals as having inherent qualities that made nurturing possible; attempting to change basic personality characteristics or behaviors was not necessary. He believed people saw the world from their own unique perspective, which is referred to as a **phenomenological** perspective Rogers believed that no matter what phenomenological view of the world people held, they were all continually attempting to actualize their best and most productive selves. This positive and optimistic view of human beings is often challenged by those who call attention to the unlimited opportunities for observing people as they think and act in ways that are harmful to themselves and others. But Rogers believed these thoughts and actions were primarily reflections of a distorted view of oneself and the world, distortions caused by trying to meet the expectations of others rather than trying to actualize one's own self.

The origins of Rogers' beliefs, their development into a major helping process, and an examination of the essential ingredients of that process will serve as a foundation for this chapter. Information on the counselor's or therapist's role in providing interventions and the methods used to carry out that role will then provide the practical base for beginning to implement the process.

BACKGROUND

Carl R. Rogers

Person-centered theory began to make an impact on psychology in the 1940s. Carl R. Rogers was the individual behind the theory, and his influence was so great that it is commonly referred to as **Rogerian theory**. The major concepts of the autonomous self, reliance on one's own unique experiences, the desire and ability to make positive personal changes, and movement toward the actualization of potentials are all observable in the personal development of Rogers.

Rogers was born in 1902 into a morally and religiously conservative family that was strictly religious, devoted to its children, and committed to the concept of hard work. Dancing, watching movies, smoking, drinking, and anything that vaguely suggested sexual interest were clearly forbidden, although little was said about them. The family was able to convey its directions in subtle ways that were generally unspoken but nevertheless clear to everyone.

The family was largely self-contained, and the young Rogers had few friends. He became a loner of sorts, spending most of his time working, thinking, and reading. His early lifestyle caused him to pay close attention to his personalized experience of the world. In later years, this concept would become better known as a phenomenological approach to counseling or psychotherapy.

Rogers' family moved to a farm 30 miles west of Chicago when he was 12 years old. It was here that his work ethic was reemphasized; he also developed an intense interest in science and experimentation. He spent much of his time studying the variety of insects and animals that were now available to him. A scientific approach to all issues was further emphasized by his father, who insisted that all farming should be as scientific and modern as possible. These concepts of hard work, scientific study, experimentation, and evaluation would later set Rogers apart from other theorists: He was the first to intentionally and creatively subject experientially recognized human development and therapeutic processes to rigorous scientific study. Those interested in his theories often overlook this aspect of his work, but it is a major contribution to the development of professionalism in counseling and psychotherapy.

Rogers left home to study agriculture in college but later turned to religious studies and eventually to clinical psychology as he became more interested in people, beliefs, and values. His religious beliefs, like those of his parents, were strong. However, the more he studied and discussed the issues, the more his views diverged from his parents'. A 6-month trip to China as part of the World Student Christian Federation Conference encouraged his change to a more liberal viewpoint.

Explaining these changes to his parents was extremely difficult and often disappointing for all concerned. Nevertheless, Rogers reported great growth in his intellectual and emotional independence from these open confrontations. Later reflection led Rogers to believe that these were the times when he was learning to pay more attention to a values system that emanated from himself and taking large steps toward overcoming parental conditions of worth that had directed much of his life. The experience with his parents left him much more confident in himself, his beliefs, and his ability to deal with difficult situations. This idea that individuals can and must rely on themselves for direction and strength was to become another major emphasis in his theory, as well as in his own life.

Rogers graduated from the University of Wisconsin, married, and in 1924 began to study for the ministry at Union Theological Seminary in New York City. His focus of attention changed during his 2 years at Union as he became more and more interested in psychology and education. Consequently, he transferred to Columbia University to study psychology and earned his PhD there in 1931.

After graduation from Columbia, Rogers worked with children in Rochester, New York, for 12 years; later he was on the faculty at Ohio State University, the University of Chicago, and the University of Wisconsin. His final stop was at the Center for Studies of the Person at La Jolla, California, beginning in 1963. This period of time until his death in 1987 was extremely productive. It included work in education and in individual and group counseling and psychotherapy. The last years of his life were spent traveling in the most troubled places in the world, using his person-centered approach to promote peace among warring groups.

Theory Background

The field of counseling or psychotherapy in the 1920s and 1930s relied on techniques that were highly diagnostic, probing, and analytic as well as unsupported by scientific research. Rogers' first major work, *Counseling and Psychotherapy* (1942), was a clear reaction to this situation and to his work with children. "So vast is our ignorance on this whole subject [counseling and psychotherapy]," he wrote, "that it is evident that we are by no means professionally ready to develop a definitive or final account of any aspect of psychotherapy" (p. 16). He presented **nondirective** counseling and psychotherapy in this work along with a clear call for a more scientific approach to research in both his nondirective and other, more directive techniques.

Client-Centered Therapy (1951) was a culmination of a decade of practice and research in which Rogers expanded his concepts and renamed his approach. This new emphasis changed the role of the counselor or therapist from an individual who only reflected the content of client statements to one who identified the client's underlying emotions in client words and through the helping relationship. The effect of this new work was to expand the dimensions of accurate empathy with the client and to force the counselor or therapist to go beyond simple reflection of client words.

In 1957 Rogers moved to the University of Wisconsin where his efforts at research on his theory increased and broadened. Here he tested his ideas on hospitalized clients with schizophrenia rather than on the primarily normal population he had been working with at the University of Chicago. His research confirmed the view that the conditions present in the helping relationship did have a significant effect on both the progress of counseling or psychotherapy and the outcomes for clients (Rogers, 1967). Rogers' work with client populations ranging from normal to extremely disturbed encouraged him to broaden the use of his ideas to include all people.

Person-centered is the term currently used to emphasize the personal nature of counseling or psychotherapy and other relationships in education, business, and government agencies. The therapeutic or helping relationship is now envisioned as one of person-to-person rather than healthy counselor or therapist to unhealthy client.

Person-centered theory developed out of a close examination of individual helping relationships, but during the 1970s and 1980s Rogers began focusing more on groups than on individuals. He was a major promoter of personal-growth groups, where individuals worked together for the purpose of self-actualizing growth rather than toward a more limited goal of overcoming psychological illnesses (Rogers, 1970). Another group adaptation saw Rogers, in the last years of his life, using person-centered concepts in a group format to deal with critical world conflicts. He traveled to areas with major social conflicts, such as Central America (Thayer, 1987), South Africa (Rogers & Sanford, 1987), Northern Ireland (Rogers, 1987b), and even the Soviet Union (Rogers, 1987a), to run growth groups with leaders and nonleaders who had fought, but never tried to understand each other. His accounts of these encounters make it clear that a person-centered orientation can be promoted in groups as well as in individual relationships. These successful experiences also gave recognition to the value of person-centered practices with people with widely different cultural backgrounds.

The enduring nature of Rogers' work can be seen in every current article or book that examines person-centered theory. Their discussions of the theory, practice, and research aspects all emphasize his work over any other, even though it is now decades old. His work continues to be the core of the theory, although many professionals have expanded it. Researchers and educators such as Barrett-Lennard (1998), Carkhuff, (1969), Hill (2004), Truax and Carkhuff (1967), and Wilkins (2003) emphasized the instruction and measurement of Rogers' core conditions in efforts to improve evaluation of counselor effectiveness and to develop more successful counselor training models. Today, virtually all counselor education programs emphasize these conditions and related techniques, beginning early in the training programs.

Modern-day issues such as managed care and medical treatment models have greatly increased the emphasis on diagnosis, symptom elimination, problem behavior reduction, and time-limited treatment, which are not conducive to a person-centered approach. The primary focus on techniques in these models, rather than on the relationship Rogers advocated, have made full compatibility difficult. At the same time, all these approaches begin with relationship, and each of these models is giving greater recognition to the importance of Rogers' core conditions (Goodman, 2004). Even such technique-driven counseling or therapy models as family counseling (O'Leary, 1999), applied behavioral analysis (Holburn & Vietze, 2000), and brief therapy (Presbury, Echterling, & McKee, 2002) are emphasizing the essential nature of these core conditions for counseling success. Contemporary counselors or therapists may not find many books with *person centered* in the title, but they will see the idea deeply ingrained in virtually every modern approach to counseling or psychotherapy.

HUMAN NATURE: A DEVELOPMENTAL PERSPECTIVE

The person-centered approach to counseling or psychotherapy implies great confidence in each client. This confidence arises from a belief that all people have innate motivation to grow in positive ways and the ability to carry out such a growth process. This highly positive view of human nature varies widely from other theories that view human nature as evil, negative, or a nonissue. Such a positive view of human nature is essential for the person-centered practitioner because of the major responsibilities clients are given in the direction, style, and content of the helping relationship. The person-centered perception of people is based on four key beliefs: (1) people are trustworthy; (2) people innately move toward **self-actualization** and health; (3) people have the **inner resources** to move themselves in positive directions; and (4) people respond to their **uniquely perceived world** (phenomenological world). The activation of these characteristics in a person's external environment brings about the most desirable aspects of development.

Trustworthiness of People

Person-centered counselors or therapists must treat their clients as trustworthy, or there will be no reason to allow them to take a leadership role in the helping relationship. From this point of view, words such as *good, constructive,* and *trustworthy* describe natural characteristics of human beings, although people also appear to take actions that demonstrate the opposite. These inappropriate actions are taken when the individual's ideal view of self does not match the **real self.** Individuals use defensive thoughts and actions to protect themselves from having to observe that they are not living the lives they believe they should. Such actions are not deceitful so much as they are direct actions based on conflicting perceptions of a person's world. All individuals are trying to improve and to act in the world as they see it in as honorable a manner as possible.

Consider the teenage girl who skips school and has been arrested for the fourth time for shoplifting. Many in society will judge her to be a bad person or one who cannot be trusted. The girl will recognize that lack of trust and consequently have little motivation to seek a productive relationship with these people. The person-centered counselor or therapist must believe that the girl will be trustworthy in their relationship if and when she is convinced that she has a meaningful relationship with a counselor or therapist who is genuine and trusting. A major part of that relationship will be the counselor or therapist conveying genuine trust through words and actions. Anything less than this trusting relationship will convince the girl that this is just another person who will not trust her and is, therefore, not to be trusted. The result is that she will have little motivation to work on her own potential for trustworthiness in the therapeutic relationship. Only when trust can be established will the girl accept the potential for an honest, respectful, and valuable relationship with the counselor or therapist.

Movement Toward Actualization

Human beings are viewed by the person-centered theorist as always striving to obtain the maximum amount from themselves. They seek any means to develop all their abilities "in ways that maintain or enhance the organism" (Rogers, 1959, p. 196). This is the driving force in the positive development of the individual. It clearly moves the individual away from control by others based on conditions of worth and toward autonomy and self-control. The movement toward **autonomy** and self-actualization provides individuals rather than outside persons (parents, counselors, therapists, teachers, etc.) with the primary motivational strength behind development. This energy source is also seen as potentially more influential than environmental factors such as socioeconomic status, hunger, or danger, which also affect how the individual perceives or seeks self-actualization.

The teenage girl discussed previously would likely be seen by many to have inadequate self-control and little desire to overcome her problems. Individuals and society as a whole will probably seek to control her and pressure her to grow in ways deemed appropriate by others. The person-centered view, however, emphasizes that the girl is actually working toward making the most of herself and that she will continue to do so regardless of what others do. What others can do is provide a safe environment where the girl can lower her defenses and anti-social behaviors without fear of being denounced for failures and nonacceptance. When this occurs, she can be expected to continue to pursue self-actualization, but now in ways that are more appropriate and socially viable.

Inner Resources

The actualizing tendency provides the motive for positive development in people. But do individuals have the capacity to carry out this motivation? Person-centered theory presumes that individuals do have that capacity (Rogers, 1961). Holding the belief that people have the motivation to grow in positive directions does not mean that counselors or therapists have confidence in client ability to follow through on that motivation. The person-centered approach emphasizes a belief that this ability to grow in positive directions is available to everyone. Certainly some of the most heartwarming stories told throughout the ages have demonstrated how people overcome tremendous odds to change and become a person that others and they themselves like better. These same stories also cause people to question why it happens for some and not others. Person-centered theory emphasizes that potential differences in degree of ability to change and overcome are not as important as persons' beliefs that they can accomplish great things on the journey to improve. In many ways, person-centered theory is based on two fairly well-accepted principles of human dynamics. The first principle states that people always have much more potential than they use most of the time. The second emphasizes that success is found in the journey rather than in a preconceived goal. Person-centered counselors or therapists must believe in these principles if they are to help clients recognize and accept their own abilities.

The person-centered counselor or therapist must have the confidence that the troubled teenage girl has the inner resources as well as the motivation to grow. Demonstration of this confidence-building belief allows for emergence of the creative ideas and actions that can expand potential options and encourage growth in new directions. When this confidence is not conveyed, both counselor or therapist and client are likely to aim for goals that are far short of the girl's potential.

Individually Perceived World

The person-centered view recognizes that events will be perceived differently by different people (Rogers, 1961). Two armies fight, two adults argue, and relationships break down because each side perceives what is "right" to be different from the other side's perception. The person-centered view of these examples is that individuals or groups relate to the world and their own actions from a unique context or **phenomenological perspective.** Therefore, words, behaviors, feelings, and beliefs are selected to match the specialized view of the world held by each individual.

The idea that no two people perceive the world in exactly the same way explains much of the variation in the previous three concepts. Cultural background and environmental factors play large parts in this variation, and individual perceptions of and reactions to experiences create even more differences. The troubled girl surely does not see the world as the safe and kind place perceived by another person who is successful in school, feels culturally accepted, and has a comfortable family life. Neither will she perceive the world as rational as the counselor or therapist is likely to see. It is quite possible that the girl is stealing, in part, because of a different perception of the world. She sees this behavior as the only one available for her to help feed herself, her mother, and her infant sister. Person-centered counselors or therapists must recognize these differently perceived worlds, work unendingly to understand them, and seek to help clients grow through their personally perceived world rather than through the world as it is perceived by the counselor, therapist, or others.

Interaction with External Factors

A person-centered view of human development gives attention to external factors that affect psychological development in addition to critical internal forces. Even as infants, people make choices that induce growth and actualize potential. They reject experiences that are perceived as contrary to their well-being. However, these naturalistic ways of making choices become confused as the developing person recognizes that other individuals may provide or withhold love based on how well the person assimilates values and behaviors set by others. This recognition can move individuals away from using their own best judgment to make personal choices and promote a method that requires taking actions based on the presumed desires of others. The two theoretical concepts used to explain this aspect of development are **unconditional positive regard** and **conditions of worth** (Rogers, 1959).

Individuals who are given unconditional positive regard by significant people in their lives receive recognition of their positive nature, including their motivation and ability to become increasingly effective human beings. The worth and value of the individual are not questioned in this case, although specific behaviors or beliefs can be rejected as inappropriate. A parent might say to the young woman who was stealing, "You are a good person and I know you want the best for us, but the stealing was just wrong and was punished."

Individuals who are given and can recognize unconditional positive regard being provided to them feel permitted to continue trusting themselves as positive human beings. The belief is conveyed to them that they will make errors of judgment and behavior, but that as positive individuals they will also strive to examine themselves continually and be able to take actions for their own improvement. Being provided with unconditional positive regard helps individuals to continue seeking their own development with the confidence that they will become increasingly effective human beings.

Many times the regard and love offered by others have strings attached, as would be the case if the girl who stole had been told by her angry parent, "You're just a common criminal and no daughter of mine!" Children faced with the type of love that is conditioned on doing only those things that a parent wants and where differences or mistakes are judged to be unacceptable can come to believe that they are only good, loved, cared for, fed, or valued if they do just as others believe they should. These conditions of worth pressure developing persons to devalue their inherent potential for making choices and for growth. They begin looking for directions and decisions that originate from external sources instead of trusting their more natural internal reactions to their environment. This process moves developing individuals away from confidence in their ability to run their own lives and pushes them to seek validation based on the lives of others who appear to be more positive than they are.

MAJOR CONSTRUCTS

The core of person-centered theory is a set of beliefs about people and relationships rather than a series of programmable verbal and behavioral techniques. Counselors or therapists interested in implementing this theory must look first to themselves and their perceptions of others rather than to what specific behaviors ought to be performed. This is a challenging task, particularly for new practitioners who are seeking to find out what they should "do" and to what extent they "do things well." The following constructs are essential beliefs involved in person-centered theory. Practitioners must have a clear perception of them before they can implement a person-centered approach effectively.

No Two People See the World Exactly Alike

According to the phenomenological approach, no two people can be expected to see things as happening in exactly the same way. Practitioners must recognize that whatever they personally believe reality to be will be different from the client's perspective and that each client will have a unique perspective. Therefore, asking the client to believe or act in a way that "everyone knows is right" is the counselor's or therapist's opinion, based on his or her own phenomenological view, rather than some ultimate "fact." Because helping someone from a person-centered approach emphasizes this concept, it is imperative to understand the client's perspective as thoroughly as possible.

Consider the case of a physically abusive husband who was court ordered into counseling. One part of his reasoning for why he hit his wife hard and so often that she needed to be hospitalized was, "I come home from work, there is no food on the table, there are dishes in the sink, and then she back talks me. Of course I hit. Anybody would!"

No counseling degree is needed to realize that, "No, anyone wouldn't hit her and certainly not like you did." For most people, the perceived world makes it clear that this is not appropriate thinking or behaving. This behavior, however, is an obvious sign that the client has a very different view of the world than the counselor and almost everyone else. Person-centered counselors or therapists know that arguing with this person will not change his mind. What will help is to obtain an accurate picture of the client's perceived world in order to gain a better understanding of why he thinks this way and what will impede or assist change.

Empathic Understanding Is Critical

Empathic understanding is critically important to the person-centered approach, because it is the counselor's or therapist's way to perceive the client's phenomenological world. Empathy refers to understanding the client's world from the client's point of view. This is no easy task because it is hard for practitioners to set aside their own biased views of the world in an attempt to see things through the client's eyes. All other actions they take will be inappropriate without empathy, as they would then be based on inaccurate perceptions of the client. The construct of empathy allows practitioners to respond effectively and assures clients that their confidence in the counselor is justified.

Knowing the content of what a client says along with the feelings behind the words are the two essential elements of empathic understanding. The reasoning for the abuser striking his wife is important information that may be revealed in his statements. The feelings, on the other hand, may come out in words like *anger, hate, frustration,* or in other ways such as reddening of the face, facial expressions, posture, laughter, or tears. Empathic understanding combines all of these verbal and nonverbal clues to understand clients.

Empathic understanding involves two tasks that practitioners must accomplish to make it a useful construct: understanding and accurately conveying that understanding. Counselors or therapists must set aside their own beliefs and enter the client's world so that they can understand. Setting aside disdain for the abusive spouse is no easy task, but not doing so will taint any understanding of the person with the practitioner's own biases.

Understanding by itself has only minimal value as counseling technique. The client must also be aware of what the practitioner understands. This second dimension is crucial for empathic understanding to be useful. Empathic understanding improves the helping relationship only when the client clearly recognizes what it is the counselor or therapist understands; therefore, the counselor or therapist must be able to effectively communicate that understanding back to the client in words and actions.

People Make Simple Mistakes in Judgment

People make simple mistakes in judgment all the time. They also make choices that appear to be right to them but that are ineffective because they are made to match the perceived world of others rather than their own best judgment. People may act in response to how they believe others would have them act (conditions of worth) rather than trusting their own positive, growth-oriented nature (i.e., their **tendency to actualize**).

Practitioners who demonstrate faith in the whole person rather than denigrating clients for mistakes of behavior allow their clients the freedom to explore their inner world without fear of rejection. Lacking such unconditional positive regard, clients may try to do what they believe the practitioner wants to achieve a better life. Such actions will only increase client beliefs that they cannot make their own effective choices and must instead look to others for what is best to do or not do. They may find more socially acceptable ways of behaving, but they will not have gained confidence in their own ability to seek more changes as needs arise.

Confidence in the Client Is Paramount

In comparison to other theories, person-centered theory places tremendous confidence in clients even knowing that they will make mistakes in judgment along the way. This confidence is based on the belief that people are innately good and continually seeking a fully functioning experience in the world even as they make mistakes. People's tendency to actualize personal potential in positive ways is the force that the person-centered practitioner recognizes and seeks to free from self-induced constraints.

The repeat history of the abusive spouse makes trusting so difficult that the courts may need to step in to protect others. That, however, is the work of the courts not of the counselor or therapist whose person-centered task is to believe in this person's desire to do the right thing, even though he is currently unable to perceive what that is or how to do it. This position contrasts with other views of human nature that do not allow the practitioner to trust because client difficulties are seen as weaknesses or deficiencies that stand in the way of personal progress unless the practitioner corrects them. Person-centered clients are treated as effective human beings who are able to grow and succeed regardless of the nature of their difficulties.

Perceived World of the Client May Not Approximate the World Sought

Individuals come to counseling or psychotherapy because of difficulties evolving from the fact that the world they perceive is not in close proximity to the world they would naturally seek for themselves. The natural, growth-oriented, self-trusting nature of these people has been pushed into conflict with their chosen world, where they continually look outside their true selves for decisions. They act based on perceptions of what others think is right, and the results of their actions are not personally fulfilling or effective. This conflict is termed **incongruence**.

It is a common occurrence, for example, to find that abusive persons have experienced an abusive environment. They have often struggled inside themselves—verbally and even physically—to reject the unnatural, hurtful, and untrusting aspects of the environment, but at some point they come to believe that this is "just the way things are" because others accept the environment. They take actions based on the acceptance of this environment by others only to find their actions conflict with the receiving and giving of love, caring, and self-trust they naturally desire. The result is increasing levels of incongruence both within themselves and between them and their relationships with others.

Congruent Individuals Trust Their Worldview

Congruent persons trust their view of the world and their ability to act on their positive nature. They feel confident about reacting in the present moment because of a belief in their organism's ability to discriminate between appropriate and inappropriate behaviors. People around them then generally verify this self-trust, because the actions of congruent persons tend to be beneficial both personally and socially. In situations where human fallibility causes errors in reactions, congruent individuals have a view of the world that allows them to evaluate the reactions of others and to make appropriate adaptive responses for the immediate and distant future. Congruent people are not infallible, but they do have the ability to recognize and use mistakes to grow without devaluing themselves or others.

The construct of congruence helps explain the concept of **anxiety** in person-centered theory. Low personal anxiety occurs when the perceived self is in line with actual experiences (congruence). Alternatively, the degree to which individuals' perceptions of themselves do not match the way they actually are (incongruence) is directly related to higher levels of anxiety. In person-centered theory, practitioners make efforts to increase congruence in the clients rather than to directly reduce anxiety.

APPLICATIONS

Overview

The person-centered concept of a growth-oriented and competent individual in need of counseling or psychotherapy presumes a scenario analogous to the growth of a simple garden bean. The bean seed has within itself all the potential to grow, but it must be provided with the proper climate for it to achieve its full potential. The seed will develop as expected if placed in fertile ground where adequate warmth, sun, and water are available. Human hands do not need to touch it under the ground, nor should those hands help pull it out of properly prepared ground. In fact, such human attempts to directly manipulate will almost surely threaten the bean's development! The effective gardener knows that arranging correct conditions and leaving the plant alone to seek its own growth is the best way to allow it to reach its greatest potential.

Fostering the natural growth of the bean suggests how to apply person-centered theory to counseling and psychotherapy. The client has all the necessary but as yet unfulfilled potential for attaining greater self-understanding, self-acceptance, self-growth, self-satisfaction, and self-actualization. The practitioner's task is to provide the essential growth conditions of a genuine human relationship in which acceptance, caring, and a deep understanding of the client are developed and communicated effectively to the client. Application of these conditions involves intervention strategies that allow persons to make changes in the direction of their greatest potential.

Goals of Counseling and Psychotherapy

Movement from incongruence to congruence identifies the cornerstone, person-centered goal for people who are having psychological or sociological difficulties. Such persons are attempting to perceive more accurately their own positive nature and to use what they have learned more effectively in their everyday lives. As this occurs, they will better accept both their strengths and weaknesses as legitimate and evolving parts of their positive nature. This acceptance reduces distortions in their view of the world and leads to greater accuracy in the match between how they see themselves and their interactions with people, ideas, and things.

Reduced distortions and a greater trust in one's evolving positive nature lead to other specific outcomes that practitioners often identify as goals of counseling or psychotherapy. People who find success in counseling or psychotherapy generally become more flexible and creative in their thoughts and actions as they free themselves from stereotypes and inappropriately imposed conditions of worth. They begin to see a wider range of feelings in themselves, gain more confidence in the expression of those feelings, and feel enthusiasm about the new aspects of life opened up by these experiences. These newfound levels of freedom to trust the accuracy of their feelings and thoughts allow them to take the actions necessary to overcome feelings of helplessness, powerlessness, and the inability to make decisions about the present and future. This new level of self-empowerment is perhaps the outcome most noted by everyone around an individual who has benefited from person-centered counseling or psychotherapy.

Process of Change

The process of change through the helping relationship is guided by the presence of three basic conditions: genuineness, acceptance and caring, and empathic understanding. As Rogers wrote, "Studies with a variety of clients show that when these three conditions occur in the therapist, and when they are to some degree perceived by the client, therapeutic movement ensues, the client finds himself painfully but definitely learning and growing, and both he and his counselor regard the outcome as successful." Rogers continued, "It seems from our studies that it is attitudes such as these rather than the therapist's technical knowledge and skill, which are primarily responsible for therapeutic change" (1961, p. 63). Over the past four decades this perspective on the significance of the relationship to the process of change has been integrated within virtually all schools of counseling and psychotherapy (Farber, Brink, & Raskin, 1996; Hazler & Barwick, 2001; See & Kamnetz, 2004).

The first of these three conditions is the **genuineness** of the counselor or therapist. Clients must perceive that this individual is a real person who has feelings, thoughts, and beliefs that are not hidden behind facades. This genuine nature allows clients to trust that whatever specifics emerge in the relationship, the practitioner can be recognized as both personal and honest. Client sees that being open and genuine, which includes revealing one's fallibility, is not a condition from which competent human beings must shrink. Most of our daily relationships are not highly genuine; instead, they are controlled by facades and roles that cause us to doubt the information we receive from people.

The second condition is **acceptance and caring** provided by the counselor or therapist, which allows clients to be less anxious about their perceived weaknesses and the prospect of taking risks. The weaknesses we perceive in ourselves generally become those things we least want others to see, so we try to hide our weaknesses whenever possible. Limitations often result in some degree of embarrassment, with an accompanying tendency to work even harder at hiding them. Persons who need assistance are working hard to hide their perceived weaknesses from others and from themselves. Often they identify a less threatening weakness as the problem to avoid examining a more personally threatening one. Acceptance and caring, if consistently felt by the client as unconditional positive regard, offer the opportunity to reduce the degree of stress caused by these fears in the relationship. In turn, acceptance and caring will increase the chance that the client can recognize, discuss, and work on problem areas rather than hiding from them.

The third condition for change is the practitioner's **empathic understanding** of the client. This deep recognition of the client's internal frame of reference must be successfully communicated to the client to be effective. Neither the practitioner nor the client can ever fully understand the client. Nevertheless, the degree to which they effectively explore the client's world together to arrive at a common understanding will improve the client's abilities to understand and, therefore, take action in his or her life.

These three basic conditions provide the necessary environment that allows individuals to implement their **actualizing tendencies**. They arrive in counseling questioning their abilities and ideas, fearing the weaknesses they recognize, and fearing even more weaknesses that they suspect but are unknown to them. They have been seeking answers from other people—those whom clients believe clearly must have better answers. All of these conditions make clients fearful of letting their true selves be seen by others or even themselves, so they wear a variety of masks to present a better picture than what they fear is there. Providing the basic therapeutic conditions allows clients to explore themselves and their fears and to experiment with new ways of thinking and behaving within a safe and growth-oriented environment.

Receiving attention and support from a genuine individual who can be trusted allows clients to explore themselves in areas and ways they cannot in less therapeutic situations. Having another person closely and consistently listen helps clients to observe and listen to themselves better: "You're right, I am angry. And now that I say it out loud, I realize I've been angry for a long time." They begin to drop masks as they recognize aspects of themselves to be not quite as bad as they thought: "I do have the right to be angry even when someone else doesn't want me to be that way. I'm not comfortable with that idea, but it is there for now." Self-recognition and self-acceptance are key first steps in the growth process.

As individuals become open to their true experiences and more trusting of their own **organism**, they begin to see the blocks to growth that have burdened them. They also gain the confidence needed to recognize and deal with their problems on their own. New levels of self-confidence allow for dropping of protective masks and for accepting strengths and weaknesses as aspects that are both real and changeable over time. An internal **locus of control** develops as clients take control of their lives instead of following the direction of others who have been running their lives.

A major part of the development process in clients is recognition that they are fallible human beings who are always in a growth process. This position is very different from the belief that a person must be perfect to be good or loved. Acceptance of this position allows people to view themselves as continuing to learn and grow throughout their lives and to see success as regular improvement rather than perfection.

Clients' confidence in their ability to evaluate themselves, decide how to change, actually change, and accept their errors as learning steps thereby reduces anxiety and the dependence on others for directing their lives. An accurate perception of the real world and their part in it will continue to recognize the importance of the reactions and beliefs of others, but this information will now be seen as more equal in significance to their own views. Consequently, clients will take more responsibility for their own existence and need less external intervention.

Traditional Intervention Strategies

The counselor or therapist who is looking for a specific list of things to say, actions to take, or diagnoses to make will not find them in this theory. Person-centered theory is much more related to who practitioners are than to what techniques they use. Practitioners focus their actions around providing the conditions of genuineness, unconditional positive regard, and empathy in the relationship. No book can say how all individuals should be genuine, because each of us is different. Likewise, how a practitioner genuinely shows unconditional positive regard or empathy is dictated to some degree by the type of person he or she is. This section highlights two general areas related to therapeutic intervention techniques: how to be genuine and specific behaviors that have consistently been identified with communication of the core conditions.

Being Genuine. To be genuine, counselors or therapists need to look closely at themselves before deciding how to be or what to do. Obviously, one cannot be genuine by thinking, saying, or doing what someone else does. Knowing oneself, then, becomes critical: It allows the practitioner's actions and words to be congruent with the way he or she really is while at the same time helping the practitioner match the client's needs. Person-centered counselors or therapists need to be knowledgeable about themselves and reasonably comfortable with this information. They must be more congruent than their clients so that they give more to their clients than they take. One clear way to deal with these issues is for practitioners to seek quality helpful relationships, including counseling or psychotherapy, for themselves and to work as hard on their own continued growth as they ask their clients to work.

Being genuine does not mean sharing every thought or feeling with the client. Such a tactic would simply take the focus off the client and put it on the practitioner, which is not a part of person-centered helping or any other type of helping. An appropriate approach involves being a helpful, attentive, caring person who is truly interested in the client and able to demonstrate that interest and involvement. Have you experienced the type of situation in which an acquaintance says, "I know how you feel," and you know very well the words coming from this near stranger are nothing more than words? Not only do you reject the words, but you also lose faith in the person's honesty. The same person might have said, "I hardly know you, but if your experience is anything like my own loss, it must hurt a great deal." The second statement recognizes the reality of the two different people; it does not try to indicate more understanding than is reasonable to believe. There are as many genuine statements or actions as there are people and situations. The right statement or action matches the person the practitioner is with the unique situation with the client at a given time.

Active Listening. The first technique emphasized in person-centered theory is active listening and its reflection of content and feelings. Demonstrating empathy for the client requires highly attentive and interactive listening skills. Counselors or therapists must first show that they are paying attention. The physical actions most common to this are facing clients, leaning toward them, and making good eye contact. This position and the use of facial and body expressions that relate to the client's comments puts practitioners and clients in physical contact. After putting themselves in the best possible position to listen, practitioners must hear and see what is communicated and turn the bits and pieces into a holistic picture. They use both the words and the actions of the client to develop an understanding of the content and feelings being presented.

Taking in information is the initial step in active listening. Practitioners must then reflect the content and feelings of clients back to them for their listening to have action value. "I hear you saying . . ."; "So you are feeling . . ."; and "You seem to be feeling . . . because of . . ." are samples of the ways practitioners can explore with the client how accurate their empathy truly is. Only in this way can they jointly discover understanding and misconceptions at one level and move on to greater understanding.

Even the genuine counselor or therapist will not always have a full understanding of the client's world and will make varied types of mistakes in trying to reflect it. The process of active listening helps both parties clarify the content and feelings of a situation and is a learning process for each. Practitioners who can treat their own mistakes and growth during this learning process in a genuine manner, as a natural part of life, help clients accept their uncertainties and weaknesses.

Reflection of Content and Feelings. The first steps in the empathy exploration process tend to be the recognition and reflection of the actual words stated and the feelings that are most obvious. As client and counselor or therapist get to know each other better, an effective practitioner becomes better able to move beyond these surface interactions to see and convey feelings that clients do not even recognize they are expressing. For example, a client may be distracted or become quieter periodically during sessions. Initially, these reactions may appear related to the specific topic at hand. Over time, however, the practitioner may be able to tie those reactions to some general concept that pulls together in meaningful ways what seemed to be very different topics.

The practitioner's description of what he or she recognized can be valuable to the client, even when the description involves as little as extended listening, observing, and reflecting of the person's world. At its most powerful, reflection can bring together complex elements of the client's world into a much more accurate picture of the client as a whole than the individual elements create separately. The process is similar to what you might experience in trying to describe your face and then looking in the mirror. The closer and longer you look in the mirror, the more detail you see and the better you can describe the overall look of your face. Counselors or therapists who accurately reflect content and feelings act like that mirror; that is, they help clients see what they are expressing so that the clients can revise and expand on perceptions of themselves based on what they see in their reflection.

Immediacy. Many of the most powerful interactions are those in which the content and feelings involved relate directly to the immediate situation between the client and the counselor or therapists; in other words, they depend on **immediacy**. The mirror analogy fits here as well, as the mirror provides immediate feedback and it would be much less useful to you each day if it only showed how you looked several hours or years earlier. Recognition, understanding, and use of feelings are seen as major problems for clients from the person-centered perspective. Immediacy provides a here-and-now approach to the relationship with the practitioner in general and to feelings in particular. The relationship between client and practitioner is considered the most important therapeutic factor in part because it is available for immediate examination. Therefore, the feelings that both client and practitioner are currently experiencing are often the most therapeutic ones available. Statements that receive primary emphasis are ones such as "How are you feeling now?" and "Your statements make me feel . . ." On the other hand, statements seen as less therapeutically useful might be these: "Why did you feel that way?" "What did the other person think?" "What did you believe then?"

A major reason for emphasis on the here and now in person-centered theory is the ability of the client and practitioner to together verify, check, and explore reactions immediately. Statements or feelings from the past make use of only the client's perspective; thus the practitioner has a reduced opportunity to be a vibrant part of the client's experience.

Appropriate Self-Disclosure. In truly genuine relationships, clients see relevant parts of the practitioners' phenomenological world as well as their own world. Appropriate **self-disclosure** allows clients to compare their view of the world with the view of another individual whom they have come to trust and value as a significant human being. Under nonthreatening circumstances, such comparisons give clients the chance to review and revise their views based on information that they might otherwise not have had available or that was too threatening to accept. A supportive relationship allows clients forward movement to try out new thoughts and behaviors based on the comparative information. Much like the growth of the bean mentioned earlier, clients are can use the supportive atmosphere and comparative information to develop at the rate and in a manner most appropriate for them.

Personalized Counselor or Therapist Actions. One of the great misconceptions among new practitioners is that simplistic listening and reflecting are all the person-centered counselor or therapist does. This reaction to his concept of an evolving and personalized theory was a major frustration to Rogers throughout his professional life. After one demonstration session, a workshop participant confronted Rogers, "I noticed that you asked questions of the client. But just last night a lecturer told us that we must never do that." Rogers responded, "Well I'm in the fortunate position of not having to be a Rogerian" (Farber et al., 1996, p. 11). Rogers used his own thoughts and personality in many creative ways, just as all quality person-centered counselors or therapists do. These are the aspects of counseling or therapy that appear as metaphor, humor, confrontation, and at times even interpretation or directiveness. Each of these seemingly directive aspects was identified by Bowen (1996) in his review of a Rogers' tape in which he was counseling a client.

Many practitioners now use Rogers' relationship development model as the foundation on which to build other cognitive, behavioral, or emotional approaches (Hill, 2004; See & Kamnetz). Boy and Pine (1999), for example, identified additional stages in which person-centered counselors or therapists use their own creative methods to help clients recognize and deal with problems after the essential relationship elements have been established. They also argued that because each client is different, person-centered practitioners must adjust their methods as much as possible to fit the preferred mode of the client. Their view is that a true person-centered approach will have a consistent foundation, but that the full range of the relationship must build on the unique aspects of the counselor or therapist, the client, and their personalized relationship together. Although Rogers did not write about this in an exact fashion, he has been considered as generally supportive of the model: "If a therapist has the attitudes we have come to request as essential, probably he or she can use a variety of techniques" (Wilkins, 2003, p. 92).

Much of Rogers' work has been so well integrated into other theories and practices that the person-centered labels have been dropped. However, there are practitioners who give more specific attention to the person-centered element of their work. They reflect a wide variety of approaches, just a sample of which includes person-centered expressive therapy (N. Rogers, 2001), person-centered family therapy (O'Leary, 1999), person-centered child counseling (Thompson, Rudolph, & Henderson, 2004), multimedia approaches to person-centered counseling, client-centered psychodrama (Brazier, 1993), person-centered psychological testing (Watkins, 1993), person-centered applied behavioral analysis (Holburn & Vietze, 2000), and person-centered art therapy (Malchiodi, 2003). Person-centered theory may not have the name recognition that it did 30 years ago, but its core concepts and their influence continue to be observed throughout the field.

Nonclient-centered Interventions. Some techniques are not true aspects of person-centered counseling. One key example is the form of diagnosis and detailed treatment planning that has become a significant part of the mental health field today. Increasingly, insurance companies and government agencies are requiring clear-cut statements of the client's so called illness, its severity, and the estimated length of time it will take to be corrected. Person-centered counselors or therapists do not view clients in an ill versus well context, so they can have a great deal of trouble working with these requirements. Person-centered theory is much more appropriate for helping people progress than for getting them over some designated level of a diagnosable condition. Person-centered practitioners who find themselves in situations where they must design extensive diagnosis and treatment models need to pay close attention to how and to what degree they can integrate these relatively ill-suited processes.

One way that person-centered practitioners have approached the assessment model is to deal with it as a joint task with the client and to determine their ability to work successfully together (Wilkins, 2003). They view assessment as a way counselor or therapist and client explore how they will work together and toward what goals. Practitioners who use the assessment model consider it part of their congruence; that is, they use it to clarify how their roles and responsibilities will influence the relationship and potential success of counseling or therapy. They see this process as similar to reaching agreement on many other ethical and practical aspects of the working relationship. The key to this approach is the joint interaction of counselor or therapist and client: the client continues to direct the counseling or therapy with recognition of how joint responsibilities with the practitioner influence their work together.

Many new counselors or therapists identify with a person-centered approach because it fits what they want to do and what has helped them grow in positive relationships. When they attempt to use the approach, however, they often get caught up in non-person-centered techniques, mostly for their own comfort. For example, there is little need for extensive **questioning** in the person-centered approach, for the task is to follow the client rather than to continually direct them toward issues to be explored. New practitioners in particular tend to question clients more than is necessary. They are likely to begin seeking extensive information in clients' pasts rather than talking about current perceptions and interactions. The questions also tend to lead them into overanalyzing client comments and reactions in order to develop elaborate rationales for why clients do what they do. These techniques may stem in part from the fact how professionals have completed many years of education where such tactics are highly effective methods for succeeding in academia. Now they are faced with doubts about their own ability to use the skills they have been taught with real clients who can be hurt. Lack of confidence and experience often causes them to fall back on the questioning and directing tactics of the traditional academic community rather than responding and following tactics of the person-centered approach. Just as clients need time and proper conditions to gain trust in their organism, new person-centered counselors or therapists need time to trust in their developing organisms.

Brief Intervention Strategies

Implementation of Core Conditions. The era of managed care, growing requests for counseling and psychotherapy, fewer resources, and the hurry-up nature of contemporary society form far less than ideal conditions for a model of therapy that promotes growth rather than immediate resolution of problems. The faith in people and personalized, patient support of their development that embody person-centered counseling or therapy may not be central to the quick-fix business model. Nevertheless, even those who prefer brief intervention have come to recognize the need for applying person-centered core conditions in their practices. The person-centered foundation of listening to, understanding, and validating clients remains essential to developing and maintaining the necessary therapeutic alliance that allows a variety of brief intervention techniques to succeed (Presbury, Echterling, and McKee, 2002; J. C. Watson & Bohart, 2001).

Brief intervention techniques do not act like an injection of antibiotics that go to work immediately on the bacteria in the body independent of any actions on the part of the patient.

Even the briefest of counseling or therapy intervention techniques require clients to have sufficient belief in the technique, recognition of its personal relevance, and confidence in the counselor or therapist before they can successfully implement the technique and derive benefits. Practitioners must promote the core conditions of the person-centered approach as part of brief interventions in order for the interventions to achieve maximum effect.

Introduction of Constraints. Person-centered counselors or therapists who choose not to use techniques from the variety of brief therapy models currently in vogue must still deal with the pressures of time caused by clients who want to get over symptoms and with business conditions. Probably the most important action these practitioners can take to meet brevity demands is to introduce the constraints under which practitioner and client must work. Doing so helps them both evaluate how to best work together under the client's direction and the constraints on their relationship. How much time is available in a session, how many sessions are allowed, and how progress will be evaluated are examples of topics in which brief time frames are involved. This process of forthright introduction of constraints is in line with other early discussions of relationships between clients and practitioners on ethical issues such as confidentiality and the nature of the counseling or therapy experience and on practical matters such as appointments and costs.

Development of Goals. The outcomes of discussions on time constraints create movement toward developing tentative goals. Naturally, goals arise early in most person-centered counseling or therapy as clients describe problems and hopes. When brevity is a concern, clarity about early goals becomes even more important so that the client has a sense of where initial thoughts and efforts should be directed. The first critical point in the development of person-centered goals is that they be set by the client instead of emphasizing the practitioner's expectations. The second key point is that clients be fully aware that goals are tentative and may well change as counseling or therapy progresses. Flexibility is essential. Person-centered counselors or therapists believe that clients can direct their own counseling or therapy. They also know, however, that effective counseling or therapy creates learning that changes client perceptions of needs, goals, and directions.

Group Work. Many counselors or therapists choose person-centered group counseling or therapy as a means of giving additional time to more people through the attention that a person-centered approach offers. Practitioners in schools, colleges, agencies, and private practice can become pressed for time because of client needs and their own qualities. The better that individual counselors or therapists become, the more clients seek their services. Group person-centered approaches were found to be effective in providing the core conditions from group members as well as the counselor or therapist to produce positive therapeutic outcomes (Page, Weiss, & Lietaer, 2002).

Honest Interactions. Integrating brief intervention strategies into person-centered counseling or therapy may not be ideal, but there are practical ways to approach the problem for adults and children (Thompson et al., 2004). One person-centered concept is essential in determining how to respond to pressures for brevity: To be genuine and trustworthy, counselors or therapists must be honest about the factors that affect the counseling or therapy process. If the practitioner does not inform the client of time or other constraints on the process, the client will likely realize the negative impact of the constraints later. Such a situation diminishes the therapeutic alliance, as the client looses faith with the practitioner and the process. The rule of thumb is to let the client know about constraints and work honestly from that point.

CLIENTS WITH SERIOUS MENTAL HEALTH ISSUES

Discussion of clients with serious mental health can be problematic for person-centered counselors who generally find that traditional assessment and assignment of mental disorder categories are not useful to treatment. Such conceptualizations encourage people other than the client to identify the problems and the direction of treatment. In the person-centered approach, on the other hand, practitioners place therapeutic attention on the client's perceptions of difficulties, goals, and treatment directions. These differences are significant because in the mental health field today assessment and diagnosis are expected elements. Person-centered counselors or therapists who want employment in most mental health agencies or who desire insurance payments for their private practice need to deal with this form of labeling, at least for communication purposes.

A meta-analysis of studies on experiential therapies, the bulk of which were person centered, showed positive effects across a wide range of disorders (Greenberg, Elliott, & Lietaer, 1994). For example, adaptations of person-centered counseling were found to be useful with diagnoses that varied from the more common depressive disorders (Elliott, Clark, Wexler, Kemeny, Brinkerhoff, & Mack, 1990) to those such as borderline personality disorder (Bohart, 1990), schizophrenia (Prouty, 1998) and dementia (Zeman, 1999).

Although person-centered counseling or therapy has been found to have value throughout the most serious diagnostic categories, there are treatment issues that are likely to make it less effective as the primary technique. Increasing knowledge about the biological aspects of serious disorders like schizophrenia and obsessive-compulsive disorder has led to drugs often being the preferred treatment (Day, 2004). Such treatment options can be expected to increase as advances are made in understanding the chemical processes in the body. Disorders that require clients to learn specific skills such as those in sex therapy call for much more counselor or therapist directness and for behavioral techniques. Also, the client-directed nature of person-centered theory requires a great degree of client motivation. Persons who are not motivated to grow through counseling or therapy become less viable candidates for person-centered counseling or therapy as the sole model for treatment.

CROSS-CULTURAL CONSIDERATIONS

Person-centered counseling or therapy has been questioned as to how well it can adapt to various cultures that may hold different values, have widely dissimilar immediate and generational experiences, and operate from social norms that are poles apart (Day, 2004). Such questions deserve attention from person-centered practitioners because the therapy originated from White, European, and American influences that emphasize individuality, self-control, and ongoing personal development more than changing the immediate forces that affect individuals. To effectively meet Cross-Cultural Competencies of the American Counseling Association the person-centered practitioners must pay particular attention to understanding themselves, being genuine in their interactions, and applying active empathy in the broadest sense with clients.

Being genuine in counseling relationships entails a prerequisite that you understand yourself sufficiently to be genuine. Exploration of your own values, beliefs, biases, and cultural norms and how you act on these is essential for the congruent communication necessary for clients to evaluate it as honest and trustworthy. Furthermore, as personal characteristics change with time, circumstances, and introductions to people with vastly different experiences from your own, the self-exploration must be ongoing. Cross-cultural counseling and therapy require even greater emphasis on such self-exploration, because when it is lacking, practitioners may see client differences from themselves as client problems rather than as cultural differences in experiences, behaviors, and worldview. Only when person-centered practitioners continually examine and expand their understanding of their own values and biases will the genuineness they attempt to present be valuable and not counterproductive.

Active empathy, an essential part of the relationship capacities of counselors or therapists, is gaining in importance as diversity and interactions between cultures increase (Montgomery & Kottler, 2005). The ability to develop full understanding of client thoughts, experiences, emotions, and worldview, along with the ability to communicate this understanding effectively to clients, is a primary requirement for breaking down barriers and misconceptions in cross-cultural counseling. The phenomenological perspective of person-centered counseling or psychotherapy in many ways parallels the multicultural worldview; both emphasize that people view the world differently and require counselors or therapists to learn about each client's world as fully as possible. Through understanding the culture of clients and the multiple influences it has on them, counselors or therapists can make sense of the words, actions, and emotions that they see and that are described by the clients. The ability of practitioners to communicate the depth and accuracy of their understanding to clients helps clients to trust the practitioners and accept the genuine relationship as positive.

Self-exploration, genuineness, and active empathy implemented effectively allow cultural adaptations that are necessary for cross-cultural counseling or therapy to be successful. These three conditions enable traditional person-centered counselors or therapists to adapt to cultures that emphasize family honor and dignity over individual desires (Tu, 1985), to counteract the potential for stigmatization of minorities (Lemoire & Chen, 2005), and to meet the unique needs of cultural entities within larger cultural groups (Sanders & Bradley, 2005). Self-exploration, genuineness, and active empathy encourage person-centered counselors or therapists to move beyond what is sometimes considered a reflection-only model to the dynamic and evolving model it is meant to be.

EVALUATION

Overview

The person-centered movement brought about innovations in research and training as well as a new approach to counseling and psychotherapy. The emphasis on objectivity in examination of the relationship between client and practitioner moved the profession forward in its evaluation of specific interaction variables. This solid research background did not, however, eliminate all problems from the person-centered appraoch. Several limitations characterize person-centered theory: (1) being considered a simplistic theory when it is actually quite complex; (2) requiring greater trust from the client than people are able to offer; and (3) having few specific tactics for new practitioners to fall back on as other theories provide. An overview of these limitations and others are summarized at the end of this section.

Supporting Research

Carl Rogers' perception of people, counseling, and psychotherapy as highly personal and individualized often gives newcomers to the field a sense that Rogers and his theory deemphasize research over personal interaction. This perception could not be further from the truth. In fact, the early research of Rogers has been recognized by some as "the birth of psychotherapy research" (Barrett-Lennard, 1998, p. 261). Rogers was a major innovator in the development of research techniques for counseling, psychotherapy, and person-centered theory. He recognized that for any theory or technique to remain credible and become more effective, solid research is essential (Rogers, 1986).

Rogers pioneered the use of taped transcripts (Cain, 1987) and other clinical measures of interacting to broaden the scope of psychological research (Hjelle & Ziegler, 1992). These techniques, along with the use of the **Q-sort** method, helped bring the more subjective aspects of people, counseling, and psychotherapy into respectability. Among Rogers' earliest significant publications were books on extensive research studies with the populations of standard mental health centers (Rogers & Dymond, 1954) and with people with schizophrenia (Rogers, 1967). All this work demonstrated his commitment to research on his theory and established his basic concepts as valid and reliable sources of client progress.

Rogers' research and teaching tool that is used most today is the tape-recording and transcribing of sessions with clients. Note taking from memory was not considered satisfactory. He wanted to hear and see as much of the interaction as possible to judge the client's reactions and his own work. Taping and evaluating sessions has become common practice today, and many of Rogers' tapes and transcripts of counseling sessions continue to be reviewed and analyzed in detail (Farber et al., 1996).

The Q-sort method of data collection became a major influence in the acceptance of Rogers' theory. Developed by William Stephenson (1953), a colleague of Rogers at the University of Chicago, the Q-sort method uses many different formats for people to sort attributes of themselves into various categories and levels. Generally, when the method is used in person-centered research, subjects are asked to perform the task once for self-description and another time for ideal self-description. These two sortings are compared to see how well their perceived and ideal selves match. The theory suggests that the closer the match of the ideal and perceived selves in a person, the more congruent the person is. Because congruence is thought to improve during effective person-centered interaction, researchers can look for increasingly closer matches between these two measures as counseling or psychotherapy continues. This procedure enabled Rogers to validate many of his theoretical constructs and procedures.

Research on person-centered counseling as a total theory motivated many studies in its early years, but the momentum for such research has declined significantly over the past 20 years (Corey, 2001). This decline appears to be due in part to the general acceptance of Rogers' basic concepts as necessary, if not sufficient, core conditions for success in counseling and psychotherapy and to the extensive research done in the 1950s and 1960s. Most of the recent research has been on these core conditions, which are widely believed to be Rogers' common factors for counseling success (See & Kamnetz, 2004). Acceptance of Rogers' ideas is so widespread that many of Rogers' concepts are no longer considered Rogerian (Goodyear, 1987).

The essentials of relationships continue to receive attention in current research efforts. Studies continue to show that variables in relationships account for much of the success variance across counseling theories (Hubble, Duncan, & Miller, 1999).

The profession has not ignored potential weaknesses in person-centered research. Some researchers have questioned the methodological aspects of some studies. Concerns about sophistication and rigor have been raised (Prochaska & Norcross, 1999). Similar comments led others to ask whether the problems raise doubts about the validity of the theory (N. Watson, 1984). These concerns deserve particular attention when considered along with the fact that less person-centered research is now being conducted at the same time that the core conditions are widely accepted.

Person-centered theory has remained relatively unchanged according to some authorities (Cain, 1986). Combs (1988) suggested that this lack of development of the basic theory is the reason for a lessening of research in the area. Whether or not a lack of theory development has brought about less research, for the theory to grow, new ideas and additional research are necessary.

Limitations

Person-centered theory may suffer most from the fact that it seems so simple to learn. The concepts are relatively few, there is no long list of details to remember, and there are no specific tactics to recall for each diagnostic problem a client might have. The counselor or therapist can be lulled into a feeling of security by this apparent simplicity. For example, simple listening and reflecting of words and surface feelings are usually beneficial at the very beginning of a session. However, continued surface-level interactions that do not consider the many dimensions of both the client and practitioner may quickly become repetitive, nondirectional, and trite.

The reality is that the few basic concepts in person-centered theory have a virtually unlimited complexity, because counselors and therapists must be fully aware of their clients' and their own changing phenomenological worlds. They must respond to the interactions between these worlds in ways that best fit the genuine natures of their clients and themselves. This is a difficult task that requires an excellent understanding and continuing awareness of oneself and the client. New practitioners in particular have a difficult time with this complexity. Persons who are working hard and feeling under pressure to remember and do a "new thing" or a "right thing" will naturally find it difficult to be genuine and aware of all that is happening around and within themselves and others. Acting on what they recognize adds yet another level of difficulty to the task.

The supportive nature of person-centered theory is often misinterpreted to mean that the practitioner should not be confrontational with clients. Counselors or therapists often need to do more than listen and reflect. People who function effectively confront themselves all the time, and practitioners must recognize that appropriate confrontation is a natural part of an effective helping relationship. Person-centered theory makes room for such confrontation, but it gives few specific guidelines as to where, when, and how it should occur.

A great deal of trust in the positive motivation and abilities of oneself and one's clients is required of the person-centered counselor or therapist. Without this trust, many of the other person-entered concepts lose their true value, and a therapeutic interaction may become little more than polite conversation. Such trust in people and a process is not easy to establish in all circumstances. Human beings have difficulty suspending their mistrust because fears, previous experiences, and preconceived notions are a natural part of the human condition. The more extreme a person's negative experiences and reactions are, the more difficult it is to act fully on the person-centered belief system. The result is that most practitioners can place confidence in a bright, college-educated, law-abiding, depressed client, but have more difficulty maintaining a similar confidence in a depressed rapist or murderer.

Person-centered practice requires a great deal of personal knowledge, understanding, and awareness, as well as a willingness to act on this information. There are few techniques or activities to fall back on if the counselor or therapist does not have or cannot act on this information about the helping relationship. Other theories provide more activities or tactics that allow the practitioner to give the process a boost when the relationship is not all it could be.

SUMMARY CHART—*Person-Centered Theory*

Human Nature

Person-centered theory emphasizes a highly positive view of human nature in which people can be trusted to be continually seeking productive directions toward maximum self-actualization. Perceptions of unconditional positive regard from their environment support people's development, whereas conditions of worth inhibit it and produce nonactualizing thoughts and behaviors.

Major Constructs

Clients have psychological and sociological difficulties to the degree that their phenomenological worlds do not match their true positive nature (incongruence) and its use in their everyday lives. Empathic understanding of the client's world is essential in helping clients find a more congruent match between their phenomenological world and their actions, feelings, thoughts, and responses from others.

Goals

Counselors or therapists provide a safe, caring environment in which clients can get in closer touch with essential, positive elements of themselves that have been hidden or distorted. Less distortion and more congruence lead clients to have greater trust that their organisms can be relied on for effective reactions to people and situations. This added trust results in reduced feelings of helplessness and powerlessness, fewer behaviors driven by stereotypes, and more productive, creative, and flexible decision making.

Change Process

The change process is stimulated when counselors or therapists provide the core conditions of genuineness, acceptance and caring, and empathic understanding. Change takes place as clients perceive these conditions and begin exploring and testing new thoughts and behaviors that are more in line with their positive, growth-oriented nature. This exploration, testing, and learning leads clients to increase their trust in their organism's ability to think and act in a wider variety of circumstances.

Interventions

Person-centered theory is marked by minimal specific intervention techniques. Practitioners are asked to be genuine in a relationship rather than to perform a rigid set of actions. Inter-actons in the immediacy of the situation and evaluation of the results through active listening, reflection of content and feelings, appropriate self-disclosure, and other personally, professionally, and situationally responsive interactions are essential.

Limitations

Success depends on practitioners maintaining high trust in the feelings and actions of clients and themselves. Lack of trust often causes practitioners to fall back on safe, passive reflection responses. These are necessary early on, but they become increasingly inadequate as the need for a more comprehensive therapeutic relationship develops—a relationship that includes the directness that comes with additional culturally, situationally, and personally relevant feelings and interactions.

THE CASE OF JONATHAN: *A Person-Centered Approach*

The use of a case study to view person-centered theory raises several problems. The standard case study concept suggests that a collection of historical factors will be used to describe and diagnose an illness. However, person-centered theory places more emphasis on clients' perceptions of and feelings about their world than on facts as seen by others. It disdains looking at work with clients as focused on illness. In addition, in person-centered theory the relationship with the counselor or therapist is much more critical to the success of therapy than a client's specific, historical case development. Many person-centered practitioners might, therefore, choose to ignore the concept of a clinical case history.

The problem with this decision, however, is that it may convey the idea that person-centered counselors or therapists do not seek to understand a client's perceived experiences or expect to observe specific progress outside the therapeutic relationship. In fact, the reason person-centered practitioners attend so closely is precisely because they want to understand the client's perceived experiences and worldview as well as possible. They then use that understanding within a therapeutic relationship that is unique to the particular phenomenological worlds of the client and the counselor. Finally, like all good counselors or therapists, person-centered practitioners must evaluate the progress of clients both inside the therapeutic relationship and in the outside world.

The modified case study that follows attempts to take each of the factors just described into account by examining potential phenomenological aspects of the client's situation as though the information had been acquired within the therapeutic relationship. Assumptions are added that might reflect other information the practitioner acquires about feelings and emotions not included in the more content-oriented case description. This case study will also emphasize Jonathan's relationship with the counselor or therapist and suggest potential directions that Jonathan's growth might take as a result of a positive therapeutic relationship.

Jonathan's Phenomenological World

As would be expected with clients entering counseling or therapy, Jonathan has a phenomenological view of the world that is incongruent with his true feelings, abilities, and potential. He has incorporated unattainable conditions of worth that come from a mixture of culture, conflicts in cultures, family, and personal relationships. In his currently perceived world, he will never be able to be a good enough son, father, Native American, employee, colleague, or partner to satisfy those whose approval he desires. The harder he tries to please others, the further he gets away from personal feelings of self-worth and the less pleasing he does of anyone, including himself. He has lost trust in his own organism's ability to feel, think, decide, and act in productive ways; consequently, he is trying to act in a world as others see it, a strategy that will not bring him the growth or success he is naturally seeking.

The fact that Jonathan's phenomenological world is frequently out of line with the world that actually affects him causes Jonathan great anxiety. He looks outside himself for ways to act, only to find that what others point to as the "right" way does not satisfy anyone, least of all himself. He knows that who he is and what he does are not working, but he cannot identify other ways to view the situation and no longer trusts himself to provide that direction.

Actualizing Tendencies

It is clear that Jonathan has never fully given in to the conditions of worth that direct him in non-actualizing ways. He keeps experimenting with new challenges and finding success for periods of time in spite of the disapproval of his actions by others. Decisions to take time away from high school to better understand himself, to return to graduate school, to try life outside the reservation, to return to the reservation and recognize its importance to him, to make different attempts at responsibility in marriages, and to seek better ways to deal with work all demonstrate an actualizing tendency that keeps Jonathan moving forward, even in the face of mounting conditions of worth placed on him by others. He was referred to counseling by his employer, but his openness to talking of his experiences, weaknesses, anxieties, and desires for growth speak positively for his motivation to get more out of himself and to take the necessary actions.

Jonathan has been seeking a variety of ways to actualize his most appropriate self and has demonstrated that he has the tools to succeed. This is a person who has seen his brother die in a car he was driving, struggled with the clash of his involvement in two very different cultures, and still found times of success at school, work, and in relationships. His abilities seem clear even as his success is frustrated due to distorted views and the absence of caring relationships in which he could be accepted for who he truly is and will work to be. This situation stops him from recognizing alternative views of himself and potential actions that could lead to much greater self-actualization. The growth Jonathan seeks will be found to the degree he gains the confidence in himself that will allow him to maintain involvement during difficult times rather than attempting to escape as he has by physically and emotionally leaving situations and through alcohol abuse.

The Counselor's or Therapist's Role

A counselor or therapist valuable to Jonathan will empathically work with his situation, see his inner strength, trust in his willingness and ability to move in positive directions, and provide the core therapeutic conditions that will allow his actualizing tendencies to flower. These conditions will help Jonathan clarify the intricacies of his own feelings and see the value in sharing his views accurately with another person. Jonathan also needs a close relationship with a counselor or therapist who is not burdened by false fronts so that he can trust the legitimacy of the human interaction (genuineness).

Unconditional positive regard for Jonathan can be conveyed in part by showing confidence in him as a competent person who can think and act effectively. The counselor or therapist will not lead Jonathan to specific topics, suggest ways for him to act, identify his problems for him, or direct, reward, or punish him. Instead, the practitioner will show attention, listen actively, and display an understanding of his cultural influences, without placing judgments on the information.

The counselor or therapist will listen and observe closely in order to grasp all of Jonathan's verbal and nonverbal thoughts and emotions. To achieve this, the counselor or therapist will convey back to Jonathan what she or he sees, hears, and feels, so that together they can check on the accuracy of their communications. Mistakes, underestimations, and overestimations are common in this process of developing accurate empathic understanding. The process should be viewed as a learning tool for both parties rather than a set of correct statements made by the counselor or therapist. Jonathan presents ideas, the counselor or therapist tries to reflect them and possibly tie them to previously recognized concepts, and both parties negotiate to reach mutual understandings. It is only from such struggle that accurate understanding arises.

Unconditional positive regard and accurate empathic understanding begin to look false and misleading to the client if genuineness is not conveyed. Jonathan needs to see himself in a relationship that is open and honest. It must be made clear to him that what the counselor or therapist thinks, does, and says are consistent and that taking on the role of counselor or therapist does not mean one cannot be a real person at the same time. Such consistency will allow Jonathan to trust the reality of the relationship, as well as the ideas, skills, and behaviors that develop from it. He will learn to use the counselor or therapist as a model for his own development of congruence. As progress continues, Jonathan will recognize that because this is a positive human relationship with a genuine person, the ideas and actions can be transferred to his life outside counseling or therapy. The relationship, therefore, will be viewed as an immediate, natural, real, and dependable experience that can be duplicated in many respects beyond the helping relationship.

The person-centered practitioner is often considered to be caring and kindly; nevertheless, the core conditions offer a great deal of challenge to the client. Jonathan will not always want to hear how the counselor or therapist is reacting to him, as this may require that he confront aspects of himself that are difficult to accept. Only the truly empathic counselor or therapist, who is also genuine, can successfully overcome such difficult issues. The many challenging times and confrontations in a person-centered approach are those that would be expected in any genuine human relationship. The added benefit in this particular relationship is that the counselor or therapist is professionally trained as well as being a caring individual.

Expectations for Progress

The person-centered counselor or therapist who adequately and consistently provides the necessary therapeutic conditions can expect Jonathan to progress in some general ways. However, Jonathan might not change in the ways that others deem to be best. Jonathan is seeking himself. Although certain other people affect that self, progress in counseling or therapy will likely reduce the impact these others have on Jonathan. This influence will be replaced by increasing trust in his organism so that Jonathan will begin to see his personal ability to control his own life while still considering the needs of others.

As Jonathan starts to trust his relationship with the counselor or therapist he becomes freer to talk of difficult issues and recognize that this person will still think well of him, no matter how inappropriate certain aspects of his feelings, thoughts, and actions appear to be. Issues will begin to appear in a light that is different from what Jonathan had envisioned previously. Generally, the new view will offer problems in a manageable form that is not nearly as terrible or insurmountable as Jonathan had perceived. Excitement about finding new ways to see the world will likely be followed by struggles to understand his new perceptions and how he will need to relate to them differently.

Jonathan will soon find a need to explore his new ways of viewing, feeling, and acting in the world outside of counseling or therapy. He will want to know how his children, family, boss, and others will respond if he chooses to act differently. Such issues will be explored in the therapeutic relationship before trying them on others. Jonathan will want to examine both the good and bad results of his actions after they have been tried in real life. The new ideas, observations, and attempted behaviors in each situation will expand Jonathan's view of the world and likely bring him back to the counselor or therapist for help in integrating the new information.

There will be pleasures, fears, successes, and disappointments in Jonathan's development, just as in everyone's. But Jonathan will come to recognize that there are important lessons in each experience and that everything learned increases the confidence in his own ability to direct himself and correct his mistakes. Eventually, he may learn to have enough confidence in his immediate reactions to use a productive combination of his own ideas and those of others to develop positive outcomes. He will also recognize that even when things do not work out as planned, he is effective enough as a human being to overcome mistakes.

CHAPTER 9

Gestalt Theory

Melinda Haley
New Mexico State University

Fritz Perls is generally considered the foremost practitioner of Gestalt counseling and psychotherapy; however, his method was influenced by the Gestalt psychologists who preceded him such as Max Wertheimer, Wolfgang Kohler, Kurt Koffka, and Sandor Ferenczi. The word *Gestalt* is a German term used to define a unique patterning in which parts are integrated into the perceptual whole. Gestalt psychology is concerned with perception and cognition, whereas Gestalt therapy focuses on personality, psychopathology, and psychotherapy.

Gestalt counselors and psychotherapists engage the whole organism (person) and operate from the perspective that human beings have the capacity and strength to grow, to develop, and to become the persons they are meant to be. Practitioners make a basic assumption that individuals can cope with their life problems, especially if they are fully aware of what is happening in and around them. Clients are directed to move from talking about experience to directly experiencing what they are focusing on at any given moment in counseling or therapy. Clients are seen as having the ability to respond to their environment appropriately and flexibly.

Most Gestalt counselors and therapists would agree the particular goal of Gestalt therapy is the phenomenological exploration of the individual rather than reconditioning of behavior or interpretation of the unconscious. The process of change in Gestalt counseling and

The author extends her gratitutde to Mary Finn Maples for her contibution to the first three editions of this chapter and to Conrad Sieber for his work on the first two editions of this chapter.

psychotherapy consists of identifying and working through a variety of blocks or interferences that prevent the client from achieving a balance. Specific interventions are the concrete behaviors of experimentation that emerge from the cooperation that exists between the client and the practitioner. They are labeled *experiments* rather than exercises because they are procedures aimed at discovery.

Generally, Gestalt therapy lacks dimensions usually associated with brief interventions such as quantifiable behavioral goals. The focus is not on facilitating behavioral changes in the client but on helping the client to develop insight and interpersonal awareness. Gestalt therapy is holistic; it does not break a person down into separate pieces or variables, so it is difficult to "classify" clients in the manner required by the American Psychiatric Association's *Diagnostic and Statistical Manual of Mental Disorders*. Gestaltists do not believe in disease but rather in *dis-ease,* and to suggest that disorders are of the mind is inimical to the Gestalt approach. Gestaltists also view "symptoms" as an individual's creative adjustment to a difficult situation in his or her life. Gestalt theory advocates that the individual cannot be understood in isolation but must be understood within his or her social and historical context, and within the uniqueness of his or her field.

BACKGROUND

Gestalt theory has a rich and varied history. Although Fritz Perls is generally credited with being the foremost practitioner of Gestalt counseling and psychotherapy (James & Gilliland, 2003), his method was influenced by the Gestalt psychologists who preceded him such as Max Wertheimer, Wolfgang Kohler, Kurt Koffka, and some would even say Sandor Ferenczi (King & Wertheimer, 2005; Serge, 2004). These psychologists laid the psychological groundwork for Perls' application of Gestaltism in counseling and psychotherapy. According to Henle (1978), the difference between Gestalt psychology and Gestalt therapy is that the former is concerned with perception and cognition, whereas the latter focuses on personality, psychopathology, and psychotherapy.

The word *Gestalt* is a German term used to define a unique patterning in which the parts are integrated into the perceptual whole (James & Gilliland, 2003). There are three parts to the definition of a Gestalt, "a thing, its context or enviornment, and the relationship between them" (p. 2; Brownell, 2003e); Gestalt "connotes the structural entity which is both different from and much more than the sum of its parts" (p. 1; Clarkson, 2004).

Frederick (Fritz) Perls

Friedrich Saloman Perls was born in 1893, the middle child and only son of middle-class Jewish parents in Berlin. He later anglicized his name, becoming Frederick, although most people called him Fritz (Thompson & Rudolph, 2000). Perls received a medical degree in 1920 after a brief stint as a medical corpsman during World War I. He found his war experience brutal in military authoritarianism and racial prejudice. These experiences influenced his humanitarianism but also left him with a deep cynicism about human nature (Seligman, 2001). His early training in psychoanalysis took place in Austria and Germany, and he became associated with neurologist Kurt Goldstein (Clarkson, 2004). While working as Goldstein's assistant at Frankfurt am Main's Institute for Brain Injured Soldiers in 1926, Perls became interested in the transforming of Gestalt psychology into Gestalt therapy (McBride, 1998; Perls, 1969b).

Henle (1978) believed that Perls viewed most of his differences with Gestalt psychology as insurmountable because he regarded himself as an organismic psychologist, or a viewer of humankind in its holistic sense. When Hitler came to power, Perls and his new wife relocated to Johannesburg, South Africa, and he shed the Freudian psychoanalytic influence. They were, in fact, the first psychologists in South Africa (Wheeler, 2004). In 1946, he immigrated to the United States, where he published *Gestalt Therapy: Excitement and Growth in the Human Personality* in 1951. Following the favorable reception of this text, he established several Gestalt Institutes throughout the country, the first in New York in 1952. His work at the Esalen Institute in California established him as a prominent practitioner of Gestalt counseling and psychotherapy.

Laura Perls

Fritz Perls' work was carried on after his death in 1970 by his wife, Laura (Lore) Posner Perls (1905–1990). It has become increasingly clear since her death in 1990 that Laura Perls contributed significantly to Gestalt counseling and psychotherapy, having studied with Max Wertheimer and gaining recognition as a Gestalt psychologist in her own right (Wheeler, 2004). She continued her work long after her husband's death and became an influential force in Gestalt therapy and the training of Gestalt therapists.

Paul Goodman

Another person who participated in the development of Gestalt therapy is Paul Goodman. When he met Fritz Perls in 1949, Goodman was an accomplished classical scholar, wrote fiction and political criticism, and had been deeply influenced by his studies of Freud, Rank, and Reich (Wheeler, 2004). It was a fortuitous meeting, as Perls was looking for a person learned in these areas to help him edit what came to be known as *Gestalt Therapy: Excitement and Growth in the Human Personality*.

Perls received recognition initially for this work, but many scholars have since come to credit Goodman with writing at least half of the manuscript, specifically the half dealing with the theory of Gestalt therapy (Serlin & Shane, 1999). His role is now seen as one of collaboration with Fritz and Laura Perls, and his own contribution to development of the theory is acknowledged. Although Fritz Perls is still credited as Gestalt therapy's most boisterous and ardent promoter, there are those who now consider Paul Goodman its chief theoretician (Meier & Davis, 2001).

Phenomenology, Existentialism, Field Theory, and Dialogue

Gestalt psychology was not the only influence that inspired Gestalt therapy. The roots of Gestalt therapy can most certainly be found in phenomenology and field theory. Nevertheless, there exists within Gestalt therapy the influential existentialist writings of Soren Kierkegaard, Friedrich Nietzsche, Martin Buber, Paul Tillich, Martin Heidegger; the writings of Aristotle, William James, John Dewey, and Immanuel Kant; the philosophies of Zen Buddhism and Taoism; and some basic principles from psychoanalytic theory, humanistic theories, and Reichian body therapy (Ginger, 2004). The coagulation of all these perspectives placed the focus on improving clients' awareness of their subjective experience, facilitating their ability to become authentic and make choices that lead to a meaningful life, and setting in motion the natural process of growth that moves toward integration within self, and between self and the environment (Brownell, 2003a).

Phenomenology. **Phenomenology** is the study of human experience through attending to the subjective observations of individuals (Fairfield, 2004). Inquiry into experience, or observing one's own experience, is inherently a subjective undertaking. The focus of inquiry may be internal (on the self) or external (on the environment), but the observations of the individual are considered to be relevant and meaningful. Phenomenology suggests a conscious awareness of the subject's own experience through self-observation (Houston, 2003).

Existentialism. Existential thought came to the fore during the 19th century when philosophers in Europe began contemplating the absolutism of prior concepts such as, What is truth and what is fact? Is the "whole" person (Gestalt) more than the sum of the parts? (Hazler, 2001). Existentialism is concerned with human existence as directly experienced. People seek to find meaning in their experience (Ginger, 2004).

Field Theory. The Gestalt therapy perspective relies heavily on field theory (Parlett, & Lee, 2005). Field theory focuses on the whole, in which all the elements found within the field are in relationship to and influence one another. Thus, no individual part operates in isolation from any of the other parts in the field.

Dialogue. The importance of dialogue in the relationship between counselor or psychotherapist and client has been recognized, and in recent years this enhanced recognition is thought to be the most important advance in Gestalt therapy (Brownell, 2003b). The main objective to the dialogue component of Gestalt therapy is to facilitate rapport and relationship building with the client (Fairfield, 2004).

The fundamental theory behind the dialogic approach is that individuals develop in relationship to other people. When a person is supported through a genuine and trusting relationship, that person grows in a positive direction and gains a positive sense of self. In contrast, when a person is not supported, he or she often experiences shame and this can thwart the growth of a positive concept of self (Brownell, 2004). Therefore, empathic understanding through dialogue is considered an important part of the change process.

HUMAN NATURE: A DEVELOPMENTAL PERSPECTIVE

Perhaps one of the most attractive features of Gestalt theory is its attention to the holistic nature of humankind. As in existentialism and phenomenology, genuine knowledge is the expected outcome of what is apparent and evident in the experience of the perceiver (Resnick, 2004). Traditional Gestalt psychologists remain focused on cognition, perception, and motivation. In contrast, Gestalt counselors and psychotherapists engage the whole organism (person) and operate from the perspective that human beings have the capacity and strength to grow, to develop, and to become the persons they are meant to be (Hazler, 2001).

A basic assumption of Gestalt therapy is that individuals can cope with their life problems, especially if they are fully aware of what is happening in and around them. Centered in the present, persons in Gestalt counseling or psychotherapy are always in the process of being what they are in the here and now, in the process of becoming the persons that they can be (Ginger, 2004).

MAJOR CONSTRUCTS

This section describes the major constructs associated with Gestalt theory and therapy. These include field theory, differentiation and contact, boundaries, dichotomies and polarities, and foreground and background. There are many more constructs associated with Gestalt therapy, but this section will provide a brief overview of the major ones.

Field Theory: Organism and Environment

The scientific paradigm forming the basis of the Gestalt therapy perspective is field theory with a view to the organism-environment as a field of activity (Fairfield, 2004). In contrast to a reductionistic, unilinear, cause and effect model, field theory focuses on the whole, in which all the elements found within the field are in relationship to and influence one another (Fairfield, 2004). Field theory is based on the principle of interdependence.

Phenomenological Field. The phenomenological field is one kind of field, the one that is the focus of Gestalt therapy (Fairfield, 2004). This field changes according to the individual's focused awareness (Yontef & Fuhr, 2005). At one moment the focus may be entirely internal, attending to self and its interrelated parts. During the next moment the phenomenological field may shift to a focus on the person in relationship to his or her external environment, which is made up of its own constituent and interacting parts. When the focus is internal, the field is represented by parts of the self, which may be broadly defined as mind and body.

Gestalt therapy is **holistic** rather than reductionistic. It is concerned with the differentiation of and interrelationship of the parts that make up the whole, rather than focusing on parts in isolation from one another (Crocker & Philippson, 2005). As the old saying goes, "The whole is greater than the sum of its parts" (McBride, 1998).

Differentiation and Contact. In Gestalt therapy, a healthy individual is one who can differentiate self while also making contact with others. Contact involves the ability to be fully present, in the moment, and available (Lobb & Lichtenberg, 2005). In fact, life is described as a constant process of contact and separation between the person and the person is in relationship to (e.g., family members and loved ones, colleagues, employers). Contact and differentiation, connection and separation, define a goal of Gestalt therapy, which is to help clients become more integrated within themselves and in relationship to others. In other words, Gestalt therapy helps to create **differentiated unity**. Differentiated unity for the client as a whole person means awareness of thoughts, feelings, and senses (i.e., taste, smell, hearing, touch, sight)—an integration of mind and body.

When people cannot become differentiated, often what happens is **confluence**. This is the process whereby a person loses sight of himself or herself by incorporating too much of the environment or others into the self (Lobb & Lichtenberg, 2005).

Boundaries. For survival, the organism, that is, the individual, must make contact with the environment. The function of the individual's boundaries is to simultaneously be firm enough to differentiate self from others yet be open or permeable enough to make contact with others (Brownell, 2003a). In this process, the individual assimilates nourishment from the environment and rejects or keeps out that which is not nourishing. For instance, in a family a teenager may have boundaries firm enough to understand that he is unique in certain ways from an admired older brother; thus he can accept pursuing his own interests yet be flexible enough to accept his brother's love and support. Therefore, differentiated contact naturally leads to health and development (Wolfert & Cook, 1999).

Boundary disturbances occur when boundaries between self and others are overly rigid—creating isolation—or are overly permeable—creating a merger in which differentiation of self is lost to confluence with the other (Clarkson, 2004). An example of a boundary disturbance is **retroflection,** an internal split within the self in which elements of the self are rejected as "not-self." In this situation, the individual does to self what is normally done to the environment, that is, differentiating between nourishing and toxic elements in the environment, assimilating the former and rejecting the latter (Lobb & Lichtenberg, 2005). The individual in this case disowns parts of self, which undermines health and functioning.

Introjection occurs when material from the environment is taken in without discrimination concerning its nourishing or toxic qualities (Ginger, 2004). **Projection** involves taking parts of self and directing them outward onto others (Houston, 2003). Some people are unaware of disowned parts of themselves and routinely project them onto others. This interferes with self-awareness, coming to terms with these disowned elements of the person, and accepting them.

Deflection is the avoidance of contact through diversion (Clarkson, 2004). Instead of being direct and genuine in a relationship, the individual may present a disingenuous, false image of himself or herself to others as a way of avoiding contact. Deflection also occurs when the individual fails to receive from, attend to, or be aware of information coming from the environment. For example, an individual pretends to listen to a colleague while his or her thoughts are actually elsewhere. The information from other to self is deflected (Yontef & Simkin, 1989).

Dichotomies and Polarities. In field theory, a distinction is made between dichotomies and polarities. **Dichotomies** are unnatural splits in which a field is made up of separate, competing, either-or parts instead of integrated elements in relationship to one another that form a whole (Brownell, 2003b). **Polarities,** however, are a natural part of fields. Fields are differentiated into polarities, opposite parts that work in tandem or contrast to one another to help clarify meaning (Crocker & Philippson, 2005).

When **integration** fails, splits occur. The parts of the person—those elements of mind and body that make him or her what he or she is—are experienced as separate, not integrated (Clarkson, 2004). A mother may dichotomize her capacity to be a caretaker from her ability to care for herself. Yet health is found in integration, where difference is accepted and various parts of the self work together.

Foreground and Background. Another principle of Gestalt therapy is that of the **foreground** and **background** in a phenomenological field, or **figure-ground.** The goal, if it can be called this, is a well-formed figure standing in contrast to a broader, less well-defined background (Brownell, 2003d). The figure is in the forefront of the individual's awareness of the phenomenological field at any one time. Problems occur when foreground and background are not well formed and clearly distinct from one another.

Yontef and Simkin (1989) stated that health defines a situation where awareness accurately represents and brings to the foreground the dominant need of the whole field. Gestalt therapy abides by the law of **homeostasis,** that is, the organism's tendency to seek balance within itself and between itself and its environment (Brown & Srebalus, 2003). Thus, if the person needs food for energy, he or she becomes hungry, the need for food comes to the foreground, and the person eats. This returns the body to a state of homeostasis where there is enough food to provide the energy needed for proper functioning.

The Gestalt psychology principle of **pragnanz** is instructive in concluding the examination of the foreground and background dynamic (Nevis, 2004). It states that the field will form itself into the best Gestalt that global conditions will allow. That is, interacting elements in a field, and their structure in relationship to one another, tend to form themselves, creating foreground and background in the best possible way. Thus, there is an innate drive toward health and growth in nature, of which humans are a part.

Awareness

Awareness is the key to Gestalt therapy. In fact, a major goal of Gestalt therapy is awareness itself (Yontef & Fuhr, 2005). Through awareness, the organism (i.e., person) naturally proceeds toward growth, integration, and differentiated unity in which the parts of the field are separate from and in contact with one another. The premise is that persons have the capacity to be aware of their own needs and priorities. Persons can accurately know themselves and the environments of which they are a part and make decisions that are congruent with their growth. Awareness, knowing the environment, and being in touch with one's self means that the individual is responsible for self-knowledge, self-acceptance, the ability to make contact, and ultimately to make choices (Hazler, 2001).

In Gestalt therapy, clients are directed to move from talking about experience to directly experiencing what they are focusing on at any given moment in counseling and therapy. For instance, experiencing and expressing feelings is different as a process from talking about those very same feelings. Thus, Perls differentiated between intellectualizing, or a tendency of people to talk about their feelings and experiences, and the direct experience and, thus, increased awareness of thoughts, feelings, and senses.

Often people have more choices or are unconsciously making choices that constrict their lives and growth potential. Children do not choose the family they are born into, but when they begin to mature they do have choices about familial values they do or do not accept as congruent with their emerging sense of self. Similarly, parents do not choose the specific child they give birth to, but they do choose how to parent.

Clearly, if the natural process of growth were going well, clients would be unlikely to seek therapy. Thus, it is helpful to understand the meaning of **impasse**. Typically, clients reach an impasse, that is, become stuck, when they doubt their ability to be self-supporting and have relied too heavily on external support, which is no longer available (Clarkson, 2004).

Responsibility

In Gestalt therapy, clients are seen as responsible, or **response-able**; they have the ability to respond to their enviornment appropriately and flexibly (Houston, 2003). Although it may be important to distinguish between true limitations and real alternatives, ultimately each client has the responsibility to choose and value, to create a healthy balance between self and surroundings (Hazler, 2001). To accomplish this, the client must address **unfinished business**— those important needs, concerns, and issues that require the client's attention (Brown & Srebalus, 2003). Through increased conscious awareness, the client also discovers disowned parts of self. These disowned parts of self are raised into awareness, considered, and assimilated if congruent with the core of the client's true self; the parts are rejected if they are alien to the client's deepest sense of self. This process of reowning and taking responsibility facilitates integration. In this therapy model, both client and counselor or therapist are self-responsible (Houston, 2003). Counselors and therapists are responsible for the nature of their presence with the client; they must have both self-knowledge and knowledge of the client. They maintain nondefensiveness while keeping their awareness and contact processes clear and in tune with the client (Yontef & Simkin, 1989).

Shoulds

Arbitrary regulation creates "shoulds" that can control clients' thoughts, feelings, actions, and relationships (Clarkson, 2004). Any counselor or therapist who has worked with clients has often seen the strong pull between clients' sense of what they should think, feel, or do and the emerging awareness of what they, in actuality, do think, feel, and want to do. Gestalt therapy places a high value on autonomy and self-determination. Although Gestalt therapy maintains a "no shoulds" ethic, there is one exception. The exception is the situation. Perls believed that when clients understand the situation they find themselves in and allow it to shape their actions, they have begun to learn how to cope with life (Yontef & Simkin, 1989).

I-Thou, What and How, Here and Now

A shorthand for Gestalt therapy is reflected in the phrase "I-thou, what and how, here and now," which was derived from the philosophical writings of Martin Buber (Brownell, 2003e). The counselor or therapist and client form an alliance based on self-responsibility and an agreement to strive to be present with one another during their time together. Furthermore, the focus of counseling and therapy is the what and how of a client's experience in the present, in the moments that counselor or therapist and client are together (Hazler, 2001). Client and counselor or therapist explore together through **experiments** that reveal what the client does and how it is done. Melnick, Nevis, and Shub (2005), stated that the experiment is one method of teaching the client in which the client can learn. A here-and-now focus on the what and how of the client's internal and external processes increases awareness, which is a necessity for growth and a focus of the experiment (Brown & Srebalus, 2003).

The counselor or therapist is aware of the centrality of the relationship between the client and counselor or therapist and tends to it by being present, respectful of the client's capacity to heal and grow, and willing to be an authentic person in the therapeutic relationship (Melnick et al., 2005). The relationship is viewed as horizontal not vertical. Thus, the two parties seek equality in relation to one another (Clarkson, 2004). In this process, the counselor or therapist may choose, when appropriate, to share his or her own experience in the moment as it helps to facilitate the client's awareness.

Direct experience is the tool used to expand awareness; the focus on the client's present experience is made deeper and broader as counseling or therapy unfolds. Awareness is viewed as occurring now; it takes place now, although prior events can be the object of present awareness (Yontef & Fuhr, 2005). Although the event took place in the past, the focus is on the awareness of it that is taking place in the now, in this moment. Therefore, the present is understood as an ever-moving transition between past and future (Yontef & Simkin, 1989).

APPLICATIONS

Overview

This section focuses on the goals and desired outcomes of Gestalt counseling or therapy, the process of change that leads to client growth, and specific strategies used in the change process.

Goals of Counseling and Psychotherapy

According to Tillett (1991), "As creativity and spontaneity are central to Gestalt, and as there is intrinsic antipathy towards the concept of therapy as technique, it can be difficult to reach an acceptable definition of Gestalt therapy" (p. 290). Practice, however, may be illuminated by examining the goals of Gestalt therapy; Tillett (1991), described some of the goals as follows:

- Development and expansion of physical and emotional awareness are emphasized. Intellectual insight and interpretation are limited.
- The relationship between client and therapist is existential and is central to the counseling or psychotherapy process.
- Conversations between client and counselor or therapist are useful only to the extent that they support enactment and experimentation.
- Change occurs as the result of heightened awareness of the interactional process between client and counselor or therapist or by the activity and experimentation in the counseling or psychotherapy process (p. 291).

Yontef (1995) suggested that Gestaltists are not concerned with a "preset end goal" (p. 273). However, they do recommend, as most Gestalt therapists would, the particular goal of phenomenological exploration rather than reconditioning of behavior or interpretation of the unconscious (Brownell, 2003c). This goal is valuable in that it places "ownership and responsibility" (Segal, 1997, p. 332) directly on the client and facilitates the client's engaging in an inherently natural process of growth. Burley and Freier (2004) suggested that the purpose of Gestalt therapy is the "process of interruption of the gestalt formation and resolution or destruction process" (p. 322).

Creative and spontaneous intervention is the method of the experienced Gestalt counselor or psychotherapist. The major goal of Gestalt counseling or psychotherapy, toward which interventions aim, is autonomy and growth of clients through increased awareness. According to Yontef (1995), this can be "microawareness"—awareness of a particular content area—and "awareness of the awareness process" (p. 275). Through heightened awareness, clients can know what they are choosing to do and can ultimately accept responsibility for these actions. They can also discover available choices and alternatives that they may not have recognized due to limited self-awareness. How the counselor or therapist intervenes to bring about this awareness is discussed in the next section.

To help facilitate client awareness and growth, the practitioner does the following:

- Identifies themes or presenting problems that are central to the client's self-organization
- Conceptualizes the issues and concerns of the client that will guide the sequence, timing, and methods of the counseling or therapy process

- Establishes and maintains a safe and professional environment
- Provides an atmosphere that invites contact between client and counselor or therapist and encourages interaction

Process of Change

Understanding the process of change from a Gestalt perspective calls for an appreciation of Perls' goal for the process: "The Gestalt approach attempts to understand the existence of any event through the way it comes about, which is to understand becoming by the how and not the why; through the all-pervasive gestalt formation; through the tension of the unfinished situation (business)" (Perls, 1966, p. 361).

One of the major differences between the process of change in Gestalt therapy and Freudian psychoanalysis, for example, is that instead of being reductionistic and deterministic as the Freudians were, Gestalt practitioners view the client as a whole person in the context of family, school, and work relationships, and as having an innate capacity for growth (Clarkson, 2004). The methods of recognition, consideration, and working within are unique to Gestalt practitioners. Thus, "there are specific skills, techniques and knowledge that should not be overlooked by the Gestalt counselor" (Shepherd, 1975, p. 196).

Specifically, the process of change in Gestalt counseling and psychotherapy consists of the identification and working through of a variety of blocks or interferences that prevent the client from achieving a balance. Perls (1969a) described clients who block as (1) those who cannot maintain eye contact, who are unaware of their own movements; (2) those who cannot openly express their needs; and (3) those who use repression, examples of which are insomnia and boredom (p. 72).

Yontef and Fuhr (2005) asserted that change in Gestalt thearpy happens through three methodological elements: field process thinking, experiment in phenomenological awareness, and existential dialogic contact and an ongoing relationship between counselor and client. According to Levitsky and Perls (1970), the process of change, which is aimed at helping clients become more aware of themselves in the here and now, involves several precepts, including the following:

- *A continuum of awareness.* Clients focus constantly on the how, what, and where in the body, in contrast to the why (Melnick et al., 2005).
- *Statements rather than questions.* Many theorists and practitioners have found the establishment of response-ability to be more helpful and respectful than expecting answers to questions (Houston, 2003).
- *Use of the first-person pronoun "I" rather than "it" or "they."* If a client says that people feel "thus and so," the counselor or therapist asks the client to restate this sentence using "I." By saying "I feel thus and so," the client owns his or her feelings instead of distancing himself or herself from them.
- *The contact issue of addressing someone directly.* Clients are helped to express themselves, their feelings, thoughts, needs, and concerns as they occur in the moment directly to the counselor or therapist. Talking about and beating around the bush are discouraged (Yontef & Fuhr, 2005).

The process of change in Gestalt counseling and psychotherapy involves experience and activity. Yontef (1981) said that all Gestalt techniques are a means of experimentation. He further stated that experimentation in the change process can be used to study any phenomenon that the client has experienced. According to Gestalt therapy as postulated by Perls, as clients change and grow, they move through five layers of neurosis (Brownell, 2003c; Clarkson, 2004):

1. *Cliché layer.* The layer of noncontact with others; the "Hello, how are you?" "Fine, how are you?" routine. Also includes acting or appearing to be what you are not (Thompson & Rudolph, 2000).
2. *Phony layer.* The role-playing layer; the boss, the victim, the good boy/bad girl layers; the superficial and pretend layers. Perls believed that people devote much of their active lives to this game-playing layer.
3. *Impasse layer.* The place between dependence on outside support (parents, for example) and the ability to be self-supportive; an avoidance of autonomy. People often become stuck while at the same time they have become aware that they do not know a better way of coping with their fears and dislikes.
4. *Implosive layer.* The layer in which all the previous roles in the process are exposed, stripped, and seen for what they are, which are just that—roles. This layer involves "pulling oneself together, contracting, compressing, and imploding" (Perls, 1969a, p. 60).
5. *Exploding layer.* The stage in which tremendous energy is released. The "death layer comes to life and this explosion is the link-up with the authentic person who is capable of experiencing and expressing his emotions" (Dye & Hackney, 1975, p. 89).

This complete process, particularly from impasse to explosion, is often difficult for clients to comprehend. Yet most people have at one time or another reached that soul-searching depth that leads to getting in touch with values and self-perceptions that form the core of existence. The process, according to Dye and Hackney (1975), is best understood "only after it has been experienced" (p. 40).

Another component to the theory of change in Gestalt therapy is the **paradoxical theory of change**, which is discussed in much of the current literature of Gestalt counseling and therapy. This theory poists that when individuals give up trying to become what they would like to become, when they stop struggling and just be what they are, change will occur (Fernbacher & Plummer, 2005). The paradox is that change cannot occur until we first accept things as they truly are (Crocker & Philippson, 2005), or as Yonetf and Fuhr (2005) stated, "The more one tries to be what one is not, the more one stays the same" (p. 82).

The process of change in Gestalt counseling and psychotherapy also contains a crucial feature that is both a valuable asset and a critical handicap: its open-endedness. Gestalt counselors and psychotherapists rarely use techniques or tools that can be quantified from a "proof of theory" perspective. However, open-endedness is the quality that encourages creativity, inventiveness, response-ability, and spontaneous change and growth by clients.

As Gestalt therapy continues to evolve, emphasis has been placed more heavily on a dialogic approach in contrast to the traditional use of experimentation. This does not mean Gestalt counselors or psychotherapists have forgone tried-and-true experiments to facilitate change. There has been a recognition, however, that the contact between client and counselor or therapist in the therapeutic relationship is a key process to change (Yontef & Fuhr, 2005). Therefore, the dialogic approach is used more today than it was used in the past when experiments took center stage (Warwar & Greenberg, 2000).

Traditional Intervention Strategies

Specific interventions are the concrete behaviors of experimentation that emerge from the cooperation that exists between the client and the practitioner. They are labeled *experiments* because they are procedures aimed at discovery; they are not exercises in the traditional sense (Resnick, 2004). Experiments are not designed to control or initiate behavior change. Instead, experiments are conducted through counselor or therapist recommendations or suggestions for focusing awareness that clients can use to heighten intensity, power, flexibility, and creativity. The action in the experiment is seen as the natural completion of awareness (Brownell, 2003a; Resnick, 2004). Yontef (1995) explained the following goals of experiments:

- To clarify and sharpen what the client is already aware of and to make new linkages between elements already in awareness
- To bring into focal awareness that which was previously known only peripherally
- To bring into awareness that which is needed but is systematically kept out of awareness
- To bring into awareness the system of control, especially the mechanism of preventing thoughts or feelings from coming into focal awareness (p. 280).

Miriam Polster (1987) described experiments as a way of bringing out internal conflicts by making the struggle an actual process. She aimed at facilitating a client's ability to work through the stuck points in his or her life. The strategies of experimentation can take many forms, according to Polster, such as imagining a threatening encounter, setting up dialogue with a significant other, dramatizing the memory of a painful event, and reliving a particularly profound past experience in the present through role-playing, exaggerated gestures, posture, body language, or other signs of internal expression.

Most theories value the personhood of the counselor or therapist. In Gestalt counseling and psychotherapy, however, practitioners are particularly important as persons because of the active nature of the helping relationship (Yontef & Fuhr, 2005). The following view about counseling and psychotherapy is particularly appropriate for Gestalt practitioners: "The most important element in counseling is the personhood of the counselor or psychotherapist. The most powerful impact on the client may be that of observing what the counselor is and does" (Gilliland, James, & Bowman, 1994, p. 7).

Perls believed that counseling and psychotherapy were means of enriching life (Dye & Hackney, 1975). From his perspective, it is clear that "well people can get better" (Bates, Johnson, & Blaker, 1982). Intervention strategies suggested in this section are for clients who are fundamentally well but who need assistance in "making it" in a complex world (Maples, 1996). According to Dye and Hackney (1975), the aim of Gestalt counseling and psychotherapy is to take advantage of all dimensions of humanness by "achieving an integration of the thinking, feeling and sensing processes. The goal is to enable *full experiencing* rather than merely a cognitive understanding of certain elements" (p. 44).

Based on the goals of completeness, wholeness, integration, and fulfillment of the essentially healthy but needy individual (in the sense of an incomplete Gestalt), the intervention strategies outlined in Table 9.1 may be used. This chapter cannot present an in-depth discussion of all the Gestalt experiments available to the practitioner. Therefore, a comprehensive chart provides details, albeit brief ones, on several of these experiments.

Table 9.1
Intervention Strategies

Experiment	Purpose	Technique
Location of feelings	To encourage the client to directly experience sensations in the body that are connected to his or her current feelings	Instead of asking the client, "What are you feeling?" the counselor or therapist says to the client, "Show me where you are feeling this anxiety, apprehension, or nervousness."
Confrontation and enactment	To help the client confront old behaviors, feelings, or expressions by acting out the various parts. This confrontation of self and then the enactment of disowned thoughts, feelings, sensations, or actions allows the client to discover and then reown neglected parts of the self.	The client is told to "be your hand," "be your sorrow," "be your hatred." This forces the client to own what has been disowned. By identifying with all his or her "parts," the client can become what he or she truly "is" and be able to take responsibility for the self.
Empty chair or two-chair strategy; also called the hot seat	To allow the client to become cognizant of how his or her behavior may be affecting others and to gain insight into all pieces of the problem or issue (an extension of the confrontation and enactment intervention). It helps the client achieve clarity.	The client is asked to play one or more roles in addition to his or her own self. The client speaks to the part of each person connected to the problem by moving back and forth between chairs. This technique can also be used for issues that are internal within the client by having the client move back and forth among opposing forces and play out all the roles pertinent to the internal conflict. For example, in a conflict making a decision, the client can role-play both the pro and the con sides of the decision-making conflict.
Making the rounds	To assist the client in a group therapy technique whereby a group member makes some form of contact with other group members or practices new ways of being with each group member	The client is asked to engage each member of the group. For example, the engagement may be soliciting feedback from each member or making a statement to each member.
Dream work	To help the client in the present to understand what may be going on in the here and now. Because images, fantasies, and dreams are the projections of the person, dreams can be seen as the metaphoric expressions of content and can reveal certain aspects of the person. The dream is not interpreted or symbolized in Gestalt therapy. The dream is simply reenacted to bring awareness to the client regarding the different paths of self.	The client is asked to reenact the dream in the present and to play out the parts of the dream as if the dream were happening in the here and now. The client is told to animate the dream and give voice to all the people and parts. This allows the counselor or therapist to help the client come into contact with, own, and accept responsibility for parts of the self that may not be well known or accepted, as every part of the dream represents some aspect of the self.

Experiment	Purpose	Technique
Unfinished business	To resolve the unresolved feelings that have been left over from interpersonal relationships, most notably feelings of worry, resentment, grief, guilt, or rage. This exercise is designed to bring incomplete gestalts to closure.	The client is helped to recognize his or her "stuck" points. The emphasis is on helping the client recognize and accept what "is" rather than what "could be."
Rehearsal	To help the client bring clarity out of confusion and enable the client to practice change. This experiment seeks to break the client from the habit of playing the prescribed roles he or she continues to play in society.	The client is asked to rehearse new sentences or actions that are different from his or her status quo.
Minimization	To eliminate the client's ability to minimize self-expression with words or phrases (e.g., the conjunction "but," in "I would like to do this, but," or "I am a good person, but"). This prevents the client from disqualifying or taking away validity by adding ambiguity.	The counselor or therapist removes the client's use of the word *but* from his or her expressions by changing to the word *and* (e.g., "I am a good person, but" to "I am a good person, and"). This removes the ambiguity that allows the client to be noncommittal.
Exaggeration	To intensify the client's awareness by asking the client to exaggerate some aspect of feeling or expressive act (e.g., a gesture, posture, voice, inflection, or verbal statement). This intensifies the client's awareness of feelings behind the gesture of expression and eliminates his or her ability to minimize. It also enables clients to become aware of subtle signals and cues they are sending through their body language.	The client is asked to exaggerate repetitively some element of his or her being, which includes, but is not limited to, a motion or speech pattern. Through exaggeration, feelings that the client has but has not been aware of can become more apparent and the focus of attention. The client gains awareness of the inner meaning of his or her experience.
Reversal	To help the client bring out polarities that exist within the self (e.g., good girl and bad girl, caring person and selfish person, puritanical person and sexual person, top dog and underdog). The client is able to directly address parts of the self that have caused anxiety and, therefore, have been repressed.	The client is asked to reverse a statement or a way of being. If the client says, "I hate myself," he or she reverses that statement to "I love myself." If the client is shy and inhibited, he or she plays the part of a gregarious exhibitionist. The truthfulness of this polarity is then explored for relevance, as overt behavior often represents latent impulses.

—Continued

Experiment	Purpose	Technique
Exposing the obvious	To bring out into the open the deep structures and processes going on within the client of which the client may be unaware.	The counselor or therapist pays close attention to the client in the here and now and exposes aspects of the client of which the client may be unaware. For example, "Are you aware that you are clenching and unclenching your hands?"
Explicitation or translation	To help the client give voice to a nonverbal expression (e.g., a bodily movement, visual image, physical symptom) that allows him or her to turn the explicit content into implicit reality. This enables the client to experience internally what has only been looked at externally.	The client is asked to verbalize or make explicit something affecting him or her. For example, "If your tears could talk, what would they say?" "If your body spoke words, what would they be?" "If the person who molested you as a child could really tell you his or her feelings, what would he or she say to you?"
Retroflection; also known as playing the projection	To help a client redirect his or her actions, thoughts, or energy and regain lost power, energy, and self-support by determining those aspects of self that have been projected onto others and then by facitilitating bringing them back to the self. This enables the client to release his or her inhibitions, stop holding back impulses and choking off behavior, and stop projecting unwanted parts or disowned attributes of the self onto others.	The counselor or therapist has the client redirect to himself or herself what he or she has previously directed outward toward others. This splits the person into two, the giver and the receiver. When projecting, a person places onto someone else the traits, feelings, motives, and so on, that he or she does not want to face within himself or herself. When a client makes a statement such as "I don't trust you," the projection is retroflected or "played with," and the client is asked to act out the role of the untrustworthy person.
Let the little child talk	To enable the counselor or therapist to talk to the client's "inner child." As part of the personality is formed in childhood, many aspects of that child are still found within the adult and influence the "adult" in all of us.	The counselor or therapist begins by asking the client's permission to speak to his or her inner child. The client is then encouraged to "be a child" and express feelings, thoughts, and behaviors that have been repressed by adulthood. This allows the "adult" to listen to the opinions and feelings of the child let go of restraints and allow the self to be nurtured.

Experiment	Purpose	Technique
Say it again; also called the repetition game	To disrupt a patterned habit of expression and to call attention to ways of perceiving. This technique disables the client's ability to get emotional distance from sensitive feelings by rote expression. The technique makes the client stop to experience the full impact of words and feelings.	The counselor or therapist instructs the client to keep repeating a sentence over and over again. For example, a client says, "Nobody likes me." Through repetition, other messages come to the forefront. The end result is that the client may become aware that what he or she was really trying to express is that he or she has never felt loved.
I take responsibility for . . .	To help clients accept and recognize their feelings and actions and take responsibility for them instead of projecting them onto others	The counselor or therapist facilitates by making the statement, "I take responsibility for . . ." and then asks the client to fill in the blank. Typically, the client will make a statement such as, "I am uncomfortable in social situations and *I take responsibility for my own feelings of dis-ease.*"
I have a secret	To explore feelings of guilt and shame and identify what attachments the client holds that keep him or her from resolving this conflict	In this group therapy technique, group members are encouraged to think of a personal, dark secret (but not disclose it to the group) and then imagine (project) how others would react to this secret if it were known.
Contact and withdrawal	To enable the client to understand the polar nature of existence and that it is okay for polarities to exist. This experiment helps the client understand that it is okay to withdraw from situations in order to preserve one's attention. For example, one must rest to have energy; one must periodically withdraw from others to maintain closeness. Just as resting enhances energy so too does temporary withdrawal enhance closeness.	The client is told that when he or she feels like withdrawing from a situation, he or she should close his or her eyes and fantasize about a place where he or she feels secure and safe. When the client feels this safety and security, the client should open his or her eyes (having rested and enhanced energy), continue on, and reestablish contact.
Can you stay with this feeling?	To keep clients from running away from uncomfortable feelings or glossing them over without examination. It prevents the client from avoiding.	When the client expresses a feeling, mood, or state of mind that is unpleasant or uncomfortable and that he or she tries to discount, dispel, or minimize, the client is asked to elaborate on the what and how of his or her feelings.

Brief Intervention Strategies

Gestalt therpay has not been known for its brevity, and it lacks dimensions usually associated with brief interventions such as quantifiabile behavioral goals (James & Gilliland, 2003). Within the setting of managed care, it is difficult for administrators to accept the types of "treatment goals" set in Gestalt therapy because insight is neither concrete nor measurable—two criteria for treatment planning in the managed-care setting (Carrier & Haley, 2006; Seligman, 2004).

The process of change and perceived progress of a client is considered a function of the whole field, which includes the client's motivation, the therpeutic relationship, the clincial setting, and the client's social world (Brownell, 2003d). Therefore, therapy can be a lengthy process and does not easily lend itself to a managed-care setting. Gestalt therapy is existential and phenomenological; therefore the focus is not on facilitating behavioral changes within the client but is on helping the client to develop insight and interpersonal awareness. The pupose is for the client to discover, explore, and experience his or her own shape, pattern, and wholeness and to integrate all of his or her separate parts (Clarkson, 2004). As a result of this insight and awareness, the client can achieve lifestyle changes (Burley & Freier, 2004).

Given that Gestalt therapy is action oriented, it can be similar in some ways to cognitive-behavioral therapies; therefore, the benefits of brief therapy can be derived (Houston, 2003). There is no one way to conduct Gestalt therapy, so the process can be flexible toward brief intervention (Brownell & Fleming, 2005). Gestalt therapy is interested in how a client does the things he or she does and in building self-awareness. This can lead to the client making different choices in his or her life (Bitter, 2004), and as Houston (2003) stated, "The aim of Gestalt therapy is to awaken or mobilize people enough for them to get on better with their lives than they were managing before coming for help" (p. 3).

Houston (2003) advocated brief Gestalt therapy (BGT) in which the client is active between sessions in applying the insight learned in sessions. Houston asserted that clients who are psychologically minded, insight oriented, motivated, and are able to develop and sustain relationships are the best candidates for BGT. In this manner, BGT can be effective in as little as eight sessions.

The focus of BGT is on (1) helping the client gain insight into his or her problems and how he or she sustains these problems and (2) helping the client identify ways in which to cope with his or her situation more effectively by exploring the here and now of his or her behavior. Houston (2003) emphasized the importance of the fore-contact of the first session, meaning that a client's or practitioner's experiences before meeting can profoundly affect the first and subsequent sessions. Houston stated that these experiences should be brought into the foreground and explored to enhance rapport and the work in the here and now. Houston also discussed the importance of explaining what will be expected of the client in BGT, the parameters of the therapy, and how the client is in charge or responsible for his or her own progress. The emphasis is on the I-thou equality and working alliance in the therapeutic relationship. An additional focus in the first session is in determining what aspects of the client's life or difficulties need to stay in the foreground (Brownell & Fleming, 2005).

Sessions can progress to exploration of the client's contact style and countertransferential responses as well as evaluation of the client holistically, which includes client strengths and assets (Brownell & Fleming, 2005). For example, the focus is not just on what is distressing the client, but what resources the client uses to cope, how he or she engages in self care, and so forth. Houston (2003) suggested setting up range scales where the client rates himself or herself on a scale of 0 (total absence of something) to 9 (extremely present). A client might rate himself or herself as currently a 3 on confidence but would like to be a 8 on this scale. Use of a scale can facilitate goal setting as well as measure progress toward goals.

So, BGT can resemble cognitive-behavioral therapy in its brevity and focus on concrete goals that are measurable, which fits the managed-care system much more effectively than long-term Gestalt therapy. Other therapeutic tools in BGT are the use of immediacy and experiments. Experiments, as described in this chapter, can enhance insight and awareness, and immediacy keeps the work in the here and now and not on the there and then.

CLIENTS WITH SERIOUS MENTAL HEALTH ISSUES

It is difficult to have a discussion of Gestalt therapy in relationship to clients with serious mental health issues because Gestalt therapy is holistic. It does not break down a person into separate "pieces" or variables; therefore, it is difficult to "classify" clients in the manner required by the American Psychiatric Association's *Diagnostic and Statistical Manual* (DSM) (Lobb, 2003). Gestaltists do not believe in disease, but rather in dis-ease, and to suggest that disorders are of the mind is inimical to the Gestalt approach. Gestaltists believe disorders are holistic and organismic. An individual is seen as ultimately healthy if that individual is striving for balance, health, and growth (Clarkson, 2004). Gestaltists also view "symptoms" as creative adjustments by the person to a difficult situation in his or her life (Lobb & Lichtenberg, 2005).

Gestalt theory relates the development of pathology to habitual self-interruption along the **contact-withdrawal continuum**. Contact-withdrawal is a concept that explains interactions with others. People make contact with others from the outside boundary of their selves. As humans, persons strive to be with others in the world (Noren, 2004). When a person has a bad experience or experiences making contact with others, he or she begins to withdraw to protect the self (Lobb, 2003). This self-protection prevents appropriate interaction with others; therefore, interactions that could be classified as pathological occur.

As a result of hindered progress along the contact-withdrawal cycle, needs are not met and people become inhibited in awareness and expression. As a consequence, they begin to internalize to satisfy needs (Mandelbaum, 1998). In the process of internalization people begin to introject that which they cannot get from themselves, and they internalize messages given to them by others that they begin to see as "truth." Believing they are bad encourages their fear of abandonment by others; they begin to block awareness, put up defenses, and retroflect (turn back upon the self) to prevent expressing their wants or needs and to keep others from leaving them (Lobb & Lichtenberg, 2005). This is the Gestalt theory of pathology.

Conversely, normal, healthy behavior occurs when people act and react as total organisms—unfragmented, self-regulating, and able to converse along the contact-withdrawal continuum by not self-interrupting (Lobb & Lictenberg, 2005). The healthy person concentrates on one need (the figure in the foreground) at any present time and delegates other needs to the background. When the need is met, the gestalt closes and is completed, and no business is left unfinished. When the need is unmet, the gestalt remains open and the person accumulates unfinished business (Clarkson, 2004).

Research indicates that Gestalt therapy works best for overly socialized, restrained, and constricted individuals who intellectualize, and have trouble clarifying their feelings (Seligman, 2004). Another constraint is that Gestalt therapy does not categorize clients according to DSM criteria. Neverthless, Gestalt therapy has not been limited by these constraints. In fact, Gestalt therapy has been adapted for use in a variety of modalities and issues: art therapy (Lobb & Amendt-Lyon, 2003), play therapy (Daniels, 2004), educational therapy (Garcia, Baker, DeMayo, & Brown, 2005), family and couples therapy (Lynch, Lynch, & Zinker, 2005), group therapy (Schoenbert, Feder, Frew, & Gadol, 2005), crisis counseling (O'Connell, 1970), career counseling (Martz, 2001), child and adolescent counseling (Reynolds & Mortola, 2005; Toman, Bauer, McConville, & Robertson, 2005), pastoral counseling (Knights, 2002) and has been foundational in many of the touch therapies (Zimmer & Dunning, 1998) as well as eye movement desinsitization and repocessing thearpy (Tobin, 2004).

Seligman (2004) stated that Gestalt therapy can be used successfully with the following disorders: mood, anxiety, somatoform, factitiousness, adjustment, and some personality disorders or personality traits such as avoidant, dependent, narcissitic, histrionic, and obsessive-compulsive. A literature review demonstrated that Gestalt therapy has been used in a variety of situations, including but not limited to alcoholism and substance abuse issues (Clemmens & Matzko, 2005), autism (Brosnan, Scott, Fox, & Pye, 2004), phobias (Imes, 1998), depression (Furnham, Pereira, & Rawles, 2001), sexual abuse (Imes, 1998), psychosomatic complaints (Wolfert & Cook, 1999), sexual dysfunction and sexuality (Melnick, 2000), body image (Kepner, 2001), issues with self-esteem (Shub, 2000), grief and mourning (Sabar, 2000), developmental issues (Wolfert & Cook, 1999), workplace enhancement and worker adjustment issues (Kirk, Wood, Burns, Howard, & Rice, 2001), terminal illness (Strumpfel & Martin, 2004), schizophrenia (Uhlhaas & Silverstein, 2005); posttraumatic stress disorder (Hardie, 2004), geriatric issues (O'Leary & Nieuwstraten, 1999), and with special populations such as those who have been institutionalized (e.g., for long-term hospitalization or for hard-core crimes) (Wolfert & Cook, 1999).

Caution is necessary in the use of Gestalt experiments. Even though these experiments may seem simple and easy to apply, many are not suitable for all clients, especially those who are emotionally fragile because most of the techniques are intense. The same cautions are espoused when counselors or therapists work with clients who are severely psychotic, severely disturbed, in crisis, or poorly motivated to change (Seligman, 2004). The skill of the Gestalt counselor or therapist is at issue when working with these types of clients. Improper methods or the inability to work with the client through the trauma, grief, rage, or other intense emotions brought up by the techniques can leave the client in a vulnerable position (Seligman, 2004). Individuals with more severe issues or disturbances need long-term, intensive counseling or psychotherapy. Although this can be done within the bounds of Gestalt therapy, it must be done with caution and skill.

Thompson and Rudolph (2000) and Lobb (2003) advised that when working with clients who are, for example, severely psychotic, paranoid, or schizoid, it is prudent to limit activities to those that strengthen a client's contact with reality. Gestalt therapy may also be contraindicated for some issues and populations, for example, for those who have a problem with impulse control, those who act out, or those who are delinquent. For these individuals, Gestalt therapy may reinforce the behaviors. In addition, Gestalt therapy may not be suited for all cultures because it is sometimes confrontational nature can make clients from some non-Western cultures uncomfortable (Seligman, 2001).

Cross-Cultural Considerations

The term *culture* today does not mean just the ethnic orientation of a client. Culture has been defined in broader terms and includes many variables. Arredondo et al. (1996) identified three dimensions that are relevant when working with clients in terms of cross-cultureal considerations:

- Dimension A includes age, culture, ethnicity, gender, language, physical ability, race, sexual orientation, and social class.
- Dimension B includes educational background, geographic location, income, marital status, religious and spritual beleifs, work experience, citzenship status, military experience, and leisure activities and interets.
- Dimension C includes the client's historical context and events.

As such, "all counseling is multicultrual counseling based on the above multidimensional model of culture (Arredondo, 1999; Arredondo & Toporek, 2004; Fernbacher & Plummer, 2005). For example, if the counselor or therapist is male and the client is female, cross-cultural counseling or therapy is involved.

Cross-cultural counseling attempts to understand clients within their sociocultural context (Constantine, 2001). Gestalt therapy, which is based in existentialism, looks at each client holistically and phenomenologically. It is concerned with the experience of the client in the here and now and with the totality of the individual's being-in-the-world. Therefore, Gestalt therapy uniquely addresses the cross-cultural variables presented by the client (Brownell, 2003d; Crocker & Philippson, 2005; Ivey, D'Andrea, Ivey, & Simek-Morgan, 2002). Lobb (2003) stated, "There is no psychotherapeutic intervention without creative adjustment to the patient's language, because language is the expression of the patient's experience" (p. 268). Therefore, even language and the manner in which a client expresses himself or herself can be a cross-cultural variable that needs attending.

Many of the techniques associated with Gestalt therapy, such as working in the here and now, the empty chair technique, and reversal, are suited to helping the client enhance his or her awareness of interpersonal and intrapersonal experiencing and to facilitating cross-cultural understanding of the client by the counselor or therapist (James & Gilliland, 2003). Gestalt counselors and therapists are trained to be aware of themselves—their biases, their assumptions, and the way they make contact with others. In Gestalt theory the individual cannot be understood in isolation; rather, the individual must be understood in his or her social and historical context and within the uniqueness of his or her field (Fernbacher & Plummer, 2005). The Gestalt approach fits well with the basic tenets of cross-cultural counseling or therapy. Nevertheless, there may be some concerns regarding use of Gestalt therapy. Gestalt therapy emphasizes individual responsibility for one's own happiness as well as advocates for the expression of emotion. Clients from cultures that are collectivistic and emphasize collective responsibility, or that do not favor the expression of emotion, may find this therapy inapplicable, unhelpful, or even harmful (James & Gilliland, 2003).

EVALUATION

Overview

Several unique contributions have been made by the Gestalt counseling and psychotherapy model. One is the emphasis on the clients' inherent wholeness and capacity for self-awareness (Bowman & Nevis, 2005). The work of the counselor or therapist is to help clients use focused awareness of their own to free up energy for health and growth. A second contribution is the application of dialogue in the counseling or psychotherapy relationship. The counseling or psychotherapy dialogue provides contact between the clients and the counselors or therapists. Dialogue is used to engage clients not to manipulate or control them. The goal of the Gestalt therapist is to embody authenticity and responsibility in conversations with clients (Daniels, 2004).

A third contribution is emphasis on the counseling or therapy process rather than reliance solely on techniques (Melnick et al., 2005). Beginning practitioners often depend on techniques more than process to help clients. In the application of Gestalt therapy, this creates difficulties because the process of counseling or psychotherapy must accommodate itself to the personalities and experiences of the counselors or therapists and clients. This makes it difficult for the novice counselor or therapist to pinpoint an appropriate technique to apply to a particular problem. In Gestalt therapy, any activity that contributes to clients' awareness of self, others, and their experience of the larger world is considered useful.

A fourth contribution of Gestalt counseling and psychotherapy involves dream work (Clarkson, 2004). The confrontation with "unfinished business" through dream work or other interventions allows the practitioner to challenge the client's past in a lively and provocative manner. The purpose of engaging the past is for the client to become aware of and work with concerns, even those from the past, that are a part of present experience and therefore undermine the client's current functioning.

The use of dream work in Gestalt counseling or psychotherapy is often confused with the technique of dream interpretation as practiced by counselors or therapists using other psychotherapy models, such as psychodynamic approaches in which dream content is interpreted by the practitioner. Dream work in Gestalt counseling and psychotherapy is action oriented. Clients are encouraged to bring specific parts of the dream to life and experience their meaning directly. They participate actively in understanding the dream's meaning while sharing significant aspects of the dream with the counselor or psychotherapist. The aim is to increase awareness of the important themes in their lives.

A fifth contribution by Gestalt counseling and psychotherpay is its evoluationary shift from constructivism to social constructivism and the ackowledgement that organisms co-create their own reality (Lobb & Lichtenberg, 2005). Wheeler (2004) stated:

> It is not enough to see these self-organizational processes as taking place "in" an "organisim," even in interaction with "the enviornment" (or even "in" the transactions themselves, of that organism and environment). Rather, they are richly co-created processes and products of an intersubjective relational field, which does arise with them, yielding behavior and experince as emergent dynamic configurations. (p. 91)

Therefore, people are reactive and cocreate their own truth and reality. Gestalt counseling or therapy has helped the field of counsleing evolve over time. Bowman and Nevis (2005) proclaimed that Gestalt therapy has increased a shared theapeutic worldview among practitioners as there "has been movement (a) from desconstructive views of the world toward holisitc models of existence; (b) from linear causality toward field theoretical paradigms; and (c) from an individualistic psychology toward a dialogical or relational perspective" (p.5).

Finally, in this age of requirements for accountability to those who pay for services (e.g., third-party payers), the Gestalt approach lends itself well to treating certain diagnoses. According to Seligman (2004), Gestalt therapy is appropriate for treating certain affective disorders, including anxiety, somatoform, and adjustment disorders as well as occupational and interpersonal problems. According to Houston (2003), Gestalt therapy can be effective as a brief therapy to fit the managed-care environment.

Supporting Research

Gestalt therapy focuses on phenomenology and the subjective experience of the client. It is largely existential, experiential, and experimental in nature. These features do not lend themselves well to nomothetic psychotherapy outcome studies (Strumpfel & Martin, 2004). Evaluation of client outcomes in Gestalt therapy is idiographic, that is, assumed to be based on individual experiences unique to the subject of evaluation. Although individuals can be questioned about their unique experience of growth in Gestalt therapy, these reports do not lend themselves well to empirical research and the summation of findings via statistical analyses of group data (Wolfert & Cook, 1999). Therefore, Gestalt therapy has often been criticized for not having adequate research to support its claims (Burley & Freier, 2004). However, Clarkson (2004) asserted, "Gestalt is concerned with the quality of practice, of learning, of making sense or meaning of experience—so is qualitative research" (p. 182).

Gestalt therapy has been shown to be as effective as any other form of therapy (Crocker & Philippson, 2005). Current studies regarding which therapies are most effective have concluded that common factors, which include the therapeutic relationship and the working alliance, are perhaps the most influential factors and that no one theory or therapy stands above the rest as more efficacious or effective as any other (Brown & Lent, 2000; Gelso & Fretz, 2001; Locke, Myers, & Herr, 2001; Sexton & Ridley, 2004; Wampold, 2001). Gestalt counseling or therapy acknowledges the powerful role of the therapeutic relationship in the success of counseling or therapy, and much time is spent in development of the I-Thou relationship and equality between counselor or therapist and client.

Research indicates a great deal of support for the efficacy of Gestalt therapy. Shane (1999) noted that several studies reported efficacy in using Gestalt therapy when working with the body on issues related to body image and to distress related to coping with rheumatoid arthritis. Johnson and Smith (1997) found Gestalt therapy to be efficacious when working with clients who had phobias. In a meta-analysis of 31 clinical studies, Strumpfel and Martin (2004) noted the greatest effect size of Gesalt therapy for affective disturbances, substance-dependence disorders, psychosomatic disturbances, personality disturbances, interpersonal problems, and chronic pain. Strumpfel and Martin stated that even though Gestalt therapy is not symptom oriented, it works as effectively on symptoms as therapies that are more symptom oriented.

Limitations

One of the limitations related to Gestalt counseling and psychotherapy has little to do with the theory itself but with Perls (Shane, 1999). Reliance on the workshop format developed during the 1960s seemed to lead to a reliance on Perls himself as a sort of guru who could answer any problem by demonstrating Gestaltism in a workshop, almost like an actor with an adoring audience.

Another limitation is the temptation for novice counselors or psychotherapists to use such Gestalt "techniques" (i.e., processes) as empty chair, top dog and underdog, figure-ground, and locating feelings, without sufficient practitioner training. These processes alone can be of little value in helping the client. In addition, the intense emotional responses that some Gestalt experiments evoke can be harmful to the client if misused or abused by an inexperienced counselor or psychotherapist (Melnick et al., 2005). Other criticisms stem from counselors who use Gestalt therapy and integrate other techniques into a hybrid form of counseling that does not fit under the Gestalt theoretical umbrella. Sometimes these "other" techniques clash with Gestalt theory and are ineffectual (Brownell & Fleming, 2005; Lobb & Lichtenberg, 2005; Tobin, 2004).

Other limitations of Gestalt counseling and psychotherapy are discussed briefly next.

- How does a counselor or therapist prove that the client has achieved "understanding," "meaning," or "organization" in the helping relationship? This question is difficult to answer with most theoretical counseling or psychotherapy approaches, but it is a particular challenge for Gestaltists.
- Perls' work is sometimes seen as a potpourri of various theories—a little Freud, a little Jung, and a lot of the Berlin school—yet Perls seldom credits them for their contributions. In addition, in her later years Laura Perls noted that there were as many ways to do Gestalt therapy as there were Gestalt therapists, which further dilutes the practice of the theory (Brownell & Fleming, 2005).
- According to Yontef (1993), some practitioners believe the client's cognitive process is important in counseling or psychotherapy work, yet many Gestaltists tend to deemphasize cognition and focus more on feeling.
- The holistic nature of Gestalt counseling and psychotherapy and its allowances for therapist creativity in developing treatments flies in the face of today's trend toward specialization in the medical field (e.g., medical specialists such as cardiovascular surgeons who treat very specific diseases). However, holism fits the human condition better, so there is something to be said for bucking this medical trend.
- Perls' here-and-now orientation could limit the freedom that a counselor or psychotherapist might like to use in exploring the history of an issue, problem, or concern more fully.
- Some current Gestalt therapists believe the issue of sexuality, historically thought to be something abused in Gestalt training programs, has been virtually left out of the current training of Gestalt therapists. Several articles have criticized this shift in focus from earlier days and claim Gestalt therapy has gone to the other extreme, and this has the potential to harm clients (Becker, 2000; Bowman, 2000; Clemmens, 2000). In addition O'Shea (2000) believes there is a strong heterosexual bias in which the issues pertaining to gays, lesbians, and bisexuals have largely been ignored.
- Gestalt therapy does not lend itself well to diagnosis using the DSM or behavioral contracting, which limits its applicability in managed-care settings (James & Gilliland, 2003).

Despite the limitations that may exist in Gestalt counseling and psychotherapy, its holistic nature is one of its most appealing features. Contrasted with more empirical scientific approaches, it offers a wide variety of opportunities to facilitate the client's journey toward greater health and development.

SUMMARY CHART—*Gestalt Theory*

Human Nature

Rooted in existentialism and phenomenology, Gestalt counseling and psychotherapy focuses attention on the holistic nature of humankind. Gestalt counselors and psychotherapists strive to encompass the whole organism and operate from the perspective that human beings have the capacity and strength to grow, to develop, and to become the persons they want to be. A basic assumption is that individuals can deal with their life problems if they are fully aware of what is happening in and around them.

Major Constructs

There are a number of major constructs connected with Gestalt counseling and psychotherapy: holism, the concept of unifying wholes, which includes mind and body, past and present, and individual and environment; field theory, the idea that the individual in his or her environment produces a psychological field in which self-regulation can take place; figure-ground, the idea that the client's unfinished business becomes "figure" or foreground during the therapeutic process and everything else temporarily recedes to "ground" or background; here-and-now orientation, emphasis on the present rather than on the past or the future for the purpose of promoting the growth process; boundaries and polarities, the client's "definition" in relation to the environment and traits existing on the opposite ends of the same continuum (Yontef & Fuhr, 2005).

Goals

- Identifying themes that are central to the client's self-organization
- Conceptualizing the issues and concerns of the client that will guide the sequence, timing, and methods used
- Establishing and maintaining a safe professional environment
- Providing an atmosphere that invites contact between client and counselor or psychotherapist

Change Process

Change results from the identification and working through of a variety of blocks or interferences that prevent the client from achieving a holistic integration of all aspects of self and the capacity to achieve responsibility for self. Clients work through the cliché, phony, impasse, implosive, and exploding layers of neurosis during this process.

Interventions

Usually labeled as *experiments* because they are procedures aimed at discovery and not exercises in the traditional sense, interventions are designed to control or initiate behavioral change (Melnick et al., 2005). Gestalt interventions may include location of feelings, confrontation and enactment, empty chair strategy, dream work, dialogue, making the rounds, unfinished business, playing the projection, rehearsal, and exaggeration.

Limitations

- Gestalt theory deemphasizes the cognitive components of the counseling and psychotherapy process.
- Gestalt theory is often seen as a potpourri of theories and philosophies.
- Holistic approaches can be incompatible with today's emphasis on time-limited, brief approaches.
- Gestalt theory places too much emphasis on the here and now.
- Gestalt confrontation and emphasis on exploring emotion may not work well with cultures that emphasize collectivistic responsibility or that do not advocate sharing emotional expression.

THE CASE OF JONATHAN: *A Gestalt Approach*

The goal of Gestalt therapy is not to facilitate direct change in the client through planned intervention; instead, the goal is to facilitate the client's awareness and insight into himself or herself using creative experiments (Daniels, 2003). Specifically, from the existential perspective the goal is to help the client become aware of his or her subjective experience as fully as possible. The desired outcome is that the client (1) becomes more authentic as a person; (2) sheds his or her "false self" and the "shoulds" that make up his or her life; (3) makes better choices that lead to a better life situation; (4) develops the ability for growth; and (5) becomes more integrated within the self, with others, and between the self and the environment. Through this enhanced awareness of the self, the client gains self-acceptance, can take responsibility for choices, and can be in charge of his or her own destiny.

The counseling or therapy objective for any client is to become response-able and break through his or her stuck points. The counseling or therapy is not directive but is experiential and is conducted through a conduit of the here and now and through the client-therapist (I-Thou) relationship. The focus is on the process and not the content.

Case Conceptualization

Jonathan is exhibiting a great deal of avoidance surrounding the issues of his brother's death, his role as a Native American within the majority White society, his role as a husband and father, his role as a man, and his obligations to his reservation and his family. These unresolved issues are creating stuck points in Jonathan's life and have left him with quite a residual of unfinished business or unexpressed feelings, which are causing him anger, depression, frustration, pain, anxiety, grief, guilt, and feelings of helplessness that he has turned into resentment and self-defeating behaviors. Corey (2001) observed that resentment left unexpressed and undealt with turns to guilt. Jonathan expresses severe guilt when he states, "I have ruined the lives of three families plus my own life and who knows what I am doing to my children."

Instead of expressing his feelings to those people directly involved, Jonathan has instead run away. He has quit (1) both his marriages, (2) the university, (3) the Bureau of Indian Affairs school, (4) his family and the reservation by running to Arizona, (5) his hospital job, and (6) his children. If he follows this same pattern, Jonathan will also quit the residential treatment facility at which he is currently employed.

There is evidence that Jonathan is avoiding his feelings and creating unfinished business for himself. He is uncertain as to whether his family blames him for his brother's death. He avoids confronting his wives regarding marital problems and instead engages in extramarital affairs and heavy drinking. He desires to avoid any other relationships with women of the type he had with his wives. He leaves the reservation and his family. This unfinished business is driving his self-defeating behaviors of anger, alcohol consumption, broken relationships, and inability to maintain employment or a permanent residence.

Adding to his burden, Jonathan is living under an umbrella of oppressing expressed and unexpressed "shoulds" that he has internalized. He should have been able to prevent the car accident that killed his brother. He should have been a better husband to his wives. He should be a better father to his children. He should be a better son to his parents. He should have the answers to "make all of this better."

Treatment Plan

Jonathan will have the following therapeutic goals:

- *Learn about himself and the situations in which he is currently enmeshed.* This goals includes exploring his unfinished business in the context of the here and now and experiencing his feelings and expressing them in real time during the session rather than just talking about them from the safe perspective of the past. This will allow Jonathan to get to the root of his frustrations and see them for what they really are.
- *Recognize that he has choices, that his choices affect his life, and that he can accept things as they are rather than for what he might want them to be.* Jonathan needs to let go of what could have been and start living in what is right now.
- *Learn that he can influence his environment rather than letting his environment control him.* He can learn this by focusing on the here and now rather than living in the past, a past that he can neither control nor change. He can only affect the right now by making choices in the present that will facilitate his own self-growth and enhance his ability to make better choices.

Experiments

Gestalt counselors and psychotherapists do not use *interventions* in the classical use of this term. Instead, in collaboration with the client, experiments are designed to bring about greater self-knowledge and insight. Experiments allow the client to complete unfinished business by bringing a situation from the past into the right now, whereby the client can use words, actions, or fantasy to complete the unfinished event (Hardie, 2004; Melnick et al., 2005). Thus, the unfinished business becomes complete and slips into the background rather than continuing to occupy the client's mind and the foreground of his or her field. Experiments that could facilitate the goals outlined for Jonathan are described next; many more experiments as can be found within the context of this chapter. The following two examples are an attempt to give insight into how these experiments might be used and how they might enhance the client's awareness.

Empty Chair. The technique of dream work can be used to help Jonathan express his feelings regarding his brother's death and deal with the unfinished business surrounding this event that continues to plague him. The counselor or psychotherapist first asks Jonathan permission to proceed with the experiment. After receiving Jonathan's approval, the counselor or therapist has Jonathan sit in one chair with another empty chair directly across from him. The counselor or therapist then has Jonathan speak both parts. This procedure allows Jonathan to express his repressed and avoided feelings regarding his brother and the events leading up to his death and also to express what he imagines his brother would say to him in response. The experiment takes the emotion out of the safety of referring to it in the past and brings it into the present where it can be worked through. Through the empty chair, Jonathan can speak directly to his brother and tell him of his pain and guilt. In this way, Jonathan can complete his unfinished business with his brother. This same technique can be used to work through his feelings of failure and rejection regarding his past relationships with his wives and family.

Dream Work. Because images, fantasies, and dreams are the projections of the person, dreams can be seen as the metaphoric expressions of the content of, and can reveal certain aspects of, the person (Clarkson, 2004). Jonathan has a particularly poignant dream that can be worked with in the counseling or psychotherapy relationship, and this work can aid him in understanding rejected aspects of himself. The counselor or therapist can set up chairs to represent the seating in a bus. After receiving Jonathan's permission for this experiment, the counselor or therapist instructs Jonathan to act out all the parts of his dream. Through this reenactment, Jonathan will gain insight into the feelings he has repressed. A clearer image should emerge that will help Jonathan understand in the here and now why he has behaved in the manner that he has. Through this gained insight into his self, Jonathan can begin to make different choices, live in the here and now, and stop letting his past control his future.

CHAPTER 10

Cognitive-Behavior Theories

Cynthia R. Kalodner
Towson University

ognitive-behavior theories are best conceptualized as a general category of theories, or a set of related theories, that have evolved from the theoretical writings, clinical experiences, and empirical studies of behavior- and cognitive-oriented psychologists and other mental health workers. The hyphenated term *cognitive-behavior* reflects the importance of both behavior and cognitive approaches to understanding and helping human beings. The hyphen brings together behavior and cognitive theoretical views, each with its own theoretical assumptions and intervention strategies. *Cognitive-behavior* is the hybrid of behavior strategies and cognitive processes, with the goal of achieving behavior and cognitive change (Dobson & Dozois, 2001).

Throughout this chapter, the blending of aspects of behavior and cognitive approaches to cognitive-behavior counseling and psychotherapy can be seen. There is no single definition of cognitive-behavior theory because there are so many different cognitive-behavior theories. All cognitive-behavior theorists value the role cognitions play in the development and maintenance of psychological problems (Dobson, 2001). For a therapy to be *cognitive-behavior*, it must be based on the idea that cognitions mediate (lead to) behavior change. Counselors or therapists who apply this model use treatments that target cognitions in the service of changes in behavior. Outcomes of treatment are based on cognitive, behavior, and emotional changes (Dobson, 2001). This chapter provides an overview of cognitive-behavior approaches to helping people. Beck's cognitive therapy (Beck, 1976; Beck, Rush, Shaw, & Emery, 1979) is described in detail.

BACKGROUND

To understand cognitive-behavior theories, it is necessary to study the development of behavior theory, various cognitive models, and the union of these approaches into cognitive-behavior theories.

Watson and the Beginnings of Behavior Theory

Early behaviorism was based on learning theory, the development of clearly defined techniques, and systematic, well-designed research (Hayes & Hayes, 1992). The behavior history of cognitive-behavior theory began with the behavior approaches developed by **John B. Watson,** who is usually recognized as the most influential person in the development of behaviorism (Craighead, Craighead, & Ilardi, 1995). **Behaviorism** was formed as a reaction against the Freudian emphasis on the unconscious as the subject matter of psychology and introspection as the method of its investigation. Watson (1930) claimed that behavior should be the sole subject matter of psychology and that it should be studied through observation. Furthermore, according to Watson, conscious processes (e.g., thinking) were determined to be outside the realm of scientific inquiry.

Using **Pavlov's** principles of classical conditioning in which unconditioned stimuli (loud bell) paired with conditioned stimuli (white rat) lead to a conditioned response (startle), Watson trained Little Albert to fear a white rat, white cotton, and even Watson's white hair! This demonstration is important because it indicates that human emotions can be learned and modified using learning principles. Several other well-known conditioning model behaviorists, including Eysenck, Rachman, and Wolpe, developed treatments such as systematic desensitization and flooding, based on classical conditioning and counterconditioning (Kazdin & Wilson, 1978). The relationship between stimulus and response is essential to these classical behavior paradigms.

A critical contribution Watson brought to psychology is the methodology for conducting research. Methodological behaviorism is concerned with procedures for scientific inquiry and data collection. It has the following characteristics: an assumption of determinism; an emphasis on observation of behavior and environmental stimuli; use of specific operational definitions of independent and dependent variables such that measurement is reliable; the necessity to be able to falsify the hypotheses through research; use of controlled experimentation; and replication of research findings that allows generalization to other subjects or situations. Methodological behaviorism continues to have a strong influence on cognitive-behavior research.

Skinner and Operant Conditioning

The work of **B. F. Skinner** on the principles of reinforcement and operant conditioning further developed the school of behaviorism. Skinner is the best-known and most controversial figure in the field of behaviorism (Craighead et al., 1995). Despite the fact that until his death, in 1991, Skinner maintained an adamant denial of the importance of cognitions and affect in understanding human behavior, his work was tremendously influential in the field of counseling and psychotherapy. Skinner developed applied behavior analysis, which is based on **operant conditioning**. In operant conditioning, reinforcers shape behavior by being contingent on the response (Kazdin & Wilson, 1978). Skinner's schedules of reinforcement (1969) defined how different amounts of reinforcement can be delivered to continue to support behavior changes. Key interventions in applied behavior analysis include reinforcement, punishment, extinction, and stimulus control, each of which involves a search for environmental variables that will lead to changes in behavior.

In operant conditioning, reinforcement is used to increase behavior. Examples of positive reinforcement are praise or money. Negative reinforcement, which also increases behavior, involves the removal of a negative stimulus, such as electric shock or a ringing bell. An example of negative reinforcement is turning off a loud bell after a rat presses a bar. Punishment and extinction decrease behavior by the addition of an aversive stimulus or the removal of a positive reinforcer, respectively. An example of punishment is administering an electric shock to a person after that person smokes a cigarette. In extinction, a behavior to be decreased is ignored; for example, a person who has the habit of interrupting conversation is ignored by friends when he or she interrupts, but friends listen when the person makes a comment in conversation without interrupting.

Wolpe and Systematic Desensitization

Joseph Wolpe is another major contributor to the development of behavior therapy. **Systematic desensitization**, a behavior procedure used to treat phobias, is the most thoroughly investigated behavior procedure to treat simple phobias (Emmelkamp, 1994). According to the theory of reciprocal inhibition, which underlies systematic desensitization, when a response incompatible with anxiety (e.g., relaxation) is paired with an anxiety-evoking stimuli (whatever the client reports as anxiety producing), the association between the anxiety-producing stimulus and anxiety will be lessened (Wolpe, 1958). Through the use of systematic desensitization, clients are "desensitized" to their fears. First, clients are taught to use progressive relaxation to become completely relaxed. Then, using a hierarchy arranged with the least anxiety-provoking stimuli first and the most anxiety-provoking stimuli last, the counselor or therapist asks the client to imagine each stimulus while remaining relaxed. Kalodner (1998) reported the details of the technique of systematic desensitization.

A Brief History of Cognitive Therapy

The earliest cognitive-behavior therapies emerged in the early 1960s, but it was not until the 1970s that major works on cognitive-behavior therapy were written (Dobson & Dozois, 2001). The cognitive revolution brought forth by Beck and Ellis and others began as clinicians found that the available systems of therapy were not satisfactory. (The contributions of Ellis are reviewed in chapter 11). **Aaron Beck** (1976) was dissatisfied with psychoanalysis and behavior therapy. Though trained as a psychoanalyst, Beck objected to the unconscious aspects of Freud's theory, asserting that people can be aware of factors that are responsible for emotional upsets and blurred thinking. Beck indicated that his work with depressed individuals did not substantiate the psychoanalytic theory (Weinrach, 1988). At the same time, he found the radical behavior explanation for human emotional disturbance to be too limited to adequately explain human emotional difficulties. For Beck, psychological disturbances may be the result of "faulty learning, making incorrect inferences on the basis of inadequate or incorrect information, and not distinguishing adequately between imagination and reality"

(1976, pp. 19–20). Beck's work in cognitive therapy has been extremely influential in the treatment of depression and has been expanded to other psychological problems. The basics of his theory will be presented later in this chapter.

HUMAN NATURE: A DEVELOPMENTAL PERSPECTIVE

Early behavior theory, with its emphasis on learning, seems somewhat antithetical to developmentalism. The view of early behaviorists' on the development of human nature was limited to the learning concepts of operant and classical conditioning. Individuals, born with a **tabula rasa** (blank slate), learn to associate stimuli and responses; development is considered the sum total of these associations.

Cognitive-behavior theories are not developmental in the same sense as are stage theories. In cognitive-behavior theories there is a stated assumption that behavior is learned (Kazdin & Wilson, 1978). This assumption applies equally to the explanation of how problem behaviors and adaptive behaviors are developed. Behavior is assumed to be developed and maintained by external events or cues, by external reinforcers, or by internal processes such as cognition. Development is based on each individual's different learning history, unique experiences provided by the environment, and the individual's cognitive understanding of the world.

The use of the here-and-now, ahistorical perspective in cognitive-behavior therapy, highlights the emphasis on the present in understanding the current problems of a client. Childhood learning experiences are not usually the variables that are functionally related to current behavior, and the functional relationship is critical to assessment and treatment. Except as they may relate to present problems, past problems are not attended to in the same way as they might be in other counseling and psychotherapy systems (Beck, Rush, Shaw, & Emery, 1979). Nevertheless, current problems are influenced by individual social learning history, so past problems are not ignored. It is clear, however, that a relative lack of importance is attributed to early childhood experiences.

MAJOR CONSTRUCTS

Cognitive-behavior theories are an amalgamation of behavior and cognitive approaches; therefore, cognitive-behavior theoretical constructs contain aspects of both behavior and cognitive theory. Consideration of the separate behavior and cognitive roots illustrates the key constructs in cognitive-behavior theories. Kendall and Hollon (1979) outlined the treatment target, treatment approach, and treatment evaluation for behavior, cognitive, and cognitive-behavior theories (see Table 10.1). For behavior interventions, purely behavior terms such as *behavioral excesses* or *deficits, learning theory,* and *observed changes in behavior* are used. Likewise, the cognitive interventions are based on purely cognitive terms such as *cognitive excesses* or *deficits, semantic interventions* (cognitive), and *changes in cognitions.*

Cognitive-behavior interventions are considered to encompass a range of approaches limited by the purer behavior and cognitive interventions (Kendall & Hollon, 1979). Treatment targets range from behavior excesses and deficits to cognitive excesses and deficits, and cognitive-behavior interventions target both cognitive and behavior excesses and deficits.

Table 10.1
General Characteristics of Cognitive-Behavioral Interventions

	Treatment Target	Treatment Approach	Treatment Evaluation
Behavioral	Behavioral excesses or deficits	Behavioral "learning theory" interventions. Environmental manipulations (e.g., token economies, contingency management)	Observed changes in behavior with rigorous evaluation
Cognitive-Behavioral	Behavioral excesses or deficits	Behavioral interventions. Skills training, information provision (e.g., modeling, role playing)	Observed changes in behavior with rigorous evaluation
	Behavioral and cognitive excesses or deficits	Broadly conceived behavioral and cognitive methods	Observed changes in behavior and cognition with methodological rigor
	Cognitive excesses or deficits	Cognitive interventions with adjunctive behavioral procedures	Examination of cognitive and, to a lesser extent, of behavioral changes
Cognitive	Cognitive excesses or deficits	Semantic interventions	Changes in cognitions, "integrative changes," often, but not always, nonempirically evaluated

Source: From Hollon, S. D., & Kendall, P. C. (1979). Cognitive-behavioral interventions: Theory and procedure. In P. C. Kendall & S. D. Hollon (Eds.), *Cognitive-behavioral interventions: Theory, research, and procedures* (pp. 445–454). New York: Academic Press. Copyright 1979 by Academic Press. Reprinted by permission.

Treatment interventions also range from an emphasis on behavior interventions, to an emphasis on cognitive interventions with some behavior strategies included, to a full integration of cognitive and behavior strategies. The evaluation strategy associated with cognitive-behavior counseling and psychotherapy interventions ranges from an emphasis on behavior changes to an emphasis on cognitive changes; in the middle are observed changes in behavior and cognition with methodological rigor. What cognitive-behavior theories provide, given this amalgamation model, is greater flexibility in treatment targets and interventions, with an emphasis on rigorous standards in measurement of change and research evaluation (Kendall & Hollon).

Importance of Cognitions

The unifying characteristic of cognitive-behavior counseling and psychotherapy approaches is the fundamental emphasis on the importance of cognitive workings as mediators of behavior change (Craighead et al., 1995; Dobson & Dozois, 2001). All cognitive interventions attempt to produce change by influencing thinking, which is assumed to play a causal role in the development and maintenance of psychological problems (Dobson & Dozois). The relationship between thoughts and behavior is a major aspect of cognitive-behavior theory and counseling and psychotherapy. Thus, all cognitive-behavior therapies share these three fundamental propositions:

- Cognitive activity affects behavior.
- Cognitive activity may be monitored and altered.
- Desired change in behavior may be affected through cognitive change (Dobson & Dozois, 2001, p. 4).

Importance of Learning

The cognitive-behavior model of psychological disturbance asserts that abnormal behavior is learned and developed the same way that normal behavior is learned and that cognitive-behavior principles can be applied to change the behavior. The importance of this statement lies in the focus on learning as the way behavior is acquired, rather than on underlying intrapsychic conflicts. The cognitive-behavior model rejects the psychodynamic and quasi-disease models of development, which assume that underlying intrapsychic conflicts cause maladaptive behavior.

Importance of Operational Definitions and Functional Analysis

In cognitive-behavior approaches, problems are viewed operationally. The definition of the presenting problem must be concrete and specific, and the problem must be observable whenever possible. Problems are assumed to be functionally related to internal and external **antecedents** and **consequences**. This assumption means that to understand behavior, one must know the events that precede (antecedents) and follow (consequences) the behavior. These events may be external and observable behaviors or internal thoughts and feelings. The functional relationship conceptualization of problems necessitates a clear understanding of the internal and external antecedents that contribute to a problematic behavior, as well as the internal and external consequences that maintain the behavior. Therefore, the causes and treatments of problems should be multidimensional. Causes might include behaviors, environmental circumstances, thoughts, beliefs, or attitudes. Treatments are addressed in the intervention section of this chapter. There is rarely a single cause for a problem, so treatments are comprehensive and designed to address the multiple issues.

Importance of Therapeutic Empathy

Often when cognitive-behavior counseling or psychotherapy is described, the techniques and theory are emphasized but the importance of the relationship between the client and the counselor or therapist is underemphasized. This is unfortunate. The use of therapy manuals, which is increasing both in psychotherapy research and in clinical practice, exacerbates this concern about an over emphasis on techniques (Connolly Gibbons, Crits-Cristoph, Levinson, & Barber, 2003). The use of therapy manuals may restrict the counselor's or therapist's ability to respond to the client's needs in the moment; however, detailed analyses of transcriptions of cognitive-behavior therapy sessions show that practitioners do vary in their responses to clients (Connolly Gibbons et al.). Practitioners cannot become so reliant on techniques that they forget that clients require a warm and supportive environment in the therapeutic process.

Although cognitive-behavior treatment manuals focus on specific treatment techniques, the helping relationship is also addressed.

A study of depressed clients who sought treatment from either therapists using a cognitive-behavior approach or therapists using an emotionally focused approach based on client-centered and Gestalt techniques showed no significant differences between client ratings of the different types of therapists on variables such as empathy, unconditional acceptance, and congruence (J. C. Watson & Geller, 2005). These results indicate that as therapists treat clients they are able to do so within a therapeutic relationship, regardless of the theory underlying their approach. Beck described the importance of the relationship and included strategies for developing a therapeutic relationship. Burns and Auerbach (1996) highlighted the necessity for a warm, empathic therapeutic relationship in cognitive therapy. They provided an empathy scale that allows clients to rate how warm, genuine, and empathic their counselors or therapists were during a recent session.

The necessary and sufficient conditions for personality change developed by Carl Rogers are included in Beck's cognitive therapy as "necessary, but not sufficient." In other words, these conditions form the basis for the relationship, but the techniques of cognitive therapy are necessary to produce therapeutic change. The efficacy of the intervention depends on a relationship that is characterized by counselor or therapist warmth, accurate empathy, and genuineness (Beck, Wright, Newman, & Liese 1993).

APPLICATIONS

Overview

There is great variability in the interventions practiced in cognitive-behavior counseling and psychotherapy. Cognitive-behavior interventions include various combinations of cognitive and behavior techniques and are aimed at changing either cognitions, behavior, or both (Kendall & Hollon, 1979; see Table 10.1). Cognitive-behavior interventions are directive, structured, goal-directed, and time-limited treatment, and most types involve the client in a collaborative relationship with the counselor or therapist. The use of homework assignments and skills practice is common, along with a focus on problem-solving ability.

The Association for the Advancement of Behavior Therapy (AABT) describes therapy as goal oriented, generally short term, and often drug-free (AABT Web page: http://www.aabt.org/ABOUTAAB/ABOUTAAB.HTM). The treatments used by counselors or therapists who use cognitive-behavior therapy are research based and designed to help clients reach specific goals. For example, AABT indicates that a goal might include the following elements:

- Acting—smoking less or being more outgoing
- Feeling—helping a person to be less scared, less depressed, or less anxious
- Thinking—learning to solve problems or get rid of self-defeating thoughts

Goals of Counseling and Psychotherapy

Before selecting a goal for counseling or psychotherapy or conducting any intervention with a client, a counselor or therapist using a cognitive-behavior orientation begins with developing a conceptualization, or understanding, of the case. Cognitive-behavior case formulation has five components: problem list, diagnosis, working hypothesis, strengths and assets, and treatment plan (Persons & Davidson, 2001). These are illustrated in the case presented at the end of this chapter.

The **problem list** is a comprehensive itemization of the difficulties stated in concrete behavior terms. Usually five to eight problems are identified in a variety of areas, such as psychological, interpersonal, occupational, medical, financial, housing, legal, and leisure (Persons & Davidson). Relationships between the problems may become clear when all of the issues are listed in this way. It is also useful to see a list of all the issues so that a prioritization of issues can be made when preparing the treatment plan. A comprehensive problem list requires a detailed assessment and involves asking clients about areas that they may not have initially discussed. For example, clients may not report substance abuse. For this reason, a global assessment is recommended. The counselor or therapist can use information derived from a standardized, structured interview, along with the initial description of the presenting problem, to develop an accurate picture of the problem. The practitioner usually begins by asking clients to describe the problem. However, clients do not always describe the most important problem in initial sessions. Sometimes they may not be ready to reveal the true problem until they have developed trust and confidence in the practitioner.

The second component in this case formulation plan is **diagnosis**, which refers to the American Psychiatric Association's *Diagnostic and Statistical Manual–IV–TR* (APA, 2000) method of presenting information along five axes. Diagnosis is not always included in cognitive-behavior conceptualizations. Nevertheless, diagnosis is important because it provides a link to the type of treatment that may be selected. (It is beyond the scope of this chapter to describe diagnosis in detail.)

The **working hypothesis** is considered the most critical part of case conceptualization. It is a way to present the connections between the issues on the problem list. Subsections of the working hypothesis are the schemas, precipitating or activating situations, and origins. The schemas section concerns the core beliefs held by the client. Core beliefs refer to those thoughts that are central to the problem, and these beliefs may cause or maintain the problems. Usually they are the client's negative thoughts about himself or herself, the world, others, or the future. Precipitating or activating situations refer to the specific external events that produced the symptom or problem. They refer to things that may have happened just before the problem began. Origins refer to early history that might be related to the problem. Origins might explain how the client learned the schemas that maintain the current situation, for example, modeling from family: A family with poor communication skills may explain why a client has problems expressing herself or himself.

Strengths and assets refer to the positive aspects of a person's current situation. For example, a client may have good social skills, the ability to work collaboratively, a sense of humor, a good job, financial resources, a good support network, regular exercise, intelligence, personal attractiveness, or a stable lifestyle (Persons & Davidson, 2001). It is always useful to know what are *not* problems in a client's life. These strengths can be used when developing the treatment plan.

The **treatment plan** is the outcome of the case conceptualization. It must be related to the problem list and working hypothesis and tell the goals for counseling or psychotherapy. Treatment plans are complex and require attention to goals and obstacles as well as modality, frequency, interventions, and adjunct therapies. The goals of treatment must be reviewed with the client, and counselor or therapist and client must agree on these goals. Cognitive-behavior counselors or therapists are often focused on measuring outcome, so it is important to know how progress in counseling or psychotherapy will be measured and monitored. For example, perhaps the counselor or therapist will ask the client to keep a diary of maladaptive thoughts or a count of episodes of binge eating. Obstacles refer to the potential difficulties that may arise during treatment. Awareness of the obstacles may assist the counselor or therapist and client cope more effectively with them. Modality refers to the type of counseling or psychotherapy that will be used—in this case, cognitive-behavior therapy. Frequency refers to the number of sessions a week; most often cognitive-behavior therapy is offered once a week. Interventions refer to the specific strategies that will be used in sessions. Adjunct therapies refers to additional therapy that might be used, for example, pharmacotherapy.

Process of Change

The process of change is concerned with understanding how the theory explains the mechanisms for therapeutic change. This is particularly important in the cognitive-behavior arena as there are many different theories and many different interventions.

Self-Efficacy. The self-efficacy theory of Bandura (1977, 1986) has been used to provide a cognitive-behavior theoretical explanation for how people change. It has been proposed as a common pathway to explain how people change despite use of different therapeutic techniques. Self-efficacy theory asserts that individuals develop expectations for their success in performing specific behaviors and that these expectations influence their decision to try new behaviors and maintain behavior changes (Bandura). Self-efficacy may be thought of as a sense of personal competence or feelings of mastery. The degree to which a person feels efficacious influences the amount of effort that he or she will apply in given situations. Thus, cognitive-behavior therapy may work through increasing self-efficacy of clients.

Bandura (1986) described four mechanisms through which self-efficacy can be developed: enactive attainments, vicarious experience, verbal persuasion, and recognition of physiological states. Enactive attainments, the most powerful contributors to self-efficacy development, refer to an individual's own experience with achieving a goal. Vicarious experiences refer to observing others as they succeed or fail. Through the process of observing, individuals are provided with a basis for making comparisons to their own competence to perform the task. Verbal persuasion is a less powerful way to influence self-efficacy. Physiological states refer to the emotional arousal or degree of apprehension a person feels. Feelings of fear may lead to a decreased performance, whereas a moderate amount of anxiety may be helpful when performing a new task.

The process of learning assertive behavior can illustrate these sources of self-efficacy. When clients are taught assertiveness skills, they practice making appropriate assertive comments. Enactive attainments are the experiences of success that lead clients to feel able to repeat the assertive behavior. In assertiveness training groups, clients watch each other perform new behaviors; this is an example of vicarious experiences. Verbal persuasion is the source of self-efficacy based on telling clients, "You can do it"; like encouragement, verbal persuasion might increase self-efficacy, but other sources are more powerful. The mechanism of physiological states can be used in assertiveness training to inform clients that a moderate amount of anxiety may be helpful as they attempt to make changes in their behavior.

When the self-efficacy model is applied to how cognitive therapy and other cognitive-behavior interventions work, all four of the sources of self-efficacy are involved. In the process of learning that cognitions contribute to behavior and affective difficulties, enactive attainments, vicarious experiences, verbal persuasion, and physiological states play major roles.

Does Changing Beliefs Lead to Change in Behavior? In addressing the question of how people change, Beck (1976) asserted that behavior and affective change occur through change in cognitions. The assumption is clearly that changing beliefs is the key to helping people. Research has demonstrated that cognitive therapy does indeed change thoughts and that there are reductions in psychological disturbances. However, it has not been clearly demonstrated that changes in cognitions cause changes in behavior and affect. In fact, changes in cognition occur in behavior programs not designed to change thoughts (DeLucia & Kalodner, 1990) and in pharmacological treatment (Hollon & Beck, 1994).

Traditional Intervention Strategies

Cognitive-behavior interventions include aspects of both behavior and cognitive interventions. The separation of behavior, cognitive, and cognitive-behavior techniques is rather artificial, because most cognitive procedures include behavior components and some behavior interventions contain cognitive elements (Emmelkamp, 1994). Nevertheless, a sample of some techniques most often associated with behavior approaches follows. In addition, cognitive interventions are described briefly. The greatest attention is devoted to providing details of several cognitive-behavior theories of counseling and psychotherapy.

Behavior Interventions.   Behavior interventions focus primarily on changing specific behaviors. Examples of purely behavior interventions include reinforcement, extinction, shaping, stimulus control, and aversive control.

Reinforcement is a well-known behavior strategy. **Positive reinforcement** is a procedure in which some behavior is increased by following it with something rewarding; for example, children who clean their room are given praise and attention, a gold star, or a new toy. Most important about reinforcement is that the receiver views the reinforcer as positive. **Negative reinforcement** is the removal of something aversive to increase behavior. The buzz most cars make when the key is put in the ignition is a negative reinforcer designed to increase use of seat belts. Both positive and negative reinforcement increase behavior and can be applied when clients want to increase a behavior.

Extinction is a behavior intervention designed to decrease a problematic behavior. In this case, a reinforcer that has followed the behavior in the past is removed, and the problem behavior decreases. Think about the child who repeatedly gets out of his or her seat in a classroom. When the teacher notices and asks the child to sit down, the child may return to the seat. However, the attention of the teacher is reinforcing and the problem of out-of-seat behavior usually continues. In the intervention of extinction, the teacher ignores the behavior until it stops. Extinction is characterized by **response burst**. In this example, the child may get out of the seat, wander around, and continue to engage in negative behavior in an increasing manner, still trying to get the attention of the teacher. If the teacher gives in and attends to the behavior now, negative behavior is actually being reinforced. Response burst is to be expected and usually subsides when the individual learns that no amount of negative behavior will get the attention that has been reinforcing.

Shaping is a behavior intervention used to gradually increase the quality of a behavior. Often used to teach a new skill, shaping works by reinforcing the behavior as it gets closer to the final goal. Shaping is used when there is a clearly identified behavior to be changed and when differential reinforcement (reinforcing the behavior that gets closer and closer to the target, while ignoring other behavior) can be applied to successive approximations of the behavior.

In **stimulus control**, some event in the environment is used to cue behavior. When a stimulus leads to behavior that is desirable and will be reinforced, the cue is called a discriminative stimulus. For example, seeing exercise shoes in the living room may act as a cue to do aerobics. The exercise shoes are a discriminative stimulus for exercise.

An example of **aversive control** is punishment, which is defined as the addition of an unpleasant event following a negative behavior to decrease the occurrence of that behavior. Punishment is not used often by behaviorists, but it has been used to eliminate dangerous behavior such as head banging or other self-mutilative behaviors in children who are severely emotionally disturbed.

Cognitive Interventions. Cognitive interventions focus on the role of cognitions in the life of clients. An excellent self-help book written by Burns (1999) can be especially useful for clients using a cognitive-behavior approach to recover from depression. This book, *Feeling Good: The New Mood Therapy,* was strongly recommended in a national study of psychologists who rated self-help books (Norcross, Santrock, Campbell, Smith, Sommer, & Zuckerman, 2003). The book is a source of information about the different types of cognitive distortions that can be identified and changed through the process of cognitive therapy, for example, all-or-nothing thinking, disqualifying the positive, and catastrophizing (Burns, 1999). **All-or-nothing thinking** is characterized by assumptions that things are either 100% perfect or absolutely terrible; there is no gray area. Few things are perfect, so all-or-nothing thinking usually leads to depression because everything is viewed as terrible. **Disqualifying the positive** involves rejection of any positive experiences (e.g., compliments) and assumption that these positive events do not really count for some reason. The person using this type of distortion may say, "I only received an A because the test was so easy" or "She is only complimenting me because she wants a ride in my new car." **Catastrophizing** is the exaggeration of a negative event so that it has much more impact that it deserves. Making a mistake at work or receiving a B on a quiz may be catastrophized into losing the job or failing the course.

Cognitive therapy works through using many kinds of procedures, including thought stopping and positive self-statements, to change negative or maladaptive kinds of thoughts. **Thought stopping** is a procedure designed to interfere with thoughts that run through the mind of the client and make it difficult to change behavior. In this procedure, the client imagines the troublesome thought running through his or her mind and the counselor or therapist shouts, "Stop!" Although the client may be a bit surprised, the shout does usually stop the thought. The client can then replace the thought with a more adaptive one: "I can handle this situation." Clients can learn to implement this procedure on their own; that is, they can stop their own thoughts and substitute more useful ones.

The use of **positive self-statements** can go along with thought stopping. Statements such as these can be practiced over and over: "My opinion is important." "I am an assertive person." These thoughts may not feel quite right at first, but the important point is that what clients tell themselves influences their feelings and behavior. The counselor or therapist may use self-statements as a way to cue assertive behavior by saying, "If it were true that your opinion was important, how might you behave?" The client might be encouraged to try acting as if the statements were true.

Cognitive-Behavior Interventions. The essence of cognitive-behavior therapies is the union of behavior and cognitive strategies to help people. Often cognitive-behavior strategies include the use of treatment manuals or guidelines for the implementation of interventions in which counseling and psychotherapy strategies are clearly described and evaluated. Other advantages of treatment manuals include facilitation of counselor or therapist training and an increased ability to replicate research (Dobson & Shaw, 1988). Treatment manuals are available for cognitive-behavior treatment for a variety of psychological problems. These manuals are specific for clinical problems; thus, there are cognitive-behavior manuals for bulimia nervosa (Fairburn, Marcus, & Wilson, 1993), chronic pain (Turk, Meichenbaum, & Genest, 1983), depression (Beck et al., 1979), anxiety disorders (Brown, O'Leary, & Barlow, 1994), and panic disorder (Barlow & Cerny, 1988). To keep up with the need for treatment manuals, Division 12 of the American Psychological Association has begun to publish a series of books called *Advances in Psychotherapy—Evidence-Based Practice*. These books focus on the description of disorders, theories, diagnosis, and treatment. Many are based on cognitive-behavior approaches. Information about the series can be found at http://www.hhpub.com/index.php?content=books/series/52.html More information about cognitive-behavior manuals can also be found at http://www.apa.org/divisions/div12/est/97report.pdf

The primary principle underlying **Beck's cognitive therapy** (CT) is that affect and behavior are determined by the way individuals cognitively structure the world. In an interview with Weinrach (1988), Beck described CT as "based on the view of psychopathology that stipulates that people's excessive affect and dysfunctional behavior are due to excessive or inappropriate ways of interpreting their experiences" (p. 160). First developed to treat depression, CT was later extended as a treatment for anxiety and is now being used to treat other psychological problems such as panic disorder and agoraphobia, drug abuse, and eating disorders. Refer to full descriptions of CT in *Cognitive Therapy of Depression* (Beck et al., 1979), *Anxiety Disorders and Phobias* (Beck & Emery, 1985), *Cognitive Therapy of Personality Disorders* (Beck, Freeman, Davis, et al., 2004), and *Cognitive Therapy of Substance Abuse* (Beck et al., 1993).

Beck and Emery (1985) identified the following 10 principles of CT:

1. It is based on the cognitive model of emotional disorders.
2. It is brief and time limited.
3. It is based on a sound therapeutic relationship, which is a necessary condition.
4. It is a collaborative effort between the client and the counselor or therapist.
5. It uses primarily the Socratic method.
6. It is structured and directive.
7. It is problem oriented.
8. It is based on an educational model.
9. Its theory and techniques rely on the inductive model.
10. It uses homework as a central feature.

The cognitive model of disturbance asserts that cognitions play a central role in human emotional problems. In CT there is an emphasis on internal thoughts, feelings, and attitudes rather than on behavior, although behavior techniques are used in conjunction with cognitive therapy to help clients test their maladaptive cognitions and assumptions. Cognitive restructuring is used to identify automatic thoughts, evaluate their content, test the hypothesis that is generated, and identify underlying assumptions.

Brief Intervention Strategies

Cognitive-behavior therapy (CBT) is by nature a brief approach to counselng. Most manualized treatment programs range from 10 to 20 sessions, often weekly for the first part of the therapy process and then less often. Follow-up sessions may be included.

Unlike some dynamic therapies, CBT is time limited. For example, treatment of anxiety disorders may take from 5 to 20 sessions (Beck & Emery, 1985) and treatment for moderate to severe depression may take 20 sessions over a 15-week period (Beck et al., 1979). The pace of intervention is rapid, and longer-term therapy is viewed as unnecessary to facilitate change. Guidelines for keeping the counseling or psychotherapy process brief include making treatment specific and concrete, stressing homework, and developing the expectation that intervention will be brief for both the client and the counselor or therapist (Beck & Emery).

The therapeutic relationship is highly valued in CBT. For the cognitive methods to work well, the counselor or therapist must work to establish good rapport with the client. Accurate empathy and warmth are necessary to enable the client to engage in a relationship with the practitioner so that cognitive techniques can be implemented. Use of CBT requires a collaboration between the counselor or therapist and the client. It is the practitioner's role to provide structure and expertise in solving the problems presented by the client, but the process involves teamwork. One aspect of CBT is collaborative empiricism, which is a continual process carried out by the counselor or therapist and the client to identify, reality test, and correct cognitive distortions. Clients are encouraged to be active in the process of learning how maladaptive thoughts interfere with desirable changes in behavior.

In the **Socratic** (or **inductive**) **method** the counselor or therapist leads the client through a series of questions so that the client becomes aware of thoughts, identifies distortions in thinking, and finds and implements more adaptive replacements for the distortion. Beck et al. (1979) presented the following interaction, which illustrates the use of questions to assist the client in disputing irrational thoughts.

> PATIENT: I think anyone who isn't concerned with what others think would be socially retarded and functioning at a pretty low level.
> THERAPIST: Who are the two people you admire most? (The therapist knew the answer from previous discussion.)
> P: My best friend and my boss.
> T: Are these two over concerned with others' opinions?
> P: No, I don't think that either one cares at all what others think.
> T: Are they socially retarded and ineffective?
> P: I see your point. Both have good social skills and function at high levels. (pp. 265–266)

This interaction shows how the counselor or therapist can use examples and questions to guide the client to the conclusion that the initial statement was inaccurate.

CBT is a structured and directive approach to counseling and psychotherapy. Treatment manuals have been developed for structuring the counseling and psychotherapy process. Treatment plans are developed for each individual, and each session has an agenda to organize the discussion of specific problems. Clearly CBT is problem oriented, which means that the focus is on solving present problems. CBT is based on an educational model: People *learn* inappropriate ways of coping with life and the process of change involves *learning* new ways of learning and thinking.

The inductive method is essential to CBT because it involves a scientific way of thinking about problems (Hollon & Beck, 1994). Clients are taught to think of their beliefs as hypotheses that require testing and verification. Counselors or therapists are trained to help clients disconfirm maladaptive beliefs by confronting them with evidence contrary to those beliefs. Hypotheses often require behavior assignments to test assumptions outside of the counseling or psychotherapy session, and clients report on their experiences. In addition, CBT requires the client to do regular homework assignments. Assignments involve applying the techniques learned in the counseling or psychotherapy office in the client's world and reporting the results to the counselor or therapist. Homework is used to reinforce learning and to give the client a place to try out new behaviors.

CLIENTS WITH SERIOUS MENTAL HEALTH ISSUES

Cognitive-behavior therapies have been developed and used with clients who have a wide range of clinical problems. A great deal of research supports the use of these therapies with a variety of clinical problems. Work on empirically supported treatments is indicative of the efficacy of CBT for people who have problems such as generalized anxiety disorder, obsessive-compulsive disorder, panic disorder, social phobia, specific phobia, depression, eating disorders, and others (Sanderson & Woody; 1995; Woody & Sanderson, 1998). The list of empirically supported treatments contains references for specific treatments and manuals for conducting each type of therapy, along with training opportunities for each of the treatments.

Some research-based examples follow. Cognitive-behavior therapy was used to treat schizophrenia (Turkington, Kingdon, & Turner, 2002). In this study, psychiatric nurses applied a brief CBT program to individuals with schizophrenia. Caregivers of the individuals were included in the program. Symptoms of schizophrenia were reduced in study participants and many expressed satisfaction with the CBT approach. Nearly 57% rated the overall program as 'it helped me more than anything previously to understand my illness' (p. 525).

CBT was studied as treatment for panic disorder (Addis, Hatgis, Krasnow, Jacob, Bourne, & Mansfield, 2004). Clients who received the CBT-based panic therapy improved more than those who received a control therapy. Applications of CBT to clients who abuse substances revealed that CBT can be an effective treatment (Baker, Boggs, & Lewin, 2001; De Wildt, Schippers, Van Den Brink, Potgieter, Deckers, & Bets, 2002). Baker et al. implemented a CBT program with users of amphetamines and found that significantly more people in the group that received therapy were abstinent from drug use at a 6-month follow-up compared with a control group.

CBT is a therapeutic approach that is diverse enough to be applied to a wide range of clinical problems. Therapy manuals and research protocols continue to be the focus of ongoing research to study the use of CBT in people who face a variety of clinical disorders.

CROSS-CULTURAL CONSIDERATIONS

Cognitive-behavioral interventions have been used with clients from varying cultural and ethnic backgrounds, especially in the past several years. As understanding of the needs of diverse clients developed, standardized CBT treatments were adapted and studied. Examples on how CBT can be used with people from diverse backgrounds follows.

When a cognitive-behavior group treatment was specially adapted for a group of depressed, low-income African American women (Kohn, Oden, Munoz, Robinson, & Leavitt, 2002), depression scores dropped significantly. In this pilot study, scores for women who received the adapted treatment dropped by 32 points, whereas scores for those who received the standard treatment dropped by 23 points. The changes made to the standard treatment for depression included structural and didactic adaptations. Stuctural changes involved limiting the group to African American women, running the group closed to new members, and adding experiential meditative exercises and a termination ritual. In addition, some changes in terminology were made, for example, *therapeutic exercises* instead of homework. When possible, anecdotes from African American literature were included to illustrate cognitive-behavior concepts. Didactic changes, such as the addition of culturally specific sections of content, were also made to the standardized CBT program. For example, a section on African American family issues was added to focus on intergenerational patterns of behavior and to reinforce the concept of families' history of strength. Family genograms were used and discussed in this section of the intervention.

Several studies focused on the application of CBT to individuals from a Chinese background (Chan et al., 2005; Chen & Davenport, 2005; Lin, 2002; Molassiotis, Callaghan, Twinn, Lam, Chung, & Li, 2002). Because the population of China is the largest in the world, it seems important to focus on this ethnic group. The studies cited reviewd assumptions that Western approaches to therapy may be inappropriate for working with Asian populations and found that CBT is a viable treatment approach, with modifications for cultural considerations. Chen and Davenport (2005) highlighted the changes that could make the application of CBT work with Chinese Americans. For example, they suggested that Socratic questioning may be less appropriate with Chinese American clients because they may feel ashamed or incompetent if they do not have the "right" answer. Instead, they recommended that practitioners avoid asking too many personal questions in the beginning of the therapeutic process. Instead, use sentence starters such as "If I let my parents down…" rather than "What thoughts come up for you when you think about letting your parents down?" (p. 106).

Two applications of CBT approaches with Chinese patients who have symptomatic HIV have been published. Both studies reported that psychological distress was reduced and quality of life was enhanced by weekly sessions of CBT (Chan et al., 2005; Molassiotis et al., 2002).

Chinese clients may expect a more directive counselor or therapists, because Chinese clients have a tendency to seek information and advice as well as ways to solve problems (Lin, 2002). Counselors or therapists using CBT may be able to connect with these needs by using problem-solving stragegies and solution-focused approaches. Other cultural characteristics of Chinese clients such as the influence of the family may not fit as well with the internal locus of control and individual focus found in Western culture. It is clear that counselors or therapists who want to use CBT with Chinese clients need to read about Chinese culture and seek appropriate supervision (Lin, 2002).

EVALUATION

Overview

There is a tremendous amount of research literature on the effectiveness of various cognitive-behavior interventions for different types of disorders. The most recent studies have focused on diverse groups. The whole continuously developing body of work on empirically supported treatments is indicative of research that demonstrates the efficacy of cognitive-behavior therapy for a variety of problems.

The following selected review is limited to research on the work of Beck and his work on depression. A review of the research that supports CBT requires a book of its own. It is simply not possible to review the research on this topic in a few pages. If you are interested in CBT applied to other clinical issues, consult the *Annual Review of Behavior Therapy and Progress in Behavior Modification*. Research on cognitive-behavior treatment is ongoing, so you may find articles published in journals such as *Behavior Therapy, Cognitive and Behavioral Practice, Cognitive Therapy and Research,* and *Addictive Behaviors*.

Supporting Research

The treatment of depression has received a great deal of attention from cognitive-behavioral researchers. Beck's CT, developed for the treatment of depression, has been the subject of many treatment outcome studies. It has been compared—with favorable findings—to waiting list controls, nondirective therapy, behavior therapy, and various antidepressant medications. In an older but often-cited study, Shaw (1977) compared Beck's CT to behavior therapy treatment for depression that was developed to restore an adequate schedule of positive reinforcement (which included activity scheduling, verbal contracts, and communication and social skill development), nondirective therapy, and a waiting list control. Those treated by CT had the best outcomes on self-reported measures of depression. In addition, ratings by clinicians who were unaware of the type of therapy received by individual clients also were more favorable for the CT treatment group.

A meta-analysis of treatment studies comparing individuals who received CT and control subjects who received no treatment yielded this finding: CT clients had lower final depression scores than 99% of the no-treatment control subjects (Dobson & Shaw, 1988). It is clear that CT is better than no treatment. The next test involved a comparison of the effects of CT with the effects of antidepressant medication. In a landmark comparative outcome study, Rush, Beck, Kovacs, and Hollon (1977) compared the use of CT to pharmacotherapy based on the tricyclic antidepressant imipramine. The clients were moderately to severely depressed individuals seeking treatment for depression. Clients were randomly assigned to CT or drug treatment. CT consisted of no more than 20 sessions in 12 weeks, and the imipramine treatment consisted of 12 weekly sessions. Weekly self-reported depression ratings were obtained. In addition, an independent clinician (who was aware of the treatment being received) interviewed the subjects to provide a clinical rating of depression. Although both interventions led to a reduction in depression, the results indicated that CT outperformed medication in self-reported ratings and in clinician evaluations. More than 78% of the clients treated with CT showed marked reductions in depression, whereas only 22% of those treated with medication experienced similar reductions in depression. In addition, there was a greater dropout rate associated with the medication treatment. These results are particularly astounding because many of the therapists were psychoanalytically oriented and were relatively inexperienced in conducting CT (however, the therapists did follow a specified CT treatment manual and received weekly supervision). It seems that CT is an effective intervention for depression.

Another study that used medication and CT to treat depression found that the use of drug treatment and CT was no better than CT alone (Beck, Hollon, Young, Bedrosian, & Budenz, 1985). The combination of CT and drug treatment was better than drug treatment alone. Beck et al. concluded that if a client needs antidepressant medication, the individual should get CT with the medication. More recently, DeRubeis, Gelfand, Tang, and Simons (1999) reanalyzed individual patient data from four studies of CT treatment for depression and concluded that CT was as effective as medication for treatment of patients who were severely depressed. Conclusions from this research indicate that CT is as effective as medication in the treatment of depression, even in cases of severe depression. Wampold, Minami, Baskin, and Tierney (2002) reported that CBT, in comparison to other therapies for depression, was as effective as other bona fide treatments and more effective than treatments considered not bona fide.

Limitations

The union of cognitive and behavior counseling and therapy into *cognitive-behavior* has been able to overcome many of the limitations of either type of therapy alone. However, individuals who are more inclined toward psychodynamic interpretations continue to object to the lack of attention to unconscious factors in determining behavior and to the absence of concepts such as ego strength and insight. In addition, experiential counselors and therapists think that cognitive-behavior strategies do not pay enough attention to feelings. Insight and an emphasis on the past are features of other types of counseling and therapy that do not fit within the purview of cognitive-behavior theory.

The behavior therapy roots of current cognitive-behavior theory may be criticized for not paying attention to the role of thoughts and feelings, ignoring the historical context of present problems, and allowing the counselor or therapist too much power to manipulate the client. The origins of behavior theory emphasized operationally defined behaviors and functional analysis, so these are features that define the approach—the things that make behavior counseling or therapy behavioral. The idea that behavior counselors or therapists are manipulative comes from the use of external reinforcers and stimulus-control types of treatments. This idea may be maintained by token economy systems. In individual practice, behavior counselors or therapists use informed consent to make changes in the contingencies of behavior.

The cognitive therapy roots may be described as too difficult to study empirically and as paying too much attention to cognitive factors while minimizing affective ones. Cognitive therapies focus to a large extent on internal events (thoughts), which cannot be directly observed. Although radical behaviorists object to this, most other types of counseling or psychotherapy also fit this criticism. Cognitive therapy researchers have continued to develop thought-listing and monitoring strategies to alleviate the criticism. In addition, cognitive strategies have been challenged for lack of sufficient attention to affective factors. Emphasis on cognitions may lead to an intellectual understanding of the problem, but may not help change the feelings associated with the thoughts. This limitation is related to the fact that the mechanism for understanding how behavior, thoughts, and feelings change is still not understood.

SUMMARY CHART—*Cognitive-Behavior Theory*

Human Nature

Cognitive-behavior theories are not developmental in the same sense as are stage theories. In cognitive-behavior theories there is a stated assumption that behavior is learned. This assumption applies equally to the explanation of how problem behaviors and adaptive behaviors are developed. Behavior is assumed to be developed and maintained by external events or cues, by external reinforcers, or by internal processes such as cognition. Development is based on each individual's different learning history, experiences, and cognitive understanding of the world.

Major Constructs

The major constructs of cognitive-behavior theories are an amalgamation of behavior and cognitive approaches. They include emphasis on behavior and cognitive excesses or deficits, learning theory, observed changes in behavior, semantic interventions, and changes in cognitions. Operational definitions, functional analysis, and therapeutic empathy also serve as major constructs.

Goals

The goals of cognitive-behavior theories are best viewed in terms of understanding the nature of the presenting problem from a behavior, affective, cognitive, and social perspective; how progress in counseling and psychotherapy can be measured and monitored; the environmental contingencies maintaining the behavior; and which interventions are more likely to be effective.

Change Process

Because there are many different theories and interventions in the cognitive-behavior arena, the process of change is best understood in terms of how theory explains the mechanisms for change. For example, Bandura's self-efficacy theory asserts that individuals develop expectations for their success in performing specific behaviors and that these expectations influence their decisions to try new behaviors and maintain behavior changes. Beck asserts that behavior and affective change occur through the change in cognitions.

Interventions

The interventions used in cognitive-behavior theories are many. Some behavior interventions are reinforcement, positive reinforcement, negative reinforcement, extinction, shaping, and stimulus control. Cognitive interventions include identification of cognitive distortions, thought stopping, positive self-statements, cognitive restructuring, use of the empathic therapeutic relationship, the Socratic method, disputing, reframing, role-playing, modeling, humor, homework, risk-taking exercises, systematic desensitization, bibliotherapy, shame-attacking exercises, self-instructional training, stress inoculation training, and relapse prevention.

Limitations

Critics of cognitive-behavior theories say theories are limited because of their lack of attention to unconscious factors in determining behavior and because of the absence of concepts such as ego strength and insight. Experiential counselors and therapists indicate that cognitive-behavior strategies do not pay enough attention to feelings. Insight and an emphasis on the past (which are often seen as important in other theories) do not fit within the purview of cognitive-behavior theory.

THE CASE OF JONATHAN: *A Cognitive-Behavior Approach*

Using Persons and Davidson (2001) case conceptualization model as the basis of this discussion, I begin with a problem list. The case study provides bits and pieces of the kind of information necessary to understand the problems faced by Jonathan. It would be best to have the client explain the problem, which Jonathan does not do in this case description, at least not directly.

Problem List

1. *Depressed, feels hopeless and lonely.* A Beck Depression Inventory score would be a useful bit of information. Depression is evidenced by sad affect, sleep disturbances, and disturbing dreams. His words are indicative of his depressed affect and sense of hopelessness: "I have little to live for. I have ruined the lives of three families plus my own life and who knows what I am doing to my children."
2. *Interpersonal difficulties at work.* Jonathan reports problems at work that involve his supervisor (who made the recommendation that Jonathan seek counseling) and his coworkers. He feels misunderstood and unliked. He perceives his work as less than what his supervisor and coworkers expect. He responds with anger to these situations.
3. *Interpersonal difficulties in relationships with women (ex-wife and second wife).* Jonathan is currently separated from his second wife and young daughter. He was previously married and has three other children. The first marriage ended in divorce when Jonathan began to drink heavily and had an affair. His second marriage is in jeopardy because of Jonathan's drinking and extramarital relationships. He feels like a failure in relationships with women and feels guilty for being an absent father.
4. *Acculturation issues.* Jonathan grew up on the Navajo reservation but left after his separation from his second wife. Currently he is living in the city. He is separated

from his culture, family, and heritage. He feels alienated, a victim of racism and prejudice, and "not wanted in the White man's world."

Note: Multicultural issues that are present when working with Native American individuals may be complicated by the view that many have that mental illness is a justifiable outcome of human weakness or the result of avoiding the discipline necessary for the maintenance of cultural values and community respect (LaFromboise, 1998). I include acculturation issues on the problem list and highlight the unique aspects of working with a client of a Native American background. Note that multicultural counseling requires a set of skills that goes beyond that which can be presented in this cognitive-behavioral case conceptualization.

5. *Alcohol abuse.* Jonathan has a history of drinking heavily and using alcohol as an escape from interpersonal problems.

6. *Grief issues.* Jonathan feels guilty about being the driver in the accident that resulted in his brother's death. This appears to be unresolved grief. In addition, he feels a loss (grief) about being away from his children.

Working Hypothesis

Schemas.   Jonathan's thoughts about self, others, the world and the future are as follows:

- I am inadequate, irresponsible, inferior, ashamed, and guilty.
- Others are demanding and disrespectful, and they do not understand me.
- The world is unfair, demanding, and racist.
- The future is hopeless.

Precipitating and Activating Situations.   The immediate precipitant was his supervisor's suggestion that he talk to someone about the problems he was having at work. Jonathan has looked for other employment but has been unable to find another job, which he attributes to prejudice toward Native Americans. When Jonathan feels helpless and lacking in control of his life, he often drinks alcohol or seeks inappropriate relationships with women, both of which create additional problems for him.

Origins.   The onset of the problems appears to be when Jonathan's brother was killed as a result of a car accident in which Jonathan was the driver. We do not know much about this accident—was Jonathan drinking? How have family members resolved their grief about this loss? How do they deal with loss in general (there was a loss of a sister in childbirth). Jonathan may have learned that feelings are not to be discussed, which leaves him with sadness and guilt and no outlet.

Summary of Working Hypothesis.   When Jonathan was challenged to take responsibility for himself, his family, and his tribe, he began to feel "less than." His cognitive schema of inadequacy, irresponsibility, inferiority, shame, and guilt brought about unhealthy coping strategies, such as alcohol abuse and seeking sexual comfort in women. He feels angry and frustrated. These patterns have occurred in his personal and professional relationships over many years.

Since Jonathan is a Native American who recently left the reservation, several issues are relevant. Feelings of inadequacy and low self-esteem are indicators of depression.

Stress is associated with relocating to an urban area among Native Americans who leave the reservation.

Strengths and Assets

Jonathan is intelligent, resilient, and caring. He has an intact family and family members appear to want him to be involved with the immediate family and the tribe. He completed two years of a nursing degree and was employed on the reservation at the Bureau of Indian Affairs hospital. He is part of a culture that values the family and social group.

Treatment Plan

Goals

1. Reduce depressive symptoms
2. Increase self-esteem and confidence
3. Increase social support through family or extra-family support
4. Reduce anger
5. Develop relaxation strategies
6. Join Alcoholics Anonymous (AA) affiliated with a reservation or tribal community
7. Return to school to finish nursing degree

Modality

1. Individual cognitive-behavioral therapy that is culturally sensitive
2. AA that is affiliated with Native American values

Initial Intervention

1. Focus on the present by assessing current depression and suicidality using the Beck Depression Inventory and clinical interview
2. Refer to culturally sensitive AA group (Alcoholism is a critical issue with Native American and it is associated with suicide and violence in this group)
3. Incorporate meditative relaxation
4. Develop an anger management plan
5. Do not discuss medication as a treatment option (many Native Americans believe that synthetic medication is not good for the health of Indians; Paniagua, 1998)

Asking Jonathan to describe his problem would help the counselor or therapist identify the primary presenting problem and provide the basis for deciding on goals for counseling or psychotherapy. This is not clearly presented in the case description, which is telling in that Jonathan may not understand what he might be able to get out of counseling or psychotherapy. A first step might be to help Jonathan describe how he wants his life to be different than it currently is. The goals can be expressed in cognitive, behavior, or affective statements. For example, Jonathan might indicate that he wants to get a new job, return to school, or move back to the reservation. He may express an interest in feeling less depressed or angry. He may want to discuss his drinking and target that for change. What Jonathan wants is not clear from the case description provided.

Features of Jonathan's Case

How can progress in counseling or psychotherapy be measured and monitored? The counselor or therapist might select cognitions, behaviors, or feelings to monitor. Jonathan could complete thought diaries or record the kinds of maladaptive thoughts he has during the day. He might be asked to keep track of how often he drinks or of some other target behavior. He could record a rating of his feelings, which would provide useful information about how his behaviors and thoughts contribute to his negative affect. The counselor or therapist could use a variety of self-report measures such as the Beck Depression Inventory to provide a record of depression.

What are the environmental contingencies maintaining the behavior? It is important to study Jonathan's issues in the particular contexts of his daily life. What happens at work that contributes to his negative thoughts and feelings? It could be that he is telling himself that he is not performing as his supervisor thinks that he should, and this contributes to his problems at work. Likewise, what are his thoughts about his children? Does he think that they miss him and want him to be present in their lives, or is he thinking that they are glad that their dad is far away? We don't know, other than that he wonders if his absence is harmful to their development.

Which interventions are likely to be effective? It seems that the cognitive-behavior interventions described in this chapter would be valuable for working with Jonathan. I selected Beck's cognitive therapy to demonstrate how a particular approach would be used. Establishing rapport is a critical part of Beck's approach. The counselor or therapist will have to take special steps to establish good rapport with Jonathan. Because of his Native American cultural background, this may be a particularly important part of the counseling or psychotherapy process. Jonathan may have difficulty with the notion of counseling or therapy. He may be more accustomed to medicine men and other Native American healers and their practices (Paniaguia, 1998). I would encourage Jonathan to bring this type of healing into our work, and I would be most interested in collaborating with a Native American healer to work with Jonathan. (Additionally, it would not be appropriate to question or interpret Jonathan's lateness to the session; rather, it is noted that the orientation to time is different among Native Americans.) Accurate empathy and warmth conveyed throughout the assessment and intervention are necessary to engage Jonathan in collaborative efforts to test some of the thoughts he identifies and to try new strategies in his work setting and personal relationships. A strong therapeutic relationship is necessary to allow therapeutic effects to be maximized.

A cognitive-behavior counselor or therapist would establish a plan to work with Jonathan that focused on developing an understanding of the role his thinking is having in his current situation. Jonathan would be challenged to identify the thoughts that go through his mind at work and at home, especially thoughts that are tied to depression, alcohol abuse, and anger. Patterns of thoughts might be classified into general categories of cognitive distortions, such as all-or-nothing thinking, overgeneralization, or disqualifying the positive. As Jonathan learns how to identify thoughts, he may begin to talk about some feelings and see that the thoughts and feelings are related to his problems. It is the primary task of the counselor or therapist to demonstrate that the thoughts, feelings, and behaviors are interrelated and that the counseling or psychotherapy will work through changing the maladaptive thoughts.

Once there is an understanding of some of the thoughts that Jonathan may be having, the counselor begins the process of changing the thoughts. Questions such as these are useful:

"What's the evidence?" "What's another way of looking at the situation?" "So what if it happens?" (Beck & Emery, 1985, p. 201) are useful. Hypothesis testing, generating alternative interpretations, and decatastrophizing are some cognitive strategies that might be used. Self-monitoring thoughts might be a homework assignment to help Jonathan focus on thoughts and how they affect his behavior and feelings.

One of the ways Jonathan copes with depression is to drink alcohol. Although this withdrawal behavior is a consequence of the depression, it ultimately increases the depressed feeling he has because it isolates him from making real connections with others. The extramarital relationships are outcomes of this situation, and they create a situation in which he feels more isolated and unhappy.

There are certainly other features of Jonathan's case study that a counselor or therapist would address, including a potential risk of suicide and his parental, family, and tribe relationships. I have focused primarily on depression as it seems to be the primary problem, and one for which there is great motivation to seek solutions. As Jonathan learns the strategies in cognitive therapy, he may be better equipped to address the other problem areas in his life.

CHAPTER 11

Rational Emotive Behavior Therapy

Ann Vernon
University of Northern Iowa

A lbert Ellis, priding himself on being somewhat of a renegade, developed a theory that has had a profound impact on the field of counseling and psychotherapy. As rational emotive behavior therapy has evolved, practitioners throughout the world have used this theory in different settings with a wide variety of clients to help clients change their thoughts, feelings, and behaviors. Today, Ellis continues to promote his theory.

BACKGROUND

Albert Ellis, the grandfather of **cognitive-behavioral therapy** and the founder of **rational-emotive therapy**, currently known as **rational emotive behavior therapy (REBT)**, is considered as a mentor by more counselors and psychotherapists throughout the world than perhaps anyone else alive (Broder, 2001). Although he has a reputation for being abrasive and abrupt and often seems to delight in being flamboyant and somewhat eccentric, comments about his harsh manner reflect overgeneralizations. In fact, there is another side to Albert Ellis that is often ignored, that is, his ability to be compassionate and personable—characteristics to which many clients, colleagues, and personal friends can attest. Although he is an energetic professional who literally never wastes a minute, he reveals his humanness by being unassuming, witty, supportive, and encouraging (DiMattia & Lega, 1990). The fact that he donates all his income from his therapy sessions, lectures, and workshops to the **Albert Ellis Institute** attests to his generous nature.

    Ellis was born in Pittsburgh in 1913 but spent most of his life in New York City. The eldest of three children, Ellis was frequently hospitalized when he was young for nephritis; he also suffered from severe headaches (Ellis, 2004a). Ellis was a bright student who began writing stories, essays, and comic poems at the age of 12. Before becoming a psychologist, Ellis worked as an accountant while he pursued his interests in philosophy, music, literature, and politics. He wrote novels and operas, and as a political activist, he overcame his fear of public speaking by giving political talks (DiGiuseppe, 1999).

As a young man, Ellis was interested in romantic and sexual relationships, in part because he was anxious about dating. In fact, he had a great deal of social phobia throughout his childhood and teen years (Nelson-Jones, 2000). At age 19, to overcome his shyness toward women, he forced himself to talk to a hundred girls in the Bronx Botanical Gardens (Ellis, 2004a). When others began asking him for advice about romance, friends encouraged him to enroll in a clinical psychology doctoral program. After graduating from Columbia University, he started intensive psychoanalytic training. Although he had reservations about Freud's theory of personality, Ellis retained his belief in the efficacy of psychoanalytic techniques and spent 2 years in intense analysis. At the conclusion of his therapy, he worked under supervision with his own clients and practiced orthodox psychoanalysis. However, he soon became disillusioned with this approach and began to question the validity of interpretation and insight as well as the effectiveness and efficiency of psychoanalysis (DiGiuseppe, 1999; Ellis, 2004b).

In 1950, Ellis began to experiment with different forms of therapy, including psychoanalytically oriented psychotherapy and eclectic-analytic therapy. Although he achieved better results with his clients, he still felt dissatisfied. He began putting his psychological and philosophical knowledge together in a different way, and between 1953 and 1955 he reread philosophy and did a comprehensive study of all the major therapy techniques (Ellis, 2002a). "As a result of this research, I came up with REBT by the end of 1954 and started practicing it in January 1955" (Ellis, 2002a, p. 14). It was first called **rational therapy** (Dryden, 2002b), then rational-emotive therapy, and is now known as rational emotive behavior therapy (Broder, 2001; Dryden, 2002b).

As an innovator, Ellis is often criticized, but he commented that he probably "gets more criticism than most because I do some original things" (Broder, 2001, p. 78). He does not let criticism stop him because he sees his motive as being effective and efficient. Therefore, he continues to change his ideas and revise his theory, striving to make it comprehensive and intensive so that "clients wouldn't just feel better, but they would also get better" (Broder, 2001, p. 78). As a therapist, Ellis sees his goal as solving personal and social problems. As a problem solver, he tries to figure out better solutions. He noted that had he not been a therapist, he would have been an efficiency expert. His intolerance for inefficiency can be summarized in his statement that he "recognized the fact that life is short and the one thing you never get back is time" (Broder, 2001, p. 78). For this reason, Ellis does most things quickly and efficiently, and often he does several things at once, such as exercising or reading while he listens to music. He is not a procrastinator, as he views that as a waste of time. As a high school student, he did his homework in the 10 minutes between classes, and to this day he always submits articles several months before they are due. Ellis attributes his ability to accomplish so much to his persistence, lack of procrastination, and the fact that he does not have to do everything perfectly (Broder, 2001).

As the founder of REBT, Ellis generally practices what he preaches. Several years ago he fell and was hospitalized for a few days. Although hospitalization was a major inconvenience because he was scheduled for an out-of-town speaking engagement, he characteristically did not complain; instead, he videotaped his lecture from his hospital room and continued reading and writing during his stay. He was diagnosed as having Type 1 insulin-dependent diabetes when he was 45, and since then he has been assiduous about testing his blood and giving himself insulin. Rather than being victimized by his fate, he deals with the disorder and makes the necessary accommodations by exercising high-frustration tolerance (Ellis, 2004a).

Rational emotive behavior therapy was the first cognitive-behavioral therapy to be introduced into clinical practice (Ellis,1957). In its over 50 years of existence, it has been applied successfully to individual, group, marital, and family therapy for a wide array of problems. It is a well-established form of counseling or therapy that has been used successfully with children and adults in hospital and mental health facilities, as well as in educational, industrial, and commercial settings (Ellis & Dryden, 1997; Vernon, 2002). Although more than 12,000 counselors or therapists throughout the world have been trained in REBT (DiGiuseppe, 1999), Ellis himself is one of the most significant promulgators of his theory. Up until 2 years ago when he was 90, he worked from 9:30 a.m. until 10:30 p.m., 7 days a week, only interrupting his schedule for a brief afternoon nap in his office. In a given week, he saw as many as 80 clients, conducted at least five group therapy sessions, supervised trainees, and gave lectures and workshops throughout the world. Shortly before his 90th birthday he developed a severe infection, lost his large intestine, and almost died. Since that time he sees fewer clients and until very recently, he also supervised fellows in training and conducted his famous **Friday night workshops**. Ellis has published more than 75 books and 800 articles, primarily on the theory and applications of REBT, and he continues to write.

Ellis has been a frequent guest on radio and television shows and has been featured on ABC, NBC, CBS, and CNN. He is a charismatic speaker who has given more than 2,500 lectures and workshops throughout the world. He is one of the most controversial figures in modern psychology and has received many awards, including Distinguished Psychologist, Scientific Researcher, and Distinguished Psychological Practitioner from various associations (DiMattia & Lega, 1990). His books have been translated into more than 20 languages, and he is famous for his **rational humorous songs**, which he has written and sung at his public talks and workshops and on radio and television programs in the United States and abroad. Ellis is president emeritus of the Albert Ellis Institute in New York City, which has affiliated training centers throughout the world.

HUMAN NATURE: A DEVELOPMENTAL PERSPECTIVE

Rational emotive behavior therapy is based on the assumption that humans have a biological tendency to think irrationally or dysfunctionally, as well as rationally or functionally (Dryden, 2002b; Dryden, DiGiuseppe, & Neenan, 2003). Therefore, even though they have an inborn propensity toward growth and actualization, human beings can readily sabotage their growth by their unrealistic, illogical, or other types of defeatist thinking (Dryden & Ellis, 2001; Ellis, 2001c; Ellis, 2002a). Ellis and Dryden (1997) noted that, although social influences exist, even people with the most rational upbringing show evidence of major irrationalities and often adopt new irrationalities after giving up previous ones. Nevertheless, REBT theory clearly asserts that despite the tendency to think irrationally, humans have the ability to construct self-enhancing thoughts, feelings, and behaviors and are strongly motivated to change things for the better (Ellis, 2001a; Ellis & Dryden, 1997).

Fundamental to REBT is the notion that our contradictory nature, along with our social upbringing, not only impels us to create happier and more fulfilling lives, but also encourages us to elevate strong goals, desires, and preferences into absolutistic and unrealistic shoulds, oughts, and musts that lead to emotional and behavioral difficulties. Dryden, DiGiuseppe and Neenan (2003) noted that these shoulds, oughts, and musts fall under three main categories: self-demandingness, other-demandingness, and world-demandingness. **Self-demandingness** refers to the idea that we must always perform well and win others' approval; and if we do not, we are incompetent, unworthy, and deserve to suffer. Self-hatred, anxiety, and depression often result from self-demandingness, along with procrastination, withdrawal, and obsessiveness. **Other-demandingness** implies that people with whom we associate must always treat us kindly, considerately, and fairly; and if they do not, they are unworthy, bad, rotten, and deserve to be punished. Anger, rage, hurt, jealousy, vindictiveness, and violence develop as a result of other-demandingness. **World-demandingness** means that the conditions in which we live must be enjoyable, hassle-free, safe, and favorable; and if they are not, the world is awful, horrible, and unbearable. This form of demandingness often leads to anger, depression, self-pity, and low-frustration tolerance, as well as withdrawal, procrastination, phobias, and addictions (Ellis, 1994).

MAJOR CONSTRUCTS

Basic Tenets

REBT has a strong philosophical basis (Dryden & Ellis, 2001; Ellis, 2002a, 2002b; Ellis, 2004b). In fact, Ellis relied heavily on the teachings of Epictetus, a Stoic philosopher who believed that "people are disturbed not by things, but by the view which they take of them" (Dryden, 2002b, p. 384). However, REBT is not a form of Stoicism because the true Stoic attempts to develop an immunity to feelings, whereas REBT recognizes that rational thinking leads to the healthy expression of feelings. Contrary to what many people believe, emotions are a significant component of this theory.

In developing REBT, Ellis was also influenced by several psychologists, including Karen Horney and Alfred Adler (Ellis, 1994; Ellis & Dryden, 1997). Horney's "tyranny of the shoulds" (Ellis & Dryden, p. 3) lead to Ellis' emphasis on how absolutistic thinking creates and maintains emotional disturbance. Adler's work was important because he used active-directive teaching and emphasized people's goals, purposes, values, and meanings, concepts inherent in REBT (Dryden & Ellis, 2001). Also, Adler was one of the first well-known therapists to focus on inferiority feelings (Ellis & Dryden, 1997), and REBT similarly addresses the concept of inferiority with its emphasis on self-rating and ego anxiety.

Developing a **rational philosophy of life** is a major construct of REBT. A rational philosophy is designed to help people increase their happiness and decrease emotional distress. Walen, DiGiuseppe, and Dryden (1992) noted that the purpose of a rational philosophy is to identify beliefs that lead to survival, satisfaction with living, positive ways of relating to others, intimate involvement with a few others, and personally fulfilling endeavors.

Commitment to the scientific method is also a central aspect of REBT. Application of the scientific method to personal life helps people give up dysfunctional beliefs that can lead to emotional disturbance and ineffectual behavior, according to Ellis (DiGiuseppe, 1999). Testing one's assumptions and examining the validity and functionality of beliefs are important, as well as is developing flexibility in adopting new beliefs to guide behavior. Ellis' theory includes some elements of constructivism, specifically in the sense that humans would be better off if they understood that they themselves create their images of how the world is or should be (Ellis, 1998, 2001c). Whereas modern constructivists assert that people should be allowed to find their own reality and develop alternative beliefs on their own, REBT posits that there are some constructions—namely, rational beliefs—that are more functional and lead to emotional adjustment. Therefore, REBT and counselors or therapists focus on helping clients develop rational, as opposed to irrational, constructions (Dryden & Ellis, 2001).

According to REBT, certain values promote emotional adjustment and mental health. These values include the following (DiGiuseppe, 1999):

1. Self-acceptance. Healthy people accept themselves unconditionally and do not measure their worth by their achievements. They try to enjoy themselves rather than try to prove themselves.
2. *Risk taking.* Emotionally healthy people take risks and tend to be rather adventurous, but not foolish.
3. *Nonutopian.* Healthy people realize they are unlikely to get everything they want, and they do not attempt to avoid everything they find painful. They accept the fact that there is no such thing as utopia and, therefore, do not strive for the unattainable or for unrealistic perfectionism.
4. *High-frustration tolerance.* Healthy people recognize that there are problems they can do something about and those they cannot change. Their goal is to modify the negative conditions that can be changed, accept those that cannot, and have the wisdom to know the difference between the two.
5. *Self-responsibility for disturbance.* Healthy individuals do not blame others, the world, or fate for their distress. Instead, they accept a good deal of responsibility for their own thoughts, feelings, and behaviors.
6. *Self-interest.* Emotionally healthy people tend to put their own interests somewhat above the interests of others. Although they sacrifice themselves to some degree for those for whom they care, they do not do this completely.
7. *Social interest.* Most people choose to live in social groups; therefore, they understand that it is important to act morally, protect the rights of others, and contribute to society in order to help create the kind of world in which they would like to live.
8. *Self-direction.* Emotionally healthy people generally assume responsibility for their own lives, but at the same time they cooperate with others. They do not need or demand considerable support or nurturance from others.
9. *Tolerance.* Healthy individuals allow themselves and others the right to be wrong, recognizing that they may not like unpleasant or obnoxious behavior but do not condemn humans for behaving that way.
10. *Flexibility.* Mature, healthy people are unbigoted, open to change, and flexible in their thinking. They do not make rigid rules for themselves or others.

11. *Acceptance of uncertainty.* Healthy individuals acknowledge and accept the fact that they live in a world where absolute certainties do not exist. Although they like some degree of order, they do not demand to know exactly what will happen.

12. *Commitment.* Individuals tend to be happier and healthier if they are involved in something outside themselves and have at least one strong, creative interest around which they structure part of their lives.

Theoretical Assumptions

Ellis would argue that REBT is more theoretical than most therapies and that the theory not only structures but also drives the entire therapeutic process (Trower & Jones, 2001). Like most generic cognitive-behavioral therapies, REBT ascribes to the notion that cognitions or beliefs cause emotions and behavior (Ellis, 2002b), and REBT theorists stress the interconnectedness of thinking, feeling, and behaving (Dryden et al., 2003; Nelson-Jones, 2000). Because people think, feel, and act simultaneously, it is logical that what people think affects how they feel, that people usually do not feel or act without thinking, and that how they behave influences what they think and how they feel (DiGiuseppe, 1999).

Central to this theory is the idea that events and other people do not make us feel bad or good (Dryden, 2003; Ellis, 2002a). Rather, emotional distress results from dysfunctional thought processes such as exaggeration, overgeneralization, oversimplification, illogic, faulty deductions, absolutistic rigid schemas, and unvalidated assumptions (DiGiuseppe, 1999). Therefore, the best way to reduce emotional distress is to change the way people think.

According to REBT, irrational beliefs emanate from multiple environmental and genetic factors. Although these factors contribute to the acquisition of irrational beliefs, they are maintained because people rehearse them and continue to reindoctrinate themselves without reevaluating their thinking (DiGiuseppe, 1999). REBT theorists emphasize that irrational beliefs can be changed, but they acknowledge that this is often difficult and takes persistent practice. Ellis (cited in Nelson-Jones, 2000) stated that "people are born, as well as reared, with greater or lesser degrees of demandingness, and therefore they can change from demanding to desiring only with great difficulty" (p. 186).

Ellis and Dryden (1997) identified five major theoretical concepts: goals, purposes, and rationality; a humanistic emphasis; the interaction of psychological processes and the place of cognition; basic biological tendencies; and fundamental human disturbances.

Goals, Purposes, and Rationality. REBT proposes that humans are happiest when they have goals and purposes that give meaning to their lives. As they strive to attain their goals, they need to adopt a philosophy of self-interest in which they put themselves first and others a close second (as opposed to being selfish and disregarding others). Given that they are interested in goal attainment, **rational** implies "that which helps people to achieve their basic goals and purposes, whereas **irrational** means that which prevents them from achieving these goals and purposes" (Dryden, 1984, p. 238).

Humanistic Emphasis. Although REBT is rational and scientific, it is not "purely objective, scientific or technique-centered, but takes a definite humanistic-existential approach to human problems and their basic solutions" (Ellis & Dryden, 1997, p. 4). The importance of human will and choice is emphasized, while at the same time a recognition is made that some behavior is biologically or socially determined (Ellis, 2001c).

Interaction of Psychological Processes and the Place of Cognition. REBT emphasizes an interactive view of psychological processes in that cognitions, emotions, and behaviors do not exist in isolation but actually overlap considerably. This theory, however, especially emphasizes the cognitive aspect of the psychological process (Dryden & Neenan, 2004). In fact, REBT is best known for the concept of rational and irrational beliefs.

Basic Biological Tendencies. REBT acknowledges that social influences have some impact on humans' tendency to think irrationally but stresses a strong biological basis to irrationality. According to Ellis and Dryden (1997), even if everyone had an exceptionally rational upbringing, all humans would eventually think irrationally and dysfunctionally to varying degrees. Ellis also noted that many self-destructive behaviors are not advocated by parents, educators, or the media, which strengthens the argument for a biological basis. For example, parents do not encourage children to procrastinate or seek immediate gratification, yet that does not stop children from doing so. Furthermore, even though people give up irrationalities, they often develop new ones, and it is easy to revert back to self-defeating behaviors even after working hard to change them. Unfortunately, it is sometimes easier to learn and practice self-defeating behaviors rather than self-enhancing behaviors.

Fundamental Human Disturbances. Dryden and Ellis (2001) identified two major categories of psychological disturbance: ego disturbance and discomfort disturbance. Ego disturbance occurs when individuals make demands on themselves, others, and the world. If these demands are not met, they put themselves down by assigning a global negative rating to themselves and identifying themselves as bad or less worthy. This category contrasts with the concept of **unconditional self-acceptance (USA)**, which does not involve rating but acknowledges human fallibility. Discomfort disturbance, or **low-frustration tolerance (LFT)**, occurs when individuals make demands on themselves, others, and the world relative to comfort and life conditions. When these demands are not met, individuals begin to "awfulize" and develop an "I-can't-stand-it" attitude.

APPLICATIONS

Overview

The following section describes the goals of the counseling or therapy process and how change occurs. Emphasis is placed on the therapeutic relationship and the **A-B-C model** that is a hallmark of REBT. A wide array of cognitive, emotive, and behavioral interventions that illustrate the multimodal nature of the theory are also presented.

Goals of Counseling and Psychotherapy

The goal of rational emotive behavior therapy is to help clients develop a rational philosophy of life that will reduce their emotional distress and self-defeating behavior and result in their ability to lead a happier and more fulfilling life (Dryden, 2002b; Ellis, 2001a; Walen et al., 1992). To achieve this goal, REBT counselors or therapists help clients identify how they prevent themselves from being happy by focusing on their irrational beliefs that lead to emotional and behavioral disturbance. They encourage clients to think more rationally (logically and flexibly), feel healthier, and act more efficiently to achieve their basic goals and purposes (Dryden, 2002b). Consequently, the counselor or therapist uses cognitive, emotive, and behavioral interventions that help clients feel better and get better.

A basic premise of this theory is that it is educative and preventive. Therefore, another goal of the REBT counseling or psychotherapeutic process is to educate clients about how they disturb themselves and to actively teach them the A-B-C model so they can ultimately help themselves (Ellis, 2002b). REBT counselors or therapists encourage clients to read self-help books and listen to tapes. They share worksheets and articles that describe cognitive distortions and emotional disturbance. They do not hesitate to use themselves as models to teach the concept of self-acceptance by self-disclosing about how they have made mistakes or learned to overcome low-frustration tolerance. With children and adolescents, they use developmentally appropriate interventions that teach young clients basic REBT concepts and how to help themselves overcome their problems (Vernon 1998a, 1998b, 1998c; 2002; 2006a, 2006b).

Process of Change

The REBT theory of change is basically optimistic; that is, although humans have a biological tendency to think irrationally, they also have the ability to choose to change their irrational thinking and self-defeating emotions and behavior (Dryden & Ellis, 2001; Ellis, 2001a). According to this theory, there are several levels of change. The most long-lasting and elegant change involves philosophic restructuring of the irrational beliefs (Dryden & Ellis, 2001, Ellis & Dryden, 1997). At this level, change can be specific or general. According to Dryden and Ellis, "Specific philosophic change means that individuals change their absolutistic demands ("musts," "shoulds") about given situations to rational relative preferences. General philosophic changes involve adopting a nondevout attitude toward life events in general" (p. 310). Dryden and Ellis also distinguished between **superelegant** and **semielegant** philosophical change at the general level (p. 310). They noted that superelegant change implies that under almost all conditions for the rest of their lives, people will not upset themselves about anything, whereas semielegant change means that most of the time people will adopt a rational emotive philosophy that will enable them not to upset themselves when bad events occur. Superelegant change rarely happens, as people "fall back to musturbating and thereby disturbing themselves" (p. 310).

DiGiuseppe (1999) stressed that it is far better to help clients change their core irrational beliefs at the philosophic level rather than their automatic thoughts. Challenging automatic thoughts or inferences, reframing, or reattributions are considered **inelegant** solutions; although they may be a coping strategy for a particular event, they are not effective across a wide range of stimuli.

The REBT theory of change is quite simple (Dryden, 1996). Specifically, if clients choose to overcome their emotional and behavioral problems, they first must acknowledge that they have a problem. They also need to realize that, to a large extent, they create their own disturbance. Although environmental conditions can significantly contribute to their problems, it is how they think about those conditions that primarily influences their degree of distur-bance (Ellis & Dryden, 1997). Second, they must identify any **meta-emotional problems,** which are secondary problems about primary problems (Dryden & Neenan, 2004). For ex-ample, clients often are depressed about being depressed or denigrate themselves for having a problem. Unless clients tackle these meta-emotional problems before they deal with the original issues, they will often fail to overcome the original disturbance. Third, they need to identify irrational beliefs and understand why a belief is illogical and irrational. Fourth, they must recognize why rational beliefs would be preferable and give them better results. Fifth, they need to learn how to challenge their irrational beliefs and replace them with rational al-ternatives. Finally, they need to keep working on their tendencies to think and act irrationally.

The Therapeutic Relationship.   For change to occur, REBT counselors or therapists are active and involved as they educate clients and help them develop a rational perspective and effec-tive problem-solving skills. According to Dawson (1991), the relationship between client and counselor or therapist is very important. While counselors or therapists are building rapport with clients, they can also begin to help clients recognize their practical and emotional problems.

Ellis (2001c) noted that "we had better be in psychological contact with our clients; be congruent, genuine, integrated persons; experience accurate, empathic understanding of clients' awareness of their own therapeutic experience" (p. 122). He said that while none of these traits is absolutely necessary, they are all highly desirable. Ellis himself prefers an active, directive therapeutic style with most clients (Dryden, 2002a; Ellis, 2002a; Ellis & MacClaren, 1998), but he does not dogmatically insist that there is one specific type of relationship between client and counselor or therapist, stressing that the degree to which one is active-directive is a choice (Dryden & Ellis, 2001; Ellis, 2002a; Ellis & MacClaren, 1998). Never-theless, Ellis and MacClaren stated that there are several advantages of an active-directive approach, including the fact that it is useful with some disturbed people who have low-frustration tolerance and will not put forth the sustained effort needed for change to occur.

Dryden and Neenan (2004) emphasized that rational emotive behavioral counselors or therapists are encouraged to be flexible. They and Ellis (1997, 2001a) concurred that even though not all REBT practitioners agree with the active-directive style, it is possible to vary the style and, at the same time, adhere to the theoretical principles on which it is based. Ac-cording to Dryden (1999), "Effective rational emotive behavioral counselors vary their ther-apeutic styles and can adopt a variety of therapeutic styles to fit with the therapeutic requirements of different clients" (p. 20).

With children and adolescents, establishing a good therapeutic relationship is particu-larly important. Being patient, flexible, and less directive are essential, as is using a wider va-riety of techniques (Vernon, 2002, 2004a).

REBT counselors or therapists believe that because clients come to counseling or ther-apy for problems and want help, part of establishing a good relationship is to help clients work on their problems immediately (DiGiuseppe, 2002). Thus, part of the rapport-building process involves coming to an agreement on the goals for change (Dryden, 2002c; O'Kelly, 2002). In addition, practitioners must be active and help clients discover what they are do-ing to upset themselves (Dryden, 2002a). As a result of those actions, clients can leave the first session with some insight and hope, which in turn enhances their relationship with the counselor or therapist.

Contrary to what many believe, REBT has been influenced by Rogers' core conditions. The concept of unconditional acceptance and genuineness is endorsed by REBT counselors or therapists (Dryden, 2002a; Ellis, 2001c). REBT counselors or therapists encourage their clients to accept themselves unconditionally as fallible human beings and endeavor to accept their clients unconditionally as well. In fact, Dryden (1996, 2002a) posited that unconditional acceptance is more important than counselor or therapist warmth, because too much warmth may inadvertently reinforce clients' demands for love and approval, which is irrational.

Because they feel free to be themselves and at times self-disclose their own fallibilities, REBT counselors or therapists are genuine (Dryden, 2002a). This genuineness has therapeutic purposes because it indicates to clients that counselors or therapists are humans, too, and it teaches them what the counselor or therapist did to overcome his or her own problems. Of course counselors or therapists should not self-disclose when they think it is inappropriate or when they think the client might use such self-disclosure against them. REBT counselors or therapists are also empathic, both affectively and philosophically; they communicate that they understand how clients feel and show clients that they understand the beliefs underlying the feelings (Dryden, 1999). They may also be appropriately humorous, as many clients tend to take life too seriously. Dryden (2002a) stressed that humorous interventions are not directed at the clients themselves but at their irrational beliefs and self-defeating feelings and behaviors. He cautioned that the use of humor may not be appropriate with all clients, which is why it is so important to be flexible.

Dryden (1999) noted that the preferred counseling or therapy relationship is egalitarian in that the client and counselor or therapist are equal in their humanity. From another perspective, however, the relationship is unequal, because the counselor or therapist has more expertise and skills and needs to help clients in their personal problem solving. The situation changes, however, as clients gain more insight and the counselor or therapist encourages them to assume more responsibility for change. Thus, as the counselor or therapist becomes less directive and clients become more effective problem solvers, the relationship becomes more egalitarian.

The A-B-C Model. Ellis developed a conceptual model to illustrate the major constructs of this theory, as well as the process of change (Dryden, 1999; Dryden & Ellis, 2001; Ellis, 2001c; Ellis & MacClaren, 1998). In essence, the nature of emotional disturbance can be explained by recognizing that as people attempt to fulfill their goals, they encounter an **activating event** (A) that either blocks or helps them achieve these goals. Activating events may be positive or negative; may refer to real or perceived events; can be past, present, or future oriented; and can be an individual's own thoughts or feelings. When individuals seek counseling or therapy, they strongly believe that the activating event has caused their negative **emotional and behavioral consequences** (C).

REBT theory posits that it is not the activating event (A) that creates the emotional and behavioral consequences (C), but rather the **beliefs** (B) people hold about these activating events. The activating event may certainly contribute to the consequence, but two individuals can experience the same event and feel and react differently, which explains the relationship between A, B, and C. For example, consider two students who both studied hard for a test and failed it. Assume that one student was devastated and the other student was just disappointed. The difference in how they felt can be attributed to what they were thinking about the event. The devastated student equated her failure with her self-worth; she thought the failure proved how stupid she was. The disappointed student wished that he would have gotten a better grade, but he realized that this failure in no way proved his ignorance.

Beliefs (B) are either rational or irrational. **Rational beliefs** are self-enhancing and help people achieve their goals; they are flexible, logical, and pragmatic (Dryden et al., 2003). Rational beliefs are realistic preferences that typically result in constructive behavioral patterns and moderate negative emotions when the activating events (A) fall short of the desired outcome (Dryden, 1999; Ellis & MacClaren, 1998). **Irrational beliefs** are rigid and emanate from absolutistic evaluations that ultimately sabotage goals. They result in negative emotions such as depression, anger, anxiety, resentment, self-pity, worthlessness, and rage, as well as in maladaptive behaviors such as withdrawal, avoidance, violence, and procrastination.

Originally, Ellis identified 11 irrational beliefs (Ellis, 1962), but now there is one core belief, which is a "must," and several derivatives.

1. I must be successful at important performances and relationships, or I am inadequate and worthless.
2. Other people must treat me considerately and fairly, or else they are bad and deserve to be punished.
3. The conditions under which I live must be absolutely comfortable and pleasurable or I can't stand it. (Ellis, 1996, p. 13)

These basic irrational beliefs share four key elements: demanding, awfulizing, low-frustration tolerance, and global rating of self or others. Irrational beliefs are illogical and are not validly inferred, whereas rational beliefs are logical and can be validly inferred from earlier premises. For instance, if a student wanted to get a good grade on his test, his rational and logical conclusion would be that studying and doing homework would help him achieve that goal. However, if he assumed that studying for tests and doing his homework meant that he absolutely must get a good grade and that the teacher cannot give him anything except a top grade, he would be thinking irrationally because his conclusions are illogical.

Counselors or therapists can detect irrational beliefs in several ways: cognitively, emotionally, and behaviorally. Cognitively, irrational beliefs can be identified by listening for "shoulds, oughts, and musts," as well as phrases such as "I can't stand it," or "that is horrible" (Nelson-Jones, 2000, p. 204). Emotionally, irrational beliefs are present when there are extreme negative emotions such as panic, depression, or intense anger. Specifically, when clients report feelings of depression, guilt, or extreme sadness, they are probably engaging in self-downing. When they are angry, "musts" and demands are generally prevalent. Frustration and anxiety are often present with low-frustration tolerance. Behaviorally, self-defeating actions signal the likelihood of irrational beliefs.

Once the emotional and behavioral consequences and the irrational beliefs have been identified, the next step in the A-B-C-model is **disputation (D)**, which is what REBT is probably best known for. Disputation is an active process that helps clients assess the helpfulness of their belief system (Ellis & MacClaren, 1998). The purpose of challenging rigid and inflexible beliefs is to replace them with rational alternatives. Various types of disputations can be used mildly or vigorously (Ellis, 2002a). Disputing can be **didactic**, which is informational. In this process, the counselor or therapist explains the difference between rational beliefs, which are flexible and adaptive and help in goal attainment; and irrational beliefs, which are rigid, illogical, and interfere with goal achievement (Dryden, 2002a; Ellis & MacClaren,

1998). The **Socratic approach**, another common form of disputation, involves questioning that gives clients insight into the irrationality of their thinking (Dryden, 2002a).

During the disputation process, several different types of cognitive disputes are useful. In a **functional dispute**, the purpose is to question the practicality of the client's irrational beliefs. Because irrational beliefs result in self-defeating behaviors and unhealthy emotions, questions such as these are helpful: "How is what you are doing helping you?" "How is continuing to think this way affecting your life?" (Ellis & MacClaren, 1998, p. 60). Another type of dispute is the **empirical dispute**, which helps clients evaluate the factual aspects of their beliefs. Examples of questions that may be appropriate in empirical disputes include these: "Where is the evidence that you are no good simply because you failed an exam?" "Where is the proof that life is not worth living if you do not get into graduate school?" "So you did not get the job you wanted. Where is it written that you will never be employed for the rest of your life?"

A third type of dispute is the **logical dispute**, which helps clients see how illogical it is to escalate their desires and preferences into demands (Nelson-Jones, 2000). Typical questions could include these: "How does it follow that just because you'd like this to be true and it would be very convenient, it *should* be?" and "How does it follow that failing at an important task makes *you*, a person who may fail at many tasks and succeed at many others, a failure? How does *it*, failing, make *you*, worthless?" (Ellis & MacClaren, 1998, p. 64). **Philosophical disputing** is another approach that helps clients look at meaning and satisfaction in life. Because clients often focus on specific problems and lose perspective on other aspects of their life, a philosophical dispute such as the following will help them develop that perspective: "Despite the fact that things will probably not go the way you want some/most of the time in this area, can you still derive some satisfaction in your life?" (Ellis & MacClaren, 1998, p. 66).

Clients readily can recognize that their beliefs are not rational, but as Dryden (1999) cautioned, even if counselors or therapists are successful in helping them achieve this understanding, it does not mean that they have a strong conviction in the rational alternative. Although intellectual insight indicates some progress, it is not sufficient to promote emotional and behavioral change. Therefore, counselors or therapists must persist in helping clients give up their irrational beliefs by continuing to use directive questions, as well as other cognitive, emotive-evocative, imaginal, and behavioral techniques to help change irrational ideas. The ultimate goal is to help clients develop **effective new beliefs or philosophy (E)** (Ellis, 1996, 2001a) and **effective new feelings (F)** (Corey, 2001).

The 18-Step Model. Dryden et al. (2003) identified 18 steps that counselors or therapists can use in each session to help them implement the critical aspects of REBT to effect client change. They noted that these steps can be applied to all age groups, even though the techniques used at each step may differ.

The first step is to ask clients to describe the problem and the second step is to reach agreement about the target problem. In each session, clients may present different issues, and it is important to have consensus on what is to be addressed. The third step is to agree on a goal with respect to the problem that was defined. The fourth step is to ask for a specific example of the target problem. Assessing emotional and behavioral consequences, and an assessment of the activating event, occur in Steps 5 and 6. In Step 7, the counselor or therapist and client agree on a goal with respect to the assessed problem. In Step 8, the counselor or therapist helps the client see the link between the problem as the defined goal and the problem as the assessed goal. Step 9 involves the counselor or therapist determining whether there are any relevant secondary emotional problems that must be dealt (e.g., being anxious about being anxious). In the 10th step, the counselor or therapist teaches the connection between beliefs, feelings, and behaviors, and this is followed by an assessment of irrational beliefs in Step 11.

Step 12 involves connecting the irrational beliefs to the disturbed emotions and behaviors and connecting the rational beliefs to the healthy emotions and behaviors. Disputing the irrational beliefs, using a combination of logical, empirical, and functional disputes, is Step 13. Proposing alternative rational ideas and using direct teaching are also appropriate. In Step 14, the counselor or therapist helps clients deepen their conviction in the rational beliefs through continued disputing and by helping clients describe how they would behave differently by adopting this new belief. Step 15 involves checking the validity of the activating event. In Step 16 clients are encouraged to practice new learning through the use of homework assignments that may include worksheets or various types of behavioral activities. Step 17 is checking homework assignments. The final step (18) is to facilitate the working-through process.

The 18-step model is particularly helpful to counselors or therapists who are just beginning to practice REBT. The steps can be written in the form of a checklist to serve as a guide throughout sessions.

Maintaining Change. REBT counselors or therapists recognize that clients will backslide; therefore, they teach clients that it will take work and practice to maintain change (Dryden & Neenan, 2004). Throughout the counseling or therapy process, they use bibliotherapy, homework assignments, and self-help materials to help clients develop skills to use inside and outside of counseling or therapy (Dryden et al., 2003; Vernon, 2002). They also help clients review the A-B-C model to determine what caused them to fall back into their old patterns; then they encourage clients to practice disputing again and again until they can replace their irrational beliefs with rational alternatives (Nelson-Jones, 2000). Recording counseling or therapy sessions so that clients can listen to them again can also be effective (Velten, 2002).

Traditional Intervention Strategies

Dryden (1999) and Ellis (2002a) pointed out that REBT has a multimodal emphasis because REBT counselors or therapists utilize so many cognitive, emotive, and behavioral interventions to bring about change. Although REBT counselors or therapists use techniques from other schools of therapy, REBT "is based on a clear-cut theory of emotional health and disturbance" (Dryden & Ellis, 2001, p. 325), and the techniques are consistent with the theory.

Cognitive Interventions. The most common cognitive intervention is the disputation of irrational beliefs, which involves helping clients detect the beliefs, debating with them about whether their beliefs are true or logical, and helping them discriminate between rational and irrational beliefs (Dryden & Ellis, 2001). Although Socratic questioning is often used to encourage clients to think about how logical and functional their beliefs are, skillful counselors or therapists use a variety of disputing methods (Ellis, 2002a), including didactic explanations, humorous exaggeraton, and the friendship dispute, to help clients see their unreasonable self-standards (Dryden et al., 2003).

In another cognitive intervention, written homework forms help clients dispute their irrational beliefs between sessions (Dryden, 2002b; Ellis & MacClaren, 1998). **Referenting** is an intervention in which clients make a list of the advantages and disadvantages of changing their irrational beliefs and behaviors (Ellis & MacClaren, 1998). **Rational coping statements,** which are factual, encouraging phrases such as, "I can accomplish this task" or "I will work toward accomplishing this task, but if I don't succeed it doesn't make me a failure as a person" (Ellis & MacClaren, p. 67) can also be effective, particularly if they are implemented after more forceful disputing has been done.

Semantic methods are also useful, for example, helping clients change "I can't" statements to "I haven't yet" (Dryden & Ellis, 2001, p. 327). Other methods to introduce or reinforce a rational philosophy include bibliotherapy or audiotherapy in which clients are assigned books and materials to read or tapes to listen to (Dryden, 2002b, Ellis, 2002a, 2002b; Ellis & Harper, 1997); use of REBT with others to practice rational arguments (Dryden & Ellis, 2001); and age-appropriate worksheets that help clients identify and dispute irrational beliefs (Vernon, 2002; 2006a, 2006b).

Emotive Interventions. As Dryden and Ellis (2001) pointed out, "REBT therapy has often been falsely criticized for neglecting the emotive aspects of psychotherapy" (p. 328). In fact, many emotive techniques are routinely used by REBT counselors or therapists. For example, humor in the form of exaggeration is often used to help clients avoid taking themselves so seriously (Dryden, 2002b; Ellis, 2001a; Nelson-Jones, 2000); however, the technique must be used cautiously (Vernon, 2002). Walen (2002) stressed that it is never appropriate to make fun of clients. Another popular form of humor is to use rational humorous songs (Ellis, 2002b) that Ellis and others have written. Songs such as the following are available at the Albert Ellis Institute and are frequently used in REBT workshops.

Love Me, Love Me, Only Me (Tune: "Yankee Doodle Dandy")

Love me, love me, only me
Or I'll die without you!
Make your love a guarantee
So I can never doubt you!
Love me, love me totally—really, really try, dear;
But if you demand love, too
I'll hate you till I die, dear!
Love me, love me all the time
Thoroughly and wholly!
Life turns into slushy slime
'Less you love me solely!
Love me with great tenderness
With no ifs or buts, dear.
If you love me somewhat less,
I'll hate your goddammed guts, dear!

Rational role-playing is also an effective emotive intervention (Ellis, 2001a; Ellis & MacClaren, 1998; Vernon, 2002). Role-playing can help clients express feelings and can help resolve various emotionally laden issues. Ellis cautioned that even though feelings are expressed through role-playing, the relief may be temporary because clients have not explored the basic beliefs that resulted in the feelings. Therefore, it is important to conduct rational role-playing that not only helps clients express feelings but also identifies the beliefs that created those feelings.

A variation of rational role-playing is a **reverse role-play** in which the counselor or therapist takes the role of the client and the client assumes the role of counselor or therapist. In this way, the client learns to dispute his or her own irrational ideas as played out by the counselor or therapist.

Rational emotive imagery (REI) is a key REBT emotive intervention (Dryden, 1999; Dryden, 2002b; Ellis, 2001a). The purpose of REI is to help clients identify more rational and appropriate emotions in a particular problematic situation as well as to provide an opportunity for clients to experientially identify self-statements and coping techniques that could work for them in stressful situations. In implementing this technique, the counselor or therapist invites the client to close his or her eyes and imagine a difficult situation that evoked strong negative emotions. After the client reconstructs this image and labels the upsetting feelings, the counselor or therapist asks the client to change the upsetting feelings to a more reasonable negative emotion. When the client signals that this has been accomplished, the counselor or therapist invites the client to return to the present and describe the healthy emotions, exploring how thoughts helped contribute to these less upsetting emotions. Clients are usually encouraged to practice REI for 30 days to help them learn how to change unhealthy negative emotions.

Another emotive intervention is **forceful coping statements.** In this intervention, clients formulate rational coping statements and practice them forcefully during and between sessions (Ellis, 1996; Ellis, 2001a; Ellis & Velten, 1992). Ellis and MacClaren (1998) noted that clients have usually practiced irrational statements for a long time; powerfully repeating such statements as "When I fail it NEVER, NEVER makes me a complete failure as a person" (p. 78) over and over helps clients replace the irrational statements with rational alternatives.

Experiential exercises are used by many REBT counselors or therapists in individual counseling or therapy as well as in classroom settings and small groups (Ellis & MacClaren, 1998; Vernon, 1998a, 1998b, 1998c, 2004b). These exercises help clients learn new skills and give them an opportunity to explore problematic areas. For example, Ellis and MacClaren described an exercise in which clients wrote irrational beliefs on one side of an index card; on the other side, they wrote five negative things that have happened to them because they think that way. Vernon (2002) discussed helping clients with procrastination by having them list things they typically put off doing and giving the list to the counselor or therapist. As the client lies on the floor, the counselor or therapist reads the items one by one. As each one is read, the counselor or therapist puts a stack of newspapers on the client's body. After the final item is read and the pile of newspapers is quite high, the client is invited to talk about how he or she feels with everything "all piled up" and what steps to take to get out from under the pile of procrastination.

Behavioral Interventions. Behavioral interventions have always played an important role in helping clients change, and they are used to supplement and reinforce cognitive and emotive interventions. Behavioral interventions are often incorporated into homework assignments or are used in conjunction with other techniques.

One of REBT's most unique behavioral interventions is the **shame attacking exercise** (Ellis, 2004a, 2004b). Ellis realized that shame is at the core of a significant amount of emotional disturbance; when people do something they consider shameful, they criticize their actions and think that they should never repeat them. Ellis (1996) said, "In REBT we try to help people to stop putting themselves, their whole person, down no matter how badly they behave and no matter how much other people look down on them for so behaving" (p. 92). To help clients understand this concept, they are encouraged to do things in public that they regard as shameful or embarrassing, such as yelling out the stops on elevators (Nelson-Jones, 2000), approaching strangers in the subway and asking them what month it is, explaining that they have just gotten out of the mental hospital (Ellis, 2004a), or singing in the street (Ellis, 2001a). Shame attack exercises should not be illegal, harmful, immoral, or bothersome to others. Rather, they are "foolish, silly, and ridiculous" (Ellis, 2001a, p. 153) and are intended to help clients understand that although they may act "bad" or "foolish," they are not bad persons. After doing shame attacks, clients often feel much less uncomfortable and anxious; at the same time, they realize that they can tolerate not having the approval of others.

Another behavioral intervention is **skills training** (Dryden, 1999). This intervention is considered an inelegant solution if clients do not work on identifying and disputing irrational beliefs. Nevertheless, many clients need practical skills to help them overcome deficits—skills that range from trade skills to interpersonal or social skills such as assertion (Ellis & MacClaren, 1998).

Behavioral interventions can include rewards and penalties. Counselors or therapists help clients arrange reinforcement (i.e., rewards) for achieving a goal or penalties if they do not (Dryden, 1999). Penalties may involve contributing money to a cause clients do not believe in as a forceful way to modify behavior (Ellis, 2001a); rewards include things the client truly enjoys. Paradoxical homework, which involves prescribing the symptom the client is attempting to work on, is used with some clients (Ellis & MacClaren, 1998). Ellis and MacClaren cautioned, however, that there are risks with this approach and it is not appropriate for all clients.

Brief Intervention Strategies

"REBT was specifically designed from the start to be brief but effective for many (not *all*) clients (Ellis, 2001c, p. 125). Although some clients are seriously disturbed and need more extensive therapy, Ellis noted that "self-neurolitizing individuals can be significantly helped in five to twelve sessions" (p. 125).

Beginning in the first session, REBT counselors or therapists teach clients the ABC's of emotional disturbance and show them how they construct and maintain their symptoms and how to ameliorate them. This explanation contributes to significant improvement, which Ellis (2001c) maintained can occur in a few weeks.

Perhaps what distinguishes REBT from many other theories and makes it briefer is that it is a self-help approach: Clients are taught how to change their irrational thinking so they can apply REBT techniques to present as well as future problems. In addition, clients learn to practice the skills and concepts between sessions by completing various homework assignments, engaging in rational emotive imagery, or using reinforcements and penalties. All these techniques, in addition to those previously described, are brief interventions.

CLIENTS WITH SERIOUS MENTAL HEALTH ISSUES

According to Seligman (2004), there has been an increase in the severity of disorders that counselors and therapists need to treat. REBT has been applied to a wide variety of the mental disorders included in Seligman's disucssion: anxiety (Ellis, 2001c; Warren, 1997), depression (Hauck & McKeegan, 1997; Walen & Rader, 1991), obsessive-compulsive disorder (Ellis, 1997), panic disorder and agoraphobia (Yankura, 1997), schizophrenia (Trower, 2003), and borderline personality disorder (Ellis, 2001c). A brief description of REBT applications to these disorders follows.

Anxiety. From an REBT perspective, clients with generalized anxiety disorder are more likely to "interpret ambiguous information as threatening, overestimate the probability of the occurrence of potentially dangerous events, and rate the feared events as more aversive or costly" (Warren, 1997, p. 14). Furthermore, they may have issues related to approval and self-worth or they may fear criticism and worry about making mistakes; therefore many life circumstances appear threatening.

After assessing the irrational beliefs, REBT practitioners lead clients through the disputation process, paying special attention to clients' anxiety about being anxious ("I can't stand this," "I shouldn't be anxious") and noting the shame and self-downing that clients often experience about their worry and anxiety (Walen & Rader, 1991). Teaching clients to differentiate between the possibility of something occurring and the probability of it happening is also an effective strategy.

Depression. Ellis (1987, 2001c) maintained that REBT is an effective therapy with individuals who are depressed because it specifically focuses on addressing irrational beliefs instead of on correcting distorted negative inferences. For this reason, REBT may result in more pervasive and long-lasting change. According to Hauck and McKeegan (1997), "Depression can be caused by (a) self-blame (the "bad me" approach), (b) self-pity ("poor me"), and (c) other-pity ("poor you")" (p. 49). Each of these factors is accompanied by underlying irrational beliefs that, if effectively disputed, can help alleviate depression. However, Hauck and McKeegan stressed that alleviation of depression generally occurs only when the depression is preceded by a negative life event as opposed to depression that is primarily organic in nature. These authors concurred with Walen and Rader (1991) that when depression is primarily biological in origin, a combination of cognitive therapy and antidepressant medication is most likely needed.

Walen and Rader (1991) suggested that the basic principle of cognitive therapy—how you feel is based on what you think—may send an erroneous message to clients with serious depressive illnesses that they are responsible for their illness. Walen and Rader strongly suggested that counselors or therapists differentiate among the different types of depression. Furthermore, they stressed the importance of letting clients with acute depression know that they have an illness and of helping them reframe depression as a disease, not a character flaw.

Obsessive-Compulsive Disorder. Ellis (1997) indicated that the need for certainty contributes to individuals' tendency to develop rituals or obsessions. He also noted that obsessive-compulsive disorder (OCD) may be the result of biological deficiencies, in which case medication may be needed in combination with REBT procedures. Although techniques such as activity homework and in vivo desensitization are often used successfully with clients who have OCD, clients with severe OCD are so obsessed with their repetitive behaviors that they find it difficult to adhere to the behavioral, emotive, or cognitive techniques and fail to persist in changing their ritualizing.

Foa and Wilson (1991) identified several important considerations in treating clients who have OCD, including helping them recognize that the anxieties that underlie their OCD behaviors are unrealistic, illogical, and self-defeating. These authors also stressed the importance of helping clients develop high-frustration tolerance so that they can work harder to overcome their repeated rituals. Ellis (1997) pointed out that these clients often put themselves down for having OCD, and he indicated that REBT counselors or therapists must help these clients accept themselves unconditionally with their OCD and use REBT techniques to help them dispute their anxiety, depression, and self-hatred about having this disorder.

Panic Disorder and Agoraphobia. Some individuals have a biological predisposition to panic disorder as a result of their genetic makeup (Clum, 1990), in which case psychotropic medications are often helpful in reducing symptoms. However, Yankura (1997) stressed that it is not sufficient to treat panic disorders with medication alone. Yankura noted that it is far more effective to also use approaches such as REBT that teach coping skills to increase clients' sense of self-efficacy.

REBT treatment for anxiety disorders "involves helping clients to identify, dispute, and replace the irrational beliefs that underpin their anxiety problems" (Yankura, 1997, p. 126). Typical irrational beliefs of clients are thinking that they must not experience uncomfortable feelings or panic attacks and that something terrible may happen if they do. For example, clients may think it would be awful if they fainted or lost control and that they could not stand the embarrassment. It follows, then, that clients would tend to avoid going to places where they have had a panic attack, which results in their agoraphobia. These clients also tend to put themselves down; they think that they should be better able to control the panic and avoidant behavior and that they are weak and inadequate if they cannot.

REBT counselors or therapists use various interventions to help clients with panic disorder and agoraphobia. For example, they help clients distribute their catastrophizing and awfulizing about their anxiety and teach them how to use distraction techniques such as focusing on their breathing or tensing and relaxing muscles (Clum, 1990). They also use approaches such as flooding in which clients are encouraged to confront what they fear (Yankura, 1997).

Borderline Personality Disorder. According to Ellis (2001c), people with borderline personality disorder seem "to be born with innate tendencies that interact with their experience to produce several deficiencies" (p. 362). They have rigid and impulsive thinking styles and inconsistent images of others; exaggerate the significance of things; are demanding, self-downing, and easily enraged; in addition, they are overdependent and often alienated (Cloninger as cited in Ellis, 2001c). Ellis (2001c) maintained that individuals with borderline personality disorders have high levels of self-downing and low-frustration tolerance. Although it is possible to help them minimize the way they disturb themselves about their condition, in reality, they can rarely be completely cured. Nevertheless, Ellis (2001c) maintained that improvement can be achieved by using REBT to teach clients how to unconditionally accept themselves, how to ameliorate the self-defeating nature of their low-frustration tolerance, and how to challenge their dysfunctional cognitions.

CROSS-CULTURAL CONSIDERATIONS

REBT has been implemented cross-culturally for years through the Albert Ellis Institute and affiliated training centers located throughout the world. In these centers, counselors and therapists receive training and supervison in using REBT with clients. Consequently, REBT is widely used in many countries.

Ellis (2002a) stressed that counselors and therapists should be multiculturally open-minded and know as much as possible about the rules of the miniority culture. He emphasized that REBT practitioners are "almost intrinsically multicultural" (p. 195) in that they accept all clients unconditionally, regardless of their cultural, religious, or political practices. He also pointed out that oppression exists in most cultures and that teaching clients unconditional other-acceptance might help diminish oppression.

Ellis (2002a) abandoned his theory that religion and spirituality do more harm than good. He acknowledged that devout faith is not irrational and self-defeating. In fact, Ellis acknowledged that faith has resulted in many emotional and behavioral benefits for individuals.

Lega and Ellis (2001) initiated cross-cultural studies and noted that such studies are an important new direction for REBT research. Lega and Ellis found that the concepts of *musts* and *demandingness* apply to several different Latin American and European cultures but vary somewhat in degree. Ellis hypothesized that cultural as well as biological factors influence how these differences are manifested. He and Lega recommended increasing emphasis on multicultural research, which would in turn promote more informed practice of REBT in different cultures.

EVALUATION

Overview

Ellis (1996) acknowledged that he was prejudiced but maintained that REBT is more likely to help people achieve "deeper and more lasting emotional and behavioral change than other methods of therapy" (p. 1). He stated that clients usually can improve significantly in 10 to 20 sessions, in individual as well as group therapy. In the following sections, supporting research and limitations are addressed.

Supporting Research

Smith and Glass (1977), in their meta-analytic review of psychotherapy outcome studies, concluded that RET was the second-most effective psychotherapy, with systematic desensitization being first. However, because Ellis focused on theory and practice rather than research, REBT has a reputation of having insufficient empirical support. In an attempt to address this limitation, Lyons and Woods (1991) reported results from a meta-analysis of 70 outcome studies. They made a total of 236 comparisons of REBT to baseline, control groups, cognitive-behavioral modification, behavioral therapy, and other psychotherapies. Results indicated that subjects who received REBT showed significant improvement over baseline measures and control groups. Many of these studies supported the efficacy of REBT for a wide array of problems including stress, depression, anger, social anxiety, alcohol abuse, weight issues, behavioral problems, problems with assertion, school underachievement, test anxiety, sexual fears and dysfunction, and performance and public speaking anxiety. However, Lyons and Woods cautioned that most studies did not report on follow-up data, which makes it difficult to determine the long-term effects of the counseling or therapy.

Several more recent studies suggested that REBT can be useful for practitioners in school or clinical settings. Sapp, Farrell, and Durand (1995) reported improved academic performance by African American children who used an REBT program. Graves (1996) demonstrated that a parent training program reduced stress and improved parenting skills in parents of children with Down syndrome. Shannon and Allen (1998) showed that students who participated in an REBT-based skill training program had better grades than peers in a control group and scored higher on a standardized math test.

Ellis (2001b) noted that there are many reasons for the lack of solid outcome studies. Because REBT endorses the use of many cognitive, emotive, and behavioral techniques, it is difficult to test the effectiveness of the techniques, and this has been discouraging for researchers. Furthermore, paper-and-pencil tests are an inadequate way to get at clients' beliefs and their unconscious shoulds and musts. A compounding problem is the fact that the Albert Ellis Institute, which could have been a significant instigator of solid outcome research, has traditionally been a counseling or therapy training institute, not an academic research institute. It has attracted mental health practitioners who are more interested in learning how to effectively help others than in doing research. At the present time, however, several efforts are underway at the institute to promote quality research.

Limitations

In an interview with Broder (2001), Ellis stated, "My basic goals are to push REBT, and to improve it so as to help more people use it.... I want REBT to be successful in the world.... I think that REBT and Cognitive Behavior Therapy (CBT) are going to help more people more of the time in an efficient manner than other therapies" (p. 85). Although he acknowledges that considerable research needs to be done, Ellis firmly stands behind two predictions he made at the American Psychological Association convention in 1956 (Ellis, 1994, p. 418): that "REBT . . . will prove more effective with more types of clients than any of the other kinds of psychotherapy that are now being widely employed" and that "a considerable amount of . . . REBT will prove to be the most effective type of psychological treatment that helps to minimize the basic neuroses . . . of many clients, and particularly of many with whom other types of therapy have been shown to be relatively ineffective."

In recognizing the limitations of REBT, Ellis (1994) stated that REBT is not alone—"even the most effective forms of psychotherapy are, as yet, distinctly limited" (p. 331) because clients continue to hold onto their irrationalities and repeatedly behave in self-defeating ways, even though they may have insight into the cause of their disturbances and improve slightly. Therefore, no matter how hard the counselor or therapist works, client resistance is often difficult to overcome.

Perhaps one of the biggest limitations of REBT has been the negative influence of Ellis himself, as he acknowledged (2001b). In his opinion, professionals have slighted or opposed REBT because "I am a charismatic individual, with characteristics which many of them find distasteful" (p. 69). He admitted that his public manner and use of four-letter words is controversial and unconventional and that his use of the term *rational* may be averse to empirically minded psychologists. Because it is irrational to demand that Ellis change his style, professionals must recognize that they can adhere to the basic principles of REBT, which has been used effectively with adults as well as with children (Vernon, 2002), without emulating Ellis' style.

SUMMARY CHART—*Rational Emotive Behavior Therapy*

Major Constucts

REBT has a strong philosophical basis as well as commitment to the scientific method. The interconnectedness of thinking, feeling, and behaving is central to this theory, as is the notion that emotional distress results from dysfunctional thought processes.

Goals

The goal of REBT is to help clients develop a rational philosophy that will allow them to reduce their emotional distress and self-defeating behaviors.

Change Process

Change occurs as counselors or therapists help clients work through the A-B-C model of emotional disturbance. Irrational beliefs are replaced with rational alternatives that result in more moderate, healthy emotions and self-enhancing behaviors.

Interventions

A wide variety of cognitive, emotive, and behavioral interventions are used in REBT: disputing, rational-emotive imagery, rational role-playing, bibliotherapy, shame attack exercises, and rational coping self-statements.

Limitations

Limitations include the lack of outcome research and the overgeneralization that REBT is Albert Ellis. Although Ellis is the founder of the theory, practitioners all over the world integrate the basic principles of this effective theory in their own style.

THE CASE OF JONATHAN: *A Rational Emotive Behavior Therapy Approach*

Following 18-step model of Dryden et al. (2003), the REBT counselor or therapist would first ask Jonathan to describe his problem and they would agree on the target problem. The counselor or therapist would use active listening skills and convey genuine interest in Jonathan by asking pertinent questions to help focus the interview. Jonathan and the counselor or therapist would come to some agreement about the goals for the session. Next, the counselor or therapist would ask for a specific example of the target problem, and an assessment of emotional and behavioral consequences would follow. In this case, Jonathan indicated that he is depressed and lonely as well as angry and frustrated. Consequently, his drinking has increased and he has taken his anger and frustration out on his coworkers and supervisor, which has resulted in suspension without pay.

After assessing emotional and behavioral consequences, the counselor or therapist would assess the activating event (A): Jonathan's difficulties at work, financial problems, marital separation, and moving off the reservation. After reaching agreement with Jonathan on the goal with respect to the assessed problem, the counselor or therapist would help Jonathan see the link between the problem as the defined goal and the problem as the assessed goal. After this, the counselor or therapist would want to determine if there are any relevant secondary problems (e.g., is Jonathan depressed about being depressed). At this point, the counselor or therapist would then want to teach Jonathan how these events themselves do not create his negative feelings and behaviors, but his thoughts about these events create the emotional upset. The counselor or therapist would then assess Jonathan's irrational beliefs (B), helping him to understand how his anger at his supervisor and coworkers is stemming from his irrational belief that they should not be so demanding and perfectionist and should not treat him so unfairly. The counselor or therapist would also help Jonathan see how his depression is related to his self-downing—that his work is never good enough, that he is not wanted in the "White man's" world, and that nothing ever seems to work out for him in terms of job and family. Even his dream reflects his self-downing: The bus driver does not hear him, laughs at him, and ignores him.

After helping Jonathan identify his irrational beliefs and how they connect to his feelings and behaviors (C), the REBT counselor or therapist would use a combination of logical, empirical, and functional disputes (D) to help him replace his irrational beliefs with rational alternatives. For example, the counselor or therapist might ask: "Where is the evidence that you are not wanted in the 'White man's' world? And even if you aren't, does that make you a bad person? Or, suppose it is true that your supervisor is expecting too much and treating you unfairly. How is getting angry helping you improve the situation?" The counselor or therapist would continue to help Jonathan dispute his irrational beliefs with the goal of helping him adopt a more effective rational philosophy (E) and reduce the intensity of the negative emotions (F), which in turn would help him behave in less self-defeating ways.

In addition to disputing, the REBT counselor or therapist would help Jonathan by using a combination of other techniques. For example, the practitioner would teach him how to be assertive rather than aggressive, implement a reward and penalty system with regard to his drinking, instruct him in using rational coping self-statements, and show him how to use rational emotive imagery.

The counselor or therapist would also help Johathan deepen his conviction in rational thinking by having him describe how he would behave differently by adopting these new beliefs. After checking the validity of the activating event, the REBT counselor or therapist would then encourage Jonathan to practice his new learnings by completing homework assignments, which will be checked at each session.

Although REBT counselors or therapists would not deal with a lot of issues regarding family of origin, they would help Jonathan deal with his guilt and self-downing relative to his parents' feelings about his decision to leave the reservation, his guilt over his brother's death, and his failure to succeed in marriages. In addition, they would deal with his low-frustration tolerance, which leads to his drinking and exacerbates his problems (e.g., life is too hard; I can't stand the pain and discomfort—I need an escape) through disputing as well as other psychoeducational approaches.

The goal of counseling or therapy is to help Jonathan learn more effective ways of thinking, feeling, and behaving that will enable him to deal not only with present problems but also with future issues. The REBT counselor or therapist supports, challenges, educates, and empowers the client through a variety of cognitive, emotive, and behavioral strategies.

CHAPTER 12

Reality Therapy Theory

Robert E. Wubbolding
Xavier University, Cincinnati

This chapter describes the validating theory for the practice of reality therapy. Choice theory states that human beings are motivated by current needs and wants and therefore are not trapped by past experiences. The delivery system, summarized by the WDEP acronym, provides a practical methodology for counselors and therapists to help clients clarify their wants, describe their behavior, evaluate their choices, and make effective action plans. Choice theory and reality therapy are used to address serious problems as well as personal growth concerns.

BACKGROUND

William Glasser, the originator of **reality therapy,** first began to develop this approach to counseling and psychotherapy while working in a correctional institution and a psychiatric hospital. A board-certified psychiatrist, Glasser had been trained in the traditional methods of psychiatry. He was taught to help clients gain insight so that after transference was worked through, they could achieve a higher degree of sanity. However, his experience had shown that even if these goals of the analytic approach were achieved, clients did not necessarily change their behavior, and many continued to have difficulty making productive decisions. With support and input from a sympathetic professor named G. L. Harrington, Glasser formulated the early principles of his new treatment modality.

The watershed year for reality therapy came in 1965, when Glasser published *Reality Therapy*. In this then-controversial book, Glasser emphasized that people are responsible for their own behavior and that they cannot blame the past or outside forces and at the same time achieve a high degree of mental health. He asserted that behavior involves choices and that there are always options open to most people. Consequently, the objective of counseling and psychotherapy should be measurable behavioral change, not merely insight into and understanding of past events or current subconscious drives.

Although not greeted enthusiastically by the medical profession, Glasser's theory was well received by many, including corrections personnel, youth workers, counselors, therapists, and educators. Glasser was asked to consult in schools to help students take more responsibility for their behaviors and to blame others less, and out of this work came his book *Schools Without Failure* (1968). In this work, he discussed how reality therapy can be used in large groups—what he called "class meetings." Although not the same as group counseling or psychotherapy, the meetings have some of the same goals, such as increased self-esteem, feelings of success, and group members' involvement with and respect for each other.

At that time, many professionals saw reality therapy as a method rather than a theory. Then Glasser (1972), in *The Identity Society,* formulated what might be called the theory's sociological underpinnings. He explained that three forces had contributed to the radical changes in Western civilization in the 1950s and 1960s: the passage of laws that guaranteed human rights, increased affluence that satisfied the basic need of survival for most people, and the advent of instant communication via electronic media. These three gradual but important changes facilitated the arrival of the "identity society"—a world in which persons are more focused on their **identity needs** than on their survival needs. Most people want an opportunity to move beyond economic and political serfdom. Therefore, reality therapy found acceptance because it is a theory that facilitates personal empowerment by means of **self-evaluation** and positive planning for the future.

Still, this pragmatic and culturally based method needed solid theoretical grounding. Such a foundation was provided by a relatively unknown theory of brain functioning. Powers (1973) described the brain as an input control system similar to a thermostat that controls the temperature of a room. Glasser (1984) extended Powers' **control theory** (or control system theory) by incorporating a system of needs to explain human motivation, and then he molded the theory to the clinical setting and the practice of counseling and psychotherapy. With the addition of these and many other ideas, it was no longer appropriate to call Glasser's theory "control theory"; consequently, the recognized name is now choice theory. The delivery system is reality therapy.

Another major development in reality therapy is the extended application described by **Wubbolding** (2000). The **WDEP** formulation (explained in following section) provides a pedagogical tool for learning and practicing the process of reality therapy. Wubbolding has also extended the theory to multicultural counseling based on his experience working in Asia, Europe, and the Middle East. Additionally, he has provided credibility for the system by emphasizing research data and scientific validation. The system now is elevated beyond the work of one man and has reached the level of universal applicability.

Most recently Glasser (2003) has challenged the psychiatric profession's overuse of medication. He has suggested the use of choice theory study groups as a prevention for mental disorders (Glasser, 2005).

HUMAN NATURE: A DEVELOPMENTAL PERSPECTIVE

Reality therapy provides a comprehensive explanation of human behavior as well as a methodology for addressing the vicissitudes of the human condition. Choice theory explains why and how human beings function; and the WDEP system (Wubbolding, 1989, 1991, 2000), which is explained briefly in the following paragraph and in greater depth later in the chapter, provides a delivery system for helping oneself and others remediate deficiencies, make better choices, and become more fully self-actualized.

The W in WDEP implies that the counselor or therapist helps clients explore their *wants*. D means that clients describe the *direction* of their lives as well as what they are currently *doing* or how they spend their time. E indicates that the counselor or therapist helps in the client's self-*evaluation* by asking questions such as, "Are your current actions effective?" Clients are then helped to make simple and attainable action *plans*, as implied by P. Thus, reality therapy is not a theory of developmental psychology per se. Still, as discussed in detail later, it contains ideas that harmonize with various stages of development.

Fundamental to reality therapy is the principle that human needs are the sources of all human behavior. An infant as well as a senior adult seeks to control or mold the world around himself or herself in order to fulfill his or her inner drives. But here the commonality among persons at various stages ends. For as persons grow, they develop specific wants unique to themselves. An infant, child, adolescent, young adult, middle-aged person, or senior adult has formulated a wide range of wants that are unique to that person, yet similar to needs experienced by others of the same age and culture.

Similarly, although the behavior of all human beings is designed to fulfill inner needs, behavior differs according to age and culture. Human behavior has an impact on the external world and, in a sense, shapes it as a sculptor molds clay. As a result, the input or **perception** that a person gets from the world—a person's worldview—is dynamic, always changing, and unique to each person depending on age and culture. A developmental implication of the principles of choice theory is that the perceptual system, or worldview, is a storehouse of memories. Because human problems at many levels of development are rooted in relationships, Ford (1979) and Wubbolding (1988) emphasized the necessity of interpersonal **quality time** as a facilitative component of healthy development. When parent and child, friend and friend, spouse and spouse, or colleague and colleague spend quality time together, they build a storehouse of pleasant and healthy perceptions of each other. For quality time to serve as a solid support for effective growth and development, it must be characterized by the following traits:

- *Effort.* The activity requires effort. Watching television and eating together can help, but they are less effective than other activities because they require little or no energy.
- *Awareness.* The persons are aware of each other. Playing a game or engaging in a hobby is useful in facilitating the relationship and individual development. Watching television without talking to each other qualifies only minimally.
- *Repetition.* The activity is not an isolated event but is performed on a regular basis. Consistent walking with a friend deepens the relationship and enhances the growth of both persons.
- *Free of criticism and complaint.* While the activity is being carried out, there should be no criticism of the other person. For instance, child development is enhanced if a parent creates an accepting atmosphere and encourages positive conversation.
- *Need fulfilling for all persons.* The activity is geared to the interest and ability of all concerned. Attending a rock concert with an adolescent might be so painful for the parent that the relationship—and, therefore, the development of both persons—fails to improve.

- *Performed for a limited time.* Persons of various age levels require various amounts of time to ensure appropriate development. A child obviously requires more quality time than an adult.

Quality time is a crucial component of human growth and development. Moreover, the application to various individuals of activities labeled "quality time" is determined by the persons' interests and levels of intellectual functioning as well as their ages and degree of mental health.

MAJOR CONSTRUCTS

The underlying theory that justifies the methodology of reality therapy is called **choice theory**. Although choice theory is separate and existed before reality therapy was developed, the terms *choice theory* and *reality therapy* are now sometimes used interchangeably. Norbert Wiener, a Harvard University mathematician, formulated many of the principles that have been subsumed under the name **control theory** (Wubbolding, 1994; Bevcar & Bevcar, 2006). Wiener described the importance of feedback to both engineering and biological systems (1948), as well as the sociological implications for human beings (1950). However, Wubbolding (1993) emphasized that the more proximate basis for the clinical applications was formulated by Powers (1973). Powers rejected the mechanism of behaviorism by emphasizing the internal origins of the human control system.

Most significant in the development of choice theory, however, is the work of Glasser (1980b, 1984, 1986, 1996, 1998, 1999, 2001, 2003, 2005), who expanded Powers' work and adapted it to the clinical setting. Human beings, Glasser stated, act on the world around them for a purpose: to satisfy their needs and wants. Glasser referred to **total behavior**, which is comprised of action, thinking, feelings, and physiology. All behaviors contain these four elements, although one element or another is more obvious at a given moment. Such behaviors, negative or positive, are the output generated from within a person to gain a sense of control or to satisfy needs.

Wubbolding (2000) summarized Glasser's choice theory as it applies to counseling and psychotherapy:

1. Human beings are born with five needs: belonging, power (competence, achievement, recognition, self-esteem, and so on), fun or enjoyment, freedom or independence (autonomy), and survival. These needs are general and universal. Preeminent among the human needs is that of belonging. Wubbolding (2005) stated, "No matter how dire one's circumstances, the human will and creativity are relentless in their pursuit of human closeness" (p. 43). Along with wants, which are specific and unique for each person, needs serve as the motivators or sources of all behavior.
2. The difference between what a person wants and what one perceives one is getting (input) is the immediate source of specific behaviors at any given moment. Thus, reality therapy rests on the principle that human behavior springs from internal motivation, which drives the behavior from moment to moment (Glasser, 1998; Wubbolding, 1985a, 2001; Wubbolding & **Brickell**, 1999).
3. All human behaviors are composed of doing (acting), thinking, feeling, and physiology. Behaviors are identified by the most obvious aspect of this total behavior. Thus,

someone counseled for poor grades in school is seen as presenting an action problem. People are labeled "psychotic" because the primary and most obvious aspect of their total behavior is dysfunctional thinking. Depression, anger, resentment, and fear are most obvious in other persons, so their behavior is called a feeling behavior. For others, the most obvious component of behavior is the physiological element, such as heart disease or high blood pressure.

Human choices are not aimless or random. They are all teleological; in other words, they serve a purpose: to close the gap between the perception of what a person is getting and what he or she wants at a given moment.

4. Because behavior originates from within, human beings are responsible for their behavior. In other words, people are capable of change. This change is brought about by choosing more effective behaviors. The aspect of human behavior over which we have the most direct control is that of acting, and secondarily, that of thinking. Therefore, in counseling and psychotherapy, the focus is on changing total behavior (1) by discussing current actions along with the evaluation of their effectiveness in fulfilling needs, (2) by discussing current wants and the evaluation of their realistic attainability, and (3) by discussing current perceptions or viewpoints along with their helpfulness to the individual.

5. Human beings see the world through a perceptual system that functions as a set of lenses. At a low level of perception, the person simply recognizes the world; the person gives names to objects and events but does not make judgments about them. At a high level of perception, the person puts a positive or negative value on the perception. Exploring the various levels of perception and their helpfulness is part of the counseling or psychotherapy process.

In summary, choice theory is a psychology built on principles that emphasize current motivation for human choices. It stands in opposition to both psychological determinism and what Glasser (1998, 2003) calls external control psychology. Human beings are free to make choices. Thus, although the past has propelled us to the present, it need not determine our future. Similarly, our external world limits our choices but does not remove them.

APPLICATIONS

Overview

Reality therapy is a practical method based on theory and research. It aims at helping people take better charge of their lives. To help clients make such changes, the counselor or therapist focuses on realistic choices, especially those touching on human relationships. It is first necessary to establish a safe therapeutic **environment** similar to that espoused in most theories, although choice theory offers some unique ways to accomplish this. The WDEP system details the specific reality therapy **procedures** used to help accomplish these goals.

Goals of Counseling and Psychotherapy

The goal of reality therapy is to help clients fulfill their needs. Consequently, the counselor or therapist helps clients explore current behaviors and choices related to belonging, power, fun, and freedom. More specifically, the precise wants related to each need are examined so as to help clients fulfill their specific objectives, or their **quality world** wants. Therefore, assisting clients to make more effective and responsible choices related to their wants and needs is the aim of the counselor or therapist. These choices are seen as motivated by current needs and wants, not by past traumas, unresolved conflicts, peer pressure, or previous training.

Process of Change

To understand how change can occur in the life of a client, it is necessary to understand the following principles in the theory and practice of reality therapy.

1. *Present orientation.* Choice theory, the theoretical basis for reality therapy, rests on the principle that the human brain functions like a control system—for example, like a thermostat—seeking to regulate its own behavior in order to shape its environment so that the environment matches what it wants. Therefore, human behavior springs from current inner motivation and is neither an attempt to resolve past conflicts nor a mere response to an external stimulus.

2. *Emphasis on choice.* One of the goals of counseling and psychotherapy for the practitioner of reality therapy is to help clients make positive choices. Therefore, it is useful to see behavior as a result of one's choices, to treat it as such, and to talk to clients as if they have choices. Even though no human being has total freedom to make better choices easily, it can still be helpful to view even severe emotional disturbance as a person's best choice for a given period of time. The work of the counselor or therapist is to reveal more choices to clients and to help clients see that better choices are possible.

3. *Control of action.* In bringing about change, it is useful to recognize that the action element is the component of a person's total behavior over which the person has the most control and, therefore, choice. Although some persons have an amazing amount of direct control over their physiology (some can choose to stop bleeding when they are cut), people seen in counseling and psychotherapy can rarely change their blood pressure, their ulcer condition, or their headaches by an act of will. People can rarely change their feelings of depression, guilt, anxiety, or worry merely by choosing to do so. And though people have some control over their thoughts, it is not easy to begin thinking differently from the way they have in the past. Because people have the most control over the action element, helping them change their actions is more efficacious than helping them think differently or helping them feel better. It is more productive to help spouses choose to talk politely to each other than to help them feel better about each other. Increasing self-esteem is possible if a client chooses to act in ways that are different from ways in which he or she has acted previously.

4. *Importance of relationship.* The specific procedures of the WDEP system are based on the establishment of an empathic relationship. As is abundantly clear from research, the relationship between the client and the counselor or therapist is critical in effecting change. Reality therapy offers specific interventions aimed at helping clients make more effective choices, and these are most effective when there is a genuine relationship established. Counselors and therapists who use reality therapy effectively use many of the same skills and possess the same qualities as other counselors and therapists: empathy, congruence, and positive regard. Reality therapy offers specific ways, some unique to

reality therapy and some incorporated from general practice, for establishing and maintaining a therapeutic relationship (Richardson & Wubbolding, 2001).

Reality therapy developed from a desire to see change happen in clients rather than to have clients merely gain insight and awareness. Contributing to the efficacy of reality therapy are its principles of present orientation, choice, action, and the relationship.

Traditional Intervention Strategies

Conventional counseling and therapy in the past often meant a long-term commitment for clients and counselor or therapist. Building rapport, obtaining and documenting a case history, and allowing appropriate catharsis and insight constituted the focus of traditional counseling and therapy. Out of these dynamics, client change would gradually develop. Reality therapy is based on different premises. Clients are encouraged to take action in an effort to satisfy their five needs regardless of their history, insight, or even whether they feel good about taking action. In fact, reality therapy had been criticized as *merely* a short-term problem-solving method. Although reality therapy can be used as a long-term method, the goal is to help clients improve rapidly.

Brief Intervention Strategies

The methodology used in reality therapy consists of establishing an appropriate environment or psychological atmosphere and then applying the procedures that lead to change: the WDEP system. Together these constitute the **cycle of counseling** (see Figure 12.1). This cycle illustrates that the specific interventions summarized as WDEP are built on a trustful relationship. Trust-destroying and trust-building ideas (**toxins** and **tonics**) are listed in Figure 12.1. The process is described as a cycle because there is no single place to start when it is applied to clients. Counselors and therapists need to use their creativity to match the system to each client.

Creating a Positive Environment. An atmosphere that provides for the possibility of change is characterized by specific guidelines and suggestions about what to do and what to avoid. These are designed for use by counselors, therapists, and case managers as well as supervisors and managers in the workplace. They can also be taught to clients, parents, teachers, and others for use in improving their interactions with clients, students, employees, and children. The specific applications vary slightly, but the principles are consistent.

Among the toxic behaviors to be avoided is arguing. The counselor or therapist is quite active when applying the procedures; thus, there is danger that in helping clients evaluate their behavior, the practitioner will overstep the proper use of reality therapy by arguing about the best choice for the clients. This mistake results in resistance. Also, bossing, criticizing, demeaning, or finding fault with clients only creates resistance and poisons the atmosphere. In fact, even constructive criticism is best avoided in relationships with most clients.

One of the most important toxic behaviors is that of accepting excuses. Too much empathy or sympathy reinforces the perceived helplessness and powerlessness of clients. Clients often describe how they did something harmful to themselves or someone else not because they made a choice, but because of an outside force. For example, the teacher gave an unfair test. Someone rejected me. Another person got me into trouble. Clients are depressed because

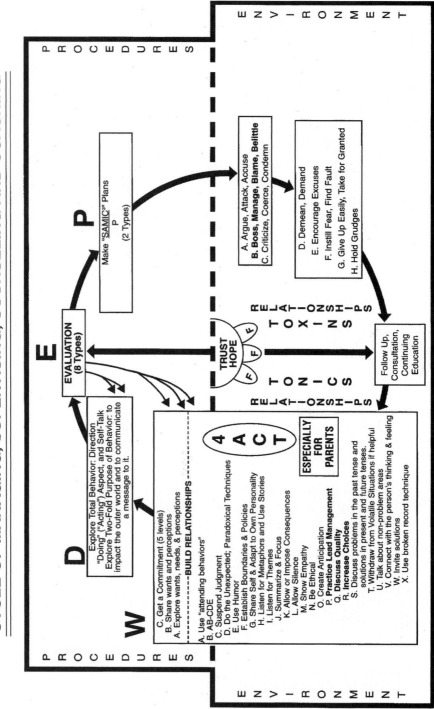

Figure 12.1 Cycle of Counseling

Adapted by Robert E. Wubbolding, EdD, from the works of William Glasser, MD. Copyright 1986 Robert E. Wubbolding, EdD. 15th Revision 2006.

SUMMARY DESCRIPTION OF THE
"CYCLE OF MANAGING, SUPERVISING, COUNSELING AND COACHING"

The Cycle is explained in detail in books by Robert E. Wubbolding:
Employee Motivation, 1996: Reality Therapy for the 21st Century, 2000
A Set of Directions for Putting and Keeping Yourself Together, 2001

Introduction:

The Cycle consists of two general concepts: Environment conducive to change and Procedures more explicitly designed to facilitate change. This chart is intended to be a **brief** summary. The ideas are designed to be used with employees, students, clients as well as in other human relationships.

Relationship between Environment & Procedures:

1. As indicated in the chart, the Environment is the foundation upon which the effective use of Procedures is based.

2. Though it is **usually** necessary to establish a safe, friendly Environment before change can occur, the "Cycle" can be entered at any point. Thus, the use of the cycle does **not** occur in lock step fashion.

3. Building a relationship implies establishing and maintaining a professional relationship. Methods for accomplishing this comprise some efforts on the part of the helper that are Environmental and others that are Procedural.

ENVIRONMENT:

Relationship Tonics: a close relationship is built on TRUST and HOPE through friendliness, firmness and fairness.

A. Using Attending Behaviors: Eye contact, posture, effective listening skills.

B. AB = "Always **Be** . . ." **C**onsistent, **C**ourteous & **C**alm, **D**etermined that there is hope for improvement, **E**nthusiastic (Think Positively).

C. Suspend Judgment: View behaviors from a low level of perception, i.e., acceptance is crucial.

D. Do the Unexpected: Use paradoxical techniques as appropriate; Reframing and Prescribing.

E. Use Humor: Help them fulfill need for fun within reasonable boundaries.

F. Establish boundaries: the relationship is professional.

4 A C T

- Affirm feelings
- Accept
- Show affection
- Action consequences
- Conversation (WDEP)
- Time together

G. Share Self: Self-disclosure within limits is helpful; adapt to own personal style.

H. Listen for Metaphors: Use their figures of speech and provide other ones. Use stories.

I. Listen to Themes: Listen for behaviors that have helped, value judgements, etc.

J. Summarize & Focus: Tie together what they say and focus on them rather than on "Real World."

K. Allow or Impose Consequences: Within reason, they should be responsible for their own behavior.

L. Allow Silence: This allows them to think, as well as to take responsibility.

M. Show Empathy: Perceive as does the person being helped.

N. Be Ethical: Study Codes of Ethics and their applications, e.g., how to handle suicide threats or violent tendencies.

O. Create anticipation and communication hope. People should be taught that something good will happen if they are willing to work.

P. **Practice lead management, e.g., democracy in determining rules**.

Q. **Discuss quality.**

R. **Increases choices.**

S. Discuss problems in the past tense, solutions in present and future tenses.

T. Withdraw from volatile situations if helpful.

U. Talk about non-problem areas.

V. Connect with the person's thinking and feeling.

W. Invite solutions.

X. Use broken record technique.

Relationship Toxins:

Argue, **Boss Manage,** or Blame, Criticize or Coerce, Demean, Encourage Excuses, Instill Fear, or Give up easily, Hold Grudges.

Rather, stress what they **can** control, accept them as they are, and keep the confidence that they can develop more effective behaviors. Also, continue to use "WDEP" system without giving up.

Follow Up, Consult, and Continue Education:

Determine a way for them to report back, talk to another professional person when necessary, and maintain ongoing program of professional growth.

PROCEDURES:

Build Relationships:

A. Explore **W**ants, Needs & Perceptions: Discuss picture album or quality world, i.e., set goals, fulfilled & unfulfilled pictures, needs, viewpoints and "locus of control."

B. Share Wants & Perceptions: Tell what you want from them and how you view their situations, behaviors, wants, etc. This procedure is secondary to A above.

C. Get a Commitment: Help them solidify their desire to find more effective behaviors.

Explore Total Behavior:

Help them examine the **D**irection of their lives, as well as specifics of how they spend their time. Discuss ineffective & effective self talk. Explore two-fold purpose of behavior: to impact the outer world and to communicate a message to it.

Evaluation – The Cornerstone of Procedures:

Help them evaluate their behavioral direction, specific behaviors as well as wants, perceptions and commitments. Evaluate own behavior through follow-up, consultation and continued education.

Make **P**lans: Help them change direction of their lives.

Effective plans are **S**imple, **A**ttainable, **M**easurable, **I**mmediate, **C**onsistent, **C**ontrolled by the planner, and **C**ommitted to. The helper is **P**ersistent. Plans can be linear or paradoxical.

Note: The "Cycle" describes specific guidelines & skills. Effective implementation requires the artful integration of the guidelines & skills contained under Environment & Procedures in a spontaneous & natural manner geared to the personality of the helper. This requires training, practice & supervision. Also, the word "client" is used for anyone receiving help: student, employee, family member, etc.

For more information contact:

Robert E. Wubbolding, EdD, Director

Center for Reality Therapy
7672 Montgomery Road, #383
Cincinnati, Ohio 45236

(513) 561-1911 • FAX (513) 561-3568
E-mail: wubsrt@fuse.net • www.realitytherapy.com

The Center for Reality Therapy provides counseling, consultation, training and supervision including applications to schools, agencies, hospitals, companies and other institutions. The Center is a provider for many organizations which award continuing education units.

of some unfavorable outside event. The alternative to the quicksand of excuses is the effective use of the WDEP system. Asking about wants or goals gets quickly beyond the discussion of a perceived external locus of control.

In the early stages of the development of the reality therapy delivery system, the advice was to never give up. A more realistic formulation is to stay with the person as a helper past the time he or she expects to be abandoned. In other words, do not give up easily. Similarly, the counselor or therapist might be tempted to give up on the WDEP system if it fails to render the desired results immediately. Wubbolding (1996) emphasized that the WDEP principles appear to be easy to practice because the vocabulary is uncomplicated. Yet to be proficient in the practice of the skills, repeated practice and supervision are required.

A positive environment that serves as the basis for the WDEP system is built not only on avoiding the uncongenial behaviors of arguing, criticizing, or giving up on the tonic behaviors. In addition, efforts to establish an agreeable and harmonious atmosphere are sustained and nourished by use of the following intervention strategies, also called tonic behaviors.

Use Attending Behaviors. **Attending behaviors** described by Ivey, D'Andrea, Bradford Ivey & Simek-Morgan (2002) are especially useful in the practice of reality therapy: eye contact, facial expression, physical posture, verbal following, and paraphrasing. These skills serve as an effective foundation for an enhanced relationship between the client and the counselor or therapist. The acronym **AB-CDEFG** stand for additional interventions:

- *Always be* **courteous.** Being courteous is a behavior that counseling theory rarely mentions, perhaps because it is assumed to exist in the helping relationship.
- *Always be* **determined.** The determination of the counselor or therapist is perceived as an explicit and implicit belief or attitude. The message, relayed to the client by the verbal and nonverbal behavior of the practitioner, is simply that no matter what the circumstances of the client's life, no matter how dreadful the past history, a better life is possible.
- *Always be* **enthusiastic.** In this context, enthusiasm is not cheerleading. Nor is it a naive belief about long-standing disturbances and the difficulty in dealing with them. Rather, it is the continuous effort to look at the bright side; to emphasize what the client can do; to discuss possibilities, not merely problems; and to take a problem-solving approach.
- *Always be* **firm.** In establishing an empathic environment, the counselor or therapist remains firm. There is no contradiction between seeing the client's point of view and taking a stand for honesty and sobriety while disclosing opposition to dishonesty, drunkenness, or abusive behaviors. Moreover, disclosure that the counselor or therapist supports the policies of the practitioner's employer and applies them unapologetically does not damage the relationship. Rather, it facilitates the establishment of boundaries. However, firmness is not intended to serve as an excuse for the authoritarian personality to impose his or her whims on clients.
- *Always be* **genuine.** Personal authenticity and congruence are seen as necessary prerequisites in reality therapy as well as in other helping methods.

Suspend Judgment. As stated earlier, all behavior is a person's best effort at a given time to fulfill his or her needs. Consequently, a counselor or therapist who keeps this principle in mind can more easily see quite harmful choices from a low level of perception, without approval or disapproval. Balancing such suspension of judgment with "always be firm" is a tightrope on which every counselor or therapist walks daily.

Do the Unexpected. Unpredictability is a quality that facilitates a helpful counseling or psychotherapy environment. Focusing on a strength, a success, or a time when the client felt good often generates the type of discussion that clients do not expect. Nevertheless, clients who are characterized by **negative symptoms** also choose **positive symptoms** (Wubbolding, 1981, 2001). Therefore, it is good to discuss in detail the circumstances when clients chose effectively, felt good, and remained in effective control of their lives. Wubbolding described other ways for doing the unexpected and incorporated **paradoxical techniques** such as reframing, redefining, and relabeling into reality therapy (1984, 1988, 2000). To be effective using these and other paradoxical techniques, it is necessary to invert one's thinking. Causes are seen as effects; the objectionable is now a strength (Dowd & Milne, 1986; Fay, 1978; Seltzer, 1986; Weeks & L'Abate, 1982). Wubbolding (1993) stated:

> A depressed child is seen as pensive, gentle, and thoughtful. An angry child is outgoing and has deep conviction. The bully is a leader and has ambition, while a submissive child is kind and cooperative. This paradoxical technique is, therefore, a technique that is useful to establish a relationship and can even serve as a procedure leading to change. However, it is not to be used indiscriminately and manipulatively. Rather, it is a psychological condiment, to be used sparingly. And like the other "guidelines" it is primarily a way to establish a safe counseling environment. Its misuse is a toxin. Its approriate use is a tonic. (p. 293)

Use Humor. A healthy and democratic sense of humor is a curative factor for the mental health specialist. The entertainer Victor Borge once remarked that laughter is the shortest distance between two people. Peter (1982) stated that laughter is helpful in dealing with anxiety, depression, and loss.

Be Yourself. Often students learning counseling and psychotherapy skills adopt the style of their teachers or of the leaders in each theory. Although this is expected, students also need to adapt the skills to fit their own personality and core beliefs.

Share Yourself. The creation and maintenance of a trusting relationship is facilitated by appropriate self-disclosure. According to a Swedish proverb, "A joy shared is twice a joy. A sorrow shared is half a sorrow." Self-disclosure by a counselor or therapist can be helpful, but caution is necessary. Cormier and Cormier (1998) warned that there can be a danger of accelerating self-disclosure to the point where the client and the counselor or therapist spend time swapping stories about themselves. As with all techniques for building a trusting relationship, self-disclosure is best used moderately.

Listen for Metaphors. Metaphors in this context are figures of speech, analogies, similes, and anecdotes that serve to quantify problems and thereby make them manageable. Barker (1985) stated that if properly constructed, stories and other metaphors offer choices to clients. He observed that they are often helpful because "psychotherapy is essentially a process of providing people with more choice in the matter of how they behave, or respond emotionally, in various situations" (p. 17). Also, stories and anecdotes can be humorous and help clients perceive their problems and decisions in a different light. Metaphors used by clients are often overlooked by counselors and therapists, or they are paraphrased. It is better, however, to use the metaphor, to extend it, and to return to it in subsequent sessions (Wubbolding & Brickell, 1998). Consider these two metaphors, which might be stated by clients or initiated by the counselor or therapist: "I feel like a floor mat." "I feel like I'm on a merry-go-round." Using these metaphors, the counselor or therapist can offer clients specific choices such as, "Would you like to get off the floor?" "Do you want to get off the merry-go-round?" "What would you be doing today if you were on solid ground, away from the merry-go-round?" As with all such techniques used to enhance the counseling and psychotherapy environment, metaphors do not constitute the essence of reality therapy. They do, however, build trust between the client and the counselor or therapist.

Listen for Themes. Tying together the ideas, feelings, and actions of clients helps them to gain a sense of direction and control. The practitioner who uses reality therapy listens carefully for themes such as previous attempts to solve problems, wants that are fulfilled, and what has helped and not helped the client. This technique is not exclusive to the practice of reality therapy, but the counselor or therapist who uses the technique listens for themes that are linked to the WDEP interventions (see Procedures: The WDEP System).

Summarize and Focus. Similar to the identification of themes, this technique helps the counselor or therapist listen carefully and communicate to clients that they are being heard. Unlike summaries in other theories, this summary concentrates on components of the WDEP system. A counselor or therapist might summarize a client's statements by responding, "You've stated that you've tried to get a promotion at work and been unsuccessful, that you've approached your boss and described what you want, that you've put in extra hours. Nothing so far has gotten you what you want." The counselor or therapist has summarized what the client has done that has not worked and has omitted many other details.

Focusing means to center the conversation on the client rather than on outside forces over which neither involved party has control. Very little can be done to cause changes in other people. Nothing can be done to change the past. Thus, it is most helpful if the counselor or therapist gently and positively assists clients to discuss their own here-and-now wants, total behaviors, plans, hopes, frustrations, and perceptions.

Allow or Impose Consequences. Professional counselors and therapists have fewer opportunities to use this element of the environment than those who wish to integrate reality therapy into their work. Probation and parole officers, halfway-house workers, and others often function in a supervisory role and are required to impose consequences. It is assumed that the consequence is reasonable and not punitive and that it is imposed to help rather than merely control the client.

Even counselors and therapists occasionally impose consequences when life-threatening or evidently dangerous situations are described by the client. The code of ethics of the American Counseling Association states:

> The general requirement that counselors keep information confidential does not apply when disclosure is required to protect clients or identified others from serious and foreseeable harm or when legal requirements demand that confidential information must be revealed. Counselors consult with other professionals when in doubt as to the validity of an exception. (Herlihy & Corey, 1996)

Allow Silence. The use of silence in reality therapy, if timed properly, allows the client to conduct inner self-evaluation, reassess wants, think about what is controllable and, therefore, uncontrollable, and in general take responsibility for the direction of the session.

Be Ethical. The ethical principle concerning clear or imminent danger is one of many that the practitioner of reality therapy practices. A trusting relationship and a professional atmosphere conducive to helping are built around solid ethical principles. Anyone using reality therapy properly knows, understands, and practices the ethical standards of various professional organizations. Professional disclosure is often required, as in Ohio (State of Ohio, 1984); thus, counselors, therapists, and social workers must provide clients with a written description of their professional qualifications. Wubbolding (1986) and Wubbolding & Brickell (2005) emphasized that counselors and therapists should provide clients with information about the nature of reality therapy. These details help clarify the boundaries of the relationship as well as indicate the advantages and limitations of the assistance that the practitioner can offer. Wubbolding (1990) also emphasized the importance of knowing how to assess suicidal threats and how this assessment is used in the practice of reality therapy. Informed consent, dual relationships, confidentiality, and proper record keeping are among the many ethical issues impinging on the relationship between counselor or therapist and client.

Be Redundant or Repetitious. Often the same questions are asked in various ways. When a client is defensive and offering excuses in the form of denial, the counselor or therapist sometimes repeats the same question in a different way. It becomes a theme aimed at helping clients evaluate their own behavior. "When you made that choice, did it help?" "Did it work for you?" "What impact did that action have on you and on others?" "Did it help you enough?" "Was the action the best you were capable of at that time?" Such questions asked at various times become a haunting theme that gradually and supportively lessens denial and facilitates the client's assumption of responsibility. Yet like the overall art of counseling or therapy, the skill of being redundant is developed through practice and self-evaluation.

Create Suspense and Anticipation. In a counselor's or therapist's effective use of reality therapy there can be an element of drama. A counseling or psychotherapy session should be a significant event in the lives of clients. An authentic buoyancy on the part of the counselor or therapist and a desire to reassure can elicit a feeling of curiosity and a sense of impending success. The ability to communicate a sense of optimism is an advanced skill and is developed with practice and training.

Establish Boundaries. There are limits within which a counselor or therapist operates, and these should be clarified. The ethical principle of dual relationships is clearly part of boundary classification. Furthermore, the client might wish to shield certain areas from discussion. A useful question for counselors or therapists to ask is, "Is there any topic you would prefer we not discuss?" Such questioning empowers clients to choose what they want to work on. If clients have many topics that are forbidden territory (which is rarely the case), the counselor or therapist can ask them if it is helpful for them to conceal or mask potential topics. In any event, the wishes of the client are paramount and are respected.

The previous strategies are designed to help the counselor or therapist using reality therapy to establish rapport, mutual trust, and a safe atmosphere in a brief and efficient manner.

The strategies involve swift and positive interventions that facilitate the client's expectation that the experience is worthwhile and significant. These environmental building blocks aimed at establishing and deepening the relationship provide a fundamental prerequisite for what is essentially the practice of reality therapy: the WDEP system.

Procedures: The WDEP System. The specific interventions that are the essence of reality therapy are based on the trusting relationship described as **environment**. The procedures or determinations (Wubbolding, 1985b) are most appropriately formulated as the WDEP system as described in Figure 12.1 (Glasser, 1990; Wubbolding, 1989, 1991, 2000, 2004; Wubbolding & Brickell, 1999, 2005). They should not be seen as steps to be used sequentially or mechanically; and although they are described in simple, jargon-free language, they can be difficult to implement. For instance, a counselor or therapist working with a student referred for a school discipline problem would probably not begin with a lengthy discussion of W (wants), but rather with an exploration of D (doing): in other words, what happened to bring about the referral? Thus, in conceptualizing the entire process, it is useful to see it as a cycle that can be entered at any point.

W: Discussing Wants, Needs, and Perceptions. Because human beings are motivated to fulfill their wants and needs, it is important for the counselor or therapist to take the time to explore the specific wants of the client. Questions might include these: "What do you want from your spouse? From your school? Your job? Your career? From your friends? Your parents? Your children? Your supervisor? From yourself? What do you want from me? From your church?" Thus, there are at least 11 generic questions that can be asked. These are multiplied threefold if the counselor or therapist asks more precisely about each category: (1) "What do you want that you are getting?" (2) "What do you want that you are not getting?" (3) "What are you getting that you don't want?" The areas for exploration and clarification become almost endless when the counselor or therapist adds, "How much do you want it?" "What would you need to give up to get what you want?" "What will you settle for?"

All wants are related to the five needs: belonging, power or achievement, fun or enjoyment, freedom or independence, and survival. Therefore, it is useful to help clients link their wants explicitly to their needs by asking, "If you had what you wanted, what would you have?" or "If your wants were met, what would that satisfy inside?" Such questioning of a parent often elicits the following: "I want my child to keep the curfew, get good grades, stay away from drugs, do the house chores, and be pleasant to the rest of the family. If I had that, I would have peace of mind. I would know that I am a good parent." The parent has specific wants and has identified the underlying need: achievement or power.

Discussing perceptions is also an important part of W. Questions about clients' perceptions are slightly different from those specifically relating to wants. A parent might be asked, "What do you see when you look at your child?" The answer might be, "I see a child who is rebellious at times and cooperative when she wants something from me." Asking about perceptions is especially useful in groups and in family counseling and psychotherapy because arguments can be prevented. A counselor or therapist can intervene by reminding all present that they are discussing their viewpoints—what they see, not what is.

Change and growth occur only if the client is committed to making changes in his or her actions. Thus, it is imperative that the counselor or therapist discuss the client's **level of commitment** to the process and its outcomes. The question "How hard do you want to work at changing your situation?" gives the client an opportunity to look inward and reflect on the degree of responsibility he or she wishes to assume. Wubbolding (1988, 2000) identified and developed five levels of commitment as described by clients:

1. *"I don't want to be here."* This statement clearly illustrates that the client is at best reluctant and resistant. He or she may have been coerced into counseling or psychotherapy.
2. *"I want the outcome, but not the effort."* This level indicates that the client does want to change and is perhaps at the first stage ("I'll do it") in gaining effective control and taking personal responsibility.
3. *"I'll try; I might."* Trying to make a change for the better constitutes the middle level of commitment to change. Still, *trying* to get out of bed early is not the same as doing it.
4. *"I will do my best."* At this level, a person goes beyond trying and commits to specific action. However, such a commitment still allows the possibility of failure.
5. *"I will do whatever it takes."* The highest level of commitment represents an outcome centered on a no-excuses level of commitment.

The levels of commitment are developmental. The higher levels are more helpful than the lower ones. Yet for some clients, "I'll try" is a major improvement. They should not be pushed too vigorously or too quickly to move to a higher level. Rather, the skillful counselor or therapist helps clients to evaluate their level of commitment and gently leads them to the next level.

D: Discussing Behavioral Direction and Doing (Total Behavior). The counselor or therapist helps the client review his or her overall direction by inquiries such as "Where do you think you're going if you continue on the same path?" A child might be asked, "If you continue to flunk in school, resist your parents' requests, and continue on the same pathway, where will you be in 2 or 3 or 12 months?"

The exploration of the overall direction is only the embarkation point for further questioning about current total behavior. More time and effort are needed to help clients examine their specific actions. The counselor or therapist helps the client verbalize exactly what he or she did for a specific amount of time.

E: Helping Clients Conduct Evaluations. In the cycle of counseling and in the WDEP system of procedures, the element of evaluation occupies the central position (Wubbolding, 1990) (see Figure 12.1). Like a keystone in an arch, its pivotal place supports the entire structure. If it is absent, the arch crumbles. The practice of reality therapy is firm and effective to the degree that the counselor or therapist assists clients in evaluating their own behavior, wants, perceptions, level of commitment, and plans. Wubbolding et al. (2004) stated, "through skillful questioning clients ask themselves whether they are living as they want to live (p. 225).

Because of the prominent place of self-evaluation in the cycle of counseling, reality therapy is properly placed among the cognitive counseling theories. It is here, especially, at the cardinal point of self-evaluation, that cognitive restructuring takes place. Clients look inward and examine the effectiveness of their lifestyle and its specific aspects. Only now, when they have concluded that some part of their control system (wants, behaviors, perceptions) is not helping them or is not as beneficial as it could be, do clients see that a change is necessary and that alternative and more effective choices are available. Because of the curative role of human relationships in reality therapy, many self-evaluation questions focus on the client in relation to others. The central questions focus on whose behavior can clients control and whether their lifestyle is taking them closer or farther away from the people around them (Glasser, 2003, 2005).

More specifically, evaluation contains the following elements.

1. *Evaluation of behavioral direction.* After helping the client describe the overall direction of his or her life, the counselor or therapist assists in evaluating the significance of this direction. Is it the best direction in the mind of the client? Is it helpful or harmful? Does the direction have what for the client is high quality, especially regarding human relationships?

2. *Evaluation of specific actions.* Questions about specific actions are geared to the descriptions provided in the client's explanation of how a specific segment of his or her day was spent. Such questions as the following might be asked: "Did sleeping until 10:00 in the morning help or hurt your effort to find a job?" "What were the consequences of hitting your brother?" "When you shout at the kids, do you get what you want?" Petersen (2005) stated, "The success of reality therapy lies in the client's ability to self-evaluate that present behaviors are not getting him/her closer to what s/he wants" (p. 13).

3. *Evaluation of wants.* The client is assisted in making judgments about the appropriateness and the attainability of his or her wants: "Is what you want truly good for you?" "How realistic is it for you to get your parents totally off your back?" "How realistic is it for your adolescent child to become 100% cooperative or perfect in your eyes?"

4. *Evaluation of perceptions or viewpoints.* Perceptions are not easily changed. Rarely are they changed by a simple decision to view a person, a situation, or an event differently. Yet they can be changed by altering behavior (Glasser, 1980b, 1984; Powers, 1973). Because perceptions involve what people want, they occupy an important place in the evaluation process. So even though they are not directly changed, their desirability and appropriateness should be evaluated. Evaluative questions for perceptions might include these: "Does it help if you see your son only as rebellious and lazy?" "What is accomplished if you see only the negative aspects of your parents' behavior?" "When you nurse a negative attitude toward your boss, does it help you to improve your situation at work or your relationship to him or her?"

5. *Evaluation of new direction.* As new possibilities unfold for clients, it is useful to help them determine whether those possibilities are satisfying needs. The rebellious student is asked, "How will cooperation at home benefit you and your family?" "If you were to make an effort to learn, do your homework, ask questions in class, and, in general, do what 'successful' students do, would you feel better?" "What impact would this approach have on your friends and family?"

6. *Evaluation of plans.* After a new direction is defined, and often even before clients have committed to a change of direction, clients can be encouraged to make plans. At first glance these plans might appear to be meager and insignificant, but often they represent the first steps toward more effective and positive need-satisfaction. In working with an adolescent, Wubbolding (1980) was able to help him make a modest plan of action. This high school student had shut himself in his room on the weekends with the curtains and drapes closed. Although resistant at first, he eventually made plans to open the blinds and let the light in. He subsequently developed a healthy social life by making

rudimentary changes in his overall direction. Thus, the evaluation of plans is based not on whether they solve the basic problem but on whether they address the problem and aim toward the more effective fulfillment of belonging, power, fun, and freedom.

P: Planning. According to one saying, "To fail to plan is to plan to fail." Glasser (1980a) stated that plans vary; some are detailed and others are quite simple, yet "there must always be a plan. People who go through life without some sort of a long-term plan, usually divided into a series of small plans to reach larger goals, are like ships floundering without rudders" (p. 52).

The procedure of planning is often mistakenly viewed as the essence of the practice of reality therapy. Although planning is important, it is effective only if based on a client's inner self-evaluation. Plans that are truly efficacious, or at least more likely to be carried out by the client, have at least eight qualities, which can be summarized by the acronym SAMI^{2}C^3 (Wubbolding, 2004):

S   *Simple:* The plan is uncomplicated.

A   *Attainable:* If the plan is too difficult or too long range, the client will become discouraged and not follow through.

M   *Measurable:* The plan is precise and exact. The client is encouraged to define a clear answer to the question, "When will you do it?"

I   *Immediate:* The plan is carried out as soon as possible.

I   *Involved:* The helper is involved if such involvement is appropriate. The involvement is, of course, within the bounds of ethical standards and facilitates client independence rather than dependence.

C   *Controlled by the client:* An effective plan is not contingent on the actions of another person but is, as much as possible, within the control of the client.

C   *Committed to:* The counselor or therapist helps the client to pledge firmly to put the plan into action.

C   *Consistent:* The ideal plan is repetitious. A single plan can be a start, but the most effective plan is one that is repeated.

The common denominator to all planning is persistence on the part of the counselor or therapist. This coincides with the injunction "Don't give up."

In summary, the cycle of counseling or psychotherapy is a design for understanding reality therapy and an outline for knowing how to apply it. The environment consists of specific recommendations for building a firm but friendly atmosphere in which a client can feel safe and confident while realizing that the counselor or therapist actively seeks to be of help. The WDEP formulation is not a system that is intended to be followed in a mechanical manner; rather, it is a system from which the proper intervention is selected at a given time because of its apparent appropriateness.

Once criticized as a short-term, problem-solving, symptom-focused method, reality therapy provides an effective tool for counselors and therapists working in the world of managed care and solution-focused counseling. The goals of the WDEP system include (1) *improvement* in need satisfaction, especially human relationships; (2) positive and productive living symbolized by employment and other signs; and (3) learning the basics of reality therapy as a range of tools for further use and self-help. Users of reality therapy should aim at achieveing measurable results in 10 sessions or less.

CLIENTS WITH SERIOUS MENTAL HEALTH ISSUES

From the point of view of reality therapy, the diagnostic labels described in the American Psychiatric Association's *Diagnostic and Statistical Manual of Mental Disorders* are not static conditions. They are negative symptoms (i.e., behaviors generated for a purpose—to fulfill wants and needs). As goal-directed behaviors, they can be replaced by more effective behaviors (i.e., positive symptoms). Seligman (2004) stated that reality therapy might be applied to disorders such as conduct disorder, oppositional defiant disorder, substance abuse, impulse control, and some personality disorders. The skilled reality counselor or therapist spends little time discussing diagnostic symptoms such as hallucinations, compulsions, psychoses, or depression (Glasser, 1998, 2003, 2005). Rather, the counselor or therapist and client search for specific solutions related to effective need and want satisfaction, especially directed toward a better sense of belonging and healthier relationships.

In the application of reality therapy, medication can assist clients to make more effective choices. The theory began in a mental hospital and a correctional institution and is widely used in corrections. Although not describing diagnostic categories, Lojk (1986) demonstrated that reality therapy is used successfully with prisoners. Bratter, Bratter, Maxym, Radda, and Steiner (1993) successfully used reality therapy for delinquent youths whose diagnoses ranged from attention deficit hyperactivity disorder and conduct disorder to affective disorders, both depression and bipolar.

The reality counselor or therapist treats all behaviors as if some element of choice is present. In this way, clients feel both hope and empowerment. They realize that a better life is accessible and they are not irretrievably doomed to a life of mental illness.

CROSS-CULTURAL CONSIDERATIONS

Reality therapy is an emminently cross-cultural method. Based on universal psychological principles, the method has been applied to cultures as diverse as Asian, Middle Eastern, South American, African, European, as well as those represented in North America. Instructors indigenous to various cultures have adapted the principles to their respective clients (Wubbolding et al., 2004). Practitioners who use the principles of reality therapy are aware of their own beliefs and attitudes about their own culture and the cultures of their clients. Their application of the WDEP system is based on their knowledge of the particular group they are working with, and like any counselor or therapist, they need to be aware of their own biases as well as the strengths and cultural differences of the individual clients (Arrendondo et al., 1996).

EVALUATION

Overview

Even though more research could be conducted to validate the use of reality therapy, the widespread interest in the theory indicates that many practitioners have confidence in its efficacy. From 1975 to 2006, more than 7,500 persons worldwide completed the 18-month training program and were certified in reality therapy. Anecdotal evidence points toward the theory's usefulness with a wide variety of issues: eating disorders, child abuse, marriage, aging, elective mutism, career satisfaction, study habits, self-esteem, assertive behavior (N. Glasser, 1980, 1989).

Supporting Research

Practitioners of reality therapy represent virtually every helping profession: counselors, therapists, educators, managers, chemical dependency workers, corrections specialists, and many others. This overview of research represents a sampling of some such studies.

Glasser (1965) described the dramatic effect of a reality therapy program in a psychiatric hospital. The average stay in a ward of 210 men was 15 years. Within 2 years, 75 men had been released and only 3 of them returned.

In a study of the effects of reality therapy in a rural elementary school, Bowers (1997) found improvements in relationships and self-concept but little change in school attendance. The author noted that school attendance was not a significant problem at this school.

Studying the effects of reality therapy in a therapeutic community in Ireland, Honeyman (1990) found significant changes in the residents' self-esteem, awareness of their inability to control their drinking, and insight into living in a more inner-controlled manner. Positive effects were also found when reality therapy was used with teachers (Parish, 1988, 1991; Parish, Martin, & Khramtsova, 1992), undergraduate students (Peterson & Truscott, 1988), graduate students (Peterson, Chang, & Collins, 1997; Peterson, Woodward, & Kissko, 1991), foster parents (Corwin, 1987), negatively addicted inmates (Chance et al., 1990), and student athletes (Martin & Thompson, 1995). Y. S. Kim (2001) found a positive correlation between the use of group reality therapy with parents and self-esteem as well as parent-child relationships. Similarly, in a 1-year follow-up study of previous research, Kim and Hwang (2001) found constant, positive, long-term effects on middle-school students' sense of internal control.

K-h Kim (2002) developed a responsible behavior choice program and tested it with 13 Korean elementary school children. Using a pretest-postest design, she measured the effectiveness of eight sessions of group counseling in reality therapy. Compared with the control group, the experimental group showed a significant change in both locus of control and sense of personal responsibility. The research supported the effectiveness of short-term reality therapy. Adding further support to the use of brief reality therapy, Lawrence (2004) used reality therapy as a group counseling modality for persons with developmental disabilities. In six sessions, participants in the reality therapy experimental group showed significant changes in self-determination compared with the control group. The self-regulation, autonomy, psychological empowerment, and self-realization scores of those in the experimental group showed the impact of short-term use of reality therapy.

This brief selection of research studies illustrates the value of reality therapy as a reliable tool for counselors and therapists. However, many areas remain for study. Researchers could investigate further the effects of reality therapy on the areas mentioned as well as on other issues dealt with by counselors and therapists.

Limitations

Reality therapy should be seen as an open system that will grow and change. It is not a narrow theory that is rigidly applied. Yet as a freestanding cognitive behavioral theory and practice of counseling and therapy, it has limitations. Some of these are inherent in the theory, and some reside in the skill of the practitioner.

Many clients believe that to make changes in their lives or to feel better they need to gain insight into their past, resolve early conflicts, describe the negative aspects of their lives, and tell how they arrived at their present state. Many of these clients could be successfully encouraged to emphasize their present behavior, but some believe that no change can result without dealing specifically with past pain. For such clients, reality therapy will appear to avoid the real issues.

The concrete language of reality therapy may be another limitation. It contains little jargon or technical terminology, and the theory and practice uses words like *belonging, power, fun, freedom, wants, plans, self-evaluation,* and *effective control.* Because the language of reality therapy is easily understood, its practice can appear to be easily implemented. Nevertheless, the effective use of reality therapy requires practice, supervision, and continuous learning.

SUMMARY CHART—*Reality Therapy Theory*

Human Nature

Human beings choose behaviors that are purposeful and designed to satisfy five basic needs: survival, belonging, power, freedom, and fun. Motivation originates from a here-and-now urge to satisfy one or more of these sources of behavior. The most important motivation is to establish relationships with other human beings.

Major Constructs

Emanating from the five basic motivators are specific wants or desires. When these are not fulfilled, people choose specific actions that are accompanied by cognition, feelings, and physiology. These four elements comprise total human behavior. The behaviors are aimed at gaining input from the world and are seen as choices. The input is called perception. People behave in order to have the perception that their wants are satisfied and their needs fulfilled. Human beings have control over their own choices not the behavior of others.

Goals

The goals of reality therapy are twofold: process goals and outcome goals. The reality counselor or therapist helps clients examine their own behavior, evaluate it, and make plans for change. The outcome is more satisfying relationships, increased happiness, and a sense of inner control of their lives. The plans are thus aimed at satisfying specific wants as well as the five motivators connected to their wants.

Change Process

Effective change occurs when clients feel connected to the counselor or therapist, that is, when there is a genuine therapeutic alliance. Experiencing an effective relationship leads to change if the counselor or therapist is skilled in helping clients clarify their wants, evaluate their behavior, and make effective plans. Clients learn that no matter what difficulties they encounter, they always have choices.

Interventions

The WDEP formula summarizes the various interventions made by counselors or therapists. They help clients identify and clarify their specific wants, including what they want from the counseling process. Counselors or therapists assist clients to describe each aspect of their total behavior and to evaluate the attainability of their wants and the effectiveness of their actions. They then help clients formulate realistically doable plans for fulfilling wants and satisfying needs.

Limitations

Reality therapy has been used with clients seeking help with decision making, facing developmental issues, dealing with crises, coerced into counseling, and with severe psychiatric diagnoses. The system is described in simple language that can lead to the misconception that the process is easy to implement. Another limitation is that reality therapy does not emphasize insight into problems. Consequently, clients who seek insight rather than change are less inclined to benefit from reality therapy.

THE CASE OF JONATHAN: *A Reality Therapy Approach*

It is evident that Jonathan feels rejected by coworkers, family, and society in general. This alienation manifests itself in his total behavior: actions, thinking, feelings, and physiology. His excessive drinking, self-talk ("They're all against me"), anger, and insomnia are symptoms of unmet wants and needs. Because he is unable to connect with other people, achieve success at work, enjoy life, and make desirable or satisfying choices, he has extracted from his internal behavioral suitcase choices that have proven to be highly ineffective and destructive.

In categorizing Jonathan's behavior as benignly as possible and yet accurately, I would give him a diagnosis of adjustment disorder with mixed anxiety and depressed mood. He would be informed of this diagnosis and its meaning. He would understand that improvement is possible if he is willing to evaluate his own behavior and alter his choices.

A skilled reality therapist would establish an empathic, ongoing but time-limited relationship with Jonathan to help him to especially satisfy his need for belonging at work and with his family, thereby resulting in an internal sense of control. A primary goal of such counseling or therapy would be to help him abandon his negative symptoms and choose positive ones. Accomplishing this might involve systemic interventions such as conferences with his employer as well as couple counseling or therapy with his estranged wife.

Establishing the Environment

As in any counseling or therapy, a warm, caring relationship is the foundation for change. It is important to listen carefully to Jonathan, allowing him to tell his story in his own words. Reflective listening and empathy are crucial at this stage. However, the user of reality therapy does not listen passively but instead attempts to identify themes related to the procedures. For example, Jonathan's frustrations can be translated into wants. Because he is a verbal client, he will probably use metaphors to describe how he feels as well as other aspects of his current plight. Such metaphors might include "I feel like I'm in prison," "I'm really down," "I'm at the end of my rope," and "I feel like a floor mat." These can be used later in the counseling or therapy to help him gain a sense of inner control.

In establishing the environment, the reality counselor or therapist intervenes directively and emphatically but does not encourage venting of feelings in such a way as to indirectly communicate that merely talking will solve a problem. Feelings are always connected to actions. Questions such as "What did you do yesterday when you felt so depressed?" are useful. The counselor or therapist also helps the client to speak of problems in the past tense and solutions in the present or future tense. This results in addressing an immediate goal—communicating hope (i.e., Jonathan can improve his life and achieve some degree of happiness).

After a friendly atmosphere has been established, the counselor or therapist uses the WDEP system more explicitly.

Using the Procedures

The use of the WDEP system is not a step-by-step process. In fact, there is no absolute delineation between environment and procedures (see Figure 12.1). At the beginning of the session, Jonathan was encouraged to talk about actions (D) when he described his anger, alienation, pain, guilt, loneliness, and depression. There are many more explicit interventions that are built on the friendly, warm, helping relationship and these interventions should not be used precipitously in the session.

Exploration of Wants and Locus of Control.   Jonathan would be asked to describe what he wants (W) from the counseling or psychotherapy process. He would discuss how he thinks the counselor or therapist could help him. The counselor or therapist would disclose how he or she can be of assistance, what is realistic, and so forth. The counselor or therapist would explain that his many problems can be less painful if his interpersonal relationships improve. Even his nightmares are normal expressions of frustrations resulting from unmet needs, especially belonging.

The counselor or therapist would help Jonathan describe what he wants from his employer, coworkers, wife, and so on, and help him describe exactly what a pleasant and satisfying day would look like. More than likely he would have difficulty describing such a day, but the counselor or therapist would patiently help him to be specific.

The exploration of his perceived locus of control is especially relevant for Jonathan. The counselor or therapist would lead him to the conclusion that his own behavior is all that he can control and that effective counseling or psychotherapy will empower him to make more need-satisfying choices. This emphasis does not minimize the impact of the external world on Jonathan or the systemic issues that limit his options.

The counselor or therapist would further elicit a high level of commitment, a willingness to try new behaviors such as communicating with his wife in new ways (e.g., using the traits of quality time with his wife and his children). Interspersing statements about the hopefulness of his future, the counselor or therapist would assure Jonathan that his reactions to his circumstances are normal and not unusual.

Exploration of Specific Actions and Self-Evaluation.   After this exploration of the overall direction of his life with emphasis on belonging, Jonathan would describe how he spends his time regarding the other psychological needs: power or achievement, fun or enjoyment, and freedom or independence.

He would go into detail about the last time he chose to do something that provided a sense of accomplishment, even if it was for a brief time. Although discussion of fun might seem superficial, there is almost always a "fun deficit" in clients who are absorbed in anger, resentment, guilt, alienation, self-pity, loneliness, shame, depression, or any other negative symptom. The counselor or therapist would ask Jonathan to evaluate his own behaviors; that is, did they work for him and were they helpful and satisfying. Self-evaluation (E) is a major part of this dialogue. If Jonathan does not allow time for fun, is he helping or hurting himself? The counselor or therapist would interject humor into the session to help Jonathan laugh. When he reflects on his laughter and says he felt better for a few seconds, he will come to realize that he can feel better for longer periods of time if he chooses to insert some fun into his schedule.

Jonathan would explore the feeling of being trapped and discouraged about his choices or options. His current actions would be the focus of the discussion. When was the last time he felt freedom or independence? What was he doing at that time? If he does not do the same things that helped him feel some degree of freedom earlier, how will anything change for him?

Planning.   The planning phase (P) always depends on the clients' judgments. Thus, it is assumed that the plans described next fit with Jonathan's wants. It is also assumed that he is committed to them and that he has made firm evaluations that his current direction and specific activities are not helping. He is, therefore, ready for a new series of choices. The planning is connected with the four psychological needs: belonging, power, freedom, and fun.

Belonging

1. He will contact his wife to see if he can spend a brief time with her and the child. He would ask her to agree that the time be free of arguing, blaming, criticism, and all discussion of divisive topics.
2. He will look for opportunities to establish friendly, casual, and temporary relationships. He will look for opportunities to go out of his way to engage as many people in conversation in church groups, stores, neighborhood, and so on.
3. Upon return to work, he will do the same: engage in agreeable conversations. The counselor or therapist explains that this is not an avoidance of unpleasantness. This plan is a temporary attempt to build relationships with coworkers.

Power

1. He will agree to an alcoholism assessment.
2. If necessary, he will join a 12-step program.
3. He will investigate opportunities for furthering his education: courses, financial aid, and so on.
4. He will begin to read for discussion during counseling books such as *A Set of Directions for Putting and Keeping Yourself Together* (Wubbolding, 2001).

5. The counselor or therapist will arrange for a conference with his work supervisor and coworkers to address cultural issues for the purpose of resolving disagreements.

Freedom

1. He will think about the counselor's or therapist's comments that nightmares are normal for him and that each nightmare experience means he will need to have one less after that. Nightmares are not a sign of sickness but are the way he releases tension.
2. He might be encouraged to try to have a nightmare when he goes to bed.

Fun

1. He will schedule brief periods of enjoyable activities. At first these might not seem like fun, but eventually he will find them need satisfying.
2. When he returns to counseling or psychotherapy, he must tell the counselor two jokes found in books, magazines, or on the Internet.

The goal of this process is to help Jonathan fulfill his needs more effectively not merely to remediate problems. The plans must be his, not those of the counselor or therapist who suggests them. The plans are also developmental. Not all of them are formulated at the same time. Perhaps in the first session only one plan is selected.

Through use of the WDEP system built on the proper atmosphere or relationship, Jonathan can make significant changes in his life in 8 to 10 sessions.

CHAPTER 13

Family Theory

Valerie E. Appleton[†]
Eastern Washington University

Cass Dykeman
Oregon State University

U p to this point, the chapters in this textbook have focused on counseling and psychotherapy with individuals. Why care about the application of counseling to families? After all, the fathers and mothers of counseling and psychotherapy did not seem to care about applying their ideas to whole families. In this chapter, we will present reasons why you should care about the familial applications of counseling and psychotherapy. In addition, we will define key terms, detail prominent theories, and discuss practical applications of these theories.

So why should you care about family counseling or therapy? The following questions suggest possible reasons: What would family therapy theories add to your clinical reasoning? What would family therapy techniques add to your clinical tool bag? At the end of this chapter, we hope you can list many answers for both questions. Let us start with the assertion that family therapy can enlarge the scope of your clinical reasoning and practice. Specifically, it can enlarge your scope from individuals to families and the larger sociocultural contexts that make up an individual's environment. Family therapy can help you look at the patterns of communication and relationship that connect people to each other and to their social and physical environments.

[†]In December of 2005, Dr. Val Appleton, Dean of the College of Education at Eastern Washington University, passed away. Dr. Appleton was a gifted scholar, teacher, and leader. She is deeply missed by all who knew her.

BACKGROUND

In elementary school education, there is a principle that in grades 1 through 3 a child learns to read, and in grades 4 through 6 a child reads to learn. In other words, literacy must precede the acquisition of ideas and their applications. This principle is especially true when it comes to learning about family therapy. Family therapists have a maddening habit of coining new terms and using common terms in unique ways. This habit can sometimes leave neophytes to family therapy in a daze. To enhance your understanding of the theoretical and applied discussions in this chapter, consider the following family therapy terms.

- **Centripetal** and **Centrifugal**. These terms were borrowed from physics to describe different relational styles in families. Centripetal families look inward to the family as the source of pleasure, joy, and satisfaction. As such, these families seek to maintain rigid boundaries and harmonious familial interaction. Centrifugal families look outside the family for pleasure, joy, and satisfaction. As such, familial boundaries and interactions are minimized (Beavers & Hampson, 1990).
- **Cybernetics.** This term refers to the study of the processes that regulate systems, especially the control of information (Barker, 2003).
- **Dyad.** This term refers to a two-person system (McGoldrick & Carter, 2001).
- **Family boundaries.** This term denotes the explicit and implicit rules in a family system that govern how family members are expected to relate to one another and to nonfamily members (Barker, 2003).
- **Family homeostasis.** This term describes a family system's tendency to maintain predictable interactional processes. When such processes are operating, the family system is said to be in equilibrium (Sauber, L'Abate, Weeks, & Buchanan, 1993).
- **Family projection process.** This term refers to the transmission of a problem in a marital dyad to one of the children. Such a process helps maintain the illusion of a harmonious marital relationship. However, the process occurs at the expense of transmitting the symptoms of the problem to one of the children. Typically, this child is presented at the beginning of family therapy as the "problem to be fixed" (Sauber et al., 1993). Among family therapists, this child is called the "identified patient," or "IP."
- **Family system.** A family system is a social system built by the repeated interaction of family members. These interactions establish patterns of how, when, and to whom family members relate (Sauber et al., 1993).
- **Family therapists.** Family therapy is practiced either as a specialty within a profession (e.g., counseling, clinical psychology) or as a stand-alone profession (e.g., marriage and family therapy). Persons who practice family therapy usually possess at least a master's degree (Dykeman, 2004).
- **Family therapy.** This is an umbrella term for therapeutic approaches in which the whole family is the unit of treatment. The term is theoretically neutral, as one can conduct family therapy using a variety of frameworks (Reber, 2002).
- **Family.** This term applies to two or more people who consider themselves family. These persons generally share a common residence and assume the obligations, functions, and responsibilities generally essential to healthy family life, such as economic support (Barker, 2003).

- **Feedback loop.** This term identifies the process by which a system gets the information required to correct itself. Self-correction is exerted either to maintain a steady state (i.e., homeostasis) or to move toward a goal (Nichols & Schwartz, 2003). A system that receives negative feedback attempts to maintain a steady state. Positive feedback increases deviation from the steady state, enabling the family to evolve to a new state (N. J. Kaslow & Celano, 2005).
- **Holon.** Koestler (1967) coined this term to name whole units nested in larger whole units, for example, the marital dyad in a nuclear family.
- **Marital dyad.** This term denotes a relationship composed of a husband and wife (Sauber et al., 1993).
- **Nuclear family.** The nuclear family is the kinship group that consists of a father, a mother, and their children (Barker, 2003).
- **Triangulation.** This is the process of a third person or thing being added to a dyad to divert anxiety away from the relationship of the twosome (McGoldrick & Carter, 2001).

Now that some key terms have been defined, let us take a closer look at major family theories and their clinical applications.

HUMAN NATURE: A DEVELOPMENTAL PERSPECTIVE

As with individual development, family systems can be seen as a developmental process that evolves over time. Developmental models of family life include the **family life cycle**, the **family life spiral**, and the **family genogram**.

Family Life Cycle

Jay Haley (1993) offered the first detailed description of a family life cycle. He identified six developmental stages, stretching from courtship to old age. Haley was interested in understanding the strengths families have and the challenges they face as they move through the life cycle. He hypothesized that symptoms and dysfunctions appeared when there was a dislocation or disruption in the anticipated natural unfolding of the life cycle: "The symptom is a signal that a family has difficulty in getting past a stage in the life cycle" (p. 42).

Over time, tension inevitably emerges in families because of the developmental changes they encounter (Smith & Schwebel, 1995). Family stress is most intense at those points where family members must negotiate a transition to the next stage of the family life cycle (Carter & McGoldrick, 2004). On one level, this stress may be viewed as part of the family's response to the challenges and changes of life in their passage through time; for example, a couple may encounter tension while making the transition to parenthood with the birth of their first child. On another level, pressures may emerge from the family's multigenerational legacies that define the family's attitudes, taboos, expectations, labels, and loaded issues; for example, over several generations a rule that men cannot be trusted to handle the money may impose stress when the woman is absent. When stress occurs on both levels, the whole family may experience acute crisis.

Family therapists can find it difficult to determine the exact sources of stress on a family. Papp and Imber-Black (1996) presented an interesting vignette describing the power of illuminating a wide spectrum of stressors for a family. In this vignette, Papp and Imber-Black connected what was viewed as the developmental struggle between a mother and an adolescent son to a three-generation theme of "footsteps." In this case, the adolescent son's grades had plummeted and he was depressed and argumentative. Furthermore, he had engaged in some stealing activity. On the surface, these behaviors can be understood as either symptomatic of family life with an adolescent or symptomatic of life after creation of a blended family. However, by identifying the underlying theme, Papp and Imber-Black discovered that the family's fears emerged as a story about the son "following in the footsteps"—in particular, the footsteps of a drug-dealing father and a larcenous grandfather. The therapists skillfully challenged three generations of the family to tell the family myth about their men who chose the "wrong path." Sorting out the current stressors on the family through the lens of the family scripts encouraged the adolescent to leave behind the old stories to develop his own story. The process also helped his mother to realize how these historic scripts hid her son from her. This multigenerational storytelling intervention worked to free the young man from a catastrophic prophecy while bringing all members of the family into better communication.

Family Life Spiral

Combrinck-Graham (1985) constructed a nonlinear model of family development called the family life spiral. The spiral includes the developmental tasks of three generations that simultaneously affect one another. Each person's developmental issues can be seen in relation to those of the other family members. For example, a midlife crisis involves the reconsideration of status, occupation, and marital state for adults in the middle years of their lives. This crisis may coincide with their adolescent children's identity struggles and their parents' plans for retirement. Similarly, when a family's childbearing experience is viewed in terms of grandparenthood, the birth of a child "pushes" the older generations along the time line, whether or not the grandparents are prepared for their new roles.

The family life spiral looks like an upside-down tornado. This spiral is compact at the top to illustrate the family's closeness during centripetal periods. It is spread out at the bottom to represent centrifugal periods of greater distance between family members.

Centripetal Periods. The close periods in family life are called *centripetal* to indicate the many forces in the family system that hold the family tightly together (Combrinck-Graham, 1985). Centripetal periods (CPs) are marked by an inner orientation that requires intense bonding and cohesion, such as early childhood, child rearing, and grandparenting. Both the individual's and the family's life structure emphasize internal family life during these periods. Consequently, the boundaries between members are more diffuse so as to enhance teamwork among the members. In contrast to diffuse internal boundaries, external boundaries may become tightened as if to create a nest within which the family can attend to itself.

Centrifugal Periods. By contrast, the distant or disengaged periods have been called *centrifugal* to indicate the predominance of forces that pull the family apart (Combrinck-Graham, 1988). Centrifugal periods (CFs) are marked by a family's outward orientation. Here the developmental focus is on tasks that emphasize personal identity and autonomy, such as adolescence, midlife, and retirement. As such, the external family boundary is loosened, old family structures are dismantled, and distance between family members typically increases.

The Family Merry-Go-Round.   The terms *centripetal* and *centrifugal* are derived from physics and indicate the push and pull of forces on and within things—in this case, families. These forces might also be compared to the process of riding a merry-go-round. On a merry-go-round, the centripetal force is the push you need to keep you on your horse. You push against the spinning ride toward the center of the rotation. The centrifugal force is what tries to pull you off and out into the world away from the spinning direction. For example, if you let go of your horse's pole, this force will pull you away from the merry-go-round. In this case your seat belt will help!

Families are in a constant process of pushing and pulling to adapt to life's events. Families move between centripetal and centrifugal forces depending on the developmental tasks required of them at various stages of the family life cycle. A family will typically move through one cycle each 25 years. This period is the time required to produce a new generation. In each family cycle, different members will experience these shifts:

- One's own childhood (CP) and adolescence (CF)
- The birth (CP) and adolescence (CF) of one's children
- The birth (CP) and development (CF) of one's grandchildren

These developmental shifts have been called *oscillations* that provide opportunities for family members to practice intimacy and involvement in the centripetal periods and individuation and independence in the centrifugal periods (Combrinck-Graham, 1985).

Implications for Practice.   Neither direction, centripetal or centrifugal, defines a pathological condition. These directions describe the relationship styles of the family at particular stages of the family life spiral. Symptom formation often occurs when the family is confronted with an event that is out of phase with the anticipated development of the family life spiral. Such events include untimely death, birth of a disabled child, chronic illness, or war. For some families, stress will develop around typical developmental demands, such as children's needs for dependency as infants or adolescents' demands for more autonomy. The intensity and duration of family anxiety will affect the family's ability to make the required transitions. The purpose of family therapy is to help the family past the transitional crisis so that they can continue toward the next stage of family life.

Family Genogram

Genograms give family therapists another useful way to conceptualize family development. Typically, a genogram is used to chart the progression of a particular family through the life cycle over at least three generations. It is like a family tree that includes information about birth order, family members, their communications, and issues of relationships. The work of Monica McGoldrick provides an excellent resource for clinicians who are not familiar with the use of genograms (see McGoldrick, Gerson, & Shellenberger, 1999). Genograms often provide the basis of clinical hypotheses in family work and offer a culturally sensitive method for understanding individual or family clients. For example, Magnuson, Norem, and Skinner (1995) recommended mapping the relationship dynamics in the families of gay or lesbian clients. They pointed out the importance of mapping the relationship markers of gay or lesbian couples that are not recognized by general society (e.g., marriage). Gibson (2005) provided excellent guidance on the effective use of genograms in school counseling settings.

Hartman (1995) developed a similar tool called an **ecomap**. The advantage of the ecomap is that it allows the client and counselor or therapist to diagram family and community interactions in tandem. Genograms and ecomaps are increasingly being used in fields beyond family therapy such as nursing (Olsen, Dudley-Brown, and McMullen, 2004) and family medicine (Wattendorf & Hadley, 2005). An ecomap is included as an organizing element in the case study presented later in this chapter.

MAJOR CONSTRUCTS

Theoretical Antecedents

Present-day family systems theories emerged out of the ideas and debates in the social and physical sciences after World War II. The next two sections outline the specific ideas that led to the development of a systems approach to counseling and psychotherapy.

Bateson. **Gregory Bateson** is acknowledged by many as the pioneer in applying cybernetic systems thinking to human interaction (Imber-Black, 2004). He saw that cybernetics provided a powerful alternative language for explaining behavior—specifically, a language that did not resort to instinct or descriptions of the internal workings of the mind (Segal, 1991). Bateson began to use these ideas to understand social interaction (Bateson, 1951). For instance, he applied cybernetic principles to the study of families of clients with schizophrenia (Haley, 1976). Bateson considered pattern, process, and communication as the fundamental elements of description and explanation. He believed that by observing human systems he could formulate the rules governing human interaction.

The Palo Alto Group. In 1952, while based in Palo Alto, Bateson received a grant from the Rockefeller Foundation to investigate the general nature of communication. He was joined on this project by Jay Haley, John Weakland, William Fry, and Don D. Jackson. This research team defined the family as a cybernetic, **homeostatic** system whose parts (i.e., family members) covary with each other to maintain equilibrium by means of error-activated negative feedback loops (Jackson, 1957). For example, whenever deviation-amplifying information is introduced (e.g., an argument between two family members or the challenge of a new stage in the family life cycle), a designated family member initiates a counterdeviation action (e.g., a family member exhibits symptomatic behavior), such that the family's existing equilibrium is restored (i.e., threatened changes are defeated). The emphasis on homeostasis prevailed in family therapy theory into the 1980s.

The recognition of the **symptomatic double bind** as a homeostatic maneuver regulating family patterns of relationship is considered the definitive contribution of the Palo Alto Group. The symptomatic double bind most often cited is Bateson's classic example of the interaction between a mother and her son who had "fairly well recovered from an acute schizophrenic episode." Bateson described this interaction as follows:

> [The son] was glad to see her and impulsively put his arm around her shoulders, whereupon she stiffened. He withdrew his arm and she asked, "Don't you love me any more?" He then blushed, and she said, "Dear, you must not be so easily embarrassed and afraid of your feelings." The patient was able to stay with her only a few minutes more, and following her departure, he assaulted an aide and was put in the tubs. (Bateson, Jackson, Haley, & Weakland, 1976, pp. 14–15)

The Palo Alto Group noted both the incongruence of the mother's message and the fact that the son could not clearly and directly comment on it. They concluded that the son's craziness was his commentary on his mother's contradictory behavior. Bateson's work in the 1950s spawned the development of many family therapy models, including the strategic model of Haley (1991) and Madanes (1991). An examination of this model follows the discussion of the ideas of another Palo Altoan—Virginia Satir.

Conjoint Theory

Virginia Satir is among the best loved of all theorists in the field of family therapy and, arguably, beyond. After leaving a career as a schoolteacher, she first practiced as a psychiatric social worker, then engaged in private practice work with families. In 1959, she joined the Mental Research Institute in Palo Alto. Satir gained international recognition with the publication of her first book, *Conjoint Family Therapy,* in 1964.

Satir acknowledged the impact of a diverse group of theorists on her life's work (Satir & Bitter, 1991). These included Fritz Perls (Gestalt therapy), Eric Berne (transactional analysis), J. J. Moreno (psychodrama), Ida Rolf (life-posturing reintegration), Alex Lowen (bioenergetics), and Milton Erickson (hypnosis). Her family therapy model reflects a growth perspective rather than a medical model for assessing and working with families. In her frame, illness was seen as an appropriate communicative response to a dysfunctional system or family context. Health, therefore, is developed when the system is changed so as to permit healthy communication and responses.

Like other communication theorists, such as Bateson, Satir defined **congruence** as the use of words that accurately match personal feelings. In other words, congruence is where direct communication and the meta-communication are the same. When using congruent communication, the person is alert, balanced, and responsive to any question or topic without needing to hold back. In contrast, **incongruence** is seen as communication wherein the nonverbal and verbal components do not match. Examples of incongruent communication include double messages, assumptions, ambiguous messages, and incomplete communication. Satir saw self-esteem as the basis for family emotional health. Her perspective was that there is a correlation between self-esteem and communication. Low self-esteem is associated with poor communication, because low self-esteem affects behavior and interactions among the members of the system. She also held that maladaptive communication can be both learned and unlearned.

To demonstrate concretely to a family how incongruence occurs and is a source of pain and poor self-esteem, Satir would ask them to join into a game. The communication game would typically be used to work with two members. She observed that when a person delivers an incongruent or mixed message there is little skin or eye contact. It is as though the sender is "out of touch" with the other person. In the communication game, Satir taught families to improve their communication through a series of interactions that concretely show people what happens when they do not look, touch, or speak congruently. Satir (1983) outlined these steps as follows:

1. Place two persons back to back and ask them to talk.
2. Turn them around and have them "eyeball" each other without touching or talking.
3. Then they eyeball and touch without talking.

4. Then they are asked to touch with eyes closed and without talking.
5. They eyeball each other without touching.
6. Finally the two talk and touch and eyeball and try to argue with each other.

By the last stage of the game the couple usually finds it impossible to argue with one another. The problem of delivering an incongruent message is clear to the family when one is touching, talking, and looking at the listener.

Besides the humor of this process, the provocative nature of this game encourages a deeper examination of the ways family members suffer and feel inadequate or devalued when engaged in incongruent communication patterns. These revelations are supported through steps toward increasing self-esteem and communication as the family moves from a "closed" to a more "open" system. Satir believed that a functional family is an **open system** wherein there is a clear exchange of information and resources both within the system and with the others outside the family. In contrast, a **closed system** is rigid and maladaptive.

Satir observed that family pain is symptomatic of dysfunction. She did not feel that the problems families brought to her were the real difficulty. Rather, she saw that methods of coping within the family and rules for behavior that were fixed, arbitrary, and inconsistent decreased the family's ability to cope over time. Her approach involves the following treatment stages:

1. Establish trust.
2. Develop awareness through experience.
3. Create new understanding of members and dynamics.
4. Have family express and apply their new understandings with each other.
5. Have family use their new behaviors outside therapy.

As the family moves through this cycle of change, they feel less anxious and more fully valued and valuing of each other (Satir & Bitter, 1991). In this way, self-esteem, communication, and caring are raised and pain is decreased.

Strategic Theory

Jay Haley left Palo Alto in 1966 and joined **Salvador Minuchin** in Philadelphia to pursue his growing interest in family hierarchy, power, and structure. In 1974, he established the Washington Institute of Family Therapy, where Cloe Madanes joined him. Their family therapy model has three roots: the strategic therapy of Milton Erickson, the theories of the Palo Alto Group, and the structural therapy of Minuchin.

Haley (1991) and Madanes (1981) asserted that a family's current problematic relational patterns were at some point useful, because they organized family members in a concerted way to solve an existing problem. These patterns persisted because they protected the family from the threat of disintegration. Haley held that therapeutic change occurs when a family's dysfunctional protective patterns are interrupted. He noted that the role of family therapists, through the use of directives, is to provoke such interruptions. Haley offered therapist provocations such as the following:

- A husband and wife with sexual problems may be required to have sexual relations only on the living room floor for a period of time. This task changes the context and so the struggle.

- A man who is afraid to apply for a job may be asked to go for a job interview at a place where he would not take the job if he got it, thereby practicing in a safe way.

For Haley (1990), therapist directives served three purposes: to facilitate change and make things happen; to keep the therapist's influence alive during the week; and to stimulate family reactions that give the therapist more information about family structure, rules, and system. Haley held that the goal of therapy was not client insight; in fact, the family need not understand the actual mechanisms of change. Furthermore, the therapist should act without trying to convince the family that the set of hypotheses guiding the therapy is valid. Haley commented, "The goal is not to teach the family about their malfunctioning system but to change the family sequences so that the presenting problems are resolved" (p. 135).

Haley's ideas have direct consequences for the family therapist wishing to practice a strategic approach. First, a strategic family therapist attends to what is defined by the family members experiencing the problem as the "nature of the problem." Second, the therapist focuses on how the family is responding in attempting to resolve the problem. The assumption here is that it is often the very ways in which families are defining a problem and responding to it that may keep it going in a vicious problem-solution cycle.

Structural Theory

Structural family therapists do not sit on the sidelines during therapy. Rather, they become involved with family members, pushing and being pushed. Minuchin put a strong emphasis on action in his own work as a family therapist. His justification for this emphasis was his belief that "if both I and the family take risks within the constraints of the therapeutic system, we will find alternatives for change" (Minuchin & Fishman, 1981, p. 7). He commented that observers of his structural family therapy work would notice (1) his concern with bringing the family transactions into the room; (2) his alternation between participation and observation as a way of unbalancing the system by supporting one family member against another; and (3) his many types of response to family members' intrusion into each other's psychological space (Minuchin & Fishman).

Minuchin's therapeutic maneuvers were based on his theoretical schema about family structure and family transformation. He carried out his vision by being uniquely himself. He stated:

> In families that are too close, I artificially create boundaries between members by gestures, body postures, movement of chairs, or seating changes. My challenging maneuvers frequently include a supportive statement: a kick and a stroke are delivered simultaneously. My metaphors are concrete: "You are sometimes sixteen and sometimes four"; "Your father stole your voice"; "You have two left hands and ten thumbs." I ask a child and a parent to stand and see who is taller, or I compare the combined weight of the parents with the child's weight. I rarely remain in my chair for a whole session. I move closer when I want intimacy, kneel to reduce my size with children, or spring to my feet when I want to challenge or show indignation. These operations occur spontaneously; they represent my psychological fingerprint. (Minuchin & Fishman, 1981, p. 7)

For Minuchin, family therapy techniques are uniquely integrated in the person of the counselor or therapist who goes "beyond technique" to wisdom, specifically, wisdom concerning "knowledge of the larger interactive system—that system which, if disturbed, is likely to generate exponential curves of change" (Bateson, 1972, p. 439).

Transgenerational Theory

Murray Bowen's approach to family therapy, like Haley's, had many roots. Specifically, Bowen merged concepts such as Freud's unconscious id and Darwin's theory of evolution with his own observations of people with schizophrenia at the Menninger Clinic and the National Institute of Mental Health. His core idea was the concept of the **differentiation** of self. It was through this concept that Bowen addressed "how people differ from one another in terms of their sensitivity to one another and their varying abilities to preserve a degree of autonomy in the face of pressures for togetherness" (Papero, 1990, p. 45).

Bowen also posited that there were two different systems of human functioning: an emotional and reactive system that humans share with lower forms of life, and an intellectual and rational system that is a more recent evolutionary development. The degree to which these two systems are fused or undifferentiated is the degree to which the individual is vulnerable to the impulses of his or her emotional system and less attentive to his or her intellectual and rational system. For example, people are more likely to react emotionally rather than rationally when they are anxious. Bowen asserted that the extent to which persons have differentiated their thinking system from their emotional system will determine how able they are to maintain a sense of self in relationships with others, particularly members of their family.

Bowen believed that emotional illness was passed from one generation to another through the **family projection process (FPP)**. FPP theory suggests that the ego differentiation achieved by children will generally approximate that of their parents. However, FPP often distributes the capacity for differentiation unevenly among family members. For example, one child may grow up with a high level of ego differentiation, but a sibling may grow up with a low level of differentiation. The hallmark of a high level is a well-defined sense of self and low emotional reactivity, whereas a low level is characterized by a poorly defined sense of self and high emotional reactivity.

Low levels of ego differentiation occur when parents "triangulate" a child into their conflicts to dissipate the stresses of their relationship. Bowen (1978) held that "triangles" were the natural consequence of two poorly differentiated people who are overwhelmed by anxiety and seek relief by involving a third party. Triangulation is how parents' low level of differentiation is passed on to the next generation. Klever (2005) presented empirical evidence supporting Bowen's theory of multigenerational transmission of family unit functioning.

Bowen's work has influenced many of present-day family therapy theorists. One of the best examples of the extension of Bowen's ideas is the work of McGoldrick et al. (1999) on genograms, which was discussed earlier in this chapter.

Narrative Theory

Long before *constructivism* or *narrative* became common terms in counseling, family therapists used story making. Papp and Imber-Black (1996) cited various names coined to identify the role of story in family work, including *family myth, family paradigm,* and more recently, *landscape of consciousness.*

The narrative therapy approach of family therapist **Michael White** (1992) was built on the writings of French philosopher and social historian Michel Foucault (1980), who described the process whereby knowledge is embedded in language and serves the values of the dominant culture. Narrative has become a popular method for therapy based on the notion that individuals, families, and entire cultures are given a different level of power as creators of their realities.

In regard to reality creation, White and Epston (1990) asserted that the social sciences classify and minimize people around a norm that becomes internalized. People take on these objective categorizations and see themselves as "a schizophrenic" or as "having a behavior disorder." Solutions to such internalized and normative problems are limited. To overcome this internalization, narrative family therapists work to help families "externalize" problems through storytelling. This **externalization** can give a family the ability to construct a story wherein the problem is subject to manipulation or change because it exists as a separate entity. Also, externalization can break the retelling of complaint-saturated stories and offer a sense of personal agency. A common question asked in narrative family therapy is "How has the problem affected your life?" Such a question works to separate the family from their problem.

Families have styles for telling their stories. Roberts (1995) defined six types of story styles: intertwined, separated, interrupted, secret, rigid, and evolving. For example, family members may offer intertwined stories so the events described at one time are used to make sense of other circumstances. Conversely, a rigid story is frozen and told over and over in the same way without interpretations. Everyone in the family knows these stories by heart because they have been told so often. Once the type and goals of the story style are determined, the counselor or therapist can work with the family to see what resources they have available and open possibilities for making new meaning out of personal histories. The work of Roberts offers another method for assessing the types of stories told and their possible therapeutic uses. Horton and Andonian (2005) have gone as far as suggesting that the family be metaphorically reconceptualized as an anthology where individual and collective voices are heard, edited, subjected, emphasized, embellished, and assembled.

The major constructs discussed in this section were developed by clinicians to understand how families function. Family theorists conceptualized the communication patterns, structures, relationship dynamics, and story-making processes of their client families. The concepts they developed reflected their own therapeutic interventions. In this way, family theory is a rich resource to students and family practitioners. Table 13.1 provides an overview and comparison of these major theoretical constructs.

APPLICATIONS

Overview

All counseling and psychotherapy approaches share a common goal of producing change in clients. In this section, we differentiate family therapy applications from the applications of the individualistic approaches you studied in the previous chapters. Our goal is to help you find ways to add systems-level interventions to both your clinical reasoning and your counseling or therapy tool bag.

Goals of Counseling and Psychotherapy

Family therapy represented a watershed in the history of counseling or therapy. Before family therapy, the focus of counselors or therapists had been solely on the individual. The goal of counseling or therapy was always to change some cognitive, affective, or behavioral

Table 13.1
Major Family Therapy Theoretical Constructs

	Conjoint	Strategic	Structural	Transgen-erational	Narrative
Major theorists	Satir	Haley, Madanes	Minuchin	Bowen, McGoldrick	White
What family members participate in therapy?	Flexible	Everyone involved in the problem	Whoever is involved and accessible	The most motivated family member(s)	Flexible
What is the theory of dysfunction?	Low self-esteem; poor communi-cation; triangulation	Confused hierarchy; rigid behavioral sequences	Enmeshed or disengaged boundaries; intrafamilial coalitions	Emotional fusion (symbiosis with family of origin); anxiety; triangulation	Disem-powerment by the dominant cultural narrative
What are the primary goals of therapy?	Improved communi-cation; personal growth	Problem solving; restoration of hierarchy	Change in the family structure; increased flexibility	Greater differentiat-ion of self; reduced anxiety	Empower-ment through reauthoring the family's life story
How is family functioning assessed?	Family life chronology	Structured initial interview; intervene and observe the reaction	Joining the family to experience its process; chart family structure	Genogram	Narration of family history and myths
What is the temporal focus of therapy?	Present	Present	Present	Past	Present and past
What are common intervention practices?	Modeling and coaching clear communi-cation; family sculpting; guided interaction	Directives to change behavior; they may be straightfor-ward, paradoxical, or ordeals	Reframing to change the perception of the problem; structure is changed by unbalancing and increasing stress	Reducing anxiety by providing rational, untriangu-lated third party; coaching to aid in differen-tiation from family of origin	Externali-zation of family problems through narration
What characterizes the therapist's approach to the family?	Active, directive, matter of fact, nonjudgmental; models open communi-cation	Active, directive, but not self-revealing; planful, not spontaneous	Active, directive, personally involved; spontaneous; humorous	Interested but detached; reinforces calmness and rationality	Active partnership; encourages the telling of family history and myths

Table 13.2
Worldview Comparison

Individual Psychotherapy	Family Systems Psychotherapy
Asks, why?	Asks, what?
Linear cause-effect	Reciprocal causality
Subject-object dualism	Holistic
Either-or dichotomies	Dialectic
Value-free science	Subjective, perceptual
Deterministic, reactive	Freedom of choice, proactive
Laws and lawlike external reality	Patterns
Historical focus	Here-and-now focus
Individualistic	Relational
Reductionistic	Contextual
Absolutistic	Relativistic

component of an individual. In contrast, family therapists aim to change systems within which individuals reside. Becvar and Becvar (2002) compared how the worldview of individual psychotherapy differed from that of family systems psychotherapy. Table 13.2 details the major differences they mentioned.

Process of Change

Family therapists use cybernetics to understand change, specifically, the cybernetic control processes involving information and feedback. Information in the form of feedback precipitates shifts that either amplify or counteract the direction of change. Family therapists differentiate between **first-order change** and **second-order change**. Lyddon (1990) succinctly defined these different types of change as follows: "First-order change is essentially 'change without change'—or any change within a system that does not produce a change in the structure of the system. In contrast, second-order change is 'change of change'—a type of change whose occurrence alters the fundamental structure of the system" (p. 122). At any given moment, counselors or psychotherapists can only bring about one or the other type of change in their clients.

First-Order Change. First-order change occurs when a family modifies problem behaviors yet maintains its present structure. An example of a first-order change intervention is a family therapist's instructing parents when they can fight with their son over bedtime. By this intervention, the family therapist hopes to give the family relief from their problem behavior; radical change of present family system is not a goal. Family therapists call the process of bringing about this type of change *negative feedback.*

Second-Order Change. In contrast to first-order change, second-order change refers to transformations in either the structure or the internal order of a system. Family therapists often seek to generate or amplify change processes that will alter the basic structure of a family system (Nichols & Schwartz, 2003). This goal embodies second-order change. An example of a second-order change intervention is a family therapist's directing the more passive parent to take over bedtime compliance responsibility with the goal of changing the power dynamics in the marital dyad. Family therapists call the process of bringing about second-order change *positive feedback*.

Traditional Intervention Strategies

The case study at the end of this chapter will illustrate in detail one way to conduct family therapy. Besides the strategies presented in the case study, two additional points on family therapy applications should be considered. The first is an understanding of the significance of nonspecific factors in family therapy outcomes. The second is how to structure the first session so that family therapy can get off to a good start.

Specific Versus Nonspecific Factors. A strong current trend in individual-focused counseling or therapy research is examination of the specific and nonspecific factors involved in treatment outcomes. **Specific factors** are those counseling or therapy activities that are specific to a particular approach, for example, a strategic family therapist's use of a proscribing-the-symptom intervention. **Nonspecific factors** are those change-producing elements present in counseling or therapy regardless of theoretical orientation. Many nonspecific factors have been proposed, but few have withstood empirical testing. One exception is working alliance. In fact, working alliance scores are the best known predictor of counseling or therapy outcomes (Horvath, 1994).

The modern transtheoretical definition of **working alliance** was promulgated by **Edward Bordin** (1994), who posited that there were three components of working alliance: task, goal, and bond. He conceptualized these three components as follows:

- *Task* refers to the in-therapy activities that form the substance of the therapeutic process. In a well-functioning relationship, both parties must perceive these tasks as relevant and effective. Furthermore, each must accept the responsibility to perform these acts.
- *Goal* refers to the counselor or therapist and the client mutually endorsing and valuing the aims (outcomes) that are the target of the intervention.
- *Bond* embraces the complex network of positive personal attachments between client and counselor or therapist, including issues such as mutual trust, acceptance, and confidence (adapted from Horvath, 1994).

Overall, Bordin's working alliance model emphasized "the role of the client's collaboration with the therapist against the common foe of the client's pain and self-defeating behavior" (Horvath, p. 110).

Family therapists have been slower to examine the nonspecific factors involved in positive treatment outcomes (Blow & Sprenkle, 2001). One exception was **William Pinsof** of the Family Institute (Evanston, Illinois). In his research, Pinsof (1994) found a positive relationship between working alliance and family therapy outcomes. The few other studies conducted on working alliance in family therapy produced similar results (Knobloch-Fedders, Pinsof, & Mann, 2004).

Given the effectiveness of working alliance concerning treatment outcomes, persons practicing family therapy would be wise to attend carefully to such alliances. However, such attention would run counter to the preeminence family therapists give to technique. Coady (1992) noted that the emphasis in family systems theory on homeostasis has led to family therapists' viewing family members as being dominated by the family system. He stated that family therapists "often expect families to exert an oppositional force against change efforts, and they feel compelled to manipulate the family into change" (p. 471). Unfortunately, such a perspective runs exactly counter to formation of strong working alliances. A commitment to build strong working alliances with client families does not mean the counselor or therapist has to dismiss technique. Rather, it means acknowledging that techniques should not be separated from the interpersonal and cultural contexts in which they occur (Coady).

In a study on the development of working alliance in couple therapy, the researchers found gender differences in alliance development (Thomas, Werner-Wilson, and Murphy, 2005). Thomas and her colleagues found that for men, negative statements made by their partner were a consistent negative predictor of working alliance. They went on to note that their results "indicate that men expect therapists to provide a refuge from what they see as a barrage of negative statements from their partners. Therapists who fail to provide this protection for men effectively contribute to the lack of therapeutic alliance" (p. 31). Thomas et al. did not find that negative statements made by a partner influenced working alliance for women. In reference to both genders, Thomas el al. found that "partner self-disclosure positively influenced the bond dimension of alliance for both men and women. When the therapist actively creates a safe place for partners to disclose their thoughts and feelings, clients feel more bonded to their therapist" (p. 33).

The Family Interview. From the start, Haley (1991) advocated brevity and clarity in counseling or therapy work with families. He stated, "If therapy is to end properly, it must begin properly—by negotiating a solvable problem and discovering the social situation that makes the problem necessary" (p. 8). To help family therapists start on a good note, Haley outlined a structured family interview for use during an initial session. The five stages of this structured family interview are as follows:

1. *Social:* The interviewer greets the family and helps family members feel comfortable.
2. *Problem:* The interviewer invites each person present to define the problem.
3. *Interaction:* The interviewer directs all members present to talk together about the problem while the interviewer watches and listens.
4. *Goal setting:* Family members are invited to speak about what changes everyone, including the "problem" person, wants from the therapy.
5. *Ending:* Directives (if any) are given and the next appointment is scheduled.

The information gained from the first interview helps the family therapist form hypotheses about the function of the problem within its relational context. Moreover, this information can help the family therapist generate directives to influence change. For Haley, "the first obligation of a therapist is to change the presenting problem offered. If that is not accomplished, the therapy is a failure" (p. 135).

Brief Intervention Strategies

Managed care's drive toward greater cost-efficiency has pushed all forms of therapy to develop brief applications of their approach. Family therapy theorists and researchers have not ignored this demand from the health care industry. The following approaches have proven effective in a brief family therapy setting: (1) cognitive-behavioral (Kazak et al., 2004), (2) solution focus (Peterson, 2005), and (3) family systems (Bishof, Richmond, & Case, 2003). More research on the efficacy of brief family therapy will surely emerge during the next few years.

CLIENTS WITH SERIOUS MENTAL HEALTH ISSUES

Family therapy has been found to be applicable to persons with mental disorders. Two major family therapy researchers, William Pinsof and Lyman Wynne (2000) conducted an exhaustive review of published family therapy research. Based on a criterion of at least two controlled studies with significant positive results and no studies with negative results, they concluded that there was sufficient scientific evidence to support the fact that couple therapy (CT) or family therapy (FT) is more effective than therapy that does not involve a family member in treating the following mental disorders:

- Adult schizophrenia (FT)
- Depression in women in distressed marriages (CT)
- Adult alcoholism and drug abuse (FT)
- Adolescent conduct disorders (FT)
- Anorexia in young adolescent females (FT)
- Childhood autism (FT)
- Aggression and noncompliance in attention deficit/hyperactivity disorder (FT)
- Dementia (FT)
- Childhood conduct disorders

Pinsof and Wynne concluded their listing with the powerful and instructive conclusion that "for most disorders, therapists are likely to be more effective if they include relevant and appropriate family members in treatment" (p. 2).

CROSS-CULTURAL CONSIDERATIONS

Family is a culturally determined phenomenon:

> The dominant American definition, reflecting white Anglo Saxon Protestant (WASP) values, focuses on the intact nuclear family unit. African Americans' definition of family refers to a wide network of kin and community. For many Italian Americans, family implies a strong, tightly knit three-or-four generation unit including godparents and old friends. The traditional Chinese definition of family includes ancestors and decedents. (Kaslow, Celano, & Dreelin, 1995, p. 622)

Thus, an effective family therapist must possess a high degree of cultural competence with diverse populations (McDowell, 2004). Otherwise, marginalizational and colonization enter and poison the family therapy process (Borstnar, Bucar, Makovec, Burck, & Daniel, 2005).

In a review of the literature on cultural competence and family interventions, Celano and Kaslow (2000) found family therapy to be the preferred treatment for culturally diverse clients. They noted that family therapists can be efficacious and culturally competent only when they

1. recognize the effects of their own culture(s) on the therapy;
2. acknowledge that family therapies, theories and techniques reflect the culture in which they were developed;
3. attend to the dynamic interplay of the cultural influences that affect the individual's and family's functioning;
4. devise and implement problem-resolution strategies that are culturally acceptable. (p. 217)

In another review, Bean, Perry, and Bedell (2001) noted that there was wide conceptual and empirical support for the use of family therapy with Latinos. Beitin and Allen (2005) demonstrated the efficacy of a family systems approach with Arab American couples facing life in the post 9/11 world.

EVALUATION

Overview

The emergence of managed care has radically altered the delivery of mental health services. Increasingly, those who pay for treatment are demanding proof of efficacy. This demand for efficacy has extended to those professionals practicing family therapy (Kaslow, 2000). In this section we review what is known about the efficacy of family therapy.

Supporting Research

Historically, empirical research has not been a strong component of family therapy (Gladding, 2001). Lebow and Gurman (1995) noted,

> At one time, most research on couples and families was conducted with little or no connection to the outstanding clinical developments in the field. Alternative modes of investigation such as inductive reasoning, clinical observation, and deconstruction have dominated in the development of methods and treatment models. Some couple and family therapists have even been reluctant to acknowledge that empirical research has an important role. (p. 29)

Fortunately, this reluctance was overcome and solid research evidence for the efficacy of family therapy now exists—evidence that professionals practicing family therapy can use to defend their work in the world of managed care.

From their review of published family therapy research, Pinsof and Wynne (2000) concluded that there was sufficient scientific evidence to support the fact that couple therapy (CT) or family therapy (FT) is more effective than therapy that does not involve a family member in treating these additional areas:

- Marital distress (CT)
- Cardiovascular risk factors (CT)
- Adolescent drug abuse (FT)

In addition, Pinsof and Wynne found that couple therapy or family therapy is more effective than no treatment for all of the previously mentioned areas as well as the following:

- Adult obesity (CT)
- Adult hypertension (CT)
- Adolescent obesity (FT)
- Anorexia in younger adolescents (FT)
- Childhood obesity (FT)
- Almost all childhood chronic illness (FT)

Based on the findings of Pinsof and Wynne and their strong recommendation regarding the inclusion of relevant and appropriate family members in effective treatment, it would seem obvious that counselors or therapists would rapidly adapt to this process. The truth, however, is that professional counselors or therapists have been slow to adopt this practice in their work. In fact, the latest study of the practice patterns of *family* therapists revealed that approximately half of their client load was *individuals* (Doherty & Simmons, 1996).

Research on treatment outcome predictors is useful to family therapy practitioners, but little credible research has been conducted in the area. One notable exception is a study by Hampson and Beavers (1996), who studied family and therapist characteristics in relation to treatment success. Their subjects were 434 families treated at an actual family therapy clinic in Dallas. Hampson and Beavers reported the following predictors of successful treatment:

- Number of family therapy sessions attended
- Third-party ratings of family competence
- Self-ratings of family competence
- Therapists' ratings of working alliance

Measure of family competence in the study of Hampson and Beavers included items on family affect, parental coalitions, problem-solving abilities, autonomy and individuality, optimistic versus pessimistic views, and acceptance of family members. The six-session mark was the breakpoint in increasing the probability of good results. However, a sizable subset of families did well with fewer than six sessions. What distinguished this subset of families was their strong self-ratings of competence. Hampson and Beavers were careful to note that family size, family income, family structure (e.g., blended), family ethnicity, and counselor or therapist gender did not predict outcome.

Limitations

One of the basic ethical principles in health care is the principle of nonmaleficence, that is, "above all, do no harm." To carry out this ethical principal, you must make yourself aware of the limitations of each counseling or therapy approach contained in this textbook. To that end, we now present two important limitations to the family therapy approaches.

First, the early language chosen for describing family systems was "combative and bellicose, often suggesting willful opposition: double bind, identified patient, family scapegoat, binder, victim, and so on" (Nichols, 1987, pp. 18–19). The choice of language emphasized the destructive power of families and contributed to an assault on the family by several pioneers in family therapy (Cooper, 1970). This assault has continued to the present because many family therapy educators and practitioners have overread this language and adopted a directive, manipulative approach to treatment. This overreading led to unfortunate consequences. For instance, Green and Herget (1991) discovered that at their family therapy clinic many families found "paradoxical prescriptions as signs of therapist sarcasm or incompetence, that engender massive resistance, sometimes destroying all together the clients' faith and cooperative attitude in therapy" (p. 323). Also, Patterson and Forgatch (1985) uncovered, in their study of families in treatment, a direct relationship between client resistance and frequency of counselor or therapist directives.

Second, family therapists have ignored the different socialization processes operating for men and women. Thus, family therapists have not adequately considered how these socialization processes have disadvantaged women (Friedlander, Wildman, Heatherington, & Skowron, 1994). Walters, Carter, Papp, and Silverstein (1988) called for family therapists to review all family therapy concepts through the lens of gender socialization to eliminate the dominance of male assumptions. Their hope was that such a review would promote the "recognition of the basic principle that no intervention is gender-free and that every intervention will have a different and special meaning for each sex" (p. 29).

SUMMARY CHART—*Family Theory*

Human Nature

Like models used to explain individual development across the life span, the creation and maintenance of a family system can be viewed as a developmental process that evolves over time. Developmental models of family life include the family life cycle, the family life spiral, and the family genogram.

Major Constructs

A variety of constructs are associated with family theory, and each theory contributes discrete concepts. Conjoint theory, strategic theory, structural theory, transgenerational theory, and narrative theory are points of departure for some of the major constructs connected with counseling and psychotherapy with couples and families.

Goals

The goals of individual counseling or therapy are usually aimed at changing cognitive, affective, or behavioral components of the individual. In contrast, family counselors and psychotherapists aim to change whole systems.

Change Process

Family counselors and psychotherapists use cybernetics to understand change. Specifically, cybernetic control processes involve information and feedback. Information in the form of feedback precipitates shifts that either amplify or counteract the direction of change. Family counselors and therapists differentiate between first-order and second-order change.

Interventions

Strategies and interventions associated with systemic change in families are varied; many were first introduced in the context of a specific family theory. Systemic change can be difficult to precipitate, so family therapists must be well schooled and supervised in the application of interventions. In addition, practitioners must be able to set boundaries and limits with couples and families and be "powerful" and strategic in their choices and development of treatment plans.

Limitations

The choice of language connected with couple and family counseling and psychotherapy often emphasizes the destructive power of families and contributes to an "assault" on the family. At times, practitioners forget that the proper use of interventions always involves consideration of cross-cultural variations that may limit applicability. Practitioners have often ignored the different socialization processes operating for men and women and how these processes have disadvantaged women.

THE CASE OF JONATHAN: *A Family Theory Approach*

Presenting Problem

Jonathan (age 36) was referred by a human resources counselor at work to a mental health service agency in Phoenix. Jonathan was suspended for difficulty at work with anger and arguments with his coworkers. It was clear during the intake process, that he was feeling overwhelmed with his life and feelings of isolation from his estranged wife and daughter. Jonathan's workplace offered to provide the cost of the counseling session as part of the employee assistance program.

Therapists

Jenny Smith and Rick Tsome were the cotherapists assigned to work with Jonathan and his family. They are both staff therapists with mental health services in Phoenix. Mrs. Smith possesses a national certification in family therapy. Mr. Tsome holds a national certification as an art therapist and is state certified in chemical dependency counseling. Both therapists have worked extensively with families in the area. Mr. Tsome is also a member of the Navajo Nation. The counseling agency is aware that counseling or therapy goals with diverse clients are better met when the client is matched with therapists with understanding of the cultural heritage of the clients.

Family Demographics and History

Jonathan Benally lives in a blue-collar neighborhood of Phoenix. His parents, Charley Benally (age 66) and Rita Benally (age 64), live on the reservation near Shiprock where his first wife and their three children reside. Jonathan's wife, Glenna (age 34) and daughter Amber also live in Phoenix. Glenna's parents, Nelson Tsossie (age 57) and Gladys Tsossie (age 55), live on the Navajo reservation near Canyon de Chelley. Both sets of grandparents interact with Jonathan's children in their respective villages and come together for community events. The children from both of his marriages know each other and visit or live with a variety of extended family members including aunts and second cousins in respective areas of the reservation. This pattern of residence is common on the reservation and reflects a different process of child rearing than is typically seen in the dominant culture. Besides these grandparents, all of Jonathan's siblings live on the reservation. These include Herbert (age 42), Slim (age 40), and Ethyl (age 37). The deaths of two siblings, L. C. and Bea, and their ages are noted on the ecomap. Jonathan's ecomap appears as Figure 13.1 and reflects purely fictional names and places developed with respect for Navajo people and customs.

Family Therapy Process

Intake Interview: Building Working Alliances.   Mrs. Smith and Mr. Tsome have both worked extensively with Native American families. This experience influenced the selection and application of their interventions. For instance, they initiated the first sessions with Jonathan and with Glenna by discussing tribal affiliation and clan names. They developed an ecomap with Jonathan of his family that includes the spiritual and types of bonds that the various members of his family have (see Figure 13.1). The ecomap is a pen-and-paper depiction of the family's existential relationship with the environmental systems (Hatman, 1995).

Case Conceptualization and Treatment Planning.   Mrs. Smith and Mr. Tsome diagnosed Jonathan as suffering from late-onset Dysthmic Disorder (Axis I: 300.4) and Alcohol Abuse Disorder without physiological dependence (Axis III: 303.00). Jonathan has experienced a growing sense of loneliness, failure, and worthlessness in life. His depression was demonstrated by the symptoms of alcohol abuse, unsatisfying liaisons with women, and anger toward others at work. Jonathan's statement of love for his wife and fear that he had ruined three families helped the counselors to determine the overarching framework for their intervention. The therapists decided to address three levels of Jonathan's family life: (1) the immediate family of Glenna and Amber, (2) the family of origin, and (3) the tribe and extended family. Mrs. Smith and Mr. Tsome prioritized the first level for immediate intervention with attention to the alcohol use. To address Jonathan's alienation from his wife and daughter, the two therapists proposed that Jonathan bring them to the next session. Mr. Tsome offered to invite Glenna to the session and successfully got her agreement to attend the following Wednesday.

Combining Conjoint Family Therapy With Art.   Art allows individuals to project both personally and culturally relevant images that can transcend the limitation of spoken language and dominant cultural frames. Art is also an effective method for assessing family interactions and communication patterns (Kwiatkowska, 1978). During her years at the National Institute of Mental Health where family therapy was being developed, Hanna Yaxa Kwiatkowska devised a series of art tasks useful for therapists to evaluate and disrupt nonproductive family structures. Later, Landgarten (1987) combined Satir's (1983) conjoint family therapy approach with Kwiatkowska's art task series to help family members examine problems in a symbolic way.

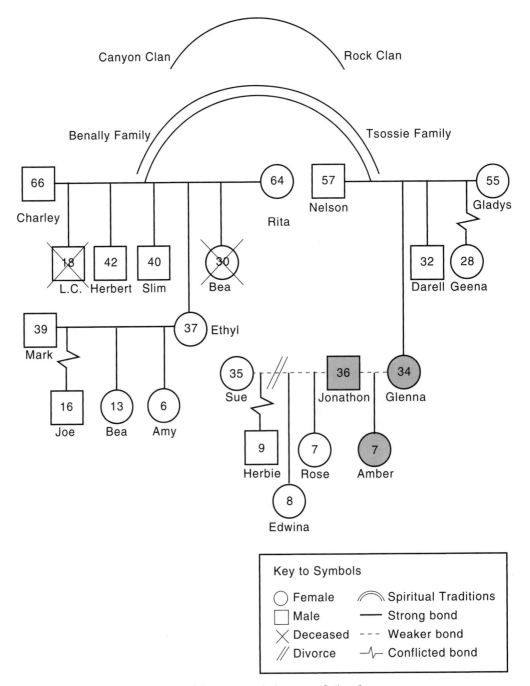

Figure 13.1   Jonathan's Ecomap (all names and places are fictional)

Mr. Tsome and Mrs. Smith used these conjoint therapy art tasks to begin their work with Jonathan and Glenna while Amber participated in a separate playgroup. The goal was to strengthen the couple's relationship to provide a foundation for supporting the next steps of counseling. As in narrative therapy approaches, the metaphors that would emerge from the art processes would provide a valuable method to help the couple to rediscover their interconnectedness. Mr. Tsome and Mrs. Smith planned that the information obtained through the art products would be used to set goals and plan directives for integrating families and tribal members as appropriate and over time.

Session 1.   The first session involved building a working relationship with the couple by engaging them in a series of four art tasks to help them reconnect and begin to communicate with each other. Mr. Tsome and Mrs. Smith alternately directed the art tasks so that both therapists would have an opportunity to direct and support and observe the couple. The first drawing task eased the couple into the art-making process by introducing the material with a warm-up process (individual free drawing). The second and third drawings focused specifically on the problems and resolutions identified by Jonathan and Glenna. The final art process put the couple together to create a family mural on one piece of paper. Through the task sequence, the couple was encouraged to move from a distant to a closer physical proximity. At the end of the art process, the therapists reviewed all of the drawings with the couple. The assignments given for each of the tasks were as follows (adapted from Kwiatkowska, 1978):

- "Make an individual free drawing of anything that comes to mind."
- "Make an individual drawing of why you think you are here."
- "Make an individual drawing on how you would like the 'problem' to change."
- "Now together, make a joint mural about your family."
- "At this time we will review the drawings you have made."

The therapists often used this series of tasks with families like Jonathan's who play lethal games with one another through hurtful communication patterns and alienation. The use of such tasks allows a family therapist to do the following:

- Elicit metaphorical information for planning future intervention
- Provide drawing tasks that disrupt dysfunctional family communication patterns (e.g., a family's covert blaming rule)
- Help family members discover and clarify values through the understanding of personal symbols

Given the tension present between the couple, they welcomed Mr. Tsome's initial suggestion that they start out by working on their own drawing. The therapists had a wide array of drawing materials available to use, including oil paint, chalk pastels, and felt-tip markers.

Free Drawing Art Task.   Jonathan's free drawing depicted a man in a hazy cloud with two tiny *Yei* figures in the left corner. The images of *Yei* figures are used in Navajo sandpaintings and represent supernatural beings translated from the Navajo word *god*. Jonathan's drawing reflected his confusion and hinted at his affiliation to tribal beliefs. Glenna drew a large heart with herself, Amber, and Jonathan inside it. Across the heart was a broken line depicting that the heart was broken. Tears fell from the heart. Her drawing reflected her feelings of abandonment and difficulty raising Amber alone.

After 20 minutes, Mrs. Smith had the couple stop their drawings and share them. As the couple discussed their drawings and the pain of their separation, they made eye contact for the first time in the session. Mr. Tsome read these nonverbal behaviors as a sign that the couple was ready for more close proximity. To concretize this new connection to Jonathan, Mr. Tsome directed Glenna to add to Jonathan's drawing through the production of a joint mural.

Couple Mural Art Task.   After the mural was completed, Mrs. Smith asked Jonathan and Glenna to discuss the feelings the mural evoked about reconciliation. Mrs. Smith helped to reflect the statements the couple made that they had fallen into a family communication style described as the blaming cycle (Satir, 1983). In this communication style, family members are stuck in a lethal cycle of blaming others for their problems. Jonathan blamed the "White man's world" for his troubles, Glenna blamed Jonathan for abandoning her and Amber, and the Benally and Tsossie families blamed Jonathan for leaving the family and tribal ways. The therapist stated that this style of communication avoids the expression of deeper feelings, which produces low self-esteem, and defeats the potential for growth and change. After the art sessions and expressing how unhappy they were, Glenna and Jonathan made a commitment to return for several counseling or therapy sessions to explore ways to communicate differently with one another. These sessions were planned to include Amber as soon as the couple was able to provide joint parental support for her. Between sessions, Mr. Tsome recommended that Jonathan examine how often he used alcohol in the next week and think about whether he would like to cut down on his drinking.

Sessions 2–5.   The next four sessions involved rebuilding family connectedness between the couple and their child by "trying on" new styles of communication. Again, the therapists used art tasks to facilitate culturally salient modes of communication as well as other techniques developed by Satir such as family sculpting. Both Jonathan and Glenna were able to declare their love for one another and commitment to the marriage. To develop dissonance about the use of alcohol, Mr. Tsome asked Jonathan to draw a picture of what he valued in his roles in his family. Jonathan's drawing reflected how important his wife and children are to him and how he misses the Benally family. Mr. Tsome then encouraged Jonathan to experience the dissonance between the use of alcohol and his view of being a good father or family member. This technique is a useful approach to encourage a motivation to change and has proven effective with addictive behaviors (Miller & Rollnick, 2002). Weeping, Jonathan declared that he wanted to change but did not know how. Mr. Tsome next worked with Jonathan to examine a menu of options for change and the underlying issues of his alcohol use.

Despite this work, Jonathan's desire to gain reentry to his family life remained blocked by his belief that he could not live in two worlds simultaneously, the White man's world, as he called it, and the Navajo Nation. This belief left Jonathan feeling marginalized from the Benally and the Tsossie families and prevented building alliances with his children from his first marriage.

During one of these middle sessions, the art tasks served as a potent stimulus for self-discovery. Jonathan's chalk pastel drawing recounted his early learning of the blessing songs and the blessing way offered in Navajo traditions and revealed in sandpaintings. Jonathan recognized that he kept putting *Yei* figures in all the drawings he made in the counseling or therapy sessions and that they were getting larger in size with each drawing. *Yei* figures, used in the Navajo sandpainting ceremonies, are believed to offer protection, strength, and healing. In viewing his own artwork, Jonathan saw clearly that to try to ignore his heritage was impossible. Glenna suggested that the *Yeis* might be offering their family a way to resolve the imbalance in their lives. Amber said she hoped the *Yeis* would bring her cousins together for a party.

Mr. Tsome asked Jonathan and Glenna to consider holding an option in mind—the idea of how Jonathan could be a member of two worlds at the same time. He asked Jonathan how he might integrate the two seemingly disconnected value systems of the White man's world and the Navajo blessing way. This question prompted a revelation about Jonathan's life. He had always imagined he might become a healer, a *hatathli* (i.e., medicine man). When he decided to go to nursing school, it was his intention to be a healer in the "outside world" away from the reservation. After his failure in the nursing program, Jonathan sought work helping others at the adolescent facility. However, the split between his first wife, his parents, and then his second wife overwhelmed his trust that he could be a healer.

With Jonathan's agreement, Mrs. Smith set up an appointment for him with a member of his tribal community, Hosteen Begay, a nurse who works with respected *hatathli* from local clans. It was decided that Jonathan would meet with Hosteen to discuss work at the Blessingway Physician's Clinic where Western medicine and Native American practices are combined in the care of patients. When the Benally and Tsossie families heard of Jonathan's meeting with the *hatathli*, they hosted a special family dinner for him, Gladys, and Amber. They invited the elders and all members of the Benally and Tsossie clans in honor of Jonathan's and Glenna's work to rebuild their family. After the dinner, Jonathan and Glenna decided to try living together to jointly support their family with their daughter.

Session 6: Termination.   As Jonathan began to reenter family life, his dysthmia lifted and he began to have more satisfaction in his work. Consequently, he stopped the abuse of alcohol. The meetings with Hosteen Begay and the *hatathli* at the clinic gave Jonathan a renewed sense of purpose and direction. He decided to finish his degree in nursing at the University of New Mexico. By the final session of family therapy, Jonathan reported that he was discovering a new peace in his life. In addition, the renewed consistency in Jonathan's parenting had begun to help the couple build a productive relationship. Glenna and Jonathan also developed a plan with the Benally and Tsossie families to set up regular coparenting sessions arranged with his first wife and their children to bring together the grandparents, cousins, aunts, and uncles.

CHAPTER 14

Feminist Theory

Barbara Herlihy
University of New Orleans

Vivian McCollum
Albany State University

Feminist counseling and psychotherapy developed as a grassroots movement to address the unique concerns and challenges faced by women in U.S. society. This approach, which has evolved from the experiencing and thinking of women, puts gender and power at the core of the counseling or psychotherapy process. Feminist therapy is a systems approach that considers clients' social, political, and cultural contexts as factors that contribute to their problems in living. Although emphasizing gender, modern feminists recognize that gender cannot be considered separately from other cultural variables such as race or ethnicity, socioeconomic class, and sexual orientation.

BACKGROUND

Feminist theory and practice evolved from the feminist movement of the 1960s, which provided a forum for women to actively articulate their dissatisfaction with their second-class citizenship in a patriarchal social system. **Feminism**, which is the philosophical basis for feminist counseling, "aims to overthrow patriarchy and end inequities based on gender through cultural transformation and radical social change" (Brown, 1994, p. 19). One of the most vocal feminists, Betty Freidan, put a face to feminism with her book, *The Feminine Mystique* (1963). The **National Organization for Women (NOW)** was instrumental in rallying the charge to reform social structures and traditional roles for women and was a strong voice for feminism during the 1960s and 1970s.

As the feminist movement grew, many women formed groups for the purpose of **consciousness-raising** and to discuss their lack of a collective voice in politics, the workplace, economics, education, and other significant sociopolitical arenas (Kaschak, 1992; Kirsh, 1987). Consciousness-raising groups began as loosely structured meetings of women who met to discuss their shared experiences of oppression and powerlessness but soon developed into sophisticated self-help groups that empowered women and challenged the social norms of the times (Evans, Kincade, Marbley, & Seem, 2005). Feminist counseling grew from these consciousness-raising groups, which played important roles in the education, radicalizing, and mobilization of women in the early 1970s. Although consciousness-raising groups were instrumental in helping women gain personal insight, they were not as effective in producing political change (Freeman, 1989). Thus, these groups became a chief mechanism for effecting personal change and support for their members (Lieberman, Solow, Bond, & Reibstein, 1979) but left a void where broader change at a societal level was needed.

As the therapeutic value of consciousness-raising groups became evident and the need for more structured groups grew, the 1970s marked the beginning of feminist counseling as a recognized approach to psychotherapy. Feminist counseling and psychotherapy evolved, however, without being founded by a specific person, theoretical position, or set of techniques (Enns, 2004; Evans et al., 2005). This early phase of feminist counseling and psychotherapy was predicated on the assumptions that women had shared experiences of oppression and victimization and that only a proactive approach could be effective. Early feminist counselors or therapists helped name other issues facing women and worked to adapt traditional therapies to meet the needs of women.

Feminist theory progressed through three distinct phases: radical, liberal, and moderate. Early feminist theory called for a radical form of counseling and psychotherapy, using techniques that were designed to help women see that a patriarchal society was at the center of many of their problems and that change would be virtually impossible until they were empowered to feel equal and act with equal voice. **Radical feminist** counselors or therapists vigorously communicated the goals and tenets of feminism, which included (1) encouraging financial independence, (2) viewing women's problems as being influenced by external factors, and (3) suggesting that the client become involved in social action (Enns, 2004). Radical feminist counseling and psychotherapy encouraged active participation in social action groups and other social justice causes to ensure societal change that embraced gender equity.

Walstedt (as cited in Enns, 1993) called feminist counseling a "radical therapy of equals" that made it dramatically different from traditional counseling with its hierarchical composition and emphasis on advocacy and activism. The radical phase of feminist counseling theory lasted approximately 10 years and was the catalyst for the development of other grassroots counterinstitutions, such as rape crisis centers, that offered a wide range of services to women (Enns, 1993).

Not all feminists welcomed the new feminist counseling and psychotherapy. Some feminists during this period implied that feminism and counseling were incompatible because counseling involved "one up/one down politics that encouraged women to focus on pleasing the therapist rather than assuming responsibility for themselves" (Enns, 1993, p. 8). Groups became the preferred method for feminist counselors or therapists because the balance of power between the counselor or therapist and clients was more equal, with both counselor or therapist and clients receiving and giving emotional support. Many more women could be reached through groups, thereby effecting more sweeping social change (Kaschak, 1981).

The 1980s saw a further infusion of feminist thought with other counseling theories in what has been termed the **mainstreaming era** (Dutton-Douglas & Walker, 1988). The idea was to put traditional theories to a political gender litmus test and remove those parts of the traditional approaches that promote a dichotomous view of men and women (Elliott, 1999). Many early practitioners of feminist counseling or psychotherapy promoted the goal of **androgyny**, integration of both traditional masculine and feminine characteristics as an ideal of mental health (Enns, 2004). Androgyny research (Bem, 1976, 1987) and behavioral skills training (Brown, 1986) became the standard for feminist counseling. Feminist counselors or therapists were encouraged to choose from all traditional intervention methods that did not support gender-biased outcomes (Enns, 1993).

Contrarily and simultaneously, during this same era feminist counseling and psychotherapy was being defined as a separate entity (Enns, 1993). During this time, stages of feminist counseling were articulated and skills for implementing feminist counseling were presented (Ballou & Gabalac, 1984; Fitzgerald & Nutt, 1986). Also, feminist personality theory was proposed to support and integrate feminist therapeutic practices (Enns, 1993).

Feminist counseling and psychotherapy became more liberal and less radical. **Liberal feminists** emphasize different goals than their radical counterparts. Liberal feminists view counseling as a process to gain self-understanding and see the necessity for flexibility in helping the client solve problems (Enns, 2004).

Since the late 1980s, there has been a movement within feminist theory that acknowledges feminine potential, focuses on equality, and acknowledges that many of the shared problems of women are created by a society that does not value them or allow them to exercise their free will. Unlike the earlier years of feminist counseling, the tone of feminist counseling or psychotherapy has become more moderate; **moderate feminists** adapt goals espoused by both radical and liberal feminists. During the 1980s the demand for groups decreased, and individual counseling became the most frequently used form of feminist practice (Kaschak, 1981). Enns (1993) and Shreve (1989) posited that a second wave of consciousness-raising is necessary to provide knowledge and resources for women and to effectively impact many of the same social issues that plagued women in the past. This third phase of feminist development in counseling and psychotherapy is in continuous development and helps to further define and clarify the work of the feminist counselor or therapist (Enns, 2004; Walker, 1990).

Contemporary feminist counselors or therapists practice from a range of theoretical perspectives. Enns, Sinacore, Ancis, and Phillips (2004) identified four feminisms that have emerged and that focus on multiple discriminations in addition to gender. **Postmodern feminists** examine how reality is socially constructed and focus on the changing contexts in which oppression occurs. **Womanists**, a term often preferred by feminists of color, consider the interactions of sexism, classism, and racism, and work to eliminate all forms of oppression. **Lesbian feminists** believe that heterosexism is at the core of women's oppression. **Transnational** or **global feminists** seek to link women's experiences throughout the world and to address the exploitation of women worldwide. Given the variety of perspectives, it is clear that there is no singular, unified feminist theory.

Like the feminist movement itself, feminist counseling or psychotherapy has its supporters and its critics. Critics are often those who are unfamiliar with the precepts of the theories and those who harbor erroneous concepts that feminist therapy is antimale just because it is profemale. According to Ballou and Gabalac (1984) and Enns (1992), a feminist counselor or therapist is a self-professed feminist who is not prejudiced based on gender or sexual preference and who works toward social equality for women.

Because many traditional counseling practices have been harmful when used with women (hooks, 2000), feminist counselors or therapists are encouraged to continually examine their theoretical orientations from a feminist perspective (Enns, 1993). Although there are a variety of perspectives, Evans et al. (2005) have described modern feminist counseling as an approach that incorporates the psychology of women, research on women's development, cognitive behavioral techniques, multicultural awareness, and social activism into a coherent theoretical and therapeutic package.

HUMAN NATURE: A DEVELOPMENTAL PERSPECTIVE

The feminist perspective is grounded in the belief that traditional theories of human nature and human development, created by Western males in their own image, are not universally applicable. Rather, feminists believe it is essential to recognize that women and men are socialized differently and that gender role expectations begin to influence human development from the moment a child is born. These expectations are strongly embedded in the fabric of society and have such a profound impact that they become deeply ingrained in the adult personality.

Gender-role socialization has been defined as a multifaceted process, occurring across the life span, of reinforcing specific beliefs and behaviors that a society considers appropriate based on biological sex (Remer, Rostosky, & Wright, 2001). This process has limiting effects on both women and men. For example, the myths and stories we tell our children abound with sex-role stereotypes that send subtle but powerful messages that men are strong, clever, and resourceful, while women are passive, dependent, and helpless. Oedipus solved the riddle of the Sphinx; David slew the mighty Goliath with only a slingshot; Arthur pulled the sword, Excalibur, from the rock to demonstrate that he was king; and Jack climbed the beanstalk to wealth and fortune. By contrast, Rapunzel was trapped in a tower with no exits, fated to await her male rescuer; Cinderella's lot in life depended on the prince to place the glass slipper on her foot; Sleeping Beauty could awaken only when kissed back to life by a man; and Little Red Riding Hood had to be saved by the brave woodsman (Polster, 1992). There are lifelong consequences for growing girls who learn that femininity is incompatible with strength, assertiveness, competence, and for boys who learn that masculinity is incompatible with expressions of fear, dependency, emotionality, or weakness (Lerner, 1988). Some of these consequences are as follows:

- Men are encouraged to be intelligent, achieving, and assertive, and to go after what they want. Women, on the other hand, may have a kind of wisdom called "women's intuition," but they are discouraged from being intellectually challenging, competitive, or aggressive. They are expected to thread their way through a middle ground where they are encouraged to be smart enough to catch a man but never to outsmart him (Lerner, 1988). Although women in today's society are less likely than they were decades ago to be discouraged from pursuing a career, they often are still expected to put family first and subordinate their careers to the male breadwinner.

- Men are encouraged to be independent; expression of dependency needs in men may be regarded as weak or "effeminate." By contrast, women's dependency on others is less likely to be viewed in a negative light. The attractiveness of "girlish" qualities in women is reflected in the common practice of affectionately referring to women as "chicks," "girls," "dolls," or "babes" (Lerner, 1988).
- Men are expected to be rational, logical, and stoic. Women, although they are expected to be emotional, may be labeled "hysterical" when they overtly express strong emotions. For men, anger may be the only emotion that can be expressed acceptably, and then primarily as a means of control; in contrast, it is more acceptable for women to cry or to ask for help.
- Stereotyped ideals of women's sexuality value naiveté and innocence, whereas "experience" enhances a man's sexual attractiveness. In the United States, our culture sends mixed messages to young women: They are expected to be sexually attractive, with their bodies on display, yet they are discouraged from making sexual choices and developing a healthy sexual identity (Elliott, 1999). Tolman (1991) described a "missing discourse of desire" in American society, in which discussion and exploration of adolescent female sexuality are absent or discouraged.

Feminist scholars have challenged the assumptions on which gender-role socialization and **sex-role stereotyping** are based. Notable among those who have reformulated understanding of human development are Nancy Chodorow, Carol Gilligan, Jean Baker Miller and other women affiliated with the Stone Center in Massachusetts, Sandra Bem, and Ellyn Kaschak. Their contributions are discussed in the following sections.

Mother-Child Relationship

Nancy Chodorow (1978) attributed the differences between women and men to the fact that women are primarily responsible for early childcare. Thus, a girl's identity formation occurs in a context of ongoing relationship; girls experience themselves as being like their mothers, which fuses the process of attachment with the process of identity development. For boys, separation and individuation are tied to gender identity; thus, separation from the mother is essential to the development of masculinity. Because masculinity is defined through separation whereas femininity is defined through attachment, "male gender identity is threatened by intimacy, while female identity is threatened by separation" (Gilligan, 1982, p. 8).

A Different Voice

Carol Gilligan's work with Lawrence Kohlberg as a research assistant prompted her interest in women's moral development. After conducting and analyzing extensive interviews with women, she concluded that Kohlberg's model of moral development was less applicable for women than for men. She saw differences in the way women and men responded to moral dilemmas. Men generally reacted with a morality of justice that emphasized individual rights. Women tended to approach the dilemmas with a morality of care and responsibility that emphasized a concern that no one would be hurt. Noting that these concerns are embedded in a cultural context, Gilligan was concerned that traits such as compassion and caring are prized in women but at the same time are seen as a deficit in their moral development. In her book, *In a Different Voice* (1982), she asserted that concern for connectedness is central to women's development. Exploring developmental crises faced by girls at adolescence, Gilligan concluded that it is difficult for girls to maintain a strong sense of identity and "voice" when doing so would be to risk disconnection to a society that does not honor their needs and desires for relatedness and connectedness. Thus, it is necessary for women to recover and reclaim their lost voices so that they can move forward along the pathway to healthy growth and development.

Toward a New Psychology of Women

Jean Baker Miller's (1976) pioneering work focused on gender inequality and the implications for personality development of membership in dominant and subordinate groups. In her view, because women are the subordinate group in society, they develop characteristics such as passivity and dependency to help them cope with this status. Focusing on relationships of dominance and subordination, Miller concluded that women differ from men in their orientation to power. Thus, the distinctive psychology of women arises from their position of inequality. She noted that psychology has no language to describe the structuring of women's sense of self, which is organized around being able to make and maintain affiliations and relationships. Miller conceptualized this difference as holding the potential for more cooperative, more affiliative ways of living. She called for a "new psychology of women that would recognize that women have a different starting place for their development that they stay with, build on, and develop in a context of attachment and affiliation with others" (Miller, 1976, p. 83).

Self-in-Relation

The self-in-relation theory of **Jordan and Surrey** (1986) reflects a collaborative effort among women at the Stone Center in Massachusetts to reformulate women's development and psychology. Their work followed in the tradition of Miller and Gilligan who argued for the development of new concepts, language, and theories to describe and understand female development. Jordan and Surrey paid particular attention to the positive, adaptive aspects of the mother-daughter relationship and offered a new model of female development that positively redefined the mother-daughter dyad and affirmed traditional female values of nurturance and connectedness. Their model challenged traditional psychoanalytic tendencies to pathologize female development, particularly the mother-daughter relationship, and to engage in mother-blaming as a way to explain adult psychological dysfunction. Postulating that mother-daughter sameness facilitates the development of empathy and the capacity for relatedness, they saw the core self of women as including an interest in and an ability to form emotional connections with others. According to self-in-relation theory, "women organize their sense of identity, find existential meaning, achieve a sense of coherence and continuity, and are motivated in the context of a relationship" (Jordan & Surrey, 1986, p. 102).

Gender Schema

Sandra Bem's gender schema theory provides another perspective on the powerful influence of gender-role expectations on identity development. *Schema* is a term used by cognitive psychologists to describe an organized set of mental associations used to interpret perceptions (Sharf, 2000). Bem (1981, 1993) argued that **gender schema** is one of the strongest perceptual sets we use when looking at society and our place in it. When children learn society's views of gender and apply it to themselves, stereotypes of masculinity and femininity are reinforced. Children learn very early that certain behaviors are desirable for girls to be considered "feminine" and boys to be seen as "masculine." In adolescence, boys and girls tend to become highly gender focused as they become concerned with physical attractiveness and exploring their emerging sexuality. By adulthood, these gender schemas are deeply ingrained and they are limiting to both sexes.

Engendered Lives

According to **Ellyn Kaschak**, gender is the organizing principle in people's lives. In *Engendered Lives* (1992), she focused on the societal impact on gender-role development. She argued that the masculine defines the feminine; that is, men determine the roles that women play. Because women are socialized to feel rather than to act, and because society values action more than feeling, women are placed in a subordinate role.

Conclusions

Feminist scholars, by positing different models of development for women and men, have provided a better understanding of relationships and a more comprehensive portrayal of human development over the life span (Gilligan, 1982). At the same time, they have been concerned that their work might be interpreted as dichotomizing the sexes. Although the validation of women's relational skills and the recognition of the needs for connectedness and individuation are important contributions of feminist scholars, Lerner (1988) noted that it is crucial to keep in mind that *all* people develop within the context of ongoing relationships and fail to thrive in the absence of human connectedness. A circular and reciprocal relationship exists between men and women, and an appreciation of the different filters through which they perceive and experience the world can broaden understanding of human nature and human growth and development.

MAJOR CONSTRUCTS

Although feminist counselors and therapists practice in various ways depending on their approach, generally they share a commitment to a core set of principles (Enns, 2004). The most fundamental of these principles is that **the personal is political**. The basis for this belief is that the personal or individual problems that women bring to counseling or psychotherapy originate in social and political oppression, subordination, and stereotyping. Thus, the goal of feminist counseling or therapy is not only individual change, but social transformation as well. Clients' responses are not viewed as dysfunctional or as having an intrapsychic origin; rather, they are seen as ways of coping with an oppressive environment in which they have a subordinate status. Because the environment is a major source of pathology in the lives of women and other oppressed minorities, the toxic aspects of the environment must be changed if individual change is to occur. "The goal is to advance a different vision of societal organization that frees both women and men from the constraints imposed by gender-role expectations" (Herlihy & Corey, 2005, p. 350).

A second principle, intertwined with the first, is that feminist counselors and therapists share a **commitment to social change**. They work to help clients achieve a "revolution from within" and a "revolution from without" (Prochaska & Norcross, 1994). Their goal is to assist women not only to make internal, psychological changes but also to join with others in working toward social change that will liberate all members of society from subordination, oppression, and gender-role stereotyping. In feminist counseling and psychotherapy, clients are encouraged to become active in furthering social change through such means as joining political action groups or confronting sexism in their workplace. Feminist counselors or therapists work with individual clients, couples, and families, but they also have an overarching commitment to broader social change. They are themselves involved in social change in their own communities and sometimes in larger spheres.

Third, feminist counselors or therapists are committed to the establishment of **egalitarian relationships** (Ballou & West, 2000; Herlihy & Corey, 2005; Remer et al., 2001). One of the roots of women's problems is the unequal distribution of power between women and men, and between other dominant and subordinate groups. Thus, it is important for feminist counselors or therapists to establish counseling relationships in which clients are viewed as equal partners in the therapeutic endeavor who have the capacity to change in directions that they themselves select and to decide on therapeutic goals and strategies. The counselor or therapist is viewed as another source of information rather than an "expert" in the relationship. Feminist practitioners use a variety of means for sharing power with the client, including demystifying the process, self-disclosing appropriately, and paying careful attention to informed consent issues. Their twofold aim in building egalitarian therapeutic relationships is to empower the client and to model collaborative ways of being in relationship. Feminist practitioners consider it important *not* to replicate in the therapeutic relationship the power disparity that the client experiences in her larger social, economic, and political worlds.

A fourth principle of feminist counseling and psychotherapy is to **honor women's experiences** and to appreciate their perspectives, values, and strengths. The belief that underlies this tenet is that only women's unique experiences can provide a foundation of knowledge for understanding women (Elliott, 1999). Forcing women's experiences into a traditional framework that ignores their voice and status would devalue and distort both the experiences and the women themselves (Ballou & West, 2000). Instead, theories of feminist counseling and therapy evolve from and reflect the lived experiences of women that include a number of gender-based phenomena such as sexual assault, domestic violence, eating disorders, and sexual harassment. The voices of the oppressed are acknowledged as authoritative, valued, and valuable sources of knowledge (Worell & Johnson, 1997).

Fifth, feminist counselors or therapists **recognize all types of oppression**, not only those based on gender. They respect the inherent worth and dignity of every individual and recognize that societal and political inequities are oppressive and limiting to *all* people. Feminist principles have been expanded to encompass an awareness of the multiple interactions of gender with other variables that affect the lives of clients who are not members of the dominant class or racial or ethnic group. Feminists strive to be cognizant of the ways in which all people, depending on their position in a complex social matrix, are both oppressed and oppressor, both dominant and marginalized. When psychological distress is placed within a sociocultural context, it is apparent that experiences of oppression based on gender—but also on race, ethnicity, class, physical ability, age, religion, and sexual orientation—are interrelated in complex ways (Ballou & West, 2000; Remer et al., 2001).

Sixth, a goal in counseling and psychotherapy is to help clients challenge the androcentric norms that compare women to men and embrace the idea of a "woman-defined woman" (Sturdivant, 1980, p. 92) rather than for women to allow themselves to be defined by others. One of the ways that society has tended to devalue women's voices has been to prize the patriarchal norm of "objective truth" over subjective experience. Feminists call for an **acceptance of feminist consciousness,** which acknowledges diverse ways of knowing. Within this new paradigm, women are encouraged to express their emotions, trust their intuition, and use their personal experience as a touchstone for determining what is reality (Herlihy & Corey, 2005).

Finally, the feminist approach calls for a **reformulated understanding of psychological distress.** Feminist counselors or therapists reject the medical or disease model of psychopathology. The notion of psychological distress is reframed so that it is viewed as a communication about the experience of living in an unjust society. From this new perspective, psychic pain is not seen as a symptom of disease or deficit. Instead, it is defined as evidence of resistance and the will and skill to survive (Worell & Johnson, 1997). According to Brown (1994), *resistance* is a term that describes a person's ability to remain alive and strong in the face of oppression. Thus, a client's problems in living are not assumed to arise from within that individual but to derive instead from multiple sources within a complex social context.

APPLICATIONS

Overview

Counselors or therapists practice multiple forms of feminist counseling today, basing their work on the unique combination of their feminist orientation and their counseling approach (Dutton-Douglas & Walker, 1988). Therefore, feminist counseling and psychotherapy is highly personal for the practitioner as it originates in the practitioner's personal beliefs concerning the empowerment of women and changing social norms that inhibit women from self-direction. The goals of feminist counseling and psychotherapy are basically twofold: (1) to help clients understand that sociopolitical forces influence their lives and (2) to understand how women's problems can be interpreted as methods of surviving rather than as signs of dysfunction. The overall purpose, however, is to help clients change by making choices based on their own personal experiences and strengths (Enns, 2004). The process of change includes the development of self-help skills and tools that allow clients to problem solve in the absence of the counselor or therapist. The feminist counselor or therapist helps the client explore how problems exist in both personal and social contexts (Enns), thereby demonstrating that change must occur at both a personal level and a social level.

Feminist counseling or psychotherapy can be particularly effective with certain "mental disorders" that are commonly diagnosed among women in our society. Feminist counselors or therapists use a feminist analysis with alternative diagnostic systems (Kincade, Seem, & Evans, 1998). They consider the social meanings of diagnosis, broadening the focus to a more complex understanding of the client's experience and distress within a cultural context. The client is the expert member of the therapeutic dyad who is knowledgeable about her or his own distress and its social meaning (Brown, 1994).

The basic tenets of feminist counseling and psychotherapy are widely accepted. Feminist counselors or therapists practice from self-chosen models developed from their philosophical views about social justice and equality coupled with their theoretical orientation to counseling. They operate from a complex knowledge base that includes the psychology of women; counseling and psychotherapy theory; perspectives on gender, race, and class; sociopolitical change strategies; and multicultural issues (Enns, 2004). This knowledge base is reflected in the goals, intervention strategies, and research agendas of feminist practitioners.

Goals of Counseling and Psychotherapy

Change often involves developing new attitudes toward the circumstances and realities of women's and men's lives, not just adjusting to those circumstances and realities. It is the responsibility of the feminist counselor or therapist to help clients explore a full range of options available to them instead of concentrating solely on what is perceived to be the right course to take because of one's gender. Exploration might take the form of self-analysis for the client, exposure to feminist literature, or participation in consciousness-raising groups or other gender-homogenous support groups. At a societal level, uncovering emotional distress, anger, or outrage to promote social change and participating in social activism may benefit the client. Involvement in community action programs and social action activities can help the client gain experience and confidence. Enns (2004) proposed six goals for feminist counseling: equality, independence and interdependence, empowerment, self-nurturance, and valuing diversity.

Equality as a goal of feminist counseling or psychotherapy is designed to help the client gain freedom from traditional gender roles. Gaining equal status in personal relationships, economic self-sufficiency, and work equity are all components of equality. It is the role of the counselor or therapist to encourage the client to negotiate greater equality in intimate relationships, with friends, and with work colleagues. This is done through exposing the client to information regarding the unequal status and power of women and men in Western society (Enns, 2004).

Balancing **independence** (personal attributes) and **interdependence** (relational skills) has proven to be one of the most difficult goals to operationalize for feminist counselors or therapists. Balancing personal attributes and relational skills moves feminist counseling and psychotherapy away from the notion of androgyny as the model for mental health and focuses on the importance of valuing the relational skills of women. To accomplish this balance, the counselor or therapist helps the client to separate traits related to independence and interdependence from traditional perceptions about gender roles and what is considered masculine and feminine.

Empowerment is a major goal of feminist counseling and psychotherapy in that it helps clients see themselves as having control over themselves and the ability to actively advocate for others. Empowerment involves recognition that powerlessness is a learned behavior. Once clients become aware of gender-role socialization and how it relates to oppression, it is important for them to develop mechanisms to counteract the effects of sociopolitical forces that have limited their choices in life.

Self-nurturance is a pivotal goal in feminist counseling and psychotherapy. A lack of self-care causes self-doubt, lack of self-esteem, inability to develop trust relationships, and difficulty in expressing needs (Enns, 2004). Development of self-nurturance involves becoming more self-aware—aware of personal needs, personal goals, desires, and self-identity. The aim of the counselor or therapist is to help the client to experience the sense of pleasure and mastery that comes with discovering self-value.

Valuing diversity is a more recent goal designed to create an inclusive feminist approach. This goal helps the counselor or therapist and client to recognize the many ways that gender intersects with other factors in a multicultural society. Historically, feminism and feminist counseling responded to the concerns of White women. However, although women of color may experience oppressive "isms" similar to those experienced by their White counterparts, they may also suffer from a lack of power and self-direction as a result of racism. Feminist counselors or therapists work to become educated about cultural plurality among the oppressed. "Learning about women of diverse backgrounds is important not only for providing non-biased treatment, but also for enriching our knowledge of women's lives in general" (Enns, 2004, p. 30).

Process of Change

Empowerment to change is the most essential aspect of feminist counseling and psychotherapy. To change, the individual must understand and remove socialized conditioning that restricts decision making based on societal expectations of what is appropriate for men and women. A process of **resocialization** allows clients to value themselves and realize that their lived experiences are important. What was once considered pathology can be renamed as *coping mechanisms*. The client then begins a process of relearning and practicing new behaviors that promotes egalitarian relationships. Indicators of change are clients' actions to advocate for themselves and for other oppressed groups while participating in social action groups that promote societal change.

Traditional Intervention Strategies

Feminist counselors or therapists use many intervention strategies that they have adapted from the more traditional theories and approaches to counseling. All feminist counseling and psychotherapy interventions seek to empower clients. The goal is to mobilize the client's resources to effect change at the personal, relational, and sociopolitical levels. Two important empowerment strategies are demystifying counseling and self-disclosure.

Feminist counselors or therapists strive to create an egalitarian relationship with their clients so that the inequities found in society are not replicated in the counseling or therapy relationship. For example, if the counselor or therapist calls the client by his or her first name, the counselor or therapist introduces herself using her first name. A strategy for empowering clients is to **demystify** the counseling or therapy process at the outset of the relationship by paying careful attention to informed consent issues. It is important that clients participate in identifying and naming their problems; understand and agree to goals and procedures; realize that they are in charge of the direction, length, and choices of techniques to be implemented; and know their rights as consumers of services. Feminist practitioners provide their clients with information about their theoretical orientation, competencies, and alternatives to counseling or therapy so that the clients can make fully informed choices (Enns, 2004).

Feminist counselors or therapists engage in **self-disclosure** and state their values explicitly to emphasize the commonalities among women, thereby decreasing the client's sense of isolation. Brief and timely self-disclosures about the practitioner's own struggles with issues serve the purposes of modeling coping responses to difficult issues and equalizing the therapeutic relationship. Feminist practitioners share with counselors and therapists of other theoretical orientations the commitment to ensuring that self-disclosures are in the client's best interests and are relevant to the client's needs.

Reframing and **relabeling** are intervention strategies frequently used in feminist counseling and psychotherapy. To *reframe* is to change the frame of reference for looking at an individual's behavior. When feminist counselors or therapists reframe a client's behavior, they consider the sociopolitical and cultural contributions to the client's issues, which shifts the etiology of the problem from the individual to the environment. This change in perspective avoids blaming the victim for her problems. Negative labeling, such as defining a behavior as "dysfunctional," is relabeled as a "positive coping strategy." "Feminine" characteristics such as sensitivity, compassion, or subjectivity, which may be devalued as weaknesses when viewed through an androcentric lens, are revalued as strengths through the feminist lens. Thus, through reframing and relabeling, symptoms can be seen as coping mechanisms and weaknesses can be seen as strengths.

Bibliotherapy, although not unique to the feminist approach, is another strategy that feminists find useful. Bibliotherapy involves reading and processing books or articles, carefully chosen by the counselor or therapist, to help the client understand societal influences that affect her personal experiencing (Remer et al., 2001). This literature may address issues such as women's body image and appearance, sexual violence, relationships, and aspects of the life span. For example, a client concerned about her relationship with a significant other might be asked to read Lerner's *The Dance of Intimacy* (1989). Such reading assignments empower the client by increasing the client's expertise on topics of concern to her.

Another intervention strategy that has been associated with feminist counseling and psychotherapy is **assertiveness training.** Because some women do not feel powerful, they may not act assertively and thus give up some control over their lives (Sharf, 2000). Feminist counselors and therapists teach these clients assertiveness skills using direct teaching methods, bibliotherapy, and role-playing. Through assertiveness training, women learn to stand up for their rights without violating the rights of others. The aim of training is to facilitate women's use of personal power to achieve personal change and effectively challenge their environments (Remer et al., 2001).

Although much of feminist counseling and psychotherapy is conducted with individual clients, **group work** is often a preferred modality for some issues that women experience (Herlihy & Corey, 2005). For example, group approaches have been recommended for dealing with incest and sexual abuse, body image issues, battering, eating disorders, and sexual functioning (Enns, 2004). Feminist counselors or therapists may also encourage clients to participate in consciousness-raising groups to increase their awareness of sexism and other forms of oppression. Consciousness-raising groups offer women a supportive environment in which they can share personal experiences with gender-role stereotyping and expectations, experience commonalities among women, and see more clearly the link between their own experiences and sociopolitical structure (Remer et al., 2001). Other types of groups, such as advocacy groups or political action groups, may also be recommended to empower women and allow them to experience their connectedness with other women.

Some interventions used by feminist counselors and therapists are unique to the feminist approach. **Gender-role analysis** is an intervention strategy used to help clients learn about the impact of culturally prescribed gender-role expectations on women and how their lives are affected by them (Israeli & Santor, 2000). In a collaborative effort, the counselor or therapist and client examine the client's values and how these values are reflected in the client's role expectations for herself and others. They identify the explicit and implicit sex-role messages the client has experienced and internalized. They then decide which of these messages the client wishes to change. According to Brown (1986), this analysis should include exploration of (1) gender meanings in light of family values and the client's life stage, cultural background, and present conditions of living; (2) past and present rewards and penalties for gender-role conformity or noncompliance; (3) how the counselor-client relationship mirrors these issues or provides insight into them; and (4) the client's history relative to victimization. During this process, clients learn that their methods of coping have been adaptive for living in an oppressive society rather than symptoms of pathology. They develop an empathic rather than self-blaming attitude toward themselves. Thus, gender-role analysis helps clients gain self-knowledge, increase their awareness of the sociocultural basis for distress, and identify areas for desired change. After the analysis, a plan for implementing changes is developed, which may draw on cognitive-behavioral or other strategies appropriate to the client's needs.

Power analysis is an assessment and intervention strategy that aims to help women understand their devalued status in society and to help clients become aware of the power difference between men and women. The counselor or therapist may begin by educating the client about various kinds of power and women's limited access to most kinds of power. Women are often uncomfortable with the term *power* because of their limited experience or exposure to only aggressive aspects of it. The counselor or therapist may help the client understand the differences among *power over* (which implies dominance or oppression), *power within* (which involves feeling that one has inner strength), and *power to* (which refers to goal-directed behavior that respects the rights of all involved) (Gannon, 1982). The client can then offer her own definition of power and consider how it fits for her and her way of being in the world. Together, the practitioner and client identify the client's usual means of exerting her power and the effectiveness of those means. Next, they identify ways in which the client's internalized gender-role messages affect her use of power, which synthesizes gender-role and power issues for the client (Remer et al., 2001). Finally, the client is encouraged to increase her repertoire of power strategies by experimenting in areas of her life where lack of power previously prevented change. Power analysis empowers clients to challenge and change the oppressive environments in which they live (Worell & Remer, 1996).

During the past 10 to 15 years, feminist counselors and therapists have developed a more complex **integrated analysis of oppression** that recognizes that "gender cannot be separated from other ways in which a culture stratifies human difference, privileging some at the expense of others" (Hill & Ballou, 1998, p. 3). In an integrated analysis, procedures used in gender analysis and power analysis are expanded to consider the impact of other variables such as race or ethnicity, class, sexual orientation, age, size, and religion. Because diversity is a central concern of the feminist approach, a multicultural, multidimensional analysis considers variables in addition to gender in examining personal, group, and institutional oppression in clients' lives.

Brief Intervention Strategies

As a general rule, feminist counselors and therapists have not embraced the recent trend toward brief therapies for two reasons. First, the goals of feminist counseling and psychotherapy are not compatible with a "brief" approach. Deeply ingrained gender biases are not easily brought into awareness, nor are they easily changed. Second, feminist counselors and therapists are cognizant that the push for brief (sometimes even single-session) therapy has been driven in large part by the managed-care movement. Cost-saving measures that benefit the largely White-male-dominated health care corporations typically are not viewed by feminist practitioners as an appropriate rationale for selecting therapeutic interventions. This is not to suggest that feminist practitioners attempt to prolong the counseling or psychotherapy relationship unnecessarily. Clients often are encouraged to make the transition from individual counseling or therapy to a group format such as joining a support group or political action group as expeditiously as possible.

CLIENTS WITH SERIOUS MENTAL HEALTH ISSUES

Feminist counselors and therapists are concerned about problems inherent in the prevailing medical model diagnostic system of the American Psychiatric Association's *Diagnostic and Statistical Manual of Mental Disorders (DSM)*. Since Phyllis Chesler, in *Women and Madness* (1972), articulated the view that the *DSM* approach pathologizes any difference from the standards established by the dominant group in society, feminists have argued that it is important to assess not just symptoms and behaviors but also the context of women's lives (Brown, 1994; Santos de Barona & Dutton, 1997). In this broader context, many symptoms can be understood as coping strategies rather than as evidence of pathology (Worell & Remer, 1996). Thus, feminist practitioners use a broad, bio-psycho-socio-cultural-structural model of assessment and diagnosis (Ballou & West, 2000). In using this broader approach to assessment, feminist counselors and therapists have obligations to familiarize themselves with the literature on gender and its relationship to clinical judgments of mental health and to examine their own gender biases and expectations. They actively inquire into the meaning of gender for the client, assess the rewards and penalties of gender-role compliance or noncompliance for the client, attend to the client's responses to the counselor's or therapist's gender and their own responses to the client's gender, and check their diagnoses to guard against inappropriately imposing gender-stereotyped values of mental health. Arriving at a diagnosis is a shared process in which clients are the experts on their distress and its social meaning. Clients' understanding of the meaning of their behaviors is considered equally with the practitioner's interpretations, and client strengths and resiliencies are identified (Evans et al., 2005). Some of the types of distress commonly experienced by women are discussed in the remainder of this section.

According to the *DSM-IV-TR* (2000) women are twice as likely as men to suffer from **depression**. From a feminist perspective, women have twice as many reasons as men to experience depression. Women, taught to be helpless and dependent and to please others, may feel that they are not in control of their lives or their environments. Their subordinate position, along with their experiences of domestic violence, sexual or physical abuse, poverty, or harassment or sex discrimination in the workplace, can result in a sense of powerlessness that can manifest as symptoms of depression. Feminist counselors and therapists view women's depression as revealing the "vulnerabilities of a relational sense of self within a culture that dangerously strains a woman's ability to meet basic needs for interpersonal relatedness while maintaining a strong sense of self" (Jack, 1987, p. 44). They work to help clients reframe their understanding of the causes of their depression so that they can move away from blaming themselves for the problem and from believing that they must "adjust" to their circumstances. They help clients become aware of external forces that limit their freedom so that clients can release self-blame and focus their energies on circumstances they can influence (Enns, 2004).

As a result of conflicting societal messages and multiple pressures and demands, women may experience symptoms of **anxiety** disorders. Ballou and West (2000) related the example of Beth, a working-class, single mother who presented with "fear, worry, and the experience of racing and jumpy energy, all symptoms of an anxiety disorder" (p. 279). Beth was struggling to juggle at least three responsibilities: parenting young children, maintaining a home, and working at a job she did not enjoy, all within a cultural context that isolated her and devalued her status. A feminist counselor or therapist, rather than recommending an antianxiety medication, might work with Beth to help her develop concrete ways of challenging her gender-role expectations, establish a self-nurturing program, join a support group for women who are experiencing role strain, develop relaxation skills, and identify and mobilize resources that are available to help her meet ongoing responsibilities and demands.

One specific anxiety disorder that has received considerable attention in the feminist literature is **posttraumatic stress disorder** (PTSD). Feminist practitioners have identified rape trauma syndrome and battered woman syndrome as women's typical responses to traumatic environmental events. They connect the personal to the political by stressing that violence influences the psychological self and that the symptoms are normal responses to abnormal events. They have proposed new diagnostic categories, such as complex posttraumatic stress disorder (Herman, 1992) and abuse and oppression artifact disorders (Brown, 1994), to describe reactions to a history of subjugation over a period of time. A feminist counselor or therapist who is working with clients who have symptoms of PTSD addresses the connection between abuse and sexism and behavioral patterns of learned helplessness, avoidance, and rescuing. The practitioner listens respectfully to the client and does not minimize the extent to which the client has been wounded (Chesler, 1990). In the therapeutic relationship, the counselor or therapist and client explore the ways in which emotions and cognitions have become constricted or distorted by fear or gender stereotyping, self-blame, or shame. The process involves naming the distress accurately, identifying the complex contextual factors that contribute to the client's problems, and transforming possibilities for oppression into opportunities for liberation and social change.

A feminist approach to working with clients with **eating disorders** focuses on messages conveyed by society, and by the mass media in particular, about women's bodies and androcentric standards for attractiveness. Feminist counselors and therapists use gender-role analysis to help clients examine the messages about body image that are found in magazines, advertisements, movies, and television. They help clients challenge the stereotyped ideal of a woman with large breasts and pencil-thin thighs that is held up as the standard toward which they should strive. Power analysis may help women understand how they relinquish their personal power when they diet and dress to please men, as well as how their preoccupation with weight, size, and shape contributes to a lack of power (Sharf, 2000). Group work can be effective with women who suffer from anorexia, bulimia, and other eating disorders because it provides a supportive environment for examining, challenging, and reframing body image.

Feminists have drawn attention to the high rate of sexual and physical abuse in the histories of women who have been diagnosed as having **borderline personality disorder** (BPD) (Brown & Ballou, 1992). In the traditional diagnostic system, the link between these traumatic experiences and the symptoms that lead to a diagnosis of BPD is ignored and the problem is placed within the individual. Viewed from a feminist framework, BPD is a long-term chronic effect of posttraumatic stress. Rather than focusing on a client's problematic behaviors, feminist counselors and therapists frame the symptoms as indicators of the client's strength as a survivor. The counseling process involves strategies such as establishing a contract that defines expectations for both counselor or therapist and client and sets limits in nonpunitive ways. Careful consideration is given to the client's level of readiness to explore past abuse to help the client strengthen her fragile sense of control over her inner and external worlds. Symptoms such as dissociation and mood swings are reframed as ways of coping. The counselor or therapist helps the client understand the needs beneath behaviors that seem impulsive and self-defeating, so that the client can find new ways to meet these needs. Feminists continue to propose new conceptualizations of reactions to abuse with the goal of changing the way the mental health professions deal with disorders that affect so many women (Enns, 2004).

CROSS-CULTURAL CONSIDERATIONS

For the purposes of this chapter, the terms *cross-cultural* and *multicultural* will be used interchangeably to describe an approach that is integrated with many theories of counseling and psychotherapy to produce equitable practice. However, feminist counseling and multicultural counseling have remained mostly separate and disconnected movements. Historically, feminist therapy has been criticized for its lack of attention to sociocultural factors other than gender and for ignoring the contributions of "women of color who . . . have made important contributions to feminist understandings of psychotherapy that provide us with insights into our understanding of both gender and race/ethnic biases" (Espin, 1993, p. 104).

Espin (1993) pointed out this lack of acknowledgement of the contributions of women of color in the development of theory in feminist counseling and psychotherapy, as well as the omission of multiculturalism as an integral part of the development of theory and practice. Over the past decade, feminist theorists have increasingly called for cultural diversity to become a central and defining characteristic of family therapy (Brown, 1994; Enns, 2004; Whalen et al., 2004; E. N. Williams & Barber, 2004) and for an integration of the feminist and multicultural approaches to counseling and psychotherapy. The multicultural competencies developed by the Association for Multicultural Counseling and Development (AMCD) (Sue, Arredondo, & McDavis, 1992; Arredondo et al., 1996) and endorsed by American Counseling Association provide a framework for inclusive thinking and behavior. The AMCD multicultural competencies consist of 31 competency statements focusing on interpersonal interactions (Arredondo & Toporek, 2004) that encompass the counselor's or therapist's awareness, knowledge, and skills related to the cultural values, biases, and worldviews of counselor or therapist and client (Arredondo et al., 1996).

According to M. K. Williams, McCandies, & Dunlap (2002), progressive changes in the field of feminist psychology are indicative of a greater awareness by European American feminists that the concerns and experiences of women who are not European American, middle class, or heterosexual are equally valid as those who are. Effective multicultural feminist counseling and psychotherapy require knowledge and understanding of the oppressions of culturally different clients and skills that are inclusive and punctuated by culturally sensitive behavior. Important to the future of feminist counseling and psychotherapy will be the ability of its theorists, scholars, and practitioners to acknowledge the additive experiences of women of color. However, awareness and knowledge without action, such as challenging the lack of diversity within feminist ideology and challenging women to shift their cultural worldviews, will stifle progress (Williams et al., 2002).

Acknowledgment of the existence and counterproductive influence of racism, classism, heterosexism, and other oppressive behaviors on the counseling or therapy process is the first step in developing the foundation of multicultural, feminist counseling and psychotherapy. A multicultural or cross-cultural approach also recognizes the need to work for social change and advocates for the empowerment of all clients by giving a voice to the unheard (McCollum & Green, 2005).

EVALUATION

Overview

The feminist approach to counseling and psychotherapy has not been researched extensively. However, studies that have been conducted generally show positive results. Additional quantitative and qualitative research is needed to clearly establish the effectiveness of feminist counseling and psychotherapy.

Feminist counseling and psychotherapy has not been defined as clearly as some of the more traditional approaches. It is difficult to find adequate training programs. Mistaken perceptions continue to exist that feminist counseling and psychotherapy is conducted only by women and for women.

Supporting Research

The theory and practice of feminist counseling and psychotherapy have grown rapidly, outpacing their empirical support (Remer et al., 2001; Worell & Johnson, 2001). Therefore, validating the effectiveness of the feminist approach remains an ongoing challenge. Studies that have been conducted, however, generally show encouraging results.

In comparison studies, feminist counseling and psychotherapy has been found to be a distinct modality (Worell & Remer, 2003) that is as effective as other, more traditional forms of counseling (Follingstad, Robinson, & Pugh, 1977; Johnson, 1976). Recently, controlled outcome studies assessed whether feminist counseling is effective in meeting the goals it espouses. Cummings (in press) found that both brief (less than four sessions) and extended (more than seven sessions) feminist counseling positively affected clients' sense of personal empowerment. In a long-term follow-up study of feminist counseling and psychotherapy outcomes, client self-ratings of improvement over time were assessed; results indicated that clients' resilience increased over time (Chandler, Worell, Johnson, Blount, & Lusk, 1999). Olson (2001) found evidence that feminist therapy using a narrative approach is helpful in treating clients with a history of anorexia. Chrisler and Ulsh (2001) reported that bibliotherapy appears to lead to a greater client satisfaction with counseling and therapy.

Israeli and Santor (2000) evaluated existing research on several components of feminist counseling and therapy practice. They concluded that consciousness-raising appeared to be the most studied feminist intervention and that the research literature suggests consciousness-raising provides therapeutic benefit by allowing women to feel supported. Israeli and Santor recommended that future studies focus on evaluating the efficacy of other interventions and tenets of the feminist approach, such as gender-role analysis and social activism.

More research is needed to assess the effectiveness of feminist counseling and psychotherapy using qualitative techniques, which are more synchronous with feminist principles than traditional empirical methods (Evans et al., 2005). A major challenge for the future of the feminist approach is to validate the efficacy of its applied practices with research that demonstrates client change (Worell & Johnson, 2001). This challenge is complicated by the fact that feminist counseling and psychotherapy looks beyond individual change (Evans et al.) and aims to achieve outcomes that are not easily quantifiable, such as improved self-esteem and quality of life, gender-role flexibility, involvement in social action, and awareness of socialization and oppression (Chandler, Worell, & Johnson, 2000; Moradi, Fischer, Hill, Jome, & Blum, 2001).

Limitations

One limitation of feminist counseling and psychotherapy is that it is not as clearly defined as some of the more traditional theories. It has been argued that the feminist approach is not so much a theory as it is a philosophy or belief system about the importance of gender (Rampage, 1998), and that it is better defined as politics than as counseling and psychotherapy. Because feminist practitioners are diverse, reaching consensus on the scope and definition of the discipline will be a challenging task.

It is difficult to obtain adequate training in feminist counseling and psychotherapy. There are few feminist training programs per se, although many education programs have faculty members who contribute feminist principles and practices to the training of prospective counselors and therapists (Rave & Larsen, 1995). There is no official credentialing of feminist counselors and therapists.

The erroneous perception continues to exist that feminist counseling or psychotherapy is conducted only by women and for women. This may discourage male clients from seeking counseling or therapy services from those who identify themselves as feminist practitioners. The historical association of feminism with some of the more radical elements of the women's movement may discourage some prospective clients, both female and male, from entering into counseling or therapy relationships with feminist counselors or psychotherapists.

A major challenge will be to build alliances between feminist therapy and multicultural counseling, which have remained mostly separate and disconnected movements. Historically, feminist therapy has been criticized for its lack of attention to sociocultural factors other than gender. During the past decade, feminist theorists increasingly have called for cultural diversity to become a central and defining characteristic of family therapy (Brown, 1994; Enns, 2004; Whalen et al., 2004; Williams & Barber, 2004) and for an integration of the feminist and multicultural approaches to counseling and psychotherapy. Equally important to the future of feminist counseling and psychotherapy will be the ability of its theorists, scholars, and practitioners to more clearly articulate its definition, make training more widely available, correct mistaken perceptions, and demonstrate its effectiveness through research.

SUMMARY CHART—*Feminist Theory*

Human Nature

Gender-role expectations have a profound impact on human development. Because women and men are socialized differently, models of psychological development based on male development fail to recognize that women's identity develops in a context of connectedness and in relationship with others.

Major Constructs

The major tenets of feminist therapy are (1) the personal is political, (2) practitioners share a commitment to social change, (3) practitioners are committed to establishing egalitarian relationships, (4) women's experiences and voices are honored, (5) all types of oppression are recognized, (6) feminist consciousness is accepted, and (7) psychological distress is reframed.

Goals

Based on the work of Enns (2004), the major goals of feminist counseling and psychotherapy are change, equality, balancing independence and interdependence, empowerment, self-nurturance, and valuing diversity.

Change Process

External forces are recognized as the root of problems for women. Clients learn self-appreciation and self-value. Women rename pathology as coping mechanisms. They learn to change their environments rather than adjust to them. They learn to advocate for social change and to develop egalitarian rather than hierarchical relationships.

Interventions

Although feminist counselors and therapists adapt interventions from a wide range of theoretical orientations, several strategies have been developed specifically for the feminist approach: empowerment, gender-role analysis, power analysis, and integrated analysis of oppression. Other frequently used interventions are reframing and relabeling, bibliotherapy, assertiveness training, and group work. Historically, group work has been used for consciousness-raising and support.

Limitations

Feminist counseling and psychotherapy is often incorrectly perceived as being for women only. It is not as well grounded in research as some of the more traditional theories. Adequate training in feminist counseling and therapy is difficult to find.

THE CASE OF JONATHAN: *A Feminist Approach*

Jonathan's presenting issues include poor relationships with his coworkers and his supervisor, anger management, depression, sleep deprivation, loneliness, stressors related to separation from his family, financial hardship, abuse of alcohol, alienation from his cultural support system, and feelings of oppression and discrimination. Jonathan appears to be subscribing to a traditional male role.

A feminist counselor or therapist will describe to Jonathan the goals of feminist counseling or psychotherapy and her personal philosophy concerning client empowerment and the need for an egalitarian client-counselor relationship. The practitioner will help Jonathan see that he has been socialized to believe things about being a man that may not be congruent with his needs or his cultural values.

During counseling, Jonathan will be allowed to articulate in his own words the anger and frustration he experiences as a result of his poor workplace relationships. Expression of this anger may be cathartic when in a controlled environment. Additionally, his anger may be representative of his overall lack of self-appreciation and powerlessness. Jonathan exhibits symptoms of poor self-esteem and a sense of powerlessness in trying to prove himself as a valued employee to his supervisor and as a good husband and father. The counselor or therapist may use **power analysis** with Jonathan so that he can see the power differential between majority members of society and minority groups. The counselor or therapist will guide Jonathan through some **empowerment exercises** based on the reality therapy approach so that he can understand the difference between what is in his personal control and what is not. She will ask Jonathan questions such as, "What in yourself or your environment can you control or change?" After some probing by the practitioner, Jonathan might say he has control over his drinking, how he sees himself, and his sleep environment.

For the drinking issue, the counselor or therapist may recommend a 12-step program and give Jonathan verbal and written information about such programs. To improve self-esteem, Jonathan can make a list of his positive attributes and positive things that other people have said about him. The counselor or therapist will encourage the client to concentrate on these positive attributes by making verbal affirmations.

A **cognitive approach** can be used to help Jonathan make some personal changes and changes in his environment. Jonathan might be instructed to name one thing that he would like to change about himself or his environment. The practitioner and Jonathan can consider the change together to ensure that what Jonathan wants to change is in his control and that the result would be evident in a relatively short time. This will show Jonathan that he can effect change and that some things can be changed immediately. Small, immediate changes will encourage Jonathan and keep him from doubting himself.

To improve sleep, the counselor or therapist can remind the client of the benefit of sleep in developing **holistic wellness**. Suggestions might include (1) referring Jonathan to a medical doctor to determine his physical fitness; (2) reserving the bed for sleep only, not for watching television or working; (3) entering the bedroom only to go to bed; (4) developing bedtime rituals; (5) abstaining from napping; and (6) reserving sleep for the bed only. **Dream analysis** is also an appropriate technique to help Jonathan understand what his dreams mean and how they effect his interactions with people in his work environment.

Group support can help Jonathan deal with many of his issues, for example, lack of job opportunities, loneliness, alienation, societal pressures, and family issues. Jonathan has problems in his important relationships. A **homogenous group** composed of Native American men would be ideal to help Jonathan reconnect with his cultural group and gain support from their shared experiences.

Jonathan feels incapable of fulfilling commitments to marriage and to his work. It seems to be easier for him to leave than to try to change his behavior or the behavior of others. Feminist family counseling or psychotherapy with Jonathan and his wife can help them both deal with family roles, childrearing practices, and visitation issues. This will help Jonathan deal with his guilt concerning his responsibility as a father.

Individual career and financial counseling may also be helpful for Jonathan as well as contact with Jonathan's tribal council, Bureau of Indian Affairs, or other advocacy group for Native Americans. Contact with advocacy groups can help Jonathan with job seeking, finances, and feelings that external pressures are responsible for his plight. Reconnection with his tribe and cultural group will also help to improve his relationship with his family and other Native Americans from the reservation. These actions may help him reconcile his departure from the reservation.

The counselor or therapist may suggest to Jonathan that he get involved with community groups that **advocate** for Native Americans and other oppressed groups so that he can make a greater impact on society at-large. His involvement can have a dual benefit, as it can increase his self-worth as well as engage him in making societal changes. Perhaps Jonathan's efforts can help with the issue of unemployment among Native Americans living on the reservation.

The most crucial thing to consider in feminist counseling and psychotherapy with Jonathan is the need for an **egalitarian relationship**. Jonathan must feel that he has some important contributions to make to the sessions. The counselor or therapist must consider Jonathan's culturally reinforced behavior and help him to reconnect with his cultural group. Jonathan's self-worth will improve when he understands that his behavior is not a symptom of pathology but in fact may be a part of the solution to some of his problems. Jonathan's successes in understanding and reframing his anger will assist him with relationship building and be helpful to him in maintaining employment. Generally, Jonathan is aware that there are sociopolitical issues that cause roadblocks to a better life for him and his family. By better understanding what these sociopolitical issues are, Jonathan will be empowered to change his behavior and encouraged to help make broader societal changes that can benefit Native Americans and other oppressed groups.

Part III

Nontraditional Approaches

Chapters

A textbook focused on counseling and psychotherapy would not be complete without the perspectives contained in part III. All of the theoretical positions presented in part II have a foundation in Western culture. Now it is important to consider orientations that stem from Eastern philosophy and religion. Such exposure will likely broaden your perspective by presenting diverse viewpoints regarding human nature, theoretical constructs, and application of constructs based on a philosophical and religious perspective too often missing from current educational programs in counseling and psychotherapy.

Chapter 15, "Body-Centered Counseling and Psychotherapy," offers a comprehensive view of selected somatic and body-centered modalities and psychotherapy methods. Highlighted is the Hakomi body-centered psychotherapy developed by Ron Kurtz. The main Eastern philosophical influences on Hakomi came from awareness practices of yoga, Taoism, and Buddhism. These traditions are meditative and contemplative and use the practice of mindfulness to explore consciousness and its relationship to life. These traditions also concentrate on using present experience and its study to inform action. They are based on a nonviolent worldview that supports the potential for change without force. Reliance on the Buddhist meditative technique of mindfulness is central to Hakomi, and it is this aspect of Hakomi for which Kurtz says he would like to be remembered for integrating into counseling and psychotherapy.

Generally known in the literature as transpersonal psychology, transpersonal theories are discussed in chapter 16 as they apply to diagnosis and treatment of psychological problems associated with normal human development, and to difficulties associated with developmental stages beyond that of the adult ego. The practices of transpersonal theories can include discussions and interventions pertaining to spiritual experiences; mystical states of consciousness; mindfulness and meditative practices; shamanic states; ritual; the overlap of spiritual experiences with disturbed mental states such as psychosis, depression, and other psychopathologies; and the transpersonal dimensions of interpersonal relationships, service, and encounters with the natural world.

CHAPTER 15

Body-Centered Counseling and Psychotherapy

Donna M. Roy
Portland State University

Ways of alleviating psychic pain and supporting the full flowering of humanness continue to evolve and change. Today there is an increasing recognition of the relationship between mind, body, emotion, and spirit and an expanding body of exploration into this connection. Thus, psychotherapeutic approaches that target reducing the "*disharmony* of body, brain, mind, and spirit within the whole person" (Frattaroli, 2001, p. 9) and that offer a "delicate admixture of evidence and intuition" (Lewis, Amini, & Lannon, 2000, p. 12) draw more and more adherents. This chapter offers an overview of some of the current integrative modalities. Although still termed *nontraditional* and *alternative,* many **holistic approaches** are currently practiced (Corsini, 2001). These approaches are grounded in years of clinical experience, and the empirical research base is beginning to grow as theorists and clinicians recognize the pragmatism of bringing science and heart together. (Kaplan & Schwartz, 2005; Lewis et al., 2000; Loew & Tritt, 2005; Marlock & Weiss, 2005).

BACKGROUND

Three overlapping categories of alternative counseling are somatic, expressive, and transpersonal. **Somatic** or body-centered counseling or psychotherapy, which is highlighted in this chapter, focuses on reuniting the body and mind and stems from both classical theories and ancient healing approaches (Caldwell, 1997; Kurtz, 1987; Mindell, 1982). **Expressive** counseling or psychotherapy centers on externalizing, understanding, and processing internal urges, trauma material, and untapped capacities through images, sound, movement, or words (e.g., art, dance, drama, poetry, sandtray, play, music, writing, and reading therapies). **Transpersonal** methods focus on the evolution of the individual in both spiritual and personal terms; these methods use meditation, shamanic healing, spiritual counseling and psychotherapy, and mystical, altered state, or trance experiences. In this chapter, expressive and transpersonal approaches to psychological and spiritual healing are discussed only as they relate to somatic counseling or psychotherapy.

Somatic approaches to healing have broad roots in classical psychological theories, in shamanism and Eastern philosophy, in physics and systems theory, in medicine, and in education and the arts (Caldwell, 1997; Kurtz, 1987, 1990; Mindell, 1982). This eclectic foundation evolved into a paradigm that stresses holism, inclusivity, and partnership (Kurtz, 1987, 1990).

Body-centered or body-inclusive counseling or psychotherapy takes various forms that share certain common principles. Among these is the idea that a return to health requires embracing the whole human being and giving special attention to the place where the body and mind meet, the **body-mind interface** (Kurtz, 1987). Another key idea is that the open channels for expression of self, or life energy, are needed for optimal health. From this perspective, disease is created when life force is repressed or unexpressed (Caldwell, 1997). Somatic counseling or psychotherapy assumes that body posture and movement, as well as the ways we speak of and imagine the body, are clues to how we organize our experience and relate to the world. Our bodies receive and communicate information. Central to the concept of the mind-body interface is a belief in the profound effect of the body's early experiences (prenatal and perinatal) on psychological and social development (Caldwell, 1997; Keleman, 1985; Kurtz, 1990; Pesso, 1997).

This chapter presents an overview of selected somatic counseling and psychotherapy methods and highlights **Hakomi body-centered psychotherapy**, developed by **Ron Kurtz**. Although a myriad of transformational methods exists, Hakomi can serve as a primer on body-centered counseling or psychotherapy. An original and highly eclectic body-centered modality, Hakomi is active and vital throughout the Americas, Europe, New Zealand, Australia, and Japan.

Roots of Somatic Counseling and Psychotherapy

Somatic counseling or psychotherapy owes part of its development to traditions outside the realm of conventional psychology, such as **shamanic healing**, the spiritual disciplines of the East, and contemporary philsophy of science. Shamanistic cultures throughout the world have operated for millennia from these premises: (1) the mind and body are not in fact divided; (2) health comes from balance of mind, body, and spirit; and (3) there is a direct relationship between mental and physical health. Shamans practice with respect for and understanding of the connection between the body, mind, and spirit and use the generation of trance and altered states of consciousness to facilitate what essentially is a journey within to the source of healing (Halifax, 1979; Hammerschlag, 1988; Harner, 1980). This view of wholeness and the use of meditative states such as **mindfulness** are also fundamental to Hakomi and some forms of somatic counseling and psychotherapy. The importance of increasing awareness through mindfulness—a nonreactive self-observation of internal experiences—is central to the Buddhist path. In a similar way, somatic counseling or psychotherapy and other current therapies such as dialectic behavior therapy (Linehan, 1993) and mindfulness-based cognitive therapy (Germer, Siegel, & Fulton, 2005; Hayes, Follette, & Linehan, 2004) recognize the value of developing nonjudgmental self-observation capacities and related self-reflection skills (Brantley, 2003; Ecker & Hulley, 1996; Fisher, 2002; Kurtz, 1990, 2005).

Body-centered counseling and psychotherapy have learned much from the East. Spiritual disciplines such as Buddhism recognize the unity and interrelationship of all things; they see a fundamental delusion in the idea of separateness on any level. This means that we are not separate from each other, our bodies are not separate from our minds, and our minds are not divided within themselves. The splits we perceive between others and ourselves, between mind and body, and even within our minds, are delusions. Our bodies are bridges to the unconscious as well as to the outside world. Somatic counseling or psychotherapy encourages communication not only between counselor or therapist and client, but also, and equally as important, between the various internal parts of the mind, all with the goal of recognizing wholeness and interconnections within and without (Johanson & Kurtz, 1991; Kurtz, 1990).

In addition to Eastern thought and shamanistic perspective, the somatic field is heavily influenced by psychology's more conventional theorists. Freud (1955) began as a physician and saw the body, through its sensations, as directly related to psychological states. The ego, according to Freud, was a body ego. With his eventual emphasis on talking in therapy, however, the body never became central to his work; the only place it remained in analysis was on the couch as a way to reduce the client's defenses (Caldwell, 1997). Some of Freud's contemporaries gave the body more attention. Josef Breuer (Boadella, 1987) was the first to connect the discharge of energy—catharsis—with analysis. Georg Groddeck, also practicing during Freud's time, recognized the relationship of physical illness and psychological states and pioneered the combined use of diet, massage, and psychoanalysis. Sandor Ferenczi used what he saw his patients doing with their bodies to create techniques that associated movement and posture with memories and the unconscious (Caldwell, 1997; Smith, 1985).

Considered by many to be the father of somatic counseling and psychotherapy, **Wilhelm Reich** (1974), a student of Freud and Ferenczi, saw a person's psychological history in his or her body. He believed that the repression of **universal life energy** (psychic and physical energy) caused neuroses and psychoses, which in turn caused **character armoring** (i.e., rigid and chronic physical manifestations of psychological defense mechanisms). To address this armoring and treat physical rigidity, he took the controversial step of having clients use deep breathing and his touch to identify and work with blocks in the flow of body energy (Caldwell, 1997).

Research on infants by Stern (1985), Siegel (1999), and Siegel and Hartzell (2003) demonstrated the centrality of the body in development, and Aron (1998) summarized how the object-relations, intersubjective, and relational schools of the psychoanalytic tradition understand the self as "first and foremost a body-as-experienced-being-handled-and-held-by-other self . . . a body-in-relation-self" (p. 20). In their comprehensive text Marlock and Weiss

(2005) agreed, and made the case that somatic psychology has been a continuous development of psychodynamic thought and practice.

Evolution of Somatic Counseling and Psychotherapy

Somatic counseling and psychotherapy have evolved since Reich, with **bodywork** one of the offshoots. The bodywork branch of the family tree grew from the work of practitioners like Frederick Alexander (1974), Ida Rolf (1978), and Moshe Feldenkrais (1972). Their work focused on body alignment in space as well as physical balance and was not counseling or psychotherapy. Bodyworkers were not trained as counselors or psychotherapists, but they held a strong belief that bodywork would improve mental as well as physical health. Their contributions significantly influenced somatic counseling and psychotherapy (Caldwell, 1997; Kurtz, 1987, 1990).

So-called **hard techniques** (Smith, 1985) of somatic counseling and psychotherapy that evolved from Reichian theory include bioenergetics and core energetics. These methods support the expression of strong emotions and are intense forms of therapy. Therapists use exercises with clients that intensify body tensions and force their release. Alexander Lowen (1976) and John Pierrakos (1987), students of Reich, together developed **bioenergetics**, based on Reich's universal life energy and armoring theories. Bioenergetics studies the personality through the body using a systemic description of five character types (schizoid, oral, psychopathic, masochistic, and rigid) based on body movement and form (holding together, holding on, holding up, holding in, and holding back). **Core energetics**, developed by Pierrakos when he later split from Lowen, also focuses on intensifying clients' core feelings and energy to release blocks to fulfillment (Caldwell, 1997).

Gentler Forms of Body-Centered Counseling and Psychotherapy

Currently, there is a profusion of "softer," less aggressive modalities such as the Hendricks' body-centered therapy (1993), the Mindells' process work (1997), Rand and Rosenberg's integrative body psychotherapy (Rand & Fewster, 1997; Rosenberg, Rand, & Asay, 1985), and Pesso Boyden system psychomotor (Pesso, 1997). These approaches use awareness techniques and rely less on counselor or therapist analysis of body structures and movement and more on the client's experience and self-awareness. Clients are *not* encouraged to work toward explosive catharsis, are *not* put into stressful physical positions or touched invasively, and are *not* led into altered states through intensive breathing, such as in Grof's holotropic breathwork (Caldwell, 1997). These less aggressive methods still assume that transformation is the goal and have faith in the human organism's natural tendency to unfold. The methods are informed by feminist theory, which seeks to create therapeutic relationships that are based on interdependence (Jordan & Surrey, 1986) and a sharing of power (Espin & Gawelek, 1992). Two of these forms of somatic counseling and psychotherapy, which evolved from Hakomi, are briefly described next.

Sensorimotor psychotherapy, developed by Pat Ogden (1997; Ogden & Minton, 2001), evolved from Hakomi body-centered psychotherapy and Ogden's personal training as a bodyworker. It has become one of the preeminent and clinically accepted methods for working with symptoms of trauma (Ogden, 2005; Van der Kolk, McFarlane, & Weisaeth, 1996). Aligned with Hakomi philosophically and methodologically, sensorimotor psychotherapy is grounded in the use of mindfulness to study present experience as well as in belief in the client's capacity for self-regulation through processing sensory and physiological sequences. Sensorimotor psychotherapy differentiates between treatments for trauma and for developmental wounds. Specific, phase-oriented interventions are used to improve regulation of physiological and affective states, a common need among traumatized individuals. The techniques are geared toward preventing retraumatization and "uncoupling physical sensations from trauma based emotions" (Ogden, 2005). Sensorimotor psychotherapy applies the mindful approach of Hakomi to what Van der Kolk et al. (1996) termed **bottom-up processing** (as opposed to top-down processing), which titrates and metabolizes the sensations steming from noncortical areas of the brain before they can cascade into a vortex that evokes the original trauma response. Trauma work requires a high level of counselor or psychotherapist skill regarding somatics, trauma and the brain-body connection, assessment of physiological arousal, attachment theory, and the use of mindfulness.

Re-creation of the self (R-CS), developed by Hakomi Institute founding trainer Jon Eisman (1995, 2000–2001), is rooted firmly in Hakomi and is taught in Hakomi/R-CS training programs in the United States, Canada, and Europe. This counseling and psychotherapeutic method adds a detailed map of the psyche and offers an existential alternative to doing regressive work. It focuses on the innate wholeness of people and sees each person as being formed from Divine wholeness yet experiencing human separateness and fragmentation. R-CS contends that the failure to integrate our Divine nature with our human nature, coupled with later unyielding life events, leads to a fragmented perception of self. As humans, we experience trancelike states of consciousness through which we perceive our lives. The R-CS approach to counseling and psychotherapy accesses and encourages a state of aware consciousness that recognizes our innate wholeness, allows the full expression of humanness and human resources, and supports freedom from trance.

These approaches, as well as Hakomi body-centered psychotherapy, represent an evolving holistic orientation toward counseling and psychotherapy. Johanson (2005) stated that previous therapies worked with how relationships (psychodynamic), dreams (Jungian), and cognitions and behaviors (cognitive-behavioral) are organized; in contrast, somatic therapies focus on how various aspects of the body such as posture, breathing, movement, and so forth are organized. Any of these body events can reveal psychological schemas and ways of organizing as well as provide direct access to the unconscious.

Hakomi Body-Centered Counseling and Psychotherapy

Hakomi therapy is one of the original "softer" somatic psychologies and is rooted in the experiential therapies of the 1960s, Eastern philosophy, and systems theory. Its founder, Ron Kurtz, has been called a therapeutic wizard and an irreverent pragmatist (Johanson, 1987). Kurtz's postgraduate work was in experimental psychology, learning, and perception; the major influences on his early professional development included experiential learning, sensitivity training, Gestalt therapy, bioenergetics, Buddhism, Taoism, yoga, and the work of Reich, Milton Erickson, Feldenkrais, Rolf, Pesso, and Pierrakos. He taught at San Francisco State University in the 1960s, immersed himself in the evolving experiential psychology community of the time, and then worked in New York for 7 years in private practice. After his first book, *The Body Reveals* (Kurtz & Prestera, 1976), was published, Kurtz and a small group of dedicated students founded the Hakomi Institute in 1980, which is headquartered in Boulder, Colorado. Kurtz began a career as a leader of workshops and professional training (Kurtz, 1987, 1990).

The word *Hakomi* comes from the Hopi language and means roughly, "How do you stand in relation to these many realms?" It emerged from a dream of one of the original founders. The distinct relevance to the heart of Hakomi inspired the founders of the institute to embrace the dream name, and it continues to both reflect and inform the work (Kurtz, 1990).

The Western psychological roots of Hakomi, including person-centered therapy and Gestalt therapy, emphasize the counseling or therapeutic relationship and the role of experience and its study. These western therapies see value in interpersonal encounter and dialogue, but unlike their Freudian and neo-Freudian predecessors, they place more value on integrating new experiences (beyond insight) of perception and expression. Perls' (Perls, Hefferline, & Goodman, 1977) encouragement of clients to exaggerate movements or voices was a way to interrupt "any attempt to head trip" (Kurtz, 1987, p. 10) and to ground people in their present experiences. Perls' and Rogers' experiential therapies and the encounter movement of the 1960s were much less about analyzing the past and more about being in and aware of the present, and making clients more responsible for their own change processes. The body therapies (e.g., Feldenkrais) of the 1980s added the study of present experience to the recipe. Their goal was to study how experience was organized to make fundamental life changes (Kurtz, 1990).

Another key aspect of Hakomi is drawn from the work of master therapists like Milton Erickson (Erickson & Rossi, 1976) and Virginia Satir (1983). They had fundamentally positive assumptions about people and their suffering. They believed that the pain of existence comes from how a person responds to the world and that changing the way he or she perceives and responds to life also changes the experience of pain. This assumption about the nonpathology of existence is critical to Hakomi and greatly influenced its development (Kurtz, 1987, 1990). It placed Hakomi squarely in the constructivist tradition (Mahoney, 2003) of assuming people are at least cocreative in developing the filters, schemas, or core beliefs that determine their perception and expression in life.

The main Eastern philosophical influences on Hakomi came from awareness practices of yoga, Taoism, and Buddhism. These traditions are meditative and contemplative and use the practice of mindfulness to explore consciousness and its relationship to life. They also concentrate on using present experience and its study to inform action. They are based on a nonviolent worldview that supports the potential for change without force. Reliance on the Buddhist meditative technique of mindfulness is central to Hakomi, and it is this aspect of the method that Kurtz says he would like to be remembered for integrating into the field of counseling and psychotherapy (Batchelor, 1997; Johanson & Kurtz, 1991; Kurtz, 1987, 1990).

Kurtz has a background in physics and information theory and a lifelong passion for systems theory, which constitutes Hakomi's third major influence. Systems theory assumes that living systems are nonlinear, fluid, interdependent, self-organizing, self-regulating, and self-correcting. Living systems are complex and actively respond to their environments by organizing themselves in relation to them. They are alive with uncertainty, participation, variety, and change. This is an organismic and contextual, nonmechanistic view; it asserts that dynamic, multiinfluenced systems concern wholes with interrelated parts, not separate parts fabricated into wholes (Capra, 1982; Kurtz, 1990). Hakomi embraces this paradigm.

HUMAN NATURE: A DEVELOPMENTAL PERSPECTIVE

Hakomi has an unabashedly optimistic view of human nature. Along with various spiritual traditions, it views creation as good, as something that can nourish and be enjoyed with gratitude. Although it recognizes the effect of fear, pain, and primitive brain processes in human behavior, it assumes that people are fundamentally whole; when they are wounded or fragmented, they have the innate capacity to redirect themselves back toward wholeness. Hakomi begins with the view that people are not problems that need to be fixed, but complex systems that are amenable to self-correction when obstacles and threats are removed. Although a particular self-correction may need periodic updating, it represents the best a person can do at any moment, given his or her disposition, level of awareness, and existing life conditions. Like the person-centered theory of Carl Rogers, Hakomi assumes that people are fundamentally trustworthy, naturally move toward greater awareness and self-actualization, have the needed inner resources to do this, and experience unique worlds (Hazler, 1999). It does not judge someone's response to life as being deficient or fault-ridden; nor does it see defects that need curing, although it does evaluate how people might be limiting their worlds in characterologically unsatisfying ways. Hakomi assumes that people can accomplish natural self-expansion through mindfully studying how they organize their experience and making choices based on the new perspective gained from this self-study, especially when they are provided a safe, nurturing therapeutic context (Kurtz, 1987, 1990).

Hakomi presumes that an underlying interconnectedness exists among people and in the natural world and that, at the individual level, humans have a self-healing capacity. Based on the interactive integration of the mind and the body, Hakomi is at home with individual complexity and mystery. It contends that the human "default" mode of interaction is to embrace partnership rather than domination and that people would rather peacefully cooperate than use violence to dominate, although fears can trigger defensive actions. Although it acknowledges the special role of early childhood in fostering strategic responses to the world, Hakomi theory rests on the premise that psychological woundings and limitations have multiple causes. Hakomi recognizes the multiplicity of influences on human development, but it celebrates the power of the individual in the creation of his or her own life (Kurtz, 1990). Human consciousness has the self-reflective capacity to take the organization of one's life under observation compassionately and thus introduce the possibility of change. Aron (1998) argued that the "clinical study of self-reflexivity (and especially the relationship among self-reflexivity, intersubjectivity, embodiment, and trauma) is among the most promising areas of psychological research . . . taking place today" (p. 4).

Like Reich, and consistent with a holistic orientation, Hakomi counselors and psychotherapists function from the premise that past experiences create a person's character. Although Hakomi counselors and psychotherapists use information about character formation to inform their interventions, the nature of character etiology, as defined in Hakomi, is currently in a state of flux. Counselors and psychotherapists have become increasingly aware of new findings, and further questions, regarding human development and the mind from researchers such as Daniel Siegel (1999). Although character strategies help clarify why and how people learned to be, feel, and act as they do, character theory remains secondary to honoring the gradual unfolding of individual uniqueness (Eisman, personal communication, September 26, 2001; Kurtz, 1990, personal communication, August 20, 2001).

From a Hakomi perspective, character strategies evolve from interruptions of natural growth; they are primarily the result of a child's natural responses to his or her environment over time. They develop for very good reasons—as ways to deal with innate dispositions and situations of childhood—and are the ghosts of early experiences. Hakomi concurs with developmentalists who suggest normal development requires having certain experiences within critical time periods in order to proceed with healthy growth. Without critical psychological or social "experiences that need and want to happen" (Kurtz, 1990, p. 30), children miss something important: They either do not learn, or inaccurately learn, or partially learn the human social skills and attitudes that childhood is meant to teach. As a result, they develop a fear of particular current experiences because of the pain associated with the original incomplete or skewed learning experiences. They organize around not being vulnerable to the same kind of hurt again. They enter a kind of trance, sustained by neuropeptide distribution and neurological receptor sites highly sensitive to clues of the former trauma (Cozolino, 2002), that keeps them blind and powerless in the face of the original experiences' present-day reflections. These **missing core experiences** cause pain, blocks, and limiting ways of being in the world. They contribute to the creation of character patterns whose purpose is to soothe the pain of the original experience or contend with the still-present, unmet natural longing around the issue (Eisman, personal communication, September 27, 2001; Kurtz, 1987, 1990, personal communication, June 20, 2000).

People are internally complicated and use a variety of character strategies to respond to the world, so individuals cannot be defined by one strategy; they are combinations of various patterns. Different character patterns develop around different developmental learning tasks so people evolve as "constellations of character," rather than as one fixed type (Eisman, personal communication, September 26, 2001). Life unfolds, beliefs develop, experimentation happens, strategies develop, and eventually character strategies reach a certain degree of homeostasis. Functionally, they are strengths, because they helped the child deal with his or her life; practically, they can become weaknesses if overused. The overuse problem with these adaptive characterological responses to early trauma, as Freud suggested, is that even when children mature, they are not able to perceive new experiences as new. In Piaget's terms, they continue to assimilate new situations into old characterological beliefs instead of accommodating their beliefs to new information. In Hakomi, character strategies are not treated as defenses to be overcome, but as processes to be understood. These "organized, habitual patterns of reaction" (Kurtz, 1990, p. 42) can be consciously used or not, once their roots are uncovered and the missing core experiences are reclaimed (Eisman, 1987; Kurtz, 1987, 1990).

Hakomi character typologies follow a developmental model influenced by both Freud and Lowen. Hakomi incorporates Freud's tactile, oral, anal, and genital stages, applied to the developmental period from in utero to about 7 years of age, as well as Lowen's body movement and form-derived types, and suggests a number of major strategic responses to the world (Eisman, 1987; Kurtz, 1990). Table 15.1 outlines Freud's and Lowen's terms and Hakomi's character typologies, developmental time frames, related core beliefs, strategies, and longings. These typologies can easily be mapped into the schemas of Erickson's psychosocial stages, or the American Psychiatric Association's *Diagnostic and Statistical Manual of Mental Disorders,* or onto other character frameworks (Johanson, 1999, pp. 688–689).

To provide further definition for what the self is and how it evolves, the aligned R-CS method is helpful. R-CS puts an emphasis on recognizing limiting psychological states of

Table 15.1
Character Strategies in Hakomi

Neo-Freudian term	Lowen's term	Hakomi term (Kurtz/Eisman)	Relevant developmental period	Core belief	Character strategy	Natural longing
Tactile	Schizoid	Sensitive/analytic (K) Hypersensitive/withdrawn (E)	in utero to 1 year	I am not safe, so I have to withdraw from experience.	Minimize self-expression and contact with others. Take refuge in thought and fantasy.	I have a right to be alive, safe, and welcome.
Oral	Oral	Dependent/endearing (K) Abandoned/endearing (E)	birth to 2 years	I cannot get what I need, so I have to depend on others.	Seek support by acting childlike.	I have a right to need.
Oral	Compensated oral	Self-reliant (K) Alienated/self-reliant (E)	birth to 2 years	No one will help me, so I have to do it myself.	Mobilize self-support and rely on yourself. Seek challenges.	I have a right to have my needs met.
Anal	Psychopathic 1	Tough/generous (K) Hurt/invulnerable (E)	2 to 4 years	My needs will be used against me, so I have to be invulnerable and in charge.	Hide your weakness, insecurity, and fear. Look tough, act important.	I have a right to be a separate person.
Anal	Psychopathic 2	Charming/seductive (K) Betrayed/manipulative (E)	2 to 4 years	If I am honest, they will trick me, so I have to maneuver secretly around them.	Hide your true intentions. Charm others and use them to get what you need.	I have a right to be a separate person.
Anal	Masochistic	Burdened/enduring	18 months to 4 years	If I do what I want, I will hurt them, so I have to control myself and resist them to feel free.	Bear up and wait it out.	I have a right to assert myself.
Genital	Phallic	Industrious/overfocused (K) Ignored/industrious (E)	3 to 7 years	They do not see my talent, so I have to work hard to show them my worth.	Work hard, keep going, and let nothing distract you. Take refuge in action.	I have a right to relax and be loved.
Genital	Hysteric	Expressive/clinging (K) Rejected/dramatic (E)	3 to 7 years	They do not appreciate me, so I have to work hard to get their attention.	Dramatize events and feelings to get attention and avoid separation.	I have a right to be heard and understood.

Derived from Eisman, J. (2000-2001, 2001-2002), *The Hakomi method and re-creation of the self: Professional training* (available from the Hakomi Institute of Oregon, 6836 HWY 66, Ashland, OR 97520) and Kurtz, R. (1990), *Body-centered psychotherapy: The Hakomi method.* Mendocino, CA: LifeRhythm.

consciousness and making existential choices. Eisman describes an **Organic Self** as the unique and true expression of individual humanity and Divine consciousness. Its purpose is to live, learn, grow in wisdom, and develop into a unique, fully human person. It does this through the ongoing pursuit of what it wants moment to moment: the **Organic Wish**—an intention rising from a reservoir of **core knowledge** about how the world is ideally supposed to be (Eisman, 1995).

In life circumstances when this core knowledge is betrayed, or the Organic Wish meets unresolvable resistance by some kind of limiting experience, the Organic Self fragments itself into several substates of consciousness. Each of these substates represents some aspect of the dilemma and is like a self-sustained trance with its own limited view of reality (Eisman, 1995). These substates can be seen as manifestations of neural network patterns created by repeated and/or intense negative and limiting life experiences. Eisman references current brain theory regarding neural patterns and emotional states, with emphasis on the use-dependent and plastic nature of neural patterns (Lewis et al., 2000; Morgan, 2004; Perry, Pollard, Blakley, Baker, & Vigilante, 1996; Shore, 1994; Siegel, 1999). Eisman suggests that the organic state of being is accessible even within highly traumatized individuals. Just as neural networks that create negative moods, painful affective states, and various "trances" are use dependent, intentionally and repeatedly accessing preferred states can help individuals re-create themselves according to the wishes of the Organic Self (Eisman, 2005). R-CS interventions focus on helping clients recognize the felt sense of a particular neural pattern (e.g., "This is my no-one-loves-me feeling state"), notice whether the particular feeling is a preferred one or not, and develop the skill of "shifting willfully into a different neural pattern" (Eisman, 2005, p.46). In other words, although R-CS acknowledges the common human experience of being wounded and reverting to perceptions of fragmentation, it focuses on helping clients reclaim their underlying innate sense of wholeness and aliveness (Eisman, 2000–2001). Eisman's work is congruent with that of Schwartz (1995) and Almass (1988), which are also being integrated into Hakomi trainings.

MAJOR CONSTRUCTS

Organization of Experience

Foundational to Hakomi is the tenet that experience is organized and has meaning. Bateson, in *Mind and Nature* (1979), described the organization of systems and suggested that experience is more than free-flowing emotion or energy: It is energy encoded or organized by information processing schemas. Bateson went on to say that everything in nature, indeed, nature itself, has mind. All organisms that exhibit the quality of mind are parts organized into wholes, or **holons**—hierarchical systems that exhibit increasing levels of complexity. What makes minds organic with a trustworthy inner wisdom, according to Bateson, is that all parts are in communication with each other within the whole. Trouble in living organic systems stems from a lack of communication, which is why Hakomi agrees with Wilber (1977) that therapy on multiple levels can be thought of as healing splits or overcoming barriers to more inclusive communication. Minds are these kinds of information processing systems (Kurtz, 1990). From a Hakomi perspective, the concept that experience is organized and has meaning leads to the celebration of creativity and complexity and underscores the importance of holding the highest order of possibility for clients.

Additionally, humans have life experiences from conception through old age that have emotional and cognitive (and spiritual) impact, and from which we make generalizations about the world. These generalized beliefs, especially those from early childhood events and traumatic or other life-altering experiences, compose **core organizing material** that resides deep in our psyches and forms a base on which we continue to perceive and act in the world. We create feeling and meaning from these events; we begin to believe we are loved or unloved, safe or unsafe, strong or weak. We gather and meld our responses into our own truths that rule our lives. Each of us gathers and groups events and experiences to keep the flow of experience moving in particular directions. Although we are each very active in this creation of our lives, we usually are unaware of much of it (Eisman, 2000–2001; Kurtz, 1990). Thus, Hakomi is in agreement with narrative therapy about the necessity of constructing meaningful story lines to organize our experience, but Hakomi is more insistent that core narratives operate at unconscious levels not easily accessible to new story lines suggested in ordinary consciousness (Fisher, 2002). Likewise, Hakomi theory is congruent with the findings of the intersubjective psychoanalytic school (Stolorow, Brandchaft, & Atwood, 1987) that "transference is an expression of the universal psychological striving to organize experience and create meaning" (p. 46) normally held in the "prereflective unconscious" (p. 12), necessitating therapy that can make the unconscious conscious.

Lack of awareness of our own role in creating our lives is not surprising. People have learned through millennia to speed progress by developing habits that reduce the time needed to attend to repetitive actions. We are skilled in many areas of our lives at responding without having to think. Many of these automatic life responses flow from memories, beliefs, images, neural patterns, and attitudes that do not need to reach consciousness to profoundly influence our actions (Kurtz, 1990). Studying this core organizing material allows us to make these automatic habits conscious and make choices about changing the actual flow of our experience, thereby affecting implicit memory (Cozolino, 2002). Hakomi works toward helping clients uncover their organizing core beliefs and influences and wake up to themselves and their creative power. Although this study is often accompanied by strong emotions, which Hakomi honors, Hakomi emphasizes the uncovering of meaning rather than the release and expression of emotion (Kurtz, 1990).

Principles

Hakomi has basic principles that inform all of its techniques and therapeutic strategies. A counselor or psychotherapist operating in congruence with these principles, even without knowing any Hakomi techniques, would still be an effective partner in healing. The principles provide a theoretical scaffolding for the counselor or therapist to understand what is at stake and construct appropriate interventions on the spot. They provide an attitudinal foundation that communicates to the client that he or she is free, alive, and of exquisite interest. The experimental attitude the principles give rise to of curiosity, invitation, acceptance of uncertainty, receptivity, and faith in the client's unfolding, invites the unconscious to reveal itself and collaborate in the process. In contrast, working outside of these principles is, as Kurtz says, like "working blind" (1990).

The **unity principle** states that everything is interconnected, participatory, and holonic and that the idea of a separation between people and within people is false. Unity is associated with belonging and bonds because, as Kurtz says, "the universe is fundamentally a web of relationships" (1990, p. 33). Unity is also reflected in primal psychic wholeness, rather than brokenness. It assumes there is a basic healing drive toward unity in all of us. This view is very different from a mechanistic orientation that focuses on separation and isolation as fundamental human constructs and the assumption of entropy (i.e., everything is losing energy and falling apart). The unity principle assumes that we have to actively split ourselves internally and from others to perceive a world of separation. The unity principle proclaims the underlying belief, in the interconnectedness of existence, which is why Hakomi trainings always encourage therapists to network and work in interdisciplinary ways to address multiple variables (Kurtz, 1990; Wilbur, 1977).

The **organicity principle**, in line with Bateson's propositions concerning living organic systems, affirms that each organism has its own organization and self-regulation when all the parts are communicating within the whole. As such, it is not possible to "heal" another person, only to assist (or hinder) his or her own self-healing through a therapeutic relationship and appropriate interventions. This principle underscores the importance of looking within the client, within the client-counselor or client-therapist relationship, and within related systems to find insight and answers. It also reminds counselors and therapists to follow natural processes that want to unfold rather than assume authority over the client's process. The organicity principle respects the client's innate capacity for health, self-determination, and personal responsibility (Kurtz, 1990).

Mindfulness is a state of consciousness that allows nonjudgmental awareness of present experience. Some have called its use in Hakomi "assisted meditation" (Kurtz, 1990, p. 23). It is also a principle that assumes the path of consciousness is the preferred way. Psychotherapy deals with the organization of experience, and Hakomi's clinical experience is that mindfulness is the most powerful tool for being able to study and encourage transformation of that organization. In Hakomi, the **mindfulness principle** involves waiting and noticing, without taking automatic action, to allow what wants to happen to actually happen. Mindfulness allows a client to stay with his or her immediate experience long enough to gather the information needed for true change to be possible, but without being at the mercy of the experience. This is a different dynamic than either talking about one's experience as an event in the past or acting out the immediacy of one's impulses. In a mindful state, a client maintains a connection to both conscious and normally unconscious experience. Awareness becomes crystallized and offers the person a broader, witnessing view of his or her inner and outer world while also allowing awareness of his or her immediate surroundings. Mindfulness is not the same as hypnosis, which intentionally bypasses the conscious mind to go straight to the unconscious. Hakomi welcomes the conscious and unconscious as equal partners, using mindfulness to witness internal events. It is in agreement with Wolinsky (1991) that ordinary consciousness is a type of self-hypnosis trance governed by habitual, automatic processes; introducing a mindful or witnessing state of consciousness is what allows freedom from the trance.

The **principle of nonviolence** involves a basic respect for life and engenders an attitude of inclusiveness and regard for the "inevitable presence of unity and organicity" (Eisman, 2000–2001). It eschews the use of force against a living system because force creates resistance, which hinders growth. Mindfulness is the central therapeutic tool of the method, and clients simply cannot turn their awareness inward if they do not feel safe or if they feel they must defend against any kind of judgement or agenda that they have not claimed as their own. Hakomi has a particular view of nonviolence that goes beyond the conventional interpretation of the term; violence, for example, does not have to be blatant. Violence can be a counselor or psychotherapist thinking he or she knows what's best for a client, failing to truly accept a client as a self-determining, whole living system (Kurtz, 1990). It can be a practitioner denigrating or ignoring some emotion or defense that arises instead of cheerleading for deeper exploration. Hakomi affirms the nonviolence or paradoxical nondoing of Taoism (Johanson and Kurtz, 1991) and implements it within the therapeutic relationship as well as in clinical interventions.

One way Hakomi operates within this principle of nonviolence is its support of, rather than active opposition to, client "defenses." By supporting the client's tried-and-true ways of managing and protecting himself or herself, Hakomi creates a safe space for exploring these possibly outdated mechanisms and does not increase the client's need to protect himself or herself further (Johanson and Kurtz, 1991). Another nonviolent aspect of Hakomi is its focus on experience over problem solving. This allows choices to unfold naturally and the client to be the "doer" of his or her own change process. Another example is the way Hakomi invites both the client's conscious and unconscious mind to be present in sessions. This ensures that the client is not tricked or manipulated and retains full power of choice (Kurtz, 1987).

The **principle of mind-body holism** recognizes that the mind and the body reflect one another and that the mind-body system is multifaceted and unpredictable in its mutual, reciprocal influence. It is an orientation that "sees patterns and interactions and non-linear influences" (Kurtz, 1990), and is intrigued and expectant about complexity and mystery. In Hakomi, the mind-body interface is the territory most explored because it is the place where information is accessible and can evolve. This is where the counselor or psychotherapist can have a direct relationship with the unconscious. Unlike words that can conceal as much as reveal, bodily postures, gestures, muscle tones, breathing patterns, and so forth reveal core beliefs tied into deep physiological mechanisms (Johanson, 1996).

Two additional principles have been added to Hakomi training literature as a result of the experience of long-time Hakomi practitioners. These are truth, proposed by Hakomi trainer Halko Weiss, and mutability. The **principle of truth** speaks to (1) the importance of not making false promises to clients, especially to those in the altered state of consciousness called the child state (see Traditional Intervention Strategies); (2) the importance of being ethical and honest; and (3) the significance of the existential pursuit of the question "What is the truth?" for both counselor or therapist and client. It assumes such values as human wholeness, goodness, worth, and right to exist are fundamental (Eisman, 2000–2001).

The **principle of mutability** assumes that change is an inherent and absolute characteristic of reality. Things change and will continue to change. Hakomi therapy is built on the assumption that people can and want to change and will do so under certain circumstances. Hakomi embraces this concept by supporting clients in transforming their core beliefs and fully embodying and acting from their truths (Eisman, 2000–2001).

Healing Relationship

The Hakomi method assumes that it is the counselor's or psychotherapist's job to create the therapeutic relationship and that the effectiveness of counseling or therapy is embedded in the context of the relationship between counselor or therapist and client. This means that maintaining the relationship and holding an emotional attitude grounded in the principles is fundamental to doing good therapy. The importance of this relational context is gaining support in scientific quarters. Lewis et al.'s (2000) rigorous and eloquent exploration of the psychobiology of love describes how the limbic system regulates human relationships, as does Siegel's work on interpersonal neurobiology (Siegel, 1999, 2003). Both past and present limbic resonance between people shapes the brain and individual experience of the world. This relational dynamic directly supports Hakomi's reliance on loving presence (Kurtz, 2000) and the psychotherapeutic relationship as the crucial container in which growth and change happens. Likewise, the research of Mahoney (1991) on human change processes underlines the importance of the therapeutic alliance as beyond method or technique by a factor of eight.

The counselor's or therapist's attitude needs to be one of "resting in nonviolence" (Kurtz, 1990) to gain the cooperation of the client's unconscious. In addition, the counselor or therapist needs to be warm, accepting, honest, nonjudgmental, and respectful of the client's self-management. This requires a level of psychological maturity on the part of the counselor or therapist that comes from deep self-awareness. It offers the client the chance to engage with someone who has the strength and trust (Johanson and Kurtz, 1991) to back off and let the process unfold. An understanding of the client's world is also needed, as is the ability to communicate that understanding to the client in a way that rings true (Eisman, 2000–2001; Kurtz, 1990).

A therapeutic relationship is also founded on self-awareness on the part of the counselor or therapist (Yalom, 2002), and the cooperation of his or her own unconscious. In Trungpa Rinpoche's words, "full human beingness" (1983) is critical to counselor and psychotherapist effectiveness. Hakomi realizes that for counselors and psychotherapists to develop skills such as intuition and holistic seeing, it is essential to be self-aware and self-trusting. Practitioners may not need to be enlightened, but it is crucial that they be on the road toward greater self-understanding and acceptance (Kurtz, 1990).

APPLICATIONS

Overview

Hakomi is a mindful or contemplative, body-inclusive approach to counseling and psychotherapy that focuses on helping people internally reorganize their experience and thereby change how they live their lives. A therapeutic relationship based on a partnership worldview is key to success, as are techniques geared toward honoring all aspects of the client and the client's world. The following sections describe Hakomi's goals, change assumptions, intervention strategies, and client characteristics.

Goals of Counseling and Psychotherapy

Hakomi's primary healing intentions are to facilitate the unfolding of a client's experience toward core material, to offer a related transforming experience (missing experience), and to support the reorganization of the self. Interventions are aimed at affecting core material's influence on a client so he or she has the chance to transform his or her life. To do this, Hakomi techniques focus on mindfully opening and enhancing communication between mind and body, as well as unconscious and conscious. The counselor's or therapist's task is to, without force, "bring together all aspects of the person: mind/mind, mind/body and self/universe" (Kurtz, 1990, p. 33), so that change happens at the level of core material, thereby fostering maximum organic wisdom through healing any splits or barriers to inclusion, harmony, and communication within the information processing system of the mind-body (Kurtz, 1990). The end result is not in taking away any defenses from the client but in rendering them optional when appropriate, as transformation happens through new possibilities being organized in.

Process of Change

Hakomi sees change as a natural life process, like a seed gracefully unfolding into a plant. Transformative change is, however, more than just simple growth. Hakomi interventions encourage the client's evolution into his or her full humanness, into his or her greatest complexity and capacity as a system, much the same way that water braids under pressure and allows more to flow through the system. Hakomi recognizes that this kind of change requires exquisite attention to safety issues that foster the willingness to be vulnerable and the courage to move forward in spite of danger, uncertainty, and past traumas. It requires the existence of a protected and caring environment for the journey and the presence of an honest, supportive, loving therapist willing to wait and call forth what is true (Kurtz, 1990). Hakomi supports change unfolding in life-affirming ways, trusts that change wants to happen, happens in the present, and occurs when the principles are honored.

Traditional Intervention Strategies

Hakomi can be thought of as the "method of evoked experiences in mindfulness" (Kurtz, 1990). Although there are many counseling and psychotherapy methods that are humanistic, client centered, partnership oriented, and supportive, Hakomi is unique for these reasons:

- Its use of systems-based principles to ground the counselor or therapist
- A compassionate and collaborative therapeutic relationship to hold the work
- Mindfulness to empower the client, not as an adjunct to therapy but as a primary tool within the sessions (Fisher, 2002)

Present Orientation. All Hakomi techniques operate in the now, whatever the actual time frame of the event or issue under study. Hakomi respects the profound effect past experiences have on a person's perception of reality and interactions in the everyday world. Nevertheless, Hakomi methods are based on the assumption that the results of past conditioning are forming the present moment where life is happening and where insight, perceptual shifts, and new intentions can be formed. Rather than talking, even in an insightful way, for an hour about the past, a client in Hakomi counseling and psychotherapy might mindfully study current physical, emotional, or energetic responses to a body event, or a statement from the counselor or therapist, or some other intentional experiment that evolves from what is happening in the session. The counselor or therapist is more interested in present-moment indicators of the storyteller than the conscious content of the infinite variations on the story that can come from unconscious core narrative beliefs. This mindful study of experience in the present is one of the aspects of Hakomi that Kurtz (2000) suggested makes it quicker than other methods.

Kurtz posited that observation and examination of present experience are more efficient than discussion and speculation in reaching core characterological material, because ordinary consciousness is already organized and the goal is to access the level of consciousness that does the organizing.

Experimental Attitude. Hakomi is a process-oriented method of assisted self-study that assumes the goal is transformation. The ebb and flow of the process involves working mindfully with presenting issues and with created experiments that help the client spiral closer and closer to the core material that wants to be uncovered and understood. As it is the client's organicity—the natural tendency to reorganize—that is being supported, an attitude of receptivity, openness, nonjudgmentalism, and flexibility is needed. The counselor or psychotherapist has to have faith in, curiosity about, acceptance of, and eagerness for the client's natural unfolding and be able to invite, not insist (Kurtz, 1990). The counselor or psychotherapist needs to be comfortable with his or her own uncertainty in the face of the complexity of another human being and be willing to table preconceived notions of what is right for the client, trusting that the person has an innate desire and propensity to evolve (Eisman, 2000–2001). Clients need to be encouraged to enter curiously and experimentally into the mystery of new experiences and expect they might discover something they do not already know (Johanson and Kurtz, 1991). The counselor or psychotherapist often has a hypothesis and then, in collaboration with the client, creates an experimental process, gets client permission to proceed, and implements the experiment designed to help the client mindfully observe how he or she organizes in relation to it. The client and counselor or psychotherapist notice what transpires and can process or adjust to the response, develop new experiments, and further access core material. There is a lot of forgiveness or grace in the process, as any result of an experiment is valid. Whether the process confirms or disconfirms the original hypothesis, it provides new data and curiosity (Johanson, 1988) for the next step.

Managing the Process. Managing the therapeutic process using a method that emphasizes the client's organicity can be tricky, but it is as important as being in relationship with the client and more important than gathering information. The main rule of the counselor or psychotherapist is to facilitate and support the client's organic unfolding, not short-circuit the process with a static diagnosis. Within this intent, the counselor or psychotherapist has to be active at times and passive at others, both following and leading. Active taking charge directs the process by offering interventions for inducing mindfulness and for contacting, accessing, deepening, processing, transforming, and integrating client experiences. Passive taking charge creates spaciousness and an environment of letting be and allowing; it responds to the client's leads and requires the counselor or psychotherapist to be silent at critical times (Kurtz, 1990). A bias in Hakomi is Lao Tsu's counsel that the best leader follows (Johanson and Kurtz, 1991).

Managing the process brings the counselor or psychotherapist fully into the therapeutic relationship as a leader, not a dictator. Phrases such as "If it's okay with you," "How about trying . . . ?" and "Is it good to stay with this?" indicate collaboration to the client. Taking charge in Hakomi is not about controlling, ordering, or being violent toward another. It is quite the opposite of violence, in fact, for it can be violent not to act when action is called for. Taking charge in the Hakomi sense is nonviolent because it provides clear support for what the client deeply wants to happen. How the counselor or psychotherapist manages the process looks different at different points in a session: He or she creates safety and cooperation of the unconscious at the start; helps the client access and deepen his or her experience and try on new options in the middle; helps him or her learn to use the new ways in his or her life toward the end; and lets go of being in charge at the completion of the session (Eisman, 2000–2001).

Managing Consciousness. Managing consciousness is critical to Hakomi because it is a state-of-consciousness-driven modality. Without the client's ability to maintain some degree of mindfulness, self-study does not happen, so being able to induce and help a client maintain mindfulness is one of the counselor's or psychotherapist's main management jobs. Mindfulness can exist with eyes closed or open, but it is usually characterized by a slowing of breathing, a suspension of habitual reaction, and the ability to perceive, describe, and choose to neutrally witness inner experiences. To manage the immersion in this state of consciousness, the counselor or psychotherapist may need to teach the client how to be mindful, consistently return him or her to inner-directed study and body experiences, remind him or her to notice whatever happens in his or her inner world, and encourage him or her to give ongoing reports without coming out of contact with inner experience to do it.

When the client is in a state of mindfulness—an already altered state and one in which minimal input has maximal results (Schanzer, 1990)—other nonordinary states that contain core material, (e.g., the child state and emotional rapids) are more likely to occur. When this happens, the counselor or psychotherapist needs to manage the client's immersion in them as well. The final management task related to states of consciousness is to ensure the client's transition back to ordinary consciousness and safe reentry into the outside world (Eisman, 2000–2001; Kurtz, 1990).

Gathering Information. Gathering information, although important in Hakomi, is secondary to supporting the client's natural unfolding. Gathering information is not only done verbally; it also comes from tracking the client, confirming accuracy of counselor or psychotherapist perceptions, getting reports from the client, and "listening" with ears and eyes, as well as energetic, intuitive, and spiritual bodies. Clients organize around every input, so their history is continuously revealed through every reaction to a greeting, handshake, room arrangement, suggestion, or question. Intake information can certainly be sought about personal history, culture, the physical and energetic bodies, thoughts, emotions, and spirituality, as well as information on life themes and beliefs, core longings and desires, automatic defenses and strategies, degrees of congruence with the self and the outside world, and expectations and assumptions (Eisman, 2000–2001).

Categories of Experience. Hakomi values experience above all else as the door into the unconscious and core material. It works with many categories of experience that people encounter in their inner journeys: thoughts, sensations, emotions, memories, images, meanings, and beliefs (Kurtz, 1990). The theory is that all these experiences are examples of how people have created their worlds. Thus, mindfully attending to them can initiate a process of deepening awareness that leads to the level of the creator, the core beliefs that fashioned these creations.

Accessing and exploring these experiences involves being aware of clues or indicators and choosing appropriate language. The counselor's or psychotherapist's question "What are you thinking?" is bound to evoke a left-brain description, theory, or justification of a thought.

Right-brain questions or directives require clients to reference their experience as the only way of responding. The statement "Notice exactly where you feel that tension" focuses the client on his or her body sensations. Emotions can be explored with statements such as "Let that sadness get as big as it wants"; memory can be elicited with a simple "Familiar, huh?" Images may be generated by the suggestion to "Notice what you see as you stay with that." The statement "Something important about that" leads to meaning and insight; beliefs show up with a phrase such as "You start believing something about the world from this." General exploration happens with asking "What are you noticing?" or "What happens when you . . . ?" Physical contact (always done with permission), such as a touch on the hand when the client is in a mindful state, may elicit a response from any of the categories of experience. Experiences come in different types, represent different aspects of a person's world, and communicate in specific ways, but they can always be used as the start of a thread that leads from surface structure (creation) to deep structure (the creator).

Flow of the Process. Hakomi has a flow to it that both varies and stays the same. It varies in that each person has his or her own way of self-exploration and expression; it stays the same in that there are common steps that typically occur in practicing Hakomi. The following sections summarize the linear process that requires the counselor or therapist to key off of what is spontaneously evoked.

Establish a Therapeutic Relationship. For a healing relationship to be established, safety, trust, and cooperation of the conscious and unconscious are required. The initial task of the counselor or psychotherapist is to create this therapeutic container. For example, the practitioner can make **contact statements** that (1) show understanding of the client, his or her story and his or her world, (2) call attention to his or her present experience, and (3) invite the cooperation of the unconscious. A contact statement may be as simple as "Sad, huh?" if it addresses the emotional import of the storyteller and not simply the content of the story being told. Meeting the client in his or her world is what is important as well as using what the client offers. The counselor or psychotherapist needs to respect the integrity of the counselor or psychotherapist and client system by establishing appropriate boundaries (Whitehead, 1994, 1995) for taking charge of the therapeutic process, while honoring the client as the ultimate controller of his or her own life in and out of the sessions. This process presumes careful, continuous **tracking** of the client's experience—what he or she is saying and doing and what he or she is consciously and unconsciously communicating. It requires going at the client's pace, holding the best interests of the whole person, not interrogating for information, and waiting for the right time to deepen experiences (Eisman, 2000–2001; Kurtz, 1990).

Establish Mindfulness. With contact and a therapeutic alliance established, a state of relaxed, inner-directed, nonjudgmental, aware, quiet mindfulness becomes possible. This may occur simply because of the calm, simple, focused, nonjudgmental, inclusive way the counselor or psychotherapist speaks and acts. It may flow from the practitioner asking questions and giving directives that ask for experiential responses. It also may require teaching the client how to be mindful. Aspects of mindfulness such as orientation in the present, internal focus, contextual awareness, nonjudgmental self-observation, nondoing, and receptivity may be described, demonstrated, and practiced. The counselor or psychotherapist needs to be in a state of inner and outer mindfulness to be fully present, able to track the client, and wisely serve the client's needs (Kurtz, 1990).

Evoke Experiences in Mindfulness. Hakomi returns again and again to the study of present experience because it faithfully leads to core material, the organizer of experience. Counselors and psychotherapists track clients' present experience and listen for themes that want attention and offer ways to mindfully explore these experiences and themes. In addition, specific types of interventions can be proposed to evoke or deepen experience, for example, little experiments, probes, and taking over (Eisman, 2000–2001; Kurtz, 1987), all of which can be considered experiments in awareness.

A **little experiment** is a way to set up a test of what happens inside a mindful client when there is an intentional input into the client's world that is somehow related to the client's core process. The experimental attitude that considers any result as valid helps insert a degree of detachment in the process of self-study, can reduce the effects of transference in the therapeutic relationship, and allows space for lightness and flexibility. A little experiment could come, for example, from a client's difficulty with eye contact. The client might experiment with noticing his or her responses to the practitioner's looking at him or her or looking away from him or her or to himself or herself slowly turning his or her eyes toward the practitioner. The client might then deepen into a memory, a sensation, a feeling, or see an image. Whatever happens is grist for the mill and an opportunity for further study (Kurtz, 1990).

A **probe** is a verbal or nonverbal experiment in awareness delivered by the counselor or psychotherapist when the client is in a mindful state. Its wording (e.g., "Your life belongs to you") or form (e.g., a gentle touch on the arm) is based on evaluating the opposite of a limiting client belief and is potentially nourishing (although it is not the primary intent of the probe to nourish). The intent is to be truthful and to give the client's unconscious the chance to either take in some important truth or notice that he or she rejects what is offered, and then deepen curiosity into how and why it is rejected. The probe should be geared toward the particular client's process and should be used to evoke further experiences worth studying.

Although probes are most effective if customized from observing body movement, gestures, posture, and listening to a client's story, there are generic probes that relate directly to specific character strategies. For example, operating from one pattern described in Hakomi character theory, hypersensitive/withdrawn, makes it very difficult to believe the following statement: "You are safe here." Upon hearing this probe, such a client may react strongly and immediately by shaking his or her head, crying, tightening up, freezing, or withdrawing into himself or herself more. Conversely, someone not stuck in this orientation, who at least feels safe in the counselor's or psychotherapist's office, would react differently, perhaps nodding, saying he or she agrees, and visibly relaxing. Whatever the response, it provides either an opportunity for conscious integration of an important truth or material for deeper study (Kurtz, 1990).

The concept of **taking over** grew from several sources: (1) the Taoist idea of supporting the natural flow of things; (2) Feldenkrais' application of physics to therapy; (3) Pesso's use of structures; and (4) Kurtz's experience of spontaneously supporting the arched back of a woman in a workshop instead of trying to collapse it in accordance with his previous training and then his feeling of his assumptions about how to work with "defenses" transformed by her beneficial response. Taking over assumes that supporting a client's defenses, which are the natural outcome of developmental struggles and serve as protection, rather than fighting them provides safety (i.e., a way of supporting what organically arises) and leads to deeper awareness without retraumatizing the client. Taking over is based in principles that respect organic wisdom. It incorporates the Taoist principle of mutual arising that says for every force there is a counterforce, namely, automatic resistance to perceived pushing. Taking over frees the client from the work of managing or blocking some past painful experience or from having to protect himself or herself from the associated feelings. It gives the client the chance to safely experience the original event and focus deeply and singularly on its effects.

Taking over is also based on the physics of the **signal-to-noise ratio.** Lowering background noise allows a signal to be detected more clearly. Think of core material as a signal you are trying to tune into and think of your worries, tensions, anxieties, and confusions as the background noise that gets in the way. It is clear that either the signal can be increased (as in Gestalt commands to exaggerate) or the noise can be lowered to access core material. Hakomi tends toward lowering noise, which is what taking over does. A counselor or psychotherapist takes over something that the client is actively doing consistently for himself or herself, for example, clenching her fist each time she talks about her spouse. Other experiences to take over might be chronic body posture, temporary body events or sensations, spontaneous gestures, familiar limiting thoughts, beliefs or inner voices, internal conflicts, or impulses or resistance to impulses. Taking over can be done verbally or nonverbally and always includes client involvement in developing and permitting the experiment (Eisman, 2000–2001; Kurtz, 1990).

Access and Deepen. Most clients' lives reflect all the categories of experience, with some clients favoring certain ways of experiencing life over others. Hakomi respects a client's natural ways of being and doing while encouraging deepening toward core material. This deepening is sought because core beliefs, meanings, and images can be said to live "underneath" memories and emotions, which are thought of as underneath sensations and thoughts (Kurtz, 1990). A deepening spiral into core material might flow from thought (*I hate my job*), to sensation (*My neck feels tense and my stomach hurts*), to emotion (*tears of sadness*), to a memory (*My father died when I was 10*), to an image (*I see my father sitting at his desk late at night, rubbing his neck; his hand looks bloodless*), to meaning (*My father's job drained his life from him*), to belief (*I believe work will kill me, just like it killed my dad*). The process of deepening varies, of course, depending on what and how the client presents himself or herself and his or her story, and may take many interconnected spirals and periods of sustaining and processing experiences.

The **3-step method** of accessing meaning and facilitating the unfolding of experience is used over and over in a Hakomi session. The method functions as ball bearing that moves the process along. It typically engenders the spiraling process that can steer the client toward deeper meaning or, at the least, toward the continuation of "what wants to happen next." The 3-step method directs the client to (1) notice the experience, (2) stay with/immerse himself or herself in the experience, and (3) study the experience (Eisman, 2000–2001).

Accessing phrases that continually direct clients to stay with their experiences serve to maintain the inward spiral, increase focus and foster broadening of awareness, encourage a deeper felt sense of an experience, uncover meaning, and lead to further experience. Staying fully engaged in this process leads to delving deeper and deeper through the categories of experience until the core is reached and a missing core experience or felt sense of inner resource is identified. Previously described techniques, such as little experiments, probes, and taking over, as well as others, can all be used to access and deepen (Eisman, 2000–2001).

Process and Work at the Core. Powerful experiences happen when core material is reached. There is a shift from thoughts, sensations, and feelings about the present to beliefs, memories, images, and holistically felt experiences that come from the past but are awakened in the moment. This occurrence is what a shaman might consider to be the creation level of existence. The actual felt sense of a limiting core belief as well as its transformation through integrating new experiences may occur. Shifts out of mindfulness into other altered states of consciousness such as the child state or the emotional rapids are common. This is where deep character issues and the client's long held habits of self-protection may arise. Finally, a felt sense of wholeness, with no awareness of brokenness, may occur as a deep core experience and may or may not come about from retracing history, accessing painful memories, or experiencing trance states.

The **child state** is a felt experience of being young and perceiving the world from a child's orientation. It can occur, for example, when the process has evoked a body memory of a childhood experience. Sometimes it is elusive and hard to maintain; sometimes it is very intense, vivid, and full-bodied. A client in this state has the chance to complete unfinished childhood business and have important missing experiences, such as being really seen or listened to, validated, or held. Because it is not really a child in the counseling or psychotherapist's office but an adult with adult capacities, the child can tap into the adult strengths and resources (and vice versa), and integration of new insights becomes possible for the whole person (Kurtz, 1990).

Emotional rapids occur regularly in Hakomi sessions because the work centers on deep pain and strongly held beliefs. Hakomi counselors and psychotherapists want emotional release to be therapeutic not just cathartic, so they support the release of feelings and provide a safe environment to express them in, but they do not force emotional expression. Any part of a client that wants to resist expressing feelings is accepted; therefore, counselors and psychotherapists offer a nonoverwhelming, balanced way of working with emotions that allows inner study to continue. However, because supporting the resistance to expression can actually communicate safety and opportunity to the unconscious, there are times when chaotic and powerful emotions of grief, terror, or rage spontaneously and naturally explode. Their expression is then vital to the client's organicity, so Hakomi encourages counselors and psychotherapists to work differently when clients are "riding the rapids" of strong feelings than when they are in a mindful state. Kurtz suggests that, because these rapids are not compatible with mindfulness, when they occur the counselor or psychotherapist needs to fully support spontaneous behavior, let go of any attempt at self-study, and offer nourishing verbal or nonverbal contact. Return to mindful study may happen after the emotional release is complete (Kurtz, 1990).

Hakomi considers character strategies to be rooted in childhood missing experiences and to be automatic and limiting responses to the world. There is a tendency for people to fixate on a few strategies in their everyday lives, the seeds of which show up when working at the core (Eisman, 2000–2001). Although overreliance on character theory can fly in the face of organicity, knowledge of Hakomi's particular slant on Freud's and Lowen's concepts can offer a counselor or psychotherapist additional resources when working at the core.

Core material is not all painful; it also includes the experience of deep aliveness and wholeness. This felt sense can come from processing painful experiences or from making choices connected to innate aliveness. It is here that the R-CS method dovetails with Hakomi by providing a map of the psyche and ways for the counselor or psychotherapist to facilitate the tapping of client aliveness and inner resources. By recognizing the degree to which he or she feels fragmented internally and the extent of his or her longing to live differently, the client has the chance to tap into his or her innate aliveness and capacity for a fully empowered life. This energy of aliveness generally supports expansion, curiosity, existential responsibility, and truth, and it provides a resource to combat fear. It is this aliveness that generates the capacity to reject limiting trances and that, combined with clear intention and action, can lead to the Organic Self moving back to be in charge of the whole person rather than the assumed adult staying mired in the trance of brokenness (Eisman, 2000–2001). A counselor or psychotherapist who is working at a client's psychic core needs to manage interrelated and complex variables, and this process has the potential of bringing about transformational life change.

Transform, Integrate, and Complete. Transformation in a Hakomi sense is reorganization that comes when the inner resources of the self are bigger than the woundedness. From the R-CS perspective, transformation can occur when aware aliveness generates the capacity to reject limiting trances. Transformation happens in both ways, and it is both an event and a process. The event may happen in a session as working at the psychic core results in clarity about something important. It is not necessarily dramatic, although it may be accompanied with awe, joy, relief, relaxation, or strong emotions. The event is not the end; in order for real change to happen, newly realized truths need integration and nurturing both in the session and over time (Eisman, 2000–2001; Kurtz, 1990).

It is not the counselor's or psychotherapist's responsibility to force change or insist on transformation. The practitioner is called to trust the client's organicity and to create an experiential context where change has a chance. When the client's inner resources seem big enough to tip the balance toward a new belief, Hakomi counselors and psychotherapists follow the same process of experimentation that is used over and over at all stages of therapeutic work. An experiment is offered that, for example, allows the client to experience the opposite of the old belief, get unexpected permission or support, have a reality check that supports the new belief, or have a missing experience. If the experiment produces an "Aha!" response on some experiential level, the counselor or psychotherapist tracks it and works to help the client stabilize the growing new belief. This requires time to anchor the new truth and to consider and work with any life challenges around the new belief. If the experiment meets resistance, the counselor or psychotherapist needs to help the client study and work with that, not push a client who is not fully ready to change beliefs. Techniques used at this stage include savoring, stitching (tying elements together), practicing new beliefs, discussion, fantasy and imagery, anchoring (reinforcing a felt sense), storytelling, rituals or ceremonies, and suggesting homework (Eisman, 2000–2001).

Sessions often have a natural flow from ordinary consciousness to nonordinary consciousness—from studying to processing to transformation to integration—and then back to ordinary consciousness (Kurtz, 1990). The term *completion* in Hakomi refers to resolution of issues, ending counseling or psychotherapy sessions, and terminating counseling or psychotherapy. Because Hakomi operates in a paradigm that does not look for "cures," completion is seen in the context of "for now." Although the point of counseling and psychotherapy is to eliminate its need in the long term, a person's life is an ongoing evolution with needs that ebb and flow throughout his or her life span (Eisman, 2000–2001).

Brief Intervention Strategies

Hakomi is a modality that lends itself naturally to deep *and* brief approaches, primarily due to its use of mindfulness, its nonviolent orientation, and its efficiency. Its here-and-now orientation integrates developmental issues without requiring a detailed exploration of the past; yet it can result in transformation of lifelong wounds within a few sessions. Hakomi's valuing of the in-the-moment therapeutic relationship and its emphasis on self-study in mindfulness allow immediate and direct processing of both conscious and unconscious material in a way that accesses the very core of presenting problems. Similar to depth-oriented brief therapy (Ecker & Hulley, 1996), an approach that grew from a depth orientation and desire to respond to the needs of the managed-care environment, Hakomi offers a technology that can be customized to specific diagnostic needs and that allows for a specificity of focus which is often required within today's pragmatic therapeutic climate. Hakomi, through its emphasis on getting quickly to the root of the problem by its use of mindfulness, as well as its goal of facilitating an "experiential shift" (Ecker & Hulley, 1996), aligns comfortably with a model of brief therapy change.

All of the techniques described in the preceding section can be used in a brief context. Choice of experiments may be more limited in managed-care environments given the dynamics around physical touch. However, working with experiments that evoke imagination and memory can be equally as powerful. The use of mindfulness to study presenting problems, client symptoms, and attitude toward change is a fundamentally sound clinical intervention strategy, as long as it is accompanied by grounding in the Hakomi principles and the clinician has adequate related training.

CLIENTS WITH SERIOUS MENTAL DISORDERS

Before Hakomi techniques are used with clients who exhibit symptoms of specific mental health disorders, assessment of the clinical nature and severity of the client's wounding is important. In addition, mapping the goals, treatment options, time frame, medication and medical assessment needs, adjunct services, and prognosis are necessary, with or without the application of Hakomi. Seligman's (2004) 12-step process offers nonmedical practitioners detailed plans for treatment that support working in collaboration with medical and psychiatric professionals and suggest the most appropriate treatment interventions to use with specific diagnoses.

Eisman's (2005) treatment assessment paradigm offers a framework that outlines three major kinds of client woundedness (neurological, fragmented states of consciousness, and derivative experiential content), two major sources of that woundedness (missing experiences and violations), and treatment approaches that address the actual need and nature of specific client wounding. Hakomi interventions can address all three types of woundedness. It works especially well with core issues derived from developmental and other life experiences, as well as with treatment of neurologically based attachment issues, through fostering a "mindful relationship with a secure other" (Eisman, 2005, p. 49). Hakomi in conjunction with R-CS works well with experiences of fragmentation of consciousness. Eisman's assessment template allows clinicians to differentiate between trauma-based wounding, when a modality such as sensorimotor processing is most appropriate, and developmental or existential wounding, when Hakomi and R-CS are appropriate.

Many body-centered clinicians in the United States and Europe are publishing their findings and experiences in the treatment of specific disorders. New literature includes applying Hakomi and other somatic approaches to depression (Tonella, 2005b), narcissistic personality disorder (Thielen, 2005), trauma recovery (Ogden, 2005), eating disorders (Goetz-Kuhne, 2005), and psychosis (Tonnela, 2005a). In the articles of the *Hakomi Forum* to date, there are reports of using Hakomi methods with eating disorders (Moyer, 2002), jail inmates who are psychotic (Whitehead, 1992), and individuals with multiple personalities (Dall, 1995), and Johanson and

Taylor (1988) reported working with seriously emotionally disturbed adolescents. Reading these findings is a must before using Hakomi to treat any severe mental health conditions.

Clients who seek Hakomi counseling and psychotherapy exhibit a wide range of presenting diagnoses and therapeutic needs. Hakomi in pure form is appropriate for a number of neurotic conditions in which clients take responsibility for their part in their condition. However, with clients with personality disorders, that is, those who project blame and responsibility on the world around them, forms of pretherapy counseling in ordinary consciousness are required. Individuals with psychotic disorders need structure-building techniques to establish self-other boundaries, which can be done within the context of Hakomi principles. Clients with psychotic symptoms or other severe disturbances need psychiatric consultation and support if the Hakomi practitioner is not a psychiatrist. Typical Hakomi clients include children, adolescents, adults, couples, and families, and they are usually seen in private practices in the United States, and in both private practice and counseling and psychotherapy centers and clinics in Europe (Schulmeister, 2000).

CROSS-CULTURAL CONSIDERATIONS

Three categories of cross-cultural competencies approved by the Association for Multicultural Counseling and Development are (1) counselor awareness of individual cultural values and biases, (2) counselor awareness of the client's world view, and (3) culturally appropriate intervention strategies. Hakomi is well suited to any inclusive paradigm that assumes the counselor's or psychotherapist's personhood and self-awareness as a cultural being is the starting point for a cross-culturally sensitive therapeutic relationship. The "beingness" of the counselor or therapist dramatically influences the outcome of working in a cross-cultural context. Awareness of the "other" is equally as important as self-awareness. Hakomi recognizes that observing and tracking the client can lead to understanding the client's phenomenological world and that no real helping can happen without true understanding of and empathy with the client. Certainly Hakomi supports the assumption that no intervention should be undertaken unless it is clearly appropriate based on accurate connecting with and respect for the client's conscious and unconscious worlds.

Some aspects of Hakomi that require careful intentionality in a cross-cultural context include physical touch, use of altered states such as mindfulness, and the basic orientation toward an individual self separate from a community context (see the case study on Jonathan at the end of the chapter). Some cultures may be more open to aspects of Hakomi, such as use of physical touch in an experimental way, because of nonmainstream perceptions in regard to body and touch. It is important for counselors and psychotherapists to be cross-culturally aware in terms of general processes and specific content.

EVALUATION

Overview

Hakomi has contributed significantly to the field of psychotherapy and counseling. Foremost among these contributions is its use of mindfulness for experiential self-study. Although Hakomi has much in common with other experiential, person-centered, and systems-oriented approaches, it has succeeded in a unique integration of a number of elements. This integration results in an efficient modality that is appropriate for a wide range of clients. Specific interconnected elements (Kurtz, 2000) include the following:

- Mindful study of experience
- Reliance on experimentation and nonviolence
- Creation of a clear and direct relationship to the unconscious while maintaining connection to the conscious mind
- Systems approach to the person, his or her world, and the process
- Development of a partnership-oriented therapeutic relationship
- Emphasis on insight over catharsis and nourishment over suffering
- Nonjudgmental framing of "defenses" as the habitual management of experience

Supporting Research

In Europe, body-psychotherapy is a scientifically validated branch of mainstream psychotherapy. In 2000, the Hakomi Institute of Europe submitted evidence to and received validation from the European Association for Body-Psychotherapy in support of Hakomi's inclusion within this framework. Criteria included (1) evidence of theoretical coherence, clarity and organization; (2) research and client assessment capacity; (3) explicit relationship between methods and results; (4) broad treatment applicability; and (5) peer review (Schulmeister, 2000).

A major contribution to the field of body-centered psychology is the *Handbook of Body-Psychotherapy* (Marlock & Weiss, 2005), published in German. Also, much of the new research on the brain (Lewis et al., 2000), attachment (Shore, 1994; Kaplan & Scwartz, 2005), and trauma (Odgen, 2005; Van der Kolk et al., 1996) strongly supports approaches that take advantage of the effects of limbic resonance, the need for safe and secure attachments, and the interconnectedness of mind, heart, spirit, and body.

Research and evaluation methods of conventional therapies are congruent with Hakomi. For example, Carl Rogers' use of session taping as a means of evaluation has been a standard tool of Hakomi counselors and psychotherapists since the Hakomi Institute's inception, and it is often used in counselor and psychotherapist certification. In addition, Hakomi professionals contribute regularly to the thinking in the field. Over the past 20 years, the **Hakomi Forum** has published scores of articles by both Hakomi practitioners and aligned professionals on topics related to the theory, techniques, and application of Hakomi and body-centered psychotherapy.

Limitations

Hakomi is a form of psychotherapy whose implementation benefits from a certain clinical maturity and psychological sophistications; clinicians need significant training to become proficient in it. The Hakomi Institute and its affiliates have succeeded in formalizing, standardizing, and teaching the theory and techniques of Hakomi in a way that meets professional and adult learning needs, turns out skilled practitioner, and reaches a wide domestic and international audience of counselors and psychotherapists. Nevertheless, the pedagogical emphasis of performance over seat time means that getting certified in Hakomi requires a firm commitment to personal and professional development and to learning a broad range of fundamental Hakomi skills. As a result of the Hakomi Institute's review of issues around Hakomi certification, a more defined process now exists for students in the certification phase. There are currently only about 350 certified Hakomi therapists in the United States, Canada, New Zealand, Australia, Japan, Germany, Austria, Switzerland, Italy, and Great Britain.

As it has developed, Hakomi has grown into and has grown out of itself and has stayed true to its open and inclusive nature. Gaps in or opportunities to improve methodology or theory have regularly surfaced, and Hakomi has either reorganized itself or given rise to new modalities. The method has not always worked well with all clients, especially those who are severely traumatized or who frequently dissociate (Ogden, 1997). As Ogden identified the need to hone classic Hakomi in a way that served traumatized clients, sensorimotor psychotherapy developed. Another master Hakomi therapist, Eisman, who was in on the ground level of launching Hakomi, used his 20-year practice with hundreds of Hakomi clients who were not psychotic to define a phenomenon not clearly delineated in Hakomi theory. Eisman's clients exhibited inner fragmentation as well as the capacity to shift into a state of wholeness. From this client-reported, persistent evidence, the complementary re-creation of the self (R-CS) was born, which resulted in an alternative model and methodology of self-transformation. Another method used by counselors and psychotherapists to address this same limitation in Hakomi's model of the self is **Richard Schwartz's internal family systems (IFS) therapy**. IFS therapy grew out of family systems theory and posits the existence in each person of a core self and internal parts. IFS therapy works to reduce polarization of these parts and to increase inner harmony and what Schwarz calls "Self-leadership" (Schwartz, 1995).

It has been about 16 years since the publication of Kurtz's seminal Hakomi text. As of the writing of this chapter, Kurtz continues to offer in-person sessions, teach, write, and explore Buddhism, the development of the mind, the new research on the brain and its connection to affect regulation, attachment theory, sociobiology, and what it means to be human (http://www.ronkurtz.com). His work reflects his ongoing exploration and expands as his thinking evolves. For an excellent outline of Kurtz's current framing of Hakomi, see the article titled "Hakomi Simplified 2004: A New View of Ron Kurtz's Mindfulness-Based Psychotherapy" (Keller, 2005). Although Hakomi as practiced, taught, and elaborated on by Hakomi Institute trainers throughout the United States and Canada is reflected in this chapter, as a result of its responsiveness to cultural context and trainer uniqueness, it continues to evolve (http://www.hakomiinstitute.com).

SUMMARY CHART—*Hakomi Body-Centered Psychotherapy*

Human Nature

Hakomi believes in the innate wholeness and interconnectedness of individuals, each a complex self-organizing system that can self-heal. Although early childhood strongly affects psychological development, psychological limitations have many causes, and each person has the capacity to create his or her own life. Past experience does inform personality, but each individual is constantly unfolding in a unique way. Increased mindful self-study can lead to increased awareness and self reorganization.

Major Constructs

Hakomi is grounded in the precept that experience is organized and has meaning. Core organizers—memories, images, beliefs—lie buried deep in our psyches and rule our lives until we wake up to their meaning and influence and transform our relationship to them. The foundational principles of Hakomi are more important than any technique. They are unity (everything is connected), organicity (organisms self-regulate), mindfulness (nonjudgmental self-observation increases awareness), nonviolence (going with the grain honors natural unfolding), mind-body holism (mind and body affect each other unpredictably), truth (be honest and seek truth), and mutability (change will happen). The healing relationship needs to be partnership oriented and is the safe container where change can happen.

Goals

Hakomi has several goals:

- Provide a safe context to do transformative work.
- Increase communication between mind and body, conscious and unconscious.
- Facilitate the unfolding of the client's experience toward core material.
- Offer therapeutic missing experiences.
- Support the reorganization of the self, the stepping out of limiting trances, and transformation.

Change Process

Change will happen, but for healthy change to occur individuals need to be courageous and vulnerable, take risks, feel safe, and experience a loving therapeutic relationship. People live and change in the present, so interventions need to be oriented to the present. Change comes when inner resources are greater than inner pain.

Interventions

All Hakomi interventions are done with an experimental attitude that is open and curious and that seeks the unfolding of experience as well as the gathering of information. The managing of the process and of client consciousness keeps the state of consciousness appropriate to what wants and needs to happen. Establishing a healing relationship comes from making meaningful client contact and tracking client experience. Helping the client turn inward comes from teaching mindfulness. Mindfulness allows accessing and deepening into core material, where processing can happen. Accessing and processing techniques include little experiments, probes, and taking over. Processing at the core and transformation can involve the child state, the emotional rapids, character issues, missing experiences, and experiences of aliveness. Integration and completion can include savoring, practicing, imagining, role-playing, and homework.

Limitations

Several limitations of Hakomi have been identified:

- More empirical research studies are needed.
- Certification requires significant postgraduate training.

- The method continues to evolve and so can be a challenge to quantify.
- The method does not work for all clients, especially those who cannot attain a state of mindfulness or who frequently dissociate.

THE CASE OF JONATHAN: *A Hakomi Approach*

Because Hakomi interventions are based on experience that wants to happen in the moment, specific case planning is always hypothetical. Furthermore, Hakomi does not use a conventional diagnostic, cure-oriented approach to counseling and psychotherapy. Rather, it views clients as always on their own paths, not as broken beings who need fixing. Nevertheless, working effectively with Jonathan requires considering a number of issues. A counselor or psychotherapist needs to assess his or her own awareness of the Navaho culture, consider Jonathan's sense of himself as a cultural being, and look at his or her own cultural self-awareness. The practitioner needs to be able to work outside the dominant cultural paradigm in shepherding the counseling and psychotherapy process, looking, for example, at factors such as his or her beliefs regarding the standard 50-minute hour, his or her assumptions about individual versus group identity, and his or her expectations regarding counseling and psychotherapy goals. Moreover, the counselor or psychotherapist needs to take the following into consideration.

- Jonathan's tribal roots are healthy, deep, and available.
- The Navaho culture is matrilineal and, like other Native American tribes, organized around the responsibility to (and interdependence of) family and community, balance of opposites, and the importance in life of wisdom and spiritual awareness.
- Indigenous cultures often see psychological, physical, family, social, and spiritual problems as interconnected. Their worldviews are holistic and organismic.
- Native American men may hesitate to express deep emotions or disclose private material, except in specially framed grieving or spiritual contexts.
- The Navaho respect healers.

Jonathan's World

As a member of the Navaho Nation, a vital and large Native American tribe (Utter, 1993), and as a human being with varied life experiences, Jonathan is a man rich in inner and outer resources, with a unique and community-connected life purpose. He has managed his life based on his degree of connection with these inner and outer resources. His heritage, experiences, choices, and the larger environment have contributed to his current state of being.

His life story reveals that he values his Navaho culture and formal education, loves his immediate and extended families, and functions responsibly as a provider. Furthermore, he is able to consider and describe his own experience, recognizes connections between his feelings and his circumstances, pays attention to dream messages, is intelligent, and is able to self-critique. We can also infer that he feels trapped, afraid, angry, misunderstood, undervalued, unsuccessful, lacking in power, alienated from the "White man's world" and his own tribe, discriminated against, and deeply guilty about his brother's death. He is a complex man, as are all humans.

His life story speaks of fragmentation and separation from his personal, community, and, perhaps, spiritual roots, as well as of bouts of self-medication with alcohol. Although he clearly longs for success in relationships, he believes he and his actions are never quite good enough for his brother, his wives, his boss, his children, his extended family, or his tribe. He persists in being a seeker of answers, even though he repeatedly leaves and returns to marriage and the reservation without finding answers that satisfy him. He hears his dreams as they speak to him of his journey and frustration at not having the power to direct his life.

Congruence with Hakomi

Hakomi has much that lends itself to working effectively with Jonathan. The emphasis on relationship is, of course, primary. The principles of unity, organicity, nonviolence, mindfulness, and mind-body holism are congruent with tribal values of interconnectedness and relationship, balance of opposites, seeking wisdom and spiritual awareness, spirit-mind-body interconnectedness, and responsibility to the whole. The idea that responsibility to the community and the family is greater than responsibility to the self is also congruent with Hakomi. The principle of organicity recognizes that wholes are made up of parts, and healing interventions done anywhere in the system affect the whole and each of the parts. Consequently, serving the community helps the individual (and vice versa).

The fact that Hakomi's main goal is uncovering information, not expressing emotions, also indicates congruence. Too much talk and emotional disclosing can go against the Navaho cultural norm and may not be seen as useful or appropriate. Thus, the centrality in Hakomi of being in experience to gain insight—not necessarily in the form of spoken words, but possibly through a felt sense, or a vision, or an inner voice—may be more acceptable, as this insight can lead to wisdom that serves the family and community.

Establishing a Therapeutic Relationship

Knowing as much about Jonathan's world as the case description reveals, the counselor or psychotherapist can immediately focus on establishing a therapeutic relationship through building trust and creating a "container" that helps Jonathan feel comfortable, valued, hopeful, and empowered. This process involves listening to and honoring his story as well as demonstrating patience, collaboration, respect, curiosity, integrity, acceptance, empathy, and awareness. Carefully tracking Jonathan's experience in the session and contacting it in ways that show understanding and intuition can help build trust.

Mindfulness, Accessing, Processing

If congruent with Jonathan's beliefs, mindfulness can be reframed as a way to gain knowledge by tapping into the dreamtime world of resources—of allies, personal memories, and tribal wisdom. The purpose, then, can become less centered on individual awareness as the presumptive counseling or psychotherapy goal and more on community hopes and needs and Jonathan's connection to them. Mindfulness can also be presented as a way to identify and listen to important body language and messages, taking care to respect Jonathan's cultural boundaries around physical contact. The use of mindfulness to explore the interconnection in Jonathan's life of his body, mind, spirit, and community would honor his ongoing attempts to seek answers while providing a life-affirming, trustworthy method.

The melding of present and past can occur in mindfulness and can be therapeutic, an experience naturally congruent with a nonlinear worldview. In a shaman's world, intervening today can change yesterday and tomorrow. This could be relevant in working with Jonathan's guilt about his brother. When the time is right, the counselor or psychotherapist might use an experiment that has Jonathan mindfully respond to a probe such as "It's not your fault that your brother died" to evoke Jonathan's experience of himself as a 16-year-old, horrified and filled with guilt over his brother's death. The practitioner might then invite Jonathan to witness this 16-year-old from the eyes and heart of his wise adult self, or another wise ally or elder. This process could provide a missing experience of compassion and understanding and allow self-forgiveness for the 16-year-old Jonathan, thereby shifting his sense of himself as responsible for his brother's death. Jonathan may also be able to align with spiritual resources in this self-forgiveness process.

Jonathan's use of alcohol, the anger that precedes it, and his pattern of quitting school, marriages, and life on the reservation, only to return to them, can also be studied mindfully, processed respectfully, and put in a larger perspective. The use of mindfulness interspersed with a sharing of stories can lead to exploration of issues of acceptance and alienation, being and producing, racism and power, connection of anger and grief to each other and to alcohol use, fears about harming himself or others, and other life-limiting or life-enhancing possibilities. To honor the dream message coming to him, Jonathan's dream can be explored through the technique of mindful dream reentry, not analysis. The purpose would be to identify the dream people and dream elements and his relationship to them all; to help Jonathan—in an awake mindful dream state—to ask for and access the help that he needs to follow his inclinations; and then (again, in a mindful dream state) to act and respond to the results of his actions.

Integrating, Completing

Work with Jonathan needs to involve helping him integrate nonlimiting beliefs and empowering ways of being, acting, and connecting into his life. One task would be to consciously tie insights from the missing experience around his brother's death, his dream journey, and other experiments in mindfulness to his everyday life. Another would be to encourage Jonathan to do reality checks with people in his life and then explore their responses in sessions. These checks might be with his extended family concerning their belief about his innocence or guilt in his brother's death, with his wife and children regarding their sense of him as a husband and father, and with tribal elders about his value and purpose as a Navaho tribal member.

CHAPTER 16

Transpersonal Theories

Jonathan W. Carrier

Nathanael G. Mitchell

The term *transpersonal* means beyond (*trans*) the personal, ego, or self (Strohl, 1998). **Transpersonalism** is a developing and controversial field that includes a group of approaches made possible only in the late 20th century as ancient Eastern religious traditions became exposed to and eventually blended with modern psychotherapies in a historically unprecedented way (Bidwell, 1999; Sutherland, 2001). Transpersonal theory stands at the interface of mental health practice and spirituality and is one of the few approaches to integrate psychological concepts, theories, and methods with the subject matter and practices of the spiritual disciplines (Davis, 2000). Transpersonal approaches have been called "the first of modern sciences to take human spirituality seriously" and attempt a synthesis that rethinks both spirituality and the practice of counseling (Kelly, 1991, p. 430).

Generally known in the literature as transpersonal psychology, transpersonal theory as it applies to mental health practice is concerned not only with the diagnosis and treatment of psychological problems associated with normal human development, but also with difficulties associated with developmental stages beyond that of the adult ego (Kasprow & Scotton, 1999). It is the idea "that there are stages of human growth beyond the ego (hence the term transpersonal) that sets these theories apart from other models of human development and psychopathology" (Kasprow & Scotton, 1999, p. 12). The practice of transpersonal theory can include discussions and interventions pertaining to spiritual experiences; mystical states of consciousness; mindfulness and meditative practices; shamanic states; ritual; the overlap of spiritual experiences with disturbed mental states such as psychosis, depression, and other psychopathologies; and the transpersonal dimensions of interpersonal relationships, service, and encounters with the natural world (Davis, 2000).

BACKGROUND

Although transpersonal approaches have only recently gained widespread acknowledgement and discussion, William James first introduced the subjects of consciousness, spiritualism, and psychical research into the mental health field more than 90 years ago (Capra, 1992; Coon, 1992; Leahey, 1994). Much is also owed to well-known contributors such as Carl Jung and Abraham Maslow (Davis, 2000; Vich, 1988). Jung (1912/1967) was the first clinician to attempt to legitimize a spiritual approach to counseling and psychotherapy; Maslow (1968) played a central role in forming humanistic approaches and lent many of these ideas to the transpersonal movement. It was Maslow (1968) who labeled transpersonal theory the **"fourth force"** among major theories. Maslow's conceptualization of self-actualization and peak experiences, during which an individual experiences a spontaneous, ecstatic, and uni-fying state of consciousness, became a catalyzing force to the budding transpersonal move-ment (Walsh, 1994).

It was from these early humanistic tenets of self-actualization and the belief in tremen-dous human spiritual potential that transpersonalism was born. After the inception and acceptance of humanistic approaches, leaders of the field such as Maslow, Anthony Sutich, and Stanislav Grof expanded the concept of self-actualization to include the more spiritual, extraordinary, and transcendent capacities of humankind (McDermott, 1993; Peterson & Nisenholz, 1995). Thus, transpersonal theories arose to explore that the possibilities for greater mental health and human psychological experience that may be incredibly farther-reaching than mainstream science or psychological practice could or would allow for.

Although the theoretical underpinnings of transpersonal theory can be credited to a num-ber of individuals, theories, and philosophical approaches to mental health and spiritual experience, **Ken Wilber** (1977, 1980, 1981, 1983a, 1983b, 1984, 1986, 1995, 1997, 2000) has emerged as the primary leader of this burgeoning field. No serious discussion on transper-sonal theory can take place without mention of Wilber and his wealth of knowledge and pub-lished material on the subject. Transpersonal theories have become somewhat varied throughout evolution of the field; currently there are as many as five major approaches: transpersonal systems theory, altered states of consciousness, Grof's holotropic model, some types of Jungian theory, and Wilber's spectrum or integral approach (Bidwell, 1999). Wilber is the primary founder of transpersonal theory as it exists today, and his approach is arguably the most inclusive and transcendent of the major transpersonal theories. Therefore, we use his conceptualization as we consider transpersonal theory and its views on human develop-ment, psychopathology, and counseling and psychotherapy.

HUMAN NATURE: A DEVELOPMENTAL PERSPECTIVE

Transpersonalism views the development of higher consciousness as being necessary for transforming our lives, a belief universally reflected in all transpersonal theories of human development. Healthy development is marked by one's advancement from personal (pertain-ing to the self) to transpersonal (outside of the self) concerns. Wilber's (1997) transpersonal developmental model is one of the most accepted among transpersonal theorists for its ex-planation of the necessary transcendence to the transpersonal. Wilber's (1986) model essen-tially incorporates the accepted developmental stages of Freud, Jung, and Piaget with the humanistic tenet of self-actualization and Eastern religious and philosophical thought. His model is hierarchical in nature: Reality and psyche are organized into distinct levels, with "higher" levels being superior to "lower" levels in a logical and developmental sense (Kasprow & Scotton, 1999). When an individual progresses to the next level of development, the problems of the previous stage are resolved, but new developmental challenges may appear. Thus, as each new level is attained, new psychological structures and abilities emerge but so do the possibilities for new pathologies, should development fail to continue (Kasprow & Scotton, 1999).

Wilber (2000) views an individual's life as being marked by the pseudoindependent progress of several developmental lines (stages) through all levels of life and consciousness. The self attempts to manage each of the lines, which are interdependent but advance at their own paces (Bidwell, 1999). These developmental lines are broadly arranged into three groups, the prepersonal, the personal, and the transpersonal. Kasprow and Scotton (1999) explained these groups as follows:

- *Prepersonal functioning* occurs in the absence of full rational competence and a healthy, intact ego. It is instinctual and centers mainly on satisfying biological needs.
- *Personal functioning* is higher than the prepersonal and is controlled by and caters to the concerns of the ego. A sense of identity is created through thoughts and feelings about one's attachments and behavior is regulated by this identity.
- *Transpersonal functioning* is the most ideal and is associated with the diminishment of personal identification and the emergence of states of being and modes of knowing associated with levels of reality beyond personal identity.

Within the broad prepersonal, personal, and transpersonal states of functioning, a number of developmental lines, or stages, exist. These are composed of (1) cognitive stages through which the individual develops greater intuitive, emotional, and interpersonal abilities; (2) the vision logic stage, characterized by the integration of mind and body, or thought and feeling; and (3) psychic stages, the heart of transpersonal development, through which the individual's consciousness extends beyond the ego and is able to merge with what is observed, attains the ability to access archetypes, and eventually learns to travel at will along all the developmental lines (Bidwell, 1999; Kasprow & Scotton, 1999).

Wilber (1997) called this process of integrating, stabilizing, and equilibrating the different developmental lines on a horizontal level *translation*. The term *transformation,* on the other hand, means the process of transcending one consciousness (line or stage) and advancing vertically to the next. Development, then, occurs in the tension between these horizontal (translation) and vertical (transformation) dimensions or lines of human existence (Bidwell, 1999). Wilber (2000) holds that defining this spiritual line is central to the development of the individual. Spiritual growth is thus measured by the individual's ability to transcend a subjective point of view and move on to higher earthly, spiritual, and even cosmic perspectives (Bidwell, 1999). This **transcendence** is the hallmark of the integrated self and stands at the center of Wilber's transpersonal model (Bidwell, 1999). Wilber (1995) stated that this is "the cosmic evolutionary process, which is 'self development through self transcendence,' the same process at work in atoms and molecules and cells, a process that, in human domains, continues naturally into the superconscious, with precisely nothing occult or mysterious about it" (p. 258).

MAJOR CONSTRUCTS

Throughout its history, transpersonal theory evolved into a number of similar, but unique forms of practice and theory; so a discussion of the major constructs of the approach is somewhat complicated. Lajoie and Shapiro (1992) examined the transpersonal literature to elucidate the root themes of the theory. Their research uncovered 30 distinct themes across the varied theories, among which five occurred most frequently: states of consciousness, highest or ultimate potential, beyond ego or personal self, transcendence, and spiritual. Based on their research, Lajoie and Shapiro (1992) devised the following definition of transpersonal theory: "Transpersonal (theory) is concerned with the study of humanity's highest potential, and with the recognition, understanding, and realization of unitive, spiritual, and transcendent states of consciousness" (p. 91).

According to Davis (2000), the core concept of this definition and transpersonal theory is nonduality; that is, transpersonal theory is **unitive**: the recognition that each part (each person) is fundamentally and ultimately a part of the whole (the cosmos). Within this core concept are two central tenets: the intrinsic health and basic goodness of the whole and each of its parts, and the validity of self-transcendence from the personal identity to a sense of identity that is deeper, broader, and more unified with the whole (Lajoie & Shapiro, 1992; Scotton, Chinen, & Battista, 1996; Walsh & Vaughan, 1993). However, in the process of fostering transcendence and unity, transpersonal counseling or psychotherapy does not annihilate the individual; rather, it seeks to integrate psychological as well as spiritual development, the personal in addition to the transpersonal, and exceptional mental health and higher states of consciousness along with ordinary experience (Davis, 2000).

It is perhaps as easy to describe transpersonalism by how it differs from other theories of counseling and psychotherapy and development than by its similarities. Transpersonalism's distinction from the major models of human functioning rests largely on its radically different philosophical worldview (McDermott, 1993). Transpersonal psychotherapies generally do not seek to challenge or supplant other models; instead, they consider an expanded view of human nature while incorporating elements of behaviorism, psychoanalysis, humanism, Jungian analysis, and Eastern philosophy (Strohl, 1998). However, it is this very expanded view of human nature that diverges transpersonalism from the mainstream. According to Ajaya (1997), there are four distinct philosophical paradigms from which the major theories of counseling and psychotherapy and development draw:

- *Reductionistic:* understands existence by breaking down a phenomenon, tenet, or behavior into its smallest parts; views consciousness as the result of interaction between these smallest parts
- *Humanistic:* emphasizes the value and dignity of each individual and refutes the reductionistic premise that human experience can be broken down into its primitive component parts; does not, however, allow for higher states of human consciousness
- *Dualistic:* accepts that consciousness can transcend human experience; considers experience to be the result of a complementary interaction of the two primary principles of material phenomena and consciousness; believes that a material-bound being can never comprehend the scope and transcendent nature of consciousness
- *Monistic:* sees all phenomena as creative, illusory expressions of a primary and unified field of consciousness. This "pure" consciousness is the fundamental source of

all that exists, including human experience itself. According to this paradigm, human experience can attain an awaked state of consciousness where the traditional concepts of space and time and cause and effect all lose their meaning.

Transpersonal theorists generally view mainstream mental health theory and practice as being largely reductionistic and generally oblivious to the greater scope of human experience and potential (Dossey, 1999; Grof, 1985; Small, 2000; Weil, 1996). Humanistic theories, like reductionism, do not account for higher states of being; nevertheless, they are more amenable to the transpersonal approach and serve as a bridge between reductionism and the tenets of dualism and monisticism (Strohl, 1998). Of the four paradigms, transpersonalism primarily encompasses the dualistic and monistic approaches in an effort to reconcile the divine and human qualities of humankind (dualistic) as well as to uncover one's true source of being and the underlying unity of all existence (monistic) (Strohl, 1998).

According to Wilber (1993), although it differs fundamentally from most of reductionism and some aspects of humanism, transpersonalism acknowledges reductionistic (psychodynamic, behavioral, and cognitive-behavioral) and humanistic (humanistic and person-centered) approaches as legitimate theories that emphasize important areas of human development and experience. In essence, according to transpersonalists, the theories of psychoanalysis, behaviorism, humanism, and all their derivatives are effective niche approaches, but they do not account for most of human experience and existence. Transpersonal theory, on the other hand, is viewed by its followers to be truly eclectic and more encompassing, because it incorporates many viewpoints from adjacent and even opposing theories while focusing on expanded human qualities largely ignored by other theories (Bidwell, 1999; Kasprow & Scotton, 1999; Strohl, 1998).

APPLICATIONS

Overview

Ultimately, the goal of transpersonal counseling or psychotherapy is not merely the removal of psychopathologies or the resolution of interpersonal difficulties but fostering of higher human development (Kasprow & Scotton, 1999). Toward this end, transpersonal counselors and psychotherapists seek to facilitate the development of a stable, cohesive ego and the exploration of the existential self (Strohl, 1998). However, according to transpersonal theory, these processes are only part of the development of a healthy self. Individuals will not be able to become whole until they awaken to the deepest levels of human existence (Wittine, 1993). Transpersonal counselors or psychotherapists deal with "normal" client problems and life difficulties, as do practitioners from any other modality. What diverges transpersonal practitioners from the mainstream, however, is the added requisite of transcendent experience. In short, individuals are not truly healthy when they have achieved a satisfactory level of everyday functioning but when they have actually transcended the normal state of consciousness and everyday being to one that is unified with the highest levels and states of consciousness, being, and existence (Rama, Ballentine, & Ajaya, 1979; Williams, 1980; Wittine, 1993).

Essentially three dimensions apply to any approach to counseling and psychotherapy: content, process, and context (Vaughan, 1979). Content refers to the subject matter dealt with, process refers to the techniques and strategies used, and context refers to the practitioner's view toward counseling, suffering, healing, and mental health. Davis (2000) examined how these dimensions pertained to transpersonal counseling and psychotherapy:

- *Content.* The content of transpersonal counseling or psychotherapy includes transpersonal and mystical experiences, peak experiences, and spiritual emergencies (Grof & Grof, 1989; Watson, 1994).
- *Process.* The processes of transpersonal counseling or psychotherapy include practices drawn from spiritual traditions such as meditation (Goleman & Ram, 1996; Miller, 1994), initiations and vision questing (Foster & Little, 1997), ritual, and shamanic inductions (Walsh, 1990).
- *Context.* Transpersonal context includes holding in view the client's intrinsic health, being mindful and present centered regardless of the particular content or processes, approaching counseling or psychotherapy as both an act of service and an act of work on oneself, and recognizing nonduality in the counseling or therapy situation (Wittine, 1989).

Throughout the content, process, and context of counseling or psychotherapy, the goals of transpersonal counseling and psychotherapy are much the same as those any other approach: to aid individuals with a myriad of mental health issues and life difficulties. However, transpersonal counselors or therapists are most concerned with fostering a deepening and integration of a person's sense of connectedness, whether it be with self, community, nature, or the entire cosmos (Bidwell, 1999; Davis, 2000; Kasprow & Scotton, 1999). Regardless of the life difficulty or psychological problem at hand, transpersonal counseling or psychotherapy will almost always seek to send the client inward (Bidwell, 1999). "The more one can introspect and reflect on one's self, then the more detached from that self one can become, the more one can rise above that self's limited perspective, and so the less narcissistic or less egocentric one becomes (or the more de-centered one becomes)" (Wilber, 1995, p. 256).

Transpersonal practitioners generally accept that most people are unwilling, unable, or simply not ready to work at a transpersonal and transcendent level. Wilber stated (1997) that in America, "a disproportionately large number of people who are drawn to transpersonal spirituality are often at a preconventional level of self development. This means that much of what American (spiritual) teachers (and counselors) have to do is actually engage in supportive psychotherapy, not transformative and transpersonal spirituality" (p. 227). Thus, one of the primary goals of transpersonal counseling or psychotherapy is to bring the client to a point where he or she can begin to work on transpersonal issues. It is simply not enough in the transpersonal counselor's or therapist's mind to bring a client to an acceptable or "healthy" level of mental health. If given the chance, the transpersonal counselor or therapist will always seek to go beyond this mark into the realm of transcendence, unity, and extraordinary mental health.

Process of Change

Mistakenly, it is often thought that transpersonal counseling or psychotherapy is oriented solely toward spiritual transcendence. Transpersonal leader Sylvia Boorstein (1996) warned against this, stating that zeal for work in the transpersonal realm should not come at the expense of overlooking relevant personal issues. If a counselor or therapist glosses over the client's personal problems without working through them and making them fully conscious, there will be no foundation from which spiritual work can begin (Small, 2000). In essence, it is impossible to transcend something that has never developed or become integrated (Small, 2000). Thus, the process of change in transpersonal counseling or psychotherapy is marked by the overcoming of personal problems and life issues, which allows for primary work toward spiritual integration. As the client moves from normal functioning to transpersonal work, the process of unification and deepening the experience of connection usually engenders the highest human qualities, such as creativity, compassion, selflessness, and wisdom, all of which are indicative of psychological health and adjustment (Kasprow & Scotton, 1999).

Traditional Intervention Strategies

Wilber (2000) called for an **integrative therapy** that takes a holistic approach: investigating and addressing each of the developmental lines (stages) and using interventions that range from changing nutrition and exercise to cognitive restructuring or Jungian individuation to specific spiritual disciplines, depending on the client's developmental stage and pathologies. The transpersonal counselor or therapist must be ready to draw from all traditions, both Eastern and Western. "A truly integrative and encompassing psychology can and should make use of the complementary insights offered by each school of psychology" (Wilber, 1977, p. 15). According to Wilber (1997), the transpersonal counselor or therapist must be an expert in most forms of intervention, regardless of the theoretical modality. This extent of expertise is necessary because guiding clients through the maze of developmental possibilities is certain to require a wide range of interventions, based on the client's personality, lifestyle, and personal experiences.

The core practice of transpersonal counseling or psychotherapy includes meditation, mindfulness, intuition, yoga, biofeedback, breath training, contemplation, inward focusing, visualization, dream work, guided imagery, and altered states of consciousness (Ajaya, 1997; Boss, 1981; Davis, 2000; Hutton, 1994). Other practices that are associated with transpersonal psychology, but are not as commonly used, include shamanism, lucid dreaming, and psychedelic drugs (Davis, 2000; Walsh & Vaughan, 1993). Arguably, of all the interventions available to the transpersonal practitioner, the most central is **meditation.** Comparing the role of meditation in transpersonal psychology to the role of dreams in psychoanalysis, Walsh and Vaughan (1993) referred to meditation as "the royal road to the transpersonal." The scope of meditation and related practices have a range of uses, including self-regulation, relaxation, and pain control; but their most common use is for self-exploration and self-liberation (Shapiro, 1994). Meditation allows clients to "disidentify" from their "masks" or egos and realize their fundamental nonduality, which leads to the liberation and transcendence of the self (Goleman & Ram, 1996).

Another key aspect of transpersonal counseling or psychotherapy, of which meditation is a part, is the exploration of human experiences known as **altered states of consciousness.** Metzner (1995) defined an altered state of consciousness as a change in thinking, feeling, and perception in relation to one's ordinary, baseline consciousness that has a beginning, duration, and ending. Delirium, hypnosis, deep meditation, and intoxication are examples of altered states of consciousness (Walsh, 1994). Historically, Western theories have been slow to recognize the wide scope and enormity of altered states of consciousness as seen by the transpersonal theorist and have viewed many of these states as being pathological (e.g., delirium and intoxication) (Davis, 2000; Walsh, 1994; Wilber, 2000). According to Walsh (1994), one of the most dramatic examples of Western resistance was the reaction to hypnosis and the British physician James Esdaile. During his service as a medical doctor in India over a century ago, Esdaile discovered the remarkable capacity of hypnosis to reduce pain and mortality in surgical patients. Esdaile's findings were so dramatic and foreign that Western medical journals refused to publish his reports. When he retured to Britain, Esdaile arranged a demonstration before the British College of Physicians and Surgeons during which he amputated a gangrenous leg while the patient, under hypnosis and without any anesthetic, lay smiling calmly. Instead of marveling at what could have been a revolutionary new find to modern psychological and medical practice, his colleagues concluded that Esdaile had paid a hardened rogue to pretend he felt no pain! Fortunately, over time, Western theory has become more accepting of altered states of consciousness, and theorists and practitioners have come to appreciate that many of these states may be beneficial to counseling and therapy practice and the enrichment of human experience (Strohl, 1998).

When she or he deems the client ready, the transpersonal counselor or therapist is likely to attempt to aid the client in experiencing a range of altered states through a variety of methods, after which they will examine and discuss together. Because these experiences can be quite varied, transpersonal counselors or therapists use a method known as **phenomenological mapping** to aid the client in organizing and understanding experiences during the altered state (Wilber, 1997). The key point to phenomenological mapping is that it allows the client and practitioner to map, compare, and differentiate states of consciousness on not one but multiple experiential dimensions and with greater precision than could be achieved by lumping them all together as one experience (Walsh, 1994). The result is that the individual can better appreciate the richness and variety of transpersonal states as well as clearly differentiate them from psychopathological states such as schizophrenia, with which they can and have sometimes been confused (Walsh, 1990). Although some theorists claim that all altered states are essentially the same, transpersonal theorists argue that different methods of attaining altered states lead to different altered states; therefore, differentiation and organization are necessary (Wilber, 2000). For example, Buddhist meditation, hypnosis, and intoxication may all lead to a different type of altered experience, so each state must be discussed and examined separately to search for differences and commonalities (Wilber, 1997). Phenomenological mapping is absolutely necessary, according to Walsh (1994), because when key dimensions such as mental control, awareness of the environment, concentration, arousal, emotion, self-sense, and content of experience are compared, multiple differences between states come into view.

Once the altered states have been experienced and mapped, the individual must undergo a process known as **deep structure analysis** (Wilber, 1997). The purpose of deep structure analysis is to make coherent sense of the various altered states of consciousness, identify possible commonalities among states, bring any developmental implications of the states into view, and reveal any hidden meanings among the states that may have an important impact on the individual's life (Walsh & Vaughan, 1993; Wilber, 2000). Deep structure analysis, according to Wilber (1997), allows the individual to cluster altered consciousness states and experiences and identify a number of deep structures, which Wilber has classified into a number of hierarchical states. Although Wilber (1993) classified altered consciousness experiences into a number of overarching deep structures, his three main deep structural states, according to Walsh (1994), are subtle states, causal states, and the ultimate condition:

- *Subtle states.* Once conscious mental activity has calmed, a person may experience a range of altered consciousness states that fit into the category of subtle states. Experiences in these states can include experiences of light or sound, emotions such as love and joy, and visions of archetypes (which can vary by culture) such as shamanistic power animals, Christian angelic figures, and a range of others.

- *Causal states.* After subtle states have deepened and stabilized, then causal states devoid of any objects, images, or phenomena can arise. Causal states are the realm of pure consciousness and the transcendental source of all existential experience. These states can be culturally described as the experience of Nirvana in Buddhism and the Tao of Taoism, among others.
- *Ultimate condition.* In this final state, objects and emotions from the subtle states reappear, but they are instantly recognized as expressions, projections, or modifications of consciousness. This is the final enlightenment and realization of consciousness in all things. It is connectedness with the entire universe and all things in it. The ultimate condition is the highest goal and greatest good in all human existence. This experience can be culturally known as Salvation, Zen's One Mind, and Hinduism's Brahman-Atman, among others.

Before advancing into the use of alternative methods of counseling or psychotherapy, such as altered states of consciousness, transpersonal counselors or therapists must gauge the readiness of clients carefully. For the unprepared individual, experiences of deep connectedness can fragment necessary ego boundaries and produce chaos, terror, and confusion (Kasprow & Scotton, 1999).

Brief Intervention Strategies

Most of what can be considered purely transpersonal interventions are not brief in nature. Even a lifetime may prove too short for most individuals to experience the highest states of connectedness. Although the complete transpersonal experience is by no means short term, transpersonal counselors and therapists can and do work with a variety of clients who have problems that easily fit into the scope of "normal" life experience and require shorter term counseling or therapy. When faced with clients who require brief interventions, transpersonal practitioners are most likely to use established methods, such as cognitive-behavioral interventions, that are proven to work in time-sensitive situations. A study by Hutton (1994) delineated transpersonal theory's liberal use of other interventions: Transpersonal counselors and therapists reported using more approaches than other therapists and were found to be more synthesizing in their approach than either psychoanalytic or cognitive-behavioral counselors or therapists. Hutton (1994) found transpersonal counselors and therapists to be similar to cognitive-behaviorists in their use of behaviorally focused visualization, biofeedback, and relaxation and similar to psychoanalysts in their use of intuition and dream work.

Transpersonal counselors and therapists believe that attitudes, expectations, and beliefs create the reality that the client experiences (Strohl, 1998). An essential part of transpersonal counseling or psychotherapy that is as effective in the short-term process as in long-term process is the uncovering, examining, and addressing of the beliefs that govern the client's reality. The transpersonal practitioner attempts to aid the client in dismissing negative beliefs, thereby cultivating positive and constructive thought patterns that lead to productive behavioral habits (Strohl, 1998). It is transpersonal theory's practical yet existential approach to human experience that makes it an effective practice in both short- and long-term counseling or psychotherapy situations (Lukoff, Turner, & Lu, 1992).

CLIENTS WITH SERIOUS MENTAL HEALTH ISSUES

Wide differences of opinion exist in the transpersonal community as to the appropriateness of doing transpersonal work with individuals who are seriously mentally ill or psychotic (Kasprow & Scotton, 1999). Jung (1960), Wilber (1984), and Grof and Grof (1989) argued that transpersonal counseling or psychotherapy is not appropriate for individuals who are seriously mentally ill or psychotic, whereas Lukoff (1996) suggested that transpersonal psychotherapy may be particularly appropriate for psychotic disorders, even serious ones. This issue is compounded by the resemblance of some altered states of consciousness (transpersonal experiences) to psychotic states, such as in schizophrenia. Differentiation between altered states of consciousness and true psychotic states is of extreme importance to optimize counseling and therapy and prevent unnecessary or harmful treatment (Kasprow & Scotton, 1999). Several theorists (Agosin, 1992; Grof & Grof, 1989; Lukoff, 1985) suggested guidelines for determining the difference. Lukoff (1985) suggested the following four criteria to establish the difference between altered states of consciousness and psychosis: Transpersonal experiences are more likely in clients with (1) good premorbid (pretranspersonal experience) functioning, (2) an acute onset of symptoms within a period of 3 months, (3) the presence of a stressful precursor that could account for the acute symptoms, and (4) a positive and exploratory attitude toward the experience. Naturally, when the question arises as to whether the client is exhibiting psychotic symptoms or transpersonal experiences, the ethical counselor or therapist will always seek supervision or clinical consultation.

Another mental health issue transpersonal practitioners must be aware of is that of **spiritual emergencies.** Spiritual emergencies, first documented by Grof and Groff (1989), are emergent transegoic experiences, or experiences, ideation, and behavior, that appear to be pathological but are in fact part of the transpersonal developmental process that can occur as an individual crosses into a new stage of development (Cortright, 2000). As previously mentioned in this chapter, as an individual accesses a new line or stage of development, greater awareness and connectedness can occur, but so can the potential for greater pathologies. Spiritual emergency occurs when the crossing to another developmental line results in a negative experience or behavior. For example, a healthy or prepared individual who experiences Wilber's (1997) psychic level, which mediates a sense of connection to something outside the ego boundary, may experience feelings of universal love and empathic understanding, whereas an individual unprepared for this loss of ego boundary may experience paranoid ideation and separation (Kasprow & Scotton, 1999). Transpersonal theorists believe that these spiritual emergencies can have powerfully transformative effects on a person's life when supported by the counselor or therapist and allowed to run their course to completion (Grof & Grof, 1989; Lukoff, Lu, & Turner, 1998; Perry, 1976).

Overall, it is the onus of transpersonal counselors and therapists to be aware of their own limits of practice as well as the limitations of transpersonal interventions with individuals who are seriously mentally ill. When faced with difficulties that may beyond the scope of transpersonal interventions, practitioners have the ethical responsibility to either use a proven counseling or therapy method or refer the client to another mental health professional. Transpersonal counselors and therapists must also be prepared to deal with spiritual emergencies and the sometimes powerful aspects of clients experiencing new altered states of consciousness and deepening feelings of connectedness.

CROSS-CULTURAL CONSIDERATIONS

It is perhaps safe to say that transpersonal theory is one of the most multiculturally mindful and aware of all the major counseling and psychotherapy theories. Transpersonal theory has been influenced at least as much by Asian and indigenous spiritual systems as by Western and European psychological and philosophical traditions (Davis, 2000). Furthermore, it has strong connections to the meditative traditions of Buddhism and Hinduism, shamanic traditions, esoteric and Gnostic European systems such as alchemy and Celtic mysticism, indigenous African wisdom, and Native American spirituality (Davis, 2000). From its very origins, as well as its growth through the work of such theorists as Wilber (2000), Grof and Grof (1989), and Lukoff (1996), transpersonal psychology has been strongly multicultural and can only continue to be so.

Perhaps the most multicultural aspect of transpersonal theory is that it values the deepening and connectedness of all human experience through the veins of many cultural traditions. It actively seeks out and integrates insights on human nature and healing from a wide variety of cultures and recognizes the role of the cultural context in the experience of individuals and groups (Davis, 2000). Wilber's (1997) transpersonal work across a myriad of cultures has further served to bring many of these cultures into the fold through their descriptions of the same transpersonal experiences through the lens of different cultural tenets (e.g., shamanistic power animals and Christian angelic figures both describe visions in the subtle state). Transpersonal counseling and psychotherapy can only broaden the perspective of practitioners by requiring them to challenge culturally defined views of mental health and therapy and to draw cross-cultural insights into their approaches (Davis, 2000).

EVALUATION

Overview

Transpersonal theory is a fascinating and dynamic field that is fundamentally different from any other major theory of counseling and psychotherapy and human development. It stands at the boundary of mental health practice and spirituality and is the lone approach in wide practice to integrate counseling and therapy concepts, theories, and methodology with the subject matter and practices of the spiritual disciplines (Davis, 2000; Kasprow & Scotton, 1999). However, transpersonalism's very uniqueness has made it difficult to examine in an ideal empirical setting; for this reason, it draws criticism from researchers and practitioners unprepared to accept on faith what many continue to view as a "fringe" and "radical" theory. As we progress further into the 21st century and explore and learn more about human experience and spirituality, transpersonal approaches will likely continue to gain more followers and greater acceptance from traditional theorists.

Supporting Research

When considering the various phenomena associated with transpersonal theory (e.g., connectedness, altered states of consciousness), the discourse can become excessively abstract, vague, or inaccessible to those unversed in its tenets and even more difficult to objectively examine (Adams, 1999). Many of the interventions used by transpersonal practitioners are established methods well examined by researchers (such as cognitive-behavioral interventions), yet studies examining the techniques considered unique to transpersonal theory are aged and sparse at best. This is primarily due to the following question: How does one test enlightenment? Some older studies attempted to answer that question with limited results. For instance, Brown, Porte, and Dysart (1984) examined advanced meditators who had reached at least the first of the four Buddhist stages of enlightenment and found they exhibited enhanced perceptual processing speed and sensitivity. However, in another dated study, "enlightened" subjects given a Rorschach test were not found to be free of the normal psychological conflicts of dependency, sexuality, and aggression, as might be expected of an "enlightened" individual (Brown & Engler, 1986).

Hutton (1994) did not assess the efficacy of transpersonal counseling or psychotherapy, but he did examine similarities and differences with cognitive-behavioral and psychodynamic approaches. He discovered that all these approaches shared the belief in a firm grounding in traditional theories and practices, but he found that transpersonal theories were more accepting of other theories, whereas cognitive-behavioral and psychodynamic theories accepted mainly their own approaches and disregarded others. Hutton also found transpersonal theory to be far more accepting of client's spiritual issues than either cognitive-behavioral or psychodynamic approaches.

Although there is a significant dearth of empirical support for the practice of transpersonal counseling or psychotherapy, practitioners are quick to point out that many of its methods have been in use for hundreds if not thousands of years, even though they do not easily lend themselves to modern empirical study. Transpersonal theory is eclectic in nature and often draws from a wide range of empirically validated interventions. Future research in the field of transpersonal theory may do well to center more on transpersonal counseling and psychotherapy outcomes than on the examination of such abstract concepts as enlightenment or altered states of consciousness.

Limitations

The primary criticism of transpersonal theory is that its methodology often delves into the highly abstract, the deeply spiritual, and what some might even consider the paranormal (a claim refuted by transpersonalists)—all of which make empirical study under controlled situations difficult at best (Adams, 1999). Secularists may perceive transpersonalism as unscientific nonsense, and Christian and other theistic thinkers may view its positions as the latest version of a spiritually misguided Gnosticism that they hoped had been vanquished centuries ago (Adams, 2002). In addition to these views, there has also been some debate as to the ethicality and effectiveness of transpersonal interventions for individuals with serious mental health issues, with some practitioners calling transpersonalism downright dangerous (Ellis, 1962). For these reasons, transpersonal theory has attracted debate from famous theorists such as Albert Ellis (1986, 1989), who spoke out against transpersonalism with articles titled "The Dangers of Transpersonal Psychology" and "Fanaticism That May Lead to a Nuclear Holocaust" and held a spirited debate in the *Journal of Counseling and Development* in the late 1980s against Ken Wilbur (1989), who responded with a sarcastically titled article "Let's Nuke the Transpersonalists."

The limitations and criticisms of transpersonal theory have done little to halt its progress as a widely used modality. The academic literature regarding transpersonal theory has continued to grow well into the 21st century and shows no signs of slowing down. Although followers of traditional theory may not be prepared to accept or understand some of the complicated spiritual tenets that lie at the core of transpersonal theory, more and more counselors and therapists and their clients who seek counseling and psychotherapy in a more deeply spiritual realm continue to be attracted to this burgeoning field.

SUMMARY CHART—*Transpersonal Theories*

Human Nature

Transpersonalism views the development of higher consciousness as necessary for transforming lives. Healthy development is marked by a person's advancement from personal to transpersonal concerns. Spiritual growth is measured by an individual's ability to transcend a subjective point of view and move on to higher earthly, spiritual, and cosmic perspectives. An individual's life is marked by the progress of developmental lines (stages)—broadly arranged into prepersonal, personal, and transpersonal—through all levels of life and consciousness, which the self attempts to manage and navigate. Each stage carries with it new developmental hurdles and pathologies that must be dealt with. Successful navigation through these developmental stages eventually results in transcendence and connection or oneness with all things.

Major Constructs

Transpersonal theory is concerned with the study of humanity's highest potential and with the recognition, understanding, and realization of unitive, spiritual, and transcendent states of consciousness. Transpersonal theory is nondual. It is unitive and carries with it the recognition that each part (each person) is fundamentally and ultimately a part of the whole (the cosmos). It does not seek to replace other models of counseling or psychotherapy; instead, it considers an expanded view of human nature while incorporating elements of behaviorism, psychoanalysis, humanism, Jungian analysis, and Eastern philosophy. Proponents of transpersonal theory hold it to be the most eclectic approach in use today; that is, it includes mainstream counseling and therapy approaches while focusing on expanded human qualities largely ignored by other theories.

Goals

The goal of transpersonal counseling and psychotherapy is similar to that of other approaches: to aid individuals with mental health issues and life difficulties. However, transpersonal counselors and therapists are additionally concerned with fostering a deepening and integration of a person's sense of connectedness, whether it be with self, community, nature, or the entire cosmos. A primary goal of the transpersonal approach is to bring clients to a point where they can begin to work on transpersonal issues. Transpersonal counselors and therapists seek to bring a client beyond a "healthy" level of mental health and into the realm of transcendence, unity, and extraordinary mental health. The overarching goal is always transcendence and deepening of connectedness with the universe.

Change Process

The process of change in transpersonal counseling and psychotherapy is marked by the overcoming of personal problems and life issues, thereby allowing for primary work toward spiritual integration. As the client moves from normal functioning to transpersonal work, the process of unification and deepening the experience of connection engenders the highest human qualities of creativity, compassion, selflessness, and wisdom.

Interventions

The core practice of transpersonal counseling and psychotherapy includes meditation, mindfulness, intuition, yoga, biofeedback, breath training, contemplation, inward focusing, visualization, dream work, guided imagery, and altered states of consciousness. Practitioners are as eclectic as possible and they are as likely to use traditional intervention strategies as they are to use those labeled *transpersonal,* particularly for shorter-term counseling. Primary interventions of the transpersonal approach are meditation and altered states of consciousness. Counselors and therapists use these strategies to bring clients to the eventual goal of transcendence and enlightenment.

Limitations

Transpersonal counseling and psychotherapy have come under fire for not having enough empirical support in the literature. Therefore, some theorists question the ethicality of the transpersonal approach. Another issue involves effectiveness and safety of the approach for use with clients who have serious mental health issues. Furthermore, transpersonal theory may be too abstract and complex for most clients who are oriented in Western philosophical traditions.

THE CASE OF JONATHAN: *A Transpersonal Approach*

The goal of transpersonal counseling and psychotherapy is to assist the individual in achieving his or her highest potential. A careful examination of themes within Jonathan's personal history and dreams can help direct the transpersonal counselor or therapist toward smaller goals and techniques that will aid Jonathan in his process toward authenticity and potential. The first issue that needs to be addressed is Jonathan's willingness to be a client and his openness to transpersonal theory and techniques. Because Jonathan's supervisor recommended counseling, Jonathan's thoughts and feelings about this recommendation should be discussed openly and honestly.

In the transpersonal approach, terms such as *maladaptive, dysfunctional, irrational,* and other negative words are avoided. Instead, the goal is to reframe the client's current condition as a time of breakthrough, the birth of Jonathan's authentic self. This reframing will facilitate Jonathan in moving through the helpless and hopeless state in which he presently finds himself. Instead of focusing on the "bad" decisions he has made, transpersonal counseling or therapy will seek to help Jonathan understand that his current discomfort may have been the impetus for him to move forward to authenticity and his highest potential.

Case Conceptualization

Throughout Jonathan's personal history and dream, we see a pervasive theme of powerlessness and identification with the victim voice within. In his dream, Jonathan is on the bus ride but he is powerless to direct the bus, stop the bus, gain a consensus as to where the bus might be headed, exit the bus, or effectively communicate with the driver. He is at the complete mercy of all of the other passengers as well as the bus driver, no matter how frustrated or angry he becomes. The bus can be seen as the real Jonathan, the container of all of the voices within him. The voice that he identifies with in the dream has no control or power to do anything.

In Jonathan's personal history, there are many examples of his identification with the victim. He was powerless to seek counseling on his own, powerless to arrive on time to the session, powerless to keep his brother from dying, powerless to find satisfactory employment, powerless to raise his children, powerless to develop healthy relationships with women, and powerless to get along with coworkers. The issue is not that there is a victim voice within him; the issue is that it seems to be the only voice to which he is listening. There were times in his life when he may have been the victim and could do nothing about it. For example, he was the unfortunate victim of a car accident with a drunk driver that resulted in the loss of his brother. The victim voice was probably the most appropriate voice for this particular incident. The victim voice should be honored and understood to be an integral part of Jonathan's journey, but it should not be placed on a pedestal above all others. Jonathan cannot reach his fullest potential if the victim is the only voice to which he listens.

Another voice that Jonathan seems to be having difficulty understanding and accepting is his feminine voice. The feminine voice tends to be intuitive, nurturing, soft, and able to express emotions. In his dream, the feminine voice is characterized as the bus driver. It seems as though Jonathan feels as though this emotional, intuitive voice is guiding the bus (the real Jonathan). This feminine voice begins by simply ignoring the victim voice and then laughing at the victim after his futile attempts at communication. The victim voice then resorts to ineffectual aggression, but this does not solve the problem. The feminine voice continues to both drive the bus and to mock the frustrated victim in Jonathan.

Jonathan seems very uncomfortable with the emotional, intuitive, nurturing side of himself, yet at some level he believes that this feminine voice may be guiding all of his activity. This conclusion may not be far from the truth. Jonathan seems to be in a great deal of emotional pain, but he refuses to honor the pain and work through it. It does not appear that Jonathan has successfully worked through the grief of his brother's death. Instead of honoring and accepting the emotional pain that resulted, Jonathan quit school, blamed himself, and began identifying primarily with the victim voice. By refusing to effectively deal with and honor the feminine voice within, Jonathan has inadvertently given all of the control to this voice; therefore, he has created resentment between the victim and the feminine voices. This situation plays out in Jonathan's relationship with women. When he begins to have difficulty in his relationship, he often "gets very angry and walks away" and feels that he is "never good enough." Rather than embracing the feminine voice within that could effectively communicate with his wife and accept the pain that comes naturally in developing relationships, he becomes aggressive, drinks alcohol, tries to replace the woman with whom he is in relationship, and strengthens his identification with the victim voice. Jonathan may also be refusing to honor the feminine voice, by ignoring the nurturing qualities that might influence him to stay on the reservation and help his parents. He may be pulled by the voice of Western culture that idealizes the individual, while simultaneously being pulled toward the more collectivistic and group- and family-oriented Native American culture's voice. In an authentic person, the feminine voice, the victim voice, and all other voices would have their proper place, would work together, and could be used to reach higher states of actualization. Jonathan's refusal to honor the feminine voice has lead to an overidentification with the victim voice and to unhealthy relationships with women.

Another issue to be examined for Jonathan is the lack of unity with a power greater than himself. He reported that he was raised in a family environment that was "held together by both cultural and tribal values." Native American traditions have a strong spiritual component, and he was undoubtedly exposed to shamanistic traditions as he was raised on the reservation. Nothing of the spiritual was mentioned in his personal history, although transpersonal theory acknowledges the importance of a spiritual component in development, actualization, and human potential. Part of Jonathan's increasing depression, alcohol use, and extramarital affairs could be interpreted as an inadequate search for intimacy and pleasure that could be fulfilled through spiritual development.

Counseling Goals and Techniques

The primary goal for assisting Jonathan in reaching his highest potential would be to empower him to identify with more than the victim voice. Once this is accomplished, the second goal would be to help Jonathan overcome his focus on the chaos of all of the voices arguing, and instead realize that each voice has its proper place in his life and that each should be honored. Meeting this goal would allow him to decide which voice or voices he would like to "drive the bus" at any given moment. The third goal would be to explore Jonathan's spiritual experiences and development.

To attain the first goal, empowering Jonathan to move beyond the victim voice, several techniques could be used. One technique would be to examine his ancestry and his culture. It is true that the Native Americans were the victims of heinous brutality and displacement, but this is not their only history. Jonathan could study and get in touch with the warrior voice that is prevalent in his culture. By listening to the warrior voice, he is more likely to stand firm and fight in the face of adversity. One way to get in touch with this warrior voice would be through guided imagery. Jonathan could be taught to relax while the counselor or therapist verbally guides him to mentally picture this warrior. Through repetition of this process, Jonathan could begin to identify with this cultural heritage and own the warrior voice as part of himself. Another technique would be for Jonathan to give the victim character in his dream a voice. What does it feel like to be powerless to stop the bus or gain a consensus as to where it is headed? What does it feel like to be laughed at by the driver? These are just some of the questions that could allow Jonathan to give voice to the victim.

For Jonathan to be able to honor all of the voices within him, and to discern which voices should be listened to at appropriate times, the counselor or therapist could encourage Jonathan to give voices to all of the characters in his dream. Jonathan could give voice to the bus driver. What was the driver thinking? Why was she laughing at him? All of the other people in the bus have opinions as to where the bus is headed; he could give those characters voices as well. Why does this individual not want to go to Albuquerque? Where does he want to go instead? Why does he want to go there? What might be better there than in Albuquerque? While exploring all of the opinions of the characters within the dream, the counselor or therapist could help

Jonathan realize the validity of each of the voices on the bus. When might it be best to go to California or New York? When might it be most appropriate to listen to one voice over another voice? Another good technique for this process toward unity of the self is bibliotherapy, which is well within the realm of transpersonal interventions.

Finally, the spiritual element of Jonathan's life needs to be addressed. An in-depth history of his spiritual development and experiences would be integral to this process. Once this is obtained, the counselor or therapist will have a good idea of how Jonathan values the spiritual and how it can be used to gain insight into his authentic self. Prayers, meditation, guided imagery, and Native American spiritual traditions are excellent tools for Jonathan to connect with something greater than himself. As he begins to continually unify himself with this power, the hopelessness and lack of intimacy that he expresses will soon dissipate.

Note that these are just a few techniques that might be used with Jonathan. Transpersonal counseling and psychotherapy can be seen as an extension of or as an umbrella over a wealth of other theories. Techniques generally characterized as belonging to other theoretical orientations are embraced in transpersonal therapy. The overarching goal is to aid Jonathan in his process toward an authentic self and to achieve his highest potential, regardless of the intervention used.

Part IV

Integrative Approaches

Chapter

Integrative approaches in counseling and psychotherapy have been widely thought of as the combination of two or more theories to more effectively provide service to clients. Many counselors and therapists branch out from a central theory, but they must first have a conceptual understanding of human nature, the role of the counselor or therapist, and the structure for the helping relationship. A personal theory is vital to being an effective counselor or therapist. Effectiveness, however, is not based on theory alone but on how much of herself or himself the practitioner is willing to integrate into the helping relationship. Some counselors and therapists believe that integrative approaches are a hodgepodge of theories and interventions designed not to meet clients' needs but to account for practitioners' lack of a theoretical foundation. In chapter 17 integrative approaches are considered as models and interventions that may be used from within any theoretical orientation to provide the client with greater therapeutic expression, awareness, and efficacy. The chapter presents an overview of three integrative approaches to counseling and psychotherapy: expressive arts, narrative, and symbolism.

Integrative Approaches: Expressive Arts, Narrative, and Symbolism

Walter Breaux III
Columbus State University

For the past two decades, **integrative approaches** in counseling and psychotherapy have been widely discerned as the combining of two or more theories to more effectively provide service to clients. Although it is common practice for many counselors and therapists to branch out from a central theory, it is imperative to first have a conceptual understanding of human nature, the role of the counselor or therapist, and the structure for the helping relationship. Having a personal theory of counseling or psychotherapy, which is vital to being an effective practitioner, is not based on theory alone but on how much of herself or himself the practitioner is willing to integrate into the helping relationship. The integrative approach has been tarnished with terms like *eclectic,* leading many counselors and therapists to believe that integrative approaches are a hodgepodge of theories and interventions designed not to meet the clients' needs but to account for practitioners' lack of a theoretical foundation. For the purposes of this chapter, integrative approaches are considered as models and interventions that may be used from within a theoretical orientation to provide the client with greater therapeutic expression, awareness, and efficacy. The chapter presents an overview of three integrative approaches to counseling and psychotherapy: **expressive arts**, **narrative**, and **symbolic**.

BACKGROUND

Art, music, dance, writing, and symbolism are not new to the fields of counseling and psychotherapy. These now **nontraditional approaches** to healing were used by cultures all over the world throughout ancient times. Western thought has made great contributions in the field of counseling and psychotherapy without integrating historical healing techniques and approaches from nonindustrialized civilizations. For centuries, medicine men, shamans, and healers have used dance, music, and other expressive arts to promote physical, mental, and spiritual well-being. The ancient Greeks embodied these concepts in their worship of Apollo, the god of music, poetry, and healing. Among some African and Native American tribes, song and dance are considered cures for mental, emotional, and spiritual illness.

Integrative approaches have been slowly accepted as equally effective approaches in the therapeutic community due, in part, to the rise in popularity of **talk therapy** as a more verifiable form of counseling. **Verbal psychotherapy** has its roots in the psychoanalytic approach with Sigmund Freud's **talking cure** and has since been further developed in the cognitive-behavioral, humanistic, and "fourth-force" perspectives of counseling and psychotherapy. These **traditional approaches** have always integrated techniques for assessing and facilitating client growth beyond **classic talk therapy**. For example, action-oriented experiments in Gestalt therapy or **mandalas** in Jungian analysis allow for greater client expression and awareness through projective techniques that acknowledge a reality that may be limited or misrepresented through mere verbal articulation. Currently, such techniques are based in clinical applications and require integration within an established theoretical framework for working with clients (Rubin, 2001). With further research and conceptual development, these integrative approaches may one day develop into theories of counseling and psychotherapy (Rubin, 2001; Levine & Levine, 1999).

Expressive Arts Approaches

Art and other expressive modalities have been practiced in counseling and psychotherapy since the early 1940s. The first use of the expressive arts as a systematic approach in counseling and psychotherapy was at **Lesley College** in Cambridge, MA, in the early 1970s (Levine & Levine, 1999). **Shan McNiff, Pablo Knill**, and **Norma Canner** developed the Expressive Therapy Program, which based its curriculum on an integrative model of expressive art modalities (Levine & Levine, 1999). Based on Knill's work, many more programs in expressive arts were introduced in colleges and universities across Europe and North America. Knill is also credited with the creation of the **community art-making approach** that has become a large part of urban development and outreach in major cities in the Western hemisphere (Levine & Levine, 1999).

Narrative Approaches

Freud is often credited with the integration of narrative into his psychoanalytic approach (Lieblich, McAdams, & Josselson, 2004). However, **Michael White** is credited as the founder of narrative therapy and a major contributor, along with **David Epston**, to the effective growth of this approach. The narrative approach as a therapeutic tool has its root in family counseling, but it has become an independent approach to counseling and psychotherapy over the past 10 to 20 years (Henehan, 2003). This approach is often used by family counselors or therapists to help clients understand their relational interactions with other family members. As the use of this approach has grown outside of family counseling and psychotherapy, narrative has become an intervention more readily grounded in viewing clients as a component of social, cultural, and structural systems (Speedy, 2004). Of the many approaches to integrative counseling and psychotherapy, the narrative approach is the most widely used and conceptually developed application (Henehan, 2003; McLeod, 2004).

Symbolic Approaches

Perhaps it was Freud who first looked at imagery as a component of client expression (Markell, 2002). **Symbolic transformation** is one of the founding principals of counseling and psychotherapy and is as old as the first word, sound, or picture created for human communication. Freud's psychosexual **phallic** is, in his theory, represented through objects like guns and gestures such as finger-pointing, although he believed that "a cigar is just a cigar." **Symbolism** is central to many theories of counseling and psychotherapy such as **object relations theory**, which states that clients seek to establish relationships that symbolize previous or primary interactions in their life. Carl Jung's early and extensive research into symbols best illustrates the therapeutic benefit of attending to the client's subjective reality. Jung believed that symbols were a reality of human existence and consciousness. "Because there are innumerable things beyond the range of human understanding, we constantly use symbolic terms to represent concepts that we cannot define or fully comprehend" (Jung, 1964, p. 4).

Theory Integration

The integration of expressive arts, narrative, and symbolism with counseling and psychotherapy theory is fundamental to the effective use of these approaches. Inclusion of integrative approaches in counseling and psychotherapy enhances the **therapeutic milieu** and in turn fosters sound theoretical practice. Counselors or therapists who combine these approaches with their theoretical orientation produce interventions that interact with the true essence of the client. The integration of nontraditional approaches with theory must include a rationale for their use with clients (Cadwell, 2005). Simple haphazard mixing and matching of theory and application can lead to measures that actually impede client growth. The use of the integrative approaches in counseling and psychotherapy ought to be based on four factors:

1. *Practitioner competency with integrative measures and techniques.* The effective and appropriate use of any counseling or therapy strategy is supported by the knowledge and familiarity of the practitioner with that approach. Competent use of integrative measures ensures maximized therapeutic benefit to the client. Postgraduate education and review are imperative to effective clinical work.
2. *Client openness to integrative approaches and styles.* Every approach is not appropriate for every client. For example, symbolic exploration as an integrative technique may be too abstract and ambiguous for more practical clients. It is best to present an integrative approach to a client by explaining its purpose and intended result. This method of intervention presentation is common in the Gestalt approach and is usually prefaced by this classic question to the client: "Would you like to try an experiment?"

Remember that a client's objection to a particular intervention is not necessarily an impediment to therapeutic work.

3. *Nature of the client issue.* Appropriate interventions address client needs. The choice to use an integrative approach must also be made based on the type of problem a client is attempting to work through. Different modalities in integrative approaches address certain client problems more directly than others. A counselor or therapist would be wise to develop a sound **case conceptualization** of the client's problems and needs to avoid making an inopportune decision to present an ineffective intervention.

4. *Therapeutic relevance to the desired outcomes for the client.* Some counselors or therapists might make the mistake of choosing an integrated approach because it appeals to their own curiosity or style of practice. Although selection and use of a theoretical orientation should be a reflection of the practitioner's beliefs about client change, the role as a therapist, the counseling relationship, and interventions ought to be established based on the client's therapeutic needs. A good question for a counselor or therapist to pose when considering an integrative strategy is this: "How will this help my client?" The insight derived from this question can lead to more intentional and effective facilitation of the client's process toward insight and change.

The application of approaches from expressive arts, narrative, and symbolism is conceptually based in the theory of counseling or psychotherapy that the practitioner follows. A few examples of integrative approaches as framed by selected theoretical orientations are presented next. These scenarios represent theoretically integrated approaches in counseling and psychotherapy.

- *Narrative integration in Adlerian theory.* An Adlerian counselor or therapist who wishes to conduct a **lifestyle assessment** of clients may select the narrative approach as a means of encouraging client awareness and responsibility. Clients share their life narrative and the counselor or therapist looks for themes centered on the three life tasks of **work, friendship,** and **love.** Clients' narratives contain valuable therapeutic information, possibly concerning feelings of inferiority, family constellation, and other elements that are useful as the counselor or therapist facilitates clients' exploration of their own uniqueness.

- *Symbolism integration in existential philosophy.* The counselor or therapist who has chosen an existential framework is likely to use the symbolic approach to uncover themes in clients' speech and behavior. Concepts of freedom, isolation, and meaninglessness will arise in sessions as symbolic references to clients' inner reality. The practitioner's attention to the symbols that clients produce will contribute toward understanding clients' **phenomenological perspective** and toward developing strategies to cope with clients' **angst.**

- *Visual art integration in Gestalt theory.* A Gestalt counselor or therapist may ask clients to draw their **impasse** as an **experiment** to increase awareness. The drawing, by its artistic design, must include a **figure** and **field,** or foreground and background, that structures clients' perspective of their issue. Working in the here-and-now perspective of Gestalt, the counselor or therapist may direct clients to make changes to their drawing by adding colors to represent the emotions that arise as they draw. By allowing clients to experience their reality in this artful form, the counselor or therapist facilitates clients' work toward resolving their **unfinished business.**

An innate link exists among the three integrative approaches. The act of writing is seen as an expressive art, just as the creation of narrative form inherently produces symbolic meaning. Art in all of its forms is symbolic. Although there is significant conceptual overlap among these three approaches, their applied uses and clinical outcomes vary greatly (Markell, 2002). Integration of the three approaches with counseling or psychotherapy theory helps in sifting out those elements that, to the naive, seem the same. As the expressive arts, narrative, and symbolism are shaped by theory, they take on their own unique purpose and function in the counseling or psychotherapy process. Through a therapeutic lens, the counselor or therapist perceives the interconnected nature of these approaches as an opportunity to holistically counsel their client (Rogers, 1999). The benefit of such interrelation means that each approach is not exclusive to the other; rather, the approaches are complementary and in their use attend to multiple levels of clients' issues. The power behind integrative approaches, and indeed counseling or psychotherapy, is in the meaning and insight clients derive from effective and purposeful use of theory and the integrative approaches.

HUMAN NATURE: A DEVELOPMENTAL PERSPECTIVE

In current educational programs, counselors and therapists are trained to attend to verbal and nonverbal cues from the client. Attending to nonverbal cues, such as clients' facial expressions and body movements, minimally addresses the deeper significance of these manifestations. There are elements of the human condition that are inexpressible through monocular dialogue (Markell, 2002). However, through the integration of approaches designed to explore and facilitate nonverbal communication, counselors or therapists are able to provide clients with more holistic mediums of expression. Greater expression enhances clients' ability to use internal resources and develop their sense of power (Hogan, 2001).

By definition, integrative approaches are not grounded in a particular theoretical orientation. In general, integrative approaches are supported by the belief that therapy is not merely a science but more accurately an art. According to **humanistic theory**, it is the open expression of self, free of interference, that allows clients to make a transition from ideal states to experiential reality. For many people self-expression is manifested through various means, and reliance on verbal disclosure may interfere with clients' process of insight building and growth. Not every aspect of the human condition can or should be expressed through words. The ability to work with clients and connect with them beyond verbal counseling or psychotherapy has led to meaningful and effective outcomes in the therapeutic relationship (Hartz & Thick, 2005).

Expressive Arts

Expressive art therapies are based on the belief that clients' dilemmas respond to the freedom of artistic expression (Levine & Levine, 1999). This response to the artistic medium aids clients in holistic expression and awareness of self beyond the limits of verbalized communication of their cognitive and emotive states. The Western assumption that talking is the best form of expression is challenged by the reality that nonarticulate clients also have a valid and meaningful reality to share and explore. Just as some people express self best through talking, others prefer to, or have no other option but to, share self through nonverbal means

(Weiss, 1984). Expressive art approaches do not abstain from verbal communication between the counselor or therapist and clients but often combine artistic interventions with therapeutic dialogue. In this way clients' expressive use of the artistic medium becomes the point of therapeutic change.

The techniques used to promote the therapeutic process from an expressive arts approach are derived from one of these four therapeutic forms:

- Art therapy (specifically visual art)
- Dance or movement therapy
- Drama therapy
- Music therapy

These therapeutic forms are often integrated with each other to produce creative interventions that stimulate awareness of clients' issues from various aspects of their expressed self. The use of two or more of these expressive arts approaches must still be based in theory. Expressive arts counseling or therapy that has no consistent theoretical structure leaves much of what is going on in the process unaccounted for (Feder & Feder, 1981). Conceptually, counselors or therapists must consider the purpose of their interventions and whether they are best suited to clients' goals for counseling or therapy. The best expressive art interventions are intended to encourage **experiential awareness** of client issues (Feder & Feder).

A central practice of expressive arts counseling or therapy is to allow clients to freely experience and alternatively define themselves beyond conventional limitations. The liberating concept of this approach is supported by the idea that clients' expression of self is currently stifled by some form of suffering (Levine & Levine, 1999). To effectively move the client along, expressive art counselors or therapists create a therapeutic environment where clients can fully and safely convey self without the constrictions that currently stifle their growth. Deriving meaning from the expressive arts approach is like asking someone the meaning behind *Mona Lisa's* smile. Invariably, meaning is derived from personal interpretation. Similarly, the meaning of a certain picture, song, movement, or object is determined by clients' personal interpretation of its value to them and their current reality (Hogan, 2001). The expressive arts counselor or therapist is aware that clients operate on multiple levels of thoughts and emotions and thus are best facilitated in their growth through various methods of experiencing and validating their process. Unique to this approach is the ability of clients to create meaning and interpretation without the counselor or therapist applying a diagnosis or definition onto the clients' suffering (Levine & Levine, 1999).

The process of change for clients is supported by the practitioner's openness and familiarity with the healing and validating aspects of the expressive arts. Counseling or therapy based on *sound therapeutic practice* suggests counselor or therapist competency with the use of and comprehension of the expansive nature of integrative approaches. The more informed of and versed the practitioner is in effective and appropriate integrative interventions, the greater the benefit is to the clients receiving services. A fluent acquaintance with the expressive arts does not require expertise in their use but apt knowledge of their function and applications and how theories best support each form.

The openness of clients toward the expressive arts is a factor in this approach to integrative counseling or therapy. Clients may have certain expectations about the process of counseling or therapy and may not be willing to risk looking foolish as they engage in artistic representations of their issues. As a rule, the use of expressive arts in counseling or therapy is dictated by clients' willingness and need to fully or alternatively expressive self through artistic means. This approach has been found to be successful in work with resistant clients who may be uncomfortable with verbally opening up to a counselor or therapist (Hartz & Thick, 2005). By offering clients an opportunity to express their reality in a way that they may find less threatening, the practitioner strengthens the efficacy and rapport of the therapeutic relationship.

In the following excerpt from a session based in the Gestalt theory of counseling and psychotherapy, the counselor uses music therapy as an integrative approach to encouraging deeper reflection on the client's grief issues. The client discloses her feelings of guilt surrounding her mother's death after listening to a song the counselor played for her in session:

CLIENT: Wow, I, um . . . I always thought of my mom as "the wind beneath my wings," but I . . . I never seemed to do much to help her. I just thought there would be more time. (*laughs*) It's really funny how a song can trigger so much . . . so much . . . (*crying*) I could have been a better daughter. (*composing herself*)

COUNSELOR: It seems like you still have some regrets. You weren't good enough?

CLIENT: Yeah, and I thought I was over this stuff. I kind of feel guilty about not being there more. (*sigh*)

COUNSELOR: This guilt you feel, tell me how do you feel it?

CLIENT: How? . . . Oh, all over I guess. Listening to that song reminds me of my sister singing it to Mama last year on her birthday. I would have joined in too, but . . . I should have.

COUNSELOR: You should have? Sing the song here as you believe you should have sung it.

The counselor integrated music into her work with the client and in turn facilitated the client's awareness of unresolved feelings. The counselor, using the trademark *directives* and *experiments* of Gestalt theory, encourages the client to attend to her *unfinished business* through further expressive art. From this intervention, the client can begin to work on acceptance and forgiveness of self, a process that may not have been accessed if the counselor had not decided to be integrative in her counseling style to better assist the client.

Narrative Approaches

Narrative approaches to counseling and psychotherapy are varied in their techniques and applications. The common philosophy underlying these different schools of thought is that clients' life experiences are internally organized into **stories** or **narratives** (Hester, 2004). Most commonly, narrative approaches involve writing in the form of poetry, bibilotherapy, storytelling, and narrative reconstruction. (Note that bibliotherapy is not considered a narrative approach, but it is often used in conjunction with narrative exercises.) Narratives are used by clients to make sense of their seemingly disordered inner and outer lives (Henehan, 2003). By encouraging clients to share these stories in a therapeutic relationship, the counselor or therapist facilitates the growth of clients through a **reauthoring** of their perceptions of their lives. For this reason, some theorists believe that narrative applications are a central therapeutic tool in counseling and psychotherapy (Sarbin, 1986).

The therapeutic value of writing is well established in the professions of counseling and psychotherapy, especially in the cognitive-behavioral approaches and techniques that use writing exercises to encourage greater insight and awareness. **Storytelling** techniques are also part of the analytic and humanistic approaches as a means to explore client desires and fears (Muntigl, 2004). The inherent link between the narrative approach and theory enables simpler integration of the approach's benefits in the counseling or therapy process. The ease of narrative integration with theory has led some narrative practitioners to support a concept called **strategic eclecticism** (Guterman & Rudes, 2005). Like other forms of eclectic theory, strategic eclecticism confuses theory and practice integration with theoretical variation as a means of helping clients.

In **family systems theory**, narrative approaches are used to promote healthy family interactions and provide an understanding for the **social construction of meaning** in the personal life of clients. (Social construction of meaning is important for clients because it enables them to become aware of and acknowledge meaning as the foundation of their reality.) Narrative counselors or therapists believe that clients perceive their world from a framework of meanings that they have constructed and supported throughout their lifetime. This construction of meaning begins in the family of origin as children are taught societal norms, values, and expectations (Richert, 2002). As people grow, they agree with and support these given meanings or they disagree with and seek to invent new meaning in their personal life, relationships, aspirations, and fears. **Alfred Adler** believed the use of narrative interventions in therapy assisted clients in making sense of their thoughts and belief systems that stemmed from early memories and interactions in life (Hester, 2004).

A central theme of the narrative approach is that clients come to counseling or therapy as a result of living a personal narrative of suffering, fear, or worthlessness. Narrative counselors or therapists often invite their clients to share their most painful or challenging narratives in hopes of opening clients to the possibilities of hope that surround their stories (Salvatore, Dimaggio, & Semerari, 2004). From the narrative perspective, clients enter counseling or therapy following an **unconscious script**. They have been following their scripts for so long that they are unaware that they can change the plot around at any time. The **social context** in which clients live is of importance when conceptualizing strategies for their growth. The stories clients share in session are shaped by the meaning they have placed on relationships, their choices, and their perspective. Each of these elements is mutable, so the goal of counseling or therapy is to garner the awareness and power needed to change elements that are holding clients back from fully enjoying life.

Narrative counseling or therapy attempts to assist clients in reauthoring their life narrative and to help them reclaim their **personal agency**. Narrative counselors or therapists conceptualize clients' issues as a product of life and seek to facilitate clients' awareness of the themes and moral lessons that they have learned in their life journey. These themes and lessons are the tools that clients bring to the counseling or therapy relationship and are the key elements of change for their problems. Think of a client as a writer suffering from writer's block. The writer struggles with the question of "What do I write next?" and the client is stuck in his or her life's narrative with questions such as these: "Where do I go from here?" "How did I even get here?" The narrative approach is seen as an opportunity for clients to continue their life narrative however they wish. The role of the narrative counselor or therapist is to offer clients avenues of exploration into their dreams, desires, aspirations, fears, regrets, and emotional wounds. Through this exploration, clients find fulfillment and meaning as they begin to reauthor their life narratives into a story with happier outcomes.

In the following excerpt from a counseling session, the counselor uses an icebreaker by asking the client to provide three adjectives to describe herself. The client has been referred to counseling for alcohol abuse, and up to this point in the initial session she has been uncooperative about talking about the issue. The counselor, working from a person-centered approach, uses **unconditional positive regard** for the client in an attempt to form a *genuine rapport* built on *mutual trust and respect*.

CLIENT: Ok, three words to describe me. Well, everybody says I'm bull-headed and mean . . . and I like to cause mess, you know messy-like.

COUNSELOR: Those are three words other people use to describe you. I want to hear three words that you would use to describe you.

CLIENT: Um, I guess I am kind of mean at times, but I'm trying to work on that. How about "I don't know." I'm kind of confused about things right now. Yeah, confused . . . and I'm tired, and well heck I'm here so I must be crazy or something right?

COUNSELOR: Confused, tired, and crazy. Those words seem pretty unpleasant.

CLIENT: Yeah, well those words are good descriptions of me like right now. I'll tell you that. I'd give anything to at least have a good night's rest. Then maybe I wouldn't be so tired and grumpy all the time.

COUNSELOR: Life must be hard right now . . . So after you had a good night's rest what three words would you use to describe yourself, or better yet your life?

CLIENT: Ha, rested, sane, and . . . um, maybe a little less confused.

Through the use of a narrative intervention, the client has disclosed feelings of confusion and displeasure with her current situation in life. From this point on in the session, a therapeutic alliance can form around what the client would ideally like to see transpire in her life. The counselor can use the information that the client has shared to help her construct a plan of action to *reauthor* her current life script. A good start for this client will be to focus on her state of confusion, as it seems to be an extended and **recurring theme** in her story. The integrative use of a narrative approach in this session reframed a potentially conflictual interaction into an opportunity for therapeutic work.

Symbolic Approaches

In the discussion of symbolism in counseling and psychotherapy, people's thoughts are often drawn to the application of dream work. Although dream work is one aspect of the symbolic approach, many more symbolic elements can be explored as part of therapeutic work with clients. Even in classic talk therapies, symbolism encompasses the totality of the session. Practitioners and clients use symbols through their speech, nonverbal communication, and even by their relationship itself (Goud, 2004). Symbolic comprehension is crucial to effective communication and conceptualization of therapeutic process.

Symbolic approaches to counseling and psychotherapy are established in the belief that clients' reality is based on their **interpretation of symbols** (i.e., words, interactions, objects) in their life. In a symbolic approach to counseling or psychotherapy, clients are in search of meaning and definition in their lives. Whether or not we are aware of it, we infuse meaning into every aspect of our daily lives. When they enter counseling or psychotherapy, clients' perceptions may be focused on symbols that, through faulty representations, create an unpleasant or unmanageable reality for them. Effective use of the symbolic approach must take into account the social context of clients. The goal of symbolic counseling or therapy is to aid clients in redefining the symbols and their interpretation of symbols in their life.

In the following excerpt from a counseling session, the client shares a situation that he perceives as the source of his problem. Using **reality therapy theory** of **William Glasser**, the counselor explores the **choices** that the client is making to satisfy his **drives**.

CLIENT: I really wish my wife would get over this car thing. A new Benz is just what I need to fit in at the agency. I keep telling her this will pay off when the "uppers" notice me, but . . . (*sigh*) I don't know. She says it's either the car or her.

COUNSELOR: Tell me what this car represents for you.

CLIENT: Well . . . status, you know, makes it look like I'm doing things with the little money they pay me. Investing and . . . nobody wants to promote someone who isn't making moves, you know.

COUNSELOR: So you want to look the part of someone with a certain status and freedom to make moves, to belong?

CLIENT: Well . . . when you put it like that its sounds a little selfish and like I'm some kid no one wants to play with so I'm trying to fit in. (*laughs*) I guess I could see why she thinks I'm nuts.

The client believes that his new car is a symbol of status and will afford him more opportunities in the future. Although a new car may be a valid interpretation of status, the client's belief is having a negative impact in his marital relationship. By integrating the symbolic approach into reality therapy, the client is presented with the meaning behind his choices, which gives him a much more realistic perspective of his issue. From a symbolic approach, the counselor facilitated the client's reevaluation of his definitions of *status*, highlighting how his *wants* and needs for *belonging* and *freedom* are coming across in the session. Through *self-evaluation* the client is able to hear the symbolic meaning he has placed on a car.

MAJOR CONSTRUCTS

Expressive Arts

The term *expressive arts* refers to the various approaches and interventions used in counseling and psychotherapy for the purposes of client art-making. The creation of art is considered an integral aspect of therapeutic growth. Not only is art seen as an expression of clients' inner truth, but it also is viewed as a mode of communication of this truth (Robbins, 1980).

Counselors or therapists working from the expressive arts approach select creative opportunities for clients to share their phenomenological insights in a way that promotes their development and sense of self (Simon, 1992).

The central concept of the expressive arts approach in is action. The focus of the approach is the client doing and experiencing as a therapeutic means; therefore, the approach is considered a component of **action therapy**. Action therapy consists of processes that involve clients in purposeful physical activities at the direction of their counselor or therapist (Wiener, 1999). In action therapy, two methods promote client expression and development:

- *Nondirective or free expression methods.* These methods form the basis of expressive arts. Clients are freely allowed to engage in artfully creating a counseling or therapy intervention designed to enhance their freedom, awareness, and vitality.
- *Directive or focused expression methods.* Clients are directed by the counselor or therapist to perform a certain art activity for the purpose of exploring a specific experience or facet of the their issues. These methods are usually used as a single intervention that is integrated into the theoretical orientation from which the counselor or therapist works.

The field of expressive arts is truly limitless in the number of techniques and applications available for therapeutic work with clients. Currently, there are four modalities within the expressive arts approach: art therapy, dance and movement therapy, drama therapy, and music therapy. Each of these artistic therapies involves an active and creative method of cultivating client change. Although there are a considerable number of different styles and theories of therapeutic art expression, the following four themes highlight the common and central belief system of the expressive arts community.

1. *The human condition parallels the breath and depth of artistic expression.* The spoken word, musical chord, dramatic performance, and cadence of dance all evoke some response in humans. The type of response reflects the energy and passion the art projects. As clients experience the creation of art, they experience specific thoughts and feelings that are infused into their artwork. This interchange between clients, their art, and their inner perceptibility creates a highly conducive environment for therapeutic exploration.
2. *Artistic expression is a liberating process.* The act of doing creates. Creation is empowering. Expressive arts counselors and therapists believe that this empowering process is natural and should be infused in therapeutic work with clients. In counseling or therapy that integrates the expressive arts, clients are released from the confinement of their perceptions by the experience of sharing their artistic self.
3. *Clients' issues are a product of limiting expression and constrictive thinking or feeling.* Freedom is an ongoing theme in the expressive arts. Counselors or therapists who use this approach believe that a natural function of human beings is freedom. Clients are bound by their rehearsal of dysfunction. Expressive art is a medium that allows clients to see, hear, and experience free expression and, in turn, explore their thoughts and feelings with a liberated insight.
4. *Art-making creates a shift in clients' perception, thereby increasing awareness and insights.* As clients develop their power, they become more aware of the freedom they have to bring about change in their lives. This change in perception means that the clients'

problems begin to take on a different form; clients are now freer to objectively examine the issues in their lives.

Narrative Approaches

Narrative therapy is based on four key beliefs.

1. *Clients are not defined by problems they present.* Clients often identify themselves by their problems. In contrast, by owning a label of dysfunction, clients begin to accept their problem as an integrated part of who they are, not an inherent characteristic. For example, clients who suffer from depression are experiencing a temporal state not a characteristic of their personality. Making the distinction between self and the problem is essential if clients are to be empowered to reauthor their life narrative.

2. *Clients are experts on their lives, so the counselor or therapist should judiciously seek their expertise.* The humanistic aspect of counseling and psychotherapy is the belief that clients have their answers. Clients have spent the most time with themselves, have experienced the totality of their lives, and are the best sources on how they have come to their present place in life. Any effective intervention with clients must take into account the great familiarity they have with self and their dilemmas.

3. *Clients have many skills, competencies, and internal resources on which to draw.* All clients, even the young child, have certain life skills that they draw from in their daily life. The competencies that clients have used to arrive at this point in their life journey should be used as resources for them in their therapeutic work and beyond. The practitioner should attend to and explore the strength that is evident in clients' life narratives.

4. *Therapeutic change occurs when clients accept their role as authors of their life and begin to create a life narrative that is congruent with their hopes, dreams, and aspirations.* Clients have many choices in how they experience and perceive their life journey. Empowering clients to accept responsibility for the authoring of their life is the role of the counselor or therapist. Once clients see the thematic patterns and characters in their life narrative, they can insightfully structure their story toward more positive and healthful goals.

Symbolic Approaches

The foundational understanding of the symbolic approach in counseling and psychotherapy is derived from Jungian analytic concepts of the **collective unconscious** and the shared archetypes the practitioner and client inherently share. In many ways, the discovery of the **numinous self**, from a symbolic perspective, is the discovery of a greater connectedness to the community of shared meaning and thought. Through synchronistic experiences, clients develop feelings of connectedness that counter feelings of isolation and feelings of loneliness (Hogenson, 2005). The following tenets of the symbolic approach form the basis for effective use of this approach with clients.

1. *Symbolic reshaping is the primary function of the counseling or therapy process.* The counseling or therapy relationship provides clients with a conducive environment for

change. Through the interaction of the counselor or therapist and clients, the clients become aware of their own definitions of the symbols in their life. For example, clients working in session on trust will gradually become aware of those symbols (e.g., relationships and people) that they interpret as embodying trustworthiness. These relationships and people are symbols as they are subject to the definitions and meanings clients impose on them.

2. *Clients experience their meaning through cognitive and emotive projection.* Definitions and perspective guide clients' understanding of self and their life. As clients experience the facets of life, they tend to externalize or project their reality on to the outside world. For example, the same client who is working on trust has learned to define relationships through internal process. Whether the client is having a good or bad day, she or he will assign those attributes to people with whom she or he consistently shares those experiences. At work is the same principle behind the lasting effect of first impressions.

3. *Therapeutic change occurs when clients accept their ability to define their lives through symbols of transformation.* Clients' growth is expedited through their awareness that they control the definitions and subsequent meaning in their life. As in narrative understanding, clients are seen as the author of their existence through the meaning they infuse into their roles, relationships, possessions, social attributes, and so on. The client working through trust issues in the previous examples will have to understand that even her or his interpretations of behaviors are symbolic and that she or he controls the symbols of life.

APPLICATIONS

Overview

The integrative approaches offer many techniques for counseling and psychotherapy. Many interventions are used as integrative tools in therapeutic work with clients. This section provides a cursory overview of some of these interventions. The use of different techniques depends on clients, their problems, the therapeutic value of a chosen intervention, and, of course, clients' willingness to engage in the proposed application.

Goals of Counseling and Psychotherapy

The first goal of the integrative approaches is to enhance theoretically based counseling and psychotherapy with more holistic means of therapeutic guidance and intervention. This goal is evident in the incorporation of many experiential concepts and interventions in the practice of counseling and therapy over several decades. The use of integrative approaches engages clients on multiple levels of reality, often simultaneously. Through these approaches, clients' issues are framed not only through thoughts and feelings, but also through imagery, creativity, and self-exploration. The second goal of the use of the expressive arts, narrative, and symbolic approaches is to facilitate greater client expression and awareness of self through active experiencing of issues based in psychically disturbed thoughts and feelings. As clients *do* they become aware of how and why their problems exist. This active reviewing of emotions and cognitions promotes insight in clients. Additional client awareness and insight are facilitated through theoretical applications by the counselor or therapist.

Process of Change

The use of the integrative approaches is based on three factors that contribute to client change:

- Clients change when their current life perspective no longer represents their desired goals.
- Clients change by accepting control, responsibility, and power for the construction and insightful living of their inner realities.
- Client change is a process of authentic reflection, accountability, and openness toward growth and resolution.

Traditional Intervention Strategies

Interventions in the integrative approaches are numerous and unstandardized. There are no set interventions that can be classified as belonging to any single approach due to the amount of overlap in the techniques of creative expression. Some counselors or therapists may consider certain techniques as specifically narrative or exclusively expressive art. The actual application and client process within interventions may access two or more of the integrative approaches, as the use of symbolism is always present. Consider the following creative interventions based on the concepts of expressive arts, narrative, and symbolism:

- *Collage and mobile crafting.* This intervention strategy is usually longitudinal in nature. Clients are provided various art supplies (e.g. glue, colored paper, pipe cleaners). In one form of this technique, clients are instructed to create a collage based on a current feeling, thought, fear, dream, and so on, that they are experiencing that day. This technique may be used at the beginning or end of each session until clients have created a mosaic-style mobile of their collages. This art-making technique serves as a reminder of the client's progress throughout the session, and the actual art serves as a focusing point for therapeutic exploration.
- *Songwriting.* As an intervention, this technique is an integrative part of music therapy with narrative features. Clients are instructed to write a song (specifically lyrics) for their life, week, or day. As this can be a time-consuming process, the assignment can be given as homework. The song's length and style are left to the imagination of the client. In session the counselor or therapist may ask the client to experiment with singing the lyrics at varying rhythms and in styles to invoke shifts in the meaning and essence of the issue portrayed in the music. As in narrative-based approaches, clients' stories are embedded in the words and in the chosen method of delivery. Whether there is a chorus, the number of verses, and the content are all explorative points for therapeutic discussion.
- *Finger painting.* This intervention is often considered child's play, yet there is a great amount of therapeutic potential in its practice. Usually it is a nondirective process; clients are provided with the basic instructions to paint a picture of a dream, their family, themselves, and so forth (Synder, 1997). The counselor or therapist acts as a process observer and notes the colors used, pace of work, fluidity of movement, and

so on. Clients are encouraged to discuss the meaning of their art, that is, to describe the feelings and thoughts that may be associated with different parts of the painting. This intervention promotes expression in free play and is ideal in work with children or clients who are mentally retarded and who may benefit from the additional tactical stimulation of the intervention (Arlow & Kadis, 1993).

Expressive Arts

Art Therapy. Art therapy is the construction of visual images for the therapeutic expression of thoughts and feelings. The use of art as a projective intervention of the client's inner reality is a common practice in analytic theory. In the field of psychology, analysts encourage their clients to produce drawings or paintings that are then interpreted by the analyst as an expression of the clients'unconscious. The therapeutic use of art as an empowering tool for clients can be traced back to the work of **Margaret Naumburg** (Rubin, 2001). Naumburg is known in the field of expressive arts for opening **Walden** in 1914, the first school to integrate art as an educational and therapeutic tool. In her early work with children at Walden, Naumburg discovered much concerning the link between art and **cathartic expression** (Naumburg, 1955). Although not the first or only analyst to use art in therapy, Naumburg is credited as the first therapist to use **dynamic art therapy** as her primary therapeutic orientation with clients. Naumburg believed that clients' art was a form of **symbolic speech** that she as an analyst could not interpret (Rubin, 2001). This belief is still central in current art therapy approaches and empowers clients to construct their own meaning through their art.

Art as a counseling or therapy intervention is grounded in the belief that the creation of visual symbols of the client's inner reality provides a framework to begin deeper exploration and awareness. This reality is expressed through the client's drawings, paintings, and sculpting. The integrative use of art in counseling or therapy is common in work with children. As a component of **play therapy**, art is used to help children express aspects of their life that may be too painful or complex to disclose through verbal means. The inclusive and expansive nature of art allows for many unique and engaging therapeutic applications.

Dance/Movement Therapy. Dance or movement therapy involves physical movement and positioning as a means of client expression of and liberation from psychodynamic trauma and stress. The techniques used in dance or movement therapy range from simple stretching exercises and physical repositioning to vigorous and rhythmic dance. The underlying principle of dance therapy is that by stimulating the body, the mind is free to objectively explore constructive thoughts and emotions. In this way, the art of free movement is seen as *cathartic* and increases *bodily awareness* in the client. Similar to the **communication stances** of **Virginia Satir** in this approach clients' mental states are represented through expressive bodily movement. People who suffer with depression tend to be lethargic; in contrast, people who are experiencing joy show more energy and enthusiasm. This concept of mind-body connectedness is also present in the Gestalt approach. Gestalt counselors and therapists encourage clients to be aware of their bodies and movement as they experience thoughts and feelings in their mind.

Harpin (1999) offered the following concepts as a summarization of the therapeutic value of dance and movement in counseling and psychotherapy:

- *Movement is an integrating process.* Movement of the legs in the form of stomping may cause the client to feel aggression. Gentle swaying of the whole body may produce feelings of serenity or calmness. In these ways, movement and emotion are integrated.

- *Movement evokes emotions and cognitions that can be used to express other feelings and thoughts.* The feelings and thoughts that form the client's inner reality are expressed during movement. As a client experiencing esteem issues engages in forceful movements, she or he may begin to feel powerful; in turn, this feeling may produce feelings of sadness as the client realizes that she or he does not feel empowered in life.
- *Movement, emotion, and form, when expressed in relation to each other, can lead to increased awareness and insight.* Movement can produce awareness of the union between mind and body. As clients become more aware of their body, posture, and gestures, they also more fully experience their mental state.
- *Movement can deepen and expand clients' sense of being and creativity.* Through the integration of movement, clients gain a sense of presence with their bodies and with the essence and flow of life. Clients are motivated and empowered to confront and move away from destructive patterns of living as they take on the new identity as a vital and creative force. Ideally, clients use this force to effect change in other areas and dynamics in their life beyond counseling and therapy.

Drama Therapy. For centuries thespians have known the therapeutic benefits of dramatic expression. The origins of drama in therapy can be traced back to **J. L. Monreno,** the father of **psychodrama.** Drama therapy is based on experiencing human emotion through dramatic performance. Dramatic expression creates an intrapsychic and interpersonal change in clients (Petitti, 1992). Becoming another provides clients with an alternative reality to their current perception of their situation (Emunah, 1999). The **active experiencing** of this approach allows clients to try out a new self or role-play a personality characteristic that they find limiting. For example, shy introverted clients can, through dramatic play, develop their assertive voice. Other clients may have a moment of insight as they role-play an abusive parent whom they have spent years trying to understand or forgive.

Counselors or therapists who practice drama therapy may also integrate the psychoanalytic approach and use a free association method in which they encourage the client to act on whatever behavior or emotions come to mind. **Improvisation** is a common element in drama therapy. As is dance or movement therapy, the dramatic approach is used in family-systems and Gestalt counseling or therapy as a means of helping the client fully experience the **latent self** to promote holistic acceptance.

Noar (1999) suggested five benefits to the use of expressive drama in therapeutic settings:

- Clients experience stratification and fulfillment of the use of their body in dramatic action and play.
- Within settings such as the **therapeutic theater,** clients may be liberated of emotional stressors, anxiety, fear, pain, erotic feelings, and so on.
- Clients gradually improve their ability to experience holistically through imagination, play, and expression.
- Dramatic play in therapy promotes processing themes, such as trust, openness, loneliness, assertiveness, control, dependency, and rejection.
- Drama therapy creates and promotes relationships through the exploration of clients' inner world and hidden areas of their personality.

Music Therapy. Music therapy is the integration of acoustic stimuli into counseling or therapy to promote the experience and recognition of latent feelings and thoughts by clients.

Music therapy is founded on the belief that sounds, melodies, and rhythms produce **ebb and flow** that clients experience internally. This experience resonates with the clients' movement between different emotional and cognitive states. Music has always been a catalyst for human response by triggering memories, feelings, and cognitions. The integration of music into counseling or therapy provides clients with an intervention with which they may be familiar and comfortable experiencing.

Practitioners, who integrate music into their work with clients usually allow clients to choose a song that holds certain significance for their current dilemma. After listening to the musical selection in the session, the counselor or therapist acts as a processor by facilitating discussion around thoughts and feelings that emerge through the music. Some practitioners use the technique of **guided music and imagery** by choosing a musical selection for clients to listen to in hopes of inducing certain emotive or cognitive states in the clients (Butterton, 2004). Both methods of music selection are called **receptive music therapy** and they are presented to clients who are in a relaxed state so that they can fully attend to feeling and thoughts as they are evoked through the music (Wärja, 1999).

Expressive music therapy is another method commonly used to stimulate the client awareness. In this method, clients create music by playing an instrument or by singing (Wärja, 1999). Clients are not required to master their talent for musical production; the method is not focused on criteria of quality, pitch, and rhythm. Rather, expressive music therapy is intended to be a free manifestation of clients' interpretation of self or their problem.

According to research conducted by Feder and Feder (1981), there are three ways in which clients come to see music as therapeutic:

- Music can facilitate the establishing or reestablishing of relationships and social activities in a client's life.
- Music can help a client develop self-esteem through self-actualized awareness.
- The rhythmic structure of music is seen as an energizing force or a soothing force that brings order.

Narrative Approaches. In narrative approaches, therapeutic interventions involve exploration of clients' perceptions and beliefs. A common intervention strategy in the narrative approach is **poetry**. Poetic creation is a deeper form of narrative therapy, because it uses the client's imagination and may focus on more abstract elements in the client's life, such as beauty, fantasy, and imagery (Fuchs, 1999). Poetry is often experienced by the reader as a stimulus to the senses. Therapeutically, the intervention strategy of poetry can produce vivid expressions of the client's life narrative. Consider this intervention based on elements of psychodynamic and existential theory:

Poetic Sentence Completion.

Clients are given three to five sentence stems that serve as the first line of each stanza in the poem they are asked to create. Clients are free to diverge from the sentence stems through progressive lines, which allows a focal expression of clients' inner psyche. Examples of sentence stems follow: "Today I hope . . .", "Today I fear . . .", and "Today I will . . .". Such an intervention is used as a catalyst for setting goals and building awareness. Practitioner and client review the poem to extract themes and explore symbolic meaning through imagery and verse.

Another major intervention strategy used in the narrative approach is **journal writing.** Journaling writing is a reflective process that is intended to slow down clients' thought process by inscribing thoughts to paper. This intervention was developed in the belief that thoughts and feelings are connected through words (Thompson, 2004). Journaling writing is often used as a homework assignment that helps to structure the clients' emotions and cognitions for the upcoming session; the process also includes several techniques that are ideal for brief interventions. According to Thompson (2004), several exercises in journaling writing help promote client insight. The following intervention can be used with various client populations:

Clustering

The technique of clustering helps focus thoughts and alleviate cognitive stress. Clients create a **mind map** of their thoughts without attending to grammar or structure. This brief approach tends to produce good results with clients who lack the academic or intellectual capacity for more formalized narrative writing but can still benefit from the expressed word.

Symbolic Approaches.   As stated earlier, the symbolic approach does not purpose any specific approaches. Its integrative use of other interventions includes symbolic imagery, themes, and meaning. The following interventions are strongly grounded in symbolism but are not exclusive to symbolic approaches:

Sandtray

This technique is based in Jungian analytic theory and can be modified to work with other theories that highlight various elements of the intervention (Castellana & Donfrancesco, 2005). Typically used as a play therapy intervention, this symbolic approach involves a literal tray of sand that is used as a canvas by clients to explore and work through social and therapeutic issues. In this nondirective approach, clients can draw in the sand using fingers or tools and place objects through play in the spatial plane. During this activity the counselor or therapist observes themes and symbols that emerge and processes the meaning of such with clients to promote dialogue around issues.

Role-play Reversal

This intervention is a modification of psychodrama and requires active performance from clients. Clients are directed to become a different role, usually someone in their lives with whom they have a conflict or for whom they have an affinity. The counselor or therapist requires clients to stay in character and act out behaviors that are troubling them. For example, a client may have conflict with her father who she feels is too judgmental. In this approach, the client is asked to be and stay in the judgmental role of her father to promote insight into the possible dynamics and experience of this person. Through this process, the client gains perspective about her relationship to her father—the person whom she is performing as. The counselor or therapist processes feelings, assumptions, and meanings derived from the exercise with the client.

Brief Intervention Strategies

Each intervention strategy presented in the previous section on traditional intervention strategies can be modified to serve clients in brief therapy settings. The selection of expressive art approaches that involve materials that may need cleaning or disposal must be made with concern for time and feasibility of use. Remember, any intervention strategy that is modified must still be conceptually based on the therapeutic needs and goals of the client.

The following interventions are brief in nature and include elements from the three integrative approaches:

Five-minute Sprint

This brief approach is designed to develop cathartic expression through narrative and symbolic means. Clients are instructed to keep a list of various topics that they can use to write their "sprint." Topics may include existential questions such as these: "Who am I?" "Why am I here?" During sessions, if a client seems stuck, the counselor or therapist may instruct the client to do a five-minute sprint to clarify his or her thoughts and feelings. Through this exercise, an expedient cathartic expression is produced of the client's deepest fears, desires, anxieties, and so forth. Incorporation of colored pencils or crayons as writing mediums creates more symbolic and artistic expressions. The counselor or therapist processes the themes and style of the written work with the client as a means of promoting reflection and deeper emotional expression. (Thompson, 2004)

Dramatic Improvisation

This intervention is considered a Gestalt-based approach to awareness, but it can be modified and integrated into other theoretical orientations, such as cognitive-behavioral theory. Clients are asked to make impromptu expressions of session topics. For example, if a client is discussing his obsession with baseball, the counselor or therapist may tell him to get up and fully express his fanaticism through movement and performance. After the exercise, counselor or therapist and client process the feelings and thoughts experienced during and after the dramatic play. This intervention leads to greater awareness of physical, emotional, and psychological states in the client, so its use is holistic.

CLIENTS WITH SERIOUS MENTAL HEALTH ISSUES

Integrative approaches have been found to be effective in working with clients who have the diagnosis of schizophrenia. Lysaker, Lancaster, and Lysaker (2003) reported that the narrative was an effective method for exploration and management of schizophrenia. The narrative approach was also used successfully in aiding clients with schizophrenia express their thoughts when dialogue was impeded by their disorder (Lysaker, Wickett, Wilke, & Lysaker, 2003). This population of clients also benefited from drama therapy (Bielanska & Cechnicki, 1991) and art therapy (Crespo, 2003) as means of expression and rehabilitation.

Hendricks, Robinson, Bradley, and Davis (1999) conducted a study in which use of music therapy with clients who have clinical depression produced a decrease in depressive symptoms. These findings are supported by other models of music and expressive art therapies that report the enlivening effects of integrative approaches.

CROSS-CULTURAL CONSIDERATIONS

According to Semmler and Williams (2000) narrative therapy is an approach to counseling and psychotherapy that naturally addresses the cultural context in which clients exist. Narrative approaches have been used successfully with various ethnic populations, specifically Asian American (Chan, 2003), Latino-American (Bermúdez & Bermúdez, 2002), and multiracial (Rockquemore & Laszloffy, 2003). The narrative approach was also highly effective when working with women in their expression of inner realities through writing and poetry (Lee, 1997; Henehan, 2003).

Symbolic approaches have been used to build understanding and rapport in cross-cultural counseling relationships. However, practitioners of this approach must be aware of cross-cultural values and norms. The symbols that a counselor or therapist may interpret as negative or even symbolic may actually be positive or literal expressions of the client (Eisenstien-Naveh, 2001). For example, simple gender differences between practitioner and client about the issue of increasing intimacy in the client's life can have variant meanings and represent different symbols in the counseling or therapy relationship. Practitioners are wise to clarify definitions and terms when working from the symbolic approach. Continuous effort must be made by the symbolic counselor or therapist to challenge assumptions of meaning and to remain open to the phenomenological presentation of the client (Eisenstien-Naveh).

EVALUATION

Overview

This part of the chapter reviews the content of previous sections. Current supporting research is also discussed, as are the limitations of the expressive arts, narrative, and symbolic approaches.

Supporting Research

Several microstudies and case reports suggest the benefits of expressive arts, narrative, and symbolic approaches. These integrative approaches were used for the past few decades in work with older persons as a successful aspect of reminiscence groups (Cadwell, 2005). Also, these approaches were helpful in working with survivors of sexual abuse (Mills & Daniluk, 2002; Mulkey, 2004), clients with eating disorders (Russell, 2000), and at-risk youth (Hartz & Thick, 2005; Ungar, 2001). Male sexual abusers (Keenan, 1998) and batterers (Brownlee, Ginter, & Tranter, 1998) received effective help through integrated narrative counseling. Narrative approaches are being used with soldiers in the Iraq War and their families (Van der Velden & Koops, 2005) and with clients affected by terrorism (Shalif & Leibler, 2002; Witty, 2002).

In school counseling, drama therapy helped counter bullying among students (Beale, 2001). Teachers facing burnout and occupational stress were aided through music therapy approaches (Cheek, Bradley, Parr, & Lan, 2003). Music intervention was also cited as having therapeutic benefits for clients experiencing grief and loss (Gallant & Holosko, 2001).

A major problem with the integrative approaches—expressive arts, narrative, and symbolism—is the severe lack of empirical research currently available. The communities of counselors and psychotherapists who use these approaches have produced many models, case studies, and specialized therapeutic modalities. However, the studies that have been conducted concerning the integrative approaches have used small groups and small populations. The statistical significance of these studies' findings is hardly generalizable to a larger population of clients.

Limitations

The expressive arts, narrative, and symbolic approaches are excellent therapeutic tools for clients. This ever-emerging field in counseling and psychotherapy is, however, seriously limited by the lack of research studies that focus on the effectiveness of integrative approaches. As means of holistic exploration and client development, these approaches have much to offer to the field of counseling and psychotherapy. Currently, the potential for greater support and development from the therapeutic community is hindered by lack of scholarly interest in the integrative approaches.

Integrative approaches are limited by their dependence on integration with theory. This situation is seen as a limitation because many counselors and therapists use these approaches in their work with clients exclusive of any theory; instead, they rely solely on the concept of client interaction with the medium. This is an ethically unsound practice that can lead to pseudoexperimental work with clients. The expressive arts, narrative, and symbolic approaches do not, as yet, have a fully developed theory of personality from which to work. Best practices dictate the use of these approaches from some theoretical base (Levine & Levine, 1999; Rubin, 2004).

SUMMARY CHART—*Integrative Approaches*

Human Nature

Integrative approaches in counseling and psychotherapy are based on the concept that art, writing, and symbolic meaning, when combined with theory, are effective methods of client expression and exploration. From an integrative perspective, clients benefit from the use of techniques and modalities that holistically address their experiential living and meaning.

Major Constructs

Unlike theoretical constructs, integrative approaches do not have universally accepted concepts of client development, role of the therapist, and so forth. The major constructs of the integrative approaches are the expressive arts, narrative, and symbolism. Each of these constructs uses different modalities as means of encouraging client awareness and expression.

Goals

The first goal of integrative approaches is to enhance theoretically based counseling or psychotherapy with more holistic means of therapeutic guidance and intervention. The second goal of using expressive arts, narrative, and symbolic approaches is to facilitate greater client expression and awareness of self through active experiencing of issues based in psychically disturbed thoughts and feelings.

Change Process

Counselors and therapists who use integrative approaches believe that (1) clients change when their current life perspective no longer represents their desired goals; (2) clients change by accepting control, responsibility, and power for the construction and insightful living of their inner realities; and (3) client change is a process of authentic reflection, accountability, and openness toward growth and resolution.

Interventions

Interventions in the integrative approaches are numerous and unstandardized. There are no set interventions that can be classified as belonging to any single approach; considerable overlap exists in the techniques of creative expression. Some counselors or therapists may consider certain techniques as specifically narrative or exclusively expressive art.

Limitations

The integrative approaches are limited by the lack of empirical research on the effectiveness and applicability of the expressive arts, narrative, and symbolism in counseling and psychotherapy. Also, these approaches depend on theoretical integration with fully developed theories of counseling or psychotherapy to be practical and effective.

THE CASE OF JONATHAN: *An Integrative Approach*

Jonathan's case contains personal and interpersonal dynamics that can be evaluated using each of the integrated approaches. For the purposes of clarity and continuity, this case study will be presented from the viewpoint of only one of the integrative approaches: the narrative perspective.

In the narrative approach, Jonathan's counselor would assess that the turmoil in Jonathan's life represents a theme-based story complete with antagonistic symbols, protagonist aspirations, plot twists, and a yet undetermined conclusion. This framework suggests an exciting story, a real page turner, but the reality for Jonathan is that his life narrative has left him with "little to live for".

In the initial interview, Jonathan shares his life story, that is, the experiences that brought him to this current place and time. The main character in Jonathan's story is himself, a being at odds with his own regrets, emotions, and relationships. Jonathan's unsuccessful choices and unfulfilled obligations reveal a struggle within his life narrative. These themes have led to life changes and stressors that have formed a pattern of guilt, frustration, hopelessness, and inner conflict as expressed through his dreams.

Jonathan's culturally competent counselor decides that the use of an integrated approach with Jonathan may produce effective results, considering his ethnic heritage as a Navajo. The Navajo people have religious traditions of rituals designed around songs, paintings, and dance to enact stories of life's origin, experiences, and culmination. The Navajo people also conceptualize the life narrative as a journey of four directions beginning in the East with the rising sun and ending not in the West but in the North as one contemplates the totality of an experience and makes new choices in preparation for a new beginning in the East. With such rich metaphors and symbols from a culture that Jonathan embraces, change and awareness for Jonathan are centered in the North with a natural progression toward a new beginning as Jonathan and his counselor reach therapeutic outcomes.

Using a simple narrative exercise, the counselor, who is working from person-centered theory, invites Jonathan to write a story in his own words about the highs and lows of his journey. In the exploration of Jonathan's narrative, the counselor and Jonathan process themes of joy, despair, hope, and fear. Through the integration of the narrative approach with person-centered theory, Jonathan becomes aware of his own actualization and growth over the years. Within Jonathan's life narrative are consistent patterns of loss and transition. Jonathan begins to see his poor management of change and its natural occurrence in life as he looks from the North in Navajo tradition. From this point on in the counseling process, Jonathan and his counselor plan strategies for managing and reauthoring Jonathan's current life script.

Jonathan begins his reauthoring with elements in his social and cultural environment. As he feels drawn to his family of origin and children, Jonathan creates goals for nourishing and reconnecting those relationships. As a proud member of the Navajo, Jonathan has expressed feelings of shame, because he believes his narrative has diverged away from the values and practices of his people. With the assistance of his counselor, Jonathan begins to see that he has the power and responsibility to create a life story that will honor his cultural and familial values.

Jonathan's dreams are a part of his life narrative as well. Ideally, as Jonathan becomes more aware of his anxieties toward change and begins to feel empowered to make changes to improve his life, the nightmares will decrease and eventually cease. These dreams are conceptualized by Jonathan and his counselor as a product of a stressful and fearful life story. Jonathan views these dreams as a manifestation of taking a wrong turn in his life journey, as they began after he left his family and the reservation. He makes plans to reestablish his core values and family as major elements in his narrative.

As Jonathan's actualizing tendency becomes stronger, he is no longer focused on the limitations of his life. He develops strategies for a better today and tomorrow. He is now in the East of his journey, looking forward to another new beginning and the possibility of a full and productive life.

References

Abrams, E., & Loewenthal, D. (2005). Responsibility and ethico-moral values in counseling and psychotherapy. *Existential Analysis, 16*(1), 73–86.

Abreu, J. M., Gim Chung, R. H., & Atkinson, D. R. (2000). Multicultural counseling training: Past, present, and future directions. *The Counseling Psychologist, 28,* 641–656.

Adams, G. (2002). A theistic perspective on Ken Wilber's transpersonal psychology. *Journal of Contemporary Religion, 17,* 165–179.

Adams, M., Bell, L. A., & Griffin, P. (Eds.). (1997). *Teaching for diversity and social justice: A sourcebook.* New York: Routledge.

Adams, M., Blumenfeld, W. J., Castaneda, R., Hackman, H. W., Peters, M. L., & Zuniga, X. (Eds.). (2000). *Readings for diversity and social justice: An anthology on racism, antisemitism, sexism, heterosexism, ableism, and classism.* New York: Routledge.

Adams, W. W. (1999). The interpermeation of self and world: The empirical research, existential phenomenology, and transpersonal psychology. *Journal of Phenomenological Psychology, 30,* 39–66.

Addis, M. E., Hatgis, C., Krasnow, A. D., Jacob, K., Bourne, L., & Mansfield, A. (2004). Effectiveness of cognitive-behavioral treatment for panic disorder versus treatment as usual in a managed care setting. *Journal of Consulting and Clinical Psychology, 72,* 625–635.

Adler, A. (1978). Cooperation between the sexes. In H. L. Ansbacher & R. R. Ansbacher (Eds.), *Writings on women, love, and marriage, sexuality and its disorders.* Garden City, NY: Doubleday.

Adler, A. (1926/2000). *Psychotherapie und Erziehung.* San Francisco: Alfred Adler Institute of San Francisco, Adler Translation Project Archives. Retrieved from http://ourworld.compuserve.com/homepages/hstein/qu-encou.htm

Adler, A. (1931/1998). *What life could mean to you.* (C. Brett, Trans.). Center City, MN: Hazelden Foundation.

Adler, A. (1935). The fundamental view of Individual Psychology. *International Journal of Individual Psychology, 1,* 1–8.

Adler, A. (2005a). In H. T. Stein (Ed.), *Journal articles: 1931–1937.* Bellingham, WA: Classical Adlerian Translation Project.

Adler, A. (2005b). In H. T. Stein (Ed.), *Lectures to physicians and medical students.* Bellingham, WA: Classical Adlerian Translation Project.

Agosin, T. (1992). Psychosis, dreams, and mysticism in the clinical domain. In F. Halligan & J. Shea (Eds.), *The fires of desire* (pp. 41–65). New York: Crossroad.

Ajaya, S. (1997). *Psychology East and West: A unifying paradigm.* Honesdale, PA: Himalayan Institute.

Albinsson, L., & Strang, P. (2003). Existential concerns of families of late-stage dementia patients: Questions of freedom, choices, isolation, death, and meaning. *Journal of Palliative Medicine, 6*(2), 225–236.

Alexander, F. M. (1974). *The resurrection of the body.* New York: Dell.

Allport, G. W. (1961). *Pattern and growth in personality.* New York: Holt, Rinehart & Winston.

Almaas, A. H. (1988). *The pearl beyond price: Integrating of personality into being: An object relations approach.* Berkeley, CA: Diamond Books.

Almond, R. (2003). The holding function of theory. *Journal of the American Psychoanalytic Association, 51,* 131–154.

American Psychiatric Association. (1994). *Diagnostic and statistical manual of mental disorders* (4th ed.). Washington, DC: Author.

American Psychiatric Association. (2000). *Diagnostic and statistical manual of mental disorders* (4th ed.). Washington, DC: Author.

Ansbacher, H. L. (1965). The structure of Individual Psychology. In B. B. Wolman (Ed.), *Scientific psychology* (pp. 340–364) New York: Basic Books.

Ansbacher, H. L. (1966). Gemeinschaftsgeguehl. *Individual Psychology News Letter, 17,* 13–15.

Ansbacher, H. L. (1968). The concept of social interest. *Journal of Individual Psychology, 24,* 131–149.

Ansbacher, H. L. (1989). Adlerian psychotherapy: The tradition of brief psychotherapy. *Individual Psychology, 45,* 26–33. (Original work published in 1972)

Ansbacher, H. L., & Ansbacher, R. (1956). *The Individual Psychology of Alfred Adler.* New York: Harper & Row.

Ansbacher, H. L., & Ansbacher, R. (1964). *Superiority and social interest.* Evanston, IL: Northwestern University Press.

Aponte, J., & Wold, J. (Eds.). (2000). *Psychological intervention and cultural diversity* (2nd ed.). Needham Heights, MA: Allyn & Bacon.

Arciniega, G. M., & Newlon, B. J. (2003). Counseling and psychotherapy: Multicultural considerations. In D. Capuzzi & D. R. Gross (Eds.), *Counseling and Psychotherapy: Theories and interventions* (3rd ed., pp. 417–441). Upper Saddle River, NJ: Merrill/Prentice Hall.

Arciniega, M., & Newlon, B. (2003). Counseling and psychotherapy: Multicultural considerations. In D. Capuzzi & D. Gross (Eds.), *Counseling and psychotherapy: Theories and interventions* (2nd ed., pp. 435–458). Upper Saddle River, NJ: Merrill/Prentice Hall.

Ardell, D. B. (1988). The history and future of the wellness movement. In J. P. Opatz (Ed.), *Wellness promotion strategies: Selected proceedings of the eighth annual National Wellness Conference.* Dubuque, IA: Kendall/Hunt.

Ariel, S. (1999). *Culturally competent family therapy: A general model.* Westport, CT: Greenwood Press.

Arlow, J. A., & Kadis, A. (1993). Finger painting. In C. E. Schaefer & D. M. Cangelosi (Eds.), *Play therapy techniques* (pp. 161–175). Northvale, NJ: Aronson.

Arredondo, P. (1999). Multicultural counseling competencies as tools to address oppression and racism. *Journal of Counseling and Development, 77*(1), 102–112.

Arredondo, P., & Toporek, R. (2004). Multicultural counseling competencies equals ethical practice. *Journal of Mental Health Counseling, 26*(1), 44–56.

Arredondo, P., Toporek, R., Brown, R., Sanchez, J., Locke, D., Sanchez, J., & Stadler, H. (1996). Operationalization of the multicultural counseling competencies. *Journal of Multicultural Counseling and Development, 24*(1), 42–78.

Aron, L. (1998). The clinical body and the reflexive mind. In L. Aron & F. S. Anderson (Eds.), *Relational perspectives on the body.* Hillsdale, NJ: Analytic Press.

Baker, A., Boggs, T. G., & Lewin, T. J. (2001). Randomized controlled trial of brief cognitive-behavioural interventions among regular users of amphetamine. *Addiction, 96,* 1279–1287.

Ballou, M., & Gabalac, N. (1984). *A feminist position on mental health.* Springfield, IL: Thomas.

Ballou, M., & West, C. (2000). Feminist therapy approaches. In M. Biaggio & M. Hersen (Eds.), *Issues in the psychology of women* (pp. 273–297). New York: Kluwer Academic/Plenum.

Bandura, A. (1977). Self-efficacy: Toward a unifying theory of behavior change. *Psychological Review, 84,* 191–215.

Bandura, A. (1986). *Social foundations of thought and action.* Upper Saddle River, NJ: Prentice Hall.

Barker, P. (1985). *Using metaphors in psychotherapy.* New York: Brunner/Mazel.

Barker, R. L. (2003). *The social work dictionary.* Washington, DC: National Association of Social Workers.

Barlow, D. H., & Cerny, J. A. (1988). *Psychological treatment of panic.* New York: Guilford Press.

Barrett-Lennard, G. T. (1998). *Carl Rogers's helping system: Journey and substance.* Thousand Oaks, CA: Sage.

Baruth, L. G., & Robinson, E. H. (1987). *An introduction to the counseling profession.* Upper Saddle River, NJ: Prentice Hall.

Batchelor, S. (1997). *Buddhism without beliefs: A contemporary guide to awakening.* New York: Riverhead Books.

Bates, M., Johnson, C., & Blaker, J. (1982). *Group leadership.* Denver, CO: Love.

Bateson, G. (1951). The convergence of science and psychiatry. In J. Ruesch & G. Bateson (Eds.), *Communication: The social matrix of psychiatry* (pp. 257–272). New York: Norton.

Bateson, G. (1979). *Mind and nature: A necessary unity.* New York: Dutton.

Bateson, G., Jackson, D. D., Haley, J., & Weakland, J. G. (1976). Toward a theory of schizophrenia. In C. E. Sluzki & D. C. Ransom (Eds.), *Double bind: The foundation of the communicational approach to the family* (pp. 3–22). New York: Grune & Stratton.

Bateson, M. C. (1972). *Our own metaphor.* New York: Knopf.

Bauman, S., & Waldo, M. (1998). Existential theory and mental health counseling: If it were a snake, it would have bitten! *Journal of Mental Health Counseling, 23,* 13–27.

Beale, A. V. (2001). "Bullybusters": Using drama to empower students to take a stand against bullying behavior. *Professional School Counseling, 4*(4), 300–306.

Bean, R. A., Perry, B. J., & Bedell, T. M. (2001). Developing culturally competent marriage and family therapists: Guidelines for working with Hispanic families. *Journal of Marital and Family Therapy, 27,* 43–54.

Beard, J. H., Propst, R. N., & Malamud, T. J. (1982). The Fountain House model of psychiatric rehabilitation. *Psychosocial Rehabilitation Journal, 5*(1), 47–53.

Beavers, W. R., & Hampson, R. B. (1990). *Successful families.* New York: Norton.

Beck, A. T. (1976). *Cognitive therapy and emotional disorders.* New York: International Universities Press.

Beck, A. T., & Emery, G. (1985). *Anxiety disorders and phobias.* New York: Basic Books.

Beck, A. T., Freeman, A., Davis, D. D., et al. (2004). *Cognitive therapy of personality disorders* (2nd ed.). New York: Guilford Press.

Beck, A. T., Hollon, S. D., Young, J. E., Bedrosian, R .C., & Budenz, D. (1985). Treatment of depression with cognitive therapy and amitriptyline. *Archives of General Psychiatry, 42,* 142–148.

Beck, A. T., Rush, A. J., Shaw, B. F., & Emery, G. (1979). *Cognitive therapy of depression.* New York: Guilford Press.

Beck, A. T., Wright, F. D., Newman, C. F., & Liese, B. S. (1993). *Cognitive therapy of substance abuse.* New York: Guilford Press.

Becker, R. (2000). La femme n'existe pas (Jacques Lacan): L'hjomme non plus. *Gestalt Review, 4*(1), 26–28.

Becvar, D. S., & Becvar, R. J. (2002). *Family therapy: A systemic integration.* Boston: Allyn & Bacon.

Beecher, W., & Beecher, M. (1966). *Beyond success and failure.* Dallas, TX: Willard & Marguerite Beecher Foundation.

Beitin, B. K., & Allen, K. R. (2005). Resilience in Arab American couples after September 11, 2001: A systems perspective. *Journal of Marital and Family Therapy, 31,* 251–267.

Belkin, G. S. (1980). *An introduction to counseling.* Dubuque, IA: Brown.

Belkin, G. S. (1984). *Introduction to counseling* (2nd ed.). Dubuque, IA: Brown.

Bell, L. (1997). Theoretical foundations for social justice education. In M. Adams, L. Bell, & P. Griffin (Eds.), *Teaching for diversity and social justice* (pp. 3–15). New York: Routledge.

Bem, S. L. (1976). Probing the promise of androgyny. In A. G. Kaplan & J. P. Bean (Eds.), *Beyond sex-role stereotypes: Readings toward a psychology of androgyny* (pp. 47–62). Boston: Little, Brown.

Bem, S. L. (1981). Gender schema theory: A cognitive account of sex typing. *Psychological Review, 88,* 354–364.

Bem, S. L. (1987). Probing the problem of androgyny. In M. Walsh (Ed.), *The psychology of women: Ongoing debates.* New Haven, CT: Yale University Press.

Bem, S. L. (1993). *The lenses of gender.* New Haven, CT: Yale University Press.

Bermúdez, J. M., & Bermúdez, S. (2002). Altar-making with Latino families: A narrative therapy perspective. *Journal of Family Psychotherapy, 13*(4), 329–347.

Berg, I. K., & Miller, S. D. (1992). *Working with the problem drinker: A solution-focused approach.* New York: Norton.

Bertolino, B. (1999). *Therapy with troubled teenagers: Rewriting young lives in progress.* New York: Wiley.

Bertolino, B., & O'Hanlon, B. (2002). *Collaborative, competency-based counseling and therapy.* Boston: Allyn & Bacon.

Beshai, J., & Naboulsi, M. (2004). Existential perspectives on death anxiety. *Psychological Reports, 95*(2), 507–514.

Bidwell, D. R. (1999). Ken Wilber's transpersonal psychology: An introduction and preliminary critique. *Pastoral Psychology, 48,* 81–90.

Bielanska, A., & Cechnicki, A. (1991). Drama therapy as a means of rehabilitation for schizophrenic patients: Our impressions. *American Journal of Psychotherapy, 45*(4), 566–576.

Binswanger, L., & Boss, M. (1983). Existential analysis and Daseins analysis. In T. Millon (Ed.), *Theories of personality and psychopathology* (3rd ed., pp. 283–289). New York: Holt, Rinehart & Winston.

Bischof, G. H., Richmond, C. J., & Case, A. R. (2003). Detoxification at home: A brief solution-oriented family systems approach. *Contemporary Family Therapy, 25,* 1–739.

Bitter, J. R. (2004). Two approaches to counseling a parent alone: Toward a Gestalt-Adlerian integration. *The Family Journal: Counseling and Therapy for Couples and Families, 12*(4), 358–367.

Blinderman, C., & Cherny, N. (2005). Existential issues do not necessarily result in existential suffering: Lessons from cancer patients in Israel. *Palliative Medicine, 19*(5), 371–381.

Blow, A. J., & Sprenkle, D. H. (2001). Common factors across theories of marriage and family therapy: A modified Delphi study. *Journal of Marital and Family Therapy, 27,* 385–401.

Boadella, D. (1987). *Wilhelm Reich: The evolution of his work.* Boston: Arkana.

Bohart, A. C. (1990). A cognitive client-centered perspective on borderline personality development. In G. Lietaer, J. Rombauts, & R. Van Balen (Eds.), *Client-centered and experiential psychotherapy in the nineties* (pp. 599–622). Leuven, Belgium: Leuven University Press.

Bohm, D. (1973). Quantum theory as an indication of a new order in physics, Part B: Implicate and explicate order in physical law. *Foundations of Physics, 2,* 139–168.

Boorstein, S. (1996). Transpersonal context and interpretation. *ATP Newsletter,* 5–8.

Bordin, E. S. (1994). Theory and research on the therapeutic working alliance: New directions. In A. O. Horvath & L. S. Greenberg (Eds.), *The working alliance* (pp. 13–37). New York: Wiley.

Borstnar, J., Bucar, M. M., Makovec, M. R., Burck, C., & Daniel, G. (2005). Co-constructing a cross-cultural course: Resisting and replicating colonizing practices. *Family Process, 44,* 121–131.

Boss, M. (1981). Transpersonal psychotherapy. In R. Walsh & F. Vaughan (Eds.), *Beyond ego: Transpersonal dimensions in psychology* (pp. 161–164). Los Angeles: Tarcher.

Bottome, P. (1957). *Alfred Adler: A portrait from life.* New York: Vanguard Press.

Bottome, P. (1962). *The goal.* New York: Vanguard Press.

Bowen, M. (1978). *Family therapy in clinical practice.* New York: Aronson.

Bowen, M. (1996). The myth of nondirectiveness: The case of Jill. In B. A. Farber, D. D. Brink, & P. M. Raskin (Eds.), *The psychotherapy of Carl Rogers: Cases and commentaries* (pp. 84–94). New York: Guilford Press.

Bowers, E. (1997). The effects of CT/RT "Quality School" programming on attendance, academic performance, student self-concept, and relationships in a rural elementary school. *Journal of Reality Therapy, 16*(2), 21–30.

Bowman. C. (2000). Commentary on Leanne O'Shea's "Sexuality: Old struggles and new challenges." *Gestalt Review, 4*(1), 29–31.

Bowman, C. E., & Nevis, E. C. (2005). The history and development of Gestalt therapy. In A. L. Woldt & S. M. Toman (Eds.). *Gestalt therapy: History, theory, and practice* (pp. 3–20). Thousand Oaks, CA: Sage.

Boy, A. V., & Pine, G. J. (1982). *Client centered counseling: A renewal.* Boston: Allyn & Bacon.

Boy, A. V., & Pine, G. J. (1999). *A person-centered foundation for counseling and psychotherapy* (2nd ed.). Springfield, IL: Thomas.

Brammer, L. M. (1985). *The helping relationship: Process and skills* (3rd ed.). Upper Saddle River, NJ: Prentice Hall.

Brammer, L. M., Abrego, P., & Shostrom, E. (1993). *Therapeutic counseling and psychotherapy* (6th ed.). Upper Saddle River, NJ: Prentice Hall.

Brammer, L. M., & MacDonald, G. (1996). *The helping relationship: Process and skills* (6th ed.). Needham Heights, MA: Allyn & Bacon.

Brantley, J. (2003). *Calming your anxious mind: How mindfulness and compassion can free you from anxiety, fear, and panic.* Oakland, CA: New Harbinger.

Bratter, B., Bratter, T., Maxym, C., Radda, H., & Steiner, K. (1993). The John Dewey Academy: A residential quality school for self-destructive adolescents who have superior intellectual and intuitive potential. *Journal of Reality Therapy, 12*(2), 42–53.

Brazier, D. (Ed.). (1993). *Beyond Carl Rogers: Toward a psychotherapy for the 21st century.* London: Constable.

Breitbart, W., Gibson, C., Poppito, S., & Berg, A. (2004). Psychotherapeutic interventions at the end of life: A focus on meaning and spirituality. *Canadian Journal of Psychiatry, 49,* 366–372.

Brems, C. (2000). *Dealing with challenges in psychotherapy and counseling.* Belmont, CA: Brooks/Cole.

Brenner, C. (1974). *An elementary textbook of psychoanalysis.* New York: Doubleday.

Bretall, R. (Ed.). (1951). *A Kierkegaard anthology.* Princeton, NJ: Princeton University Press.

Broder, M. S. (2001). Dr. Albert Ellis—in his own words—on success. *Journal of Rational-Emotive and Cognitive-Behavior Therapy, 19*(2), 77–88.

Brosnan, M. J., Scott, F. J., Fox, S., & Pye, J. (2004). Gestalt processing in autism: Failure to process perceptual relationships and the implications for contextual understanding. *Journal of Child Psychology and Psychiatry, 45*(3), 459–569.

Broussard, B. (2005). Women's experiences of bulimia nervosa. *Journal of Advanced Nursing, 49*(1), 43–51.

Brown, D., & Engler, J. (1986). The stages of mindfulness meditation: A validation study: Part II. Discussion. In K. Wilber, J. Engler, & D. Brown (Eds.), *Transformations of consciousness: Conventional and contemplative perspectives on development.* Boston: Shambhala.

Brown, D., Porte, M., & Dysart, M. (1984). Differences in visual sensitivity among mindfulness meditators and nonmeditators. *Perceptual and Motor Skills, 58,* 727–733.

Brown, D., & Srebalus, D. J. (1988). *An introduction to the counseling profession.* Upper Saddle River, NJ: Prentice Hall.

Brown, D., & Srebalus, D. J. (2003). *Introduction to the counseling profession* (3rd ed., pp. 39–62). Boston: Allyn & Bacon.

Brown, J. A., & Pate, R. H. (1983). *Being a counselor: Direction and challenges.* Monterey, CA: Brooks/Cole.

Brown, L. S. (1986). Gender role analysis: A neglected component of psychological assessment. *Psychotherapy: Theory, Research, and Practice, 23,* 243–248.

Brown, L. S. (1994). *Subversive dialogues: Theory in feminist therapy.* New York: Basic Books.

Brown, L. S., & Ballou, M. (Eds.). (1992). *Personality and psychopathology: Feminist reappraisals.* New York: Guilford Press.

Brown, S. D., & Lent, R. W. (2000). *Handbook of counseling psychology* (3rd ed.). New York: Wiley.

Brown, T., O'Leary, T., & Barlow, D. H. (1994). Generalized anxiety disorder. In D. H. Barlow (Ed.), *Clinical handbook of psychological disorders* (pp. 201–223). New York: Guilford Press.

Brownlee, K., Ginter, C., & Tranter, D. (1998). Narrative invention with men who batter: An appraisal and extension of the Jenkins model. *Family Therapy, 25*(2), 85–96.

Brownell, P. (2003a). Gestalt global's Gestalt therapy construct library: Constructs from "A" through "C." *Gestalt, 7*(1). Retrieved March 7, 2005, from http://www.g-gej.org/7-1/a-c.html

Brownell, P. (2003b). Gestalt global's Gestalt therapy construct library: Constructs from "D" through "F." *Gestalt, 7*(1). Retrieved March 7, 2005, from http://www.g-gej.org/7-1/d-f.html

Brownell, P. (2003c). Gestalt global's Gestalt therapy construct library: Constructs from "G" through "P." *Gestalt, 7*(1). Retrieved March 7, 2005, from http://www.g-gej.org/7-1/g-p.html

Brownell, P. (2003d). Gestalt global's Gestalt therapy construct library: Constructs from "Q" through "Z." *Gestalt, 7*(1). Retrieved March 7, 2005, from http://www.g-gej.org/7-1/q-z.html

Brownell, P. (2003e). Gestalt global's Gestalt therapy construct library: Preamble and preliminary considerations. *Gestalt, 7*(1). Retrieved March 7, 2005, from http://www.g-gej.org/7-1/librarypreamble.html

Brownell, P. (2004). Perceiving you, perceiving me: Self-conscious emotions and Gestalt therapy. *Gestalt, 8*(1). Retrieved March 7, 2005, from http://www.g-gej.org/8-1/selfconscious.html.

Brownell, P., & Fleming, K. (2005). Gestalt therapy in community mental health. In A. L. Woldt & S. M. Toman (Eds.), *Gestalt therapy: History, theory, and practice* (pp. 257–277). Thousand Oaks, CA: Sage.

Buber, M. (1970). *I and thou.* New York: Scribner.

Buchheimer, A. (1959). From group to "gemeinschaft." In K. A. Adler & D. Deutsch (Eds.), *Essays in individual psychology* (pp. 242–247). New York: Grove Press.

Bugental, J. (1978). *Psychotherapy and process: The fundamentals of an existential humanistic approach.* Reading, MA: Addison-Wesley.

Bulkeley, P., & Bulkley, K. (2005). *Dreaming beyond death.* Boston: Beacon.

Burley, T., & Freier, N. C. (2004). Character structure: A Gestalt cognitive theory. *Psychotherapy: Theory, Research, Practice, Training, 41*(3), 321–331.

Burns, D. D. (1999). *Feeling good: The new mood therapy* (Rev ed.). New York: Avon Press.

Burns, D. D., & Auerbach, A. (1996). Therapeutic empathy in cognitive-behavioral therapy. In P. M. Salkovskis (Ed.), *Frontiers of cognitive therapy* (pp. 135–164). New York: Guilford Press.

Butterton, M. (2004). *Music and meaning: Opening minds in the caring and healing professions.* Oxford, England: Radcliffe Medical Press.

Buxton, A. (2005). Conceptualisation and existential therapy. *Existential Analysis, 16*(1), 131–143.

Cain, D. J. (1986). A call for the "write stuff" [Editorial]. *Person-Centered Review, 1*(2), 117–124.

Cain, D. J. (1987). Carl R. Rogers: The man, his vision, his impact. *Person-Centered Review, 2*(3), 283–288.

Caldwell, C. (1997). *Getting in touch: The guide to new body-centered therapies.* Wheaton, IL: Theosophical Publishing.

Caldwell, R. L. (2005). At the confluence of memory and meaning—life review with older adults and families: Using narrative therapy and the expressive arts to remember and re-author stories of resilience. *Family Journal: Counseling and Therapy for Couples and Families, 13*(2), 172–175.

Campbell, J. M. (2000). *Becoming an effective supervisor: A workbook for counselors and psychotherapists.* Philadelphia: Accelerated Development.

Cannon, B. (1991). *Sartre and psychoanalysis: An existentialist challenge to clinical metatheory.* Lawrence: University Press of Kansas.

Cappiliez, P., & O'Rourke, N. (2002). Personality traits and existential concerns as predictors of the function of reminiscence in older adults. *Journals of Gerontology Series B: Psychological Sciences & Social Sciences, 57B*(2), 116–124.

Capra, F. (1982). *The turning point: Science, society and the rising culture.* New York: Simon & Schuster.

Capra, F. (1992). Newtonian Psychology. *Mind Field, 1,* 41–66.

Capuzzi, D., Gross, D. R., & Stauffer, M. D., (Eds.) (2006). *Introduction to group work* (4th ed.). Denver, CO: Love.

Carkhuff, R. (1969). *Helping and human relations: A primer for lay and professional helpers* (Vols. 1, 2). New York: Holt, Rinehart & Winston.

Carkuff, R. R., & Barenson, B. G. (1967). *Beyond counseling and psychotherapy.* New York: Holt, Rinehart & Winston.

Carkhuff, R. R., & Berenson, B. G. (1977). *Beyond counseling and therapy* (2nd ed.). New York: Holt, Rinehart & Winston.

Carlson, J., Watts, R. E., & Maniacci, M. (2006). *Adlerian therapy: Theory and practice.* Washington, DC: American Psychological Association.

Carrier, J. W., & Haley, M. (2005). Psychotherapy groups. In D. Capuzzi, D. Gross, & M. Stauffer (Eds.), *Introduction to group work* (4th ed.). Denver, CO: Love.

Carter, B., & McGoldrick, M. (2004). Overview: The expanded family life cycle: Individual, family and social perspectives. In B. Carter & M. McGoldrick

(Eds.), *The expanded family life cycle* (pp. 1–26). New York: Gardner Press.

Cass, V. C. (1979). Homosexual identity formation: A theoretical model. *Journal of homosexuality, 4*(3), 219–235.

Castellana, F., & Donfrancesco, A. (2005). Sandplay in Jungian analysis: Matter and symbolic integration. *Journal of Analytic Psychology, 50*(3), 367–385.

Celano, M. P., & Kaslow, N. J. (2000). Culturally competent family interventions: Review and case illustrations. *American Journal of Family Therapy, 28,* 217–228.

Chan, D. W. (2003). Multicultural considerations in counseling Chinese clients: Introducing the narrative. *Asian Journal of Counseling, 10*(2), 169–192.

Chan, I., Kong, P., Leung, P., Au, A., Li, P., Chung, R., Po, L. M., & Yu, P. (2005). Cognitive-behavioral group program for Chinese heterosexual HIV-infected men in Hong Kong, *Patient Education and Counseling, 56,* 78–84.

Chance, E., Bibens, R., Cowley, J., Prouretedal, M., Dolese, P., & Virtue, D. (1990). Lifeline: A drug/alcohol treatment program for negatively addicted inmates. *Journal of Reality Therapy, 9,* 33–38.

Chandler, C. K., Holden, J. M., & Kolander, C. A. (1992). Counseling for spiritual wellness: Theory and practice. *Journal of Counseling and Development, 71,* 168–175.

Chandler, R., Worell, J., & Johnson, D. (2000, August). Process and outcomes in psychotherapy with women. Joint task force final report. In J. Worell (Chair), *Feminist therapy: Is it just good therapy?* Symposium held at the meeting of the American Psychological Association, Washington, DC.

Chandler, R., Worell, J., Johnson, D., Blount, A., & Lusk, M. (1999, April). *Measuring long-term outcomes of feminist counseling and psychotherapy.* Paper presented at the annual meeting of the American Psychological Association, Boston.

Cheatham, H., D'Andrea, M., Ivey, A., Ivey, M., Pedersen, P., & Rigazio-DiGillio, L. (2002). Multicultural counseling and therapy II: Integrative practice. In A. Ivey, M. D'Andrea, M. Ivey, & L. Simek-Morgan (Eds.), *Theories of counseling and psychotherapy: A multicultural perspective* (pp. 329–362). Boston: Allyn & Bacon.

Cheek, J. R., Bradley, L. J., Parr, G., & Lan, W. (2003). Using music therapy techniques to treat teacher burnout. *Journal of Mental Health Counseling, 25*(3), 204–218.

Chen, S. W., & Davenport, D. S. (2005). Cognitive-behavioral therapy with Chinese American clients: Cautions and Modifications. *Psychotherapy: Theory, Research, Practice, and Training, 42,* 101–110.

Chesler, P. (1972). *Women and madness.* New York: Doubleday.

Chesler, P. (1990). Twenty years since *Women and Madness:* Toward a feminist institute of mental health and healing. *Journal of Mind and Behavior, 11,* 313–322.

Christopher, J. C. (1996). Counseling's inescapable moral visions. *Journal of Counseling and Development, 75,* 17–25.

Chodorow, N. J. (1978). *The reproduction of mothering.* Berkeley: University of California Press.

Chrisler, J., & Ulsh, M. (2001). Feminist bibliotherapy: Report on a survey of feminist therapists. *Women and Therapy, 23,* 71–85.

Chung, R., & Bemak, F. (2002). The relationship of culture and empathy in cross-cultural counseling. *Journal of Counseling and Development, 80,* 154–60.

Clarkson, P. (2004). *Gestalt counseling in action* (3rd ed.). Thousand Oaks, CA: Sage.

Clemmens, M. C. (2000). Response to Leanne O'Shea's "Sexuality: Old struggles and new challenges." *Gestalt Review, 4*(1), 35–37.

Clemmens, M. C., & Matzko, H. (2005). Gestalt approaches to substance use/abuse/dependency: Theory and practice. In A. L. Woldt & S. M. Toman (Eds.), *Gestalt therapy: History, theory, and practice* (pp. 279–300). Thousand Oaks, CA: Sage.

Clum, G. A. (1990). *Coping with panic: A drug-free approach to dealing with anxiety attacks.* Pacific Grove, CA: Brooks/Cole.

Coady, N. F. (1992). Rationale and directions for the increased emphasis on the therapeutic relationship in family therapy. *Contemporary Family Therapy, 14,* 467–479.

Cohn, H. (2002). *Heidegger and the roots of psychotherapy.* London: Continuum Press.

Coker, E. (2004). The construction of religious and cultural meaning in Egyptian psychiatric patient charts. *Mental Health, Religion and Culture, 7*(4), 323–358.

Colaizzi, P. (2002). Psychotherapy and existential therapy. *Journal of Phenomenological Psychology, 33*(1), 73–112.

Combrinck-Graham, L. (1985). A developmental model for family systems. *Family Process, 24,* 139–150.

Combrinck-Graham, L. (1988). Adolescent sexuality in the family life spiral. In C. J. Falicov (Ed.), *Family transitions* (pp. 107–131). New York: Guilford Press.

Combs, A., & Snygg, D. (1959). *Individual behavior* (Rev. ed.). New York: Harper.

Combs, A., Soper, D., Gooding, C., Benton, J., Dickman, J., & Usher, R. (1969). *Florida studies in the helping professions.* Gainesville: University Press of Florida.

Combs, A. W. (1986). What makes a good helper? A person-centered approach. *Person-Centered Review, 1,* 51–61.

Combs, A. W. (1988). Some current issues for person-centered therapy. *Person-Centered Review, 3*(3), 263–276.

Combs, A. W., & Avila, D. (1985). *Helping relationships: Basic concepts for the helping professions.* Boston: Allyn & Bacon.

Combs, A. W., & Gonzalez, D. M. (1994). *Helping relationships: Basic concepts for the helping profession* (4th ed.). Needham Heights, MA: Allyn & Bacon.

Comstock, D. (2005). *Diversity and development: Critical contexts that shape our lives and relationships.* Belmont, CA: Brooks/Cole.

Connolly Gibbons, M. B., Crits-Cristoph, P., Levinson, J., & Barber, J. (2003). Flexibility in manual-based psychotherapies: Predictors of therapist intervention in interpersonal and cognitive-behavioral therapy. *Psychotherapy Research, 13,* 169–185.

Constantine, M. G. (2001). Multicultural training, theoretical orientation, empathy, and multicultural case conceptualization ability in counselors. *Journal of Mental Health Counseling, 23*(4), 357–372.

Coon, D. J. (1992). Testing the limits of sense and science: American experimental psychologists combat spiritualism, 1880–1920. *American Psychologist, 47,* 143–151.

Cooper, D. (1970). *The death of the family.* New York: Pantheon.

Cooper, J. F. (1995). *A primer of brief psychotherapy.* New York: Norton.

Cooper, M. (2003). *Existential therapies.* London: Sage.

Corey, G. (1996). *Theory and practice of counseling and psychotherapy* (5th ed.). Pacific Grove, CA: Brooks/Cole.

Corey, G. (2001). *Theory and practice of counseling and psychotherapy* (6th ed.). Belmont, CA: Brooks/Cole.

Corey, G. (2005). *Theory and practice of counseling and psychotherapy* (7th ed.). Belmont, CA: Brooks/Cole.

Corey, G. (2004). *Theory and practice of group counseling.* (6th ed.). Belmont, CA: Brooks/Cole.

Corey, M. S., & Corey, G. (1993). *Becoming a helper* (2nd. ed.). Pacific Grove, CA: Brooks/Cole.

Cormier, W., & Cormier, L. (1998). *Interviewing strategies for helpers.* Pacific Grove, CA: Brooks/Cole.

Cormier, W. H., & Cormier, L. S. (1991). *Interviewing strategies for helpers: A guide to assessment, treatment, and evaluation* (3rd ed.). Pacific Grove, CA: Brooks/Cole.

Corsini, R. J. (2001). *Handbook of innovative therapy* (2nd ed.) New York: Wiley.

Cortright, B. (2000). An integral approach to spiritual emergency. *Guidance and Counseling, 15,* 12–18.

Corwin, N. (1987). Social agency practice based on reality therapy/control theory. *Journal of Reality Therapy, 7,* 26–35.

Coster, J. S., & Schwebel, M. (1997). Well-functioning in professional psychologists. *Professional Psychology: Research and Practice, 28,* 5–13.

Counselors for Social Justice. (2005). *Advocacy competencies.* Retrieved March 31, 2005, from http://www.counselorsforsocialjustice.org/advocacycompetencies.html

Cozolino, L. J. (2002). *The neuroscience of psychotherapy: Building and rebuilding the human brain.* New York: Norton.

Craighead, W. E., Craighead, L. W., & Ilardi, S. S. (1995). Behavior therapies in historical perspective. In B. Bongar & L. E. Beutler (Eds.), *Comprehensive textbook of psychotherapy: Theory and practice* (pp. 64–83). New York: Oxford University Press.

Crespo, V. A. (2003). Art therapy as an approach for working with schizophrenia patients. *International Journal of Psychotherapy, 8*(3), 183–193.

Crocker, S. F., & Philippson, P. (2005). Phenomenology, existentialism, and Eastern thought in Gestalt therapy. In A. L. Woldt & S. M. Toman (Eds.), *Gestalt therapy: History, theory, and practice* (pp. 65–80). Thousand Oaks, CA: Sage.

Cummings, A. (1999). Assessing the process and outcome of short-term feminist therapy. Paper presented at 107th Annual Convention of American Psychological Association, Boston.

Dahl, S. (1971). Who is building the bridges? *The Personnel and Guidance Journal, 49*(9), 693–697.

Dall, M. (1995). Dancing in Neverland: Hakomi therapy from a client's perspective. *Hakomi Forum, 11,* 37–40.

D'Andrea, M. (2000). Postmodern, constructivism, and multiculturalism: Three forces reshaping and expanding our thoughts about counseling. *Journal of Mental Health Counseling, 22,* 1–17.

Daniels, V. (2004). The working corner: Dimensions of dialogue. *Gestalt, 8*(1). Retrieved March 7, 2005, from http://www.g-gej.org/8-1/corner.html

Daniels, V. (2003). The working corner: "Making the rounds," or the "go-around." *Gestalt, 7*(1). Retrieved March 7, 2005, from http://www.g-gej.org/7-1/corner.html

Dass, R. (2000). *Still here: Embracing aging, changing, and dying.* New York: Riverhead Books.

Dass, R., & Bush, M. (1992). *Compassion in action: Setting out on the path of service.* New York: Bell Tower.

Dass, R., & Gorman, P. (1985). *How can I help?* New York: Knopf.

Davis, J. (2000). We keep asking ourselves, what is transpersonal psychology? *Guidance and Counseling, 15,* 3–9.

Davis, J. (2003). An overview of transpersonal psychology. *Humanistic Psychologist, 31*(2–3), 6–21.

Dawson, R. W. (1991). REGIME: A counseling and educational model for using RET effectively. In M. E. Bernard (Ed.), *Using rational-emotive therapy effectively: A practitioner's guide* (pp. 112–132). New York: Plenum Press.

Day, S. (2004). *Theory and design in counseling and psychotherapy.* New York: Lahaska.

De Jong, P., & Berg, I. K. (2002). *Interviewing for solutions* (2nd ed.). Pacific Grove, CA: Brooks/Cole.

de Shazer, S. (1985). *Keys to solution in brief therapy.* New York: Norton.

de Shazer, S. (1991). *Putting difference to work.* New York: Norton.

De Vries, S. (2005). *Close encounters with Alfred Adler.* Alfred Adler Institute of San Francisco. Retrieved March 22, 2005, from http://ourworld.compuserve.com/homepages/hstein/newslett.htm

De Wildt, W. A. J. M., Schippers, G. M., Van Den Brink, W., Potgieter, A. S., Deckers, F., & Bets, D. (2002). Does psychological treatment enhance the efficacy of acamprosate in patients with alcohol problems? *Alcohol and Alcoholism, 37,* 375–382.

DeCastro, A. R. (2003). In search of the elusive nature of clinical psychoanalytic theory. *Psychoanalytic Quarterly, 72,* 131–155.

DeLucia, J. L., & Kalodner, C. R. (1990). An individualized cognitive intervention: Does it increase the efficacy of behavioral interventions for obesity? *Addictive Behaviors, 15,* 473–479.

DeRubeis, R. J., Gelfand, L. A., Tang, T. Z., & Simons, A. (1999). Medications versus cognitive behavioral therapy for severely depressed outpatients: Meta-analysis of four randomized comparisons. *American Journal of Psychiatry, 156,* 1007–1013.

Deurzen-Smith, E. (1991). Ontological insecurity revisited. *Journal of the Society for Existential Analysis, 3,* 15–23.

DiGiuseppe, R. (1999). Rational emotive behavior therapy. In H. T. Prout & D. T. Brown, *Counseling and psychotherapy with children and adolescents: Theory and practice for school settings* (pp. 252–293). New York: Wiley.

DiGiuseppe, R. (2002). Idiosyncratic REBT. In W. Dryden (Ed.), *Idiosyncratic rational emotive behaviour therapy* (pp. 32–45). Ross-on-Wye, UK: PCCS Books.

DiMattia, D., & Lega, L. (Eds.). (1990). *Will the real Albert Ellis please stand up?* New York: Institute for Rational-Emotive Therapy.

Dinkmeyer, D. C., Pew, W. L., & Dinkmeyer, D. C., Jr. (1979). *Adlerian counseling and psychotherapy.* Monterey, CA: Brooks/Cole.

Dobson, K. S. (2001). *Handbook of cognitive-behavioral therapies* (2nd ed.). New York: Guilford Press.

Dobson, K. S., & Dozois, D. J. A. (2001). Historical and philosophical bases of the cognitive-behavioral therapies. In K. S. Dobson (Ed.), *Handbook of cognitive-behavioral therapies* (2nd ed., pp. 3–39). New York: Guilford Press.

Dobson, K. S., & Shaw, B. F. (1988). The use of treatment manuals in cognitive therapy: Experience and issues. *Journal of Consulting and Clinical Psychology, 56,* 673–680.

Doherty, W. J., & Simmons, D. S. (1996). Clinical practice patterns of marriage and family therapists: A national survey of therapists and their clients. *Journal of Marital and Family Therapy, 22,* 9–25.

Dossey, L. (1999). *Reinventing medicine.* New York: HarperCollins.

Dowd, E., & Milne, C. (1986). Paradoxical interventions in counseling psychology. *Counseling Psychologist, 14*(2), 237–282.

Dreikurs, R. (1950). *Fundamentals of Adlerian psychology.* New York: Greenberg.

Dreikurs, R. (1956). Adlerian psychotherapy. In F. Fromm-Reichmann & J. L. Moreno (Eds.). *Progress in psychotherapy* (pp. 111–118). New York: Grune & Stratton.

Dreikurs, R. (1961). The Adlerian approach to psychodynamics. In M. Stein (Ed.). *Contemporary psychotherapies.* New York: Free Press of Glencoe.

Dreikurs, R. (1967a). Psychotherapy as correction of faulty social values. In R. Dreikurs, *Psychodynamics, psychotherapy, and counseling: Collected papers of Rudolf Dreikurs, M.D.* (p. 39). Chicago: Alfred Adler Institute of Chicago. (Originally published in 1956 in *Journal of Individual Psychology, 13,* 150–158.)

Dreikurs, R. (1967b). The function of emotions. In R. Dreikurs, *Psychodynamics, psychotherapy, and counseling: Collected papers of Rudolf Dreikurs, M.D.* (pp. 205–217). Chicago: Alfred Adler Institute of Chicago.

Dryden, W. (1984). *Rational-emotive therapy: Fundamentals and innovations.* Kent, UK: Croom Helm.

Dryden, W. (1996). Rational emotive behaviour therapy. In W. Dryden (Ed.), *Handbook of individual therapy* (pp. 306–338). London: Sage.

Dryden, W. (1999). *Rational emotive behavioural counselling in action* (2nd ed.). London: Sage.

Dryden, W. (2002a). *Fundamentals of rational emotive behaviour therapy: A training handbook.* London: Whurr.

Dryden, W. (2002b). Rational emotive behaviour therapy. In W. Dryden (Ed.), *Handbook of individual therapy* (4th ed., pp. 347–372). London: Sage.

Dryden, W. (2002c). Idiosyncratic REBT. In W. Dryden (Ed.), *Idiosyncratic rational emotive behaviour therapy* (pp. 2–14). Ross-on-Wye, UK: PCCS Books.

Dryden, W. (Ed.). (2003). *Rational emotive behaviour therapy: Theoretical developments.* New York: Brunner-Routledge.

Dryden, W., DiGiuseppe, R., & Neenan, M. (2003). *A primer on rational emotive therapy* (2nd ed.). Champaign, IL: Research Press.

Dryden, W., & Ellis, A. E. (2001). Rational emotive behavior therapy. In K. S. Dobson (Ed.), *Handbook of cognitive behavioral therapies* (pp. 295–348). New York: Guilford Press.

Dryden, W., & Neenan, M. (2004). *The rational emotive behavioural approach to therapeutic change.* London: Sage.

Dupree, P. I., & Day, H. D. (1995). Psychotherapists' job satisfaction and job burnout as a function of work setting and percentage of managed care clients. *Psychotherapy in Private Practice, 14,* 77–93.

Dutton-Douglas, M. A., & Walker, L. E. (Eds.). (1988). *Feminist psychotherapies: Integration of therapeutic and feminist systems.* Norwood, NJ: Ablex.

Dye, A., & Hackney, H. (1975). *Gestalt approaches to counseling.* Boston: Houghton Mifflin.

Dykeman, C. (2004). Counseling couples and families. In D. Capuzzi & D. R. Gross (Eds.), *Introduction to the counseling profession* (pp. 357–385). Boston: Allyn & Bacon.

Ecker, B., & Hulley, L. (1996). *Depth oriented brief therapy: How to be brief when you were trained to be deep— and vice versa.* San Francisco: Jossey-Bass.

Egan, G. (1975). *The skilled helper.* Monterey, CA: Brooks/Cole.

Egan, G. (2002). *The skilled helper* (7th ed.). Pacific Grove, CA: Brooks/Cole.

Eisenstein-Naveh, A. R. (2001). Therapy: The use of task, imagery, and symbolism to connect the inner and outer worlds. *Family Journal: Counseling and Therapy for Couples and Families, 9*(3), 314–324.

Eisman, J. (1987). Character typologies. In R. Kurtz (Ed.), *Hakomi therapy* (pp. 19/1–19/14). (Available from the Hakomi Institute, PO Box 1873, Boulder, CO 80306)

Eisman, J. (1995). *The re-creation of the self.* Unpublished manuscript.

Eisman, J. (2000–2001). *The Hakomi method and re-creation of the self: Professional training.* (Available from the Hakomi Institute of Oregon, 6836 HWY 66, Ashland, OR 97520)

Eisman, J. (2005). Categories of psychological wounding, neural patterns, and treatment approaches. *Hakomi Forum, 14–15* (Summer), 43–50.

Ellenberger, H. F. (1970). *The discovery of the unconscious: The history and evolution of dynamic psychiatry.* New York: Basic Books.

Elliott, J. M. (1999). Feminist theory. In D. Capuzzi & D. R. Gross (Eds.), *Counseling and psychotherapy: Theories and interventions* (pp. 203–229). Upper Saddle River, NJ: Merrill/Prentice Hall.

Elliott, R., Clark, C., Wexler, M., Kemeny, V., Brinkerhoff, J., & Mack, C. (1990). The impact of experiential therapy of depression: Initial results. In G. Lietaer, J. Rombauts, & R. Van Balen (Eds.), *Client-centered and experiential psychotherapy in the nineties* (pp. 549–577), Leuven, Belgium: Leuven University Press.

Ellis, A. (1962). *Reason and emotion in psychotherapy.* Secaucus, NJ: Citadel.

Ellis, A. (1986). Fanaticism that may lead to a nuclear holocaust: The contributions of scientific counseling and psychotherapy. *Journal of Counseling and Development, 65,* 146–150.

Ellis, A. (1989). Dangers of transpersonal psychology: A reply to Ken Wilber. *Journal of Counseling and Development, 67,* 336–337.

Ellis, A. E. (1957). *How to live with a neurotic: At home and at work.* New York: Crown. (Rev. ed., Hollywood, CA: Wilshire Books, 1975.)

Ellis, A. E. (1962). *Reason and emotion in psychotherapy.* Secaucus, NJ: Citadel.

Ellis, A. E. (1987). A sadly neglected cognitive element in depression. *Cognitive Therapy and Research, 11,* 121–146.

Ellis, A. E. (1994). *Reason and emotion in psychotherapy: A comprehensive method of treating human disturbances* (Rev. ed.). New York: Carol.

Ellis, A. E. (1996). *Better, deeper, and more enduring brief therapy: The rational emotive behavior therapy approach.* New York: Brunner/Mazel.

Ellis, A. E. (1997). REBT with obsessive-compulsive disorder. In J. Yankura & W. Dryden (Eds.), *Using REBT with common psychological problems: A therapist's casebook* (pp. 197–222). New York: Springer.

Ellis, A. E. (1998). How rational emotive behavior therapy belongs in the constructivist camp. In M. F. Hoyt (Ed.), *The handbook of constructive therapies: Innovative approaches from leading practitioners* (pp. 83–99). San Francisco: Jossey-Bass.

Ellis, A. E. (2001a). *Feeling better, getting better, staying better.* Atascadero, CA: Impact.

Ellis, A. E. (2001b). Reasons why rational emotive behavior therapy is relatively neglected in the professional and scientific literature. *Journal of Rational-Emotive and Cognitive-Behavior Therapy, 19*(1), 67–74.

Ellis, A. E. (2001c). *Overcoming destructive beliefs, feelings, and behaviors.* Amherst, NY: Prometheus Books.

Ellis, A. E. (2002a). *Overcoming resistance: A rational emotive behavior therapy integrated approach.* New York: Springer.

Ellis, A. E. (2002b). Idiosyncratic REBT. In W. Dryden (Ed.), *Idiosyncratic rational emotive behaviour therapy* (pp. 16–29). Ross-on-Wye, UK: PCCS Books.

Ellis, A. E. (2004a). *Rational emotive behavior therapy: It works for me—it can work for you.* Amherst, NY: Prometheus Books.

Ellis, A. E. (2004b). *The road to tolerance: The philosophy of rational emotive behavior therapy.* Amherst, NY: Prometheus Books.

Ellis, A. E., & Dryden, W. (1997). *The practice of rational emotive behavior therapy* (2nd ed.). New York: Springer.

Ellis, A. E., & Harper, R. A. (1997). *A guide to rational living* (3rd rev. ed.). North Hollywood, CA: Melvin Powers.

Ellis, A. E., & MacClaren, C. (1998). *Rational emotive behavior therapy: A therapist's guide.* Atascadero, CA: Impact.

Ellis, A. E., & Velten, E. (1992). *When AA doesn't work: Rational steps for quitting alcohol.* New York: Barricade Books.

Emmelkamp, P. M. (1994). Behavior therapy with adults. In S. L. Garfield & A. E. Bergin (Eds.), *Handbook of psychotherapy and behavior change* (4th ed., pp. 379–427). New York: Wiley.

Emunah, R. (1999). Drama therapy in action. In C. J. Wiener (Ed.), *Beyond talk therapy: Using movement and expressive techniques in clinical practice* (pp. 99–123). Washington, DC: American Psychological Association.

Enns, C. Z. (1992). Self-esteem groups: A synthesis of consciousness-raising and assertiveness training. *Journal of Counseling and Development, 71,* 7–13.

Enns, C. Z. (1993). Twenty years of feminist counseling and therapy: From naming biases to implementing multifaceted practice. *The Counseling Psychologist, 21,* 3–87.

Enns, C. Z. (2004). *Feminist theories and feminist psychotherapies: Origins, themes, and variations* (2nd ed.). New York: Haworth.

Enns, C. Z., Sinacore, A. L., Ancis, J. R., & Phillips, J. (2004). Toward integrating feminist and multicultural pedagogies. *Journal of Multicultural Counseling and Development, 32,* 414–427.

Epple, D. (2003). Encounter with soul. *Clinical Social Work Journal, 31*(2), 173.

Erikson, E. (1963). *Childhood and society.* New York: Norton.

Erikson, E. H. (1968). *Identity: Youth and crisis.* New York: Norton.

Erickson, M. H., & Rossi, E. S. (1976). *Hypnotic realities.* New York: Irvington.

Espin, O. M. (1993). Feminist therapy: Not for or by White women only. *The Counseling Psychologist, 21,* 103–108.

Espin, O. M., & Gawelek, M. A. (1992). Women's diversity: Ethnocity, race, class, and gender in theories of feminist psychology. In L. S. Brown & M. Ballou (Eds.), *Personality and psychopathology: Feminist reappraisals* (pp. 88–107). New York: Guilford Press.

Evans, K. G. (1996). Chaos as opportunity: Grounding a positive vision of management and society in the new physics. *Public Administration Review, 56*(5), 491–494.

Evans, K. M. (1997). Wellness and coping activities of African American counselors. *Journal of Black Psychology, 23*(1), 24–35.

Evans, K. M., Kincade, E. A., Marbley, A. F., & Seem, S. R. (2005). Feminism and feminist therapy: Lessons from the past and hopes for the future. *Journal of Counseling and Development, 83,* 269–277.

Evans, T. D. (1995). The encouraging teacher. In G. M. Gazda, F. S. Asbury, F. M. Blazer, W. C. Childers, & R. P. Walters (Eds.), *Human relations development* (5th ed., pp. 261–270). Boston: Allyn & Bacon.

Evans, T. D. (1996). Encouragement: The key to reforming classrooms. *Educational Leadership, 54,* 81–85.

Evans, T. D. (1997a). The tools of encouragement. *Reaching Today's Youth: National Educational Service, 1*(2), 10–14.

Evans, T. D. (1997b, February). *Establishing goals in counseling.* Paper presented at the University of Texas Permian Basin Spring Counseling Workshop, Odessa.

Evans, T. D., & Milliren, A. P. (1999). Open-forum family counseling. In R. E. Watts & J. Carlson (Eds.), *Interventions and strategies in counseling and psychotherapy* (pp. 135–160). Levittown, PA: Accelerated Development.

Ezell, M. (2001). *Advocacy in the human services.* Belmont, CA: Brooks/Cole.

Fairbairn, W. R. D. (1941). A revised psychopathology of the psychoses and psychoneuroses. *International Journal of Psychoanalysis, 22,* 250–279.

Fairburn, C. G., Marcus, M. D., & Wilson, G. T. (1993). Cognitive behavioral therapy for binge eating and bulimia nervosa. In C. G. Fairburn & G. T. Wilson (Eds.), *Binge eating: Nature, assessment, and treatment* (pp. 361–404). New York: Plenum Press.

Fairfield, M. A. (2004). Gestalt groups revisited: A phenomenological approach. *Gestalt Review, 8*(3), 336–357.

Farber, B. A., Brink, D. C., & Raskin, P. M. (Eds.). (1996). *The psychotherapy of Carl Rogers: Cases and commentary.* New York: Guilford Press.

Fay, A. (1978). *Making things better by making them worse.* New York: Hawthorne.

Feder, E., & Feder, B. (1981). *The expressive arts therapies.* Upper Saddle River, NJ: Prentice Hall.

Feinauer, L., Middleton, K., & Hilton, G. (2003). Existential well-being as a factor in the adjustment of adults sexually abused as children. *American Journal of Family Therapy, 31*(3), 201–214.

Feldenkrais, M. (1972). *Awareness through movement: Health exercises for personal growth.* New York: Harper & Row.

Fenichel, O. (1945). *The psychoanalytic theory of neurosis.* New York: Norton.

Ferguson, E. D. (1984). *Adlerian theory: An introduction.* Chicago: Adler School of Professional Psychology.

Ferguson, E. D. (1989). Adler's motivational theory: An historical perspective on belonging and the fundamental human striving. *Individual Psychology, 45,* 354–362.

Ferguson, E. D. (2000a). Individual Psychology is ahead of its time. *Journal of Individual Psychology, 56,* 14–20.

Ferguson, E. D. (2000b). *Motivation: A biosocial and cognitive integration of motivation and emotion.* New York: Oxford University Press.

Ferguson, E. D. (2001). Adler and Dreikurs: Cognitive-social dynamic innovators. *Journal of Individual Psychology, 57,* 324–341.

Fernbacher, S., & Plummer, D. (2005). Cultural influences and considerations in Gestalt therapy. In A. L. Woldt & S. M. Toman (Eds.), *Gestalt therapy: History, theory, and practice* (pp. 117–132). Thousand Oaks, CA: Sage.

Finch, E. S., & Krantz, S. R. (1991). Low burnout in a high-stress setting: A study of staff adaption at Fountain House. *Psychological Rehabilitation Journal, 14,* 15–26.

Fine, R. (1979). *A history of psychoanalysis.* New York: Columbia University Press.

Fisch, R. (1990). Problem-solving psychotherapy. In J. K. Zeig & W. M. Munion (Eds.), *What is psychotherapy?: Contemporary perspectives* (pp. 269–273). San Francisco: Jossey-Bass.

Fisch, R. (1994). Basic elements in the brief therapies. In M. F. Hoyt (Ed.), *Constructive therapies* (pp. 126–139). New York: Guilford Press.

Fisch, R., Weakland, J. H., & Segal, L. (1982). *Tactics of change: Doing therapy briefly.* San Francisco: Jossey-Bass.

Fisher, G. (2005). Existential psychotherapy with adult survivors of sexual abuse. *Journal of Humanistic Psychology, 45*(1), 10.

Fisher, R. (2002). *Experiential psychotherapy with couples: A guide for the creative pragmatist.* Phoenix, AZ: Zeig, Tucker & Theisen.

Fisher, S., & Greenberg, R. (1977). *The scientific credibility of Freud's theories and therapy.* New York: Basic Books.

Fitzgerald, L. F., & Nutt, R. (1986). The division 17 principles concerning the counseling/psychotherapy of women: Rationale and implementation. *The Counseling Psychologist, 14,* 180–216.

Floyd, M., Coulon, C., Yanez, A., & Lasota, M. (2005). The existential effects of traumatic experiences: A survey of young adults. *Death Studies, 29*(1), 55–64.

Foa, E. B., & Wilson, R. (1991). *Stop obsessing: How to overcome your obsessions and compulsions.* New York: Bantam.

Folligstad, D. R., Robinson, E. A., & Pugh, M. (1977). Effects of consciousness-raising groups on measures of feminism, self-esteem, and social desirability. *Journal of Counseling Psychology, 24,* 223–230.

Fonagy, P., Gergely, G., Jurist, E. L., & Target, M. (2002). *Affect regulation, mentalization and the development of the self.* New York: Other Books.

Ford, E. (1979). *Permanent love.* Minneapolis, MN: Winston.

Foster, S., & Little, M. (1997). *The roaring of the sacred river: The wilderness quest for vision and self-healing.* Big Pine, CA: Lost Borders Press.

Foucault, M. (1980). *Knowledge/power: Selected interviews and other writings.* New York: Pantheon.

Frankl, V. (1975). *The unconscious god.* New York: Simon & Schuster.

Frankl, V. (1984). *Man's search for meaning.* New York: Washington Square Press.

Frattaroli, E. (2001). *Healing the soul in the age of the brain: Why medication isn't enough.* New York: Penguin Books.

Freeman, J. (1989). Feminist organization and activities from suffrage to women's liberation. In J. Freeman (Ed.), *Women: A feminist perspective* (4th ed., pp. 541–555). Palo Alto, CA: Mayfield.

Freidan, B. (1963). *The feminine mystique.* New York: Dell.

Freud, A. (1966). *The ego and the mechanisms of defense.* New York: International Universities Press.

Freud, S. (1930). *Civilization and its discontents* (J. Strachey, Trans. & Ed.). New York: Norton.

Freud, S. (1940). *An outline of psychoanalysis* (Vol. 23). Standard Edition (J. Strachey, Trans.). London: Hogarth Press. (Original work published 1938)

Freud, S. (1955). *The interpretation of dreams.* New York: Baisc Books.

Freudenberger, H. (1983). Hazards of psychotherapeutic practice. *Psychotherapy in Private Practice, 1*(1), 83–89.

Friedlander, M. L., Wildman, J., Heatherington, L., & Skowron, E. A. (1994). What we do and don't know about the process of family therapy. *Journal of Family Therapy, 8,* 390–416.

Fromm, E. (1955). *The sane society.* New York: Rinehart.

Fuchs, M. (1999). Between imagination and belief: Poetry as therapeutic intervention. In S. K. Levine & E. G. Levine (Eds.), *Foundations of expressive arts therapy: Theoretical and clinical perspectives* (pp. 195–221). London: Jessica Kingsley.

Furnham, A., Pereira, E., & Rawles, R. (2001). Lay theories of psychotherapy: Perceptions of the efficacy of different "cures" for specific disorders. *Psychology, Health and Medicine, 6,* 77–85.

Furtmueller, C. (1946). Part VI: Alfred Adler: A Biographical Essay. In A. Adler (1979), *Superiority & Social Interest* (pp. 311–394). New York: Norton.

Gallant, W., & Holosko, M. (2001). Music intervention in grief work with clients experiencing loss and bereavement. *Guidance & Counseling, 16*(4), 115–122.

Gannon, L. (1982). The role of power in psychotherapy. *Women and Therapy, 1,* 3–11.

Garcia, C., Baker, S., DeMayo, R., & Brown, G. I. (2005). Gestalt educational therapy. In A. L. Woldt & S. M. Toman (Eds.), *Gestalt therapy: History, theory, and practice* (pp. 301–317). Thousand Oaks, CA: Sage.

Gardner, J. (1971). Sexist counseling. *The Personnel and Guidance Journal, 49*(9), 705–714.

Gay, P. (1988). *Freud: A life for our time.* New York: Norton.

Gazzola, N., Iwakabe, S., & Stalikas, A. (2003). Counselor interpretations and the occurrence of in-session client change moments in non-dynamic psychotherapies. *Counseling Psychology Quarterly, 16*(2), 81–94.

Gelso, C. J., & Fretz, B. R. (2001). *Counseling psychology* (2nd ed.). Belmont, CA: Thomson/Wadsworth.

George, R. L., & Cristiani, T. S. (1990). *Counseling theory and practice* (3rd ed.). Upper Saddle River, NJ: Prentice Hall.

Germer, C. K., Siegel, R. D., & Fulton, P. R. (Eds.). (2005). *Mindfulness and psychotherapy.* New York: Guilford Press.

Gibbs, S. (2005). Islam and Islamic extremism: An existential analysis. *Journal of Humanistic Psychology, 45*(2), 156.

Gibson, D. M. (2005). The use of genograms in career counseling with elementary, middle, and high school students. *Career Development Quarterly, 53,* 353–362.

Gill, M. (1996). Discussion: Interaction III. *Psychoanalytic Inquiry, 16*(1), 118–135.

Gilligan, C. (1982). *In a different voice.* Cambridge, MA: Harvard University Press.

Gilliland, B., James, R., & Bowman, J. (1994). *Theories and strategies in counseling and psychotherapy.* Upper Saddle River, NJ: Prentice Hall.

Gilliland, B. E., James, R. K., & Bowman, J. T. (1989). *Theories and strategies in counseling and psychotherapy* (2nd ed.). Upper Saddle River, NJ: Prentice Hall.

Ginger, S. (2004). Sandor Ferenczi, the grandfather of Gestalt therapy. *Gestalt Review, 8*(3), 358–368.

Giovacchini, P. (1987). *A narrative textbook of psychoanalysis.* London: Aronson.

Gladding, S. T. (2001). *Becoming a counselor: The light, the bright, and the serious.* Alexandria, VA: American Counseling Association.

Gladding, S. T. (2001). *Family therapy: History, theory, and practice* (3rd ed.). Upper Saddle River, NJ: Merrill/Prentice Hall.

Gladding, S. T. (2003). *Counseling: A comprehensive profession* (5th ed.). Upper Saddle River, NJ: Prentice Hall.

Gladwell, M. (2005). *Blink: The power of thinking without thinking.* New York: Little, Brown.

Glasser, C. (1990). *My quality world workbook.* Los Angeles: The William Glasser Institute.

Glasser, N. (Ed.). (1980). *What are you doing?* New York: Harper & Row.

Glasser, N. (Ed.). (1989). *Control theory in the practice of reality therapy.* New York: Harper & Row.

Glasser, W. (1965). *Reality therapy.* New York: Harper & Row.

Glasser, W. (1968). *Schools without failure.* New York: Harper & Row.

Glasser, W. (1972). *The identity society.* New York: Harper & Row.

Glasser, W. (1980a). Reality therapy. In N. Glasser (Ed.), *What are you doing?* (pp. 48–60). New York: Harper & Row.

Glasser, W. (1980b). *Stations of the mind.* New York: Harper & Row.

Glasser, W. (1984). *Control theory.* New York: Harper & Row.

Glasser, W. (1986). *A diagram of the brain as a control system.* Los Angeles: Institute for Reality Therapy.

Glasser, W. (1996). *Programs, policies, and procedures of the William Glasser Institute*. Los Angeles: The William Glasser Institute.

Glasser, W. (1998). *Choice therapy: A new psychology of personal freedom*. New York: HarperCollins.

Glasser, W. (1999). *Choice theory*. New York: Harper-Collins.

Glasser, W. (2001). *Fibromyalgia: Hope from a completely new perspective*. Los Angeles: William Glasser Institute.

Glasser, W. (2003). *Warning: Psychiatry can be hazardous to your mental health*. New York: HarperCollins.

Glasser, W. (2005). *Treating mental health as a public health problem*. Chatsworth, CA: William Glasser Institute.

Glosoff, H. L. (2005). Early historical perspectives. In D. Capuzzi & D. R. Gross (Eds.), *Introduction to the counseling profession* (4th ed., pp 3–55). Boston: Allyn & Bacon.

Goetz-Kuhne, C. (2005). The role of body-psychotherapy in the treatment of eating disorders. In G. Marlock & H. Weiss (Eds.), *Handbuch der Koerperpsychotherapie*. Goettingen, Germany: Hogrefe Verlag.

Goldberg, L., (2005). Introductory engagement with the perinatal nursing relationship. *Nursing Ethics, 12*(4), 401–414.

Goldfried, M. R., Greenberg, L. S., & Maramar, C. (1990). Individual psychotherapy: Process and outcome. *Annual Review of Psychology, 41*, 659–688.

Goleman, D., & Ram, D. (1996). *The meditative mind: varieties of meditative experience*. Los Angeles: Tarcher.

Goodman, D. J. (2001). *Promoting diversity and social justice: Educating people from privileged groups*. Thousand Oaks, CA: Sage.

Goodman, R. F. (2004). Treatment of childhood traumatic grief. In N. B. Webb (Ed.), *Mass trauma and violence: Helping families and children*. New York: Guilford Press.

Goodman, L. A., Liang, B., Helms, J. E., Latta, R. E., Sparks, E., & Weintrab, S. R. (2004). Training counseling psychologists as social justice agents: Feminist and multicultural principles in action. *The Counseling Psychologist, 32*(6), 793–837.

Goodyear, R. (1987). In memory of Carl Ransom Rogers. *Journal of Counseling and Development, 65*, 523–524.

Goud, N. H. (2001). The symbolic identity technique. *Journal of Humanistic Counseling, Education and Development, 40*(1), 114–122.

Graves, D. (1996). *The effect of rational emotive parent education on the stress of mothers of young children with Down's syndrome*. Unpublished doctoral dissertation, University of Melbourne, Australia.

Green, R., & Herget, M. (1991). Outcomes of systemic/strategic team consultation: III. The importance of therapist warmth and active structuring. *Family Process, 30*, 321–335.

Greenberg, J. (1996). Psychoanalytic interaction. *Psychoanalytic Inquiry, 16*(1), 25–39.

Greenberg, L. S., Elliott, R., & Lietaer, G. (1994). Research on humanistic and experiential psychotherapies. In A. Bergin & S. Garfield (Eds.), *Handbook of psychotherapy and behavior change* (4th ed., pp. 509–542). New York: Wiley.

Greenson, R. (1967). *The technique and practice of psychoanalysis*. New York: International Universities Press.

Grof, S. (1985). *Beyond the brain*. Buffalo, NY: SUNY Press.

Grof, S., & Grof, C. (1989). *Spiritual emergency: When personal transformation becomes a crisis*. Los Angeles: Tarcher.

Grunbaum, A. (1984). *The foundations of psychoanalysis: A philosophical critique*. Berkeley: University of California Press.

Guterman, J. T., & Rudes, J. (2005). A narrative approach to strategic eclecticism. *Journal of Mental Health Counseling, 27*(1), 1–12.

Hackney, H., & Cormier, L. S. (1994). *Counseling strategies and interventions* (4th ed.). Upper Saddle River, NJ: Prentice Hall.

Hackney, H., & Cormier, L. S. (1996). *The professional counselor: A process guide to helping* (3rd ed.). Needham Heights, MA: Allyn & Bacon.

Haley, J. (1976). Development of a theory: A history of a research project. In C. E. Sluski & D. C. Ransom (Eds.), *Double bind: The foundation of the communicational approach to the family* (pp. 59–104). New York: Grune & Stratton.

Haley, J. (1990). *Strategies of psychotherapy*. New York: Norton.

Haley, J. (1991). *Problem-solving therapy*. San Francisco: Jossey-Bass.

Haley, J. (1993). *Uncommon therapy*. New York: Norton.

Halifax, J. (1979). *Shamanic voices: A survey of visionary narratives*. New York: Dutton.

Halverson, S., & Miars, R. (2005). The helping relationship. In D. Capuzzi & D. Gross (Eds.), *Introduction to the counseling profession* (4th ed., pp. 56–74). Boston: Allyn & Bacon.

Hammerschlag, C. A. (1988). *The dancing healers: A doctor's journey of healing with Native Americans*. New York: HarperCollins.

Hampson, R. B., & Beavers, W. R. (1996). Measuring family therapy outcome in a clinical setting: Families that do better or do worse in therapy. *Family Therapy, 35*, 347–361.

Hanna, F. J., & Bemak, F. (1997). The quest for identity in the counseling profession. *Counselor Education and Supervision, 36,* 194–206.

Hanna, F. J., Hanna, C. A., & Keys, S. G. (1999). Fifty strategies for counseling defiant, aggressive adolescents: Reaching, accepting, and relating. *Journal of Counseling and Development, 77*(2), 395–405.

Hanna, F. J., & Ottens, A. J. (1995). The role of wisdom in psychotherapy. *Journal of Psychotherapy Integration, 5,* 195–219.

Hanna, F., Bemak, F., & Chung, R. (1999). Toward a new paradigm for multicultural counseling. *Journal for Counseling and Development, 77,* 125–134.

Hannigan, B., Edwards, D., & Burnard, P. (2004). Stress and stress management in clinical psychology: Findings from a systematic review. *Journal of Mental Health, 13*(3), 235–245.

Hansen, J. C., Rossberg, R. H., & Cramer, S. H. (1994). *Counseling: Theory and process* (5th ed.). Needham Heights, MA: Allyn & Bacon.

Hansen, J. T. (1999). A review and critical analysis of humanistic approaches to treating disturbed clients. *Journal of Humanistic Counseling, 38,* 29–39.

Hardie, S. (2004). Literature review [PTSD and gestalt therapy]. *Gestalt, 7*(1). Retrieved March 7, 2005, from http://www.g-gej.org/8-1/litreview.html

Hardiman, R., & Jackson, B. (1997). Conceptual foundations for social justice courses. In M. Adams, L. Bell, & P. Griffin (Eds.), *Teaching for diversity and social justice* (pp. 16–29). New York: Routledge.

Harner, M. (1980). *The way of the shaman: A guide to power and healing.* New York: Harper & Row.

Harpin, D. (1999). Living artfully: Movement as an integrative process. In S. K. Levine & E. G. Levine (Eds.). *Foundations of expressive arts therapy: Theoretical and clinical perspectives* (pp. 133–149). London: Jessica Kingsley.

Hartman, A. (1995). Diagrammatic assessment of family relationships. *Families in Society, 76,* 111–123.

Hartz, L., & Thick, L. (2005). Art therapy strategies to raise self-esteem in female juvenile offenders: A comparison of art psychotherapy and art as therapy approaches. *Art Therapy, 22*(2), 70–80.

Harville, M., Stokes, S., Templer, D., & Rienzi, B. (2004). Relation of existential and religious variables to the death depression scale-revised. *Omega, 48*(2), 165–184.

Hauck, P. A., & McKeegan, P. (1997). Using REBT to overcome depression. In J. Yankura & W. Dryden (Eds.), *Using REBT with common psychological problems: A therapist's casebook* (pp. 44–73). New York: Springer.

Hayes, C. H., Follette, V. M., and Linehan, M. M. (2004). *Mindfulness and acceptance: Expanding the cognitive-behavioral tradition.* New York: Guilford Press.

Hayes, S. C., & Hayes, L. J. (1992). Some clinical implications of contextual behaviorism: The examples of cognition. *Behavior Therapy, 23,* 225–249.

Hazler, J. H. (1999). Person-centered theory. In D. Capuzzi & D. Gross (Eds.), *Counseling and psychotherapy: Theories and interventions* (pp. 179–201). Upper Saddle River, NJ: Merrill/Prentice Hall.

Hazler, R. J. (2001). Humanistic theories of counseling. In D. Locke, J. Meyers, & E. Herr (Eds.), *The handbook of counseling* (pp. 151–158). Thousand Oaks, CA: Sage.

Hazler, R. J., & Barwick, N. (2001). *The therapeutic environment: Core conditions for facilitating therapy.* Philadelphia: Open University Press.

Heidegger, M. (1949). *Existence and being.* South Bend, IN: Regnery.

Heidegger, M. (1962). *Being and time.* New York: Harper & Row.

Heisel, M., & Flett, G. (2004). Purpose in life, satisfaction with life, and suicide ideation in a clinical sample. *Journal of Psychopathology and Behavioral Assessment, 26*(2), 127–136.

Hellman, I. D., & Morrison, T. L. (1987). Practice setting and type of caseload as factors in psychotherapist stress. *Psychotherapy, 24*(3), 427–432.

Helm, F. L. (2004). Hope is curative. *Psychoanalytic Psychology, 21*(4), 554–566.

Helms, J. E. (1995). An update of Helms' white and people of color racial identity models. In J. G. Ponterotto, J. M. Casas, L. A. Suzuki, & C. M. Alexander (Eds.), *Handbook of multicultural counseling* (pp. 181–191). Thousand Oaks, CA: Sage.

Helms, J. E., & Cook, D. A. (1999). *Using race and culture in counseling and psychotherapy.* Needham Heights, MA: Allyn & Bacon.

Hendricks, C. B., Robinson, B., Bradley, L., & Davis, K. (1999). Using music techniques to treat adolescent depression. *Journal of Humanistic Counseling, Education and Development, 38*(1), 39–47.

Hendricks, G., & Hendricks, K. (1993). *At the speed of life: A new approach to personal change through body-centered therapy.* New York: Bantam.

Henehan, M. P. (2003). *Integrating spirit and psyche: Using women's narratives in psychotherapy.* Binghamton, NY: Haworth Pastoral Press.

Henle, M. (1978). Gestalt psychology and Gestalt therapy. *Journal of the History of Behavioral Sciences, 14,* 23–32.

Herlihy, B., & Corey, G. (Eds.). (1996). *ACA ethical standards casebook.* Alexandria, VA: American Association for Counseling and Development.

Herlihy, B., & Corey, G. (2005). Feminist therapy. In G. Corey, *Theory and practice of counseling and psychotherapy* (7th ed., pp. 380–381). Pacific Grove, CA: Brooks/Cole.

Herman, E. (1995). *The romance of American psychology: Political culture in the age of experts.* Berkeley, CA: University of California Press.

Herman, J. L. (1992). *Trauma and recovery: The aftermath of violence.* New York: Basic Books.

Hester, R. L. (2004). Early memories and narrative therapy. *Journal of Individual Psychology, 60*(4), 338–347.

Hettler, B. (1984). Wellness: Encouraging a lifetime pursuit of excellence. *Health Values, 8*(4), 13–17.

Heuscher, J. (1987). Love and authenticity. *American Journal of Psychoanalysts, 47*(1), 21–34.

Hill, C. E. (2004). *Helping skills: Facilitating exploration, insight and action* (2nd ed.). Washington, DC: American Psychological Association.

Hill, M., & Ballou, M. (1998). Making feminist therapy: A practice survey. *Women and Therapy, 21,* 1–16.

Hillman, J. (1996). *The soul's code: In search of character and calling.* New York: Random House.

Hinterkopf, E. (1998). *Integrating spirituality in counseling: A manual for using the experiential focusing method.* Alexandria, VA: American Counseling Association.

Hjelle, L. A., & Ziegler, D. J. (1992). *Personality theories.* New York: McGraw-Hill.

Hoffman, E. (1994). *The drive for self: Alfred Adler and the founding of Individual Psychology.* Reading, MA: Addison-Wesley.

Hoffman, I. (1991). Discussion: Toward a social-constructivist view of the psychoanalytic situation. *Psychoanalytic Dialogues, 1,* 74–105.

Hogan, S. (2001). *Healing arts: The history of art therapy.* London: Jessica Kingsley.

Hogenson, G. (2005). The self, the symbolic and synchronicity: Virtual realties and the emergence of the psyche. *Journal of Analytic Psychology, 50*(3), 271–285.

Holburn, S., & Vietze, P. (2000). Person-centered planning and cultural inertia in applied behavior analysis. *Behavior and Social Issues, 10*(1), 39–70.

Hollon, S. D., & Beck, A. T. (1994). Cognitive and cognitive-behavioral therapies. In S. L. Garfield & A. E. Bergin (Eds.), *Handbook of psychotherapy and behavior change* (4th ed., pp. 428–466). New York: Wiley.

Honeyman, A. (1990). Perceptual changes in addicts as a consequence of reality therapy based on group treatment. *Journal of Reality Therapy, 9*(2), 53–59.

Hooks, B. (2000). *Feminist theory: From margin to center* (2nd ed.). Cambridge, MA: South End Press.

Hooper, A., & Holford, J. (1998). *Adler for beginners.* New York: Writers & Readers.

Horney, K. (1950). *Neurosis and human growth.* New York: Norton.

Horton, S. L., & Andonian, J. M. (2005). Family as anthology: Towards a metaphoric reconceptualization. *American Journal of Family Therapy, 33,* 85–95.

Horvath, A. O. (1994). Empirical validation of Bordin's pantheoretical model of the alliance: The Working Alliance Inventory perspective. In A. O. Horvath & L. S. Greenberg (Eds.), *The working alliance* (pp. 109–130). New York: Wiley.

Houston, G. (2003). *Brief Gestalt therapy.* Thousand Oaks, CA: Sage.

Hoyt, M. F. (1995). *Brief therapy and managed care: Readings for contemporary practice.* San Francisco: Jossey-Bass.

Hoyt, M. F. (2000). *Some stories are better than others: Doing what works in brief therapy and managed care.* Philadelphia: Brunner/Mazel.

Hubble, M. A., Duncan, B. L., & Miller, S. D. (1999). *The heart and soul of change: What works in therapy.* Washington, DC: American Psychological Association.

Hutton, M. S. (1994). How transpersonal psychotherapists differ from other practitioners: An empirical study. *Journal of Transpersonal Psychology, 26,* 139–174.

Ibrahim, F. (1991). Contribution of cultural worldview to generic counseling and development. *Journal of Counseling and Development, 70,* 13–19.

Imber-Black, E. (2004). Meaningful voices, old and new. *Family Process, 43,* 411–412.

Imes, S. (1998). Long-term clients' experience of touch in Gestalt therapy. In E. Smith, P. Clance, and S. Imes (Eds.), *Touch in psychotherapy: Theory, research, and practice* (pp. 170–200). New York: Guilford Press.

Imes, S., Rose Clance, P., Gailis, A., & Atkeson, E. (2002). Mind's response to the body's betrayal: Gestalt/existential therapy for clients with chronic or life-threatening illnesses. *Journal of Clinical Psychology, 58*(11), 1361.

International Psychoanalytical Association. *Roster of the International Psychoanalytical Association.* (1992–93). London: Author.

Israeli, A. L., & Santor, D. A. (2000). Reviewing effective components of feminist therapy. *Counseling Psychology Quarterly, 13,* 233–247.

Ivey, A. E. (1998). *Intentional interviewing and counseling: Facilitating client development in a multicultural society.* Pacific Grove, CA: Brooks/Cole.

Ivey, A. E., D'Andrea, M., Ivey, M. B., & Simek-Morgan, L. (2002). *Theories of counseling and psychotherapy: A multicultural perspective.* Boston, MA: Allyn & Bacon.

Ivey, A. E., D'Andrea, M. D., Ivey, M. B., & Simek-Morgan, L. (2002). *Theories of counseling and psychotherapy:*

A multicultural perspective (5th ed., pp. 262–287). Boston: Allyn & Bacon.

Jack, D. (1987). Self-in-relation theory. In R. Formanik & A. Gurian (Eds.), *Women and depression: A lifespan perspective* (pp. 41–45). New York: Springer.

Jackson, D. D. (1957). The question of family homeostasis. *Psychiatric Quarterly Supplement, 31*, 79–90.

Jackson, M. L. (1995). Multicultural counseling: Historical perspectives. In J. G. Ponterotto, J. M. Casas, L. Suzuki, & C. M. Alexander (Eds.), *Handbook of multicultural counseling* (pp. 3–16): Thousand Oaks: Sage.

Jacobsen, B. (2003). Is gift-giving the core of existential therapy? A discussion with Irvin D. Yalom. *Existential Analysis, 14*(2), 345–353.

Jahoda, M. (1958). *Current concepts of positive mental health.* New York: Basic Books.

James, R. K., & Gilliland, B. E. (2003). *Theories and strategies in counseling and psychotherapy* (5th ed., pp. 42–68). Boston: Allyn & Bacon.

Johanson, G. (1987). Forward. In R. Kurtz, *Hakomi therapy* (pp. i–vii). (Available from the Hakomi Institute, PO Box 1873, Boulder, CO 80306)

Johanson, G. (1988). A curious form of therapy: Hakomi. *Hakomi Forum, 6*, 18–31.

Johanson, G. (1996). The birth and death of meaning: Selective implications of linguistics for psychotherapy. *Hakomi Forum, 12*(Summer).

Johanson, G. (1999). *Making grace specific.* Ph.D. diss. Drew University, Madison, NJ. (UMI Microform 9949072)

Johanson, G. (2005). The organization of experience: A systems perspective on the relation of body psychotherapies to the wider field of psychotherapy. In G. Marlock & H. Weiss (Eds.), *Handbuch der Koerperpsychotherapie.* Goettingen, Germany: Hogrefe Verlag.

Johanson, G., & Kurtz, R. (1991). *Grace unfolding: Psychotherapy in the spirit of the Tao-te-ching.* New York: Bell Tower.

Johanson, G., & Taylor, C. (1988). Hakomi therapy with seriously emotionally disturbed adolescents. In C. E. Schaefer (Ed.), *Innovative interventions in child and adolescent therapy.* New York: Wiley.

Johnson, M. (1976). An approach to feminist therapy. *Psychotherapy: Theory, Research, and Practice, 13*, 72–76.

Johnson, W. R., & Smith, E. W. L. (1997). Gestalt empty-chair dialogue versus systematic desensitization in the treatment of a phobia. *Gestalt Review, 1*(2), 150–162.

Jordan, J., Baker, J., Matteis, M., Rosenthal, S., & Ware, E. (2005). The grief evaluation measure (GEM): An initial validation study. *Death Studies, 29*(4), 301.

Jordan, J. V., & Surrey, J. L. (1986). The self-in-relation: Empathy and the mother-daughter relationship. In T. Bernay & D. W. Ballou (Eds.), *The psychology of today's women: New psychoanalytical visions* (pp. 81–104). Hillsdale, NJ: Analytic Press.

Jordan, J. V., & Surrey, J. L. (1986). The self-in-relation: Empathy and the mother-daughter relationship. In T. Bernay & D. W. Cantor (Eds.), *The psychology of today's woman: New psychoanalytic visions* (pp. 139–168). Hillsdale, NJ: Analytic Press.

Jorgensen, C. (2004). Active ingredients in individual psychotherapy—searching for common factors. *Psychoanalytic Psychology, 21*(4), 516–540.

Jung, C. G. (1953a). Two essays on analytical psychology. In *The collected works of C. G. Jung* (Vol. 7). Princeton, NJ: Princeton University Press.

Jung, C. G. (1953b). *Collected works 12: Psychology and alchemy.* New York: Pantheon.

Jung, C. G. (1954). *Collected works 16: The practice of psychotherapy.* New York: Pantheon.

Jung, C. G. (1954). *The development of personality.* Princeton, NJ: Princeton University Press.

Jung, C. G. (1959). *Collected works 9: The archetypes and the collective unconscious.* New York: Pantheon.

Jung, C. G. (1960). *Collected works 8: The structure and dynamics of the psyche.* New York: Pantheon.

Jung, C. G. (1960). *The psychogenesis of mental disease.* Princeton, NJ: Princeton University Press.

Jung, C. G. (1963). *Memories, dreams, reflections.* New York: Pantheon.

Jung, C. G. (1964). *Man and his symbols.* Garden City, NY: Doubleday.

Jung, C. G. (1966). *Collected works 16: The practice of psychotherapy.* New York: Pantheon.

Jung, C. G. (1967). *Collected works 13: Alchemical studies.* New York: Pantheon.

Jung, C. G. (1967). *Symbols of Transformation.* In *Collected Work* (Vol. 5). R. F. C. Hall (Trans.) Princeton, NJ: Princeton University Press. (Original work published 1912)

Jung, C. G. (1968). *Collected works 18: Symbolic life.* New York: Pantheon.

Kalodner, C. R. (1998). Systematic desensitization. In S. Cormier & B. Cormier (Eds.), *Interviewing strategies for helpers* (4th ed., pp. 497–529). Pacific Grove, CA: Brooks/Cole.

Kalpana, R. (2005). Phantom limbs: South Indian dance and immigrant reifications of the female body. *Journal of Intercultural Studies, 26*(1/2), 121–138.

Kaplan, A., & Schwartz, L. (2005). Issues of attachment and sexuality: Case studies from a clinical research study. *Hakomi Forum, 14–15*(Summer), 19–31.

Kaschak, E. (1981). Feminist psychotherapy: The first decade. In S. Cox (Ed.), *Female psychology: The emerging self* (pp. 387–400). New York: St. Martin's.

Kaschak, E. (1992). *Engendered lives*. New York: Basic Books.

Kaslow, F. W. (1986). Therapy with distressed psychotherapists: Special problems and challenges. In R. R. Kilburg, P. E. Nathan, & R. W. Thoreson (Eds.), *Professionals in distress: Issues, syndromes, and solutions in psychology* (pp.187–210). Washington, DC: American Psychological Association.

Kaslow, F. W. (2000). Continued evolution of family therapy: The last twenty years. *Contemporary Family Therapy, 22,* 357–386.

Kaslow, F. W., & Schulman, N. (1987). How to be sane and happy as a family therapist, or the reciprocal impact of family therapy teaching and practice and therapists' personal lives and mental health. *Journal of Psychotherapy and the Family, 3*(2), 79–96.

Kaslow, N. J., & Celano, M. P. (2005). The families therapies. In A. S. Gurman & S. B. Messer (Eds.), *Essential psychotherapies* (pp. 343–402). New York: Guilford Press.

Kaslow, N. J., Celano, M., & Dreelin, E. D. (1995). A cultural perspective on family theory and therapy. *Cultural Psychiatry, 18,* 621–633.

Kasprow, M. C., & Scotton, B. W. (1999). A review of transpersonal theory and its application to the practice of psychotherapy. *Journal of Psychotherapy Practice and Research, 8,* 12–23.

Katz, J. H. (1985). The sociopolitical nature of counseling. *The Counseling Psychologist, 13,* 615–624.

Kaut, K. (2002). Religion, spirituality, and existentialism near the end of life: Implications for assessment and application. *American Behavioral Scientist, 46*(2), 220–235.

Kazak, A. E., Alderfer, M. A., Streisand, R., Simms, S., Rourke, M. T., Barakat, L. P., Gallagher, P., & Cnaan, A. (2004). Treatment of posttraumatic stress symptoms in adolescent survivors of childhood cancer and their families: A randomized clinical trial. *Journal of Family Psychology, 18,* 493–504.

Kazdin, A. E., & Wilson, G. T. (1978). *Evaluation of behavior therapy: Issues, evidence, and research strategies*. Lincoln: University of Nebraska Press.

Keenan, M. (1998). Narrative therapy with men who have sexually abused children. *Irish Journal of Psychology, 19*(1), 136–151.

Keleman, S. (1985). *Emotional anatomy: The structure of experience*. Berkeley, CA: Center Press.

Keller, R. (2005). Hakomi simplified 2004: A new view of Ron Kurtz's mindfulness-based psychotherapy. *Hakomi Forum, 14–15*(Summer), 5–18.

Kelly, E. W., Jr. (1995). Counselor values: A national survey. *Journal of Counseling and Development, 73,* 648–653.

Kelly, S. M. (1991). The prodigal soul: Religious studies and the advent of transpersonal psychology. In K. K. Klostermaier and L. W. Hurtado (Eds.), *Religious studies: Issues, prospects and proposals* (pp. 429–441). Atlanta, GA: Scholars Press.

Kendall, P. C., & Hollon, S. D. (1979). Cognitive-behavioral interventions: Overview and current status. In P. C. Kendall & S. D. Hollon (Eds.), *Cognitive-behavioral interventions: Theory, research, and procedures* (pp. 1–9). New York: Academic Press.

Kendler, H. (2005). Psychology and phenomenology: A clarification. *American Psychologist, 60*(4), 318–324.

Kepner, J. (2001). Gestalt approaches to body-oriented theory: An introduction. *Gestalt Review, 4*(4), 262–264.

Kernes, J., & Kinnier, R. (2005). Psychologists' search for the good life. *Journal of Humanistic Psychology, 45*(1), 82.

Kern, R., Snow, J., & Ritter, K. (2002). Making the lifestyle concept measurable. In D. Eckstein & R. Kern (Eds.), *Lifestyle interventions*. Dubuque, IA: Kendall/Hunt.

Kerr, B., Cohn, S. J., Webb, T., & Anderson, T. (2001). *Smart boys: Talent, manhood, and the search for meaning*. Scottsdale, AZ: Gifted Psychology Press.

Kierkegaard, S. (1944). *The concept of dread* (W. Lowrie, Trans.). Princeton, NJ: Princeton University Press.

Kim, K-h. (2002). The effect of a reality therapy program on the responsibility for elementary school children in Korea. *International Journal of Reality Therapy, 22*(1), 30–33.

Kim, R. I., & Hwang, M. (2001). The effects of internal control and achievement motivation in group counseling based on reality therapy. *International Journal of Reality Therapy, 20*(2), 12–15.

Kim, Y. S. (2001). The development and effects of a reality therapy parent group counseling program. *International Journal of Reality Therapy, 20*(2), 4–7.

Kincade, E. A., Seem, S., & Evans, K. M. (1998, April). *Feminist therapy theory and practice: A model for social and individual change*. Paper presented at the American Counseling Association World Conference, Indianapolis, IN.

King, D. B., & Wertheimer, M. (2005). *Max Wertheimer and Gestalt theory*. New Brunswick, NJ: Transaction.

Kinnier, R. T. (1997). What does it mean to be psychologically healthy? In D. Capuzzi & D. R. Gross (Eds.), *Introduction to the counseling profession* (2nd ed., pp. 48–63). Boston: Allyn & Bacon.

Kirk, J. J., Wood, C., Burns, N., Howard, S., & Rice, M. (2001). *Workplace counseling tools.* Cullowhee, NC: Western Carolina University. (ERIC Document Reproduction Service No. ED 455441.)

Kirsh, B. (1987). Evolution of consciousness-raising groups. In V. Franks (Series Ed.) & C. M. Brady (Vol. Ed.), *Springer series: Focus on Women: Vol. 10: Women's therapy groups: Paradigms of feminist treatment* (pp. 43–54). New York: Springer.

Kiselica, M. S., & Robinson, M. (2001). Bringing advocacy counseling to life: The history, issues, and human dramas of social justice work in counseling. *Journal of Counseling and Development, 79*(4), 387–398.

Kiser, S. (2004). An existential case study of madness: Encounters with divine affliction. *Journal of Humanistic Psychology, 44*(4), 431.

Kissane, D., Grabsch, B., Clarke, D., Christie, G., Clifton, D., Gold, S., Hill, C., Morgan, A., McDermott, F., Smith, G. (2004). Supportive expressive group therapy: The transformation of existential ambivalence into creative living while enhancing adherence to anti-cancer therapies. *Psycho-Oncology, 13*(11), 755–769.

Kissane, D., Grabsch, B., Love, A., Clarke, D., Bloch, S., & Smith, G. (2004). Psychiatric disorder in women with early stage and advanced breast cancer: A comparative analysis. *Australian and New Zealand Journal of Psychiatry, 38*(5), 320–327.

Klever, P. (2005). The multigenerational transmission of family unit functioning. *American Journal of Family Therapy, 33*, 253–264.

Kluckhohn, F., & Strodtbeck, F. (1961). *Variations in value orientation.* Evanston, IL: Row, Peterson.

Knights, W. A. (2002). *Pastoral counseling: A Gestalt approach.* New York: Haworth Pastoral Press.

Knobloch-Fedders, L. M., Pinsof, W. M., & Mann, B. J. (2004). The formation of the therapeutic alliance in couple therapy. *Family Process, 43*, 425–442.

Koestler, A. (1967). *The ghost in the machine.* London: Hutchinson.

Kohn, L. P., Oden, T., Munoz, R. F., Robinson, A., & Leavitt, D. (2002). Adapted cognitive behavioral group therapy for depressed low-income African American women. *Community Mental Health Journal, 38*, 497–504.

Kohut, H. (1977). *The restoration of the self.* New York: International Universities Press.

Kopp, S. (1972). *If you meet the Buddha on the road, kill him.* New York: Bantam.

Koss-Chioino, J. (2000). Traditional and folk approaches among ethnic minorities. In J. Aponte & J. Wold (Eds.), *Psychological intervention and cultural diversity* (2nd ed., pp. 149–166). Needham Heights, MA: Allyn & Bacon.

Kottler, J., & Brown, R. (1992). *Introduction to therapeutic counseling* (2nd ed.). Pacific Grove, CA: Brooks/Cole.

Kraus, N., & Shaw, B. A. (2000). Role-specific feelings of control and mortality. *Psychology and Aging, 15*, 617–626.

Krueger, M. J., & Hanna, F. J. (1997). Why adoptees search: An existential treatment perspective. *Journal of Counseling and Development, 75*, 195–202.

Kubler-Ross, E. (1975). *Death: The final stage of growth.* New York: Simon & Schuster.

Kuiken, D. (1995). Dreams and feeling realization. *Dreaming: Journal of the Association of the Study of Dreams, 5*(3), 129–157.

Kurtz, R. (1987). *Hakomi therapy.* (Available from the Hakomi Institute, PO Box 1873, Boulder, CO 80306)

Kurtz, R. (1990). *Body-centered psychotherapy: The Hakomi method.* Mendocino, CA: LifeRhythm.

Kurtz, R. (2000). *Highlights from a four-day advanced seminar: Melbourne, Australia.* (Available from Rosemary McIndoe, 395 Station St., North Carlton, Victoria, Australia. 3054)

Kurtz, R. (2005). Mindfuless-based self-study. *Hakomi Forum, 14–15*(Summer), 1–3.

Kurtz, R., & Prestera, H. (1976). *The body reveals.* New York: Harper & Row.

Kwiatkowska, H. Y. (1978). *Family therapy & evaluation through art.* Springfield, IL: Thomas.

Kwong-Liem, K. (2001). Models of racial and ethnic identity development: Delineation of practice implications. *Journal of Mental Health Counseling, 23*, 269–277.

LaFromboise, T. (1998). American Indian mental health policy. In D. R. Atkinson, G. Morten, & D. W. Sue (Eds.), *Counseling American minorities* (pp. 137–158). New York: McGraw-Hill.

Lajoie, D. H., & Shapiro, S. I. (1992). Definition of transpersonal psychology: The first 25 years. *Journal of Transpersonal Psychology, 24*, 79–98.

Landgarten, H. (1987). *Family art therapy.* New York: Brunner/Mazel.

Längle, A. (2004). The search for meaning in life and the existential fundamental motivations. *International Journal of Existential Psychology and Psychotherapy, 1*(1), 28–37.

Lantz, J. (2004). World view concepts in existential family therapy. *Contemporary Family Therapy, 26*(2), 165–179.

Lantz, J., & Gregoire, T. (2003). Couples, existential psychotherapy, and myocardial infarction: A ten year evaluation study. *Contemporary Family Therapy, 25*(4), 367–379.

Laplanche, J., & Pontalis, J. B. (1973). *The language of psychoanalysis.* New York: Norton.

Lawrence, D. (2004). The effects of reality therapy group counseling on the self-determination of persons with developmental disabilities. *International Journal of Reality Therapy, 23*(2), 9–15.

Leahey, T. H. (1994). *A history of modern psychology.* Philadelphia: Temple University Press.

Lebow, J. L., & Gurman, A. S. (1995). Research assessing couple and family therapy. *Annual Review of Psychology, 46*, 25–57.

Lecours, S., Bouchard, A.-M., & Normandin, L. (1995). Countertransference as the therapist's mental activity: Experience and gender differences among psychoanalytically oriented psychologists, *Psychoanalytic Psychology, 12*(2), 259–281.

Lee, C., & Chuang, B. (2005). Counseling people of color. In D. Capuzzi & D. Gross (Eds.), *Introduction to the counseling profession* (4th ed., pp. 465–481). New York: Pearson Education.

Lee, J. (1997). Women re-authoring their lives through feminist narrative therapy. *Women and Therapy, 20*(3), 1–22.

Lega, L. L., & Ellis, A. E. (2001). Rational emotive behavior therapy (REBT) in the new millennium: A cross-cultural approach. *Journal of Rational-Emotive and Cognitive-Behavior Therapy, 19*(4), 201–221.

Lemoire, S. J., & Chen, C. P. (2005). Applying person-centered counseling to sexual minority adolescents. *Journal of Counseling and Development, 83*(2), 146–154.

Lerner, H.G. (1988). *Women in therapy.* New York: Harper & Row.

Lerner, H. G. (1989). *The dance of intimacy.* New York: Harper & Row.

Lester, D., & Abdel-Khalek, A. (2003). Reliability of a scale to measure existential insecurity. *Perceptual and Motor Skills, 96*(3), 1152.

Letunovsky, V. (2004). Existential therapy in working with the body. *Existential Analysis: Journal of the Society for Existential Analysis, 25*(2), 307–333.

Levine, S. K. & Levine, E. G. (Eds.). (1999). *Foundations of expressive arts therapy: Theoretical and clinical perspectives.* London: Jessica Kingsley.

Levitsky, A., & Perls, F. S. (1970). The rules and games of Gestalt therapy. In J. Fagan & I. Shepherd (Eds.), *Gestalt therapy now: Theory, techniques, and applications* (pp. 140–149). Palo Alto, CA: Science & Behavior Books.

Lewis, J., Arnold, M. S., House, R., & Toporek, R. (2005). *Advocacy competencies.* Retrieved March 31, 2005, from http://www.counselorsforsocialjustice.org/advocacycompetencies.html

Lewis, R. (2005). Individual counseling: Brief approaches. In D. Capuzzi & D. Gross (Eds.), *Introduction to the counseling profession* (4th ed., pp. 173–193). Boston: Allyn & Bacon.

Lewis, T., Amini, F., & Lannon, R. (2000). *A general theory of love.* New York: Vintage Books.

Lewis, T. F., & Osborn, C. J. (2004) Solution focused counseling and motivational interviewing: A consideration of confluence. *Journal of Counseling and Development, 82*(1), 38–48.

Lewis-Fernandez, R., & Kleinman, A. (1995). Cultural psychiatry: Theoretical, clinical, and research issues. *Psychiatric Clinics of North America, 18*, 433–448.

Lieberman, M. A., Solow, N., Bond, G. R., & Reibstein, J. (1979). The psychotherapeutic impact of women's consciousness-raising groups. *Archives of General Psychiatry, 36*, 161–168.

Lieblich, A., McAdams, D. P., & Josselson, R. (Eds.). (2004). *Healing plots: The narrative basis of psychotherapy.* Washington, DC: American Psychological Association.

Lin, Y. (2002). The application of cognitive-behavioral therapy to counseling Chinese. *American Journal of Psychotherapy, 56*, 46–58.

Linehan, M. (1993). *Skills training manual for treating borderline personality disorder.* New York: Guilford Press.

Lipchik, E. (2002). *Beyond technique in solution-focused therapy: Working with emotions and the therapeutic relationship.* New York: Guilford Press.

Lister, J. L. (1964). The counselor's personal theory. *Counselor Education and Supervision, 3*, 207–213.

Lobb, M. S. (2003). Creative adjustment in madness: A Gestalt therapy model for seriously disturbed patients. In M. S. Lobb & N. Amendt-Lyon (Eds.), *Creative license: The art of Gestalt therapy* (pp. 261–277). New York: Springer-Verlag Wien.

Lobb, M. S., & Amendt-Lyon, N. (2003). *Creative license: The art of Gestalt therapy.* New York: Springer-Verlag Wien.

Lobb, M. S., & Lichtenberg, P. (2005). Classical Gestalt therapy theory. In A. L. Woldt & S. M. Toman (Eds.), *Gestalt therapy: History, theory, and practice* (pp. 21–39). Thousand Oaks, CA: Sage.

Locke, D. C., Myers, J. E., & Herr, E. L. (Eds.) (2001). *The handbook of counseling.* Thousand Oaks, CA: Sage.

Loew, T., & Tritt, K. (2005). Empirical research in body-psychotherapy. In G. Marlock & H. Weiss (Eds.), *Handbuch der Koerperpsychotherapie.* Goettingen, Germany: Hogrefe Verlag.

Lojk, L. (1986). My experiences using reality therapy. *Journal of Reality Therapy, 5*(2), 28–35.

Lowen, A. (1976). *Bioenergetics.* New York: Penguin Books.

Loy, D. (1996). *Lack and transcendence: The problem of death and life in psychotherapy, existentialism, and Buddhism.* Atlantic Highlands, NJ: Humanities Press.

Luborsky, L., & Spence, D. P. (1978). Quantitative therapy. In S. L. Garfield & A. E. Bergin (Eds.), *Handbook of psychotherapy and behavior change* (2nd ed., pp. 220–246). New York: Wiley.

Lukoff, D. (1985). The diagnosis of mystical experiences with psychotic features. *Journal of Transpersonal Psychology, 17,* 155–181.

Lukoff, D. (1996). Transpersonal psychotherapy with psychotic disorders and spiritual emergencies with psychotic features. In B. W. Scotton, A. B. Chinen, & J. R. Battista (Eds.), *Textbook of transpersonal psychiatry and psychology* (pp. 271–281). New York: Basic Books.

Lukoff, D., Turner, R., & Lu, D. (1992). Transpersonal psychology research reviews: Psychological dimensions of healing. *Journal of Transpersonal Psychology, 24,* 41–60.

Lukoff, D., Lu, D., & Turner, R. (1998). From spiritual emergency to spiritual problem. *Journal of Humanistic Psychology, 38,* 157–186.

Lum, D. (Ed.) (2003). *Culturally competent practice: A framework for understanding diverse groups and justice issues.* Pacific Grove, CA: Brooks/Cole.

Lyddon, W. J. (1990). First- and second-order change: Implications for rationalist and constructivist cognitive therapies. *Journal of Counseling and Development, 69,* 122–127.

Lynch, J. E., Lynch, B., & Zinker, J. C. (2005). Family and couples therapy from a Gestalt perspective. In A. L. Woldt & S. M. Toman (Eds.). *Gestalt therapy: History, theory, and practice* (pp. 201–217). Thousand Oaks, CA: Sage.

Lyon, D., & Younger, J. (2005). Development and preliminary evaluation of the existential meaning scale. *Journal of Holistic Nursing, 23*(1), 54.

Lyons, L. C., & Woods, P. J. (1991). The efficacy of rational-emotive therapy: A quantitative review of the outcome research. *Clinical Psychology Review, 11,* 357–369.

Lysaker, P. H., Lancaster, R. S., & Lysaker, J. T. (2003). Narrative transformation as an outcome in the psychotherapy of schizophrenia. *Psychology and Psychotherapy: Theory, Research and Practice, 76,* 285–299.

Lysaker, P. H., Wickett, A. M., Wilke, N., & Lysaker, J. (2003). Narrative incoherence in schizophrenia: The absence agent-protagonist and the collapse of internal dialouge. *American Journal of Psychotherapy, 57*(2), 153–167.

Mackey, R. A., & Mackey, E. F. (1994). Personal psychotherapy and the development of a professional self: Families in society. *Journal of Contemporary Human Services, 75,* 490–499.

Madanes, C. (1981). *Strategic family therapy.* San Francisco: Jossey-Bass.

Madanes, C. (1991). Strategic family therapy. In A. S. Gurman & D. P. Kniskern (Eds.), *Handbook of family therapy* (Vol. 2, pp. 396–416). New York: Brunner/Mazel.

Maddi, S. (2004). Hardiness: An operationalization of existential courage. *Journal of Humanistic Psychology, 44*(3), 279.

Maglio, A., Butterfield, L., & Borgen, W. (2005). Existential considerations for contemporary career counseling. *Journal of Employment Counseling, 42*(2), 75–93.

Maglo, D. (2002). Kierkegaard and Foulkes: The advantages of group therapy in treatment of despair. *Group Analysis, 35*(1), 27–43.

Magnuson, S., Norem, K., & Skinner, C. H. (1995). Constructing genograms with lesbian clients. *The Family Journal: Counseling and Therapy for Couples and Families, 3,* 110–115.

Mahoney, M. J. (1991). *Human change processes: The scientific foundations of psychotherapy.* New York: Basic Books.

Mahoney, M. J. (1997). Brief moments and enduring effects: Reflections on time and timing in psychotherapy. In W. J. Mathews & J. H. Edgette (Eds.). *Current thinking and research in brief therapy: Solutions, strategies, narratives* (pp. 123–142). New York: Brunner/Mazel.

Mahoney, M. J. (2003). *Constructive psychotherapy: A practical guide.* New York: Guilford Press.

Mak, Y., & Elwyn, G. (2005). Voices of the terminally ill: Uncovering the meaning of desire for euthanasia. *Palliative Medicine, 19*(4), 343–352.

Makinson, L. S., & Myers, J. E. (2003). Wellness: An alternative paradigm for violence prevention. *Journal of Humanistic Counseling, Education, and Development, 42,* 165–177.

Malchiodi, C. A. (2003). *Handbook of art therapy.* New York: Guilford Press.

Manaster, G. J. (1989). Critical issues in brief psychotherapy: A summary and conclusion. *Individual Psychology, 45,* 243–247.

Mandelbaum, D. (1998). The impact of physical touch on professional development. In E. Smith, P. Clance, and S. Imes (Eds.), *Touch in psychotherapy: Theory, research, and practice.* (pp. 211–219). New York: Guilford Press.

Maples, M. (1996). Cornerstones of a civilized society: Law, morality, faith and spirituality. *Juvenile and Family Court Journal, 47*(3), 41–60.

Markell, M. J. (2002). *Sand, water, silence—the embodiment of spirit: Explorations in matter and psyche.* London: Jessica Kingsley.

Marlock, G., & Weiss, H. (Eds.). (2005). *Handbuch der Koerperpsychotherapie.* Goettingen, Germany: Hogrefe Verlag.

Martin, S., & Thompson, D. (1995). Reality therapy and goal attainment scaling: A program for freshmen student athletes. *Journal of Reality Therapy, 14*(2), 45–54.

Martz, E. (2001). Expressing counselor empathy through the use of possible selves. *Journal of Employment Counseling, 38,* 128–134.

Mascaro, N., & Rosen, D. (2005). Existential meaning's role in the enhancement of hope and prevention of depressive symptoms. *Journal of Personality, 73*(4), 985–1005.

Maslow, A. (1954). *Motivation and personality.* New York: Harper & Row.

Maslow, A. (1968). *Toward a psychology of being* (2nd ed.). New York: Van Nostrand.

Maslow, A. H. (1970). *Motivation and personality* (2nd ed.). New York: Harper.

Maunder, R., & Hunter, J. (2004). An integrated approach to the formulation and psychotherapy of medically unexplained symptoms: Meaning- and attachment-based interventions. *American Journal of Psychotherapy, 58*(1), 17–34.

May, R. (1953). *Man's search for himself.* New York: Dell.

May, R. (Ed.). (1961). *Existential psychology.* New York: Random House.

May, R. (1969). *Love and will.* New York: Norton.

May, R. (1979). *Psychology and the human dilemma.* New York: Norton.

May, R. (1983). *The discovery of being.* New York: Norton.

May, R. (1992). *The cry for myth.* New York: Delta.

Mayers, A., Naples, N., & Nilsen, R. (2005). Existential issues and coping: A qualitative study of low-income women with HIV. *Psychology and Health, 20*(1), 93–114.

McBride, M. C. (1998). The use of process in supervision: A Gestalt approach. *Guidance and Counseling, 13,* 41–49.

McCollum, V. J., & Green E. J. (2005). *Teaching advocacy counseling: A social justice paradigm.* Manuscript submitted for publication.

McDermott, R. A. (1993). Transpersonal worldview: Historical and philosophical reflections. In R. Walsh & F. Vaughan (Eds.), *Paths beyond the ego: The transpersonal vision* (pp. 206–212). Los Angeles: Tarcher/Perigee.

McDowell, T. (2004). Exploring the racial experience of therapists in training: A critical race therapy perspective. *The American Journal of Family Therapy, 32,* 305–324.

McFadden, J., & Lipscomb, W. D. (1985). History of the association for non-white concerns in personnel and guidance. *Journal of Counseling and Development, 63*(7), 444–447.

McFadden, J. (1988). Cross-cultural counseling: Caribbean perspective. *Journal of Multicultural Counseling and Development, 16,* 36–40.

McFadden, J. (1996). A transcultural perspective: Reaction to C. H. Patterson's "Multicultural counseling: From diversity to universality." *Journal of Counseling and Development, 74*(3), 232–235.

McGoldrick, M., & Carter, B. (2001). Advances in coaching: Family therapy with one person. *Journal of Marital and Family Therapy, 27,* 281–300.

McGoldrick, M., Gerson, R., & Shellenberger, S. (1999). *Genograms: Assessment and intervention.* New York: Norton.

McLeod, J. (2004). The significance of narrative and storytelling in postpsychological counseling and psychotherapy. In S. K. Levine & E. G. Levine (Eds.), *Foundations of expressive arts therapy: Theoretical and clinical perspectives* (pp. 11–27). London: Jessica Kingsley.

McWhirter, E. H. (1991). Empowerment in counseling. *Journal of Counseling and Development, 69*(3), 22–27.

Meier, S. T., & Davis, S. R. (2001). *The elements of counseling* (4th ed.). Belmont, CA: Brooks/Cole.

Meissner, C., Brigham, J., & Butz, D. (2005). Memory for own- and other-race faces: A dual-process approach. *Applied Cognitive Psychology, 19*(5), 545–568.

Melnick, J. (2000). Sexual issues in therapy consultation and training [Editorial]. *Gestalt Review, 4*(1), 1–7.

Melnick, J., Nevis, S. M., & Shub, N. (2005). Gestalt therapy methodology. In A. L. Woldt & S. M. Toman (Eds.), *Gestalt therapy: History, theory, and practice* (pp. 101–115). Thousand Oaks, CA: Sage.

Meredith, C. W., & Evans, T. D. (1990). Encouragement in the family. *Individual Psychology, 46,* 187–192.

Metzner, R. (1995). Therapeutic use of altered states of consciousness. In M. Schiliclitiny & H. Leunes (Eds.), *Worlds of consciousness.* Berlin: VWB.

Miars, B. D., & Halverson, S. (2001). The helping relationship. In D. Capuzzi & D. Gross (Eds.), *Introduction to the counseling profession* (3rd ed., pp. 50–68). Needham Heights, MA: Allyn & Bacon.

Miars, R. (2002). Existential authenticity: A foundational value for counseling. *Counseling and Values, 46,* 218–225.

Miller, D. (1997). New physics at last? *Nature, 385,* 768–769.

Miller, G. (2001). Changing the subject: Self-construction in brief therapy. In J. F. Gubrium & J. A. Holstein (Eds.), *Institutional selves: Troubled identities in a postmodern world* (pp. 64–83). New York: Oxford University Press.

Miller, J. (1994). Contemplative practice in higher education. *Journal of Humanistic Psychology, 34,* 53–69.

Miller, J. B. (1976). *Toward a new psychology of women.* Boston: Beacon Press.

Miller, R. (2004). Some aspects of Kierkegaard's works of love: Precious words for the existential therapist? *Journal of the Society for Existential Analysis, 15*(2), 275–375.

Miller, W. R., & Rollnick, S. (2002). *Motivational interviewing: Preparing people to change addictive behavior.* New York: Guilford Press.

Milliren, A. (1995). Foreword. In T. Reed, *Lost days: Children from dysfunctional families in school.* Salt Lake City, UT: Northwest.

Milliren, A., & Eckstein, D. (2005, October). "Thin-slicing": Relationship implications. Workshop presented to the South Carolina Conference of Adlerian Psychology, Myrtle Beach.

Milliren, A., & Wingett, W. (2004). *Conversations in the style of Alfred Adler: RCI/TE.* Unpublished workshop handout at the West Texas Institute for Adlerian Studies, Odessa.

Milliren, A., & Wingett, W. (2005). *In the style of Alfred Adler.* Unpublished manuscript.

Mills, L. J., & Daniluk, J. C. (2002). Her body speaks: The experiences of dance therapy for women survivors of child sexual abuse. *Journal of Counseling and Development, 80*(1), 77–86.

Mills, M. A., & Coleman, P. G. (2002). Reminiscence and life review interventions with older people. In A. Maercker (Ed.), *Pschotherapy with the elderly and clinical geriatric psychology.* New York: Springer.

Mindell, A. (1982). *Dreambody: The body's role in revealing the self.* Boston: Sigo Press.

Mindell, A., & Mindell, A. (1997). Dreams and the dreaming body. In C. Caldwell (Ed.), *Getting in touch: The guide to new body-centered therapies* (pp. 61–70). Wheaton, IL: Theosophical Publishing.

Minuchin, S., & Fishman, C. (1981). *Family therapy techniques.* Cambridge, MA: Harvard University Press.

Mishara, A. L. (1995). Narrative and psychotherapy: The phenomenology of healing. *American Journal of Psychotherapy, 49,* 180–195.

Mitchell, S. (1988). *Relational concepts in psychoanalysis.* Cambridge, MA: Harvard University Press.

Molassiotis, A., Callaghan, P., Twinn, S. F., Lam, S. W., Chung, W. Y., & Li, C. K. (2002). A pilot study of the effects of cognitive-behavioral group therapy and peer support/counseling in decreasing psychologic distress and improving quality of life in Chinese patients with symptomatic HIV disease. *AIDS Patient Care, 16,* 83–96.

Montgomery, C. (1991). The care-giving relationship: Paradoxical and transcendent aspects. *Journal of Transpersonal Psychology, 23,* 91–104.

Montgomery, M., & Kottler, J. (2005). The developing counselor. In D. Comstock (Ed.), *Diversity and development: Critical contexts that shape our lives and relationships* (pp. 91–110). Belmont, CA: Thomson Brooks/Cole.

Montuori, A., & Fahim, U. (2004). Cross-cultural encounter as an opportunity for personal growth. *Journal of Humanistic Psychology, 44*(2), 243.

Moradi, B., Fischer, A. R., Hill, M. S., Jome, L. M., & Blum, S. A. (2000). Does "feminist" plus "therapist" equal "feminist therapist"? An empirical investigation of the link between self-labeling and behaviors. *Psychology of Women Quarterly, 24,* 285–296.

Moreman, R. (2005). What is the meaning of life? Women's spirituality at the end of the life span. *Omega: Journal of Death and Dying, 50*(4), 22.

Morgan, M. (2004). *Born to love: Hakomi psychotherapy and attachment theory.* New Zealand: Hakomi Institute.

Morita, T., Kawa, M., Honke, Y., Kohara, H., Maeyama, E., Kizawa, Y., Akechi, T., & Uchitomi, Y. (2004). Existential concerns of terminally ill cancer patients receiving specialized palliative care in Japan. *Supportive Care in Cancer, 12*(2), 137–141.

Mosak, H., & Dreikurs, R. (1976). Adlerian psychotherapy. In R. J. Corsini (Ed.), *Current psychotherapies.* Itasca, IL: Peacock.

Mountgomery M. & Kottler, J. (2005). The developing counselor. In D. Comstock (Ed.), *Diversity and devel-*

opment: *Critical contexts that shape our lives and relationships* (pp. 91–110). Belmont, CA: Thompson Brooks/Cole.

Moursund, J. M., & Kenny, M. C. (2002). *The process of counseling and psychotherapy* (4th ed.). Upper Saddle River, NJ: Prentice Hall.

Moyer, L. (2002). The context for Hakomi in the treatment of eating disorders. *Hakomi Forum, 4*(Summer), 33–41.

Mozdzierz, G. J., Lisiecki, J., Bitter, J. R., & Williams, A. L. (1986). Role functions of Adlerian therapists. *Journal of Individual Psychology, 42*(2), 154–177.

Mulkey, M. (2004). Recreating masculinity: Drama therapy with male survivors of sexual assult. *Arts in Psychotherapy, 31*(1), 19–28.

Muntigl, P. (2004). *Narrative counseling: Social and linguistic processes of change.* Discourse Approaches to Politics, Society, and Culture Series. Amsterdam: John Benjamins.

Murphy, B. C., & Dillon, C. (2003). *Interviewing in action: Relationship, process, and change* (2nd ed.). Pacific Grove, CA: Brooks/Cole.

Myers, J. E. (1991). Wellness as the paradigm for counseling and development: The possible future. *Counselor Education and Supervision, 30*(3), 183–193.

Myers, J. E., Mobley, A. K., & Booth, C. S. (2003). Wellness of counseling students: Practicing what we preach. *Counselor Education and Supervision, 42*(4), 264–274.

Myers, J. E., Sweeney, T. J., & Witmer, J. M. (2000). The Wheel of Wellness counseling for wellness: A holistic model for treatment planning. *Journal of Counseling and Development, 78,* 251–266.

Naor, Y. (1999). The theater of the holocaust. In S. K. Levine & E. G. Levine (Eds.), *Foundations of expressive arts therapy: Theoretical and clinical perspectives* (pp. 223–235). London: Jessica Kingsley.

Naumberg, M. (1966). *Dynamically oriented art therapy: Its principles and practices.* New York: Grune & Stratton.

Nelson-Jones, R. (2000). *Six key approaches in counseling & therapy.* London: Continuum Press.

Nevis, E. (2004). Introduction to the case study of organization and system interventions by Gestalt-trained practitioners. *Gestalt Review, 8*(3), 260–262.

Nichols, M. P. (1987). *The self in the system: Expanding the limits of family therapy.* New York: Brunner/Mazel.

Nichols, M. P., & Schwartz, R. C. (2003). *Family therapies.* Boston: Allyn & Bacon.

Nietzsche, F. (1889). *Twilight of the idols* (W. Kaufmann, Trans.). New York: Viking.

Norcross, J. C., Santrock, J. W., Campbell, L. F., Smith, T. P., Sommer, R., & Zuckerman, E. L. (2003).

Authoritative guide to self-help resources in mental health (Rev. ed.). New York: Guilford Press.

Noren, A. M. (2004). Commentary of the story of Daniel: Gestalt therapy principles and values. *Gestalt Review, 8*(1), 100–105.

O'Connell, V. F. (1970). Crisis psychotherapy: Person, dialogue, and the organismic event. In J. Fagan & I. L. Shepherd (Eds.), *Gestalt therapy now: Theory techniques applications* (pp. 243–256). Palo Alto, CA: Science and Behavior Books.

O'Connor, M. (2004). Finding boundaries inside prison walls: Case study of a terminally ill inmate. *Death Studies, 28*(1), 63–77.

Ogden, P. (1997). Hakomi integrated somatics: Hands on psychotherapy. In C. Caldwell (Ed.), *Getting in touch: The guide to new body-centered therapies* (pp. 153–178). Wheaton, IL: Theosophical Publishing.

Ogden, P. (2005). Sensorimotor processing for traumatic recovery. In G. Marlock & H. Weiss (Eds.), *Handbuch der Koerperpsychotherapie.* Goettingen, Germany: Hogrefe Verlag.

Ogden, P., & Minton, K. (2001). Sensorimotor psychotherapy: One method for processing traumatic memory. *Traumatology, VI,* Issue 3, Article 3. Retrieved from http://www.fsu.edu/~trauma/v6i3/v6i3a3.html

O'Hanlon, W. H. (1999). *Do one thing different: And other uncommonly sensible solutions to life's persistent problems.* New York: Morrow.

O'Hanlon, W. H., & Weiner-Davis, M. (1989). *In search of solutions: A new direction in psychotherapy.* New York: Norton.

O'Kelly, M. (2002). Idiosyncratic REBT. In W. Dryden (Ed.), *Idiosyncratic rational emotive behaviour therapy* (pp. 90–104). Ross-on-Wye, UK: PCCS Books.

Olsen, S., Dudley-Brown, S., & McMullen, P. (2004). Case for blending pedigrees, genograms, and ecomaps. *Nursing and Health Sciences, 6,* 295–308.

Olson, M. E. (2001). Listening to the voices of anorexia: The researcher as an "outsider witness." *Journal of Feminist Family Therapy, 11,* 25–46.

Okun, B. (1992). *Effective helping: Interviews and counseling techniques* (4th ed.). Pacific Grove, CA: Brooks/Cole.

Okun, B. F. (1987). *Effective helping: Interviewing and counseling techniques* (3rd ed.). Monterey, CA: Brooks/Cole.

O'Leary, C. J. (1999). *Counseling couples and families: A person-centered approach.* Thousand Oaks, CA: Sage.

O'Leary, E., & Nieuwstraten, I. M. (1999). Unfinished business in Gestalt reminiscence therapy: A discourse analytic study. *Counseling Psychology, 12*(4), 395–412.

Ord, G. (2005). Bohr, Bohm and entwined paths. *Chaos, Solutions and Fractals, 25*(4), 769–775.

Orlinsky, D. E., & Howard, K. I. (1978). The relation of process to outcome in psychotherapy. In S. L. Garfield & A. E. Bergin (Eds.), *Handbook of psychotherapy and behavior change* (2nd ed., pp. 283–330). New York: Wiley.

Orlinsky, D. E., & Howard, K. I. (1986). Process and outcome in psychotherapy. In S. L. Garfield & A. E. Bergin (Eds.), *Handbook of psychotherapy and behavior change* (3rd ed., pp. 311–381). New York: Wiley.

Osborn, C. J. (2004). Seven salutary suggestions for counselor stamina. *Journal of Counseling and Development, 82,* 319–328.

O'Shea, L. (2000). Sexuality: Old Struggles and new challenges. *Gestalt Review, 4*(1), 8–25.

Osipow, S. H., Walsh, W. B., & Tosi, D. J. (1980). *A survey of counseling methods.* Homewood, IL: Dorsey.

Oyserman, D., Coon, H., & Kemmelmeier, M. (2002). Rethinking individualism and collectivism: Evaluation of theoretical assumptions and meta-analyses. *Psychological Bulletin, 128,* 3–72.

Page, R. C., Weiss, J. F., & Lietaer, G. (2002). Humanistic group psychotherapy. In D. J. Cain & J. Seeman (Eds.), *Humanistic psychotherapies: Handbook of research and practice* (pp. 339–368). Washington DC: American Psychological Association.

Palmatier, L. L. (1996). Freud defrauded while Glasser defreuded: From pathologizing to talking solutions. *Journal of Reality Therapy, 16,* 75–94.

Paniagua, F. A. (1998). *Assessing and treating culturally diverse clients* (2nd ed.). Thousand Oaks, CA: Sage.

Papero, D. V. (1990). *Bowen family systems theory.* Boston: Allyn & Bacon.

Papp, P., & Imber-Black, E. (1996). Family themes: Transmission and transformation. *Family Process, 35,* 5–20.

Parish, T. (1988). Helping teachers take more effective control. *Journal of Reality Therapy, 8*(1), 41–43.

Parish, T. (1991). Helping students take control via an interactive voice communications system. *Journal of Reality Therapy, 11*(1), 38–40.

Parish, T., Martin, P., & Khramtsova, I. (1992). Enhancing convergence between our real world and ideal selves. *Journal of Reality Therapy, 11*(2), 37–40.

Parker, W. M. (1991). From ANWC to AMCD. *Journal of Multicultural Counseling and Development, 19*(2), 52–65.

Parlett, M., & Lee, R. G. (2005). Contemporary Gestalt therapy: Field theory. In A. L. Woldt & S. M. Toman

(Eds.), *Gestalt therapy: History, theory, and practice* (pp. 41–63). Thousand Oaks, CA: Sage.

Passons, W. R. (1975). *Gestalt approaches in counseling.* New York: Holt, Rinehart & Winston.

Patterson, C. H. (1958). The place of values in counseling and psychotherapy. *Journal of Counseling Psychology, 5,* 216–223.

Patterson, C. H. (1974). *Relationship counseling and psychotherapy.* New York: Harper & Row.

Patterson, C. H. (1989). Values in counseling and psychotherapy. *Counseling and Values, 33,* 164–176.

Patterson, C. H. (1996). Multicultural counseling: From diversity to universality. *Journal of Counseling and Development, 74*(3), 227–231.

Patterson, G. R., & Forgatch, M. S. (1985). Therapist behavior as a determinant for client noncompliance: A paradox for the behavior modifier. *Journal of Consulting and Clinical Psychology, 53,* 846–851.

Pedersen, P. (1987). Ten frequent assumptions of cultural bias in counseling. *Journal of Multicultural Counseling and Development, 15,* 16–22.

Pedersen, P. (1996). The importance of both similarities and differences in multicultural counseling: Reaction to C. H. Patterson. *Journal of Counseling and Development, 74*(3), 236–237.

Pedersen, P. (2000). *A handbook for developing multicultural awareness* (3rd ed.). Alexandria, VA: American Counseling Association.

Perls, F. (1966). *The meaning of Gestalt therapy.* Workshop presented in Atlanta, GA. Cited in J. Fagan & I. Shepherd, 1970, pp. 360–362.

Perls, F. (1969a). *Gestalt therapy verbatim.* Lafayette, CA: Real Person Press.

Perls, F. (1969b). *In and out of the garbage pail.* Lafayette, CA: Real Person Press.

Perls, M., Hefferline, R., & Goodman, P. (1977). *Gestalt therapy.* New York: Bantam.

Perry, B., Pollard, R., Blakley, T., Baker, W., & Vigilante, D. (1996). Childhood trauma, the neurobiology of adaptation and use-dependent development of the brain: How states become traits. *Infant Medical Health Journal.*

Perry, J. (1976). *Roots of renewal in myth and madness.* San Francisco: Jossey-Bass.

Persons, J. B., & Davidson, J. (2001). Cognitive-behavioral case formulation. In K. S. Dobson (Ed.), *Handbook of cognitive-behavioral therapies* (2nd ed., pp. 86–110). New York: Guilford Press.

Pesso, A. (1997). PBSP—Pesso Boyden system psychomotor. In C. Caldwell (Ed.), *Getting in touch: The guide to new body-centered therapies* (pp. 117–152). Wheaton, IL: Theosophical Publishing.

Peter, L. (1982). *The laughter prescription.* New York: Ballantine.

Petersen, S. (2005). Reality therapy and individual or Adlerian psychology: A comparison. *International Journal of Reality Therapy, 24*(2), 11–14.

Peterson, A., Chang, C., & Collins, P. (1997). The effects of reality therapy on locus of control among students in Asian universities. *Journal of Reality Therapy, 16*(2), 80–87.

Peterson, A., & Truscott, J. (1988). Pete's pathogram: Quantifying the genetic needs. *Journal of Reality Therapy, 8*(1), 22–32.

Peterson, A., Woodward, G., & Kissko, R. (1991). A comparison of basic week students and introduction to counseling graduate students on four basic need factors. *Journal of Reality Therapy, 9*(1), 31–37.

Peterson, V. P., & Nisenholz, B. (1995). *Orientation to counseling* (3rd ed.). Needham Heights, MA: Allyn & Bacon.

Peterson, Y. (2005). Family therapy treatment: Working with obese children and their families with small steps and realistic goals. *Acta Paediatrica, 94*(Suppl. 448), 42–44.

Petitti, G. (1992). Brief report: The operational components of drama therapy. *Journal of Group Psychotherapy, Psychodrama and Sociometry, 45*(1), 40–45.

Pierrakos, J. C. (1987). *Core energetics.* Mendocino, CA: LifeRythm.

Pine, F. (1990). *Drive, ego, object, and self.* New York: Basic Books.

Pines, A., & Maslach, C. (1978). Characteristics of staff burnout in mental health settings. *Hospital and Community Psychiatry, 29,* 233–237.

Pinsof, W. M., & Wynne, L. C. (2000). Toward progress research: Closing the gap between family therapy practice and research. *Journal of Marital and Family Therapy, 26,* 1–8.

Pinsof, W. M. (1994). An integrative systems perspective on the therapeutic alliance: Theoretical, clinical, and research implications. In A. O. Horvath & L. S. Greenberg (Eds.), *The working alliance* (pp. 173–198). New York: Wiley.

Polster, E., & Polster, M. (1973). *Gestalt therapy integrated.* New York: Vintage.

Polster, M. (1987). *Every person's life is a novel.* New York: Norton.

Polster, M. E. (1992). *Eve's daughters.* San Francisco: Jossey-Bass.

Ponterotto, J. G., Casas, J. M., Suzuki, L., & Alexander, C. M. (Eds.). (1995). *Handbook of Multicultural Counseling.* Thousand Oaks, CA: Sage.

Pope, M. (1995). The "salad bowl" is big enough for us all: An argument for the inclusion of lesbians and gay men in any definition of multiculturalism. *Journal of Counseling and Development, 73*(3), 301–304.

Pope-Davis, D. B., Coleman, H. L. K., Liu, W. M., & Toporek, R. L. (Eds.). (2003). *Handbook of Multicultural Competencies in Counseling and Psychology.* Thousand Oaks, CA: Sage.

Powers, W. (1973). *Behavior: The control of perception.* New York: Aldine.

Powers, W. (1975). *Behavior: The control of perception.* New York: Aldine.

Powers, R. L., & Griffith, J. (1987). *Understanding lifestyle: The psycho-clarity process.* Chicago, IL: Americas Institute of Adlerian Studies.

Presbury, J. H., Echterling, L. G., & McKee, J. E. (2002). *Ideas and tools for brief counseling.* Columbus, OH: Merrill/Prentice Hall.

Prochaska, J. O., & Norcross, J. C. (1994). *Systems of psychotherapy: A transtheoretical analysis* (3rd ed.). Pacific Grove, CA: Brooks/Cole.

Prochaska, J. O., & Norcross, J. C. (1999). *Systems of psychotherapy: A transtheoretical analysis* (4th ed.). Pacific Grove, CA: Brooks/Cole.

Prochaska, J. O., & Norcross, J. C. (2003). *Systems of psychotherapy: A transtheoretical analysis* (5th ed.). Pacific Grove, CA: Brooks/Cole.

Prouty, G. (1998). Pretherapy and pre-symbolic experiencing: Evolutions in person-centered/experiential approaches to psychotic experience. In L. S. Greenberg & J. C. Watson (Eds.), *Handbook of experiential psychotherapy* (pp. 388–409). New York: Guilford Press.

Purkey, W., & Siegel, B. (2003). *Becoming an invitational leader.* Atlanta, GA: Humanics.

Purkey, W. W., & Schmidt, J. J. (1987). *The inviting relationship: An expanded perspective for professional counseling.* Upper Saddle River, NJ: Prentice Hall.

Qin, D., & Comstock, D. (2005). Traditional models of development: Appreciating context and relationship. In D. Comstock (Ed.), *Diversity and development: Critical contexts that shape our lives and relationships* (pp. 1–20). Belmont, CA: Brooks/Cole.

Rabin, H. (1995). The liberating effect on the analyst of the paradigm shift in psychoanalysis. *Psychoanalytic Psychology, 12*(4), 467–483.

Rama, S., Ballentine, R., & Ajaya, S. (1979). *Yoga and psychotherapy: The evolution of consciousness.* Honesdale, PA: Himalayan Institute.

Rampage, C. (1998). Feminist couple therapy. In F. M. Dattilio (Ed.), *Case studies in couple and family therapy: Systemic and cognitive perspectives* (pp. 353–370). New York: Guilford Press.

Rand, M., & Fewster, G. (1997). Self, boundaries, and containment: Integrative body psychotherapy. In C. Caldwell (Ed.), *Getting in touch: A guide to the new body psychotherapies* (pp. 71–88). Wheaton, IL: Theosophical Publishing.

Rapaport, D., & Gill, M. M. (1959). The points of view and assumptions of metapsychology. *International Journal of Psychoanalysis, 40,* 153–162.

Ratts, M., D'Andrea, M., & Arredondo, P. (2004). Social justice counseling: A "fifth force" in the field. *Counseling Today, 47,* 28–30.

Rave, E. J., & Larsen, C. C. (1995). *Ethical decision making in therapy: Feminist perspectives.* New York: Guilford Press.

Raveis, V., & Pretter, S. (2005). Existential plight of adult daughters following their mother's breast cancer diagnosis. *Psycho-Oncology, 14*(1), 49–51.

Reber, A. S. (2002). *Dictionary of psychology.* New York: Penguin.

Reed, T. L. (1995). *Lost days: Children from dysfunctional families in school.* Salt Lake City, UT: Northwest.

Reich, W. (1974). *Character analysis.* New York: Touchstone Books, Simon & Schuster.

Remer, P., Rostosky, S., & Wright, M. (2001). Counseling women from a feminist perspective. In E. R. Welfel, & R. E. Ingersoll (Eds.), *Mental health desk reference* (pp. 341–347). New York: Wiley.

Remley, T. P., Jr., & Herlihy, B. R. (2005). *Ethical, legal, and professional issues in counseling* (2nd ed.). Upper Saddle River, NJ: Merrill/Prentice Hall.

Resnick, S. (2004). Somatic-experiential sex therapy: A body-centered Gestalt approach to sexual concerns. *Gestalt Review, 8*(1), 40–64.

Reynolds, A. L., & Pope, R. L. (1991). The complexities of diversity: Exploring multiple oppressions. *Journal of Counseling and Development, 70*(1), 174–180.

Reynolds, C., & Mortola, P. (2005). Gestalt therapy with children. In A. L. Woldt & S. M. Toman (Eds.), *Gestalt therapy: History, theory, and practice* (pp. 153–178). Thousand Oaks, CA: Sage.

Richards, P., & Bergin, A. (2002). *A spiritual strategy for counseling and psychotherapy.* Washington, DC: American Psychological Association.

Richardson, B., & Wubbolding, R. (2001). Five interrelated challenges for using reality therapy with challenging students. *International Journal of Reality Therapy, 20*(2), 35–39.

Richardson, T. Q., & Molinaro, K. L. (1996). White counselor self-awareness: A prerequisite for developing multicultural competence. *Journal of Counseling and Development, 74,* 238–242.

Richert, A. J. (2002). The self narrative therapy: Thoughts from a humanistic/existential perspective. *Journal of Psychotherapy Integration, 12*(1), 77–104.

Ridley, C., & Lingle, D. (1996). Cultural empathy in multicultural counseling: A multidimensional process model. In P. Pedersen, J. Draguns, W. Lonner, & J. Trimble (Eds.), *Counseling across cultures* (4th ed., pp. 21–46). Thousand Oaks, CA: Sage.

Robbins, A. (1980). *Expressive therapy: A creative arts approach to depth-oriented treatment.* New York: Human Sciences Press.

Roberts, J. (1995). Exploring story styles. *The Family Journal: Counseling and Therapy for Couples and Families, 3,* 158–163.

Robinson, T. L. (2005). *The convergence of race, ethnicity, and gender: Multiple identities in counseling* (2nd ed.). Upper Saddle River, NJ: Merrill/Prentice Hall.

Rockquemore, K. A., & Laszloffy, T. A. (2003). Multiple realities: A relational narrative approach in therapy with black-white mixed race clients. *Family Relations, 52,* 119–128.

Rodriguez, L. (2004). Ars moriendi: Existential analysis. *Journal of the Society for Existential Analysis, 15*(2), 370–377.

Rogers, C. (1942). *Counseling and psychotherapy.* Boston: Houghton Mifflin.

Rogers, C. (1951). *Client-centered therapy.* Boston: Houghton Mifflin.

Rogers, C. (1959). A theory of therapy, personality, and interpersonal relationships, as developed in the client-centered framework. In S. Koch (Ed.), *Psychology: A study of a science* (Vol. 3, pp. 184–256). New York: McGraw-Hill.

Rogers, C. (1961). *On becoming a person: A therapist's view of psychotherapy.* Boston: Houghton Mifflin.

Rogers, C. (Ed.). (1967). *The therapeutic relationship and its impact: A study of psychotherapy with schizophrenics.* Madison: University of Wisconsin Press.

Rogers, C. (1970). *Carl Rogers on encounter groups.* New York: Harper & Row.

Rogers, C. (1986). Carl Rogers on the development of the person-centered approach. *Person-Centered Review, 1*(3), 257–259.

Rogers, C. (1987a). Inside the world of the Soviet professional. *Counseling and Values, 32*(1), 47–66.

Rogers, C. (1987b). Steps toward peace, 1948–1986: Tension reduction in theory and practice. *Counseling and Values, 32*(1), 12–16.

Rogers, C., & Dymond, R. (1954). *Psychotherapy and personality change.* Chicago: University of Chicago Press.

Rogers, C., & Sanford, R. (1987). Reflections on our South African experience. *Counseling and Values, 32*(1), 17–20.

Rogers, C. R. (1957). The necessary and sufficient conditions of therapeutic personality change. *Journal of Consulting Psychology, 21*, 95–103.

Rogers, C. R. (1961). *On becoming a person: A therapist's view of psychotherapy.* Boston: Houghton Mifflin.

Rogers, N. (1999). The creative connection: A holistic expressive arts process. In S. K. Levine & E. G. Levine (Eds.), *Foundations of expressive arts therapy: Theoretical and clinical perspectives* (pp. 113–131). London: Jessica Kingsley.

Rogers, N. (2001). Person-centered expressive arts therapy. In J. A. Rubin (Ed.), *Approaches to art therapy: Theory and technique* (2nd ed., pp. 163–177). Philadelphia: Brunner-Routledge.

Rolf, I. (1978). *Rolfing: The integration of human structures.* New York: Barnes & Noble.

Rosenberg, J., Rand, M., & Asay, D. (1985). *Body, self, and soul: Sustaining integration.* Atlanta, GA: Humanics.

Rosenblatt, A., Greenberg, J., Solomon, S., Pyszczynski, T., & Lyon, D. (1989). Evidence for terror management theory: I. The effects of mortality salience on reactions to those who violate or uphold cultural values. *Journal of Personality and Social Psychology, 57*, 681–690.

Roysircar, G. (2004). Child survivor of war: A case study. *Journal of Multicultural Counseling and Development, 32*(3), 168–180.

Rubin, J. A. (Ed.). (2001). *Approaches to art therapy: Theory and technique* (2nd ed.). Philadelphia: Brunner/Routledge.

Rusca, R. (2003). An existentialist approach to anorexia nervosa. *American Journal of Psychotherapy, 57*(4), 491.

Rush, A. J., Beck, A. T., Kovacs, M., & Hollon, S. (1977). Comparative efficacy of cognitive therapy and pharmacotherapy in the treatment of depressed outpatients. *Cognitive Therapy and Research, 4*, 17–37.

Russell, S. (2000). A narrative approach to treating eating disorders: A case study. *Guidance and Counseling, 5*(4), 10–14.

Sabar, S. (2000). Bereavement, grief, and mourning: A gestalt perspective. *Gestalt Review, 4*(2), 152–159.

Salvatore, G., Dimaggio, G., & Semerari, A. (2004). A model of narrative development: Implications for understanding psychopathology and guided therapy. *Psychology and Psychotherapy: Theory, Research, and Practice, 77*, 231–254.

Samler, J. (1960). Change in values: A goal in counseling. *Journal of Counseling Psychology, 7*, 32–39.

Sanders, J. L., & Bradley, C. (2005). Multiple-lens paradigm: Evaluating African American girls and their development. *Journal of Counseling and Development, 83*(3), 299–304.

Sanderson, W. C., & Woody, S. (1995). *Manuals for empirically validated treatments.* Retrieved April 9, 2006, from http://www.apa.org/divisions/div12/est/manualsforevt.html

Santos de Barona, M., & Dutton, M. A. (1997). Feminist perspectives on assessment. In J. Worell & N. G. Johnson (Eds.), *Shaping the future of feminist psychology: Education, research, and practice* (pp. 37–56). Washington, DC: American Psychological Association.

Sapp, M., Farrell, W., & Durand, H. (1995). Cognitive behavior therapy: Applications for African American middle-school at risk students. *Journal of Instructional Psychology, 22*(2), 169–177.

Sarbin, T. (1986). The narrative as a root metaphor for psychology. In T. Sarbin (Ed.), *Narrative psychology: The storied nature of human conduct* (pp. 3–21). New York: Praeger.

Satir, V. M. (1983). *Conjoint family therapy.* (3rd. ed.) Palo Alto, CA: Science & Behavior Books.

Satir, V. M., & Bitter, J. R. (1991). The therapist and family therapy: Process model. In A. M. Horne & J. L. Passmore (Eds.), *Family counseling and therapy* (pp. 13–45). Itasca, IL: Peacock.

Sauber, R. S., L'Abate, L., Weeks, G. R., & Buchanan, W. L. (1993). *The dictionary of family psychology and family therapy.* Newbury Park, CA: Sage.

Schanzer, L. (1990). *Does meditation-relaxation potentiate psychotherapy?* Psy.D. Dissertation, Massachusetts School of Professional Psychology. Boston, MA.

Schmidt, J. J. (2002). *Intentional helping: A philosophy for proficient caring relationships.* Upper Saddle River, NJ: Merrill/Prentice Hall.

Schmidt, J. J. (2006). *Social and cultural foundations of counseling and human services: Multiple influences on self-concept development.* Boston: Allyn & Bacon.

Schoenbert, P., Feder, B., Frew, J., & Gadol, I. (2005). Gestalt therapy in groups. In A. L. Woldt & S. M. Toman (Eds.), *Gestalt therapy: History, theory, and practice* (pp. 219–236). Thousand Oaks, CA: Sage.

Schulmeister, M. (2000). *Hakomi Institute of Europe's answers to the EAP's 15 questions about scientific validation of body-psychotherapy.* Retrieved from http://www.eabp.org/scient_validity_hakomi.html

Schulz, R., Greenley, J. R., & Brown, R. (1995). Organization, management, and client effects on staff burnout. *Journal of Health and Social Behavior, 36*, 333–345.

Schwartz, R. C. (1995). *Internal family systems*. New York: Guilford Press.

Scotton, B.W., Chinen, A.B., & Battista, J.R. (1996). *Textbook of transpersonal psychiatry and psychology*. New York: Basic Books.

See, J., & Kamnetz, B. (2004). Person-centered counseling in rehabilitation professions. In F. Chan, N. L. Berven, & K. R. Thomas (Eds.), *Counseling theories and techniques for rehabilitation health professionals* (pp. 76–97). New York: Springer.

Segal, L. (1991). Brief therapy: The MRI approach. In A. S. Gurman & D. P. Kniskern (Eds.), *Handbook of family therapy* (Vol. 2, pp. 171–199). New York: Brunner/Mazel.

Segal, M. (1997). *Points of influence: A guide to using personality theory at work*. San Francisco: Jossey-Bass.

Seligman, L. (2001). *Systems, strategies, and skills of counseling and psychotherapy*. Upper Saddle River, NJ: Merrill/Prentice Hall.

Seligman, L. (2004). *Diagnosis and treatment planning in counseling* (3rd ed., pp. 191–223). New York: Kluwer.

Seligman, L. (2004). *Selecting effective treatments: A comprehensive, systemic guide to treating mental disorders* (Rev. ed.). New York: Wiley.

Seligman, L. (2006). *Systems, strategies, and skills of counseling and psychotherapy* (2nd ed.). Upper Saddle River, NJ: Merrill/Prentice Hall.

Seligman, M. (2004). Can happiness be taught? *Daedalus, 133*(2), 80–87.

Seltzer, L. (1986). *Paradoxical strategies in psychotherapy*. New York: Wiley.

Semmler, P. L., & Williams, C. B. (2000). Narrative therapy: A storied context for multicultural counseling. *Journal of Multicultural Counseling and Development, 28*(1), 51–61.

Serge, G. (2004). Sandor Ferenczi, grandfather of Gestalt therapy. *Gestalt review, 8*(3), 358–368.

Serlin, I. A., & Shane, P. (1999). Laura Perls and Gestalt therapy: Her life and values. In D. Moss (Ed.), *Humanistic and transpersonal psychology: A historical and biographical source book* (pp. 374–384). Westport, CT: Greenwood Press.

Sexton, T. L., & Ridley, C. R. (2004). Implications of a moderated common factors approach: Does it move the field forward? *Journal of Marital and Family Therapy, 30*(2), 159–163.

Sexton, T. L., & Whiston, S. C. (1994). The status of the counseling relationship: An empirical review, theoretical implications, and research directions. *Counseling Psychologist, 22*, 6–78.

Shalif, Y., & Leibler, M. (2002). Working with people experiencing terrorist attacks in Israel: A narrative perspective. *Journal of Systematic Therapies, 21*(3), 60–70.

Shane, P. (1999). Gestalt therapy: The once and future king. In D. Moss (Ed.), *Humanistic and transpersonal psychology: A historical and biographical source book* (pp. 49–65). Westport, CT: Greenwood Press.

Shannon, H. D., & Allen, T. W. (1998). The effectiveness of a REBT training program in increasing the performance of high school students in mathematics. *Journal of Rational-Emotive and Cognitive-Behavior Therapy, 16*(3), 197–209.

Shapiro, D. (1994). Examining the content and context of meditation. *Journal of Humanistic Psychology, 34*, 101–135.

Sharf, R. S. (1996). *Theories of psychotherapy and counseling: Concepts and cases*. Pacific Grove, CA: Brooks/Cole.

Sharf, R. S. (2000). *Theories of psychotherapy and counseling: Concepts and cases* (3rd ed.). Pacific Grove, CA: Brooks/Cole.

Shaw, B. F. (1977). Comparison of cognitive therapy and behavior therapy in the treatment of depression. *Journal of Consulting and Clinical Psychology, 45*, 543–551.

Shepherd, M. (1975). *Fritz*. New York: Saturday Review Press.

Shoben, E. J., Jr. (1962). The counselor's theory as a personality trait. *American Personnel and Guidance Journal, 40*, 617–621.

Shore, A. (1994). *Affect regulation and the origin of the self: The neurobiology of emotional development*. Hillsdale, NJ: Erlbaum.

Shreve, A. (1989). *Women together, women alone*. New York: Viking.

Shub, N. (2000). Gestalt therapy and self-esteem. *Gestalt Review, 4*(2), 111–123.

Shulman, B. H. (1951). Review of L. Way: Adler's place in psychology. *Individual Psychology Bulletin, 9*, 31–35.

Shulman, B. H. (1962). The meaning of people to the schizophrenic versus the manic-depressive. *Journal of Individual Psychology, 18*, 151–156.

Shulman, B. H. (1973). Confrontation techniques in Adlerian psychotherapy. *Contributions to Individual Psychology: Selected papers by Bernard H. Shulman, M.D.* Chicago: Alfred Adler Institute of Chicago. (Originally published in 1971 in the *Journal of Individual Psychology, 27*, 167–175)

Shulman, B. H. (1989). Some remarks on brief therapy, [Special Issue: Varieties of brief therapy]. *Individual Psychology: Journal of Adlerian Therapy, Research and Practice, 45*(1–2), 34–37.

Shulman, B. H., & Mosak, H. H. (1977). Birth order and ordinal position. *Journal of Individual Psychology, 33,* 114–121.

Shulman, B. H., & Mosak, H. H. (1988). *Manual for life style assessment.* Levittown, PA: Accelerated Development.

Siegel, D. J. (1999). *The developing mind: Toward a neurobiology of interpersonal experience.* New York: Guilford Press.

Siegel, D. J., & Hartzell, M. (2003). *Parenting from the inside out.* New York: Tarcher.

Simon, R. M. (1992). *The symbolism of style: Art as therapy.* London: Tavistock/Routledge.

Skinner, B. F. (1969). *Contingencies of reinforcement: A theoretical analysis.* New York: Appleton Century Crofts.

Skovholt, T. M. (2001). *The resilient practitioner: Burnout prevention and self-care strategies for counselors, therapists, teachers and health professionals.* Needham Heights, MA: Allyn & Bacon.

Skully, M. (1995). Viktor Frankl at ninety: An interview. *First Things: The Journal of Religion, Culture, and Public Life, 52,* 39–43.

Slattery, J. (2004). *Counseling diverse clients: Bringing context into therapy.* Belmont, CA: Brooks/Cole.

Small, J. (2000). A psychospiritual approach to healing. *Guidance and Counseling, 15,* 9–12.

Smith, G. B., & Schwebel, A. I. (1995). Using a cognitive-behavioral family model in conjunction with systems and behavioral family therapy models. *American Journal of Family Therapy, 23,* 203–212.

Smith, E. (1985). *The body in psychotherapy.* Jefferson, NC: McFarland.

Smith, M. L., & Glass, G. V. (1977). Meta-analysis of psychotherapy outcome studies. *American Psychologist, 32,* 752–760.

Smith, T., & Kehe, J. (2004). Glossary. In T. Smith (Ed.), *Practicing multiculturalism: Affirming diversity in counseling and psychology* (pp. 325–337). Boston: Pearson Education.

Smith, T. B. (2004). *Practicing multiculturalism: Affirming diversity in counseling and psychology.* Boston: Allyn & Bacon.

Solomon, S., Greenberg, J., & Pyszczynski, T. (1991). A terror management theory of social behavior: The psychological functions of self-esteem and world views. In L. Berkowitz (Ed.), *Advances in Experimental Social Psychology, 24,* 93–159.

Speedy, J. (2004). The contribution of narrative ideas and writing practices in therapy. In G. Bolton, S. Howlett, C. Lago, & J. K. Wright (Eds.), *Writing cures: An introductory handbook of writing in counseling and psychotherapy* (pp. 25–34). East Sussex, England: Brunner/Routledge.

State Of Ohio. (1984). *Counselor and Social Worker Law* (Chap. 4757, Rev. code). Columbus, OH: Author.

Stein, H. T. (1991). Adler and Socrates: Similarities and differences. *Individual Psychology, 42*(2), 241–246.

Stein, H. T., & Edwards, M. E. (1998). Classical Adlerian theory and practice. In P. Marcus & A. Rosenberg (Eds.), *Psychoanalytic versions of the human condition: Philosophies of life and their impact on practice* (pp. 64–93). New York: New York University Press.

Stephenson, W. (1953). *The study of behavior: Q-technique and its methodology.* Chicago: University of Chicago Press.

Stern, D. N. (1985). *The interpersonal world of the infant.* New York: Basic Books.

Stolorow, R. D., Brandshaft, B., & Atwood, G. E. (1987). *Psychoanalytic treatment: An intersubjective approach.* Hillsdale, NJ: Analytic Press.

Stone, L. (1954). The widening scope of indications for psychoanalysis. *Journal of the American Psychoanalytic Association, 2,* 567–594.

Strachey, J. (1934). The nature of therapeutic action in psychoanalysis. *International Journal of Psychoanalysis, 15,* 127–159.

Strasser, F., & Strasser, A. (1997). *Existential time-limited therapy: The wheel of existence.* San Francisco: Jossey-Bass.

Strohl, J. E. (1998). Transpersonalism: Ego meets soul. *Journal of Counseling and Development, 76,* 397–403.

Strumpfel, U., & Martin C. (2004). Research on Gestalt therapy. *International Gestalt Journal, 27*(1), 9–54.

Sturdivant, S. (1980). *Therapy with women: A feminist philosophy of treatment.* New York: Springer.

Sue, D. W., Arredondo, P. A., & McDavis, R. J. (1992). Multicultural competencies and standards: A call to the profession. *Journal of Counseling and Development, 70*(4), 477–486.

Sue, D. W., & Sue, D. (2003). *Counseling the culturally diverse: Theory and practice* (4th ed.). New York: Wiley.

Sue, S. (1997). Community mental health services to minority groups: Some optimism, some pessimism. *American Psychologist, 32,* 616–624.

Sue, E. W., & Sue, D. (2002). *Counseling the culturally different: Theory and practice* (4th ed.). New York: Wiley.

Sullivan, H. S. (1953). *The interpersonal theory of psychiatry.* New York: Norton.

Sutherland, M. (2001). Developing a transpersonal approach to pastoral counseling. *British Journal of Guidance and Counseling, 29,* 381–390.

Sweeney, T. J., & Witmer, J. M. (1991). Beyond social interest: Striving toward optimal health and wellness. *Individual Psychology, 47,* 527–540.

Synder, B. A. (1997). Expressive arts therapy techniques: Healing the soul through creativity. *Journal of Humanistic Counseling, Education and Development, 36*(2), 74–83.

Szasz, T. (2005). What is existential therapy not? *Existential Analysis, 16*(1), 127–130.

Tart, C. (2005). Future psychology as a science of mind and spirit: Reflections on receiving the Abraham Maslow award. *Humanistic Psychologist, 33*(2), 131–144.

Tatum, B. (2000). The complexity of identity: Who am I? In M. Adams, W. Blumenfeld, R. Castaneda, H. Hackman, M. Peters, & X. Zuniga (Eds.). *Readings for diversity and social justice: An anthology on racism, anti-semitism, sexism, heterosexism, ableism, and classism.* New York: Routledge.

Terner, J., & Pew, W. L. (1978). *The courage to be imperfect: The life and work of Rudolf Dreikurs.* New York: Hawthorn.

Thayer, L. (1987). An interview with Carl R. Rogers: Toward peaceful solutions to human conflict, Part I. *Michigan Journal of Counseling and Development, 18*(1), 58–63.

Thielen, M. (2005). Body-psychotherapy and the narcissistic personality disorder. In G. Marlock & H. Weiss (Eds.), *Handbuch der Koerperpsychotherapie.* Goettingen, Germany: Hogrefe Verlag.

Thomas, S. E. G., Werner-Wilson, R. J., & Murphy, M. J. (2005). Influence of therapist and client behaviors on therapy alliance. *Contemporary Family Therapy, 27,* 19–35.

Thompson, C. L., & Rudolph, L .B. (2000). *Counseling children* (5th ed.) Belmont, CA: Brooks/Cole.

Thompson, C. L., Rudolph, L., & Henderson, D. A. (2004). *Counseling children* (6th ed.). Belmont, CA: Thomson Brooks/Cole.

Thompson, K. (2004). Journal writing as a therapeutic tool. In G. Bolton, S. Howlett, C. Lago, & J. K. Wright (Eds.), *Writing cures: An introductory handbook of writing in counseling and psychotherapy* (pp. 72–84). East Sussex, England: Brunner/Routledge.

Thompson, R. W. (1996). *Counseling techniques.* Washington, DC: Accelerated Development, Taylor & Francis.

Tillett, R. (1991). Active and non-verbal therapeutic approaches. In J. Holmes (Ed.), *Textbook of psychotherapy in psychiatric practice.* Edinburgh: Churchill Livingstone.

Tillich, P. (1980). *The courage to be.* New Haven, CT: Yale University Press.

Tillich, P. (1987). *Paul Tillich: Theologian of the boundaries* (M. Taylor, Ed.). San Francisco: Collins.

Tobin, S. (2004). The integration of relational gestalt therapy and EMDR. *International Gestalt Journal, 27*(1), 55–82.

Tolman, D. L. (1991). Adolescent girls, women, and sexuality: Discerning dilemmas of desire. In C. Gilligan, A. Rogers, & D. Tolman (Eds.), *Women, girls, and psychotherapy: Reframing resistance* (pp. 55–70). New York: Haworth.

Toman, S. M., Bauer, A., McConville, M., & Robertson, B. (2005). Adolescents: Development and practice from a Gestalt orientation. In A. L. Woldt & S. M. Toman (Eds.), *Gestalt therapy: History, theory, and practice* (pp. 179–199). Thousand Oaks, CA: Sage.

Tonella, G. (2005a). Body-psychotherapy and psychosis. In G. Marlock & H. Weiss (Eds.), *Handbuch der Koerperpsychotherapie.* Goettingen, Germany: Hogrefe Verlag.

Tonella, G. (2005b). Oral depression. In G. Marlock & H. Weiss (Eds.), *Handbuch der Koerperpsychotherapie.* Goettingen, Germany: Hogrefe Verlag.

Torres-Rivera, E., Phan, L. T., Maddux, C., Wilbur, M., & Garret, M. (2001). Process versus content: Integrating personal awareness and counseling skills to meet the multicultural challenge of the twenty-first century. *Counselor Education and Supervision, 41*(1), 28–40.

Trower, P. (2003). Theoretical developments in REBT as applied to schizophrenia. In W. Dryden (Ed.), *Rational emotive behaviour therapy: Theoretical developments* (pp. 228–246). New York: Brunner-Routledge.

Trower, P., & Jones, J. (2001). How REBT can be less disturbing and remarkably more influential in Britain: A review of views of practitioners and researchers. *Journal of Rational-Emotive and Cognitive-Behavior Therapy, 19*(1), 21–30.

Truax, C., & Carkhuff, R. (1967). *Toward effective counseling and psychotherapy: Training and practice.* Hawthorne, NY: Aldine.

Truax, C. B., & Carkhuff, R. R. (1967). *Towards effective counseling and psychotherapy: Training and practice.* Chicago: Aldine.

Trungpa Rinpoche, C. (1983). Becoming a full human being. In J. Welwood (Ed.), *Awakening the heart: East/West approaches to psychotherapy and the healing relationship* (pp. 126–131). Boulder, CO: Shambhala.

Typpo, M. H., & Hastings, J. M. (1984). *An elephant in the living room.* Minneapolis, MN: CompCare.

Tu, W. (1985). Selfhood and otherness in Confucian thought. In A. J. Marsella, G. DeVos, & F. L. Hsu

(Eds.), *Culture and self: Asian and Western perspectives* (pp. 231–251). London: Tavistock.

Turk, D. C., Meichenbaum, D., & Genest, M. (1983). *Pain and behavioral medicine: A cognitive-behavioral perspective.* New York: Guilford Press.

Turkington, D., Kingdon, D., & Turner, T. (2002). Effectiveness of a brief cognitive-behavioural therapy. *British Journal of Psychiatry, 180,* 523–527.

Uhlhaas, P. J., & Silverstein, S. M. (2005). Phenomenology, biology, and specificity of dysfunctions in Gestalt perception in schizophrenia. *Gestalt Theory, 27*(1), 57–70.

Ungar, M. T. (2001). Constructing narratives of resilience with high-risk youth. *Journal of Systematic Therapies, 20*(2), 58–73.

U.S. Census Bureau (2004). *U.S. interim projections by age, sex, race, and Hispanic origin.* Retrieved August 20, 2004, from http://www.census.gov/ipc/www/usinterimproj/natprojtab01a.xls.

Usher, C. H. (1989). Recognizing cultural bias in counseling theory and practice: The case of Rogers. *Journal of Multicultural Counseling and Development, 17,* 62–71.

Utne, N. (2004). The flow of intention. *Utne, 125,* 68–70.

Utter, J. (1993). *American Indians: Answers to Today's Questions.* Lake Ann, MI: National Woodlands.

Van der Kolk, B. A., McFarlane, A. C., & Weisaeth, L. (Eds.). (1996). *Traumatic stress: The effects of everwhelming experience on mind, body, and society.* New York: Guilford Press.

Van der Velden, I., & Koop, M. (2005). Structure in word and image: Combining narrative therapy and art therapy in groups of survivors of war. *Intervention: International Journal of Mental Health, Psychosocial Work and Counseling in Areas of Armed Conflict, 3*(1), 57–64

Van Deurzen, E. (2002). *Existential counseling and psychotherapy in process.* London: Sage.

Van Kaam, A. (1966). *The art of existential counseling: A new perspective in psychotherapy.* Denville, NJ: Dimension Books.

Vaughan, F. (1979). Transpersonal psychotherapy: Context, content, and process. *Journal of Transpersonal Psychology, 11,* 25–30.

Velten, E. (2002). Idiosyncratic REBT. In W. Dryden (Ed.), *Idiosyncratic rational emotive behaviour therapy* (pp. 76–88). Ross-on-Wye, UK: PCCS Books.

Ventegodt, S., Kandel, I., Neikrug, S., & Merrick, J. (2005). Clinical holistic medicine: The existential crisis—Life crisis, stress, and burnout. *Scientific World, 5,* 300–312.

Vera, E. M., & Speight, S. L. (2003). Multicultural competence, social justice, and counseling psychology: Expanding our roles. *The Counseling Psychologist, 31*(3), 253–272.

Vernon, A. (1998a). *The passport program: A journey through emotional, social, cognitive, and self-development* (Grades 1–5). Champaign, IL: Research Press.

Vernon, A. (1998b). *The passport program: A journey through emotional, social, cognitive, and self-development* (Grades 6–8). Champaign, IL: Research Press.

Vernon, A. (1998c). *The passport program: A journey through emotional, social, cognitive, and self-developing* (Grades 9–12). Champaign, IL: Research Press.

Vernon, A. (2002). *What works when with children and adolescents: A handbook of individual counseling techniques.* Champaign, IL: Research Press.

Vernon, A. (2004a). Applications of rational-emotive behavior therapy with children and adolescents. In A. Vernon (Ed.), *Counseling children and adolescents* (3rd ed., pp. 140–157). Denver, CO: Love.

Vernon, A. (2004b). Rational emotive education. *Romanian Journal of Cognitive and Behavioral Psychotherapies, 4,* 23–37.

Vernon, A. (2006a). *Thinking, feeling, behaving: An emotional education curriculum for children.* Champaign, IL: Research Press.

Vernon, A. (2006b). *Thinking, feeling, behaving: An emotional education curriculum for adolescents.* Champaign, IL: Research Press.

Vich, M. A. (1988). Some historical sources for the term "transpersonal." *Journal of Transpersonal Psychology, 20,* 107–110.

Vontress, C. (1988). An existential approach to cross-cultural counseling. *Journal of Multicultural Counseling and Development, 16,* 73–83.

Vontress, C., Johnson, J., & Epp, L. (1999). *Cross-cultural counseling: A casebook.* Alexandria, VA: American Counseling Association.

Vontress, C. E. (1988). An existential approach to cross-cultural counseling. *Journal of Multicultural Counseling and Development, 16*(2), 73–83.

Walen, S. R. (2002). Idiosyncratic REBT. In W. Dryden (Ed.), *Idiosyncratic rational emotive behaviour therapy* (pp. 62–73). Ross-on-Wye, UK: PCCS Books.

Walen, S. R., DiGiuseppe, R., & Dryden, W. (1992). *A practitioner's guide to rational-emotive therapy* (2nd ed.). New York: Oxford University Press.

Walen, S. R., & Rader, M. W. (1991). Depression and RET: Perspectives from wounded healers. In M. E. Bernard (Ed.), *Using rational-emotive therapy effectively* (pp. 219–264). New York: Plenum Press.

Walker, L. E. (1990). A feminist therapist views the case. In D. W. Cantor (Ed.), *Women as therapists: A multi-theoretical casebook* (pp. 78–95). New York: Springer.

Walsh, R. (1990). *The spirit of shamanism.* Los Angeles: Tarcher.

Walsh, R. (1994). The transpersonal movement: A history and state of the art. *Journal of Transpersonal Psychology, 25,* 1–17.

Walsh, R., & Vaughan, F. (1993). *Paths beyond ego: The transpersonal vision.* New York: Putnam.

Walter, J. L., & Peller, J. F. (2000). *Recreating brief therapy: Preferences and possibilities.* New York: Norton.

Walters, M., Carter, B., Papp, P., & Silverstein, P. (1988). *The invisible web: Gender patterns in family relationships.* New York: Guilford Press.

Walton, F. X. (1996a, March). *Most memorable observation.* Paper presented at the University of Texas Permian Basin Spring Counseling Workshop Odessa.

Walton, F. X. (1996b, March). *Overview of a systematic approach to Adlerian family counseling.* Paper presented at the University of Texas Permian Basin Spring Counseling Workshop, Odessa.

Walton, F. X. (1996c, March). *Questions for brief life style analysis.* Paper presented at the University of Texas Permian Basin Spring Counseling Workshop, Odessa.

Wampold, B. E. (2001). *The great psychotherapy debate: Models, methods, and findings.* Mahwah, NJ: Erlbaum.

Wampold, B. E., Minami, T., Baskin, T. W., & Tierney, S. C. (2002). A meta-(re)analysis of the effects of cognitive therapy versus "other therapies" for depression. *Journal of Affective Disturbances, 686,* 159–165.

Wärja, M. (1999). Music as mother: The mothering function of music through expressive and receptive avenues. In S. K. Levine & E. G. Levine (Eds.), *Foundations of expressive arts therapy: Theoretical and clinical perspectives* (pp. 171–193). London: Jessica Kingsley.

Warren, R. (1997). REBT and generalized anxiety disorder. In J. Yankura & W. Dryden (Eds.), *Using REBT with common psychological problems: A therapist's casebook* (pp. 6–43). New York: Springer.

Warwar, S., & Greenberg, L. S. (2000). Advances in theories and change of counseling. In S. D. Brown & R. W. Lent (Eds.), *Handbook of counseling psychology* (3rd ed., pp. 571–600). New York: Wiley.

Watkins, C. E. (1982). A decade of research in support of Adlerian psychological theory. *Journal of Individual Psychology, 38,* 90–99.

Watkins, C. E. (1983). Some characteristics of research on Adlerian theory. *Journal of Individual Psychology, 39,* 99–110.

Watkins, C. E. (1992). Research activity with Adler's theory. *Journal of Individual Psychology, 48,* 107–108.

Watkins, C. E. (1993). Person-centered theory and the contemporary practice of psychological testing. *Counseling Psychology Quarterly, 6*(1), 59–67.

Watson, J. B. (1930). *Behaviorism* (2nd ed.). Chicago: University of Chicago Press.

Watson, J. C., & Bohart, A. (2001). Humanistic-experiential therapies in the era of managed care. In K. J. Schneider, J. F. T. Bugental, & J. F. Pierson (Eds.), *The handbook of humanistic psychology* (pp. 503–520). Thousand Oaks, CA: Sage.

Watson, J. C., & Geller, S. M. (2005). The relations among the relationship conditions, working alliance, and outcome in both process-experiential and cognitive-behavioral psychotherapy. *Psychotherapy Research, 15,* 25–33.

Watson, K. (1994). Spiritual emergency: Concepts and implications for psychotherapy. *Journal of Humanistic Psychology, 34,* 22–35.

Watson, N. (1984). The empirical status of Rogers' hypotheses of the necessary and sufficient conditions for effective psychotherapy. In R. F. Levant & J. M. Shlien (Eds.), *Client-centered therapy and the person-centered approach: New directions in theory, research, and practice* (pp. 17–40). New York: Praeger.

Wattendorf, D. J., & Hadley, D. W. (2005). Family history: The three generation pedigree. *American Family Physician, 72,* 441–448.

Watts, R. E. (2000). Adlerian counseling: A viable approach for contemporary practice. *TCA Journal, 28,* 11–23.

Waugh, W. (2004). The existentialist public administrator. *International Journal of Organization Theory and Behavior, 7*(3), 432–452.

Way, L. (1962). *Adler's place in psychology.* New York: Collier Books.

Weeks, G., & L'Abate, L. (1982). *Paradoxical psychotherapy.* New York: Brunner/Mazel.

Weil, A. (1996). *Spontaneous healing.* New York: Random House.

Weiner, N. (1948). *Cybernetics.* New York: Wiley.

Weiner, N. (1950). *The human use of human beings: Cybernetics and society.* Boston: Houghton Mifflin.

Weinrach, S. G. (1988). Cognitive therapist: A dialogue with Aaron Beck. *Journal of Counseling and Development, 67,* 159–164.

Weinrach, S. G., & Thomas, K. R. (1998). Diversity-sensitive counseling today: A postmodern clash of values. *Journal of Counseling and Development, 76*(4), 115–122.

Weinrach, S. G., & Thomas, K. R. (2002). A critical analysis of the multicultural counseling competencies: Implications for the practice of mental health counseling. *Journal of Mental Health Counseling, 24*(1), 20–35.

Weiss, J. C. (1984). *Expressive therapy with elders and the disabled: Touching the heart of life.* New York: Haworth Press.

Wertz, F. (2005). Phenomenological research methods for counseling psychology. *Journal of Counseling Psychology, 52*(2), 167–177.

Whalen, M., Fowler-Lese, K. P., Barber, J. S., Williams, E. N., Judge, A. B., Nilsson, J. E., & Shibazaki, K. (2004). Counseling practice with feminist-multicultural perspectives. *Journal of Multicultural Counseling and Development, 32,* 370–389.

Wheeler, G. (2004). Lineage and identity: Gestalt psychology and gestalt therapy—A reply to Paul Shane. *International Gestalt Journal, 27*(1), 83–95.

Whiston, S. C., & Sexton, T. L. (1993). An overview of psychotherapy outcome research: Implications for practice. *Professional Psychology: Research and Practice, 24,* 43–51.

Whitaker, R. (2002). *Mad in America.* Cambridge, MA: Perseus.

White, M. (1992). Deconstruction and therapy. In D. Epston & M. White (Eds.), *Experience, contradiction, narrative, and imagination: Selected papers of David Epston and Michael White, 1989–1991* (pp. 105–151). Adelaide, Australia: Dulwich Centre Publications.

White, M., & Epston, D. (1990). *Narrative means to therapeutic ends.* New York: Norton.

Whitehead, T. (1992). Hakomi in jail: A programmatic application with groups of psychotic, disruptive jail inmates. *Hakomi Forum, 9*(Winter), 7–14.

Whitehead, T. (1994). Boundaries and psychotherapy: Part I. Boundary distortion and its consequences. *Hakomi Forum, 10*(Fall), 7–16.

Whitehead, T. (1995). Boundaries and psychotherapy: Part II. Healing damaged boundaries. *Hakomi Forum, 11,* 27–36.

Wiener, C. J. (Ed.). (1999). *Beyond talk therapy: Using movement and expressive techniques in clinical practice.* Washington, DC: American Psychological Association.

Wilber, K. (1977). *Spectrum of consciousness.* Boulder, CO: Shambhala.

Wilber, K. (1977). *The spectrum of consciousness.* Wheaton, IL: Quest Books.

Wilber, K. (1980). *The Atman project: A transpersonal view of human development.* Wheaton, IL: Theosophical Publishing.

Wilber, K. (1981). *Up from Eden: A transpersonal view of human evolution.* Garden City, NY: Anchor Press/Doubleday.

Wilber, K. (1983a). *Eye to eye: The quest for the new paradigm.* Garden City, NY: Anchor Press/Doubleday.

Wilber, K. (1983b). *A sociable god: A brief introduction to a transpersonal sociology.* New York: New Press.

Wilber, K. (1984a). *Quantum questions: Mystical writings of the world's great physicists.* Boston: Shambhala New Science Library.

Wilber, K. (1984b). The developmental spectrum and psychopathology: Treatment modalities. *Journal of Transpersonal Psychology, 16,* 137–166.

Wilber, K. (1986). The spectrum of psychopathology. In K. Wilber, J. Engler, & D. Brown (Eds.), *Transformations of consciousness* (pp. 65–159). Boston: New Science Library.

Wilber, K. (1989). Let's nuke the transpersonalists. A response to Albert Ellis. *Journal of Counseling and Development, 67,* 332–335.

Wilber, K. (1993). *The spectrum of consciousness.* Wheaton, IL: Quest.

Wilber, K. (1995). *Sex, ecology, spirituality: The spirit of evolution.* Boston: Shambhala.

Wilber, K. (1997). *The eye of spirit: An integral vision for a world gone slightly mad.* Boston: Shambhala.

Wilber, K. (2000). *A theory of everything: An integral vision for business, politics, science, and spirituality.* Boston: Shambhala.

Wilber, K. (2000). *Integral psychology: Consciousness, spirit, psychology, therapy.* Boston: Shambhala.

Wilber, K. (2004). *The simple feeling of being.* Boston: Shambhala.

Wilkins, P. (2003). *Person-centered therapy in focus.* Thousand Oaks, CA: Sage.

Williams, E. N., & Barber, J. S. (2004). Power and responsibility in therapy: Integrating feminism and multiculturalism. *Journal of Multicultural Counseling and Development, 32,* 390–401.

Williams, M. K., McCandies, T., & Dunlap, M. R. (2002). In L. H. Collins, M. R. Dunlap, & J. C. Chrisler (Eds.), *Charting a new course for feminist psychology* (pp. 65–90). Westport, CT: Praeger.

Williams, T. P. (1980). *Transpersonal psychology: An introductory guidebook.* Greeley, CO: Lutney.

Williamson, E. (1958). Value orientation in counseling. *Personnel and Guidance Journal, 36,* 520–528.

Willingham, W. K. (1986). Adlerian psychology: Background, current status, and future. *Texas Tech Journal of Education, 13,* 161–169.

Wilson, E. O. (1998). *Consilience: The unity of knowledge.* New York: Knopf.

Winnicott, D. W. (1958). *Collected papers*. New York: Basic Books.

Wisman, A., & Koole, S. (2003). Hiding in the crowd: Can mortality salience promote affiliation with others who oppose one's worldviews? *Journal of Personality and Social Psychology, 84*(3), 511–526.

Witmer, J. M., & Sweeney, T. J. (1992). A holistic model for wellness and prevention over the life span. *Journal of Counseling and Development, 71*, 140–148.

Wittine, B. (1989). Assumptions of transpersonal psychotherapy. In R. Valle & S. Halling (Eds.), *Existential-phenomenological perspectives in psychology* (pp. 269–297). New York: Plenum.

Wittine, B. (1993). Assumptions of transpersonal psychology. In R. Walsh and F. Vaughan (Eds.), *Paths beyond ego: The transpersonal vision* (pp. 165–171). Los Angeles: Tarcher/Perigee.

Witty, C. (2002). The therapeutic potential of narrative therapy in conflict transformation. *Journal of Systematic Therapies, 21*(3), 48–59.

Wolberg, L. (1977). *The technique of psychotherapy*. New York: Harcourt Brace Jovanovich.

Wolfe, W. B. (1930). Adler and our neurotic world. In A. Adler, *The pattern of life*. New York: Cosmopolitan.

Wolfert, R., & Cook, C. A. (1999). Gestalt therapy in action. In D. Wiener (Ed.), *Beyond talk therapy: Using movement and expressive techniques in clinical practice* (pp. 3–28). Washington, DC: American Psychological Association.

Wolpe, J. (1958). *Psychotherapy by reciprocal inhibition*. Palo Alto, CA: Stanford University Press.

Wolinsky, S. (1991). *Trances people live*. Falls Village, CT: Bramble.

Wong, P. T. (2004). Existential psychology for the 21st century. *International Journal of Existential Psychology and Psychotherapy, 1*(1), 1–2.

Woody, S. R., & Sanderson, W. C. (1998). *Manuals for empirically supported treatments: 1998 update*. Retrieved April 9, 2006, from http://www.apa.org/divisions/div12/est/manual60.pdf

Worell, J., & Johnson, D. (2001). Therapy with women: Feminist frameworks. In R. K. Unger (Ed.), *Handbook of the psychology of women and gender* (pp. 317–329). New York: Wiley.

Worell, J., & Johnson, N. G. (Eds.). (1997). *Shaping the future of feminist psychology: Education, research, and practice*. Washington, DC: American Psychological Association.

Worell, J., & Remer, P. (1996). *Feminist perspectives in therapy: An empowerment model for women*. London: Wiley.

Worell, J., & Remer, P. (2003). *Feminist perspectives in therapy: Empowering diverse women* (2nd ed.). Hoboken, NJ: Wiley.

Worthen, V., & McNeill, B. W. (1996). A phenomenological investigation of "good" supervision events. *Journal of Counseling Psychology, 42*, 25–34.

Wrenn, C. G. (1962). The culturally encapsulated counselor. *Harvard Educational Review, 32*, 444–449.

Wulbbolding, R. (1980). Teenage loneliness. In N. Glasser (Ed.), *What are you doing?* (pp. 120–129). New York: Harper & Row.

Wulbbolding, R. (1981). Balancing the chart: Do it person and positive symptom person. *Journal of Reality Therapy, 1*(1), 4–7.

Wulbbolding, R. (1984). Using paradox in reality therapy: Part I. *Journal of Reality Therapy, 4*(1), 3–9.

Wubbolding, R. (1985a). Characteristics of the inner picture album. *Journal of Reality Therapy, 5*(1), 28–30.

Wulbbolding, R. (1985b). Counseling for results. *Not Out of Sight, 6*, 14–15.

Wubbolding, R. (1986). Professional ethics: Informed consent and professional disclosure in reality therapy. *Journal of Reality Therapy, 6*(1), 30–35.

Wulbbolding, R. (1988). *Using reality therapy*. New York: Harper & Row.

Wulbbolding, R. (1989). Radio station WDEP and other metaphors used in teaching reality therapy. *Journal of Reality Therapy, 8*(2), 74–79.

Wulbbolding, R. (1990). Evaluation: The cornerstone in the practice of reality therapy. *Omar Psychological Series, 1*(2), 6–27.

Wulbbolding, R. (1991). *Understanding reality therapy*. New York: HarperCollins.

Wulbbolding, R. (1993). Reality therapy. In T. Kratochwill (Ed.), *Handbook of psychotherapy with children* (pp. 288–319). Boston: Allyn & Bacon.

Wulbbolding, R. (1994). The early years of control theory: Forerunners Marcus Aurelius and Norbert Wiener. *Journal of Reality Therapy, 13*(2), 51–54.

Wulbbolding, R. (1996). Working with suicidal clients. In B. Herlihy & J. Corey (Eds.), *ACA ethical standards casebook*. Alexandria, VA: American Association for Counseling and Development.

Wulbbolding, R. (2000). *Reality therapy for the 21st century*. New York: Brunner-Routledge.

Wulbbolding, R. (2004). *Reality therapy training manual* (13th rev.). Cincinnati, OH: Center for Reality Therapy.

Wubbolding, R. (2005). The power of belonging. *International Journal of Reality Therapy, 24*(2), 43–44.

Wubbolding, R., & Brickell, J. (1998). Qualities of a reality therapist. *International Journal of Reality Therapy, 17*(2), 47–49.

Wubbolding, R., & Brickell, J. (1999). *Counseling with reality therapy.* Bicester, UK: Speechmark.

Wubbolding, R., & Brickell, J. (2001). *A set of directions for putting and keeping yourself together.* Minneapolis, MN: Educational Media.

Wubbolding, R., & Brickell, J. (2005). Reality therapy in recovery. In *Directions in Addiction Treatment and Prevention,* Vol. 9, Lesson 1, pp. 1–10. New York: Hatherleigh.

Wubbolding, R., Brickell, J., Imhof, L., In-za Kim, R., Lojk, L., & Al-Rashidi, B. (2004). Reality therapy: A global perspective. *International Journal for the Advancement of Counseling, 26*(3), 219–228.

Yalom, I. (1980). *Existential psychotherapy.* New York: Basic Books.

Yalom, I. (1992). *When Nietzsche wept.* New York: Basic Books.

Yalom, I. (1999). *Momma and the meaning of life.* New York: Basic Books.

Yalom, I. (2002). *The gift of therapy: An open letter to a new generation of therapists and their patients.* New York: HarperCollins.

Yalom, I. (2005). *The theory and practice of group psychotherapy* (5th ed.). New York: Basic Books.

Yalom, I. D. (2002). *The gift of therapy.* New York: HarperCollins.

Yankura, J. (1997). REBT and panic disorder with agoraphobia. In J. Yankura & W. Dryden (Eds.), *Using REBT with common psychological problems: A therapist's casebook* (pp. 112–157). New York: Springer.

Yeh, C., Hunter, C., Madan-Bahel, A., Chiang, L., & Arora, A. (2004). Indigenous and interdependent perspectives of healing: Implications for counseling and research. *Journal of Counseling and Development, 82,* 410–419.

Yiu-kee, C., & Tang, C. S. (1995). Existential correlates of burnout among mental health professionals in Hong Kong. *Journal of Mental Health Counseling, 17,* 220–229.

Yontef, G. (1981). *Gestalt therapy: Past, present, and future.* Paper presented at the International Council of Psychologists conference, London.

Yontef, G. (1993). *Awareness, dialogue, and process: Essays on Gestalt therapy.* Highland, NY: Gestalt Journal Press.

Yontef, G. (1995). Gestalt therapy. In A. Gurman & S. Messer (Eds.), *Essential psychotherapies: Theories and practice.* New York: Guilford Press.

Yontef, G., & Simkin, J. (1989). Gestalt therapy. In R. Corsini & D. Wedding (Eds.), *Current Psychotherapies* (4th ed., pp. 323–361). Itasca, IL: Peacock.

Yontef, G. M., & Fuhr, R. (2005). Gestalt therapy theory of change. In A. L. Woldt & S. M. Toman (Eds.), *Gestalt therapy: History, theory, and practice* (pp. 81–100). Thousand Oaks, CA: Sage.

Zeman, S. (1999). Person-centered care for the patient with mid- and late-stage dementia. *American Journal of Alzheimer's Disease, 14*(5), 308–310.

Zhao, G. (2005). Playing as adaptation? Layered selfhood and self-regard in cultural contexts. *Culture and Psychology, 11*(1), 5–28.

Zimmer, E., & Dunning, T. (1998). Change agents. *Village Voice, 43*(24), 76–82.

Name Index

Subject Index